7

CIM

PRACTICE & REVISION KIT

Diploma

Integrated Marketing Communications

BPP Publishing
September 2002

First edition September 1999
Fourth edition September 2002

ISBN 0 7517 4887 0 (previous edition 0 7517 4898 6)

British Library Cataloguing-in-Publication Data
A catalogue record for this book
is available from the British Library

Published by

BPP Publishing Limited
Aldine House, Aldine Place
London W12 8AW

www.bpp.com

in association with
Nottingham Business School
Nottingham Trent University

We are grateful to the Chartered Institute of Marketing for permission to reproduce the syllabus, Secimen Paper and past examination questions. The suggested solutions to past examination questions have been prepared by BPP Publishing Limited.

Authors
Chris Fill and Geraldine McKay

Series editor
Paul Brittain, Senior Lecturer in Marketing and Retailing at Nottingham Business School, Nottingham Trent University

CONTENTS

BPP PUBLISHING

The headings indicate the main topics of questions, but questions often cover several different topics.

Tutorial questions, listed in italics, are followed by **guidance notes** on how to approach the question, thus easing the transition from study to examination practice.

A date alone (6/99, say) after the question title refers to a past examination question.

Questions marked by ★ are **key questions** which we think you must attempt in order to pass the exam. Tick them off on this list as you complete them.

BPP PUBLISHING

BPP
PUBLISHING

ABOUT THIS KIT

You're taking your professional CIM exams in December 2002 and June 2003. You're under time pressure to get your exam revision done and you want to pass first time. Could you make better use of your time? Are you sure that your revision is really relevant to the exam you will be facing?

If you use this BPP Practice & Revision Kit you can be sure that the time you spend revising and practising questions is time well spent.

The BPP Practice & Revision Kit: Integrated Marketing Communications

The BPP Practice & Revision Kit, produced in association with Nottingham Trent University Business School, has been specifically written for the syllabus by experts in marketing education, Chris Fill and Geraldine McKay.

- We give you a **comprehensive question and answer checklist** so you can see at a glance which are the key questions that we think you should attempt in order to pass the exam, what the mark and time allocations are and when they were set (where this is relevant)

- We offer **vital guidance** on revision, question practice and exam technique

- We show you the **syllabus** examinable in December 2002 and June 2003. We **analyse the papers** set so far, with summaries of the examiner's comments

- We give you a **comprehensive question bank** containing:

  ○ *Do You Know* checklists to jog your memory

  ○ *Tutorial questions* to warm you up

  ○ *Exam-standard questions*, including questions set up until December 2001 and the specimen paper

  ○ *Full suggested answers* - with summaries of the examiner's comments

- A **Test Your Knowledge quiz** covering selected areas from the entire syllabus

- A **Test Paper** consisting of the June 2002 exam, again with full suggested answers, for you to attempt just before the real thing

- A **Topic Index** for ready reference

The Study Text: further help from BPP

The other vital part of BPP's study package is the Study Text. The Study Text features:

- Structured, methodical syllabus coverage

- Lots of case examples from real businesses throughout, to show you how the theory applies in real life

- Action programmes and quizzes so that you can test that you've mastered the theory

- A question and answer bank

- Key concepts and full index

There's an order form at the back of this Kit.

Help us to help you

Your feedback will help us improve our study package. Please complete and return the Review Form at the end of this Kit; you will be entered automatically in a Free Prize Draw.

BPP Publishing
September 2002

To learn more about what BPP has to offer, visit our website: www.bpp.com

---

REVISION

This is a very important time as you approach the exam. You must remember three things.

> **Use time sensibly**
> **Set realistic goals**
> **Believe in yourself**

Use time sensibly

1   **How much study time do you have?** Remember that you must EAT, SLEEP, and of course, RELAX.

2   **How will you split that available time between each subject?** What are your weaker subjects? They need more time.

3   **What is your learning style?** AM/PM? Little and often/long sessions? Evenings/ weekends?

4   **Are you taking regular breaks?** Most people absorb more if they do not attempt to study for long uninterrupted periods of time. A five minute break every hour (to make coffee, watch the news headlines) can make all the difference.

5   **Do you have quality study time?** Unplug the phone. Let everybody know that you're studying and shouldn't be disturbed.

Set realistic goals

1   Have you set a **clearly defined objective** for each study period?

2   Is the objective **achievable**?

3   Will you **stick to your plan**? Will you make up for any **lost time**?

4   Are you **rewarding yourself** for your hard work?

5   Are you leading a **healthy lifestyle**?

Believe in yourself

Are you cultivating the right attitude of mind? There is absolutely no reason why you should not pass this exam if you adopt the correct approach.

* **Be confident** - you've passed exams before, you can pass them again

* **Be calm** - plenty of adrenaline but no panicking

* **Be focused** - commit yourself to passing the exam

QUESTION PRACTICE

Do not simply open this Kit and, beginning with question 1, start attempting all of the questions. You first need to ask yourself three questions.

> **Am I ready to answer questions?**
> **Do I know which questions to do first?**
> **How should I use this Kit?**

Am I ready to answer questions?

1   Check that you are familiar with the material on the **Do you know?** page for a particular syllabus area.

2   If you are happy, you can go ahead and start answering questions. If not, go back to your BPP Study Text and revise first.

Do I know which questions to do first?

1   **Start with tutorial questions**. They warm you up for key and difficult areas of the syllabus. Try to produce at least a plan for these questions, using the guidance notes following the question to ensure your answer is structured so as to gain a good pass mark.

2   Don't worry about the time it takes to answer these questions. Concentrate on producing good answers. There are 8 tutorial questions in this Kit.

How should I use this Kit?

1   Once you are confident with the Do you know? checklists and the tutorial questions, you should try as many as possible of the exam-standard questions; at the very least you should attempt the **key questions,** which are highlighted in the **question and answer checklist/index** at the front of the Kit.

2   Try to **produce full answers under timed conditions**; you are practising exam technique as much as knowledge recall here. Don't look at the answer, your BPP Study Text or your notes for any help at all.

3   **Mark your answers to the non-tutorial questions as if you were the examiner**. Only give yourself marks for what you have written, not for what you meant to put down, or would have put down if you had had more time. If you did badly, try another question.

4   Read the **Tutorial notes** in the answers very carefully and take note of the advice given and any **comments by the examiner**.

5   When you have practised the whole syllabus, go back to the areas you had problems with and **practise further questions**.

6   When you feel you have completed your revision of the entire syllabus to your satisfaction, answer the **test your knowledge** quiz. This covers selected areas from the entire syllabus and answering it unseen is a good test of how well you can recall your knowledge of diverse subjects quickly.

7   Finally, when you think you really understand the entire subject, **attempt the test paper** at the end of the Kit. Sit the paper under strict exam conditions, so that you gain experience of selecting and sequencing your questions, and managing your time, as well as of writing answers.

BPP
PUBLISHING

EXAM TECHNIQUE

Passing professional examinations is half about having the knowledge, and half about doing yourself full justice in the examination. You must have the right approach to two things.

> **The day of the exam**
> **Your time in the exam hall**

The day of the exam

1   Set at least one alarm (or get an alarm call) for a morning exam.

2   Have something to eat but beware of eating too much; you may feel sleepy if your system is digesting a large meal.

3   Allow plenty of time to get to the exam hall; have your route worked out in advance and listen to news bulletins to check for potential travel problems.

4   Don't forget pens, pencils, rulers, erasers.

5   Put new batteries into your calculator and take a spare set (or a spare calculator).

6   Avoid discussion about the exam with other candidates outside the exam hall.

Your time in the exam hall

1   **Read the instructions (the 'rubric') on the front of the exam paper carefully**

Check that the exam format hasn't changed. It is surprising how often examiners' reports remark on the number of students who attempt too few - or too many - questions, or who attempt the wrong number of questions from different parts of the paper. Make sure that you are planning to answer the right number of questions.

2   **Select questions carefully**

Read through the paper once, then quickly jot down key points against each question in a second read through. Select those questions where you could latch on to 'what the question is about' - but remember to check carefully that you have got the right end of the stick before putting pen to paper.

3   **Plan your attack carefully**

Consider the order in which you are going to tackle questions. It is a good idea to start with your best question to boost your morale and get some easy marks 'in the bag'.

4   **Check the time allocation for each question**

Each mark carries with it a time allocation of 1.6 minutes (including time for selecting and reading questions). A 20 mark question therefore should be completed in 32 minutes. When time is up, you must go on to the next question or part. Going even one minute over the time allowed brings you a lot closer to failure.

5   **Read the question carefully and plan your answer**

Read through the question again very carefully when you come to answer it. Plan your answer to ensure that you keep to the point. Two minutes of planning plus eight minutes of writing is virtually certain to earn you more marks than ten minutes of writing.

6 **Produce relevant answers and use examples**

Make sure that you answer the question set, and not the question you would have preferred to have been set. If the question asks for examples you will fail the question if you do not include any. Examples are always useful to explain the points you wish to make. Use them where relevant.

7 **Gain the easy marks**

Include the obvious if it answers the question and don't try to produce the perfect answer.

Don't get bogged down in small parts of questions. If you find a part of a question difficult, get on with the rest of the question. If you are having problems with something, the chances are that everyone else is too.

8 **Produce an answer in the correct format**

The examiner will state in the requirements the format in which the question should be answered, for example in a report or memorandum.

9 **Follow the examiner's instructions**

You will annoy the examiner if you ignore him or her. The examiner will state whether he or she wishes you to 'discuss', 'comment', 'evaluate' or 'recommend'.

10 **Present a tidy paper**

Students are penalised for poor presentation and so you should make sure that you write legibly, label diagrams clearly and lay out your work neatly. Markers of scripts each have hundreds of papers to mark; a badly written scrawl is unlikely to receive the same attention as a neat and well laid out paper.

11 **Stay until the end of the exam**

Use any spare time checking and rechecking your script.

12 **Don't worry if you feel you have performed badly in the exam**

It is more than likely that the other candidates will have found the exam difficult too. Don't forget that there is a competitive element in these exams. As soon as you get up to leave the exam hall, forget that exam and think about the next - or, if it is the last one, celebrate!

13 **Don't discuss an exam with other candidates**

This is particularly the case if you still have other exams to sit. Even if you have finished, you should put it out of your mind until the day of the results. Forget about exams and relax!

BPP PUBLISHING

APPROACHING MINI-CASES

What is a mini-case?

The mini-case in the examination is a description of an organisation at a moment in time. You first see it in the examination room and so you have 64 minutes to read, understand, analyse and answer the mini-case.

The mini-case (Part A of the paper) carries 40% of the available marks in the examination.

As mini-cases are fundamental to your exam success, you should be absolutely clear about what mini-cases are, the CIM's purpose in using them, and what the examiner seeks; then, in context, you must consider how best they should be tackled.

The purpose of the mini-case

The examiner requires students to demonstrate not only their knowledge of the fundamentals of marketing, but also their ability to use that knowledge in a commercially credible way in the context of a 'real' business scenario.

The examiner's requirements

The examiner is the 'consumer' of your examination script. You should remember first and foremost that a paper is needed which makes his or her life easy. That means that the script should be well laid out, with plenty of white space and neat readable writing. All the basic rules of examination technique discussed earlier must be applied, but because communication skills are fundamental to the marketer, the ability to communicate clearly is particularly important.

An approach to mini-cases

Mini-cases are easy once you have mastered the basic techniques. The key to success lies in adopting a logical sequence of steps which, with practice, you will master. You must enter the exam room with the process as second nature, so you can concentrate your attention on the marketing issues which face you.

Students who are at first apprehensive when faced with a mini-case often come to find them much more stimulating and rewarding than traditional examination questions. There is the added security of knowing that there is no single correct answer to a case study.

Suggested mini-case method

You have about 64 minutes in total.

Stage		*Minues*
1	Read the mini-case and questions set on it very quickly.	2
2	Read the questions and case again, but carefully. Make brief notes of significant material. Determine key issues in relation to the questions etc.	5
3	Put the case on one side and turn to your notes. What do they contain? A clear picture of the situation? Go back if necessary and concentrate on getting a grip on the scenario outlined.	4
4	Prepare an answer structure plan for question (a) following exactly the structure suggested in the question, highlighting your decisions supported by case data and theory if appropriate. Follow the process outlined for question (b), etc.	3
5	Prepare a timeplan for each part of the question, according to the marks allocated.	1
6	Write your answer.	44
7	Read through and correct errors, improve presentation.	5
		64

A good answer will be a document on which a competent manager can take action.

Notes

(a) It is not seriously suggested that you can allocate your time quite so rigorously! The purpose of showing detailed timings is to demonstrate the need to move with purpose and control through each stage of the process.

(b) Take time to get the facts into your short term memory. Making decisions is easier once the facts are in your head.

(c) Establish a clear plan and you will find that writing the answers is straightforward.

(d) Some candidates will be writing answers within five minutes. The better candidates will ignore them and concentrate on planning. This is not easy to do, but management of your examination technique is the key to your personal success.

(e) Presentation is crucial. Your answer should be written as a final draft that would go to typing. If the typist could understand every word and replicate the layout, then the examiner will be delighted and it will be marked highly.

Handling an unseen mini-case in the examination

The following extract is taken from a Chartered Institute of Marketing's Tutor's/Student Guide to the treatment of mini-cases.

Tutor's/Student Guide to the treatment of mini-cases

'It needs to be stated unequivocally that the type of extremely short case (popularly called the mini-case) set in the examinations for Certificate and Diploma subjects cannot be treated in exactly the same way as a long case study issued in advance. If it could there would be little point of going to all the trouble of writing an in-depth case study.

'Far too many students adopt a maxi-case approach using a detailed marketing audit outline which is largely inappropriate to a case consisting only of two or three paragraphs. Others use the SWOT analysis and simply re-write the case under the four headings of strengths, weaknesses, opportunities and threats.

'Some students even go so far as to totally ignore the specific questions set and present a standard maxi-case analysis outline including environmental reviews through to contingency plans.

'The "mini-case" is not really a case at all; it is merely an outline of a given situation, a scenario. Its purpose is to test whether examinees can apply their knowledge of marketing theory and techniques to the company or organisation and the operating environment described in the scenario. For example answers advocating retail audits as part of the marketing information system for a small industrial goods manufacturer demonstrate a lack of practical awareness. Such answers confirm that the examinee has learned a given MIS outline by rote and simply regurgitated this in complete disregard of the scenario. Such an approach would be disastrous in the real world and examinees adopting this approach cannot be passed, ie gain the confidence of the Institute as professional marketing practitioners. The correct approach to the scenario is a mental review of the area covered by the question and the *selection* by the examinee of those particular parts of knowledge or techniques which apply to the case. This implies a rejection of those parts of the student's knowledge which clearly do not apply to the scenario.

'All scenarios are based upon real world companies and situations and are written with a fuller knowledge of how that organisation actually operates in its planning environments. Often the organisation described in the scenario will not be a giant fast moving consumer goods manufacturing and marketing company since this would facilitate mindless

BPP PUBLISHING

regurgitation of textbook outlines and be counter to the intention of this section of the examination.

'More often the scenarios will involve innovative small or medium sized firms which comprise the vast majority of UK companies which lack the resources often assumed by the textbook approach. These firms do have to market within these constraints however and are just as much concerned with marketing communications, marketing planning and control and indeed (proportionately) in international marketing, particularly the Common Market, as are larger enterprises.

'However, as marketing applications develop and expand and as changes take root, the Institute (through its examiners) will wish to test students' knowledge and awareness of these changes and their implication with regard to marketing practice. For example in the public sector increasing attention is being paid to the marketing of leisure services and the concept of "asset marketing" where the "product" is to a greater extent fixed and therefore the option of product as a variable in the marketing mix is somewhat more constrained.

'Tutors and students are referred to Examiners' Reports which repeatedly complain of inappropriateness of answer detail which demonstrates a real lack of *practical* marketing grasp and confirms that a leaned by rote textbook regurgitation is being used. Examples would include:

- the recommendation of national TV advertising for a small industrial company with a local market;

- the overnight installation of a marketing department comprising Marketing Director, Marketing Manager, Advertising Manager, Distribution Manager, Sales Manager, etc into what has been described as a very small company;

- the inclusion of packaging, branded packs, on-pack offers, etc, in the marketing mix recommendations for a service.

'It has to be borne in mind that the award of the Diploma is in a very real sense the granting of a licence to practice marketing and certainly an endorsement of the candidate's practical as well as theoretical grasps of marketing. In these circumstances such treatments of the mini-case as described above cannot be passed and give rise to some concern that perhaps the teaching/learning approach to mini-cases has not been sufficiently differentiated from that recommended for maxi-cases.

'Tutors/distance-learning students are recommended to work on previously set mini-cases and questions and review results against published specimen answers. They are also advised to use course-members' companies/organisations as examples in the constraints/limitations of marketing techniques and how they might need to be modified.

'Students are also advised to answer the specified questions set and if for example a question was on objectives, then undue reference to market analysis and strategies would be treated as extraneous.'

THE EXAM PAPER

Format of the exam

	Number of marks
Part A: one compulsory mini-case study (report format)	40
Part B: three questions from six (equal marks)	60
	100

Time allowed: 3 hours

Analysis of past papers

June 2002

Part A (Compulsory, 40 marks)

1   JTA Foods: consultancy report

    (a)   Positioning
    (b)   Promotional mix recommendations
    (c)   Marketing communications over life cycle

Part B (Three questions from six, 20 marks each)

2   Internet and offline marketing communications
3   Attitude change
4   Low cost airline

    (a)   Differentiation
    (b)   Internal marketing communications
5   Integrated marketing communications
6   Branding through

    (a)   Advertising
    (b)   Other methods
7   Global agencies

This paper forms the Test Paper at the end of this Kit.

The exam paper

Examiner's comments

Overall performance was improved yet again as candidates focussed on key strategic areas. The format for the first question was changed and the 5 sections prohibited production of a marketing communications plan. The requirement to produce a core message allowed creative candidates to perform well but generally this question was poorly answered.

A critical approach is essential at this level and candidates who rely on description will not be successful.

Examiner's comments

Results this year are up, there has been a noticeable upward shift in performance. I am also pleased to report that many more students are now presenting answers that are essentially strategic and not tactical. Students did well on Internal Marketing and Internet Marketing but sadly, too many students failed to rise to the challenge concerning financial matters (SOV) and the linkage between marketing communications and branding. I will need to test these areas again in the future.

Subject areas of relative strength	Subject areas in need of attention
Positioning	SOV and related financial matters
Promotional strategy (concepts)	Marketing channels
Internet and marketing communications	Branding and the role of marketing communications
Promotional objectives	Direct marketing and evaluative techniques
Internal marketing communications (and IMC)	Corporate branding (and IMC)
Tools of marketing communications	Purpose, role and use of marketing communications
	B2B Relationships

Most students tried to structure their answers according to the format requested in the question. It is very important for students to understand the need to structure their answers and to present their responses in a clear professional manner.

Many students are well prepared and had a range of examples but too many of them used their materials descriptively and failed to discuss or evaluate as requested.

The most important aspect that tutors need to work on with their students concerns the development of a more critical approach to their answers. Purely descriptive answers are not good enough at postgraduate level. Students must be encouraged to practice skills that enable them to challenge and suggest new ways of achieving desired outcomes. The strategic aspect requires an imaginative, different view of a problem in order that differentiation (through the communications) be achieved for effective positioning.

Critical evaluation can be developed in two main areas. First, the academic or theoretical knowledge component which is an essential part of any answer. The second concerns the examples which are always going to be an integral part of this module.

Sadly, the most common reason for failing a question is that students do not answer the question set. For example, they described what internal marketing communications is but did not explain how it is an integral part of corporate branding (Question 6). Some students talked competently about promotional objectives but made no mention of charities or the context of the question (Question 3). I still believe many students would benefit from more practice at past questions.

December 2000

BPP
PUBLISHING

Examiner's comments

Candidates must demonstrate their understanding from a strategic perspective and be able to apply theory to practice. A portfolio of examples will help develop this evaluative skill. Stronger students included technological aspects, external environment and direct marketing. More attention is needed in the areas of IMC as an applied concept, corporate identity, evaluation, globalisation and attitudes.

Candidates should NOT use bullet points, but if they cannot avoid this then each significant point must be elaborated on.

Question number in this Kit

June 2000

Part A (Compulsory, 40 marks)

Part B (Three questions from six, 20 marks each)

Examiner's comments

There was some improvement in the answers to this paper with evidence of better understanding and wider reading.

Answers continue to be tactical in their approach, and lack the rationale and logic that would be necessary to make the answers strategic. The paper reflected the increased emphasis on branding, and answers should have mentioned how IMC contributes to branding strategy through positioning, creating added value and differentiation.

A more critical approach is needed in the answers, which can be obtained from two sources – using academic theoretical knowledge to evaluate the situation, and using examples to demonstrate an understanding of the strategic issues.

December 1999

Part A (Compulsory, 40 marks)

Part B (Three questions from six, 20 marks each)

Examiner's comments

There was an overall improvement in the answers to this paper.

Candidates need to know what a strategic issue is. Message, media strategy, marketing segmentation, positioning and branding are all strategic issues.

Many candidates did not know what a marketing channel was. Strong subjects included internal marketing communications, loyalty and perceived risk. Students should avoid Tesco as an example of a loyalty scheme, though!

Candidates should avoid reproducing diagrams in answers unless they are relevant. They are usually too time-consuming to draw. Again, many candidates failed to relate their answers to the context of the question or give examples when required.

SYLLABUS

Aims and objectives

- To develop students' understanding of the formulation and implementation of integrated marketing communication plans and associated activities

- To enable students to appreciate and manage marketing communications within a variety of different contexts

- To encourage students to recognise, appreciate and contribute to the totality of an organisation's system of communications with both internal and external audiences

- To enable students to be aware of the processed, issues and vocabulary associated with integrated marketing communications in order that they can make an effective contribution within their working environment.

Learning outcomes

Students will be able to:

- Determine the context in which marketing (and corporate) communications are to be implemented in order to improve effectiveness and efficiency, understand the key strategic communication issues arising from the contextual analysis and prepare (integrated) marketing communications plans

- Determine promotional objectives, explain positioning and develop perceptual maps, and suggest ways in which offerings can be positioned in different markets

- Formulate marketing communications strategies with particular regard to consumers, business-to-business markets, members of the marketing channel and wider stakeholder audiences such as employees, financial markets, environmental groups, competitors and local communities

- Determine specific communication activities based upon knowledge of the key characteristics of the target audience. In particular, they will be able to suggest how knowledge of perception and attitude, levels of perceived risk and involvement can impact upon marketing and corporate communications

- Select, integrate and justify appropriate promotional mixes to meet the needs of the marketing communication strategies

- Determine appropriate levels of marketing communications expenditure/appropriation

- Evaluate a variety of promotional campaigns drawn from different sectors

- Be aware of the impact and contribution technology makes to marketing communications. Be appreciative and sensitive to uses associated with cross-border marketing communications

- Advise on the impact corporate communications can have on both internal and external audiences and their role in the development of integrated marketing communications

1 STRATEGIC MARKETING COMMUNICATIONS (20%)

1.1 A definition and appreciation of the scope and dimensions of marketing and corporate communications.

1.2 A contextual analysis understanding and justification for marketing and corporate communication strategies.

1.3 The strategic significance and impact of integrated marketing communications.

1.4 Identify key strategic communication issues that might influence an organisation's marketing communications.

1.5 The appreciation and recognition of the importance of ethical and technological influences on promotional activities and an awareness of the social responsibilities organisations have towards the way they communicate with their target audience.

2 DEVELOPING A THEORETICAL UNDERSTANDING OF MARKETING COMMUNICATIONS (20%)

2.1 Understanding the key drivers associated with information processing and buyer decision making processes.

2.2 Communication issues for internal and external audiences.

2.3 The role of personal influences on the communication process.

3 MANAGING THE MARKETING COMMUNICATIONS PROCESS (40%)

3.1 The determination and appreciation of the prevailing and future contextual conditions as a means of deriving and developing promotional strategies and plans.

3.2 The target marketing process as a means of identifying significant promotional opportunities.

3.3 Determining promotional objectives and selecting positioning opportunities.

3.4 Identify, select and formulate promotional strategies, ensuring reference is made to:
(i) push, pull and profile strategies
(ii) any existing or proposed branding strategies
(iii) the Internet and e-commerce activities relating to both consumer-to-business and business-to-business markets.

3.5 Selecting appropriate promotional mixes.

3.6 Determining message styles and key media goals.

3.7 Deciding upon the level and allocation of the promotional spend.

3.8 Managing internal and external resources necessary for successful promotional activities.

3.9 Managing and developing product and corporate brands.

3.10 Evaluating the outcomes of promotional activities.

4   EVALUATION OF DIFFERENT TYPES OF MARKETING COMMUNICATION CAMPAIGNS (10%)

4.1   Knowledge and understanding of different campaigns from different context (including FMCG, business to business, services and public sectors, and not for profit organisations).

4.2   Consideration of the competitive conditions, available resources, stage in the product life cycle and any political, economic, social or technological factors that might be identified as influencing the development of a campaign.

5   CROSS BORDER MARKETING COMMUNICATIONS (10%)

5.1   Cultural, social and media influences.

5.2   Organisational type and communication approaches.

5.3   The adaptation/standardisation debate.

5.4   Agency structure and support.

Question bank

DO YOU KNOW? - STRATEGIC MARKETING COMMUNICATIONS

- *Check that you know the following basic points before you attempt any questions. If in doubt, you should go back to your BPP Study Text and revise first.*

- The word *strategy*, in very broad terms, can be seen as a natural follow-on from objective setting and as a process of providing a short-term guide to the specific actions of the marketing plan. Alternatively, strategy is concerned with the long-term plans for the organisation's positioning, growth, profitability and so on. It is helpful to accept that there are *multiple* definitions and qualify each more carefully, as Mintzberg does.

- Marketing communications strategies cannot be formulated and analysed in isolation from the strategies of the organisation as a whole or from its marketing strategies. Marketing activities can be defined in terms of the 12Ps of the extended marketing mix and each of the 12 elements can be linked directly to marketing communications - each of them says something about the organisation.

- Marketing communications strategy must be integrated with the overall strategy of the business, and with all the other aspects of the marketing strategy. The promotional tools used for communication must also be used in an integrated way.

- The integrated approach will be adopted by organisations in the future because of pressure on expenditure, fragmentation of the media, client sophistication, the higher profile of marketing communications itself, and increasing market segmentation.

- The marketing communications process as a whole must be properly planned, implemented and controlled.

- There are three main marketing communication strategies: pull, push and profile.

  - Pull strategies are those marketing communications directed at consumers. Push based strategies are aimed at members of the marketing channel and supply network. Both push and pull strategies tend to be product orientated.

  - Profile based communication strategies are aimed at a wide array of stakeholders, both internal and external to the organisation. The message tends to have a corporate (rather than product) orientation.

- Integrated Marketing Communications is about blending all forms of communications which are directed at different stakeholder audiences.

1   TUTORIAL QUESTION: DEFINING MARKETING COMMUNICATIONS

(a) Define marketing communications.

(b) Define marketing communications in terms of its constituent elements.

Guidance note

For (b) you may like to reproduce the 'promotional tool kit' diagram shown in the BPP Study Text *Marketing Communications Strategy.*

2   MARKETING COMMUNICATIONS STRATEGY   *32 mins*

Prepare an outline of a talk you are to give to a group of Marketing Managers on the subject of Marketing Communications Strategy. Describe the key elements of the communications planning process, showing how marketing communications strategy is distinguishable from, though part of, overall marketing strategy. Plan to illustrate your talk with examples of strategy drawn from your experience.   **(20 marks)**

3   TUTORIAL QUESTION: STRATEGY AND OBJECTIVES

(a) Mintzberg suggests that there are five definitions of strategy: plan, ploy, pattern, position and perspective. Explain what each definition entails.

(b) A marketing communications strategy involves decisions about what, in outline?

(c) Suggest three objectives for each element of the promotional mix (advertising, sales promotion, public relations, personal selling).

Guidance notes

1   You may be able to answer (a) from your studies for other Diploma papers. The point is to remind you that, like those, this is a *strategy* paper. *Apply* this knowledge when you see the word 'strategy' in an examination question.

2   Answer (b) in the form of a flow diagram if you can. This is a *communications* paper too, and visual presentation is a highly effective method of communicating.

3   For (c) suggest *more* than three objectives if you can.

4   INTEGRATED MARKETING COMMUNICATIONS   *32 mins*

In a memorandum to the managing director of an organisation of your choice explain the concept of 'Integrated Marketing Communications'. In particular you are asked to describe, with a diagram and with examples, how marketing communications strategy should be integrated into the organisation's business strategy.   **(20 marks)**

5   IMC-STRATEGY AND IMPLEMENTATION (12/00)   *32 mins*

As marketing manager in a medium sized company (in a sector and/or country of your choice) prepare a report about how you propose to develop and implement an Integrated Marketing Communications strategy.   **(20 marks)**

6 TUTORIAL QUESTION: TECHNOLOGY

(a) Explain how telemarketing may be used as an integrated marketing activity.

(b) What impact are the Internet and digital TV likely to have on marketing communications?

Guidance notes

1 We list seven areas in which telemarketing has an important role. Just think about an average telephone conversation with a (potential) customer.

2 Technological developments are good meat for exam questions and, more importantly, they are *your* future. Communications is by far the most exciting area of technological development and you should be an avid consumer of any media coverage of the subject.

3 It is important to try and think about the positive and negative impact of technology on the strategic relationships.

7 OBJECTIVES (12/99)   *32 mins*

You have decided to speak to your marketing team in order that they better understand the role of objectives in the integrated communication planning process.

Prepare notes for your presentation explaining the role of objectives, and identify which of the different elements of the communication process might be influenced by the objectives set.   **(20 marks)**

8 CHARITY OBJECTIVES (6/01)   *32 mins*

You work as a Marketing Assistant for a charity organisation and you have been asked to explain why the use of objectives in an integrated marketing communications plan is important. You should consider different types of objective and use examples to illustrate your answer.   **(20 marks)**

DO YOU KNOW? - DEVELOPING A THEORETICAL UNDERSTANDING

- *Check that you know the following basic points before you attempt any questions. If in doubt, you should go back to your BPP Study Text and revise first.*

  'Marketing communications is a management process through which an organisation enters into a dialogue with its various audiences. To accomplish this, the organisation develops, presents and evaluates a series of messages to identified stakeholder groups. The objective of the process is to (re)position the organisation and/or its offerings in the mind of each member of the target audience. This seeks to encourage buyers and other stakeholders to perceive and experience the organisation and its offerings as solutions to some of their current and future dilemmas.' (Fill, 1999)

- Marketing Communications has a number of roles. It can be used to **D**ifferentiate and organisation or product, it can be used to **R**emind or **R**eassure past or current customers. It can be used to **I**nform customers and stakeholders or it can be used to **P**ersuade people to take particular actions. This can be memorised as DRIP.

- Models can be used to help simplify and provide a framework for the understanding of complex processes, such as consumer buying behaviour. The overall aim of marketing communication is to reach and influence those individuals or groups that have been defined as target customers. In order to reach and influence these target customers the marketing communicator must have as clear an understanding of their attitudes, beliefs and motives as possible.

- It is vital for marketers to have an understanding of the processes that customers go through when buying a product, whether this product is being bought by a consumer for individual consumption or by an organisation for production of other products or for resale. The thought processes of the buying process, both organisational and consumer can be simply summarised as follows:

  - Recognition of problem/need
  - Information search
  - Evaluation of alternatives
  - Purchase decision
  - Post purchase evaluation

- The extent to which a consumer engages in all these stages will depend on the size complexity and specific circumstances of the buying situation and a range of influencing factors can be identified which could possibly affect the process. Such factors need to be recognised by marketers in order that they are taken into account in marketing and promotional activity.

9 TUTORIAL QUESTION: CONSUMER BUYING BEHAVIOUR

(a) Describe the general stages in the buying process.

(b) What makes a new product successful?

Guidance notes

1   The stages identified by Kotler and described in our answer are need recognition, information search, evaluation of alternatives, purchase decision, and post-purchase evaluation. We have answered at some length.

2   For (b) we identify and briefly describe five characteristics, following Rice.

10 TUTORIAL QUESTION: ORGANISATIONAL BUYING BEHAVIOUR

(a) Identify and briefly describe four types of organisational market.

(b) How does the American Marketing Association explain the main influences and participants in the process of organisational buying behaviour?

Guidance notes

1   PRIG is a good acronym for Dibb *et al*'s types of organisational market. What does it stand for?

2   The AMA framework deals with influences within or outside the organisation, and within/outside the department.

3   Other frameworks are also useful, for example Kotler's four forces (environmental, organisational interpersonal, individual); the DMU; Dibb *et al*'s six stages (recognise the problem, develop product specifications, search, evaluation relative to specifications, select and order, and evaluate product and supplier performance) and so on.

11 TWO PRACTICAL MODELS   *32 mins*

Write a short report on the practical use of two communication models in developing marketing communication plans. Illustrate your answer with examples.   **(20 marks)**

12 ATTITUDES (12/00)   *32 mins*

Prepare notes for a presentation to be given to colleagues explaining the nature and role that attitudes play in buyer behaviour. You should explain how marketing communications can be used to influence these attitudes. In particular you should:

(a) Explain the different components of an attitude.   (5 marks)

(b) Describe ways in which marketing communications can be used to shape or change attitudes held by a target market. Use examples.   (10 marks)

(c) Suggest reasons why the development of positive attitudes in the target audience is important for those involved in the management of brands.   (5 marks)
(20 marks)

13 PERCEIVED RISK (12/01)   *32 mins*

You are the Marketing Manager for a charity and the concept of perceived risk has been brought to your attention. Identify the main types of perceived risk and evaluate the influence of marketing communications on the management of risks, as they might affect your organisation.   **(20 marks)**

14   CLIENT NEEDS (12/98)   *32 mins*

It has been noted that many advertising agencies have failed to adapt and restructure themselves in order to keep pace with the increasing demands and international communications strategies of their clients. What are the reasons for this apparent incompatibility and suggest how agencies might adjust to better meet their client needs.

(20 marks)

15   OPINION LEADERS (6/00)   *32 mins*

Many marketing communication campaigns make use of opinion leaders and opinion formers. Using examples to illustrate your points, explain how and why these personal influencers might be used.   **(20 marks)**

16   POSITIONING (12/01)   *32 mins*

As Brand Manager with a telecommunications company, and as part of a management of change process, you have been invited to explain the positioning concept to colleagues in the finance department.

Prepare notes which:

(a) Explain what positioning means.   (8 marks)

(b) Evaluate the importance of the concept, illustrating your points with examples from a sector of your choice.   (12 marks)
(20 marks)

DO YOU KNOW? - MANAGING THE MARKETING COMMUNICATIONS PROCESS

- *Check that you know the following basic points before you attempt any questions. If in doubt, you should go back to your BPP Study Text and revise first.*

- Before it can formulate a marketing plan and a complementary communications strategy an organisation must regularly carry out a comprehensive, systematic and independent examination of its marketing environment, objectives, strategies and activities. Much marketing planning is based on the concepts of segmentation and positioning.

- The main requirement in today's modern markets is better *targeting*. To determine whether a segment is worth pursuing the marketer needs to consider its size, measurability, access, uniqueness of response and stability. The basic options in targeting are undifferentiated or mass marketing, differentiated marketing, concentrated marketing and customised marketing. *Positioning* is concerned with how products create and establish an image in the minds of consumers and how they are evaluated against competing products.

- Marketing communication strategy starts with a thorough understanding of the current context within which the communication campaign is to operate. By examining the marketing strategy and market conditions, the nature of the target audiences, brand performance and other external and internal issues, it becomes possible to determine the correct promotional objectives. From this point an overall strategy emerges (3Ps of communication strategy, push, pull and profile). The organisation then has to identify which elements of the promotional mix are to be deployed: an integrated approach is becoming more and more common. Other considerations at this point are whether a push or a pull strategy is appropriate, the nature and constitution of the target market and the characteristics of the product. The *creative* aspects are a vital ingredient for success.

- The promotional strategy must be monitored and controlled to see whether it is working. Possibilities include pre-testing and post testing, coupon redemption rates, and electronic monitoring. Budgeting is usually done on an annual basis, with monthly reviews. Seasonal factors must be taken into account and some organisations have contingency funds for one-off opportunities. There are a variety of methods of budgeting, the most important of which is the objective and task method.

- Media strategy is determined by asking what is the message to be communicated, who is the audience, what is the desired response and how much is there to spend. Market, product and target audience characteristics; budget and client preferences need to be taken into account when planning media campaigns, as do the attributes of each individual media option. A multi-media campaign is likely to achieve a greater level of synergy than one which concentrates on options within one medium.

- Marketing communicators need to be fully aware of the range of qualitative and quantitative research data that is available and of the limitations of research. The process of selecting a new *agency* involves initial search; credentials presentation and shortlist; competitive pitch and final selection. The client will gauge competing agencies against set criteria such as expertise in the client's field of business, previous work handled, resources provided and costs. Personal chemistry between the individuals involved will also play a part.

- Achieving integration requires acceptance of the *need* for it, the establishment of a genuine two way communications, and the development of a useable model. Relationship marketing has many links with integrated marketing communications: both are shaped by the need to get closer to the customer.

- Marketing communication strategies (eg 'inform the consumer') specify the reasons why the communication is taking place in relation to business objectives. Tactics (eg public relations, sponsorship) specify where and how to reach the target groups that can take or influence the decision to purchase.

- A successful brand is a name, symbol, design or some combination of these things which identifies the product of a particular organisation as having a sustainable differential advantage over similar products. A variety of branding strategies are possible, such as family branding, brand extension, and multi-branding. The strength of retailers is now such that own label brands threaten manufacturer's brands.

BPP PUBLISHING

> • Marketing communications will only be able to sustain a brand if the product itself consistently lives up to the image created. A successful **branding strategy** requires careful initial research in all markets and a long-term commitment to sustaining the brand. Once established brands can be transferred to other products, even if they are quite unrelated to the original product. **Brand valuation** is a means of analysing and measuring the effectiveness of marketing expenditure. It can play a significant part in overall strategy formulation and in the management of the organisation.

17 TUTORIAL QUESTION: AUDITING, SEGMENTATION AND POSITIONING

(a) A marketing audit looks for problems and opportunities. What specific matters might be studied?

(b) What are the stages of segmentation?

(c) Describe six approaches to developing a positioning strategy.

Guidance notes

1 The three principal areas of study in a marketing audit are likely to be the marketing environment, marketing objectives, strategies and plans and marketing activities (organisation, systems, productivity). See how many points you can get under each of these headings.

2 Only an outline answer is wanted for (b) (we give a diagram). If you are not sure about what is involved in any of the stages it is time for more revision.

3 The positioning of a product or service is concerned with how it creates and establishes an image within the minds of the consumer and how it is subsequently evaluated against alternative product offerings.

18 PROMOTIONAL MIX (Specimen) *32 mins*

In your capacity as an entrepreneur who has established a successful regional marketing communications agency you have been asked to make a presentation to an audience of local business people.

Prepare notes for this presentation entitled 'The Strategic Significance of the Promotional Mix'. You aim to cover each of the main tools of the promotional mix and provide brief examples to illustrate each point. **(20 marks)**

19 PROMOTIONAL MIX AND BRANDING (Specimen) *32 mins*

The Promotional Mix developed for a branded consumer product is different to that developed for an industrial or technological product aimed at the business-to-business market.

Using an example from each sector to illustrate your answer, write a report about:

(a) The nature of these differences and the impact they each might have on an organisation's integrated marketing communication activities. (10 marks)

(b) Suggest how these two mixes might evolve in the future. (10 marks)

(20 marks)

20   FUTURE TRENDS IN THE PROMOTIONAL MIX (12/00)   *32 mins*

As an Account Manager at a direct marketing agency, explain why many of your clients have decided to redistribute a greater percentage of their marketing communications budgets away from mass media advertising to other promotional methods. You should also comment on future trends and use examples to illustrate your points.   **(20 marks)**

21   INTERNET BASED COMMUNICATIONS (6/00)   *32 mins*

For many organisations, business to business marketing communications have been transformed by the development of the Internet and related digital technologies. Prepare notes for a meeting at which you are expected to argue the case for the development of Internet based marketing communications for a business or company of your choice.

(20 marks)

22   DIFFERENT SECTORS (6/01)   *32 mins*

Using consumer and business to business marketing communication campaigns to illustrate your answer, explain the differences in the purpose and use of marketing communications in these two different sectors.   **(20 marks)**

23   PLAN LINKS (6/99)   *32 mins*

Your manager has asked you to explain how the different parts of a marketing communications plan are linked together. In response to this request:

(a)   Prepare a set of notes indicating how the different parts of the plan are interconnected.
(10 marks)

(b) Highlight a single element of the plan that you feel is of paramount importance to the success of such plans. Justify your selection.   (10 marks)

(20 marks)

24   MARKETING COMMUNICATIONS OBJECTIVES   *32 mins*

Show, with specific examples, how marketing communications objectives are derived from an organisation's mission statement. In particular demonstrate how objectives, strategies and tactics are related in a communications plan.   **(20 marks)**

25   MARKETS AND STRATEGIES   *32 mins*

Although the principles of marketing communications are the same for both consumer and industrial markets there are significant differences in the details of how promotion is carried out. Describe the characteristics of the two types of markets and the implications for choosing marketing communications strategies for industrial markets.   **(20 marks)**

26   PUSH AND PULL (12/01)   *32 mins*

An office furniture manufacturing company is about to launch a new range of products.

(a)   Explain what is meant by a push communication strategy and contrast this with a pull communication strategy.   (10 marks)

(b) Briefly outline the main characteristics of the marketing communications mix used to reach members of the marketing channel.   (10 marks)

(20 marks)

27   INTERNAL MARKETING COMMUNICATIONS (12/98)   *32 mins*

The increasing awareness and emphasis given to internal marketing communications suggest that an organisation's employees are an important market segment in their own right. Write a report explaining why this group is now perceived as important and suggest how such internal communications might be used to improve communications with other externally based stakeholder groups.   **(20 marks)**

28   CORPORATE INTERNAL MARKETING (6/01)   *32 mins*

As a Marketing Assistant, prepare a brief report for your marketing manager explaining the significance of internal marketing communications and suggest why they might be an integral part of the organisation's corporate brand.   **(20 marks)**

29   PLANNED COMMUNICATIONS (12/99)   *32 mins*

The use of planned communications in marketing channels is an important aspect of most communications strategies.

Write brief notes explaining why it is important to communicate with channel members, and suggest what might be the key influences that shape the design and implementation of such communication activities.   **(20 marks)**

30   INTERNAL MARKETING COMMUNICATIONS : TECHNOLOGY (12/99)   *32 mins*

The increased recognition and use of internal marketing communications by organisations throughout the world suggests that an organisation's employees can be regarded as an important, if often neglected, target audience.

Prepare a draft memorandum to be sent to your immediate colleagues for comment, explaining why internal marketing communications are important, and suggest how the use of technology might assist management to communicate effectively with this particular audience.   **(20 marks)**

31   DEVELOPING MEDIA STRATEGY (6/00)   *32 mins*

As Marketing Communication Manager for a global financial services organisation, you have decided to ask your assistant to attend a meeting with your full service agency. Prepare a briefing note advising your assistant of the key media concepts to be considered when developing media strategy.   **(20 marks)**

32   INTERNET CHANNELS (6/01)   *32 mins*

Prepare a briefing paper for your marketing department colleagues, describing how utilisation of the Internet (and related technologies) can change the way members of a marketing channel communicate with one another. What might be the impact of this change on the relationships between channel members?   **(20 marks)**

33   ONLINE AND OFFLINE (12/01)   *32 mins*

As the owner and manager of a company that rents holiday apartments to members of the public:

(a)   Explain the advantages of using Internet-based communications.   (10 marks)

(b)   Evaluate the role of offline communications when pursuing an online branding strategy.   (10 marks)
                                                                      (20 marks)

34   BRANDING AND MARKETING COMMUNICATION   *32 mins*

Branding is a common strategy adopted by both manufacturers and retailers in consumer markets. Using examples of brands from a country of your choice, evaluate the effectiveness of branding as a marketing communication strategy.   **(20 marks)**

35   INTERNET   *32 mins*

Evaluate the ways in which the rapid growth of the Internet is changing the way businesses communicate with their customers, suppliers and within their own organisations.

                                                                      (20 marks)

36   RETAIL STRATEGY (12/01)   *32 mins*

You are reviewing the communication policies of large retail organisations (eg supermarkets) in a country of your choice. Using examples to illustrate your answer:

(a)   Discuss the advantages of using an above-the-line branding strategy.   (10 marks)

(b)   Compare this strategy with one that focuses on sales promotions.   (10 marks)

                                                                      (20 marks)

37   BRAND DEVELOPMENT (6/00)   *32 mins*

Write a report for your Senior Managers, explaining how marketing communications can contribute to the development of EITHER a consumer OR business to business brand. Use examples to illustrate your points.   **(20 marks)**

38   BUSINESS-TO-BUSINESS BRANDING (12/98)   *32 mins*

Many organisations in the business-to-business sector have begun to use branding as a significant part of their marketing communications strategy. Write a report explaining this development. Use examples to illustrate your points and comment whether this trend is likely to continue.   **(20 marks)**

39   CORPORATE IDENTITY (6/00)   *32 mins*

In 1999 British Airways decided to reverse a decision concerning the design of their corporate identity used on the tail fins of many of their aircraft. The controversial designs were said to be disliked by overseas customers. At the same time, the redesign had been criticised by many staff who had been in conflict with the organisation about a cost cutting campaign introduced previously by management at the airline.

Prepare a report in which you identify the main theoretical elements of corporate identity/branding and use examples to illustrate how corporate communications can be used to reach important internal and external audiences. Use organisations of your choice to answer this question.   **(20 marks)**

40   BRANDING STRATEGY (6/01)   *36 mins*

A soft drinks manufacturer has decided to undertake a consumer branding strategy for the first time. Using examples to illustrate your answer:

(a)   Explain the role that advertising might play in brand development.   (10 marks)

(b)   Evaluate the role of the other marketing communication tools in branding. (10 marks)

                                                                        (20 marks)

41   TUTORIAL QUESTION: INTER AND INTRA-MEDIA DECISIONS

(a)   Describe the factors that govern media choice.

(b)   (i) What is a media schedule?

      (ii) Distinguish between a burst campaign and a drip campaign.

Guidance notes

1   For (a) we describe the nature of the medium, the positioning of ads within the medium, the way in which people use media, the amount of time spent with the medium, the creative opportunities offered, lead times and quantitative considerations. Expand upon these points.

2   For (b) you might like to practise sketching out a media schedule diagram, too, since your exam may well require you to do this. There are examples later in this Kit.

42   BUDGET PROCESS (6/99)   *32 mins*

You are a newly appointed marketing manager for a company that makes hair care products which are sold through supermarkets and major national distributors. You have identified the need to review the process by which the marketing communications budgets are determined each year.

Prepare an internal paper for the marketing and sales departments reviewing the available methods and outline your proposals by which these budgets should be set in the future.

                                                                        (20 marks)

43   MARKETING COMMUNICATIONS EXPENDITURE (12/98)   *32 mins*

As a marketing manager write a short article for inclusion in a company magazine suggesting how the amount of money spent on marketing communications might be strategically important. Use examples to illustrate your article.   **(20 marks)**

DO YOU KNOW? - EVALUATION

- *Check that you know the following basic points before you attempt any questions. If in doubt, you should go back to your BPP Study Text and revise first.*

- It is vitally important that you get into the habit of studying and analysing examples of marketing communications. You should aim to build a varied portfolio of examples that you can use in your examination.

- The following comments may help you to focus your efforts in particular areas.

- *Industrial* marketing communications strategies can be very different from consumer campaigns. There are differences in such areas as purchase motivation, customer needs, product specifications, level of customer service needed and so on. This calls for different approaches in employing the various promotional tools.

- The marketing of *services* is similar to the marketing of products in many ways, but there can be differences due to such factors as professional and legal constraints, the nature of capacity available, and the buying process itself. Personal selling is more important.

- In *non profit marketing* communications there is likely to be less money available, messages are likely to be subjected to greater scrutiny and the objectives of the communication will be quite different from those applying in consumer marketing. The major categories of non-profit communicators are political parties, social causes, the government, religious bodies and professional bodies.

- The main feature of marketing communications for *small businesses* is that resources are limited. This will mean that more is done in-house and at a local level, though all of the usual promotional tools can still be employed.

- In attempting to understand the impact of communications it is important realise that every variable interacts with other variables and cause and effect cannot easily be distinguished. Effective communications are those that increase brand *awareness*, stimulate *trial purchase* and *reinforce* brand loyalty. The amount of communication to which people are now being subjected means that it is becoming increasingly difficult to communicate successfully.

BPP PUBLISHING

44   AN ACTUAL STUDENT'S ANSWER   *32 mins*

For any charity or government campaign of your choice write an outline report which describes the campaign and specifies its objective and target audiences. Evaluate the effectiveness of the chosen campaign.   **(20 marks)**

45   BRANDING STRATEGIES (12/00)   *32 mins*

You have been invited to visit a local business school to talk to postgraduate students about marketing communications strategies.

Using brands from sectors of your choice and with which you are familiar, prepare notes which explain why such strategies need to change and set out some of the different strategies that might be adopted over the lifetime of a brand.   **(20 marks)**

46   EXAMPLES OF PLC (6/99)   *32 mins*

Using examples, prepare a memorandum to be sent to your manager explaining how useful the product life cycle might be when developing promotional strategy.   **(20 marks)**

47   CUSTOMER RETENTION (12/99)   *32 mins*

Using two examples form the consumer market to illustrate your answer, prepare a short report for your Manager explaining how customer retention schemes might add value to your communications strategy.   **(20 marks)**

48   INFLUENTIAL FORCES (6/00)   *32 mins*

Many marketing communication campaigns are influenced and shaped by competitive and wider external environmental forces. Using examples, explain how such forces might influence and shape the marketing communications for a brand (or brands) of your choice.

(20 marks)

49   EVALUATING MARKETING COMMUNICATIONS (12/00)   *32 mins*

Explain the principal means by which marketing communication campaigns for fast moving consumer products, should be evaluated. Consider the effectiveness of three main evaluation techniques.   **(20 marks)**

50   MEASURING SUCCESS (6/01)   *32 mins*

As manager of a small/medium sized direct marketing business, producing and distributing toiletries for a number of niche markets, prepare a short report for your managing director evaluating the methods available to measure the success of your promotional strategy.

(20 marks)

DO YOU KNOW? - CROSS-BORDER MARKETING COMMUNICATIONS

- *Check that you know the following basic points before you attempt any questions. If in doubt, you should go back to your BPP Study Text and revise first.*

- Different viewpoints exist concerning the globalisation of markets. On the one hand, there is the argument that consumers are converging in tastes and that companies have an opportunity to market standardised products worldwide. An alternative view is that consumer markets are fragmenting and that products and services need to be adapted to individual preferences.

- The international marketing communicator needs to decide whether or not it is appropriate to standardise communications across markets.

- Companies operating outside their home markets need to be aware of the implications of cultural differences for all aspects of the marketing mix. Verbal and non verbal communications, aesthetics, dress and appearance, family roles and relationships, beliefs, learning and work habits are dimensions of culture of particular relevance to communications.

- Planning and buying media across borders can be a complex task. Media availability can vary greatly from country to country. Media conventions which apply in a home market may not apply elsewhere.

- Laws and regulations governing marketing communications must obviously be observed Each country will have its own set of restrictions which apply to advertising, packaging, sales promotion and direct marketing.

- Research should be used to support decision making before a campaign is planned. Research can also help evaluate whether objectives have been met at the conclusion of a campaign. However, obtaining accurate, unbiased, up to date information can be difficult. Conducting primary research on an international basis requires the help of experts.

- Clients and their agencies can choose to handle international advertising campaigns in a number of ways. Although a variety of factors will influence the management of any particular campaign, the organisational structure of the client company will play an important role.

- Some agencies have expanded abroad by setting up their own subsidiaries overseas. Others have established alliances with local agencies already in existence.

- There are arguments both for and against using the services of an international advertising agency. The current preference amongst large clients is to centralise advertising with an internationally based agency, rather than choose local agencies on a country by country basis.

- The standardisation versus adaptation debate has implications for agency management. If campaigns are totally standardised across markets, the lead market agency office will take the major role in designing and implementing the global campaign; local agency subsidiaries will have minimal input.

- The process of selecting an international advertising agency involves initial search, credentials presentation and shortlist, competitive pitch and final selection. The client will gauge competing agencies against criteria such as response to the brief, types of communication service provided, expertise in handling local and international campaigns, and similarity of management style and culture to that of the client.

51 TUTORIAL QUESTION: DIFFERENCES

(a) What are the arguments for and against standardising communications internationally?

(b) What dimensions of culture are relevant to the marketing communicator?

(c) For each of the following media identify one key consideration regarding its use internationally.

    (i) Press
    (ii) TV
    (iii) Outdoor
    (iv) Cinema
    (v) Radio

Guidance notes

1 We have answered in a word or phrase for (b). Try to expand on this and give some examples if you can.

2 For (c) several points could be made under each heading.

52 WITH OR WITHOUT? *32 mins*

Choose a country with which you are familiar. Write a short report to a manufacturer of tea and coffee who is considering entering the beverage market in the country of your choice. Outline relevant cultural and social trends, the likely target end user, the retailing structure and the choice or appropriate media in the country through which to promote the company.
(20 marks)

53 MANAGING GLOBAL COMMUNICATIONS (12/00) *32 mins*

Determine and explain the key issues that an international advertising agency might advise a client about when discussing the development of an integrated marketing communications strategy for consumer products across several countries. **(20 marks)**

54 ADVANTAGES AND DISADVANTAGES OF INTERNATIONAL AGENCIES
32 mins

The multinational full service advertising agency has grown in importance. However, the present structures have been attacked as being too large, inefficient and relatively unproductive. Write note on the advantages and disadvantages of such international agencies, and the changes that they face in the next five years. **(20 marks)**

55 INTERNATIONAL BUSINESS (12/01) *32 mins*

Appraise the role and significance of marketing communications for organisations operating in international business to business markets. Use examples to illustrate your points. **(20 marks)**

56   DUTTON ENGINEERING (12/99)   *64 mins*

During the 1990s Dutton Engineering's impressive growth was based on a strategy that was focused on the development and maintenance of strong customer relationships. Rather than spend money speculating about the generation of new customers, Dutton's policy has been to invest and build relationships with current customers.

Dutton manufacture steel and aluminium components, and in order to help realise their strategy they removed their middle management and devolved responsibility to teams of production orientated personnel, who focus upon their client's total requirements. Clients talk directly to these 'Production Cells' who are empowered to make decisions and manage all aspects of their client's requirements. There are no appointed cell leaders, managers or even secretaries, as each cell manages itself organically and recruits its own new staff.

The role of senior management has been to manage time and resources through the use of management information systems. They are able to identify areas across and within Production Cells where productivity might be improved, and help ensure that 85% of the man hours in each Production Cell are used to generate revenue. As a result of this approach revenue has doubled to £2.3m, profits are stable at 6.5%, sales per worker are double that of the national average in the sector, yet staff numbers have remained relatively stable. Not surprisingly, Dutton have become the centre of attention for its innovative and seemingly successful approach.

The company's success has been built around 42 client companies, some of whom are very loyal. Part of the company's philosophy has been to 'meet and beat customer's expectations', and the attitude of staff in each Production Cell reflects this perspective. Through high levels of quality production and customer involvement, new orders have been won. However, the growth experienced to date has been based on new orders from existing clients and very little new business has been acquired. Senior management are regarded (by the Production Cells) as responsible for generating new customers, yet they see their role as managing and teaching the 'Dutton Way'.

Little effort appears to have been made to attract new customers and there is no Marketing Department or sales force. These are costs that do not fit the current culture and are regarded as activities that would add little value and merely create high overheads. The company currently outsources transport, cleaning and payroll, so outsourcing a sales operation would be a compatible activity.

There has been little planned use of marketing and/or corporate communications, and the primary emphasis has been on strong word of mouth communications, supported by some limited public relations activities. However, a rudimentary web site, some use of telemarketing, the unplanned use of some out of date sales literature, and attendance at exhibitions, constitutes the main thrust of the communications to date. However, the organisation needs to address the balance of its current customer portfolio and attract new clients if it is to achieve ambitious growth targets - to be achieved in the first few years of the new millennium.

Source: material adapted from Sumner-Smith, D. (1998) 'Selling Without a Sales Force', Sunday Times, 25 October, p15.

Required

As a Marketing Communications Advisor you have been asked to consider the information available and to prepare a report which:

(a) Identifies the key communications issues facing the company.   (20 marks)

(b) Makes recommendations for Dutton's Marketing Communications Strategy for the next two years.   (20 marks)

(40 marks)

You have been asked specifically **not** to present a marketing communications plan but to focus on the key strategic issues that Dutton Management need to consider. You should justify your recommendations and state any assumptions made.

57 WOODSTOCK FURNITURE (6/00)   *64 mins*

Woodstock Furniture is a privately owned company located in a fashionable area in London. The company makes bespoke, high quality kitchen and bathroom furniture. Kitchens account for 80% of sales and the average order value is £25,000.

The general kitchen furniture market in the UK is worth over £800 million but of this the bespoke market is only worth a static 1 %. Woodstock's sales have fluctuated over its 22 years of trading and currently stand at £1.7 million per annum with net profit at 6.9%. However, the balance sheet is weak and there is little opportunity to attract finance for promotional investment. Staff are very supportive of the company, appear to identify strongly with the customised approach and many have been with the company since its start up. However, many of the internal systems and procedures are old, slow and in need of updating - perhaps a reflection of the slower, detailed craftsmanlike culture that identifies the Woodstock Furniture Company.

In recognition of some of the problems facing the company, the management has developed a marketing plan which seeks growth of 15% per annum to be achieved by market penetration and in particular, the attraction of new customers. It now needs a marketing communication programme to develop a strong corporate brand. The problem is that profit margins are small and there is little to invest in developing the brand and competing with well known high street outlets.

The competition, as Woodstock see it, have huge resources which can be used to invest in promotional campaigns to drive awareness and action. For example, these companies have authentic web sites, unlike Woodstock's site which is little more than an online brochure. Many of the large national standardised companies can produce promotional literature in large production runs and are happy to ignore wastage. Using expert photography of 'pretend' kitchens, the quality and impact of the literature is high. Woodstock's smaller budgets dictate that photographs of real customers' kitchens are required, which seldom look perfect and can even appear amateurish. It costs £4 to produce each of the Woodstock brochures so vetting of each request for literature is important to avoid those people who ask for brochures but buy nothing. A high conversion rate is necessary and although 50% of quotations are converted into sales, Woodstock cannot afford this figure to be lowered.

Woodstock's customers do not want the standardised kitchen units provided by the larger, more dominant players in the market They want kitchens made to measure and which complement the character of their homes. They look for attention to detail, design, craftsmanship and support when commissioning bespoke companies such as Woodstock. The target market is affluent, often has more than one home and relies on word of mouth recommendation when drawing up a shortlist of possible providers. For many, price is not the key issue - rather it is the capability to craft suitable furniture to match the required decor and house style. This requires a high degree of trust, which successful companies in this market are able to reciprocate and in turn generate commitment. Many of Woodstock's customers are celebrities but because discretion and privacy is important to them, they often refuse to allow their names (and kitchens) to be used for Woodstock publicity. However, customer loyalty is extremely important with over 60% of new business being driven from existing customers.

In recognition of this, Woodstock now believes that it is in the business of craftsmanship and the design and construction of customised furniture rather than the business of making and installing kitchen and bathroom furniture. It has improved levels of support and service (having, for example, introduced annual maintenance contracts) and has high levels of customer satisfaction. The marketing plan states that prices are to be raised to capitalise on premium pricing opportunities and the high levels of demand inelasticity. The marketing plan involves forming relationships with architects and developers and creating cross promotions and alliances with firms operating in similar markets, such as conservatories, studies and staircases.

Source: Adapted from an article in the Sunday Times, 15 August 1999.

Required

As a Marketing Adviser you have been asked to help the company achieve its objectives. In particular you are to prepare an Integrated Marketing Communications Plan for Woodstock Furniture covering the next two years. It is important to justify your recommendations and state any assumptions made in order to prepare the plan.

(40 marks)

58 APOLLO DATA LOGGERS (12/00) *64 mins*

Apollo Data Loggers manufactures and distributes a range of equipment (both hardware and software) designed to monitor and capture data concerning temperature, humidity, damp and shock. For example, growers of fresh produce need an accurate record of temperatures experienced during the growth, preparation and transportation of their produce. For freight carriers and transporters, data logging provides a means of verifying the conditions in which their customers' products are carried.

Apollo has established itself in the market partly through superior technology which, unlike its competitors, is capable of downloading data whilst it continues to record. Sales revenues have grown to approximately £3m but profitability, whilst respectable, remains unexciting at around 6%. The market is becoming more competitive which in turn impacts on price. To avoid price competition and discounting which eventually leads to an erosion of profitability, Apollo's marketing strategy requires a move to niche markets where premium pricing can be sustained.

To reach its markets Apollo has developed a global network of over 40 distributors. These channel intermediaries provide their customers with solutions but the decision making is often complex involving all three parties; Apollo, the distributor and the client. This network can require vast amounts of information and the development of customised products to meet client requirements. For example, Apollo's distributors need information about the range of 42 mainstream products and the product revisions which occur with increased frequency. These revisions can be caused by customers buying equipment to support their own businesses which is not compatible with the data logging equipment.

Apollo is required therefore to update its own equipment constantly and communicate information about the revisions more frequently.

In order to communicate with and support its distributors Apollo produces sales literature manuals, product specifications, brochures and data sheets. In addition, data capture software needs to be made available and updated as necessary. Contract with the distributors is maintained by telephone, fax, email and through visits by members of the sales force. Apollo is also well represented at leading exhibitions, either directly or indirectly through agents and distributors. There is little advertising apart from some in the trade press and public relations has been largely ignored.

In order to retain clients, build longer term relationships and reduce costs, many manufacturers are looking to develop positive life-long relationships with their distributors. One way in the past has been to increase the switching costs for distributors. However, this is difficult unless there is some distinct and sustainable competitive advantage or reason to be aligned with a particular manufacturer. Correspondingly, distributors are looking for improved reliability, manufacturer commitment and integrity as well as product expertise. To meet these requirements a shift in the form of the relationship between Apollo and its distributors is necessary and to do this a more effective and efficient communication system needs to be introduced.

To date, Apollo's marketing communications strategy has been to use its distributors to present Apollo's products to their markets. This has often resulted in a fragmented and varied set of messages which are largely product oriented and based on the provision of information, product attributes and benefits. The strategy is now being questioned as some people claim that the current approach is slow and inefficient due to duplication and repetition which drives up communication costs. With increasing competition, a requirement for faster information flows and a need to present a more unified and focused identify to clients and distributors means that the marketing communications strategy is in need of review.

Source: The information provided in this case is based on a case in Bickerton, Bickerton and Simpson-Holley 1998, Cyberstrategy, Butterworth-Heinemann. Information has also been provided by the company, whose name has been disguised. Some of the material has been adapted in order to provide a suitable context for the min-case study and in no way is intended to imply good or bad management or even actual situations or current practice.

Required

As Marketing Manager for Apollo you have embarked upon the process of reviewing the company's marketing communications. You are required to make a report to the Directors about the following points.

(a) Identify and prioritise the key strategic issues concerning the communications between Apollo and its distributors and clients. (20 marks)

(b) In view of the issues you have identified, recommend and justify a means by which technology might be used to develop Apollo's marketing communications strategy.

(20 marks)

(40 marks)

It is important to answer both these questions separately and **NOT** write a marketing communications plan.

59 BREAKFAST CEREALS (6/01)   *64 mins*

The UK Ready-to-Eat breakfast cereal market is worth £1,080 million and is dominated by three main manufacturers, Kellogg's, Weetabix and Cereal Partners. They hold 69% market share but are faced with a number of competitive pressures, one of which is the 21% share held by the own label distributors which is growing at 5% each year. The market is mature and is characterised by strong competition. Growth in the market has been slow with only product innovation and segmentation activities (eg chocolate flavours and children's products) showing above average performance. Branding in the RTE sector is extremely important.

Manufacturer	Market share by volume %	UK Advertising spend £m
Kellogg's UK	42	55
Weetabix Ltd	15	15
Cereal Partners Ltd	12	18
Own label	21	0
Others	10	14
Total	**100%**	**£102m**

Table 1: Market share and advertising spend for three leading UK Cereal manufacturers.

With high penetration levels (90% of households holding stock and 73% of consumers claiming to eat them for breakfast) opportunities for real growth appear to be limited. However, research has shown that regular eating of the right sort of breakfast can help us get the correct balance of foods we need. The nutritional value of breakfast cereals and their impact on health, diet and weight, combined with their convenience, suggest that there are new opportunities for product development and marketing communications. This health orientation has helped broaden market opportunities through new products (eg the very successful launch of Nutigrain cereal bars from Kellogg's for those who need to eat a mobile breakfast, for example when travelling to work) and the promotion of breakfast cereals as an all-day snack food (which has been referred to as guilt-free snacking). The development of the Nutrigrain bars also demonstrates how Kellogg's has moved into new marketing channels (eg petrol forecourts) and is reaching new audiences. The different strategies adopted by the leading brand manufacturers suggest that there is no single best way to use marketing communications in this market.

Kellogg's is the leading brand manufacturer but has been most affected by the growth of own label brands. Faced with declining market share it has just announced an aggressive marketing policy, slashing prices by 12% on its top 6 brands. It also intends to increase its advertising spend by 40%. In the past its advertising has been based around a benefit oriented message which aims to educate audiences about the nutritional values of its products. In doing so Kellogg's acknowledges the role parents play in the decision making process. Kellogg's also collaborates with the Government's Health Education Authority to raise awareness of the need for a balanced diet and the important role breakfast plays in our daily food intake.

The **Weetabix** company is privately owned and discloses very little about its activities. The Weetabix biscuit, the company's main brand, has a unique characteristic in that it turns very soft and mushy when milk is poured on it. Rather than work as a product disadvantage it increases the product's utility as it makes it a suitable food for all ages; from babies as a weaning food, to young people as a quick and convenient snack food, through to those in their later years. In addition to specific brand advertising which has been attribute based, Weetabix aims to add value to its brands through the use of sales promotions rather than focus on price reductions and discounts. For example, one promotion used 40 free drawstring tea bags banded on top of Weetabix 48 pack whilst another linked into an offer with Maxwell House coffee. Weetabix has been very profitable and the company does not want to be drawn into a price war.

Cereal Partners was formed through an alliance between General Mills and Nestlé and is the single largest producer of own label products. The core of its activities in the market has been brand extensions and relaunches of established brands. This is demonstrated through the extensions of its largest single brand, Shredded Wheat, into Fruitful, Honey Nut and Bitesize. It does not see price as a significant factor in the decision making process as it claims that research indicates that breakfast cereals are perceived to be a good value food. Its advertising messages are often directed at children and stress the taste and fun properties of its main line brands.

Manufacturer	Leading brands	Brand market share of value (%)	UK advertising spend £m
Kellogg's UK	Kellogg's Cornflakes	9	8
Weetabix Ltd	Weetabix	7	9
Cereal Partners Ltd	Shredded Wheat	4.5	5

Table 2: Market share and advertising spend for three leading UK cereal brands

Note: *Information for this case has been collected from a variety of public sources. The figures have been adjusted to enable clearer relationships to be observed. The material is not intended to imply good or bad management practice. This mini case is presented as illustrative material and is suitable for teaching purposes only.*

Required

As a Marketing Communications Adviser for a major marketing consultancy organisation prepare a short report in answer to the following two questions:

(a) Evaluate the marketing communications strategy of each of the three main brand manufacturers. (25 marks)

(b) Suggest how Weetabix Ltd might use marketing communications to counter the new promotional strategy announced by Kellogg's. (15 marks)

(40 marks)

You should base your report upon the information provided in the mini case (about the companies' approach to promotional investment and brand development).

Do not attempt to write a marketing communications plan.

60   AP ENGINEERING (12/01)   *64 mins*

AP Engineering (AP) is a privately owned civil engineering company, employing approximately 4,200 people in the Asia Pacific region. The company designs and manages the building of major civil engineering projects in a variety of vertical market sectors.

The company wins contacts by bidding for client-specified projects and offering the best (perceived) value for money. The problem with this approach is that the appointed civil engineering company has limited input to the original requirements/specification and, as soon as the project is completed, its involvement is normally terminated. Perhaps even more importantly, the margins earned on such projects are notoriously slim, so in order to grow the business, higher margins need to be generated.

Following a review of the business, AP's new strategy is based upon a total engineering service, one which centres on client needs and their total project requirements, rather than the previous engineering/product focus. In other words, the company now adopts a relationship marketing approach. The emphasis is upon providing added value by shifting the offering both upstream and downstream. Therefore, AP Engineering now provides three connected offerings.

(a)   The front-end work, which involves undertaking the planning and risk analysis work for its clients

(b)   The core work, which is about the design and build aspect of the project

(c)   The tail-end work, which is essentially Facilities Management

Among the many advantages this strategic approach presents, there are two significant benefits. The first lies in the substantially higher margins that the front and tail-end work attracts. The second concerns the reduced 'resource' wastage by being able to help accurately define the client problem at the earliest possible stage in the project life cycle.

In order to develop and implement this strategy, AP has had to evolve a new skills mix, namely Asset Management and Facilities Management skills. AP chose to purchase a number of small consultancies and formed alliances with other targeted companies specialising in these particular skill areas.

Whilst this might sound reasonably straightforward, AP has had to address further issues concerning the development of a suitable commercial culture for the established employees and those new to the enlarged organisation. The company now views each project as a commercial activity and all employees must adopt increased levels of commercial awareness (eg project risk assessment, the importance of working within budget and invoicing on time). In addition, the employees of the newly acquired organisations have to be incorporated into the values and corporate philosophy of the new company culture. A further issue concerns the way the company presents itself to clients and other key stakeholders.

The organisation is deliberately seeking to develop closer client relationships based upon trust and empathy. It has done this by improving understanding of its clients' business, by getting involved right from the start of a new project, by completing projects on time and within budget, and by a willingness to share sensitive information. It also helps that the AP Engineering brand is highly visible and has developed a credible reputation based upon clients' perceived value.

The level of communication frequency between client and AP Engineering varies across the life of a project. There is a great deal of communication at the outset of a project as the brief is determined by all parties. As the project moves to the design phase, the level of communication tends to fall. However, projects often run tight on their deadlines; hence interorganisational, and even intraorganisational communication levels intensify in an attempt to resolve on-site problems as quickly as possible.

The company realises that personal contact is the most significant communication tool used in the development and maintenance of client relationships but the company is undecided about its communication strategy, and has asked you, in your capacity as Marketing Communications Consultant, for your advice.

Required

As a Marketing Communications Consultant, advise AP with regard to the following questions:

(a) Identify a communication strategy that AP should pursue in the next year.   (5 marks)

(b) What is the justification for your strategy?   (10 marks)

(c) Which tools of the promotional mix might best be used to implement this strategy? Why?   (10 marks)

(d) What might be the core message that needs to be delivered over the next year?(5 marks)

(e) Make a list of the issues that AP might consider before implementing an integrated marketing communications policy.   (10 marks)

(40 marks)

Answer bank

1 TUTORIAL QUESTION: DEFINING MARKETING COMMUNICATIONS

(a) Marketing communications is all forms of communications between an organisation and its customers and potential customers. More broadly, it is all forms of communications by an organisation with its environment, including internal communication. More narrowly, it can be defined in terms of constituent elements such as sales promotion, advertising, PR, direct marketing and so on.

(b) The promotional toolkit illustrated in the BPP Study Text includes the following elements.

- Word of mouth
- Sales promotion
- Public relations
- Merchandising
- Direct marketing
- Exhibitions
- Internal marketing
- Corporate image
- Packaging
- Sponsorship
- Advertising
- Personal selling
- Branding

These are the most obvious communication methods, though other parts of the marketing mix, including the product itself, pricing policy and distribution channels will also have significant parts to play.

2 MARKETING COMMUNICATIONS STRATEGY

Tutorial note. This challenging question requires a well structured answer. Students are required to have a thorough knowledge of:

(a) the business and marketing planning processes;

(b) the marketing communications planning process;

(c) how to integrate the two processes;

(d) examples of practical and successful communication strategies derived from such an integrated process.

REPORT

To: Marketing Managers
From: Marketing Communications Manager
Date: December 2001
Ref: Presentation on the subject of marketing communication strategy

1 Audience/objectives

The audience consists of marketing managers. We can assume therefore that they are reasonably well versed in the actual marketing planning process.

Although they will be knowledgeable about the planning process their involvement in the detail will vary from person to person. Some will have a close working knowledge; others will only have limited experience of planning directly themselves.

There will also be degrees of scepticism. Some will be committed planners others will not.

Even more important to our specific talk is the fact that the marketing managers can be assumed to have relatively less detailed knowledge of the marketing communications planning process.

The objectives of the talk can therefore be defined as follows.

(a)   To show how marketing communication planning is an integral part of the overall company planning process.

(b)   To demonstrate that without this link communications planning would be less effective.

(c)   To describe the SOSTAC model as a way of bringing about this integration.

(d)   Lastly, to illustrate the talk with practical examples of strategy.

2   **The total planning process**

It is vital that we as marketing managers understand the corporate planning process and the role of marketing planning within it. Furthermore, because marketing communications accounts for a significant share of the marketing mix it is important also to understand the integration of the marketing communications planning process.

Each level of the organisation has a hierarchy of:

(a)   Objectives
(b)   Strategy
(c)   Tactics.

The tactics of the upper level then become the objectives of the next level down in the organisation. The levels we can consider usually are:

(a)   Corporate
(b)   Functional (including marketing)
(c)   Activity (including marketing communications).

These relationships are shown in more detail in the diagrams below. The first is Simon Majaro's Planning Hierarchy. The second shows the relationship of corporate, marketing and communications planning in more detail. The third shows the operational planning stages of marketing communications.

Clearly each of these diagrams of the real situation will vary from company to company according to size, nature of business, and experience of planning. In some predominantly marketing organisations the link between corporate and marketing objectives will be a very close one.

In larger companies with separate operating divisions another level of planning will be introduced. These operation divisions are often called 'strategic business units'.

The planning hierarchy

The planning hierarchy by Simon Majaro

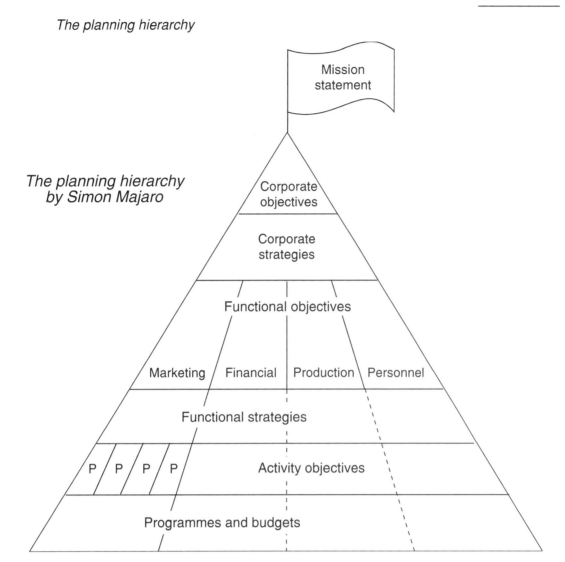

BPP
PUBLISHING

*The strategic marketing and tactical communications planning
process within the overall strategic marketing planning process*

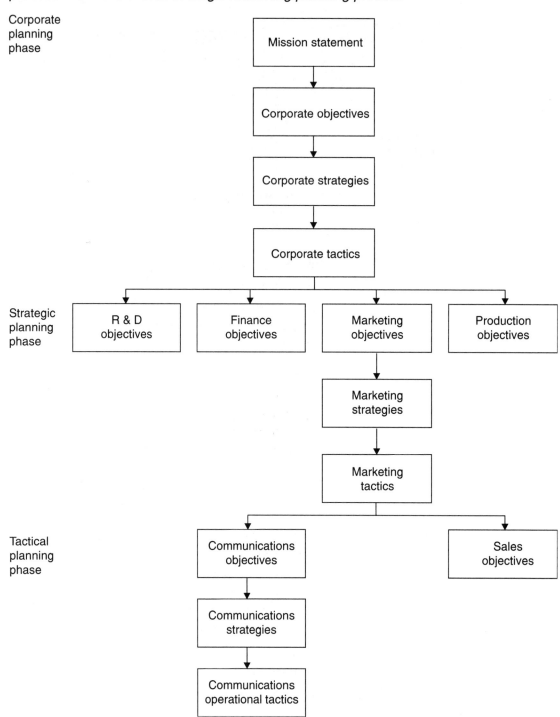

The operational planning stages of marketing communications

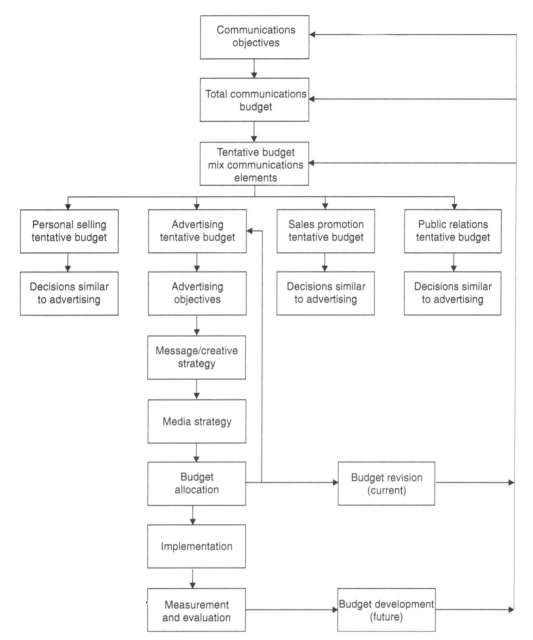

3 The SOSTAC communications planning process

Because marketing communications planning is less well developed and less well understood it is important to demonstrate the vital link to business and marketing planning. It is also important to have a rigorous, memorable and easy to apply marketing communications planning model. Such a model which I would like to recommend to you is that being developed by Smith, Pulford and Berry called the SOSTAC model.

S = Situation analysis
O = Objective setting
S = Strategy development
T = Tactics
A = Action
C = Control

This model is capable of being used in many planning situations but it is being developed specifically for marketing communications planning.

The situation analysis which starts the process can be seen as part of the overall corporate and marketing analysis and audit process. Four areas of analysis are carried out.

(a) Internal company analysis of 4Ps or 7Ps
(b) Analysis of the market and customers
(c) Analysis of competitors using Porter's five forces
(d) Analysis of the external environment evaluating changes in the following areas.

    (i) Sociological
    (ii) Technological
    (iii) Economic (macro)
    (iv) Political/legal
    (v) Environmental

In the case of marketing communications planning in particular, note is made of any strengths, weaknesses, opportunities or threats which have a direct bearing on possible communication solutions

SOSTAC planning model

Stage	Planning elements	Strategic direction
Stage 1	Situation analysis ↓	Where are we now?
Stage 2	Objective setting ↓	Where do we want to go?
Stage 3	Strategy development ↓	How do we get there - broad direction?
Stage 4	Tactics development ↓	How do we get there - individual steps
Stage 5	Action planning ↓	How do we take people with us?
Stage 6	Controls and review	How do we know when we have arrived?

Each of the following elements of the SOSTAC model can then be developed specifically for the communications process as follows.

Objectives

Objectives can be developed under the headings on the Ansoff matrix.

(a) Market penetration
(b) Market development
(c) Product development
(d) Diversification (strategic alliances)

Each of these broad areas will require a different communications objective.

Strategy

Strategy in communication terms is then best developed by reference to particular target audiences. The most useful approach to this is to work through the steps of:

(a) Segmentation
(b) Targeting
(c) Positioning

Positioning is achieved by a judicious choice of the marketing mix including promotions or marketing communications.

Tactics

To help to remember a systematic approach to the tactics of marketing communications we can use 3Ms.

(a)   M = methods
(b)   M = media
(c)   M = messages

Action

To help us develop action plans we consider a different set of 3Ms.

(a)   M = manpower (responsibilities)
(b)   M = minutes (timescales)
(c)   M = money (budgets)

Control

Finally it is necessary to control the effectiveness of the marketing communications process by measuring the achievement of the business, marketing and marketing communications objectives.

4   Examples of strategies

The most powerful examples of marketing communications strategies are those linked directly to the corporate and marketing strategies. A number of such examples are given below.

(a)   *Boddington's beer*

Whitbread's marketing objective was to launch the beer nationally in a controlled manner. The communication strategy was to promote the brand as an authentic regional beer brewed in Manchester using the slogan 'The Cream of Manchester'. This reflected the creamy full head obtained from this cask conditioned beer. The media strategy was to use the rear covers of colour magazines to promote the golden colour of the product. Television was not used initially in part because of limited brewing capacity.

(b)   *PPP Healthcare*

PPP were facing increasing competition in the health insurance market especially from the commercial insurance companies especially Norwich Union. The PPP management decided to plan for an increase in market share, to distinguish themselves from their rivals and to rebrand themselves. Marketing communications obviously had an important role to play in this. To increase the awareness of the new company name (PPP Healthcare) and to reposition itself as a healthcare company not an insurance company the company chose to use a television and national press campaign stressing the support it provides to customers.

(c)   *BMW cars*

BMW cars were exported to the UK mainly as performance cars. BMW (GB) was established in 1979 with the ambitious aim of tripling UK sales by 1990, whilst maintaining high profit-margins. The 'Ultimate Driving Machine' campaign was developed and is still running 17 years later. The marketing communications objectives were:

       (i)   To enrich the image of the vehicle

       (ii) To build positive aspects of the image

       (iii) To raise the brand's image

These objectives have been met over a prolonged period in spite of the sales targets meaning that there would be more of the less exclusive models on the road. An advertising strategy was developed partly through TV but mainly through quality colour magazines.

5 Conclusions

These are examples of successful marketing communications strategies which have produced outstanding business results. This has only been possible because the management of those companies have had clear business and marketing objectives which in turn have provided the drive for clear marketing communications plans.

The marketing communications planning process has therefore to be a close and integrated component of the overall planning process. One way of achieving this is to use the SOSTAC planning framework which is memorable, easy to apply and powerful in its effect.

3 TUTORIAL QUESTION: STRATEGY AND OBJECTIVES

(a) (i) *Strategy as a plan:* strategy is a consciously intended course of action, a set of guidelines to deal with a given situation. Strategy is seen, in this case, as 'a unified, comprehensive, and integrated plan designed to ensure that the basic objectives of the enterprise are achieved'.

(ii) *Strategy as a ploy.* A ploy is a manoeuvre intended to attack an opponent or competitor. A marketing company may threaten to enter a rival's market or to discount prices heavily as a way of threatening a rival's plan to enter the company's established market. In another case a company may develop a 'fighting brand' alongside its already established, possibly higher priced mainline brand.

(iii) *Strategy as pattern.* Strategy is seen as a 'consistency in behaviour whether or not intended'.

(iv) *Strategy as position:* a means of locating an organisation in its environment. This may be thought of as a niche in a market place. Another aspect of a position strategy is whether a company chooses to be a leader or a follower in its chosen market.

(v) *Strategy as perspective:* an established way of perceiving the company and its markets. Thus McDonald's employees are trained to emphasise 'quality service, cleanliness and value' whereas Kwiksave employees see themselves as part of a 'no frills' organisation.

(b) See diagram below.

The Communication Strategy Process

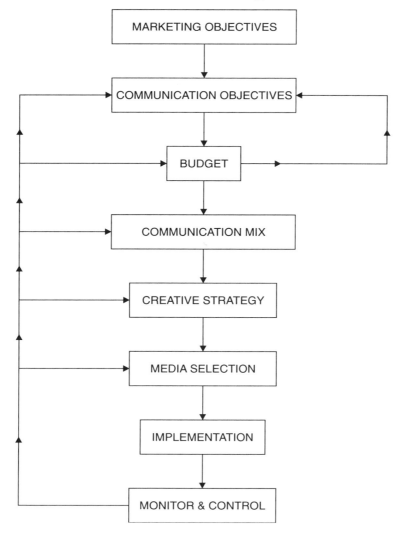

(c) Possible objectives are as follows. You may have thought of others.

(i) *Advertising*

(1) To increase sales.
(2) To inform the public of a new product launch.
(3) To announce a sales promotion.
(4) To raise the level of awareness amongst the target audience.
(5) To act as a reminder to purchase the product.
(6) To generate new business leads (integrated with direct marketing).
(7) To maintain brand awareness, position and price premium.

(ii) *Sales promotion*

(1) To reward loyal customers and ultimately keep them.
(2) To act as an incentive to purchase a new product launch.
(3) To acquire other brand users.
(4) To gain shelf space within a retail outlet.
(5) To act as a spur towards short term sales.

(iii) *Public relations*

(1) To build corporate identity.
(2) To create customer confidence.
(3) To build credibility with the City, financiers and suppliers.
(4) To build internal morale within the company.

BPP
PUBLISHING

(5) To establish good press relations.

(iv) *Personal selling*

(1) To increase sales by sales person, product group, region, outlet type.
(2) To increase market penetration of specific customer groups.
(3) To increase average order value.
(4) To improve sales to call ratios.
(5) To target new customer groups.
(6) To improve after-sales care.
(7) To provide market data and identify new product opportunities.

4 INTEGRATED MARKETING COMMUNICATIONS

Examiner's comments. This question follows my predecessor's campaign for greater understanding and application of integrated marketing communications. The need for this knowledge has not decreased, indeed the need can be said to be even greater now with the increasing fragmentation of the media and the realisation that all elements of the communications mix must work together.

This proved to be a popular question among both UK and international students. Given the expected nature of the question, students were generally well prepared and achieved good marks. There were three components to the question. Firstly, the description was well done. Second, implementation was less well done. More diagrams could have been used. Third, the illustration of a student's own organisation was only done well by the best students. However, those students who failed to provide examples probably failed the question, as the practical or applied aspect of the programme is very important.

Besides defining integrated marketing communications, as the strategic choice of all marketing communications elements to meet business objectives, good students were able to describe the factors influencing the importance of the subject. Among the diagrams that might have been included in an answer are Majaro's Hierarchy of Objectives, Strategies and Tactics, and Pulford's Seven Levels of Integration, besides the more usual ones integrating the marketing mix and the promotional mix.

MEMORANDUM

To: Managing Director
From: CIM Student
Date: 4 June 2002
Ref: Integrated Marketing Communications

The purpose of this memorandum is to present a case for the development, implementation and maintenance of Integrated Marketing Communications (IMC) at Cult International Plastics.

Situation Analysis

Cult International Plastics is launching a new product into a relatively new market and has set ambitious market share and business objectives. In addition to achieving a market share of 10% of the domestic market in 2003, Cult is aiming to become the preferred supplier for leading builders' merchants supplying the building trade and DIY stores supplying the domestic sector.

It aims to do this with a stronger, lighter and more flexible plastic extrusion that can be shaped and cut on site. This will provide greater opportunities for customised products and lower costs.

Marketing communications has a major role to play not only in informing target markets but also in positioning Cult as a leading and innovative supplier to the building sector. It is vital that any proposed communication programme should be fully *integrated,* both in terms of delivering messages and providing efficiency and effectiveness.

This paper sets out the advantages of IMC, some initial ideas about how it could be implemented at Cult and provides examples with a view to establishing its credibility as a leading edge approach to communications management.

Definition of IMC

The development and acceptance of IMC over the past few years, as a term synonymous with good marketing practice, has been wide and rapid. However, it is apparent that there is little uniform agreement about what it means and how it should be implemented.

IMC involves:

'The strategic choice of elements of marketing communications, which effectively and economically influence transactions, between an organisation and its existing and potential customers, clients and consumers'

'The management and control of all marketing communication elements'

'Ensuring that the brand positioning, proposition, personality and messages are delivered synergistically across every element of communication and are derived from a single consistent strategy'.

This presents a view of IMC.

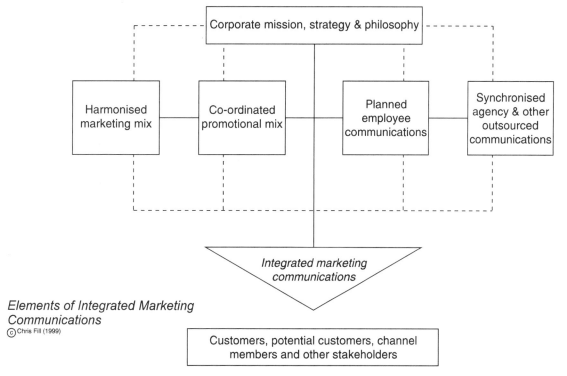

Elements of Integrated Marketing Communications
© Chris Fill (1999)

Benefits of adopting IMC

The benefits of moving towards the adoption of IMC are quite clear in my opinion and even if we are unable to achieve all of them in the medium term the fact that we are able to consider the totality of our communications will give us the opportunity to achieve a competitive advantage.

(a) With increasing inflation in media costs IMC gives us a chance to reduce our communication expenditure and achieve greater effectiveness.

(b) The technological advances that have been made in the past few years means that there are new ways to reach our customers and potential customers. If we do not consider them then we may risk losing some of our customers.

(c) IMC means that there are opportunities to link our communications with our distribution channel partners and provide a more co-ordinated and two-directional flow to our promotional activities.

(d) Internal communication opportunities exist and by linking our internal and external communications we may be able to promote increased understanding of the needs of our employees, customers, channel partners and a range of other important stakeholders.

(e) Our customers are changing their lifestyles and are using a wider range of media to achieve their goals. By utilising IMC we will be in a better position to reach our customers and deliver consistent messages that do not confuse them or drive them to our competitors.

(f) Our growth in international markets places greater emphasis upon the need to control and co-ordinate our marketing and corporate communications. IMC provides that opportunity and this will be important when dealing with customers who are located in many different overseas markets.

(g) The establishment of IMC will enable us to appoint a single advertising agency to handle all of our above-the-line work in different countries and to bring together our other agencies in Public Relations, Direct Marketing and Sales Promotion to develop co-ordinated and consistent campaigns.

Levels of IMC

There are a number of levels associated with IMC and the diagram below sets these out succinctly.

Elements of Integrated Marketing Communications
©Chris Fill (1999)

Action Plan for Cult Plastics International

Should we agree to commence the implementation of IMC, an action plan will be required to ensure that not only do we achieve the benefits set out earlier but that we plan events in such a way that we are able to overcome any resistance to this new approach.

I propose that the following be considered as a possible action agenda.

(a) Launch the IMC concept

(b) Train teams throughout the organisation

(c) Develop plans to deliver IMC at different levels

(d) Test plans for viability

(e) Implement

(f) Review implementation, adjust and control activities

The success or failure of IMC will, like other major strategic developments, rest with employees' perception of top management's involvement and endorsement of IMC. I urge you to make your self visible over this matter and to be seen as a firm believer in IMC.

It appears that the development of IMC by other companies has been limited because of the narrow perspective they have taken to the subject and of the need to reorganise the allocation and control of resources. I suggest that as a first step we attempt to coordinate the activities of the promotional mix and the marketing mix with the corporate goals. Integration with some of our external partners should follow at a later date. It is better to achieve a set of restricted goals rather than achieve only partial success with a wide range of goals.

Examples of IMC

To illustrate how IMC has been used by other organisations I include the following examples. It should be remembered that the context in which these campaigns were developed varied widely and there may have been internal and external conditions that framed the way the communications were developed. Our situation is unique: our approach will need to accommodate the different forces acting upon us and so should not attempt to replicate all the actions of these organisations.

(a) *Walkers Crisps* embarked upon a series of campaigns that incorporated a consistent communications mix. The objective was to revive and reposition the brand and this has been achieved using television with Gary Lineker as the central spokesperson to appeal to both adults and teenagers.

    (i) Lineker has been a consistent element throughout all the campaigns and is presented and perceived as a cheeky but fun endorser for the brand. Advertisements with a number of related spokespersons such as Paul Gascoigne and the Spice Girls have been mixed with messages with unrelated spokespersons such as everyday people and even a nun. These campaigns have been used in association with sales promotions such as competitions from which a tremendous amount of PR media coverage has been generated.

    (ii) The market grew by 11%, but Walkers achieved growth of 21%. They have revived their brand, achieved market leadership and profitability and repositioned themselves as the number one snack food brand in the UK through the use of IMC.

(b) *Häagan Dazs* demonstrated the effective use of IMC when they entered the UK market. Ice cream was traditionally a seasonal children's food and the market had experienced little growth or innovation. The business strategy adopted was to create a new market segment, one that is now referred to as the 'super-premium segment'.

    (i) The positioning intention was to present Häagan Dazs as a luxury, fashion-orientated food for adults. To achieve the business goals, the entire marketing mix was coordinated: the product reflected high quality, the high price induced perceived quality, the distribution in the launch was through up-market restaurants in prestige locations and 5-Star hotels, where Häagan Dazs was the only branded ice cream on the menu.

(ii)   The promotional campaign used celebrities from many walks of life as opinion leaders to create a word-of-mouth ripple effect. The quality of the media used and messages themselves reflected the same quality theme. The brand has since become firmly established and, although the arrival of Ben & Jerry's and other up-market brands has increased competition and rivalry, the brand remains distinctive and continues to use an integrated approach to its communications.

Conclusions

To conclude I should like to reaffirm that in future our communications should be based upon an integrated approach drawing together the goals, the strategies, the tools and all those involved in our communications with all stakeholders.

5   IMC-STRATEGY AND IMPLEMENTATION

> **Examiner's comments.** This question calls for the development and implementation of IMC, not just an explanation of what this is. Issues concerning the introduction of new concepts and the management of change are vital. Barriers to change in this particular example are the managers themselves and so this answer does not criticise them directly. The role of senior management to take this forward is crucial to offer credibility.

To: Regional Managers, XYZ Building Society

From: Marketing Manager

Re: Integrated Marketing Communications

Introduction

This report will consider the importance of an Integrated Marketing Communications Strategy as we enter our new era of business using the relatively new business model of an Internet banking facility.

Present situation

Our present marcomms strategy is to achieve two main objectives

(a)   To establish our brand as offering a greater service than other financial service brands which are largely commodities

(b)   To encourage traffic to our Tele banking and branch networks

However the new service (Internet banking) which is to be launched under the same brand name now needs to be launched. This will replace the telephone system and also allow us to enter a new market with better products for those searching for an on line bank.

The new service may well cause some anxiety amongst branch staff who may fear for their jobs. Consumers wanting to know about the new services will approach them. Although the service is somewhat different from that available through branches it must carry the same corporate and brand values of being the most professional financial service provider available to our target markets.

IMC- a definition

Integrated Marketing Communications can be seen as the strategic choice of elements of marketing communications that effectively and efficiently informs and influences all stakeholders. This involves the management and control of all marcomms activity and ensures that a synergistic message is presented across all elements of communication and these will go towards the achievement of corporate and marketing objectives.

Introducing IMC

Our society has a traditional branch based network which continues to be successful. However the new customers demand that they be serviced through a number of different methods, including branch, telemarketing and Internet service delivery. We are now working towards the integration of all computer systems to ensure a single touch point delivery of service, so that a single customer's records can be updated, no matter how they do business with us.

This needs to be explained to customers and other stakeholders (including staff) who need to be trained about the new technology and how it can help them provide a better service. The message we put out must be consistent through above the line, below the line and Internet activity.

Our integrated approach must be across the whole marketing mix (our technology has now changed to allow this to happen) and our pricing and promotions must all say the same.

Our promotional mix must also be integrated. As we wish to use a number of different methods they must all offer the same message – that our society is the most professional, however we do business.

Our marcomms strategy must also be vertically integrated so that all messages help us achieve our marketing objectives- i.e. to ensure that we keep our customers (members) and gain 4% more. This will help us achieve our corporate objectives of guaranteeing a return to our members whilst retaining mutuality.

Implementing IMC

Our strategy makes sense but will not come to fruition by itself and it is important that it is implemented throughout the society.

Of course we have top management support who have committed £100 million pounds to ensure that our systems are up to date. We will be using a new full service advertising agency to produce an above the line strategy and develop our new Internet site. In addition we now need to ensure that all staff are told about the changes and this will be done via meetings, e-mail and internal training videos and workshops. These will be followed up after implementation to ensure that the new approach is working and to gain feedback from staff.

Branch managers like yourselves will need to ensure that your own staff are fully up to date on the new marcomms activity, and we will be inviting you on to the implementation working party to ensure that the activity suits your own needs.

Conclusions

In order to ensure an integrated approach it is important to talk to all players concerned. Existing customers will be told about the new service via direct mail and an integrated public relations campaign will be used in which staff will be involved. The unions are also involved on the implementation planning committee.

The objectives will not be achieved overnight and the achievements will be incremental. They will be measured and methods changed if they are not working. A multi million pound budget has been set aside to achieve this important process and we are sure that with your help we can implement an integrated approach to position ourselves as the most professional supplier of financial services.

6 TUTORIAL QUESTION: TECHNOLOGY

(a) When combined within the marketing and selling functions, telemarketing plays an important role in the following areas.

   (i) *Building, maintaining, cleaning and updating databases*. The telephone allows for accurate data-gathering by compiling relevant information on customers and prospects, and selecting appropriate target groups for specific product offerings.

   (ii) *Market evaluation and test marketing*. Almost any feature of a market can be measured and tested by telephone. Feedback is immediate so response can be targeted quickly to exploit market knowledge.

   (iii) *Dealer support*. Leads can be passed on to the nearest dealer who is provided with full details.

   (iv) *Traffic generation*. The telephone, combined with postal invitations, is the most cost effective way of screening leads and encouraging attendance at promotional events.

   (v) *Direct sales and account servicing*. The telephone can be used at all stages of the relationship with the prospects and customers. This includes lead generation, establishing buying potential for appropriate follow-up and defining the decision-making process.

   (vi) *Customer care and loyalty building*. Every telephone contact opportunity can demonstrate to customers that they are valued.

   (vii) *Crisis management*. If for example there is a consumer scare, immediate action is essential to minimise commercial damage. A dedicated hotline number can be advertised to provide information and advice.

(b) The emergence of the *information superhighway* will potentially have a huge impact upon the marketing of products and services together with associated communication techniques.

The ability to shop from home and choose items directly with the use of scanners can be integrated with direct advertising. Infomercials (which combine information with a commercial) which the consumer has chosen from a databank will be relayed directly to the home down cable links. These may take the form of recipes, DIY hints, car repairs and so on. Consumers will also be able to purchase the necessary ingredients or parts simultaneously, simply by pointing a mouse on a computer screen at the desired goods and clicking its buttons

It is estimated by Verdict Research that home shopping will become a £300m market in the UK within the next few years. US operator QVC (Quality, Value and Convenience) launched television shopping in 1993 in the UK through satellite, which is available to cable and Sky subscribers.

The speed of adoption will depend upon how readily the public accept and use the new technology and to what extent they will be deterred from actively browsing around the shops. This will vary from country to country and community to community.

The superhighway will also enable viewers to interact directly with the television programmes they watch. It may be the case that certain channels with specialist broadcasts (for example a channel devoted to golfing, cookery or motor sport) will be characterised solely by advertisements from within those areas of interest. Viewers will then be able to conduct a dialogue with the screen to find out more information about the particular programme, product or service which is being covered.

Advertising opportunities will abound as advertisers choose individual channels to suit the special interest and viewer profile.

However, as the packaged goods manufacturers responsible for big name brands are aware, the need to communicate your product to the widest possible audience is the key to maintaining a brand's position. It may be possible in the future to *reward* the viewer for watching your commercial. Machines placed on top of televisions could print out money-off coupons for specific products which the viewer has just watched. These would be redeemable against that product over a specified time period.

Taking this a step further, it could be possible to tailor advertisements to individual requirements, as information on individual viewing habits is monitored through interactive television.

7   OBJECTIVES

> **Examiner's comments.** Most candidates knew the role objectives play in a marketing communications plan. However, a number of candidates saw the word 'integrated' and went on to write on integrated marketing communications without relating it to the question.
>
> A number of students did badly on the second part of the question. Note that this area is likely to come up again. Students who can show that they have understood the concept of linkages in the marketing communication planning process will do well in this subject.

Introduction to Objectives

1   The use of objectives in any management related activity is essential. Within marketing communications the derivation and use of objectives can be critical for a number of reasons. They can provide the following:

- Direction

- Consistency in decision making

- The time period for the activity to be completed

- A means by which the values and scope of the activity are communicated to all participants

- A means of evaluation

2   These general roles highlight the scope and importance of objectives. An organisation however, can have a number of different goals, many of which can be seen as hierarchically aligned.

3   An integrated marketing communications (IMC) plan requires that all the goals of an organisation be incorporated or at least reflected in the lower level communications. For example, the mission of an organisation provides a framework for the organisation's objectives which in turn should be represented in the business and marketing objectives. The goals for a marketing communications plan (or campaign) should be similarly aligned.

Different Types of Promotional Goals

4   The goals for a marketing communications plan can be referred to as the promotional goals. They consist of three main elements: Sales, Communications and Corporate related issues.

5   The Sales goals refer to the market share, sales value and ROI figures that commercial organisations generate on a regular basis and to which all managers can easily refer. These figures can be drawn down easily from the marketing plan. Unfortunately, these

do not account for the communication task facing each Marketing Communication or Brand Manager. They fail to incorporate a customer perspective and give little or no direction to the creative team assigned to the advertising aspect.

6   In response to the short comings of the Sales goals it is necessary to incorporate a set of Communication related goals. These refer to tasks concerning awareness levels, the provision of information (developing knowledge/understanding) and changing perceptions and attitudes towards a brand.

7   Finally, it is my belief that if we are to generate IMCs then it is absolutely imperative that these product related goals are counterbalanced by goals relating to how the organisation itself is perceived by the other stakeholders. This refers to corporate identity and image issues and the nature of the task facing an organisation depends on the gap between what stakeholders think about the organisation and how the organisation would like to be perceived.

Linkages with Other Parts of the Marketing Communication Planning Process

8   The Promotional Goals are developed through the Contextual Analysis, either through market research, the marketing plan or through analysis and understanding. As an integrated plan it is important to understand that these goals impact on nearly all the other parts of the planning process.

- They constrain the number of promotional strategies to be considered and selected.

- They impact on the type of message to be formulated and delivered to the target audience(s). This in turn affects the development of the brand.

- The choice of media to be used to convey the message will also be influenced by what is to be achieved and how quickly. For example, if the plan requires the development of prompted awareness then a reach media strategy is more likely to be appropriate than a frequency strategy.

- The amount of resources that can and are allocated to the plan will reflect, in part, the nature of the task that needs to be accomplished.

- The goals will also impact on the schedule and timing of the implementation of the marketing communication activities. Good integration requires that there be consistency and harmonisation across the promotional mix.

- The promotional objectives will be used to evaluate how successful the plan/campaign has been.

9   There is no doubt that the use of carefully specified (SMART) objectives is a crucial part of the development of an Integrated Marketing Communications plan.

8   CHARITY OBJECTIVES

Examiner's comments. This question proved to be popular with students and most understood the different types of objective and were able to give examples. Many chose to use charities as the background for their examples and scored higher marks. I was pleased that so many students knew the structure of the IMC plan and were able to relate their answer to this framework.

At some point in all of these IMC examinations, there will be an opportunity for students to work with the marketing communications planning framework. I am increasingly reluctant to set a 'write a plan' question for the mini case. However, it is important that students do understand the key components and how the parts are linked together.

Why are objectives are so important in the Integrated Marketing Communications Plan?

A briefing note for the Marketing team

Introduction

As a charitable organisation Barnardos has an extremely important role to play in protecting vulnerable young people in Britain and helping prevent circumstances that will mean that they are in danger in the future. Today we wish to focus on the role and nature of objectives and discuss why they are important to us as a charity in our planning, implementing and measuring marketing communications strategy.

What are Objectives?

Put simply objectives are what we are aiming to achieve by when. However there are many types of objectives in marketing communications planning and need to be investigated. Objectives become the pivotal link pin between the corporate, business, marketing plans and the marketing communications strategy.

A hierarchy of objectives exist. Starting with the mission statement for our charity, which sets the framework for all of the charity activity. (For example this could be to protect vulnerable young people and prevent future situations, which could endanger young people).

This allows business objectives to be set enabling the work to be carried out. (To generate an income of £xxx and employ the right mix of skills to ensure delivery of our service).

Marketing objectives can now be set. (To recruit a core of 50,000 supporters who will commit to £200 per annum to support the work).

Marketing communications objectives can now be identified (To gain 50% awareness about the charity amongst First time parents who are known to be keen on the future development of young people and position the charity as the most effective at protecting vulnerable young people).

It can be seen that each objective makes a contribution to the next level in the planning hierarchy.

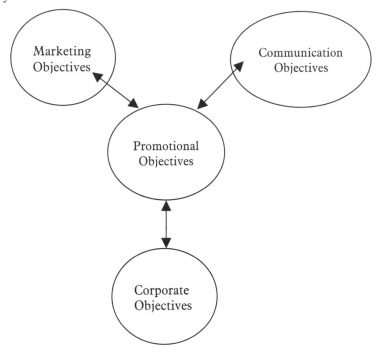

SMART objectives

Objectives must be specific, measurable, achievable, realistic and timed. This is particularly important for the charity since it has limited resources and will be judged by the many stakeholders, including the charities commission to ensure it has been efficient in its operations.

Communication objectives

Tend to be expressed in terms of affecting

- Attitudes and perception
- Awareness
- Action

What do they do?

They provide a number of different benefits including

(a) **Direction and focus** for the whole charity. This means that all activity will be co-ordinated to achieve the set objective leading to an integrated campaign of activity. This means that wastage of activity is avoided, particularly as we are on a tight budget and we wish to keep funds for our works.

(b) They communicate the **values and scope** of the activity for all participants. This is particularly important for a charity since there are many stakeholders. It is important that the volunteer manning our charity shop has a similar understanding to all other members of staff so that a cohesive approach is taken to fund raising.

(c) **Benchmark** for measuring success. SMART Objectives will indicate what is to be achieved by when and by whom. For example each piece of fundraising direct mail will be measured against our objectives for level of donations within a specific cost. Objectives can be long term or shorter milestones along the way.

(d) Determine the best strategy. By knowing what we must achieve, the methods we must use become fairly obvious. For example in order to achieve the awareness levels set for Barnardos the choice of P.R and advertising become important. If the objectives were more direct- for example to persuade each supporter to pledge a donation of £200 then direct marketing activity would be used.

The very process of setting objectives ensures that the context and current situation is reviewed which is a helpful activity to go through and also target markets are considered, in this case any one of a number of stakeholders. As a charity this is particularly important when many of our staff are volunteers and may not have the professional training to help them organise their activities.

Concluding remarks

Setting objectives is vitally important to ensure the success of any organisation but is particularly important in the charity business. Without knowing where we are going as a charity it would be impossible to determine how we are going to get there. Objectives are set to set the strategic direction of the charity and enable all stakeholders to be pulling together to achieve the stated outcomes in the most efficient and effective manner.

9 TUTORIAL QUESTION: CONSUMER BUYING BEHAVIOUR

(a) The general stages in the buying process have been identified by Kotler as follows.

    (i) Need recognition
    (ii) Information search

(iii) Evaluation of alternatives

(iv) Purchase decision

(v) Post purchase evaluation

(i) The process begins when the buyer *recognises a need* or problem. This can be triggered by internal stimuli, such as hunger or thirst, or external stimuli, such as social esteem. If the need rises to a *threshold level* it will become a *drive*, and, from previous experience the buyer will know how to satisfy this drive through the purchase of a particular type of product.

The task for the marketer is to identify the circumstances and/or stimuli that trigger a particular need and use this knowledge to develop marketing strategies that trigger consumer interest.

(ii) Once aroused the customer will *search for more information* about the products that will satisfy the need. The information search stage can be divided into two levels. The first is 'heightened attention', where the customer simply becomes more receptive to information about the particular product category. The second stage is 'active information search'. The extent of active search will depend on the strength of the drive, the amount of information initially available, the ease of obtaining additional information and the satisfaction obtained from the search.

The task for the marketer is to decide which are the major information sources that the customer will use and to analyse their relative importance. According to Kotler consumer information sources fall into four groups.

(1) *Personal sources*: family, friends, neighbours, work colleagues

(2) *Commercial sources*: advertising, salespeople, packaging, displays

(3) *Public sources*: mass media, consumer rating organisations

(4) *Experiential sources*: handling, examining, using the product

Through this information-gathering process the consumer will learn about competing brands and their relative pros and cons. This will enable the consumer to narrow down the range of alternatives to those brands that will best meet his or her particular needs - what has been called the 'choice set'. The marketer's task is to get his brand into the customer's *choice set*.

(iii) Most current models of *evaluation* are cognitively oriented - in other words they take the view that the customer forms judgements largely on a *conscious and rational basis*. Kotler states that, as the consumer is trying to satisfy some need with the buying process, he will be looking for certain benefits from the product chosen and each product will be seen as a 'bundle of attributes' with varying capabilities of delivering the benefits sought and hence satisfying the need. The composition and the relative importance of the components of this bundle of attributes will differ between customers, and therefore the marketer should determine what importance the customer attaches to each attribute.

In order to ensure that the brand has the best chance of being chosen by the consumer, the marketer has a range of options for action.

(1) *Modifying the brand.* Redesigning the product so that it offers more of the attributes that the buyer desires. Kotler calls this 'real repositioning'.

(2) *Altering beliefs about the brand.* Kotler recommends that this course of action be pursued if the consumer underestimates the qualities of the brand, and calls it 'psychological repositioning' ('Not just for breakfast').

(3) *Altering beliefs about competitors' brands.* This course of action would be appropriate if the consumer mistakenly believes that a competitor's brand

has more quality than it actually has, and can be referred to as 'competitive repositioning'.

(4) *Altering the importance weights of attributes.* The marketer would try to persuade consumers to attach more importance to the product attribute in which the brand excels.

(5) *Calling attention to neglected attributes,* particularly if the brand excels in these attributes. ('Have you forgotten how good they taste?').

(6) *Shifting the buyer's ideals.* The marketer would try to persuade consumers to change their ideal levels for one or more attributes.

(iv) The *decision processes* involved in a major purchase such as a car are very different from the decision processes involved in the purchase of chocolate confectionery. Assael presents a typology of consumer decision making based on the *extent of decision making* and the *degree of involvement* in the purchase.

Assael's typology comprises four types of decision-making.

(1) *Complex decision-making* occurs when *involvement is high* and the consumer *searches and considers alternatives,* such as in the purchase of major items like cars, brown goods, white goods etc.

Complex decision making will not occur every time and if the brand choice is repetitive the consumer learns from experience and purchases a brand known from previous experience with little or no decision making (*brand loyalty*).

(2) *Low involvement decision making*

- Customers sometimes go through a decision making process even if not highly involved in the purchase because they have little experience of the product area (*limited decision making*). In this case the customer will go through the process of information search and the evaluation of alternatives, albeit to a lesser extent than for complex decision making.

- Limited decision making may also occur when the *customer seeks variety;* for example, customers may be likely to switch between low involvement brands in a quest for interest in the product area. Such *variety-seeking behaviour* is likely to occur when the customer perceives minimal risk and has little commitment to a particular brand. The brand switch is unlikely to be preplanned and may occur at the place of purchase: for example, while he is actually going round the supermarket the customer may decide to try a new type of biscuit.

(3) '*Inertia*', comprises low involvement with the product and no decision making. Inertia implies that the customer is buying the same brand, not out of any brand loyalty, but because it is not worth the time or trouble to search for an alternative.

(v) *Post purchase* of the brand the consumer will experience some level of satisfaction or dissatisfaction, depending on the closeness between the consumer's product expectations and the product's perceived performance. These feelings will influence whether the consumer buys the brand again and also whether the consumer talks favourably or unfavourably about the brand to others.

(b) Rice identifies five characteristics associated with the success of new products.

(i)   *Relative advantage:* the extent to which the consumer perceives the product to have an advantage over the product it supersedes, implying that, the greater the perceived advantage, the greater the probability of adoption.

(ii)   *Compatibility:* the degree to which the product is consistent with existing values and past experiences of the potential customers, the assumption being that the less a product is compatible with consumer values, the longer it will take to be adopted.

(iii)   *Complexity:* the degree to which a new product is perceived to be complex and difficult to use. The more difficult it is perceived to be, the harder it will be for the product to be accepted.

(iv)   *Trialability.* It is believed that new products are more likely to be adopted when customers can try them out on an experimental basis.

(v)   *Observability:* a measure of the degree to which adoption of the product, or the results of using the product, is visible to friends, neighbours and colleagues. This seems to affect the diffusion process by allowing potential customers to see the benefits of the product, and thus increase (or even create) a 'want' for themselves. This process can be given added impetus if the product is seen to be used by celebrities or other role models. This factor obviously lends itself more to some products than others.

10   TUTORIAL QUESTION: ORGANISATIONAL BUYING BEHAVIOUR

(a)   Dibb *et al* identify four types of organisational markets - producers, resellers, governments and institutions.

(i)   *Producer markets* comprise those organisations that purchase products for the purpose of making a profit by using them to produce other products or by using them in their own operations. This may include buyers of raw materials and of semi-finished and finished items used to produce other products.

(ii)   *Reseller markets* consist of intermediaries such as retailers and wholesalers who buy the finished goods in order to resell them to make a profit. Other than minor alterations, resellers do not change the physical characteristics of the products they handle.

(iii)   *Government markets* comprise those national and local governments who buy a variety of goods and services to support their internal operations and to provide the public services that are within their remit, normally making their purchases through bids or negotiated contracts.

(iv)   *Institutional markets* comprise those organisations that seek to achieve charitable, educational, community or other non-business goals.

BPP PUBLISHING

Departmental influences

Within the
organisation

Cell 1
Purchasing
agent

Cell 2
Buying
centre

Within the
buying
department

In
other
departments

Cell 3
Professionalism

Cell 4
Organisational
environment

In other
organisations

(b) *Cell 1: the purchasing agent.* This represents the buyer, located in the quadrant which is within the organisation and within the purchasing department. Various factors will influence the buyer, including social factors, price and cost factors, supply continuity and risk avoidance.

(i) *Social factors* include the relationships, friendships and antipathies that exist between buyer and suppliers and the extent to which these impinge on purchasing decisions. Whilst in an ideal world such social factors should not influence decision making, they are, in reality, an important factor in the equation.

(ii) *Price and cost factors* are obviously important and can include such things as the economic state of the buying organisation, the level of competition among suppliers, any cost/benefit analyses that might have been conducted, the purchasing budget and the personality and background of the purchasing agent (for example, an agent with an accountancy background may be more cost conscious).

(iii) *Supply continuity* is a function of the number of suppliers that are available and the importance of the purchased item to the organisation.

(iv) *Risk avoidance* is a common motivation for organisational buyers. Buyers can typically cope with risk in a number of ways.

(1) Exchanging technical and other information with their customers and prospects.

(2) Dealing only with those suppliers with which the company has previously had favourable experiences.

(3) Applying strict (risk reducing) rules.

(4) Dealing only with suppliers who have a long-established and favourable reputation.

(5) Introducing penalty clauses, for example for late delivery.

(6) Multiple sourcing to reduce the degree of dependence on a single supplier.

Cell 2: the buying centre. This cell equates to the Decision Making Unit, where the focus is within the firm but between departments. Some of the influencing factors in this cell include organisation structure and policy, power, status and conflict procedures, and gatekeeping.

(i) With regard to organisational structure and policy, the place of the purchasing department within the organisation is very important as it will determine such matters as the level of influence and the reporting relationships. Policy and history will determine the extent to which the buyer can take autonomous action.

(ii) Power, status and conflict procedures relate to the degree to which the buyer or purchasing department wishes to change or maintain the status quo. For example, decentralisation and divisionalisation of the organisation may motivate outside departments to initiate their own buying decisions.

(iii) Gatekeeping controls the flow of information in the organisation and the person who acts as the gatekeeper can exert considerable influence.

Cell 3: professionalism. This cell examines the influence of professional standards and practice in other organisations, the main factors being specialist journals, conferences and trade shows, word of mouth communication and supply-purchase reciprocity.

(i) Specialist journals, conferences and trade shows are likely to be the source of much professional knowledge and provide a good vehicle for the updating of such knowledge. In addition, professional organisations usually attempt to set standards for professional conduct.

(ii) Word of mouth communication, or the professional 'grapevine' can act as a potent force within the profession.

(iii) Supply-purchase reciprocity refers to arrangements whereby two organisations reach an agreement to supply each other.

Cell 4: the organisational environment. This cell is concerned with factors outside of both the purchasing department and the organisation, including economic, commercial and competitive forces, the political, social and legal environment, technological change, co-operative buying (through, for example, the formation of consortia), and the nature of the supplier. It is often assumed that large organisations make inflexible suppliers as their size enables them to adopt a 'take it or leave it' attitude. However, they probably offer a more reliable and less risky service.

11 TWO PRACTICAL MODELS

Examiner's comments. Unfortunately, very few students were able to illustrate their answers with meaningful applications. This reflects previous answers to similar questions. It appears that whilst models are well used in *marketing* strategy thinking, this is not the case with *communications* strategy.

What are models?

A model is a simplified interpretation of a system or process which can be used to assist understanding, develop calculations and scenarios and predict the occurrence of events. In subjects such as communication and buyer behaviour there are a number of complex variables that need to be understood in order to anticipate likely outcomes to events. For example, these events may be advertising messages, word-of-mouth communications, attitudes and brand or purchase experiences.

There are a number of different types of model as defined by the Market Research Society.

- Micro or Macro

- Data-Based or Theory Based
- Descriptive or Predictive
- Behavioural or Statistical
- Qualitative or Quantitative
- Static or Dynamic

Strengths and Weaknesses of Models

Marketing communications models have a number of strengths and weaknesses which impact on marketing managers.

Advantages

(a) They provide a succinct range of parameters which managers can use to aid their planning, strategy and tactics. Research topics can be prompted as a result of the use of suitable models and frameworks.

(b) Models help ensure that managers ask the right questions and that the totality of an issue is covered.

(c) Models can help the planning and implementation process by ensuring that a logical sequence of activities is adopted.

(d) The use of models to assist understanding of complex activities is important when different variables can be the cause for concern or under performance.

(e) Models are of particular use when they can be used to predict events (such as behaviour), as a response to a stimulus (such as a sales promotion or DRTV campaign).

Weaknesses

Just as models have a number of strengths they also contain a number of drawbacks.

(a) One danger is that they can encourage managers to adopt a prescriptive approach such that they ignore the context in which the event is currently situated.

(b) The use of models may discourage lateral thinking and team work, with the consequence that opportunities are overlooked or ignored.

(c) Some models may be inaccurate or such a simplification that they do not really represent the system or process they were originally designed to interpret. For example, the linear models of communication fail to consider the context in which communication occurs, the interaction and behaviour of the people involved or the influence of the intervening variables in the process.

Example 1

The attitude construct, *Cognitive - Affective - Conative*, is a very simple model which suggests that communications aimed at changing behaviour need to first be rooted in the provision of knowledge and information, then stimulate a feeling or degree of preference and then motivate an individual to act or behave in a particular way.

$$\text{Cognitive} \qquad \text{Affective} \qquad \text{Conative}$$
$$\text{Learn} \longrightarrow \text{Feel} \longrightarrow \text{Do}$$

Many advertising campaigns and subset models have been built around this construct. The AIDA model and the Hierarchy of Effects models such as those of Lavidge and Steiner, have been developed around this sequential progression.

When new products or brand variants are launched the first task is to make the target audience aware of the availability of the offering and to provide them with sufficient information.

The next task for these brands, and those that are already established in the market, is to stimulate interest and/or remind potential or current buyers of the brand so that they form particular (positive) feelings towards it.

This can be seen in terms of marketing communication messages that suggest that people (like you) prefer this brand over another, or that this brand matches your requirements, or that the rewards obtained from using this brand will match the individual's expectations. The Oxo series of advertisements seek to identify with the target audience by portraying a typical family in action, so that the viewer sympathises with the family predicament and associates the context with Oxo as the only gravy-cube brand worth buying.

Behaviour, or the conative construct, is manifest in messages that instruct a particular course of action such as requesting a brochure, buying a product or requesting a trial.

This model is useful in that different promotional tools can be seen to be of particular use at particular stages. Advertising and direct marketing to develop awareness, public relations and advertising to generate preference and feelings, with personal selling, direct marketing, sales promotion and point of purchase activities aimed at provoking action.

Example 2

The second model to be considered is the linear model of communication developed originally by Wilbur Schramm.

The communication process

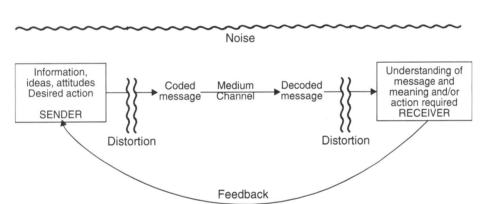

This is an early descriptive model that explains how communication was thought to work. A source devised a message that was transmitted through a channel of communication that is then noticed, decoded and interpreted. Feedback to the source may occur and noise in the communication system may prevent reception or distort interpretation.

This model is useful in that it can encourage managers to identify correctly the problem that exists and then devise and construct messages that they feel their target audiences will be able and willing to understand and act upon as necessary. This model impacts upon the source credibility, message design, media planning and market research (feedback) to understand whether the correct message has reached, and been interpreted correctly by, the target.

Whilst this model is a useful tool it suggests that communications operate in a vacuum (despite the noise element) and does not take into account the behaviour and interaction of the people involved.

Conclusion

Models play a particularly useful role in marketing communications through their ability to simplify the different processes and to educate individuals not only about how the process works but also what actions need to be undertaken at each stage in the development of marketing communication activities.

However, they are not good predictive tools and are certainly not a replacement for management judgement.

12   ATTITUDES

> **Examiner's comments**. It was important here to recognise the theoretical components of attitude and include examples to illustrate the practical use of this in designing marcomms activity. Better answers demonstrated some of the difficulties in changing attitudes.

Presentation to Marketing Colleagues and Brand Managers

By: Marketing Research Manager

Using Marcomms to Influence Attitudes and Buyer Behaviour

I have been asked by the marketing director to give a short presentation to you to highlight the importance of understanding the attitudes held by our consumers. In order to ensure that our marketing communications are effective it is important to establish

- What an attitude consists of

- Whether attitudes affect buyer behaviour and in what way

- If marketers can shape attitudes to achieve a more positive buyer response to our marketing activity

I intend to use examples from our own and other businesses to illustrate my presentation. Please ask questions as we go through the presentation.

What is an Attitude?

A simple way of looking at attitude is to look at the three components that make up an attitude. These are as follows

(a) **Cognitive**. This is the knowledge and beliefs that we have about a brand or product and can be acquired through past experience, learnt from what we have been told, or read. Obviously much of our marcomms activity, for example our advertising, aims to inform the customer. For example the Toyota Prius advertising told of its unique product features i.e. dual fuel technology and the improved running costs that this would bring. However for some customers the most important information to help them make their decision to buy is the guarantee to buy back after 5 years. As marketers we need to know what knowledge customers have about our products and where they found this information from.

(b) **Affective**. This is how our customer feels about the product or brand in question. It is their evaluation of the information offered. By showing the environmental benefits of the new model using "nice" family images we are hoping that the idea of using cleaner fuels will be accepted by the customer as a good thing and they will feel well disposed to our product. Therefore we need to try and understand what our customers feel about our product, brand and company. A negative view is not likely to translate to positive sales.

(c) **Conative**. This is how our customer will decide to act and refers to our individual's predisposition to act in a certain way. This behaviour can be observed through market research, which should be carried out pre and post purchase.

When looking at attitudes it is important to try and understand whether the attitude to the product, the brand or the company is most important. In addition Fishbein suggested that the attitude to the act of buying was more important than the attitude to the actual product. This is very important in our own car market where attitudes to act of buying a brand new car will be affected by other people's attitudes, and not just our customers.

Much of the press advertising done by our dealers in August is stressing the benefits of being the first person to have a car with the brand new number plate.

Do Attitudes Affect Behaviour?

It is suggested that the three components are hierarchical and sequential. In other words consumers first must have knowledge of the brand, then they must like the brand and then they will then act in a positive way. However we know from our own experience that there are times when we will behave in a less pre determined way. For example although many of our potential customers have a positive feeling and knowledge about our brand they still buy a cheaper competitor product. Sometimes our affective component is formed after purchase and sometimes we act without liking or having knowledge about a product, particularly with impulse purchase of products. Sales people in our dealers may often try to incentivise a sale by including optional extras at no extra charge. The consumer may take these without fully understanding the features or liking them but may grow to like them after use.

Therefore it is important for us as marketers to determine not just attitudes to the product or brand, but attitudes to the act of buying that product or brand and also the sequence of events in consumer choice.

Attitudes can be difficult to change, since they may have been formed over a long period of time. They are often inter-linked and so before we can persuade a sceptical customer to buy the new Prius we must first un-ravel their attitudes to Toyota as a brand and even their attitudes to buying Japanese cars. In addition different customers may have different attitudes- it is important to try and discover segments with similar attitudes in order to direct the most appropriate marcomms activity to suit their needs.

Shaping Attitudes to Affect Buyer Purchase

As shown attitudes are fairly complex but now I wish to mention some of the methods that we can use as marketers to help shape attitudes to help achieve a more positive outcome towards our products.

A   **Change the cognitive element (knowledge and beliefs about the brand)**

This can be done in several ways

- **Demonstrate a new attribute**

  Littlewoods have recently promoted the fact that customers can have free home delivery of any product, no matter what the price and that they are always open via the Internet. This new feature for a retail company has set a new standard by which other companies will be judged and they will appear poor in comparison.

- **Change the Salience of an attribute**

  Traditionally cars have been sold on features like styling, speed, safety and so on. We are now teaching the consumer that something else should be high on their agenda in car choice- particularly during the time of fuel shortages i.e., gas fuel will reduce pollution.

- **Change beliefs**

  Volkswagen have been relatively successful with their surprisingly ordinary prices campaign which have helped change attitudes of consumers who had believed that their cars were too expensive to be considered. Kellogg's have also been successful in changing beliefs about the usage of their product so that it is now seen as a healthy "weight reducing" product after their campaign which used dieters in Scotland taking part in the 2 week diet challenge.

- **Change beliefs about a competitor's product**

  This will work if your product has true benefits compared to the competitors offering. Burger King has stressed that their burger is much bigger than a competitor! Pepsi came out best in taste tests compared to their nearest rival.

B **Change the Affective Element**

Using messages that allow your customers to like your brand can do this. Corporate branding activity, the use of cause related marketing and public relations could help here. A good example is the Tesco computers for Schools campaign, which encouraged us to believe that Tesco, was a "good" company. In addition using advertising that is fun and likeable may play a role although some companies prefer to irritate in order to get noticed!

Companies may use individual's that are liked by their customers in the hope that the warm feeling towards the individual may have a halo effect on the brand itself- a good example here is using Robbie Williams in the Pepsi advertising.

Many products find that showing their product being used in a fun environment will ensure affection is proffered. An example can be seen when looking at Gap advertising, using positive images and nice music to present their clothes to a young and vibrant consumer.

Sales promotion activity, free samples etc can reward consumers and make them feel valued by the company. Boots Advantage points reward and pamper customers and make people feel positive towards the retail brand.

C **Change behaviour**

This is more difficult but can be achieved through point of sale promotions, free trial offers or price incentives to encourage behaviour change before altering beliefs or affect. This will then lead to hopefully a change of attitude once knowledge about the product has been obtained through trial.

Conclusion

As can be seen the importance of customer attitudes in shaping behaviour is of interest. Marketers should consider attitudes when designing marcomms activity, since they can affect the best message, media, and method to be used.

However the relationship is complex and attitude change may be more difficult to achieve than the above would suggest. It is important to discover for each brand which components are important. Although attitudes in total are fairly consistent changing the individual components can go some way towards creating a more positive attitude to the brand. Skoda is a great example of how attitudes to a brand can be changed considerably.

The job here should be less difficult and I welcome your discussions on the nature and role of attitudes for our own brand. Market research can help identify the components of attitudes to our brands at the present time and monitor the changes in beliefs, affect and action throughout our campaigns.

13   PERCEIVED RISK

Memorandum

Perceived risk and its impact on our charity – Teen scope

To: Senior Management
From: Marketing Manager

December 2001

The concept of perceived risk is important when understanding any decision. **Stakeholders** may have a fear of supporting our charity, whether this support is in the form of donations, volunteering, buying a product from our shops or coming to work for us. This report poses a set questions for discussion at our next meeting, and makes some suggestions about the role that marketing communications can play in **managing risk**.

What is perceived risk?

The way in which people perceive the world is influenced by their age, education, experience and other complex psychological factors. Any area of **decision making** carries consideration of risk, but is particularly strong when large sums of **money** are involved and when the decision is being made for the **first time**.

Perceived risk is likely to be higher during the **information search** stage of the decision making process, and at the time when the decision is actually made. Therefore different communications tools may be needed at each stage, so that sufficient information can be provided. For example if we were trying to get donors to support us in their will, then a simple **branding message** to raise awareness could be followed by a substantial **direct marketing** pack and inbound telephone marketing to explain any issues of concern.

Types of risk

(a) **Financial risk** – Can I afford to give my money to this charity? We can overcome this with marcomms by showing that support can cost from just £2.00 per week- or less than the cost of a daily newspaper. Will my on line donation be secure? Encryption services will help allay such fears.

(b) **Performance risk** – Will the charity do what it says it will? Will my money be wasted on administration costs? Marketing communications can emphasise that the £2 per week is sufficient to run the help line for 24 hours, and answer another 25 calls from distressed teenagers. PR can be used to spread case studies showing where our work has been successful. In addition producing mailings that do not look too glossy or expensive will help promote the image that we are frugal. Users of the service can be reassured that the service is confidential. Branding is vital here, so that all stakeholders know what the charity does.

(c) **Physical risk** – Volunteers may feel concerned about their safety, so good internal marketing, operational handbooks and training can help allay any fears. Door to door collections will be organised so that they work in groups. People buying goods from our store can be reassured that they are of good quality, and be offered guarantees to allay fears over faulty goods.

(d) **Social risk** – Will my volunteering impress friends and colleagues or will I be seen as a an interfering "do gooder"? Building the brand so that it stands for something positive is essential, so that donors will wear their yellow ribbons with pride. The NSPCC has done extremely well in this regard. Endorsements by celebrities for our cause could be used. Internal marketing can be used to bring our paid staff and volunteers together to encourage a sense of belonging. Advertising can be used to show that volunteers come from all walks of life

(e) **Ego risk** – Involvement in the charity, whether through donation, volunteering or working must make the individual feel good about themselves. Incentives (simple thank you gifts) for donors raising a certain amount of money, or award ceremonies for volunteers who have made a special contribution, along with an internal newspaper to feature employees involvement, could all be considered.

(f) **Time** – Many supporters may be concerned about the amount of time this will take. Calls for volunteers will state what can be achieved in just a small amount of time. Direct marketing will use methods such as direct debit and pre-filled forms to reduce the effort of donating. Envelopes can be left for donors to fill at their convenience. On line facilities can also add convenience. Branding instruments that keep top of mind awareness allow consumers to decide quickly which charity that they will support.

Charities- a special case?

As a low involvement decision for some of our supporters who drop a few pennies into our collection tin, perceived risk may be minimal. However charities are a special case since they have many **stakeholders with differing expectations** about what the charity can do for them. These include donors, employees, volunteers and agencies including commercial sponsors that can provide a great boost to our income. We need to evaluate the perceived risk for all stakeholders and act to reduce this.

There are many competing causes, and stakeholders will become involved with the ones that give them maximum benefits and where the gain outweighs the risks

We therefore require our communication to do a number of different jobs, and we have a relatively **small budget**. Our branding has to be strong and our marcomms activity must be integrated to ensure that we are efficient and effective.

In short our marketing communication activity and brand needs to:

(a) **Differentiate** our charity so that performance risk is reduced

(b) **Reinforce** and add credibility to our work, to reduce social and performance risk

(c) **Inform** all stakeholders sufficiently to reduce all areas of risk

(d) **Persuade** them to get involved by reducing time and financial risk, and offering social and ego benefits that outweigh the risk perceived.

Conclusions

As with all services consideration of perceived risk throughout the decision making process is important and our marcomms plans must ensure that the right strategies address this important area . Please send any further ideas and questions for discussion at the next meeting.

14   CLIENT NEEDS

Introduction

Advertising agencies have been subjected to a number of significant external pressures in the last ten to fifteen years. Their response to these pressures has been mixed and in many cases cautious, perhaps mindful of the need to monitor and avoid fashion swings and management fads.

Reasons for possible incompatibility

The reasons why some of these organisations have failed to keep pace with their clients' needs are as follows.

1   Hierarchical structures
2   Market complexity
3   Reliance on the commission payment scheme
4   Failure to implement integrated marketing communications
5   The plethora of new media and subsequent fragmentation
6   Audience fragmentation
7   The variable quality of overseas support
8   Poor positioning
9   Agency complacency

Many of these points are interrelated and the causality factor often hard to determine. Time does not permit a full examination of all these issues, so I shall select a few and consider some of the points in more detail.

The *structure* adopted by many advertising agencies is *hierarchical* and in many ways ill-suited to flexibility and the necessary speed of reaction required by many clients. These structures have strong historical roots, and in that sense are hard to change. International operations demand consideration and preferably experience of *cross cultural issues*, networking and, in many cases, *delegation* to country agencies, some of whom may require more support and guidance than others. Hierarchies require authority and control in order that they function appropriately. Such conditions may not always exist overseas, may be incompatible with client structures and may hinder the decision making process.

Developing international and global brands is a *complex activity* which requires special skills, from both a client and agency perspective. These may be hard to secure. When looked at in terms of the level of investment associated with international brand support, the issue becomes increasingly more complex and difficult.

Management consultancies have taken a lot of strategic work away from many advertising agencies. This has had a knock-on effect in terms of international brand support. Poor positioning therefore has been a contributory factor to this problem of incompatibility.

The plethora of *new media and subsequent fragmentation* of both audiences and media have proved problematic. Some traditional full service agencies have developed central media buying units in order to provide added value for clients but the issue of media planning and scheduling has become more complex. When an international dimension is superimposed, so the degree of complexity increases.

Complacency and a lack of drive to change is a contributory factor in many cases. A predilection to preserve the status quo regarding their relationships with clients suggests that some agencies lack strategic vision and may also not be fully aware of their *clients' goals*. The fault may, perhaps, lie with clients not communicating their marketing communication strategies effectively. Matters are certainly not helped by the willingness of many clients to change agencies mid term, or as a result of merger and acquisition activity.

How might agencies adjust?

There are therefore, many potential gaps between the expectation of clients and their respective agencies. One of the choices agencies need to make is whether to anticipate client needs internationally or whether to remain orientated to the domestic arena and make ad hoc arrangements to support any client who develops an overseas requirement.

How integrated does the agency need to be? Full integration for all agencies is obviously not practical, feasible or strategically viable. However, in terms of meeting client needs, restructuring and adaptation to the new environment with a view to establishing differing levels of integration, and in this case international support, may be useful. Gronstedt and Thorson (1996) suggest five different agency structures, ranging from the Consortium of agencies at one level through the Dominant Agency, the Corporation, the Matrix and the Integrated Organisation at the other level. These represent different means by which agencies might structure themselves in order that they might develop across international markets and meet the needs of their clients. It is interesting to note that at each end of this spectrum of integrated structures, the levels of integration and staff expertise are inversely related. The consortium allows for high levels of expertise but little integration whilst the integrated agency offers high levels of integration, obviously, but low levels of expertise. Agencies need to establish the right balance to suit their client needs.

At the heart of this problem about incompatibility there seem to lay three main issues. These are about Structure, Strategy and Relationships. Agencies and clients need direction and knowledge in order that they can manage these three variables and in doing so reduce or at least minimise any gap in expectations and support.

15   OPINION LEADERS

> **Examiner's comments.** This was a fairly popular question but many students did not really understand the difference between an opinion leader and former, which could form the start of the answer. The use of diffusion of innovation models can help, providing a link with the marcomms strategy can be made, but this is not the only issue to be considered. Word-of-mouth campaigns could have been discussed, but not many did so.

Introduction

My response to this question will be based around an understanding of communication flows and then an appraisal of opinion former and opinion leader concepts.

Multi-step Flows of Communication

The flow of communication in a campaign was first considered to be linear in that information flowed from a source through a channel to a receiver who then provided feedback. This interpretation proved to be inaccurate in that it failed to account for the many variables that can impact on the communication process. One of the main variables is the influence of other people, shaping and redirecting the flow, content and intended meaning of messages.

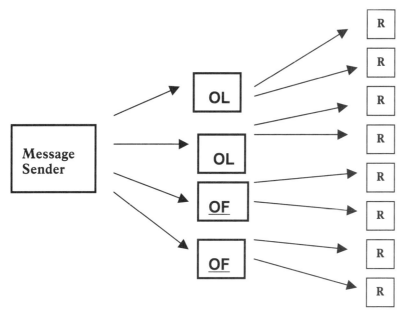

Figure 1
The Two-Step Model
of Communication

The Two-Step Model (see Figure 1) and multi-step flow models of communication reflect the potential impact that these individuals might have on communications.

Types of Influencers

There are two main types of influencer, opinion leaders and opinion formers. The first are usually members of a peer group who have a particular interest and knowledge about a product category or area of interest. They may be friends, family or work colleagues to whom others (opinion followers) turn for advice and reassurance when contemplating a particularly significant purchase. They believe the information they receive is both credible and unbiased when considered in the light of many commercial messages.

Opinion Formers on the other hand are people who are designated as expert and knowledgeable about a particular topic or subject. Very often these people are public figures and it is the nature of their work that bestows the perceived expertise. Opinion formers therefore help shape the thoughts of others by providing information and advice that opinion followers value and believe is credible. Pharmacists, motoring journalists and qualified accountants for example, can provide credible information about medicines, cars and taxation issues respectively for those active in the decision making process. This information may be communicated person to person or through broadcast or print media.

In a marketing context this is an important factor because if it is possible to identify and direct marketing communication messages to those people that are capable of influencing other people then the implications for the efficiency and effectiveness of marketing communications activities is enormous. A popular advertising format is to use a slice of life approach where typical members of the target market are observed discussing issues and one of the characters uses the sponsors product to resolve the difficulty (soap powders, shampoo (for dandruff removal) and furniture).

Opinion leaders provide information for a number of reasons. People like to talk about their product purchases because it can relieve post purchase tension, bestow status on them and provide a means of advising and showing care for others (in this case those considering a similar purchase). Whilst it is difficult to isolate opinion leaders and target them directly, many are known to be innovators or part of the early adopters group within the process of diffusion. These people are actively interested in their topic/area and seek out information in advance of the general population. Identification therefore is helped because they are more likely to attend exhibitions, access specific web sites and read the specialist press. For example, when Sony launched the mini disc they targeted specialist music equipment

BPP PUBLISHING

retailers and held premium prices. The hi-fi enthusiasts (opinion leaders) were keen to buy the latest technology (regardless of price) and they then told others (followers) about their discovery which fed further demand which then allowed Sony to release the product through other high street (mainstream) outlets.

Opinion formers provide information because they are required to do so either because it is part of the job or because they have been contracted to do so or because it is a means of maintaining their own position. Some forms of sponsorship and celebrity endorsement can be regarded as opinion forming if only because they might be regarded as supporting the central act or object of the sponsorship itself. So, David Ginola may act as an endorser for L'Oreal haircare products but he is not known as an expert in haircare, he is seen as supporting the brand, in return for a specific (financial) reward. Opinion formers pass on information because it is part of the job and may only be known to a discrete number of people.

Conclusion

Recognition of the role that opinion leaders and formers can play in assisting the marketing communication process is important if the potential of a brand, and especially new brands and product launches, is to be fulfilled.

16 POSITIONING

> **Examiner's comments.** The presentation format used is important as it can allow a lot of material to be put across. A depth of understanding about the strategic nature of the concept was required here and this was achieved through the examples given. Direct application to the telecomms market was useful.

POSITIONING

What is it?

Why it is so important?

A presentation to the Finance Department

December 2001

Note: This presentation is being made to a non marketing audience, and so jargon will be kept to a minimum. The audience does have company and product knowledge however, and may have an important role in releasing funds to support marketing programmes in future.

Introduction Market background Purpose of talk	As a **brand building** telecom business, it is important that our brand is perceived by customers and other stakeholder groups in a clear and consistent way that **differentiates** us from our many competitors. Our market is now extremely crowded, and many of our **competitors** have a similar offering and are servicing the same market.

One of the key elements of success will be an increased emphasis on the concept of **positioning**. This talk will try and explain what positioning means, evaluate its importance and consider some of the ways that we can use this in our business.

(a)

Segmentation Targeting Positioning	**Positioning** is the final stage of the strategic process. • **Segmentation**-This divides the total market into groups of homogenous people who have similar needs (e.g. business customers employing 500 office based workers or domestic users with ISDN for Internet access). • **Targeting**-Where we choose which segments we can best serve with our appropriate marketing mix. • **Positioning**- designing the company's offering and image, so that it occupies a unique positioning in the customer's mind that is meaningful and distinct.

This is particularly important in crowded market places like ours. It is important to see that **positioning is relative**- it is **how the consumer places us** vis a vis our competitors.

Positioning methods	A number of different methods can be used to position a brand. They tend to be **market** related, **customer** related or **product** related. Explicitly:

(i)   **User**- the brand is positioned according to its user. For example Brewster's restaurants are seen as the family restaurant, Milky Bars are a children's brand

(ii)   **Usage occasion**- The brand for a special occasion e.g. Roses chocolates are promoted as a thank you present.

(iii)   **Disassociation**- Away from the traditional product class. For example Nationwide Building society emphasises that it is not a bank.

(iv)   **Product features**- technological advancement of BMW cars.

(v)   **Benefits**- Direct Line rescue insurance emphasises that in 80% of cases their mechanic will fix your car at the roadside, Babyliss Whisper hairdryers are seen as quieter.

(vi)   **Emotional appeal**- e.g. Volkswagen's "Lupo"- their new baby.

Ask now how the company is perceived by those present. Then show the following positioning by customers.

Innovative

X Ideal
Position

X BT

X Competitor A

High Price ←   → Low Price

C Competitor C

X Present Position

Out of date

This **perceptual map** shows where we are presently perceived by our target market, compared to our competitors, based on research. Although our products are in fact technically more advanced than all of our competitors, they are not seen to be so.

(b)

Why is Positioning important? The Benefits of positioning	The concept of positioning is important for the following reasons.

(i) It makes us focus on the **customer's perception** of our brand relative to the competition. This ensures that we look at our offering from the customer's point of view, and saves us from the trap of our own self importance.

(ii) Positioning allows **differentiation in the market place** and allows competitors to sit side by side, even if they are serving the same target market. For example in the luxury car market there is room for both Mercedes and BMW.

(iii) Desired positioning dictates the most suitable **marketing mix**.

(iv) Positioning means that the **emphasis on price is removed,** and offers a source of sustainable competitive advantage.

(v) If a brand can dominate a position in the consumer's mind, then competitors will find it hard to move them from this position. Therefore positioning acts as a **barrier to entry** and some guarantee of loyalty.

(vi) Can be used to identify **gaps in the market** (for new product development) and allow an analysis of **threats**.

(vii) Shows us that our **perceived position** is not as we might have intended, and therefore suggests that we need to reposition ourselves using integrated marketing communications both to achieve growth plans and to show customers that we are technological leaders in this market.

(viii) Positioning can also be looked at from the point of view of **other stakeholders,** so that any gaps between the different audiences can be seen and acted upon (for example, staff perceptions versus customer views).

(ix) The **customer** will have a clear expectation of our company, and this will dictate **service** and **brand strategy**. Technological superiority gives the expectation of a **premium price,** and this could lead to higher profits.

Conclusions

Questions

As you see, positioning is an important concept, and the adoption of this is a source of competitive success for many companies. It is particularly important since it focuses on the customer's perception and will help determine our strategy for the future.

Marketing communications is vital for positioning, and if integrated properly can be an investment that improves the **efficiency** and **effectiveness** of our whole business. This will bring financial success, and so I hope that you will now wish to be involved and offer support to our marcomms plans for the future.

Any questions?

17 TUTORIAL QUESTION: AUDITING, SEGMENTATION AND POSITIONING

(a) A marketing audit might look for problems and unexpected opportunities in the following areas.

(i) *The marketing environment*

   (1) What are the organisation's major markets, and what is the segmentation of these markets; what are the future prospects of each market segment?

   (2) Who are the customers, what is known about customer needs, intentions and behaviour?

   (3) Who are the competitors, and what is their standing in the market?

   (4) Have there been any significant developments in the broader environment (eg economic, or political changes, population or social changes etc)?

(ii) *Marketing objectives, strategies and plans*

   (1) What are the organisation's marketing objectives and how do they relate to overall objectives? Are they reasonable?

   (2) Are enough (or too many) resources being committed to marketing to enable the objectives to be achieved; is the division of costs between products, areas etc satisfactory?

   (3) Is the share of expenditure between direct selling, advertising, distribution etc an optimal one?

   (4) What are the procedures for formulating marketing plans and management control of these plans; are they satisfactory?

   (5) Is the marketing organisation (and its personnel) operating efficiently?

(iii) *Marketing activities: organisation, systems and productivity*

   (1) A review of sales price levels should be made (eg supply and demand, customer attitudes, the use of temporary price reductions etc).

   (2) A review of the state of each individual product (ie its market 'health') and of the product mix as a whole should be made.

   (3) A critical analysis of the distribution system should be made, with a view to finding improvements.

   (4) The size and organisation of the personal sales force should be studied, with a view to deciding whether efficiency should be improved (and how this could be done).

   (5) In the light of all of the above, a review of the effectiveness of *marketing communications* activities should be carried out.

(b) *Stages of segmentation*

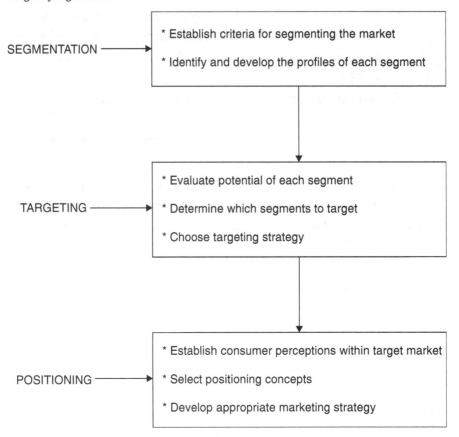

SEGMENTATION
* Establish criteria for segmenting the market
* Identify and develop the profiles of each segment

TARGETING
* Evaluate potential of each segment
* Determine which segments to target
* Choose targeting strategy

POSITIONING
* Establish consumer perceptions within target market
* Select positioning concepts
* Develop appropriate marketing strategy

(c) There are a number of approaches to developing a positioning strategy. These include positioning by:

(i)   Attribute
(ii) Price and quality
(iii) Use or application
(iv) Product user
(v)   Product class
(vi) Competitor

Positioning by *attribute* involves positioning the product by clearly identifying it with a distinct set of attributes which distinguish the product within the market. BMW, the German car manufacturer, whilst positioned within the luxury end of the car market, make constant reference to the engine performance and design as part of their positioning statement. Likewise, Volvo the Swedish car manufacturer have for many years positioned themselves on safety features incorporated into the design of the car. Although most manufacturers have now adopted these techniques, a recent RAC survey (1994) found that 28% of the UK car buying public placed Volvo at the top of the league for safety.

Price and quality are becoming increasingly important as companies attempt to offer more features, better value and improved quality at competitive prices. J. Sainsbury the retail food multiple, promote themselves by stating that 'Good food costs less at Sainsbury's'.

In the third case, the company attempts to position their product or service by deliberately associating it with a specific *use or application*. Kellogg's, the cereal manufacturer, in striving to defend their market position and increase sales, have positioned their main product Corn Flakes as any time of day food, and not just to be eaten at breakfast.

Positioning by virtue of *product user* associates the product with a particular class of user. SmithKline Beecham have positioned 'Lucozade Sport' with the sporting fraternity, and have strengthened this through endorsement advertising using major sporting personalities. Leyland paints, a division of Kalon plc, advertise their paint products as 'The paints the professionals use'.

It is possible to position a company brand within a *product class* or an associated product class. Kraft foods, who produce 'Golden Crown', have positioned their product with respect to the associated product class, butter. Heinz, who produce a range of 'Weight Watcher' foods, position these against normal but more calorific foods.

A *competitor's position* within a market may be used as a frame of reference in order to create a distinct positioning statement. Avis car rental use the slogan 'We're number 2, so we try harder'. Here the market leader is being used as a reference point to create a competitive statement. The key determinant for the marketer is whether claims made within a promotional campaign which use blatant comparisons can be substantiated through better quality, service, value, cost and so on.

18 PROMOTIONAL MIX

'The Strategic Significance of the Promotional Mix'

by

CIM Student

Slide 1 – Introduction and Welcome

Good evening ladies and gentlemen, my name is Sam Smithers from Grubb, Allen and Pollen. May I take this opportunity to thank you for inviting me to talk to you about marketing communications and in particular the strategic impact of the various elements of the promotional mix.

Slide 2 – Agenda

As you can see, my plan for this session is to first consider the elements of the promotional mix before examining the strategic significance and benefits of an integrated approach to marketing communications practice.

The promotional plan
Strategic significance
Integration
Benefits and difficulties
Conclusions
Question time

I shall be using a few examples to illustrate my points and, of course, I welcome questions at any time, although there will be some time at the end to discuss points of interest. I shall aim to finish at 2045hrs.

Slide 3 – The Promotional Mix

Marketing communications is just a part of the total marketing plan or marketing mix. Indeed the two elements are often confused but in order for clarity the marketing mix is composed of a number of different elements such as price, product, distribution, people and promotional activities. It is these elements in combination that provide the overall marketing plan.

One of these elements, promotion, provides a powerful means by which a marketing mix is presented to its target audience. The successful communication of the marketing mix is paramount if target markets are to understand the offer being made to them.

In order to affect this communication there are a number of promotional tools that are used or 'mixed' together. These are:

> advertising, sales promotion, public relations,
> personal selling and direct marketing.

These are the tools of the promotional mix.

By mixing the tools together in different ways to meet the needs of the marketing plan, it is possible to achieve one of a number of goals. These are to:

> Create awareness
> To persuade
> To remind/reassure
> To differentiate

The first of these is to make an audience aware of an offering, existence or benefits. Before anyone can form an opinion or attitude, it is necessary to be informed of a product's existence.

Alternatively, awareness levels may be adequate so the task may be to persuade an audience to try a product or resist defecting to a competitive product offering.

A third requirement may be to remind and/or reassure an audience of a product or of the experiences associated with a previous purchase.

Finally, communications can be used to differentiate a product offering, to set it aside from the competition.

Slide 4 – Strategic Significance

The word strategy is often used to mean different things to different people. To me, strategy is not about planning or the development of plans. Plans are the articulation of strategy, a means of bringing together the various means by which a strategy is implemented and goals achieved.

Promotional strategy is about the overall direction and focus of communications. There are three main options: a pull strategy, a push strategy and a profile strategy.

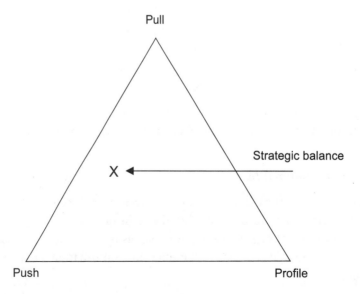

A pull strategy is concerned with communications directed at end users or customers. A push strategy concerns those channel partnerships formed to deliver products and services to end users, commonly referred to as the trade or distributors. A profile strategy concerns the way an organisation is presented to a range of stakeholder audiences and is essentially about corporate image and reputation management.

These three strategies are not used independently of each other, indeed it is important to appreciate that these 3Ps need to work together, and management need to make a judgement about the appropriate balance. As we can see from the diagram, the strategic triangle requires the three approaches to be combined, integrated in such a way that the overall goals will be achieved.

Please remember that this balance need not be static, but must be expected to shift as the context within which each communication campaign changes and evolves, as the environment inside and outside an organisation reshapes itself.

Slide 5 – Integration

Much time and consideration has been given by academics and practitioners to the concept of integrated marketing communications (IMC). Whilst time does not allow me to go into full detail about IMC tonight, may I just say that if IMC is to be achieved then understanding and setting the strategic balance of an organisation's communications is very important.

For successful implementation of each of the 3Ps it is necessary to utilise a different promotional mix. The tools have different properties and enable different goals to be achieved. For example, when launching a new consumer product such as Sunny Delight, it is first necessary to create distribution (push) through the major grocery multiples. This involves personal selling and direct marketing. Once distribution is secured awareness needs to be established in the target audience. This strategy (pull) requires the use of mass communications (in this example) which involves the use of television, poster and print advertising. This can be supported with public relations activities designed to create credible third party comment, and endorsement, about the brand.

Procter and Gamble do not use a profile strategy to any greater degree partly because of their multi-brand policy. However, other companies, such as the AA or British Airways focus a great deal of their communications on raising and sustaining their corporate brands. The corporate brand can act as an umbrella under which product brands can be infused with the corporate ideal and values, saving investment and human resources.

Slide 6 – Benefits and Difficulties

The promotional mix should be integrated if the same consistent message is to be conveyed to each of the various audiences a brand and its parent organisation interacts. By adopting a strategic approach promotional activities can be targeted, streamlined, made efficient and effective.

If the goal is to differentiate through positioning then by using the different tools of the promotional mix and by delivering clear messages positioning can be used as a form of sustainable competitive advantage and thus be difficult for a competitor to replicate.

Communications used by Procter and Gamble enabled Sunny Delight to be positioned as a distinct new refreshing drink for kids. The communications also informed people where to find it in supermarkets (chiller cabinets) and where it should be stored at home (in refrigerators).

A strategic approach can be difficult to establish, particularly when management have little experience of using communications in this way. The structure and form of many communications agencies do not actively encourage a strategic approach to the use of the promotional mix although I am pleased to observe that there does appear to be movement towards a recognition of IMC and the benefits it can bring clients and agencies.

Slide 7 – Conclusions

The promotional mix consists of different tools which are each capable of undertaking different tasks. By setting a communication strategy and then by using the right mix of tools in the right way, it is possible to create awareness, persuade, remind/reassure and differentiate a product brand or a corporate brand.

Slide 8 – Question Time

Thank you for listening to me tonight, have you any questions?

19   PROMOTIONAL MIX AND BRANDING

(a)   The nature of these differences and the impact they each might have on an organisation's integrated marketing communication activities.

To: The CIM Senior Examiner

From: A CIM Student

Date: December 2001

Ref: Promotional Mixes

1.0   Introduction

1.1   This brief report seeks to outline some of the differences between the promotional mixes used in consumer and business-to-business markets.

The promotional mixes developed for these two types of audiences have to be different for a number of reasons. Because of time restrictions I have used three here but there are many others.

2.0   Differences

2.1   Number of decision maker: In consumer markets the number of decision makers is limited to a single or perhaps a couple of people. In business markets (btob) there may be many members of the DMU. Therefore, the promotional mix needs to convey a simple consistent message in consumer markets but in btob markets different messages need to be conveyed to a variety of different people in the DMU. This will put pressure on IMCs to ensure that the variety of messages is correct, that they are being conveyed effectively and that the communication budget is appropriate.

2.2   Message content: Messages in consumer markets are (generally) based more on emotion and imagery rather than rational product benefits used in the btob market. This impacts on the media selected and the way messages are presented.

2.3   Balance of the mix: In view of the above it is not unsurprising that the advertising and sales promotions tend to dominate the mix in consumer markets. In btob personal selling has greater share. Recently however, it can be seen that there is a move from above to below the line work in consumer markets. This is because markets and media are more fragmented and that there are more possibly effective and efficient means of reaching consumers than through the use of mass media. The impact on IMC is huge as it means that customers are coming into contact with the brand in a variety of ways which puts pressure on clients to be consistent with the messages they communicate.

Direct marketing has had a tremendous impact on both markets with particular emphasis on the btob market. Direct marketing, in its various guises, enables organisations to communicate more effectively, frequently and more cost efficiently with their business end users and so reduces the cost of the sales force and enables them to focus the efforts of the specialist sales force more effectively.

For a long time the btob markets have practised the use of integrative approaches to communication. Only recently have those operating in consumer markets started to pay concerted attention to developing IMC.

(b)

3.0 Consumer markets

3.1 The mix used to reach consumer markets will continue to evolve away from a reliance on the use of mass media. With rapid technological developments, and in particular, Internet and digital related technologies, clients operating in consumer markets will look to change the pattern of the communications by incorporating a greater proportion of eCommerce related communications (and distribution patterns). Direct marketing will establish a correspondingly important part of the mix. For example, Amazon books have invested in eCommerce as their total communication and distribution platform and established a large share of the retail book market. Other companies have decided to balance their high street retail presence with Web Site approaches. Chains such as Arcadia and Dixons (Freeserve) have adopted this approach very profitably.

3.2 Business to Business Markets

In the btob markets direct marketing and eCommerce are set to become an even more important part of the promotional mix. The drive for more efficient communications and to be able to account for communication budgets and investments means that the UK can be expected to follow the huge growth in eCommerce established in North America.

3.3 The emphasis on personal selling will not disappear but there will be greater use of direct marketing and eCommerce to complement the promotional activities. For example, IBM have developed their strategy around eBusiness and have been enormously successful as a result. If this is compared with the performance of Compaq Computers who have continued to operate through value added resellers, and all things being equal, technologically related communications appear to be well placed.

4.0 Conclusion

4.1 It seems as if the development of the promotional mixes in both markets will be influenced by technology. The death of mass media communications in the consumer market has long been predicted by a few commentators but in my opinion this is unlikely. New methods will be used to supplement, not replace current methods. New brands in both markets will arise to take advantage of the Internet whilst established brands and products will seek to incorporate and integrate a greater proportion of eCommerce activities as part of a portfolio of communication methods.

4.2 More personalised and integrated communications and associated messages will be adopted by consumer markets. In business to business markets a greater use of emotion and imagery can be expected along with the development of brands (such as Intel) and a more flexible promotional mix where the field sales force does not play such a dominant role.

20 FUTURE TRENDS IN THE PROMOTIONAL MIX

> **Examiner's comments.** This question requests that examples are provided so not doing so will result in a fail. It is important to answer the question and not just write all that is known about direct marketing, but take a broader perspective.

To: Marketing Director

From: Account Director, Direct Marketing Inc.

Date: December, 2000

Re: Moving Away from Mass Advertising

Introduction

This report will highlight the reasons for many of our own clients considering alternatives to mass advertising in order to achieve their marketing communications objectives. It will demonstrate the benefits of using a number of below the line methods and give examples of where this new approach has worked for a number of different clients. It will also consider the likely future scenario for the promotional mix.

Why the change?

1 Cost and wastage

The cost of mass advertising has escalated and many of our clients have been feeling that they are not getting the value for money that is required. The cost for a national TV campaign, achieving perhaps 450 housewives TVR's could be as much as ten million pounds, using television. Production costs have also risen as advertising messages need to be more sophisticated to gain the awareness required.

Research costs to monitor the effectiveness are high and mass techniques have a high wastage factor- why speak to all housewives when your target market is only a small subset of these?

2 Audience and media fragmentation

The introduction of numerous satellite channels, radio networks and a vast array of press titles has meant more choice for the customer who is more selective in terms of viewing. The old days of advertising during a soap to gain a high number of your target market are gone as audiences now wish to be treated as individuals and segments are smaller.

Magazines such as FHM have offered opportunity to reach the male 18-35 markets and have been used by advertisers for beer and spirits.

3 Measurability and accountability

Below the line methods like direct marketing allow far greater targeting, control and measurability. This appeals to most marketing directors (and their financial colleagues) who wish to see what's working and what is not. Direct marketing can be tested on a very small number of potential clients with roll out happening only when the best test pack has been identified. For example Barclaycard have used a different bill stuffer for their male and female customers after tests showed that they were likely to be interested in different special offer events.

Measurements such as cost per enquiry, cost per conversion and gross profitability per mailing are possible along with customer lifetime value.

4 **Competitive forces**

Greater competition has meant for many clients that clutter negates the effect of advertising messages. The company using a different method will stand out as being innovative. Cadbury have had good success with their foray into direct marketing, using direct mail to bring customers to their Internet site and take part in their survey on whether the customer is an optimist or a pessimist (is the glass half empty or half full?)

5 **Technological change**

Costs of technology are being driven down giving access to database marketing for even small companies, using desktop publishing to produce reasonable quality price lists, newsletters etc. The increased information held on customers means a better understanding and more on target message. For example the Boots advantage card, smart card technology allows customers to come in store and gain sales promotion for product that they will find suitable- a far more efficient approach than blanket distribution of sales promotion.

Internet, mobile communications, and database technologies have allowed a seamless and integrated approach for customers. This offers more personalization and tailored messages. It also gives access to customers that would not be contacted via the traditional media.

6 **Globalisation**

The increased amount of international business suggests a shift away from a-t-l approaches because cultural and language differences imply costly changes and inappropriate advertising for some communities. Alternatively a bland approach that serves nobody is often in evidence.

7 **Dynamic markets**

Lead times for advertising and above the line methods can be long and so new methods like Internet and so on offering much more flexibility. Also new markets like internal markets and other stakeholders increase in importance and these will need to be served with the best possible method.

The future

It is likely that fragmentation will continue as new technology will allow different forms of communication, and a far better understanding of the customers needs and communications requirements. Customers will expect a greater use of technology and companies will require cost effective methods.

However the use of the internet and other related technologies cannot operate in isolation- customers need to be directed to the new technologies and mass media techniques are likely to offer an efficient method of corporate branding, profile strategies and also creating awareness.

Other methods like sponsorship will become more available but they will be even more effective when combined with PR and some advertising- an integrated approach.

What is now required is an integrated approach- and our direct marketing experience will allow us to ensure the most effective and efficient method of taking this forward. Agencies will need to incorporate all aspects of the promotional mix and become integrated in terms of their structures so that they have a full understanding of the client's corporate values

A great example of a company using a variety of old and new techniques is Boots. Through their advantage card they are utilising database technology with sales promotion techniques. They are key players in the Well being DRTV channel and have an active web-site. They still spend on A-t-l to ensure awareness of their special offers and to direct traffic to their interactive methods.

To conclude, therefore we would suggest that your company consider in depth a combination of new and old technology, a-t-l and b-t-l to achieve a cost effective, integrated approach to achieve you marcomms objectives. Our company can offer the skills to deliver this effectively and successfully.

21 INTERNET BASED COMMUNICATIONS

> **Examiner's comments.** This is a straightforward question with an easy format. Many students wrote good answers, but the depth was not always sufficient. Facts were presented about the internet, but these were not always related to the context of the question. Better answers recognised the development of relationships as an important factor, and addressed the strategic aspects.

In business-to-business (b2b) markets organisational buying behaviour is more complex than that observed in consumer markets. This is because of the increased number of people involved in the decision making process and the nature of the relationships between organisations. As a result of this and other factors marketing communications in the b2b market is traditionally characterised by the predominance of personal selling and the relatively little use of advertising. In fact it is the complete reversal of business to consumer based promotional activity (b2c) where mass media based communications have tended to be the most important route through to the target audience.

The development of the Internet and related digital technologies has introduced new ways in which audiences in both sectors can be reached. There are many other ways in which organisations can benefit from these developments but these notes will concentrate on communications in the b2b sector.

Very briefly, the Internet and digital technologies can lead to faster communication, more information, lower costs, more effective transactions, a reduction in sales force personnel costs, improved relationships with intermediaries, the development of new/revised types of intermediary, potential for improved levels of customer satisfaction, speedier problem resolution, greater accuracy and less noise in the communication system, provision of exit barriers for intermediaries and an improved use of the communication mix. I will not go into these in detail but will highlight some of the points made.

In the b2b sector the development and maintenance of profitable relationships is important. Part of marketing communications role is to develop these relationships by reducing perceived risk and uncertainty. It also needs to provide clarity and provide fast, pertinent and timely information in order that decisions can be made.

Loyalty

Loyalty between organisations can be improved therefore by targeting information and customised messages at the right people within the partner organisation. Speed of response to customer questions and the clarity of the information provided is important for the development of trust and loyalty.

Productivity

Productivity should be increased as electronic communication not only saves time but also shortens the time between order and delivery.

Reputation

The reputation of our organisation should be enhanced considerably, not only through our web site but also through the way we are perceived to meet the needs of our customers. Subject to the actions of our competitors in this area we may also have a competitive advantage.

Costs

The costs of our communications can also be considerably reduced. Just as sales literature and demonstration packs take time to prepare, even longer to change/update and are quite expensive with a great deal of wastage, brochure ware on the Web site is fast, easily accessible and adaptable. One step further into Web site development will enable us to collect names and addresses, respond to email questions and provide rich data for our sales force. If we develop the Web site still further, then eCommerce transactions will enable routine orders to be completed quickly and at a lower cost, freeing up the sales force to visit established customers more often and opportunities to open new accounts and manage those accounts that are strategically important, more attentively.

Marketing Communications Mix

Digital technologies enable the collection of data for use through on and offline sources. So our direct marketing activities can be improved, our sales promotions targeted to provide real and valued incentives. Even our public relations activities can benefit by placing suitable material on our web pages.

Effectiveness

Finally, digitally-based communications can improve the accuracy of the information we provide and also enable us to measure the effectiveness of our marketing communication activities. However, we must not forget that offline communications are going to still be important and these new communication formats should be considered as an addition to rather than a substitution of our current marketing communications.

Now, whilst I have set out the advantages we must be aware of some of the drawbacks.

Traditional Customers

Internet access for some of our smaller business partners may be restricted and they may prefer to continue having face-to-face contact with our sales force. This we must respect and so deploy our new marketing communications mix carefully and not impose it on unwilling organisations.

Investment /Set Up costs

The set-up costs will be expensive and an appropriate investment approach needs to be adopted. Some parts of this technology can also lock us into relationships which might be difficult to get out off, should conditions change. In effect these are barriers to exit for each party.

Legal and Security

There will also be some legal and information security issues that we need to address in order to reduce any risk our partners might perceive.

End Notes

In order to conclude and summarise our marketing communications with business partners will improve through improved efficiency and effectiveness which in turn will be reflected in the nature and quality of the relationships we hold and ultimately be reflected in our overall performance and meeting our corporate goals.

Improved trust, commitment and a higher propensity to share information must lead to increased business performance. The development of the Internet based communications is a strategic decision that needs to be thought through in terms of the impact it will have on the way we and our partners do business. This in turn will require significant changes in the way we currently communicate and do business in the b2b market.

22 DIFFERENT SECTORS

> **Examiner's comments.** This was a popular question and many students used grids to highlight the difference between the two sectors. Some explained the differences in the communications used but too few answered the question fully.
>
> The question required students to explain how the purpose and use of marketing communications differs, not just explain what the differences are between the two sectors. I feel this reflects the variation between the depth of learning some students are prepared for or expect to make, and the level of attainment this award represents. This is a postgraduate qualification yet some of the examination answers are of a much lower standard. I urge all tutors to impress upon students the need not only to read in their spare time but also to write answers that are reflective and which suggest a quizzical (critical approach).
>
> Good answers discussed marketing communications by exploring what the tasks are in the two sectors, how the sector characteristics demand a different approach and how strategy and tactics can be accommodated through different approaches and the deployment of marketing communication tools.

Introduction

This essay sets out to identify the main differences between business to business and business to consumer sectors and highlights the impact of these differences on the marketing communications strategies. It offers examples of each sector and concludes that the differences are perhaps becoming less pronounced as companies from both sectors are using a variety of promotional tools and pay considerable attention to the role of branding.

	Consumer Markets	*Business Markets*	*Impact on Marketing Communications*
No of buyers	Many	Few	Personal selling more relevant in b-t-b markets. Mass communication methods like advertising more often used in consumer markets
Decision making unit	The family	Gatekeepers Influencers Deciders Buyers	Targeting is easier for the consumer markets. Many different types of media and message may be necessary to reach the different members of the DMUs in b-t-b markets.
Buyer Behaviour	Influenced by intangible and tangible differences	Rational, based on benefits	Branding important in consumer markets. May also be important in business markets if the buyer is a risk avoider and where there are not many perceived functional differences
	Impulse purchase	Likely to be extended decision making	Sales promotion less relevant in b-t-b markets
	Price may be more important	Functional benefits more important	Impact on marcomms messages

Main Differences

The main difference between business to business communications can be seen in the choice of marcomms methods and messages. This becomes clear when we consider the communications strategies for the following companies

Siebel selling in customer relationship management systems into businesses

This company will use personal selling, with sales team made up of a number of different experts. Each expert will communicate with his or her opposite number in the Client Company. They may do some trade advertising but in different magazines- the marketing manager will hear about the benefits of data mining systems in a direct marketing magazine, whereas the IT manager will hear about the technicalities of the system in the IT trade press. Public relations activity will concentrate on press releases using a case study approach to reduce perceived risk. Direct marketing methods will be used alongside exhibitions and road shows. The buying of a full system is extremely extensive and so the amount spent prior to and post purchase will be high. As the distribution chain is likely to be short the push strategy will concentrate on personal selling, allowing control of message and methods. The message will vary, depending on the role in the decision-making unit but is likely to be technical. Profile strategies are becoming increasingly important here since by having a good profile (and brand name) the initial approach to a new customer will be eased.

Thomsons Holidays

Much above the line activity and sales promotional activity will be used to stimulate interest and get a booking form the decision- making unit. The whole family is involved and Thompson has recognised this by providing special videotapes for the youngsters showing them what the holiday will be like to them. Branding is very important and as this is a service trust must be established at the beginning. Membership of trade bodies will help. Exhibitions are less s likely to be used although they may attend lifestyle shows at relevant times. Communications with channel and a push strategy is important here, along with possibly some direct marketing activity. The adoption of new methods of promotion and booking via the Internet has removed some of the reliance on distributors. PR is important and sponsorship of shows like 'Wish you were here?' develop the profile of the company.

Conclusion

It can be seen that there are differences between the two sectors but these differences are becoming blurred as Business to business markets realise the importance of branding and profiling and consumer markets start to adopt crm techniques through the opportunities offered by new technologies such as e commerce, telephony, m- commerce and so on.

23 **PLAN LINKS**

> **Examiner's comments.** This question required a clear answer, which element is the most important. It was not important that students select a particular element, just that they selected one and justified their selection.
>
> Many students chose to select 'integration' which although important is not an element of the plan as previously established.

To: Ms Alice Davis: Manager
From: CIM Student: Marketing Manager
Ref: How parts of a marketing communications plan are linked together.

Further to your request to know more about the linkages within marketing communication plans I have set out what the parts of a marketing communication plan are, and then indicated some of the main linkages. In the second part I argue that we should particular importance to the context analysis as the most important part of the plan.

(a) A marketing communication plan is a sub plan of the marketing plan which in turn feeds the business plan. In other words, these plans are all related to each other and in order to improve the chances of business success these plans must be integrated.

Marketing communications planning framework

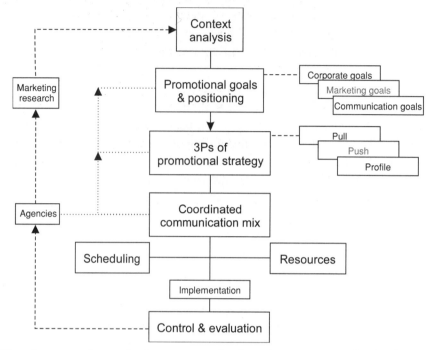

The elements of a marketing communication plan are set out in the following diagram. Whilst the plan may appear to be linear in format, in actual practice many of the elements are actioned in parallel rather than sequentially. In some case parts of these plans are formulated in the minds of those responsible whereas in many large organisations these plans are a formalised articulation of an agreed course of action. Marketing communications can consume large financial and time resources so it is absolutely important that the plans are correct and satisfy the objectives set out.

We know that individually these elements are rather meaningless, it is only by binding them together as a system of inter-related parts do we know that the elements work together and the plans actually work.

At the hub of these plans is a Context Analysis. I shall explain the working in more detail later, but by understanding the situation in which the communication campaign needs to work, for example is it a new or established product, what is the nature of the target audience, is the market growing or declining etc, is it possible to design a plan that will work. The original communication theory stated that in order to be successful it was important for the source of a message to be able to understand and define the problem accurately in order that they formulate a message using symbols and expressions that could be decoded and understood by the target audience. Well, this principle is still important here, we must understand the problem and then feed the other elements of the plan.

Linkages

In the following table I set out some of the main linkages.

Table 1

Objectives	From the marketing plan, from the customer, stakeholder and competitor analysis
Strategic balance	From an understanding of the brand, the needs of the target audiences and relevant stakeholders
Brand positioning	From perceptions, motivations, attitudes or own brand and those of competitors
Message content/style	Involvement, risk, DMU analysis, processing styles and positioning intentions
Promotional tools and media	Target audience media habits, involvement, preferences and resource analysis.

The marketing plan provides the marketing and corporate objectives. The marketing plan also indicates the positioning intentions.

By understanding the target audience the communication objectives can be derived, positioning confirmed and the overall approach for the creative brief and media plan determined.

By understanding the needs of the different stakeholders it is possible to determine the right balance for the strategic direction. Developments in the external environment can influence the goals, the positioning and the message and media formats. Even the level of financial resources can be affected by swings in economic or political conditions.

The goals themselves determine the positioning, the strategy and the promotional mix plus the budget. It could also be argued that the schedule of activities is also influenced by the goals and the timescale within which the promotional goals are to be accomplished. Additionally, the promotional mix determines the financial resources to be allocated and the shape and pattern of the overall campaign.

The control and evaluation stage is important to ensure that the campaign itself stays on course and in that sense helps bind the plan together. The role of the various agencies engaged in the campaign can also be influential and help ensure all aspects are considered on a pre and post campaign basis.

(b) The most important element of the plan is the contextual analysis. In order to analyse situations in a systematic way it is helpful to consider five main areas: business context, customer context, stakeholder context, external context, organisational context.

Review of the *business context* serves to integrate the marketing plan, understand the market and competitor conditions and develop the segmentation analysis in order that a viable positioning strategy might develop.

Understanding the *customer context* is vital. What are the buying characteristics of the target market, when, how and why do they buy? This information can be used to feed the promotional goals, the positioning intentions, the balance of the strategy and the promotional mix and resource requirements.

The *stakeholder context* is important as it extends our view of marketing communications to suppliers and distributors in the marketing channel. It also opens up the wider non-buying audiences and suggests we should consider the corporate image held of our organisation.

Changes in the external environment may influence the tone of the message. For example Levis sensed a social move to be 'friendly' amongst the younger generation. As a result the Sta Pres campaign featured a puppet character referred to as Flat Eric, companion for the human central character.

Finally, the organisation itself can have a huge influence on a campaign. The Procter and Gamble traditional hierarchical 'safe' approach has led to product features being the mainstay of their advertising. Unilever however have a more structure which is reflected in their more emotional advertising messages. The organisation will determine the general amount of financial resources to be allocated and will also influence to what degree employees are to be integrated within the marketing communication activities. Internal marketing communications can be a considerable influence as it is at the staff/customer interface that brand values can really be communicated.

Conclusion

All aspects of the marketing communication plan are interlinked. Through interlinking integration can develop which can lead to more effective marketing communications. The most important element to consider is the Context Analysis which if not accurate, can affect the success of the rest of the plan.

24   MARKETING COMMUNICATIONS OBJECTIVES

Tutorial note. Note that the senior examiner uses a sort of report style even though the question does not explicitly ask you to do so. This helps to give the answer a structure. The use of diagrams and bullet points is also encouraged.

Examiner's comments. Students were expected to answer this question in two ways. Firstly by accurately demonstrating the relationship between objectives, strategies and tactics in terms of a communications plan. Secondly by showing, with specific examples, how to apply the process to their own organisation or an organisation of their choice. Many students were able to carry out the former task but few students carried the process through with carefully chosen examples. This was clearly a question where the use of diagrams and bullet points would give the examiner a good feel for students' knowledge.

REPORT

To: Managing Director
From: Marketing Manager
Date: June 2002
Ref: Developing marketing communications objectives from the organisation's mission

1   Introduction

A key to successful, marketing communication strategy is a complete integrated programme. It is necessary for every element of the programme to contribute in a consistent and synergistic manner. This has the benefits of:

(a)   Being highly effective
(b)   Being cost efficient
(c)   Reinforcing messages to consumers

In this report we show how a hierarchy of objectives may be developed from an organisation's mission statement. The relationship of objectives, strategies and tactics is also discussed.

To demonstrate these principles in practice examples are taken from the launch of a new lager, Carling Premier Lager, by the Carling Brewing Company. Carling is part of Bass plc one of the largest brewery companies in Britain.

> *Tutorial note.* Students will, of course, choose examples from organisations with which they are familiar.

2 Development of objectives

An organisation's mission statement is a description of long-term vision and values. Mission statements have become increasingly common because they provide clear guidance to managers and employees on the future direction of the organisation.

In particular the mission statement can be used to develop a hierarchy of objectives which link the long-term vision and values with specific objectives at each level of the organisation.

The linkage between the mission and *marketing communication* objectives in particular can be seen from the following diagram.

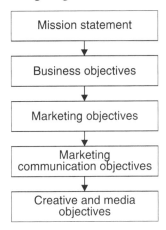

3 Example of Carling Premier Lager

Carling Brewing Company is a subsidiary of Bass plc which is a large leisure and brewing company. Carling is best known for its major product, Carling Black Label, which is Britain's best-selling lager brand. It achieves sales of over 2.5 million barrels per year, nearly 70% more than its nearest rival.

Carling Black Label sales are estimated at £900 million per year, supported by a marketing investment of over £20 million. Carling has undertaken a high profile sponsorship of the Football Association's Premier League. Carling has had a consistent high impact advertising campaign using the theme 'I bet he drinks Carling Black Label'.

In 1995 Carling launched a premium lager called Carling Premier to compete in the growing premium lager sector. The market for standard lager is declining at the rate of about 5% per annum whereas premium lagers are growing at a rate of 5%.

Having given this description it is now possible to show how the marketing communications objectives for Carling Premier Lager can be developed from the business mission of Bass plc.

Bass plc mission

We shall assume that the Bass mission is as follows.

To be the leading provider of leisure and hospitality products and services and to achieve benefits for all Bass stakeholders including:

(a)   Shareholders
(b)   Customers
(c)   Employees

(d)   Suppliers

(e)   The communities which Bass serves

Carling's business objectives

We shall assume that Carling's business objectives are as follows.

(a)   To be the UK's leading lager provider.

(b)   To earn targeted profits for Bass plc.

(c)   To develop new products to meet consumers' needs.

These objectives can be seen to relate to the mission of the Bass Group. Whereas Bass is concerned with the complete leisure field, Carling is concerned with one business sector, lager.

It should be noted that in reality these business objectives will be carefully quantified and will then be used within the company's management control system.

Marketing objectives

Having monitored the decline in standard lager sales and the growth in premium lager sales Carling saw an opportunity for a new Carling premium lager to exploit the brand values and high recognition of Carling. Carling therefore set three marketing objectives.

(a)   To enter the growing premium lager sector with an innovative and original product.

(b)   To bring new premium values to the lager market. (Carling Premier combines cool refreshment with unique smoothness).

(c)   To help the Carling brand access key new drinkers, outlets and occasions.

Marketing communication objectives

We are now in a position to state the key communication objectives which have derived directly from the mission of the parent company Bass plc.

(a)   To position Carling Premier as a completely new type of 'smooth chill', premium draught lager with a unique look feel and flavour.

        (i)   Less gassy, smoother and easy to drink

        (ii) Never loses its creamy head

        (iii) Served at a special low temperature

(b)   To target key customers with certain characteristics.

        (i)   Aged 18-34, predominantly male, BC_1C_2 social class

        (ii) Individuals who are cool and stand out in a crowd

        (iii) People who already drink premium lagers and ales

(c)   To target key outlets and occasions.

        (i)   Special occasions, group drinking

        (ii) City bars

        (iii) Young venues

        (iv) Up-market destinations

(d)   To support the product with a heavyweight TV campaign, a major PR launch, and wide coverage in the trade press.

(e)   To support every act with a comprehensive package lasting for eight weeks.

4   **Relationship of objectives, strategies and tactics**

The following diagram illustrates how objectives, strategies and tactics can be linked together.

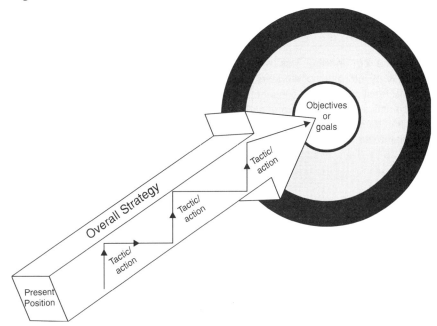

(a)   An objective is an end point or goal to be reached and is usually quantified. The following acronym more accurately defines the characteristics of objectives (SMART).

S pecific

M easurable

A chievable

R elevant

T imed and targeted

(b)   A strategy describes the broad direction of an organisation's actions. It represents a pattern of actions which cumulatively take us in the direction of the objective.

(c)   Tactics are the individual short-term actions that are taken. They are represented in the diagram above as a series of short steps.

5   **Examples from Carling Premier Lager**

The marketing communication *objectives* of Carling Premier have been defined above.

The *strategy* can be seen to include a number of key elements.

(a)   The use of the Carling brand name

(b)   The development of awareness of an innovative new product

(c)   The use of product characteristics of 'smooth' and 'chill'

(d)   The use of a heavyweight campaign with both above the line and below the line components

The *tactics* are the more detailed choices of:

(a)   Particular media

BPP
PUBLISHING

    (b)   The timing of the campaign

    (c)   The decision not to link the product directly to the football sponsorship

    (d)   The development of point of purchase material

25 MARKETS AND STRATEGIES

> **Examiner's comments.** This was a reasonably popular question that was well tackled especially by international students. Good students were able to describe well the differences in characteristics between consumer and industrial markets. Such students presented these characteristics well in the form of grids of factors. Particularly good students were than able to go on and demonstrate the implications for choosing marketing communications strategies for industrial markets. Some six elements of strategy would have gained high marks particularly if backed up by practical examples.

REPORT

To: Managing Director
From: Marketing Communications Manager
Date: 11 June 2002
Ref: Marketing communication strategies for industrial markets

1 Introduction

The principles of marketing have been developed in considerable detail over the last three decades and are now well practised in the field of consumer marketing. The acceptance of marketing principles, however, has been faster among consumer goods producers than in those concerned with industrial marketing, sometimes called business to business marketing.

The amounts of money spent on consumer marketing communications are considerable and perhaps they account for a larger proportion of the marketing budget. This is one of the reasons why marketing communications practice has developed less in industrial marketing situations.

Although the principles of marketing communications are the same for both consumer and industrial marketing there are significant differences in how the marketing is carried out. This report describes the characteristics of the two types of markets and the implications for choosing marketing communication strategies for industrial markets.

2 Characteristics of consumer and industrial markets

In order to be able to plan marketing communications strategies for industrial markets it is important to understand the characteristics of such markets. Also, if we are to use our knowledge and expertise gathered from the more advanced field of consumer marketing we need to be able to compare the characteristics of the two types of market.

The table below summarises and contrasts the characteristics between industrial and consumer marketing.

Major differences between industrial and consumer marketing

	Area	Industrial marketing	Consumer marketing
1	Purchase motivation	Multiple buying influences Support company operations	Individual or family need
2	Nature of demand	Derived or joint demand	Primary demand
3	Emphasis of seller	Economic needs	Immediate satisfaction
4	Customer needs	Each customer has different needs	Groups with similar needs
5	Nature of buyer	Group decision	Purchase by individual or family unit
6	Time effects	Long term relationships	Short term relationships
7	Product details	Technically sophisticated	Lower technical content
8	Promotion decisions	Emphasis on personal selling	Emphasis on mass media advertising
9	Price decisions	Price determined before Terms are important	Price substantially fixed Discounts important
10	Place decisions	Limited number of large buyers Short channels	Large number of small buyers Complex channels
11	Customer service	Critical to success	Less important
12	Legal factors	Contractual arrangements	Contracts only on major purchases
13	Environmental factors	Impact sales both directly and indirectly through derived demand	Impact demand directly

3   Business decision-making process

Perhaps the most significant differences are the nature of the buying motivation and the linked nature of the buying decision process. In industrial buying there are many motivations. These stem partly from the technical use of the product but also from financial, security of supply and, to a lesser degree, emotional reasons. The decision-making unit can be equally multi-faceted.

Decision makers and buying motivation

Decision makers		Buying motivation
1	Operations Manager	Uses the product in the organisation's processes - wants efficiency and effectiveness.
2	Technical Manager	Often has to test and approve the product - wants reliability.
3	The Managing Director	May approve major expenditure or change of supplier.
4	The Purchasing Manager	Approves conditions of purchase. Monitors supplier performance.
5	Legal Manager	Draws up or approves legal contracts with supplier.
Decision makers		Buying motivation
6	Finance Manager	Approves expenditure and controls debt payment.
7	Health and Safety Manager	May have a role to play with hazardous supplies.

It will be immediately obvious that marketing communications strategy for industrial marketing must reflect this considerably more complex decision-making process.

4 Implications for marketing communications strategy

4.1 *Strategic importance*

Business or industrial marketing can be regarded as involving more strategic decisions in its implementation. Consumer products, by definition, are mass market products often purchased in a routine and habitual manner. This is unlikely to be the case in industrial marketing. Business customers have differing needs and in some cases these needs may be conflicting within the organisation. Identifying business needs is complicated by having to deal with different decision-makers within the company.

4.2 *Impact of time*

The length of time involved for the purchase evaluation and for the life of the product is much greater in industrial markets. Consumers often make buying decisions on the spur of the moment. Industrial buying decisions may take over one year. This then alters both the type of marketing communications and the relationships between the buying and selling organisations.

4.3 *The buying organisation*

Business buyers have several different methods of organising purchasing, and this can affect communication strategy. Some firms purchase on a highly centralised basis. This allows for maximum price advantage and negotiation strength because of economies of scale. Other organisations allow decentralised purchases which leads to local needs being better met. In these cases, two different forms of selling organisation are needed and the communication strategy will be different.

4.4 *Variety of products and services:*

The variety of products in business markets is extremely large. Business products vary from product inputs to items for resale. They can be broken down into three main types.

- Capital equipment (major purchases of fixed assets)
- Production inputs (becoming part of the buyer's process)
- Business supplies/services (ongoing use by the buyer)

Again, each type of purchase will need a different communications strategy.

5   **The industrial communications mix**

Relative importance of promotional elements.

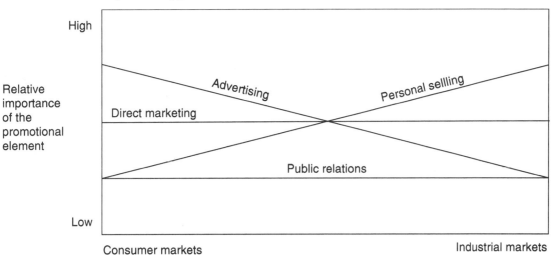

The above chart shows the relative importance of differing elements of the promotional mix between consumer and industrial markets. These differences are reflected in developing marketing communication strategies for industrial markets.

The clearest difference is the importance of personal selling in industrial markets because of the complexity of the decision-making process, the differing industrial needs and the higher value of individual purchases. Advertising, though still important in industrial marketing, is less so than for consumer marketing.

The diagram also shows that both public relations and direct marketing have important continuing roles in both consumer and industrial marketing.

6   **Methods of industrial marketing communications**

It is clear that the methods to communicate with industrial markets will be of a much greater variety than for consumer markets. This in turn means that industrial marketing decisions can be really challenging and the need for effective integrated marketing communications is important. The range of promotional methods is described below.

1   *Personal selling*

     This is a major component of industrial marketing because of the need to deal with technical and other issues on a face-to-face basis.

2   *Internal selling*

     Increasingly it is recognised that a salesperson has an internal role to play in representing his customer needs to the company.

3   *Advertising*

     A wide variety of publications exist which can be used to target industrial market sectors including:

     • Trade journals
     • Business press
     • Directories

     Advertising is used to create awareness, provide information, generate leads, assist channel members and sometimes to sell off the page.

BPP PUBLISHING

4   *Telemarketing*

Telemarketing has been proved to be a very cost effective method of order processing, customer service, sales support and account management.

5   *Direct mailing*

Direct mail, another form of direct marketing, has been used by industrial marketers for a long time but its use has substantially increased. It can be used to provide information and generate enquiries. It can be tailored to individual customer needs.

6   *Public relations*

Sometimes in industrial markets this is referred to as publicity. It often focuses on getting editorial coverage in appropriate magazines but has a wider role of building customer relations.

7   *Sales promotion*

Sales promotion is an important area of communication in industrial markets. There is a wide range of methods that are of well established use in industrial campaigns, including the following.

- Literature
- Videos
- Events
- Trade shows
- Exhibitions
- Discounting
- Business gifts

Technical literature is clearly important in specifying the product. Complicated equipment can be captured on video and applications shown. Trade shows and exhibitions continue to grow in importance. Discounting and special price promotions are used extensively in industrial markets. Business gifts continue to have their value if not used excessively.

7   Conclusions

It can be seen that the process of developing effective marketing communication strategies for industrial markets is a complex but rewarding one. The principles of industrial marketing communications are the same as for consumer marketing but the strategies are different. The table below summarises some of the strategic implications.

Principles of industrial marketing communications strategy

Major principles	Strategic implications
Purpose of industrial promotion	Builds up the company's image in the mind of the purchaser.
Communication objectives	Must be geared to specific business objectives.
Communication methods	Different balance than for consumer markets. Personal selling more important.
Choice of media	Important to determine the best media to reach the complex decision-making process.
Measuring effectiveness	Essential to measure the contribution of communications in achieving business objectives.

Finally, it should be stressed that the concept of Integrated Marketing Communications is equally, if not more, important in industrial marketing. This is because there is likely to be a more complex promotional mix and definitely a more complex audience. Consistent delivery of images on a limited budget is therefore important.

26   PUSH AND PULL

> **Tutorial note.** This question was fairly straightforward and answered well. A contrast between push and pull should be made in part (a) and part (b) should emphasise the importance of key account management and long term support.

(a) There are three strategies that can be used by this company when launching a new range. They can be used independently, or together, depending upon the resources available, the target audiences, the objectives set , the competition and the present reputation of the company.

   (i)   **Push**- to influence the distributor to stock the new range and develop our relationship. They, in turn, will encourage the end user to buy our range at point of sale.

   (ii)   **Pull**- Communications aimed at the end consumer so that they be aware of the range and wish to buy.

   (iii)   **Profile**- aimed at all relevant stakeholders, including internal audiences, to build company reputation.

Our company has an established reputation amongst office retailers, but the new range because of its design makes it appropriate for home office use. Therefore a mix of push and pull strategies should be used to. Firstly, distributors will be encouraged to take the full range and display it well and include it in their catalogues and own promotions (push). Secondly, a pull strategy aimed at end users (both purchasing managers and home customers) will create awareness, generating demand and store traffic. This will in turn encourage distributors to support the launch.

(b) Suggested mix to reach channel members

   (i)   **Personal selling** is important in business to business relationships since it builds trust. The sales force can demonstrate the product benefits and negotiate discounts and local promotional support. They will also advise on **merchandising** ,displays and give training.

   (ii)   **Point of purchase** material will be made available, stressing the quality of the product, along with literature that can be used by the distributor to mail out to their customers or distribute in store.

   (iii)   **Non personal direct marketing.** This might include a secure **extranet** site, so that distributors can get information on stock availability, order status and product specifications. **Direct mail** to launch the range may be used to pre-warn distributors or initially to tell new retailers about the range, and the special benefits of stocking the range.

   (iv)   **CD ROMs** could be mailed out to distributors with room design software included, so that distributors can offer this benefit to their customers when selling the new range. The disk will carry the catalogue.

    (v)   **Sales promotions.** Special discounts for large orders or pre launch discounts will encourage sales into the distributor. Incentives and competitions for distributor sales teams will encourage their support at the point of sale.

    (vi)   **Exhibitions** supported by corporate hospitality will create interest in the new range and facilitate dialogue between the company and its distribution network.

    (vii)   **Advertising** in trade journals will create awareness and may encourage opportunities for PR support.

    (viii)   **Public relations** will feature the new range and tell of the support that will be offered to the distributors on taking the new range

Conclusion

Support from members of the supply chain is extremely important for a furniture manufacturer such as ours. The push strategies must therefore be undertaken to encourage dialogue with channel members and ensure that have the right tools to sell on the products. The mix will be used to create awareness, persuade distributors to take stock, develop relationships and create sales. The push strategies must be integrated with pull techniques to ensure long term success for the new range.

27   INTERNAL MARKETING COMMUNICATIONS

> **Examiner's comments.** This was a popular question and many answers were of a high standard. To do well the student had to link internal and external aspects. Corporate communication and corporate identity are increasingly important elements of the syllabus.

Introduction

The notion that employees constitute an important market segment is relatively recent but has been gaining increasing acceptance by both organisations and academics. Employees are seen as important because they have particular needs and wants some of which are satisfied by work which they exchange for pay and intrinsic benefits such as belonging, self esteem and self identity.

It is only through employees that management are really able to achieve their corporate goals. Therefore, the direction and philosophy of an organisation, whether it be in the private or public sector, is an integral part of an organisation's strategy and its communications with externally based stakeholders.

The benefits of internal marketing communications

- Staff motivation
- Staff retention
- Resource utilisation
- Developing competitive advantage
- Moving towards integrated marketing communications

Staff motivation

Involvement and participation within the organisation and its strategic and operational activities improves motivation and organisational identity improves. By encouraging employees to identify with the mission and values of an organisation, any gap between an organisation's external identity and its internal identity is narrowed.

Staff retention

In a period when staff skills are at a premium and difficult to replace it makes good sense to preserve the current work force. Good communications are therefore important to retaining qualified and valued member of the workforce. This in turn can breed experience and contribute to the development of better products and services and improved, credible external communications. B&Q, a DIY warehouse in the UK, feature their own staff in their television advertising. This helps develop employee identification as they are perceived to be valued, and externally it provides a point of differentiation from the other DIY stores in the sector and a form of trust as these staff know what they are selling.

Resource utilisation

Good communications can help identify areas where there is duplication of effort and, where possible, improve the level of resource utilisation.

Competitive advantage

The service element of the product offering is important so there must be increased attention given to training and skills. Associated with this is the competitive shift as more and more product offerings become less distinctive in their own right. Differentiation through the service component has provided companies such as KwikFit, TNT Express and British Airways with competitive advantage.

Links with external communications

The development and increased focus on integrated marketing communications means that internal marketing communications cannot be ignored.

Many external stakeholders communicate on a regular basis with the employees of an organisation. Customers are obviously a very important group and need to be treated in the right manner in order to build levels of customer satisfaction. Suppliers and distributors, shareholders, financial service providers and members of the local community also communicate. All receive messages from the organisation, interpret them in particular ways and through the images formed develop, maintain or alter the reputation of the focus organisation.

Employees are essentially *opinion formers* and through 'word of mouth' communications and behaviour they help shape the views external stakeholders have of them as an organisation as a whole. In this sense therefore, internal marketing communications are an integral part of the move toward integrated marketing communications and therefore cannot be ignored or left alone. The way an organisation is perceived by *employees* may differ to the way the organisation is perceived by *external stakeholders*. The extent of any such *gap* is said to be reflected in the strength of the organisation's overall identity. It follows that management should assist their employees to understand what is *central* to the business, what is *distinctive* about the business and what is *enduring*.

28   CORPORATE INTERNAL MARKETING

> **Examiner's comments.** It appears to me that many students were prepared for a question on Internal Marketing Communications and to a lesser extent, Corporate Branding. Unfortunately too few were able to put the two topics together coherently. In particular, it is noticeable that knowledge about Corporate Branding is weak and time should be spent in class helping students understanding corporate personality, identity and image.
>
> Despite these comments there were some excellent answers where it was evident that students knew the subject well.

Internal Marketing Communications and its Impact on Corporate Branding

To: Marketing Manager

From: Marketing Assistant

June, 2001

Contents

1 What is Corporate Branding?
2 What is Internal Marketing?
3 The integration of marketing communication to achieve success

Introduction

This report looks at the significance of internal marketing communications on the organisations corporate brand. It uses a number of examples to define what is meant by the terms Corporate Branding and Internal Marketing and shows how they must b integrated to achieve corporate and business goals. There are several aspects that must be linked in order to present strong corporate brand including:

- Co-ordinated marketing strategy
- Consistent on-message information
- Integrated marcomms
- Planned internal communications

The latter is the main emphasis of this report.

What is Corporate Branding?

Branding is becoming increasingly important within marketing, as it is often the point of difference between different products. The same can be said of corporate branding- many companies offer similar products and services and it is the corporate brand, which differentiates the company. Corporate branding relies on profile strategies to ensure a consistency to all stakeholders. A good corporate brand can be extended allowing diversification in a number of industries. For example the Virgin brand can be applied to many sectors where the under dog fights the staid traditional companies.

It can take years to build a credible corporate brand and this brand could be pulled down so easily through inconsistent messages, particularly if the originators of the message, the employees are inconsistent. Corporate branding is portrayed by what the company looks like, what the company does and how it behaves- a mixture of tangible and intangible elements.

Logos, literature and web-sites tell us what the company looks like. Corporate identity is important but so is the ethical behaviour and social responsibility to all its stakeholders, including employees.

What is Internal Marketing?

Many companies concentrate their marketing communications effort on the external audiences such as customers and channel members. However the internal stakeholders can play a vital role to ensure the success of any activity. And they should be treated in the same way as external customers.

Although internal marketing communications seeks to adhere to the normal DRIP factors i.e. to differentiate employees, remind and reassure them, inform our staff so that all internal departments know what is happening, they have a much wider role.

(a) **Transactional**

By communicating with all staff they can co-ordinate their actions, use resources more efficiently and provide direction for the organisation. A very simple example of this might be the use of e- mail to inform staff about the arrival of an important customer. Or the use of an Intranet allowing internal access to relevant information to ensure consistency and collaboration.

(b) **An affiliation role**

This is evident particularly when it is a dialogue that is established. Employees will buy in to strategy, adopt it as their own and then be happy to co-ordinate activities with other, possibly external parties. This role adds to the motivation of staff and creates a sense of belonginess. The use of staff uniforms, team meetings, suggestion boxes and other dialogue creating methods can be used here.

There are many examples where internal communications has not been carried through successfully as shown by the criticism by BA staff when the new wing designs were painted- staff did not know it was happening and they did not know the reasons behind the re branding exercises. Therefore they complained that the money being spent here was wasted especially since they were in negotiation about pay.

An example where internal and external campaigns were integrated successfully was the Barclays 'Big Bank' campaign. The advertising positioned the bank as a global player, a one-stop shop for all banking needs. In parallel to the external campaign an internal campaign was conducted to educate all employees about the full range of their products, the benefits and how to implement them. The campaign was successful and cross selling to existing customers was raised substantially.

A recent survey put Timpson, the high street cobblers, in the top 10. The corporate brand stood for friendly people within a family atmosphere. Employee satisfaction was high, not because of the high pay or long holidays but because the company was still run like a family business in spite of its size. Staff were kept regularly informed of what the company were doing and had the ear of senior management on a regular basis. This is also extended to marcomms for external audiences- letter headings and signages are cheerful and friendly.

Tesco pay regard to their staff by empowering them to help customers. This supports the brand slogan of 'every little helps', and allows staff to gain more job satisfaction than if they were not allowed to use their own initiative.

The full integration of all marcomms activity must include internal stakeholders for without their support the company culture will be at odds with corporate brand objectives.

29   PLANNED COMMUNICATIONS

> **Examiner's comments.** Students did not know what a marketing channel was and marks suffered accordingly. This area will become more important in the next few years.
>
> Students should ensure that they understand communications and relationships between intermediaries: the push approach.

Organisations need to work with other organisations if they are to achieve their own goals. Manufacturers need to work with wholesalers and agents and distributors, retailers and value added resellers if they are to be able to present their products and services to their potential end user customers.

Manufacturers also need to work closely with their suppliers, those upstream from their current position in the marketing channel. All these organisations may be independent of each other but they all need each other to complete activities that they themselves do not have the skills or resources to accomplish. Therefore, the members of a marketing channel are said to be interdependent.

As organisations need to work together it follows that communications between the members of the channel are also of vital importance. Communications are necessary in order to help differentiate their products and services in the minds of the member, to persuade them to take stock, to provide information to enable them to understand the technicalities of the product and to inform their customers and finally communications are necessary to remind and reassure the partner organisation.

Contemporary thought suggests that the development of trust and commitment is absolutely imperative if a cooperative relationship is to be shaped such that any two organisations in the network are able to understand each other and work to support one another as necessary.

In addition to the points noted above there is a need for organisations to help motivate and to direct the activities of other partner organisations. These communications with channel intermediaries are referred to as push related communications. They are known as push because the information is being pushed through the channel down towards the end users.

The question refers to the identification of the key influences that shape the design of communication activities in the marketing channel. The problem with this is that what is key in one situation may not be key in another. Key influences will vary according to markets and certain trading and competitive conditions. However, some factors may be common across channels.

1   The Type of Intermediary
2   The Balance of Power in the Channel
3   Type of Product/Service
4   Buyer Characteristics
5   The Competition
6   The Structure Exchanges in the Channel
7   Resources
8   The PEST Factors
9   Current Strategy
10 Strength of Corporate Identity.

This list cannot be regarded as complete although these are the common factors that should be considered. The four main elements are expanded below.

The Type of Intermediary

The distinction here is between whether the intermediary is a retailer, wholesaler of distributor. The role and function of the intermediary will influence the type of information they need and the frequency and style in which the communication needs to be provided.

The Structure Exchanges in the Channel

This refers to whether the members of the channel regard transactions between each other as necessary just to get the job done or whether there is a long term view and a relationship that is important to both parties.

The Competition

The communication campaigns of a competitor can have a strong impact on the communications between channel members. For example, should a competitor offer a discount then there is pressure upon others in the channel, especially from distributors, to also reduce prices in order to maintain a competitive position. The launch of new products and services by competitors can also influence promotional campaigns. New positioning strategies might be developed, information about which needs to be passed through to all members.

Resources

The current type and form of communication may have become embedded in the channel and expected by other members. Whilst this is not a key influence, what lies behind it might be. For example, current operating methods and strategy may be indicative of the prevailing business strategy, organisational culture and the amount of marketing communication resources that are made available.

Personal selling is an important part of the promotional mix in inter-organisational communications. Changes due to new technology may result in a reduction in the size of the sales force and in the calling patterns and frequencies of the revised sales force. Advertising support for joint campaigns may be increased or reduced as budgets change as will the level of training and across company project team support, where appropriate.

As a final comment, the willingness of channel partners to share information with others in the channel indicates the degree to which members trust and support each other and suggests what level of commitment between members of the marketing channel there may be.

30 INTERNAL MARKETING COMMUNICATIONS: TECHNOLOGY

> **Examiner's comments.** Some candidates produced good answers, realising that this question was closely related to the mini-case in the exam.
>
> Candidates failed to underline the importance of technology, especially for multi-national companies whose employees can be continents apart. Many answers lacked substance. Various technological advances, including email, were mentioned but not put into the context of effective communication.

Memorandum

Comments welcomed by 21 December 2001

Importance of Internal Marketing Communications

The drive to develop integrated marketing communications and the increased interest in corporate branding and associated communications has focused attention on the role of employees as an internal stakeholder. The potential impact they have on an organisation's external stakeholders and on organisational performance appears to have been underestimated for a long time.

One of the benefits of developing integrated communications is that if achieved it is likely that all stakeholders will perceive a consistent and harmonious set of identity cues and form more uniform images.

The role of internal marketing communications can be seen from three perspectives.

1   The **DRIP** factors whereby:

   D   Employees need to understand how the organisation is *differentiated* to the others in the sector and how different they are as a workforce.

R   Employees need to be *reminded* how good they are and what the overall targets are that they are all striving to achieve. They also need to be *reassured* that they are valued and that they are supported and appreciated.

I   It is important that this audience is kept *informed* of company developments and that they understand how, when and why the company is acting in the way it is.

P   Sometimes they need to be *persuaded* to undertake certain tasks or actions.

2   There are also **transactional** impacts where good internal communications can help coordinate the actions of staff and project teams, improve the use of resources and direct developments within the organisation.

3   Finally, internal marketing communications is an important mechanism through which **affiliation** with the organisation can be encouraged. For example, it provides identification with the company, can motivate employees and promote and coordinate activities with those external to the organisation.

Impact of Technology

It appears that internal marketing communications is important and can lead to improvements for the company and for us as individuals. The recent advances in technology have enabled many organisations to reduce the amount of paper and time spent on internal communications and made the process far more efficient.

The use of the Internet has not only changed the way many organisations communicate with their customers, especially in the business-to-business sector, but has also enabled communications with discrete audiences. Intranets and web pages only accessible by staff provide a fast and effective way of delivering information, reminding staff of their role and the company's position and providing a means of enhanced identification. Some organisations provide their mission and corporate objectives, staff handbook, address book details, internal catalogues, notice boards, chat rooms and other company information which is accessible by everyone internally.

Email provides for global communication which is both quick, inexpensive and accurate in the sense that there is little chance of message corruption en route. Electronic files containing spreadsheets and reports can be transmitted at electronic speeds and enable savings to be made in terms of labour and printing costs.

Training materials can be standardised and this can help ensure that all staff are trained in the same way and assist in the delivery of uniform messages. British Airways use video conferencing on a regular basis for management communication and they also used the same technology for the simultaneous launch of their now infamous "new" corporate identity in 1997.

The final benefit to be mentioned is that product information and updates can be communicated more efficiently and effectively through intranets either to employees or members of the market channel (internal members).

Conclusion

The rapid development of technology has enabled management to communicate more effectively and efficiently with their employees. It has also allowed employees an opportunity to communicate more effectively with other employees and management. If two way communication is valued by management then increased use of technology will be an important and necessary requirement.

31   DEVELOPING MEDIA STRATEGY

To :   A N Other Marketing Communications Assistant
From :   A J Smith Marketing Communications Manager
Date :   13 June 2000

Ref : Media Concepts

Prior to your forthcoming meeting with our agency XYZ I would like to set out some of the key media concepts and then see how they are associated with media strategy.

Concepts

Two of the important concepts are Reach and Frequency. Reach refers to the percentage number of people in the target market who are reached once with the message. Frequency refers to the percentage who are exposed to the message two or more times within a given budget and time frame. Of course it is possible to develop both coverage and frequency but this will normally require separate campaigns.

Gross rating points, or ratings, are the number of impacts made in a campaign (simply put this is coverage x frequency) and is a useful measure as it indicates the total effect of a campaign. Very often the media plan will state the ratings to be achieved and this will relate to the cost of the campaign. Obviously the higher the ratings, which can be guaranteed by the media, the heavier our investment will need to be.

Now, as you know, our target markets around the world do not buy a single newspaper or magazine nor do they see a single television programme. Therefore our media plan should state the level of overlap between people who are likely to be exposed more than once to our campaign. This is referred to as duplication and the agency will have duplication tables so as to improve the efficiency of our investment.

The only other concepts are Opportunities–to–See (OTSs) which refers to the number of people who buy the vehicle (magazine, paper) but does not necessarily mean they actually see our message, Cost per Thousand (CPT) which is a measure of the cost incurred to reach each thousand people in our target audience. You might like to look out for the point that CPT can only be used to compare the media costs within a media vehicle not to compare costs across media (for example television and magazines). The final concept is flighting which refers to the pattern of advertising: is the advertising to be transmitted in a concentrated period of time (burst) or is it to be fed out over a longer period (drip)?

There are a number of other concepts which are not media specific. However, if we are to undertake a global campaign we need to be aware of target markets, and the local conditions that may impair or assist the way in which we communicate with our audiences.

Media Strategy

Media strategy is about trying to get the best fit between media vehicles and the target audience, at the lowest possible price.

The media strategy will be dependent to a large extent on what we are trying to achieve. If we are rolling out a new brand then awareness will be a prime objective. If awareness is the goal then a coverage based media strategy is likely to be more appropriate. Here we will be trying to make as many people as possible aware of the new brand. If our goal is to reposition or remind people about our brand then a frequency strategy may be more appropriate. When people are required to learn something about our brand we may need three hits with our message. The first to make them aware, the second to make the point and the third to remind them about the point in order for them to memorise it. Now this approach is questionable and we should be open to new views. The level of education and the social fabric in each of the geographical areas in which we operate varies and so the media strategy needs to be flexible and we should not necessarily dictate a rigid media approach.

What we can expect is that the media plan itself needs to be efficient and effective. We need to be sure that as far as media buying is concerned that the agency buys the media on our behalf at the most advantageous rates (discounts) that can be reasonably expected. If we are not happy with the rates we may need to centralise all our media buying into a media house (dependent or independent). This of course will impact on all our brands so we will need time to carefully consider this decision.

Most of these notes have concentrated on advertising but we need to be aware of the integrated nature of our campaign and the need to harmonise the activities of the other parts of the promotional mix. We will be using sales promotions and direct marketing together with our web site. The messages that these deliver must be the same in order to not confuse our target customers, many of whom travel and will see our messages in different locations.

The media strategy will need to take account of the message standardisation or adaptation debate. I think we need XYZ to update us on their views on this subject although I think our current globalisation approach is the best way forward.

Final Comments

I hope these notes are of some help but you will come across a raft of others during the meeting. Overall, it is the strategic approach to media planning that is important and the degree to which XYZ tries to take an integrated approach to the media planning activities. Please look out for the level and quality of the skills and resources that they have available throughout the different country regions in which we have a presence.

32 INTERNET CHANNELS

> **Examiner's comments.** This was a popular question and generally it was answered well. Most students were able to refer to Internet related issues (although there is a need for increased depth of understanding at this level) but were less able to answer in the context of the question. That is, if they did know what a marketing channel is, they did not (as a rule) round the answer off by discussing the impact on relationships.
>
> This was an easy question to pick up good marks in, but the opportunity was missed by many because they did not answer the full question.
>
> Tutors, please note the continued need for students to understand what a marketing or distribution channel is, and the need for communications to help built fruitful relationships. I am looking for knowledge about trust and commitment (however brief).

To: Marketing Department

From: Marketing Manager

Date: June 2001

The Impact of Technology on our Channel Relationships – a briefing paper

Introduction

The growth of the Internet and related technologies has had a big impact on the way that many businesses have developed. This paper outlines how the use of these technologies might affect the way that we communicate with our channel members and change the relationship that we have with them. A number of different examples will be used to elaborate.

The technology

For the purpose of this paper the term Internet will be used to cover the following:

(a) Websites – here this will mean posting information such as the company brochure for general access at any time without having to call or phone

(b) Intranets – internal websites with interactivity for use within the company. This can ensure that up to date information is available to employees for relaying to channel members as requested

(c) E-mail – message system

(d) Extranets – Interactive website with limited access to specific channel members and other external parties

(e) EDI – electronic data interchange- a fully integrated system allowing all purchase related activity to be done on line, including invoicing and payment.

Other technologies include telemarketing, cd-rom, m- commerce, database and MKIS systems

The Impact on communications

The positive impacts on communications are as follows.

(a) It allows us to communicate with distant channel members e.g. globally very cheaply and accurately. This will allow a closer relationship with those far away than had been possible through less modern methods of communication.

(b) Increased speed of communication e.g. through e mail means that all channel members can be briefed simultaneously and respond more quickly.

(c) EDI will allow transactions to be processed immediately and speed response times for distributors which will allow them to serve their customer better.

(d) Frequency of communication will rise perhaps leading to a better relationship. Special offers will be updated all of the time.

(e) There will be greater opportunity for dialogue with information provided more relevant to help both sides of the channel relationship. For example email can be used by channel members to interrogate our customer service teams.

(f) The database of channel members will allow more accurate targeting and lead to better relationships.

(g) End users of the product will be able to visit our website and be linked to the most appropriate distributor's web site.

(h) Our catalogue can be supplied and updated on cd rom- this will save money for us and ensure that our distributors are kept up to date.

(i) By allowing access to our extranet, offering a different level of service to individual distributors, we can allow some to feel valued.

(j) Brand Building can be helped via technology, as distributors will be able to discover as much as they wish about our brand, choosing their own level of involvement. In addition our brand can now be seen as innovative with the extra benefits brought by the technology.

(k) Technology such as database can offer the opportunity to measure effectiveness of each campaign aimed at distributors on the channel. Internet activity can be monitored so that sections of obvious interest are developed and those of less use dropped.

(l) On line Training packages can help distributors sell on our product and make them more confident partners in the future.

The related technologies will be an additional communication channel, which must be managed. It may eventually replace existing methods of communication but in the meantime it must be consistent with the existing communication channels. For example a price offered to a distributor by the sales team should be the same price offered on the Internet if all other aspects of the mix are the same. Telemarketing teams must know if the distributor has requested information by e-mail or the Internet.

Impact on relationships

As can be seen from above most of the changes arising from new technology have a positive impact on the relationship with channel members. The free access to relevant information and training will allow distributors to concentrate on providing a better service.

They will also be able to choose which communication channel they use to contact us and so they will feel more in control than before.

Understanding should be improved as a dialogue emerges and the opportunity to build trust is obvious, for example if the channel member gets an immediate response to enquiries or if EDI allows same day delivery. Commitment will also be secured as special distributors are entitled to get further information by being included on the extranet.

Partnerships can be encouraged through information sharing and as distributors are brought on line and end users are directed to them.

Beware

Not all technology enhances relationships between distributors. Before we commit to a fully representational internet presence we must be aware that our channel members be frightened by the technology – they may also fear that we will use this to go direct to our customers and by pass them (disintermediation).

In addition we must be careful not to oversell the benefits of our system since any problems will have a negative effect on our relationship.

Technology must not replace the existing relationship we have with our sales force, but be complementary, using the technology for the communication activity it can do well.

Conclusions

This paper has looked at some of the implications of adopting some new technologies to improve the communication between our important distribution network and ourselves. There are many benefits possible but it is also important to realise the negative aspects when adopting this interactive method of communication. It must be integrated with our existing strategies for maximum effect and managed in a dynamic way, being kept up to date at all times.

33 ONLINE AND OFFLINE

Examiner's comments. This question cried out for an applied answer. The importance of brand development and an integrated approach cannot be under estimated.

Country Cottages.com

(a) As the owner of a small holiday let company in Wales there are a number of advantages of using Internet and other technology based communications.

   (i)   **Cost savings**. The Internet has reduced the number of printed brochures needed since I now provide an online brochure with pictures of all properties. I now deal direct with my customers, and no longer have to pay the 10% intermediary fee.

   (ii) **Tangibility**. Some of the properties allow the customer to see a number of different views, and take a virtual walk through the property- this tangibilises the service we offer. I am working to make the site more interactive and trying to use a number of tools to give a taste of the quietness guests might experience at some of our cottages!

   (iii) **Dialogue**. Through email I can now speak directly with my customers, confirming their booking, providing directions and answering any other questions they might have.

   (iv) **Database**. I have been able to build a database of customer characteristics and preferences which has been useful to me in marketing campaigns. I can also tell them of any last minute deals to encourage demand at less busy times.

   (v)   **24 hour service**. Customers can book online at any time and this encourages overseas visitors.

   (vi) **Dynamic**. The site is updated on a regular basis so information is relevant and useful, even showing the weather forecast and availability.

   (vii) **Global access**. Our site is accessible through a number of global search engines and customers can book using their native language.

   (viii) **Service**. Our company can now act as a service provider to our clients, since we link with appropriate providers of information in the local area. For example places to visit, road maps, transport providers , cheap flight providers and language learning sites!. Eventually this may become an income stream for us.

   (ix) **Interactivity**. Our search engine allows customers to select a property according to their needs and its availability, and therefore saves them time.

   (x)   **Relationship building**. The Internet allows me to build relationships with my customers and also allows them to tell me what they thought of their holiday. We run a visitors' book, where customers can post their impressions about the company or the property they have visited.

   (xi) **Viral marketing**. Customers tell their friends about the utility of the site and the properties we manage- recommendation is the best promotion and email makes this very easy.

   (xii) The **website** offers control and measurement and enables us to see immediately the popularity of the site and properties. It can help us track visitors and provides data for pricing, promotion and future website design.

(b) Pursuing an **online strategy** requires **offline communications** to support and enhance the online presence.

   We need to make people aware of our new business model and build site traffic. Direct marketing to our existing database of customers will be useful to remind them about us. Direct marketing could also be used to find customers with a similar profile to ours e.g. leaflet drops and loose inserts in relevant publications.

Brand building through offline methods builds trust in our company and reduces perceived risk. Brand values can be related to a number of audiences, including non customers and other opinion leaders.

Tools such as **PR and advertising** are needed to say what our company stands for (quality properties, tailored to the needs of our customers with value added service). Editorial coverage will offer many benefits to us and so I have entered a small business competition.

Differentiation is important in this market since many Internet based businesses are known purely for their cheap prices- we do not wish to compete from this platform. Advertising in travel magazines and targeted media will ensure that the right type of customer is warmed to our service. Once visitors try our website they will see that we offer superior service, but we need to inform them that we are here in the first instance. Attendance at some **specialist exhibitions** may boost awareness and provide a human face to our company.

Press advertising may also be necessary on a tactical basis at certain types of the year, featuring availability and price promotions and encouraging first time visitors.

Every medium reinforces the website address, and shows the telephone number for those who prefer human interaction. Since we use an integrated **customer relationship management** system, all of our customer service staff can see the status of each customer (whether they have booked before and so on). This allows a more personal and relevant dialogue. Telemarketing can also boost conversion rates.

Offline support is important because it does give a feeling that the company is not just a virtual presence. Some customers may also need a brochure. This may take the form of a small brochure showing the type, but not all properties available.

With all communication a **consistent message** will be used to build the brand values. These will be reflected on our website.

In conclusion, both online and offline approaches are required (both tools emphasising core values) with offline primarily driving site traffic and raising awareness. The Internet will offer a more complete communication experience, from promotion to booking and interactive dialogue. Each will complement the other, providing an integrated and cohesive experience for our customers.

34   BRANDING AND MARKETING COMMUNICATION

> **Tutorial note.** The depth of understanding that students have of the branding concept will be significant indicator when answering this question. Branding as a strategy is central to marketing communications and a rounded understanding is important.
>
> **Examiner's comments.** Too few related their knowledge to marketing communications strategy.

Branding is an important *consumer marketing tool* and companies such as Nike, Cadbury's, Procter & Gamble, Virgin and British Airways have developed sophisticated means of managing and developing their brands. Many business-to-business organisations are starting to recognise the power of branding and are utilising the approach themselves.

A brand is a term, logo, name, symbol or design that identifies the product or service within particular markets. It may be that these elements are combined together in some way to provide a *distinguishing facility* within a competitive environment. Branding therefore is a primary means of *differentiating* a product or service. As product content, quality and facilities continue to converge, the importance of distinguishing one product from another becomes more and more important. Branding allows for the development of competitive advantage and adds value to the core product. This value may not be understood and or appreciated by all members of the population, but what is important is that members of the target audience appreciate and value the brand and its associated values.

Branding brings many advantages to both consumers and a brand's owners. These are set out in Table 1. However, it is only through *communication* that the essence of a brand is conveyed and maintained. Therefore, marketing and corporate communications are absolutely essential for effective branding to be developed.

British Airways have used branding to help achieve the corporate goals. BA use branding at a *corporate level* by differentiating the airline from all other airlines. They also use product based branding to differentiate particular routes and ancillary services. The recent launch of their cut price airline 'Go' is significant in that the name (symbol, mark) of British Airways is not immediately associated with the primary means of identification. One might assume that the brand values of the parent company are not to be associated with those of the start-up fledgling airline. When British Gas wanted to launch a credit card and move into the financial services market the name (mark, symbol) of British Gas was not appropriate in that the wrong values and cultural associations were tied into British Gas that might have prevented or impeded a successful launch. They selected the name Goldfish and used a variety of different means to distinguish and separate the brand form the parent.

Customer benefits from branding	*Supplier benefits derived from branding*
★ Assists the identification of preferred products ★ Can reduce levels of perceived risk and so improve the quality of the shopping experience ★ Easier to gauge the level of product quality ★ Can reduce the time spent making product based decisions and in turn reduce the time spent shopping. ★ Can provide psychological reassurance or reward ★ Provides cues about the nature of the source of the product and any associated values	★ Permits premium pricing ★ Helps differentiate the product from competitors ★ Enhances cross-product promotion and brand extension opportunities ★ Encourages customer loyalty/retention and repeat purchase buyer behaviour ★ Assists the development and use of integrated marketing communications ★ Contributes to corporate identity programmes ★ Provides for some legal protection ★ Provides for greater thematic consistency and uniform messages and communications

Table 1

Benefits of Branding
Source: Fill (1999)

Conversely, *Virgin* have *developed and extended* the Virgin brand into many different markets, mainly because of the strength of the equity associated with Virgin. The marketing strategy of Virgin to enter new markets and to develop new products, often simultaneously, has been possible only because of the strength of the Virgin brand. Marketing communications strategy therefore has been based around maintaining and developing the strength of the Virgin brand.

There *are* different types of brand and numerous listings and topologies of brands.

(a)   There *are manufacturers' brands* such as IBM, Cadbury's and Ford, *retailer* brands such as Marks and Spencer, Tesco and Sainsbury's and Generic brands as practised in the pharmaceutical industry where a very low price and the absence of promotional materials is the prime characteristic.

(b) Brands however are a reflection the relationship between the corporate body, the product itself and the competitive context within which it is positioned. As a result of these variables a number of different brands types can be identified.

(i) Pirelli, Gillette and Kwik-Fit have a single product group offering so that the name of the organisation is the same as the lead name of individual products.

(ii) Companies such as Lever Brothers have followed a multi-brand strategy so that products in the company's portfolio are branded without reference to the parent company. Marketing communications therefore are required to maintain this policy and to build values associated with each and every product in different ways. Should a single brand experience a crisis then the other brands in the portfolio need not be damaged, unlike the Family brand approach as followed by Kellogg's and Cadbury's where the organisation's name is a visible and imperative part of the name of each and every product in the portfolio.

Marketing communications needs to build the strength of the brand over the long term and it needs to be flexible in order to adapt to changing market conditions. However, many of the long-term successful brands such as Shell have been able to maintain core values and develop a level of consistency in their communications. Brands carry a measure of **goodwill**, which can be the prime attraction of predators. When Nestlé bought Rowntree, the value of brands such as KitKat led to a price far in excess of the traditional asset value of the company. A view of the future stream of earnings a brand is likely to generate is a major factor when determining the take-over price. The Rolls Royce brand is extremely attractive with strong equity and future earnings potential. Volkswagen have just paid a price premium to snatch the purchase of Rolls-Royce away from fellow German company BMW.

Branding is part of marketing communication strategy and needs to be developed and nurtured over the long term. It can be extremely effective and provide competitive advantage through increased customer satisfaction and retention.

35 INTERNET

> **Examiner's comments.** About 40% of UK students and 30% of international students tackled this question. High marks were earned by UK students and relatively poorer ones by international students. Good answers stuck closely to the question asked - ways in which the Internet is being used - and will be used - by suppliers, customers and internally in organisations. Ideas that were realistic were rewarded. Unfortunately, some answers copied previous lists of advantages and disadvantages of the Internet generally, rather than the specific uses. General answers were less well rewarded.

What is the Internet?

The Internet is a world-wide network of computer networks. These are linked together so that users can search for and access data and information provided by others, linked through the different networks.

The World Wide Web is the multimedia element which provides facilities such as full-colour, graphics, sound and video. Web sites are points within the network created by members who wish to provide an information point for searchers to visit and benefit by the provision of information and/or by entering into a transaction.

Current uses and development issues

There are an increasing number of interactive uses that the Internet can be used for:

(a) Communication (information provision)
(b) Product development
(c) Facilitating transactions
(d) Fostering dialogue and relationships with different stakeholders

The attributes of the Internet that allow for these uses also need to be considered.

(a) High speed of interaction
(b) Low cost provision and maintenance
(c) Ability to provide mass customisation
(d) Global reach and wide search facilities
(e) Instant dialogue
(f) Multi-directional communications (eg: to suppliers, customers and regulators)
(g) High level of user control
(h) Customer (Visitor) driven
(i) Moderate level of credibility

Use with customers

The use of the Internet by organisations with their customers has in the initial years been focussed upon the business-to-business sector rather than consumer end users. Those customers that have used the Internet do so primarily in search of entertainment and information. Web sites have become increasingly sophisticated and are a useful means of meeting the needs of customers and organisations.

Businesses can communicate more cost-effectively with their customers and provide a wide range of facilities. The volume of customer traffic that can be handled is far larger and quicker than through traditional means. Sales literature, product designs and innovations, ideas, price lists, complaints, sales promotions such as competitions, and orders and sales can all be undertaken over the Internet. The objectives are essentially two-fold. The first is to generate the first steps of a relationship (or maintain one already established). The second is the collection of customer profile information to be added to the database. Names, addresses and other demographic and psychographic data can be collected without any human intervention and/or the associated costs.

The execution of financial transactions over the Internet has been a deterrent due to the fear of fraud and misappropriation of funds. More secure systems and protection devices are now becoming available and this will spur the growth of purchasing activities over the Internet in the future.

A further development is to integrate the Internet with other elements of the marketing and promotional mix. For example the Tesco and Sainsbury's initiatives to develop home shopping have met with limited success but further investment will generate new shopping patterns and purchasing behaviours.

Use with suppliers

The use of the Internet with suppliers will provide a more dynamic form of communication exchange. Problem identification, the formation of solutions and constant dialogue opportunities will enable suppliers to forge closer relationships in the marketing channel.

Marketing communications opportunities will arise where, for example, new products can be presented to suppliers much more quickly, sales literature and product specification data can be relayed instantly and, in some cases, advertising materials presented more effectively.

Sales order processing and lead management systems are already providing marketing channel members (and end-user customers) with greater efficiency and speed of information retrieval. Suppliers also benefit from being able to contribute to product modifications and fault-finding processes can be speeded up. Perhaps one of the more exciting opportunities the Internet provides is greater customisation - more tailored products for specific customers.

Use within organisations: intranets

Internally the greatest advance is the development of intranets. The provision of internal, password-protected communication networks allows for the rapid dissemination of corporate and marketing information. For global organisations this represents a tremendous step forward as an intranet can overcome time barriers and allow for the transmission of materials to all parts of a company instantaneously. It provides a wealth of information for members to keep themselves informed of company news.

The development and interest in *internal marketing* has been assisted by this new form of internal communications. The involvement of staff and the motivational opportunities afforded by intranet technology enable employees and management to work more closely together.

Future of the Internet

The future of the Internet is bounded only by imagination and technological advances. Essentially there will be greater interactive opportunities which will enable a range of stakeholders to interact with organisations as a community to provide information, education, entertainment, products, services and financial transactions quickly, efficiently and so release more time for leisure and recreational activities.

36   RETAIL STRATAGY

> **Examiner's comments.** On the face of it this question appears to be very simple but in order to gain good marks some understanding about the strategic role of advertising and below the line methods is essential as is a knowledge of branding. More important though is a good knowledge about the associations that can be created through branding

This paper will review the communications policies of UK based supermarkets, operating in an extremely competitive market. It will start by analysing the advantages of using **above the line strategies** to build the brand, and then will go on to compare this method with **below the line strategies**, with particular emphasis on sale promotion, an approach adopted by Safeway with some success. Marketing communications turn supermarkets into **differentiated brands,** so that Kwik Save is seen as a low cost provider, whilst Waitrose is seen as a provider of quality goods.

(a)   **Above the line strategies**

Above the line promotion consists of advertising in the **mass media,** and is defined as paid-for promotion where the sponsor is easily identifiable. The term arises from how agencies were traditionally paid to develop and place advertising (by commission, paid as a percentage of the amount paid for the space). Traditionally this was 15%, but this method of payment is now being used less. The term remains, and advertising is still an important tool when it comes to building brands.

Advertising offers the following advantages when it comes to building brands.

(i)   **Positive brand associations** can be developed through advertising on an emotional or rational level. A rational message can be seen in Iceland's approach to genetically modified foods, when compared to the emotional presentation of Jamie Oliver's friendships portrayed in Sainsbury's advertising. Both are effective, but in different ways.

(ii) As a **mass communication method** it has a far wider reach than most other tools, and therefore **dispersion of the message** is fast. As most of the supermarkets serve a very wide audience, this is important to create awareness very quickly.

(iii) Although costs can be quite high, the **cost per thousand reach is low** so it is an **efficient** means. Frequent ads ensure that the brand is continuously in the public domain.

(iv) The **message is under the control of the advertiser** and a range of media can be used depending on the message to be put across. For example Sainsburys have used demonstration in TV advertising to show how their range of food can be cooked. The advertiser can choose which aspects of the brand they wish to put across and in which way.

(v) Advertising can stimulate **word of mouth** and press discussion. For example Safeway's award winning 'Harry and Molly' campaign in the late 1990's stole the hearts of customers with its cute actors and message.

Advertising therefore builds the retail brand so that it can be **differentiated** and **positioned** in the customer's mind. It could be argued that only supermarkets with sufficient resources to command a significant **share of voice** will be successful. Advertising is not the only means by which brands can be built but it can pull things together in a simple message.

(b) **Below the line**

Below the line activities include methods like **sales promotion, merchandising** and **packaging**. Sales promotions are good at prompting purchase, shifting stock and features like competitions can increase involvement with the brand.

Too much sales promotion is often thought to erode **brand equity**, with customers buying purely because of the offer and not because of inherent brand values. Customers that only use the supermarkets to buy the **loss leader** products will not provide long term profits.

When budgets are limited, the use of advertising may not be an option, particularly when all competitors are competing along the same lines. For a **follower**, brand sales promotion may be a more suitable strategy

Sales promotion does have a role to play in building brands. For example Safeway's recent campaign using weekly door drops to promote **in-store special offers** has been successful. It allowed the supermarket to be differentiated from the competition, it raised awareness of the low prices in store and generated the association that Safeway is a good value retailer. In addition store traffic was created and the offers appeared so good that they generated word of mouth communication amongst neighbours.

Promotions like **free gifts** with purchases can enhance brand associations if the promotion is relevant (for example, Sainsbury's giving away recipe packs with goods, designed by Jamie Oliver).

Sales promotions can be targeted more closely than mass advertising, and can develop loyalty amongst some groups of customers which means that brand association with users can be made.

Tesco's **loyalty card** has also developed the idea that the brand does wish to help the customer, by offering money off coupons to loyal customers. This boosts their brand message of "every little helps". In fact their loyalty card has been very successful, and some retailers (including Safeway) have dropped their card because they could not create differential advantage.

An important benefit of sales promotion is that it can be **measured** through sales increases, coupon return, usage and so on. Advertising is more difficult to measure since its impact is more qualitative.

Conclusion

The roles of sales promotion and advertising differ, but both can create positive brand associations. The effect of sales promotions may have a shorter life, but if a programme of activity continues then the longevity of the message can be increased.

Advertising has many long term benefits. Neither method can work in isolation and in reality the two methods need be used together for maximum effect.

37 BRAND DEVELOPMENT

> **Examiner's comments.** Many students saw the word 'brand' and proceeded to write all they knew, without concentrating on the question or providing relevant examples. Candidates needed to focus their attention specifically on how marketing communications can help to develop a brand from product, via:
>
> • Differentiation
> • Added value
> • Positioning opportunities
>
> I recommend that future students should explore branding from a marketing communications perspective, as this topic will be examined again.

To: **Marketing Management**
From: **A CIM Student**
Date: **13 June 2000**

Reference : The Contribution of Marketing Communications to Brand Development

1.0   Introduction

The development of a strong brand is important for business performance. The role of marketing communications in the branding process is also important and one that should not be underestimated.

According to Doyle, a brand is a name, symbol, design or some combination which identifies the 'product' of a particular organisation as having some differential advantage'. Brands can apply equally to products and organisations. This report will examine the role marketing communications has in developing a brand, whether it be for an organisation or product, in the business-to-business sector (b2b).

2.0   What are the Benefits of a Brand?

Before examining the impact of marketing communications it is necessary to establish the benefits that branding can bring. There are numerous advantages and they apply to both customers as well as the brand owner. Fill (1999) cites the following benefits for customers.

• Identify preferred products
• Reduce levels of perceived risk and so improve the quality of their shopping experience
• Determine levels of product quality

- Reduce shopping time
- Derive psychological rewards of status, ownership, etc

Benefits to brand owners include the following:

- Normally allows for premium pricing
- Helps differentiate the product from competitors
- Enhances cross-product promotion and brand extension opportunities
- Encourages customer retention and possibly loyalty
- Promotes the development of integrated marketing communications
- Contributes to corporate identity programmes
- Provides some form of legal protection

What emerges from this is that branding is important because if brands are managed properly then marketing performance is likely to improve.

3.0 The Strategic Perspective of Branding

From a strategic perspective, there are three key aspects of branding, differentiation, added value and integration.

Differentiation

Brands provide the means by which a product can be seen to be different from a competitor's product. Branding is a method of separation and positioning so that customers can recognise and understand what a brand stands for, relative to other brands.

Added Value

The second key aspect is that of added value. Brands enable customers to derive extra benefits as one brand can provide different advantages to another. These advantages might be in the form of rational attribute based advantages (eg whiter, stronger or longer) or they may be more emotionally based advantages derived through the augmented aspects of the products (eg the way you feel about a brand).

Integration

For a brand to be maintained and to work it is important that the communications used to develop and maintain the brand are consistent and meaningful. Part of the essence of integrated marketing communications is that all the tools used to support a brand and the messages that are used to convey brand values must be consistent, uniform and reinforcing. Therefore, successful branding is partly the result of effective integrated marketing communications.

4.0 The Role of Marketing Communications

Marketing communications plays a vital role in all three of these strategic aspects. Marketing communications is the means by which products are turned into brands, by which customers can see how the product is different and understand what a brand stands for and what its values are.

Black and Decker discovered that they were losing sales in the trade sector because their products were perceived to be more suitable for consumers and the do-it-yourself market. Their response was to develop a separate brand for this particular trade sector. They used a new name 'Matika', identified the product range through the colour yellow and made it available through different trade channels. The promotional materials and support documentation needed a different "tone of voice" to reflect a more rugged and stronger position. The messages were integrated in order to reinforce the desired positioning.

A b2b brand is often tied closely to the company itself as opposed to b2c brands which often take preference to the manufacturer or company name. For example, a Rolls Royce power turbine is branded Rolls Royce because of the perception of tradition, high quality, performance and global reach that are associated with the Rolls Royce name.

The marketing communications should be developed so that they incorporate and perpetuate the personality of the brand. So, all the Rolls Royce advertising materials should be in corporate colours and contain the logo. All copy should be in the house style and reinforce brand perceptions.

Conclusion

Marketing communications are the means by which products become brands. By communicating the strengths and differences of a brand, by explaining how a brand brings value to a customer and by reinforcing and providing consistency in the messages transmitted a level of integration can be brought to a brand.

38   BUSINESS-TO-BUSINESS BRANDING

> **Examiner's comments**. The word 'branding' led to reams of information on branding but few candidates related it to the question set.
>
> Students **must** read the question properly before they start their answer. Pass marks were earned by relating branding to the business-to-business sector and seeing branding as a form of communication.

To :   **The Marketing Director**
From :   **A CIM Diploma Student**
Date :   **8 December 1998**
Ref :   **Branding within The Business-to-Business Sector**

1.0   Introduction

This report seeks to identify what branding is, establishes what business-to-business communications consist of and then attempts to consider how branding can assist this form of marketing communications in this sector.

2.0   What is a brand?

A *brand* is a design, name, sign, symbol or logo that differentiates one product from another and which is valued by customers. A brand is a composite of tangible and intangible elements mixed together in such a way that the resultant mix is not only meaningful but possesses values that are relevant and pertinent to customers.

Brands have many advantages for both the manufacturer and the buyer. Essentially, a brand *enables the brand owner to maintain some control* over how the products are sold through retailers and other distributors. It prevents the onset of commodification, allows for premium pricing, speeds purchase decisions, generates familiarity, reassurance and most importantly trust. It is through trust that loyalty can be developed, which in turn can bring increased profits and competitive advantage for the brand owner.

3.0   The business-to-business sector (BTB)

Branding has been an integral part of the consumer market for a long time. However, the BtB market is characterised by longer decision-making times, generally high involvement decision processes, the involvement of many people in the decision (DMU), large sums of money and potential risk. In the past, rational informative benefit based communications were regarded as important. However, the merits of using *emotional imagery* in the messages communicated to organisational buyers and by bringing together a number of identity cues under a brand umbrella has been seen to be attractive to many BtB organisations. In many of the markets in the BtB sector, competition is *priced based* and only through communication of the augmented product can the totality of the services and the value that a particular supplier can provide have the roots of branding started to be established.

Businesses buy benefits just as consumers do but they also willingly buy *relationships*. Branding provides for the establishment of a long-term relationship. Personal selling, sales support and packaging are part of the overall 'product' that organisations buy. When combined with guarantees and risk free finance deals, it appears that the embryo of a brand is under development.

In addition to the business benefits of branding, organisations have witnessed the value that some brands in the consumer sector have attained. The value of some brands far exceeds the total tangible asset value and adds to the appeal to create strong business-to-business brands. the recent takeover of Rover cars by BMW, the battle by VW and BMW to buy Rolls Royce and the value placed by Nestlé on Rowntree all testify to the value of the brand and the anticipated future income streams that reflect the overall strength of the brand. In addition, brands have a balance sheet value again an attractive option for many organisations.

4.0   Examples of business to business brands

The *Intel brand* has received a high level of promotional support and represents an attempt to develop a brand that has value for both the BtB and consumer sectors. Hewlett Packard has developed brand strength in the different markets in which it operates. IBM, Dell and Compaq have realised the benefits of brand strength when dealing with trade customers and the leverage it can bring in getting high distributor visibility or 'shelf-space'.

Newcourt Automotive Services is one of the largest leasing companies in the world. NAS supplies contract hire and leasing solutions specifically to business fleets. Through the provision of technology and consultancy Newcourt is beginning to establish a brand. Newcourt's strategy is to promote a consistent identity, values and a reputation that will help differentiate it from its competitors in the longer term.

Dexion is a strong brand in the partitioning and shelving market. Little known in the consumer world, Dexion enjoys a very strong position in the BtB market. What these two examples serve to demonstrate is that branding in the BtB sector has to be market specific otherwise funds are wasted. Therefore the identity cues used need to be managed tightly and focused upon the principal stakeholders.

5.0   The future of branding

The use of branding in the BtB sector will probably continue to increase as organisations seek to differentiate themselves, extend their brands into new products/markets and seek to find new ways of reach key members of DMUs. Some consumer brands are becoming much more flexible and allow their owners to stretch or extend into new markets, for example, Virgin. It is unlikely that this will be possible with BtB brands but opportunities to straddle consumer and BtB markets, as demonstrated by Intel, will be attempted by an increasing number of brands in the future.

39   CORPORATE IDENTITY

Examiner's comments. Many of the answers were unable to show significant knowledge of corporate branding and were unable to point to corporate identity as a mix of behaviour, symbolism and communication which showed an over reliance on the promotional mix. Highlighted integration between messages for internal and external stakeholders is useful here.

To   **Whom it may Concern**
From : **A CIM Student**
Date: **13 June 2000**
Ref: **Report about Corporate Identity**

1.0   Introduction

In this report I will explain the main concepts concerning corporate identity and proceed to explain how internal and external audiences can be reached using corporate communications. From this I will suggest that the development of Integrated Marketing Communications can be based around this orientation to multiple audiences and the need for consistent brand values.

2.0   Theoretical Aspects of Corporate Identity

It now appears to be generally accepted that Corporate Identity consists of three main elements, Corporate Personality, Identity and Image.

Corporate personality is about the nature and characteristics of the organisation itself. To a large extent it is made up of the dominant culture in an organisation and the strategies the organisation is pursing. Personality is about what the organisation actually is.

From this base, management select corporate identity cues which are used to signal particular aspects to selected target audiences. I will explain later about the range and types of cues that can be used. However, at this stage it is important to understand that identity cues can be planned and timed and they can also be unplanned and accidental and yet have a more damaging effect. Corporate identity therefore is how the organisation wants to be seen and understood.

Corporate Image is the perception each person has of the organisation as a result of interpreting the cues they receive. It is clear that people hold a variety of images of organisations and it is this multiplicity of images that represents a major challenge to those responsible for the management of corporate identity. There is a further aspect which is referred to as corporate reputation. This is the deeper, more ingrained set of images that accumulate through time and often through direct transactional experience with an organisation. Corporate image is about how the organisation is actually perceived.

The management of corporate identity can be considered in terms of reducing the gap between the way an organisation wants to be seen and understood, and the actual image that they have. These perception gaps may be large or small, they may affect a large or small number of stakeholders and they may be trivial or they may concern strategically important issues. The recent attempt to force management of Standard Life to float on the stock market (to demutualise their status) resulted in a publicly held debate through the news media. The image and understanding of the issues in favour of the action and the large personal windfalls were vigorously counteracted by the management who did not want this policy adopted. This required them to put forward their arguments in an attempt to correct their members' perception of the short and long term benefits.

These corporate communications are normally targeted at a range of different stakeholders and involve the transmission of a range of different messages. For example, the messages sent by Standard Life to the financial markets would have been orientated heavily towards encouraging them to resist the buy out and look to the long term interests of the organisation. The messages sent to their members would have stressed the financial implications but would not have been technically complex or obtuse. Messages sent to staff might have been geared to keeping them informed of events, to prime them of news that was about to break nationally and to keep them supporting the resistance.

This last group of stakeholders, the employees are increasingly being considered as an important, if not an essential part of the total communication process. With many organisations seeking to provide a high level of personal service as part of their brand's added value, it is absolutely vital that this group of stakeholders is informed, trained and has a strong customer orientation.

3.0 Corporate Identity Cues

The cues used by organisations to reach stakeholders are many and varied and should reflect the media vehicles stakeholders use. However, the diversity of cues can best be seen through the corporate identity mix as framed by Birkigt and Stadler.

- Behaviour
- Communication
- Symbolic

The behaviour of the organisation refers to the actions undertaken, what an organisation actually does, how it performs and how it reacts to environmental events. This also concerns how the people in the organisation interact with those externally and how they are observed to interact among themselves.

Communication refers to the visual and verbal messages which are more immediate and quicker to instigate than learning through behaviour. The style and tone of the promotional mix and the way the company presents itself is an important part of the overall corporate identity mix.

Symbolic cues refer to the logo and letterhead design, normally associated with corporate identity. In reality these symbolic aspects are used to harmonise and pull together the behaviour and communication aspects.

4.0 Internal Communications

Communications used to reach employees have changed a great deal over the past few years. In particular technological advances and the use of the Internet, coupled with Extranets and Intranets have enabled organisations to keep their employees informed. Many new corporate branding launches use video conferences to prime and to simultaneously inform employees across the world in many different locations. For example, British Airways used video conferencing for staff when launching their now infamous tail-fin design in 1997.

One of the main staff based communication issues is increasingly that management now appear to accept that employees play a critical role of interaction with those stakeholders who are external to the organisation. The quality of this interaction is perceived by customers as a means of determining what they think and feel about the organisation as a whole. It is during this service encounter that images are crystallised and the closer these two groups understand each other the stronger the corporate identity is likely to be. Many retail brands have put great emphasis on their customer service training and more recently financial services organisations have attempted to lift this aspect of their brands. B&Q use staff in their television (and print) ads as part of their positioning. This provides motivation and a means by which staff can identify with the brand. However, this needs to be managed carefully as the expectations customers have of B&Q (and their staff) are raised and need to be met in order not to cause customer dissatisfaction and disappointment.

The blend between internal and external communications, another indication of the role integrated marketing communications has to play, suggests that staff act as a strong cue that signals corporate brand values.

40   BRANDING STRATEGY

(a)   A brand is the combination of a term, logo, name, symbol or design that identifies the product or service within a particular market. A soft drinks brand is a combination of the tangible or functional aspects such as the flavour, the shape of the bottle, the price and the intangibles such as service, warranties and guarantees. The final element the augmented product consists of the beliefs that a consumer has about the drink. They may position it as a thirst quencher (Tizer) or a drink to make them look trendy (Red Bull) or help build their strength (Lucozade).

Branding is extremely important in the soft drinks market since it can help differentiate the product from its many competitors. There are many famous brands in this market and it is the brand that adds value to the core product.

A good example is Pepsi. In a taste test- a blind product tasting-revealed that the consumers preferred Pepsi but when asked about their preferred brand they said Coca Cola.

The many benefits of branding are clear but it is through communications that the brands' added values become pertinent to the target market. The soft drinks market is extremely congested and a new brand will need to gain awareness before it can be seen as a brand with unique characteristics in its own right.

(i)   It is effective at building awareness. However, since advertising spend is large in this market to create an impact either a large budget is necessary or very creative advertising. This can be illustrated by Tango, which used an ironic approach to be noticed by its teenage audience.

(ii)   Differentiation. Advertising is good at positioning products to help differentiate them from the competition. Using a particular advertising message or using a certain person to endorse the brand can position it in a certain way. For example Lucozade has been re positioned as sports drink after years of it being seen as a tonic to help you get over an illness. Tango is now perceived as youth product.

(iii)   Advertising can be used to inform customers about specific aspects of the brand tangible features- for example that it now comes in a 2-litre PET bottle for family use. As a visual medium T.V advertising can demonstrate the physical properties as well as creating a mood or style.

(iv)   Advertising can be used to persuade the customer to buy the product perhaps through reducing the risk of purchase and detailing the positive elements of buying that particular brand. For example Sunny Delight advertising emphasised the vitamin c content of their drink to reassure mums that it was healthy for their children.

(v)   Advertising can be used to protect market share by keeping top of mind awareness through consistent and constant advertising.

(vi) Positive brand associations are often achieved only through advertising. Another good example is the Robinson fruit squash advertisements using children's' sayings along with crude illustrations so that the brand becomes associated with the naivety of children.

The role of advertising becomes clear then. Since it can use a number of different media and the message put out is controlled by the advertiser it becomes an important tool in developing branding strategy, particularly for a soft drink where the market is crowded by many well-known brands. It could be argued that gaining a share of the advertising voice is vital for a new company in this market.

(b) Advertising alone cannot establish a differentiated brand alone. There is a role for the other tools in the promotional mix including public relations, direct marketing, personal selling and sales promotion.

Intelligent use of a variety of integrated tools can have a synergistic effect on advertising. A good example is Tango, which used advertising in conjunction with sales promotion. The advertisements advertised a telephone number where you could get hold of the orange megaphone. Here advertising created interest and desire, but the sales promotion created the action impetus.

The role of public relations is to create a mutual understanding between an organisation and its publics. Advance publicity about a forthcoming advertising campaign or on going mention of this can give instant and continued credibility. Sponsorship of a suitable event such as a teenage rock concert might be appropriate. Although costly if the correct match is found between the event and how you want the brand to be perceived it can be very useful. A good example is Sunny Delight who has recently sponsored school basketball leagues and has conveyed the right associations with the Sunny delight brand.

Personal selling in conjunction with trade sales promotions can be used to gain shelf space in the right channels to suit brand values. Ribena have recently offered a free fridge bottle as an incentive and Coca Cola have given away free retro glasses to remind customers that their brand is the 'Real Thing'.

Direct marketing may not seem to have much use in this market but it can be used to encourage trial through distribution of coupons, recipe books for fruit cocktails and so on. If the style of the direct marketing is consistent with those reflected in the advertising it can serve to provide consistency and squeeze a little more juice from the advertising.

To summarise- advertising in conjunction with other elements of the mix will serve to reinforce brand values and position the drink in the consumers mind in an appropriate way, encourage trial and to ensure that when the consumer goes for a drink they reach for 'the Real Thing'.

41 TUTORIAL QUESTION: INTER AND INTRA-MEDIA DECISIONS

(a) Media choice is governed by a number of factors arising from the different properties of the various media options.

The *nature* of the medium in its own right is an important consideration. People purchase magazines for their entertainment value, or because they serve as an information source. The fact that the magazines carry advertising may be of little importance to the reader. However, in terms of information value, editorial stance, style, language and personality, the magazine environment will tend to rub off onto the advertising and particular magazines will be chosen for their compatibility with the products and services being promoted.

Similarly, the *positioning* of adverts within television, radio or cinema contexts can make a difference to how they are perceived. An advert scheduled in the middle of a TV game show will deliver an audience with a different mind set from one scheduled in the centre break of a documentary.

Another consideration is the way in which *people use media*. For instance, many popular radio stations are used as a background to other activities (driving a car, talking to friends, carrying out activities at work or in the home). People are generally unlikely to be giving their main attention to listening to the radio (unless it is 'talk radio'). By contrast, reading a newspaper is a main activity in its own right. Whether the medium is used as sole activity or minor activity will affect the ability of that medium to deliver the advertising it contains.

The amount of *time* spent with the medium can be a factor. Daily newspapers are a relatively quick read in the busy environment of the working week. Saturday and Sunday papers are a more leisurely read in the relaxed environment of the weekend.

Some media options lend themselves to particular *creative opportunities*.

(i)   A number of recent TV ads have taken advantage of the 'pause' button on the video recorder.

(ii)   Television and cinema allow advertisers to use the power of sound and vision together to create an impression. Special effects originally created for film or pop video production can be used to give adverts an up to the minute feel.

(iii)   Other characteristics that must be considered when judging a medium on its *creative* scope are as follows.

        (1)   Potential for colour advertising
        (2)   Potential for movement and sound
        (3)   Space and time limitations
        (4)   Reprographic standards

Booking and production *lead times* may rule out the use of certain media. Magazine space is generally booked months in advance. Television and cinema commercials with high production values will take months to prepare, film and edit.

As well as taking into account the inherent features of each medium, media channels must be evaluated *quantitatively* for their ability to deliver against criteria such as coverage, frequency and cost.

(b) (i)   A media schedule is the formal listing of which adverts are to appear where.

     (ii)   A very small budget may dictate that advertising is limited to certain key times of the year (eg pre Christmas; peak sales periods). A large budget which allows for year round advertising is usually allocated in one of two ways.

             (1)   A *burst campaign* concentrates expenditure into promotional bursts of three or four weeks in length.

             (2)   A *drip campaign* allows for a continuous but more spread out presence.

42   BUDGET PROCESS

Examiner's comments. This is a relatively easy question. It asks for a display of knowledge (what are the methods) and then asks for a proposal (evaluation and reflection).

To: Marketing and Sales Departments - Pantella Hair Care
From: Marketing Manager
Subject: Marketing Communication Budget Determination

As part of my new role for Pantella I wish to review the methods used to determine our marketing communication budgets. Following on from this I will outline proposed methods for determining budgets in future. I welcome your comments prior to our next departmental meeting.

Methods of budget determination

Before presenting the methods that are used by different organisations I need to point out that the theoretically optimal model is marginal analysis. By determining the point at which an extra pound sterling spent on communications generates an extra marginal pound sterling in profit it is possible to state that the optimal budget has been achieved. However, this is difficult if not impossible to determine in the real world for a number of reasons. The main drawbacks are that we do not have perfect and timely information and sales are driven by a variety of factors not just communications (or advertising as first proposed).

The main real world methods are these.

1 *Percentage of last year's sales (or next years)*

   This method involves calculating the budget as a percentage of last year's sales. For example, this may be 5% or 10% but it is not customer orientated, it is retrospective and does not take into account any support that brands may need. For example, to counteract particular competitive behaviour, to launch a product or revive a declining brand.

2 *Case rate*

   This method uses a standard rate which is applied to each unit of sales. For example, case rate × no of sales = budget

   This raises the question of how the rate is actually calculated and once again is retrospective and doesn't consider the market conditions or that an increase in the marketing communication budget could actually increase sales.

3 *Affordable*

   Under this approach we need to work out all the other costs, and after assigning an amount for profit, what is left can be spent on communications. This approach appears to be adopted by product-orientated organisations and those that perceive communications as a cost rather than as an investment. Best avoided in my opinion.

4 *Share of voice*

   This approach requires a measurement of our market share and the total spend on marketing communications by all players in the market. Therefore, share of market and share of voice statistics can be determined and the relationship between the two expressed as a ratio. For example, we hold a 12% market share and the total communication spend (above-the-line) for the market was £87m last year. Therefore, the SOV should be around 12% of £87m or £10.44m. Although this does ensure we have an appropriate 'share of voice' it does not consider our objective to increase market share.

5 *Advertising to sales ratio*

   Closely allied to the SOV concept is the A/S ratio. In each market there is an average ratio of sales to communications spend. In engineering sectors this may be 0.2%, in food 4% and in fragrances 12.3%. The point is that in our sector the A/S ratio is about

15% so we need to understand whether the Pantella brand's A/S ratio is under, on or over the 15% and be able to justify the result.

6   *Media inflation*

This simply takes prior year budget and adds the media inflation rate. This does not consider competitor activity by our organisation.

7   *Objective and task*

This is considered in more detail later.

Proposal for determining promotional budgets for Pantella

So after considering the above I would like to propose the objective and task method of budget determination, in association with other bench marking methods such as SOV and A/S ratios.

Objective and task method works by identifying each communication objective for the forthcoming year. For example, 'raising awareness by 15% in our target market in the next six months' and the appropriate promotional tasks assigned to achieve it. For example, our TV work, print magazines and instore promotions need to be costed. If the resultant figure is not acceptable internally then the objectives need to be reworked or a different promotional strategy determined.

Whilst the objectives and tasks approach needs to be used for both the push and pull areas of our promotional work, one of the main benefits of this method will be that it will enable us to measure our results more productively and control the implementation of each campaign more effectively.

By using the other approaches (SOV, A/S ratio, competitive parity) as a series of bench marking opportunities it will be possible to have a feel for competitive conditions and to retain competitive performance. It is also possible to buy data from PIMS. This is a large database through which we would be able to understand the sector's performance and to invest in communications in such a way that might generate an optimal return on investment. This last point needs to be explored in greater detail before any commitment is made.

43   MARKETING COMMUNICATIONS EXPENDITURE

> **Examiner's comments.** This question was phrased in such a way that it could have been answered in one of two main ways. The first of these is the role and strategic impact of marketing communications whilst the other was to consider how the marketing communications budget was strategically important. Either interpretation was equally acceptable. The answer that follows attempts to consider both of these approaches.

Using our Money Wisely on Marketing Communications

by

A Marketing Manager

The amount of money any company spends on marketing communications, and advertising in particular, is absolutely crucial. Are the communications working, are they effective, are we getting good value, could we get it more cost effectively? These are all good questions, which that all management teams must ask themselves regularly and be able to respond to when challenged.

What I intend to do here is to provide some information about how we decide how much to spend on marketing communications. Before we look at these specific areas it is useful to consider what marketing communications is and what it is supposed to do. Then it will be possible to look at the different approaches to budgeting or *setting the right appropriation*, as it is called when considering the overall amount of investment in communications.

If you think about the key areas where, each and every day, we communicate with various audiences, it should come as no surprise that marketing communications is important to our success and can cost a great deal. Broadly, we communicate with the following.

- Customers
- Dealers
- Employees
- Shareholders
- Financial advisers

- Suppliers
- Local communities
- Competitors
- Media
- Many other interested parties

Of course the level of interaction will vary in intensity with each of these audiences throughout each year, depending upon a number of variables. However, marketing communications is about creating and sustaining a *dialogue* with each of these stakeholder audiences but *not just with our customers*. We need to *inform* audiences about new developments within the company, about new products and services and about what we as a company believe and value. We need to *persuade* audiences, especially customers and potential customers, we need to *demonstrate how we are different* and of value to each of them and we need continually to *remind and reassure* our customers not only about who we are but also about our products and services so that they will keep coming back to us.

BA invested over £60m in their corporate rebranding exercise in order to be identified as a global, not British, airline. Kellogg's, Nestle, Cadbury's, Unilever and the many other *fmcg* manufacturers invest millions each year on advertising in order to maintain and/or grow their market shares. Organisations in the business-to-business sector spend much less on advertising but more on personal selling and sales support. The area where the investment is made is not important to this paper. We are, however, interested in the effective and efficient use of limited resources.

In order to inform, differentiate, persuade and/or remind, we need to invest and allocate some of *our finances to marketing communications*. Choosing the right level of investment is important but unfortunately it is not a science. Yes, we have learnt over the years and we have a good idea about what the right level of investment might be. Some companies allocate a percentage of sales as the appropriation whilst others just take last years figure and add a percentage for inflation. Others allocate what they can afford whilst a few just guess. All of these methods have flaws in that they are neither customer-focused nor designed to do the right job.

Some other techniques involve investing the same as our competitors. Well, which competitor and how can we be sure that we are achieving real competitive parity? The Advertising/Sales Ratio provides an industry benchmark in order that we can understand whether we are investing above or below the industry average. For example, 1996 the A/S ratio for female fragrances was 8.7%, for cold treatments 14.2% and for cars 2.3%.

This ratio has proved useful but it does not provide the answer we are looking for as it focuses only on advertising. As we also use sales promotion, direct and interactive marketing, public relations, the sales force plus all the internal marketing communication activities, there are severe limitations to this approach. However, if our communications are predominantly above-the-line then this might be a useful method strategically.

It was reported that Procter & Gamble wanted to reduce their amount of advertising from 25% to 20% and use the 'savings' to fund price-offs in order to compete more effectively (on price) with their own-label competitors. A counter view from the company was that they wanted use their advertising and media expenditure much more efficiently yet maintain their overall visibility. This was a strong strategic approach and it courted much criticism and debate. Which ever way this policy is interpreted it is the strategic perspective that is interesting and significant.

By gauging the percentage of our communication spend against the total spent by all others in the market we are able to determine what is known as *Share of Voice*. These figures can be compared to our *Share of Market* and through analysis determine how much we should spend to achieve the market share we set ourselves. Whilst this is intuitively appealing there are some real difficulties in making this work and it does not really apply to our growing market.

PIMS (*Profit Impact of Marketing Strategy*) is a database system that uses actual data from real organisations across a variety of industries and market sectors. Through analysis of the database it is possible to determine what return on investment can be achieved based upon a number of variables. Depending upon whether a company is market leader, *number 2* or just another player it is possible to make judgements about, for example, the level of above and below-the-line promotional expenditure, or the right amount of trade communications.

We can use a number of these methods and compare the outcomes. We also determine what it is we want to achieve (*goals*) and how we think our various push (trade), pull (consumer) and profile (corporate) communication strategies will work. We then determine the actual (real) costs of putting it all into action and then make changes as necessary. This objective and task approach is perhaps the soundest technique of them all but it does require a great deal of time and accurate prediction in order to make it work.

Pedigree Petfoods said that after the tins and the cost of the meat the third most important factor to be measured and evaluated was the cost of the media and level of discounts used to advertise their dog and cat food products. This further serves to demonstrate that the level of communication spend can be a very significant part of an organisation's activities and needs a strategic perspective.

To be wise when spending or investing money is important. Our company is important and in order to grow and thrive in the next century it will be even more important not only to make good use of marketing communications but to also invest in communications in order that we maintain dialogue with the right audience using with the right message at the right time.

44   AN ACTUAL STUDENT'S ANSWER

Examiner's comments. I have chosen to reproduce an answer actually written by a student in the examination, including all spelling and grammatical errors. I will make comments about the answer and advise how it could be improved. This answer earned a pass but there is much room for improvement and many lessons to be learnt from this response.

Students do necessarily have to provide material other than that specified as a requirement in the question. For example, the question makes no mention of budgets, strategies and promotional methods. It may be that in order to answer the question students may wish to refer to these elements and display the depth of their knowledge and understanding. However, there are severe time restrictions in the examination and I wish to encourage students to focus their answers upon those parts of the question actually stated.

This question was the second most popular for international students. It was answered by 60% of international students and less than 30% of UK based students. A wide range of interesting campaigns was chosen and some reasonable results were achieved. The key to high marks was the ability to specify evaluation criteria. Clearly, this required a detailed and not superficial knowledge of the campaign.

Outline Report on the RSPCA's Communications Campaign

1 *Introduction - The Campaign*

The RSPCA is currently running a direct mail campaign sending information and requesting for a questionnaire to be completed and returned as well as requesting for a donation.

The mailing is in 3 colours, black, white and green, has the look and feel of recycled materials and interestingly, includes what they call "an inexpensive pen" to be used to complete the questionnaire and a prepaid reply envelope.

The questionnaire asks about awareness of cruelty, whether it has been witnessed and general facts about the RSPCA which may or may not have been known. They also give information about the volume of cruelty cases/workload etc and ask whether this was higher/same or lower than expected.

2 *Campaign Objectives*

The objectives are as follows.

To increase awareness of the RSPCA and its work with animals
To improve understanding that they don't just work with domestic pets
To gauge current levels of awareness
To gauge levels of concern about these issues
To improve their database
To generate income from donations

The objectives are many, however, being a registered charity with relatively low budgets they are making the best use of their approach and therefore their budget. They are not in a position to be able to use many differing approaches for each objective.

3 *Target Audience*

The audience targeted were:
People with established links with the RSPCA
Previous known donators
People known to be sympathetic to animal concerns
Families known to own pets
People known to have been sympathetic to other charitable organisations

4 *Effectiveness*

Although the true effectiveness is yet to be known (as the campaign is still running) my evaluation of its effectiveness is as follows:

Positive: presentation looks inexpensive
            pen enclosed - would people feel guilty not using it?
            reply envelope (encouraging use of stamp)
            effective use of resources 'feel'
            powerful stories and pictures

Negative: pen damaged envelope in post

            lots of different messages and lots of different questions - information overload

            targeted at people already likely to have donated id not to RSPCA then to other charity - are they getting fed up?

            possibly upsetting or could cause offence

BPP PUBLISHING

assumptive close about donation means that non-donors are unlikely to return questionnaire.

5   *Conclusion*

Whilst I understand the considerable budget restraints charities have to contend with I feel the effectiveness is lost in that there are just too many messages. Information overload results in messages just not being heard.

I also believe that they should target outside the obvious with a campaign to change attitude - so that they become people likely to support.

They also need to get research on these people - linking a questionnaire with a donations misses this vital area. All they are likely to get is info about supporters' views and understanding.

> **Tutorial note.** Now read the analysis of this answer by Chris Fill, the senior examiner, on pages (xv) to (xvi).

45   BRANDING STRATEGIES

> **Examiner's comments.** It is important in this answer to think about the internal and external influences and how the answer is structured. The use of a product lifecycle diagram can be useful to get a lot of information across, particularly since this is a presentation scenario.

Brand Dynamics and IMC
Notes for a talk to postgraduate students

Introduction

Thank you for inviting me to talk to you about the dynamic nature of brands. I would like to concentrate today on the impact of this on the marketing communications strategy that companies will need to take, using several examples from my own experience to illustrate my talk.

Why do strategies need to change?

There are many reasons why marcomms strategies may need to evolve throughout the lifetime of the brand even though an integrated approach might suggest that messages and methods remain consistent in order to maintain brand values and positioning. I will start by talking through the brand lifecycle a concept with which you are familiar

Brand Maturity

For brands a cycle of life may be seen which will dictate the most suitable marcomms strategy. For example as can be seen in the diagram below brand are introduced, they start to grow, they then mature and finally will probably go into decline.

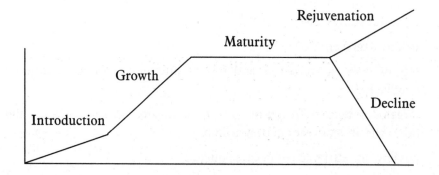

Introduction Phase

Markets: The main buyers of this product will be the innovators at this stage who are willing to take a risk in order to be the first buyers of the product

Strategy: A pull strategy is likely so that some demand is created before major distribution is sought with some push to retailers to allow availability to the next adopters

Marcomms mix: This may well concentrate on a low-key strategy to gain awareness amongst the opinion leader and formers. Public relations through use of media relations might be most beneficial here, or alternatively the use of the Internet supported by media coverage and possibly selective direct marketing to key potential users. When the game Trivial Pursuits was launched providing the game to people on the dinner party circuit enabled the product to be launched without any advertising to be spent. Of course the media will only be interested if the product is a true innovation

Message: The message will appeal to those looking for innovation and originality. Exclusive aspects of the product will be emphasised

Spend: A small budget will be needed to allow us to test the market at this stage

Growth Phase

Markets: The target markets are initially the early adopters and then the early majority. They will require some re assurance about the brand's technology and will want to find the product more widely available

Strategy: A mixture of push, pull and some profile is important at this stage

Marcomms Mix: Wide awareness and comprehension of the brand and its benefits are now needed amongst retailers and end users. So mass advertising will commence to try and capture market share before competition becomes strong along with personal selling to advertisers and possibly some sampling of the brand. An example of this is when Dove, a liquid cosmetic cream dropped samples to selected households throughout the UK in conjunction with a TV advertising campaign to raise awareness and understanding of the brand and its benefits. Also direct response advertising to enable database development may commence

Message: The message will now concentrate on telling as many people as possible about the product benefits and establishing the profile of the brand to reassure buyers through the use of guarantees or money back if not delighted.

Spend: The majority of the budget will be spent during this phase with this initial burst of activity

Maturity Phase

Markets: The buyers will be the more cautious, the late majority who will have seen the product around and will now be willing to try it. Penetration is required at this stage. As late maturity approaches there may well be an opportunity to reposition the brand so that anew market is aimed at. A good example is Johnson's baby shampoo who now position their brand as a gentle, frequent use product for the whole family, not just the children

Strategy: A mixture of pull with some profiling to reassure the new buyers, beat off the competition and develop brand equity so that the brand can be extended in the future.

Marcomms Mix: Some reminder advertising (pulse) along with relevant sales promotions for new customers. A good example here is in the financial services industry that may offer a special interest rate for first time customers. They must be careful not to alienate existing customers by excluding them from very good deals. Direct marketing may be used to distribute sales promotions to those who have not yet purchased. An example of this can be seen in the car industry where Ford have used an extensive advertising campaign backed up by direct methods to stimulate purchase of their Focus brand

Message: Reinforcing brand values to allow safe purchase

Spend: Drip to keep message in the public eye

Decline Phase

Markets: Consumers are laggards who will only now buy because the product is reduced in price or those brand loyal customers who are very used to buying the product. A decision needs to be taken as to the best target group

Strategy: If the product is to be phased out then very little marcomms will be needed. This will concentrate on a limited pull strategy. If the brand is to be repositioned or extended then some profile activity will be necessary

Marcomms Mix: For loyal customer direct marketing may be considered. For others little activity like sales promotion will be needed.

Message: Cheap and cheerful

Rejuvenation – see introduction. The product will now need to be repositioned, using a mixture of push, pull and profile strategies.

It should be noted that although the marcomms strategy will evolve over the lifetime of the brand the pattern is not clear-cut. The strategy chosen will depend on the existing equity in the brand, whether it is completely new or just a new product under the brand name. It could also be argued that the choice of strategy affects the lifecycle and not all brands are destined to die- many will remain in maturity for many years and some, e.g. Weetabix, through clever repositioning will be able to continue beyond their normal life- a good example of this is Lucozade, now positioned as an energiser for active people not a pick me up for the sick. This was achieved through using sports personalities in advertising and sponsorship of sporting activities and events

External Events

Often external environmental influences will affect the marcomms strategy. A competitor may decide to spend a vast amount of money and in doing this steal your market share. Therefore a more dominant pull and push strategy may be adopted- offering retailers promotions to maintain shelf space, or spending more above the line to keep out competition or switching your spend to a new medium to stand out from the crowd.

Economic circumstances may also change. For example during the 80's demand for TV advertising space went up considerably along with prices. Companies decided then to use other methods such as sponsorship to maintain their awareness as shown by Cadbury sponsorship of Coronation Street and Heinz getting involved with direct marketing for the first time since this was seen as a measurable and more efficient method

Technology changes have affected very much the marcomms activity and the use of new media such as the Internet; Tele marketing and mobile communications have affected the level of advertising activity. Budgets now need to be spread across a number of media and an integrated approach is necessary to ensure consistency across the media. The new media allow an individual one to one communication and brand owners need to work out the way to get the best out of this technology that will enable a consistent and integrated approach whilst tailoring their brand to meet individual needs. Getting value out of the brand is important giving rise to the trend towards corporate branding which allows the introduction of new products and brand extensions.

Legal Changes affect what can be done in terms of message and media availability. Cigarette advertisers have changed their approach, heavily using billboard advertising and direct marketing as the only options open to them. Their message has also been affected by legislation and the health warning now dominates. For other companies the sponsorship of TV and radio programmes is now acceptable and been use to good effect by a number of brands- for example the post office sponsoring "Wish you Were Here" holiday programme

Social Changes

There have been a vast number of changes that affect the marcomms approach. For example the trend towards the use of irony as shown in the Tango campaigns. Also the changes in the status of women in society. Messages must always be relevant otherwise they will be selectively ignored. In addition the changes in customer's acceptance of multinational dominant brands may be changing and an ethical profile is needed to succeed. Customers require more information about ingredients; the corporation's ethics and so on and much of this can be put across on new media like the Internet. An example is the clothing retailer Gap that used internal marketing communications to quickly train their shop assistants how to answer difficult questions about the use of child labour after a negative TV programme. In store posters and Internet information was integrated to offer a consistent message

Conclusion

So as can be seen from the many examples given here it is difficult for a brand to maintain a communications approach that is always the same. The challenge is therefore to allow some flexibility in the marcomms methods used, whilst maintaining brand values relevant to target markets. The introduction of interactive methods will allow us to get closer to our customers and this will affect our marcomms strategy in the future. Globalisation also needs to be considered, as the approach taken will affect branding and all subsequent marcomms strategies.

46   EXAMPLES OF PLC

Examiner's comments. This is a deceptive (not trick) question. Students saw the words product life cycle and leapt into an answer describing the concept but failed to focus on the promotional strategy with any depth of understanding. This should be an easy question but many failed to capitalise on the opportunity.

Memorandum

To: Marketing Manager
From: Marketing Assistant
Re: The Use of the Product Life Cycle concept (PLC)

Introduction

In this memorandum I shall set out what the product lifecycle (PLC) concept is and then determine whether the PLC is of any use when formulating and implementing promotional strategy. I hope the following points are of interest.

Definition of the PLC

The PLC is an attempt to explain and map the sales and profits that a product generates throughout its life time. The analogy drawn is that rather like a human being, a product is born, grows, matures and then declines towards death (or with drawl from the market place). As a result of defining these four stages in a products life, it has been suggested that it requires different strategies and tactics at each stage, in order that it flourish and achieve its potential.

This analogy is intuitively appealing and has been used a great deal to explain and interpret events. Whether it has a role to play in defining strategy is debatable, as will be seen later.

When the PLC was first proposed it was intended to refer to the life of generic products such as cars or telephones. However, it has become popularised to refer to particular products, brands and even fashion and more short-term events. The original idea therefore was that the strategies and tactics that evolved from the PLC were industry related rather than orientated to an individual product.

Four distinct phases of the PLC exist.

1	Introduction	the product's launch onto the market
2	Growth	rapid growth of sales volume as the product becomes known
3	Maturity	the product is in a mature competitive market - is no longer considered new
4	Decline	shrinking sales and profits, as the market declines and products are supplanted by new technology.

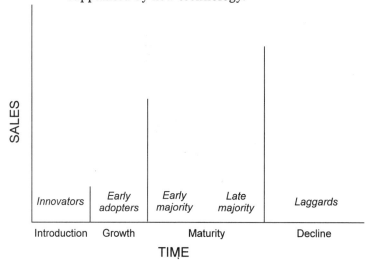

For the purposes of this memorandum I will refer to the PLC as a means of interpreting the lifecycle of individual products.

The PLC and developing promotional strategy

According to the theory each of the four stages have different strategic requirements and the focus here will only be on the promotional aspects.

Promotional Activities	*Introduction*	*Growth*	*Maturity*	*Decline*
Strategic focus	Strong push then pull for awareness	Pull to differentiate	Pull and push to sustain loyalty and exposure through reassurance	Some pull to remind core users
Public relations	x		x	
Advertising	x	x	x	
Direct marketing		x	x	x
Personal selling	x	x	x	x
Sales promotion	x		x	

The table above sets out the strategic focus for each phase and the main promotional activities to be considered. What the table does not show is the way the promotional tools are used to support a push as opposed to pull approach. One particular benefit of the PLC is that it is possible to overlay the various stages of the process of diffusion. Through this it is possible to identify the different types of buyer involved with the product at each stage and through this fine tune the appropriate message and media.

Introduction

For consumer brands this phase is critical as the primary need is to secure trade acceptance (and hence shelf space) and then build public (target audience) awareness. Sunny Delight was developed by Procter and Gamble in consultation with major multiple grocers. When the product was launched the multiples accepted the brand as had been developed partly to their specification, or least to particular category needs including price, ingredient and packaging/size specifications.

Digital TV has just been launched and there is strong competition between the two main players, Sky Digital and OnDigital. Both are using heavy weight advertising campaigns although both have resorted to sales promotion activity by giving away the set-top decoders free of charge where previously the price had been set at £200.

Growth

During growth promotional activity is used competitively to build market share. Customers are normally willing to buy having been made aware, their problem is one of brand choice. Marketing communications should therefore be used to differentiate and clearly position product such that it represents significant value for the customer. The mobile phone market has experienced tremendous growth in the UK in recent years. The four main players have sought to maintain (grow) their respective share of the growing market. Advertising and dealer support have been of paramount importance in meeting these needs.

Maturity

Once the rapid growth in a market starts to ease the period of maturity commences. The primarily characteristic of this stage is that there is little or no growth. The battle therefore is to retain customer loyalty and to do this sales promotions are often used to encourage trial by non-users of a brand and as a reward for current users.

Hoover have had to reposition themselves due to the market entry by Dyson with a technically superior product. Sales promotions alone therefore may not be sufficient and a whole repositioning programme may be necessary to sustain a brand in competitive conditions.

Decline

As sales start to decline it is normal practice to withdraw a great deal of promotion support. Direct marketing and a little well targeted advertising to remind and reassure brand loyals is the most commonly used.

Usefulness of the PLC

One of the main difficulties with the PLC is that the market is always interpreted in retrospective. It is very difficult to anticipate when different stages will be encountered and a lot depends upon the timing of the availability of sales figures. Returning to the original idea of the lifecycle, all children enter stages of puberty and adolescence but the timing will vary and their needs will often depend upon their personality and those of their parents. The same can be applied to products. The timing of the movement between stages will vary and the needs of the parent company (brand strategy) will also influence the promotional strategies that are implemented.

The PLC can help to:

1   Understand variations in demand
2   Account for different profit cycles and hence assist budgeting and control
3   Assist understanding of a products development
4   Assist teaching and understanding of marketing problems.

However, the PLC should not be used as a self-fulfilling prophecy and should not be used to develop marketing communication strategy in isolation of other tools and methods. Yes it can be of some limited general use but competitive conditions and environmental factors are constantly changing and the PLC is not rigorous enough to incorporate the complexities facing brand management.

47   CUSTOMER RETENTION

> **Examiner's comments.** Most students gave the two answers required. Good answers differentiated loyalty from retention; they went on to explain where value was added. It was not enough to describe two schemes. These schemes needed to be assessed for their ability to add value.
>
> It was evident that many students failed to read the question properly.

To: **The Marketing Manager**
From: **CIM Student**
Date: **7 December 1999**

Ref: Customer Retention Schemes

1.0   Introduction

This report explores the suggestion that the development of a customer retention scheme might add value to our marketing communications. To do this I will discuss issues concerning loyalty and retention and then provide two examples where in my opinion the communications strategy has been improved as a result of including the retention scheme.

2.0   Customer Retention

In many consumer markets the number of customers who switch to competing brands is very high. As the level of profitability appears to be directly linked to the number of customers retained it is important for organisations to minimise the number of customers lost each period. 20% of customers provide 80% of profit and according to Kotler, the bottom 30% absorb 50% of the profits.

Financially therefore, it is imperative to control the levels of retention/defection. A brand's health is also indicated by the level of retention as this can be regarded as a surrogate measure of customer satisfaction, albeit a crude one. The UK mobile telephone market is subject to a rate of customer churn (defection) of around 30% but this is spread fairly evenly across the four main players. This figure has been reduced through the introduction of new products such as pay-as-you-go services which introduced new customers to the market and provide an element of stability.

Customer retention is not customer loyalty. These terms are often interchanged but regular purchase may be indicative of convenience and instrumental buyer behaviour which is based around satisficing and the search for valued rewards such as Air Miles and Reward Vouchers.

Loyalty in its true form means that customers might need to make sacrifices in order to remain loyal to a brand. This rarely happens, as consumers readily switch brands among their repertoires and are prepared to trial new retail brands (grocery multiples) if levels of customer convenience and satisfaction fall below acceptable thresholds. Retention should be regarded as a matter of overall product acceptability or at least satisfaction across salient attributes.

Management are now in a far stronger position to manage levels of customer satisfaction and retention through technology. Through customer profiling and profitability analysis based upon transaction data collected through POS systems and reward cards it is now easy to shape the product offerings to meet customer needs more accurately. To a large extent, many supermarket reward schemes are based on the use of their data in this way.

3.0   Impact on Communication Strategy

The development of a customer retention programme could have a number of benefits. It would serve to direct the attention of staff towards the need to be vigilant about standards and the need to drive up satisfaction levels. In that sense it could be part of an integrated marketing communication programme. A retention scheme would also serve as a focal point of a pull based strategy and perhaps reduce the level of fragmented communication activities. Retention schemes are to a large extent customer focused and enable rewards to be offered to different types of customers and in doing so reflect their levels of involvement with the brand. British Airways reward their frequent fliers through a tiered scheme according to the benefits sought by their customers. For example, Blue members are more interested in Reward (for their custom) with a little lounge service, whilst Silver members are interested in service, exclusivity and reward in roughly equal proportions. Finally, Gold members are more interested in exclusivity and service, reward for them is not important.

Our communication strategy would be enhanced as it would enable us to use our resources more effectively and reduce the level of our above-the-line spend. Through the use of direct marketing techniques we can personalise our communications and introduce a more customised approach to our entire operations. Tesco have developed their direct mail operations so that it is now a powerful and important part of their marketing communications. By understanding individual buying patterns and preferred products it has become possible to develop targeted sales promotions, delivered through direct mail, which serve to retain customers and improve satisfaction levels.

One of the difficulties however, is that customer expectations rise, competitors imitate schemes and there is a need to be innovative and find new ways of retaining and satisfying customers. This requires resources and an organisational culture which, if to be successful requires the development of good internal marketing communications.

All of these activities have the potential to affect our corporate image so we would be better able to change our positioning and develop a more robust and contemporary corporate brand. Tesco have moved from a market position based upon relatively inexpensive products and poor value to one that represents excellent value and quality across their operations and has enabled them to become market leader. Their above the line work reinforces the Tesco brand and little effort is spent communicating product offers and particular discounts.

4.0   Conclusion

The development of Customer Retention schemes is an important part of many consumer marketing communication plans. To maintain and grow levels of profitability it is necessary to keep a greater number of customers. To do this properly it appears that an organisation's communication programme benefits from schemes that rewards its customers and deliberately seeks to add value to staff, customers and all those associated with the programme.

48 INFLUENTIAL FORCES

> **Examiner's comments**. This question was very popular, and most made a sound attempt at answering it. Many however just used the PEST framework and failed to show the link between the environment and marketing communications. High marks went to those who did achieve this. There were many opportunities to discuss positioning, defending market share and using SOV, but this depth was missing from many answers.

Introduction

The purpose of this answer is to explain the nature of the influences of the wider largely uncontrollable environment and to evaluate their possible impact on an organisation's marketing communications.

The externally driven forces acting on an organisation vary in size and immediacy. It is not possible to be specific about how a force might affect an organisation's marketing communications but it is possible to make some judgements about the form and general response an organisation should make. For the purposes of this report I will use the PEST framework after first examining the competitive forces.

Competitive Forces

The impact competitors can have on an organisation can be quite critical. Very often new entrants, a new marketing strategy, brand extensions, use of new technology or new products can cause an organisation to review the way it operates, its marketing strategy and/or its marketing communications strategy. One of the most significant forces is a competitor's communications which may either directly or indirectly refer to your brand. One of the responses that needs to be considered is a repositioning exercise or at the least a review of the way your brand is communicated (mix, message, media) and the way in which a brand is perceived, relative to the competition. For example, some manufacturers brands have felt it important to respond to the development and packaging of some competitive retail brands (Coca-Cola and Sainsbury's cola, Penguin and Puffin bars) by taking legal action to protect the way in which their brand is positioned.

A competitor may attempt to use particular product attributes to position themselves which may intrude upon another brand's position. The response will be either to reinforce the communication of the strength of the attribute or move to a new attribute that is thought to be of worth to the target audience.

PEST Forces

Of the wider external environment the Political, Economic, Social and Technological forces are the most prominent.

The **Political (and legal)** environment may change in such a way that an organisation is powerless to control or influence them in any meaningful way. Some industry sectors such as pharmaceuticals are active lobbyists and seek to prevent the introduction of policies and regulations that might harm the way they communicate with their audiences (and influence other aspects of their businesses) Changes in the EU regulations are threatening the use of certain types of sales promotion and direct selling. This will cause organisations to review their promotional mix and to find new ways of communicating. Advertising to children is under threat and if it becomes EU law, will cause organisations in the sector to adapt their communication strategy.

Comparative advertising regulations have changed recently such that Sky Digital launched a campaign that compares their brand to that of their main competitor On Digital. In response and recognition of the potential harm to the On Digital brand, the organisation has had to address the Sky Digital statements and so divert them from their brand building strategy.

Changes to the **economy** can influence levels of disposable income and in turn change perceptions about value for money. In times of recession, price driven promotional campaigns are (in general) perceived to be more effective, while a return to relative affluence can enable brands to return to communicating brand values that do not influence price. Many organisations tend to reduce the level of their above-the-line work during periods of economic downturn but recent research suggest that the brands that survive and recover fastest are those that continue to use advertising to build brands during the depressed periods.

The impact of **social** changes should of course always be incorporated in the marketing strategy. Such influences need to be reflected in the communications used by organisations if they are to be perceived sympathetically and be regarded as 'in touch'. Of course this is very applicable to fashion brands but social views about GM foods have been adopted by Iceland food group as a means of differentiating themselves from their larger competitors. Marks & Spencer, once high street market leaders failed to keep in touch with changing social trends (and the reactions of competitors) and the brand became outdated and of little value (relative to its past). This was reflected not only in the way the promotional mix was deployed but also in the clothing ranges and the style of products, which of course is an intrinsic part of the way a retail brand communicates. The response has been to revise the product strategy as well as use above-the-line and through-the-line strategies in a more contemporary way.

Of all the forces in the external environment, it could be argued that changes in **technology** can, and do, have the biggest impact. The development of the Internet and new methods of interactive communication have forced brands to have an on-line presence and dot.com identity. This requires a new strategic approach which some are mastering but others are not, such as www.boo.com, which went into liquidation. The balance between off-line and on-line communications is important as the need to drive site traffic is imperative for commercial success. During the late 1990s outdoor advertising experienced huge growth mainly as a result of on-line brands generating traffic and top-of-mind awareness as a run up to privatisation (www.lastminute.com) It is not just the Internet however that can impact on organisations. Developments in database technology have influenced the way in which organisations can undertake direct marketing and sales promotions. They have helped drive a move towards integrated marketing communications. The current developments concerning WAP facilities and mobile convergence will undoubtedly affect the way some consumer brands are positioned.

Conclusion

Changes in the wider environment can have a significant impact on the way in which a brand is communicated. These forces are not constant and brand managers need to monitor and keep abreast of the changes if they are to meet the challenges they present and enable their brands to be successful. An effective marketing information system can be of help but there is an overall need for organisations to be flexible and if possible anticipate changes so that their brand values can be retained.

49 EVALUATING MARKETING COMMUNICATIONS

Examiner's comments. It is important to consider a number of different promotional methods and their related measurement techniques in order to be successful at this question. A depth of understanding is looked for along with a link to the objectives that are trying to be achieved.

A good answer will question the validity of measuring and validation techniques, including problems and costs of doing so.

Introduction

This essay will consider a range of marketing communications methods that could be used for the promotion of a fast moving consumer good and try and assess the best methods to evaluate their effectiveness. It is very important to try and evaluate the techniques we use to ensure that we are being both efficient and effective- reaching the right target market in the best possible way to achieve our objectives. Obviously push, pull and profile strategies will need to be judged in different ways.

We will concentrate on post campaign evaluation, rather than pre testing techniques. We will assume that our company are using a range of above the line and below the line methods and concentrate on evaluating the effectiveness of our pull strategies.

Evaluation Methods

The main methods of evaluation can be split into 2- quantitative measures and qualitative methods. The methods used will depend on the objectives we are aiming to achieve. If our methods are more direct then quantitative methods are most suitable like looking at sales effects. Indirect methods may require a more qualitative approach, for example trying to assess attitude change and motives for purchase.

Quantitative Methods

(a) **Sales Promotion**- methods like coupon redemption rates are useful. However they do not tell us in isolation how much extra sales they have promoted. Therefore EPOS data before and after the sales promotion period will be necessary. Another issue is to decide how long measurement should go on for- an initial increase in sales may indicate a pulling forward of purchase which is countered by slow sales as stock is used up.

(b) **Press Relations** - These may be judged through the number of column centimetres or media space has been devoted to our company. Sometimes a qualitative weighting is adopted to try and assess how much of this publicity is deemed positive or negative.

(c) **Advertising** - Audience research for a particular tool can be useful and is available for a number of advertising methods including press, cinema and television. However by itself it does not tell us whether the message has had any effect- only that in theory the audience were there.

Advertising recall will give us an indication of how many people remember our ad. This will not necessarily judge whether the ad has been effective but gives us a crude idea on awareness. Purchase does not just require awareness but also comprehension, conviction, desire and action so this method- although quantitative does not tell the whole story.

(d) **Direct Marketing** - The most 'measurable' method- this allows us to look at issues like cost per order or inquiry, order, profitability and customer lifetime value. However for a fast-moving consumer good the main role of direct marketing is to distribute sales promotion materials rather than generating direct sales so this may not be the most suitable measure.

DRTV linked to free phone numbers can show general levels of interest as calls are monitored. The campaign for Tango soft drinks measured the number of calls to claim a Tang megaphone after their advertising campaign.

Loyalty card info- at present held by the retailer may offer more qualitative insight, even though it used quantitative methods. For example this helped discover the off license sale of wine and beer to couples with young children is correlated- because they no longer have the same opportunity to go out for social occasions.

Tools like data mining have enabled a greater understanding of customer motivation, albeit quantitatively.

(e) **Sponsorship** - This is one of the most difficult tools to measure quantitatively since it is often used to achieve corporate branding. Although awareness of the sponsorship can be judged whether attitudes have changed is difficult to do in a quantitative manner. In addition to look at the effect must be done over time and managers often expect a much shorter return of information.

Qualitative Methods

These more detailed methods like in depth interviewing, focus groups and other "deeper" methods like psycho dram can help establish people's beliefs and brand associations. However due to their expense and often non-generalisability they are not used as often as the well-established techniques. However they are particularly useful to help develop campaigns and establish how campaigns have gone wrong. They should also be undertaken beforehand after in order to look at changes. Observation techniques allow a qualitative interpretation on how people behave at point of purchase.

Conclusions

Campaign Evaluation is extremely important for all products- in particular fast moving consumer goods. However the methods used will be influenced by availability of time, money and expertise. Waiting for results can hinder the roll out of an innovative campaign.

The strategic objective must be considered when deciding on the measurement technique and an appropriate measure taken. For example a new product being launched will need to gain shelf space and so sales to retailers must be an early indication of success. A profile strategy is more difficult to measure since it will take more time and success will use a number of different promotional techniques and therefore measures. Integrated marcomms activity aims to be synergistic so an atomistic measure is not always suitable.

Finally, new methods such as internet activity will allow a mixture of qualitative and quantitative measures as companies can watch visitors interact with the site to enable a greater understanding, and a quicker reaction to customer behaviour. The measurement methods need to be developed alongside the new methods in order that they achieve credibility.

Marketing metrics is a hot topic for most companies but measurement that predicts or interprets behaviour is not always possible. This must be borne in mind when considering the best method to investigate the effectiveness of investment in marcomms activity.

50   MEASURING SUCCESS

> **Examiner's comments.** This question was the least popular on the grounds that it was attempted by the lowest number of students. The key in the question was the phrase direct marketing. Unfortunately, many students failed to recognise this and proceeded to discuss evaluation for any type of mass communication campaign. This reduced their marks considerably.
>
> On a brighter note, a number of students developed grids and matrices to list out the direct tools and media and then listed the appropriate measurement techniques. They then followed the grid with an evaluation of the actual techniques. This type of imaginative response is welcome as it provides clarity and originality.

How successful is our direct Marketing?

To: Managing Director

From: Manager
Bubbles Aromatherapy Ltd

June 2001

Contents

1   Introduction and Background
2   Direct Marketing Methods
3   Evaluation Methods
4   Appraisal of Methods
5   Conclusions

Introduction

Since our launch last year it is now time to formalise the effectiveness of our direct methods of marketing in this end of year report. This will enable us to review our plans for the next few years and also provide a yardstick to measure subsequent activity by. The report will look at each method in turn and evaluate them to see if a better method could be used.

Background

Bubbles Aromatherapy is a relatively small company offering a range of up market toiletries, which have aromatherapy properties. Direct marketing has been the main method of distribution and communication since the launch.

(a)   The target market consists of a relatively small niche of prosperous buyers who are involved in alternative products, seeing aromatherapy as an important part of their lifestyle.

(b)   Distribution via chemists and supermarkets would be impossible to achieve without a fairly heavy investment in mainstream advertising. This would negate our positioning as 'real' aromatherapy products.

(c)   The launch has been supported by some fairly successful P.R. activity.

(d)   It was felt that on a small budget effectiveness could be more easily tested via direct marketing methods.

Direct marketing methods

The following direct marketing methods have been utilised at various stages throughout the year. The method used to evaluate the campaign is stated in each section.

Direct Response Advertising to stimulate interest and build database in a number of different publications including female titles, some specialist alternative therapy magazines and also small classifieds in some more mainstream titles like the Guardian. Direct Response ad offering free catalogue.

These have been evaluated through number of catalogue enquiries and then subsequent sales. Analysis has been undertaken on an ad -by -ad basis and a title by title basis.

Direct Mail of catalogue to British association Of Retail Therapists list and subscribers to Alternative today and own list of previous buyers. Mailed twice a year.

Evaluated through no of orders, value of orders and cost of order.

Internet Banner advertising within 2 similarly minded manufacturers. Orders not taken on line but no of hits established and also monitor flow-through on the site.

Telemarketing - customer rings order through and telemarketing team are charged with order admin, encouraging up-sell and also undertaking customer satisfaction surveys.

Evaluated through sales conversions, length of time of call, successful questionnaire etc.

Personal Selling - 10 demonstrations are held each year at women's Institute meetings to sell products.

Evaluated by looking at sales per event, per no of attendees and demonstrator.

Method Appraisal

It would appear that much of our direct marketing activity is wasted since the evaluation suggests that much of our activity yields little in the way of sales. However this may be due to a flaw in the evaluation methods used which are largely quantitative. The following suggestions are made to compliment our existing evaluation methods.

(a) Customer lifetime value might be a more strategic measurement method.

(b) Conversion rates and cost per sale would demonstrate where effort is wasted in the long term.

(c) Measurement must be related to objectives. Only direct methods have been used so far i.e. based on sales which is a fairly crude measure.

(d) Perhaps some measurement on the qualitative issues should be undertaken. This would give some understanding on why they bought (or did not buy) what they did. This method may be equally valid for a product of this type.

(e) Methods should be tested before they are rolled out. Testing of list, media used, message, promotional offer and all elements of our direct marketing is possible as we become more sophisticated and we now have some history of what has been successful in the past.

(f) Direct marketing is just one aspect of our overall IMC strategy. Therefore the other communications strategies that we use must also be evaluated. For example Press relations.

(g) More use could be made of our on line presence and it is hoped that this method can be used to pre test and post test our strategies through on line surveys etc.

(h) Our direct selling activity is an ideal activity to run focus groups to evaluate the qualitative issues of our own and competitors marcomms strategy.

Conclusions

Evaluation of direct marketing activity is crucial and many methods can be used to complement our existing methods of evaluation. However as a smallish company we should not be too sophisticated and use evaluation to help identify the best possible future strategies and save us money on the worst ones.

51   TUTORIAL QUESTION: DIFFERENCES

(a) *Arguments for standardising communications*

    (i)   Economies of scale can be generated. A single worldwide advertising, packaging or direct mail execution will save time and money.

    (ii)   A consistent and strong brand image will be presented to the consumer. Wherever users see the brand, they will be reassured because the messages received will be the same.

    (iii) A standardised communications policy allows for easier implementation and control by management.

    (iv) Good communications ideas are rare and should be exploited creatively across markets.

Arguments against standardising communications

    (i)   Any standardisation policy assumes consumer needs and wants are identical across markets. This may be a false assumption, as the example below illustrates.

    (ii)   Centrally-generated communications concepts may prove to be inappropriate for the specific culture of the local market.

    (iii) Media channel availability and infrastructure varies widely from country to country.

    (iv) A country's level of economic and educational development may prevent a standardised approach. For instance, a press campaign featuring detailed copy would be a non starter if literacy levels were low.

    (v)   Legal restrictions may prove to be a stumbling block. For example, France does not allow any advertising of alcohol on television; cashback sales promotion offers are not allowed in Italy or Luxembourg.

    (vi) Standardisation may encourage the 'not invented here' syndrome, so that local management become lacklustre about creative ideas and communications policies imposed from above.

(b) The following dimensions are of particular relevance to the *international marketing* communicator.

- Verbal and non verbal communications
- Aesthetics
- Dress and appearance
- Family roles and relationships
- Beliefs and values
- Learning
- Work habits

(c)   (i)   Press may not be appropriate in countries where levels of literacy are low.

(ii)   TV ownership may not be widespread. There may be no commercial stations.

(iii)   Outdoor tends to rely on visuals and it is therefore a good international medium.

(iv)   Cinema is experienced in different ways (drive-ins etc). The quality of films (and hence the audience) varies considerably.

(v)   Radio is mainly a support medium across the world. Commercial stations may not be available.

52   WITH OR WITHOUT?

> **Examiner's comments.** This was a relatively popular question with 40% of international students. This contrasts sharply with only 20% of UK students. Those that did attempt it did relatively well. Tea and coffee afforded candidates a reasonable opportunity to explore various communication issues and demonstrate their strategic knowledge. The concept of breaking into a saturated market appeared to be less well understood. Very good answers were able to demonstrate an intimate knowledge of the cultural/social and market conditions in their chosen country and draw strategic linkages between the different components of the question.

REPORT

To: F W Smith – Managing Director of Super Beverages Ltd
From: T Leaf
Date: 4 June 2002
Ref: UK tea and coffee market conditions

1   **Executive summary**

This report suggests that the tea and coffee *market* in the UK is large but competitive. There is a range of target markets, depending upon convenience or real product preference.

Cultural and social trends are considered: the indications are that the market is unlikely to decline but consumption may be static.

Growth within the market is dependent upon brand switching, which is difficult and can be expensive to achieve.

The *retail structure* reflects concentration in five main supermarkets for the convenience market. The independent sector deals with specialist beverages and each sector requires an entirely different marketing communications strategy.

The availability of a wide range of sophisticated *media* allows many opportunities to reach target audiences.

The report concludes by recommending that entry will depend upon positioning and brand development.

2   **Situation analysis**

This report has been prepared in order to assist you with your decision about whether or not to enter the UK market for tea and coffee. Various aspects of the market are considered, in particular the social and cultural trends, the retail structure and media opportunities.

3   **Target end users**

There are a number of segments that could be investigated further to determine the depth of potential.

•   Convenience coffee users
•   Real coffee users

- Tea bag users
- Real tea users
- Specialist tea users

The majority of tea is consumed by users spread across the socio-economic profile with coffee users skewed more to the ABC1 profile. Real coffee has become more popular in recent years, particularly in the 30 to 45 age range.

Opportunities may exist to position a new instant coffee or tea product by real differentiation. The market is currently dominated by a number of key brands, who use taste and smell (rich aroma), lifestyle (up-market and affluent) and usage (tea bag shape) as the principal means of differentiation. However, the market is relatively static and experiencing little real growth.

4   **Cultural trends**

Traditionally tea is drunk at the end of the afternoon and first thing in the morning and coffee is drunk at the end of a lunchtime or evening meal. These traditions are giving way as new products such as decaffeinated coffee and specialist teas become more popular. There are no significant regional differences to the consumption of either drink although more tea is drunk than coffee.

Consumption of tea in the UK is probably high in comparison to other European markets and from that point of view the UK market is attractive to new entrants. However, margins are tight and profitability is only likely to be generated by developing niche markets or by finding a new market segment.

5   **Social trends**

It is estimated that by the year 2000 over 50% of the UK population will be over retirement age (65). This may mean that the number of cups of tea consumed may well continue to rise. Tea is a relatively low-involvement product decision and it is important to establish brand loyalty, as taste deters switching.

The traditional family unit continues to be eroded as divorce rates continue to climb and the number of single parent families also increases. At the same time there is an increasing awareness of the need to eat a healthy diet, take more exercise and lead a more sympathetic lifestyle. Because of this decaffeinated coffee products have taken a substantial foothold in the UK market.

Associated with this point about lifestyle is the increased attention being given to green and ethical issues. In particular the exploitation of third world workers has been highlighted by a number of pressure groups and in this sector there has been negative publicity directed at tea producers in India.

6   **Retail structure**

The retail structure has changed dramatically over the past 10 years. Five major supermarkets dominate 65% of food purchases. Manufacturer and own-label branded tea and coffee products are bought from these outlets, in packages that suggest a purchase cycle of 2 to 3 weeks. Tea bags are packaged in card based cartons; instant coffee is distributed in glass jars, which adds to weight and cost. To secure sufficient market coverage it will be necessary to gain a listing with at least one of these main supermarkets. A strong promotional support package will be expected, incorporating trade allowances, joint promotions and price deals to remain competitive and provide strategic leverage.

There are a number of specialist retailers who deal with high quality teas and coffees for those segments who prefer high grade, unbranded products. Depending upon the target market, attention will need to be paid to negotiations with central buyers for the supermarket sector or a variety of individual buyers in the independent sector.

7 Media factors

The UK is a media rich country and the choice of media opportunities is expanding. With 98% of the population having access to at least a single television, it is possible to reach a mass market to develop a branded product.

There are numerous newspapers and consumer magazines in which advertising is possible. The development of a branded tea or coffee will be based partly around suitable print formats to reach different target audiences.

In addition to this, billboards, transport and cinema media will be an integral part of mass market campaigns.

With a purchase cycle of 2 to 3 weeks it will be necessary to generate and maintain top-of-mind awareness. Whilst this will incur high absolute costs the relative costs associated with reaching each member (or 1,000 members) of the target market will be quite small.

To promote tea and coffee in this market it will be necessary to use peripheral cues as consumers are not particularly interested or involved. The use of long copy formats is not a requirement and so the media used to prompt awareness and preference will favour television and billboards rather than print.

The are a number of trade magazines, such as *The Grocer*, in which it will be necessary to communicate with the central supermarket buyers and, more importantly, the independent specialist buyers who run their own retail outlets will have access to this publication. Unlike the consumer market, these buyers are highly involved and it will be necessary to provide detail about the product and its constituents and origins if credibility is to be established.

8 Conclusion and recommendations

The UK consumes huge quantities of tea and increasing quantities of coffee. The instant beverage market is driven by a number of major brands so successful entry will be dependent upon accurate positioning and communication with the target segments.

53 MANAGING GLOBAL COMMUNICATIONS

> **Examiner's comments.** This question requires a detailed look at the effect on marcomms strategy of the issues of globalisation. It is often tempting to repeat the typical International marketing theory without considering the impact of these on the management of the campaign.

Presentation to Client, McVitie biscuits

By

Global Advertising

Going Global- the Pitfalls and Opportunities

Introduction

Our agency has been fortunate to help develop your advertising for your UK business since 1998. Now we would like you to consider us as you expand your operations further into international markets. Today we would like to present to you some of the issues that you might wish to consider when developing your international marcomms strategies. Our presentation this morning will cover the following

- Strategic issues International Marketing Communications
- Pitfalls and Opportunities
- How Global Advertising Agency can help

Strategic Issues

Branding

Although your brand is extremely well established in UK markets it is relatively unknown in the new regions. A decision must be made on the branding strategy- should the brand be positioned in a different way in the new markets or should it be similarly positioned as a premium but family accessible brand? As an imported brand there may be an opportunity to position the product as a "luxury" which will command a much higher price than the cheaper home bands. This will affect the promotional mix, media (target markets will be exposed to a different media) and message.

Your marketing communications objectives will tend to focus on creating awareness rather than developing brand values to maintain market share. This will require a potentially large share of voice.

Push Or Pull?

As a new player a push strategy will need to be considered, particularly in markets with strong distribution networks. However shelf space is not necessarily the only challenge and local custom and legislation must be considered. For example would sampling by door drop be allowed, could coupons be offered to allow a trial of the product, what merchandising is possible?

Standardisation or Adaptation?

The marcomms debate needs therefore to reflect whether a standardized global strategy is acceptable or alternatively whether an adapted campaign is more suitable to reflect tastes, culture, and market trends. Obviously a standardised approach offers benefits in terms of global synergy, economies of scale and allows a corporate branding approach but there are disadvantages in the brand message becoming bland and irrelevant to local markets. The communications must take account of the political, legal, economic, social and technological differences in the new markets.

The following must be considered before a solution to this question is found.

Pitfalls and Opportunities

1   Market differences
2   Internal Organisation
3   Message
4   Media
5   Measurement and Research

1   **Market differences**

    (a)   **Social and Cultural Aspects**

          As your product range is in the food arena the product will be culturally bound and may not be eaten in the same context as in domestic markets. The message will therefore be affected, along with packaging.

    (b)   **Language**

          Checks will be needed to ensure that your brand names and labeling do not offend local tastes and whether promotional material needs to be translated in full and whether the translation causes offence. Messages using music and non-verbal content are often considered better if a globalised-standardised approach is going to be taken.

(c) **Competition**

The level and nature of competition may well affect the best tactics to use in terms of promotional mix. If sales promotion is the norm for this type of product then some use of this may be necessary to enter distribution and consumers awareness set

(d) **Economic Aspects**

This may affect the positioning of the brand- if a premium positioning is to be taken then the message and media must be consistent with this message even if the actual price is lower than may be expected in home markets. Promotional costs may be much higher if advertising opportunities are restricted.

(e) **Legal Aspects**

As referred to above we must ensure that no legal rules are broken- for example- knocking copy would not be tolerated in some countries.

(f) **Technology**

The use of and access to technology does vary and although the website in the UK has been extremely good at gaining involvement from the children this may not be available in all countries. Aspects like the address of the website need to be considered to suit local tastes- if a standardised campaign is to be considered then a local domain name may not be suitable.

2 **Internal Organisation**

Your company will not be manufacturing in overseas markets at the present time but there will be local sales and marketing people on the ground it is important that you use an agency with a parallel structure, which has local offices and contacts in the countries in which you operate. They will be able to advise on the issues above and also feed back information on how the campaign is being received. It will be important not to alienate the local managers and so one way to manage the campaign would be to circulate the strategy in advance to gain approval or allow them an opportunity to brief local agencies on their own needs, sharing the best ideas for adaptation by other countries managers. There will be some aspects of the McVities brand position that you will wish to keep constant and the use of a brand manual showing what can and cannot be altered will be essential

3 **Message**

This should be appropriate to the local market needs; method and media used but reflect consistent brand values

4 **Media**

Availability of media for advertising varies from country to country. Cinema Advertising and the use of radio may be more appropriate in rural India but the use of press advertising may be significant elsewhere. The availability of media research to help with media selection is potentially less sophisticated and so local guidance about the best space to buy will be necessary. Although there are many more global media available e.g. satellite stations like MTV these may not be appropriate for all audiences and very local advertising opportunities might exist and should be used. It can work to set an objective in terms of share of voice expected and then allow local representatives to buy media locally, taking account of last minute opportunities, within pre-determined budget parameters.

5   **Measurement and Research**

Access to relevant measurement methods and market research could be sketchy at least and so decisions may need to be based on less scientific method. However objectives must be measured appropriately and so care must be taken when setting these

How can we help?

As an agency Global Advertising have offices or associates in the first countries that you will be investigating with skilled local personnel to handle your business. Although they will liaise with your own local staff you will have access to what is going on through our own account directors who will be able to consolidate all local activity on your behalf.

We can advise on local legal, economic and cultural differences and we understand local media buying conditions. In addition our full service capability stretch to the overseas markets through our creative and other associates. This will save cost in the long term since a single contact ensures that communication is more direct and less likely to be distorted.

Most importantly however because of our great existing relationship with you we feel that we understand your brands and will ensure an integrated brand strategy, albeit with local differences. This will protect your corporate brand position and allow you to think global, act local!

54   ADVANTAGES AND DISADVANTAGES OF INTERNATIONAL AGENCIES

Examiner's comments. Some students were clearly aware of the topical issues and were able to describe the advantages and disadvantages of international agencies. The best students were able to go on and describe the changes that the agencies are facing in the future.

Full service multinational agencies

Over the last forty years many companies have expanded their operations internationally. Initially advertising strategies would have been controlled centrally from the company's head office. With growing size and confidence a policy of 'Think globally - act locally' would be developed. One consequence would then be the appointment of local advertising agencies in each of the operating countries. In time, dozens or even (in the case of very large companies) hundreds of agencies, each with their own specialisations, could become involved. This obviously has many potential difficulties.

Fortunately over the same period as companies expanded their operations internationally so too have advertising agencies. Many international agencies have grown either by setting up branch offices overseas or by merging with or acquiring local agencies. Key among world wide agencies have been groups with headquarters in London eg Saatchi and Saatchi and the WPP Group (which includes J Walter Thompson and Ogilvy and Mather). Another mechanism for growing international advertising services is the formation of international networks or alliances of autonomous companies.

As the trend among advertisers has been towards international brands and global integrated campaigns, the need for the international full service agency has also grown. By 'full service' we mean the offering of a range of communication services: advertising, public relations, direct marketing. It has been suggested that agency structure tends to mirror the structure of their clients. This is shown below.

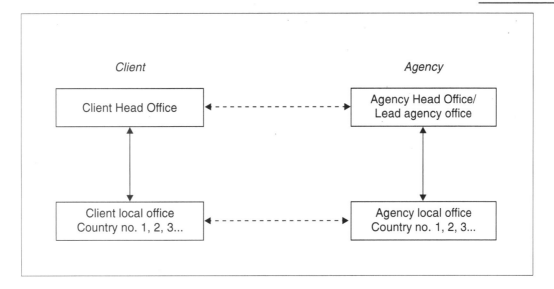

Advantages of multinational agencies

(a)   Centralised control of all advertising effort
(b)   Less duplication and dilution of effort
(c)   Speedy response across markets
(d)   Consistency of presentation
(e)   Pooling of ideas and talents from throughout the agency
(f)   Specialist resources can be made available
(g)   Standardised working methods by the agency
(h)   Reduced costs due to economies of scale

Disadvantages of multinational agencies

(a)   Antagonism is caused at local level
(b)   Possible loss of local knowledge
(c)   Uneven quality in their different branches
(d)   Bland campaigns can sometimes be produced
(e)   Local cultures and styles may be lost
(f)   Quality control can suffer because of complex logistics
(g)   Campaigns are tailored to suit the conventions of the agency
(h)   Smaller clients suffer from lack of attention of senior local staff
(i)   There is a tendency for large agencies to suffer from a high turnover of creative staff
(j)   'Not invented here' syndrome

The changes they are facing

Multinational full service advertising agencies will face many changes in the next five years.

(a)   International client companies are likely to continue to grow, placing even more demands on their multinational agencies.

(b)   Forms of transnational media such as satellite television and the Internet will pose challenges in terms of media status.

(c)   Media buying and selling power is becoming more concentrated. This has lead to the continuing growth of international media independents.

(d)   Advertisers are likely to become more sophisticated and more demanding of their agencies.

(e)   Agencies will need to become more accountable. There is some movement to payment by results systems.

BPP
PUBLISHING

(f)   There is likely to be a continuing concentration of ownership of agencies with fewer larger global organisations.

(g)   There will be a growth of agency branches in developing countries such as Russia, Eastern Europe and China.

55   INTERNATIONAL BUSINESS

> **Examiner's comments**. This was a difficult question and could have been approached from an angle of business to business marketing and/or from an International dimension. The use of examples is essential to pass this question.

To: Marketing Director, JCB
From: Marketing Communications Manager
Date: December, 2001

The role of marketing communications in international markets

Introduction

Marketing communications has an important strategic role in our **business-to-business** market. It is the aspect of marketing which requires a true understanding of our customers' needs and behaviour. It requires a dialogue with our customers and other stakeholders, and integrates all elements of the marketing mix so that they can be presented in an appropriate way.

Marketing communications has an even more complex role within the international arena, and this report aims to highlight the issues that we might experience. Examples from a number of industries will be used to illustrate the main points.

Marcomms Decision Area	International Issues	Solution
Target audiences. Small numbers in business markets	Governments may well be an important stakeholder in some regions	Ensure a variety of appropriate methods are used to reach relevant target audiences.
Buyer behaviour – Decision making unit And extended decision making process.	More complex DMU each requiring unique method of communication. British Airways have used many special promotions for secretaries who book their managers' flights, allowing air miles for the executive and the buyer. Social relationships may be very important	Listen to local managers and provide a number of different styles of promotional material, each emphasising relevant benefits for member of the DMU. Corporate hospitality and personal selling may be useful. Cultural needs training for sales reps.
Promotional strategy- traditionally push and profile in business to business markets but pull becoming more important.	Approach will vary if dealing through agents (push) or direct to the end user (pull). Profile needed to establish the corporate brand and do internal marketing	Recruit global agency with full service capability
Budget allocation	Costs will vary internationally	Set objectives and allocate budget according to task of marcomms and costs in the individual markets. Consider share of voice objective

Marcomms Decision Area	International Issues	Solution
Positioning	Brand may well be perceived differently throughout the international market. For example Mercedes, an exclusive brand in the U.K. is seen as a taxi driver's car in some markets. However Microsoft is truly global with its innovative and young positioning standardised.	Positioning based on best technology can be global.
Branding strategy Corporate branding likely more likely in business to business markets since individual products may well be bespoke	More likely to be standardised in international markets to achieve economies of scale.	Global branding to create feeling of size and importance
Mix- role of personal selling is important in these markets.	Personal selling is affected greatly by cultural and language differences. Importance of establishing personal relationship in high context cultures must be considered. Legalities of using certain methods for promotion is important.	Use local representatives where appropriate and adapt message and method to suit cultural norms
Promotional objectives	Awareness of the JCB name in many countries is very poor where there is massive local and global competition e.g. Caterpillar in US. Our objectives will theretofore vary through out the world. Marcomms may well need to Differentiate, Remind, Inform or persuade.	Set objectives in consultation with local managers, based on market conditions and choose relevant tools to achieve these objectives.
Media	Availability of media is not consistent throughout the world. Lever used cinema based infomercials in India as TV not available. In addition government control of advertising may affect costs and availability. In the West trade magazines more available.	Use agencies with local knowledge to buy relevant media, setting objectives in terms of target audience and coverage required but allowing them to choose the methods.

Marcomms Decision Area	International Issues	Solution
Message- tends to be more rational in business to business, high involvement markets. Different messages for each member of the DMU	Problems of translation and language e.g. Nova in Spain meant doesn't go so not a suitable name for a car. Company name may be difficult to pronounce English language may not be spoken	Allow adaptation of message so as not to offend local sensitivities and ensure that message is put across in a meaningful way. Avoid humour which may be interpreted in different way, For brand awareness and corporate identity rely on visual approach. Test appropriate names and take local advice. Translate literature and have local URL for websites.
Measurement	Research infrastructure may not be in place.	Set objectives where measurement is possible.
Management	Local managers may wish to avoid communications campaign invented elsewhere.	Control the brand by using a brand book to show elements which must not be changed. Circulate good ideas. Allow some choice.

Conclusion

The difficulties of dealing in a business to business market are exacerbated when operating internationally. The above grid describes the area of marcomms where the differences are greatest, and makes some suggestions to help overcome these difficulties.

The decision to standardise or adapt the marcomms will depend on whether the need for communication to play a DRI orP role is consistent throughout the world . Standardisation may well bring economies of scale, and suggest a more integrated and strong company, but tactical issues may need to be more sensitive of local nuances.

56 DUTTON ENGINEERING

> **Examiner's comments**. Some candidates tried to write a marketing communications plan which showed they did not know what key strategic communications issues were.
>
> Candidates should have set out the issues and then dealt with each one. Many candidates failed to see that each point was linked by the integrated marketing communications concept. Few students attempted to work out a budget for marketing communications.

To: Dutton Management
From : Marketing Communications Advisor
Date: 7 December 1999
Ref : Marketing Communication Issues facing Dutton

Summary

Introduction

(a) Key Communication Issues

The Key Communication Issues (KCIs) facing the company are drawn from the change in marketing strategy and the need to harness the current culture and strong customer orientation that staff have. The search for new customers, in current markets, represents a significant shift away from the tight current customer orientation where the communication strategy (or approach) is based upon the need to retain customers through high levels of satisfaction. The practice of Customer Relationship Management has been successful and should not be abandoned. What is required is a complementary and integrated marketing communications strategy that builds on what the company already has.

KCIs will be:

1. The characteristics of the targeted market segments. What are the perceptions and attitudes of current non-customers towards Dutton and their current suppliers? Such information will be essential to the message and media decisions necessary to position Dutton.

2 How are competitors' communicating with the target market? Once again there are implications for the positioning strategy.

3 How many new customers are required and what will be their geographic spread? If a small number of new customers are to be located in a tight accessible region then there may be message and media savings.

4 One of the prime KCIs concerns the branding strategy. It would appear that Dutton have a certain reputation for innovation and management style. Is this Dutton brand to be developed as part of a corporate brand or is branding to be more product orientated?

5 Following on from the branding position decision are issues concerning the content of the messages to be communicated. This is partly derived from the positioning statement but the relative balance of rational and emotional message style will have a strong bearing upon how Dutton is perceived.

6 A further KCI concerns the media to be used to reach the target audience. It would seem that the use of new media technologies would be useful if the personalised customer focus is to be perpetuated. Issues concerning the configuration of the promotional mix and the implications of possibly deploying a sales force need to be examined. If a small sales force is to be appointed, how will they interact with the current customers?

7 The revised communication strategy will represent an investment. Therefore, it will be important to determine the right level of human and financial resources that are to be used and consider where any new resources are to be obtained. For example, it may be possible to outsource the task to find new customers, to a field marketing organisation or employ agents. Alternatively, Dutton may wish to retain a high level of control over the search and new customer acquisition process in which case it may be better to employ a small sales force.

8 The final KCI concerns the need to plan and integrate the new marketing communications strategy. It appears that this aspect of planning and consequent liaison with other outsourced providers (eg advertising agencies) will require a set of skills that the current management team may not possess. This could mean the recruitment of a senior marketing manager or a current manager taking on new responsibilities. This decision will also impact on the culture of the organisation.

(b)   Recommendations for Dutton's Marketing Communications Strategy

Once the KCIs have been addressed it is important that any responses and answers be implemented as necessary. These recommendations are presented as a means of indicating the scale and direction of the communication strategy, based on the information provided. However, further research would be advisable.

9 In order to maintain and build upon their reputation for customer care, Dutton should be positioned as a Corporate Brand whose identity is based around the care concept.

10   In order to develop new business it would appear that the recruitment of a traditional field force selling team would not be compatible with the current culture or business philosophy. Outsourcing the operation or appointing agents may be more appropriate. However, new business can also be developed through the use of eCommerce facilities and this would also be of benefit to the current customer base. It is recommended that Dutton develop an eCommerce facility and project their identity through new technology.

11   It is also recommended that an integrated approach be adopted. This would allow for the following:

(a)   A consistency of messages reflecting a coherence between the philosophy and culture of the company.

(b)   The maintenance of current customer goodwill.

(c)   Lower media and management costs.

(d)   Potentially higher impact of all communications (product, price, place and promotion).

(e)   The continued involvement of staff as an integral part of the communication activities.

12   One member of the senior management team be assigned to be responsible for Dutton's overall communications, both internal and external. This will involve the development of the eCommerce facility and the appointment of a suitable local agency to be responsible for the creative and media planning work.

13   A sum of £115,000 be allocated to marketing communications over each of the next two years. This represents 5% of this year's turnover. This figure needs to be revised as necessary, although further investment will be required to develop the eCommerce facilities and associated activities. Once installed there will be substantial transaction cost savings, some of which could be redeployed into eCommerce.

Conclusions

Dutton are in a strong position to develop and to exploit their market position to generate new business. Through the use of an integrated approach to marketing communications and the incorporation of eCommerce facilities, Dutton should be able to leverage their current strengths in order to grow the company.

57   WOODSTOCK FURNITURE

Examiner's comments. The compulsory question will be used to challenge students about strategic marketing communications issues. The following terms should be highlighted in this context.

- Positioning
- Differentiation
- Added value
- Strategic approaches (pull, push, profile)
- Resources (especially financial)
- Objectives
- Audience
- Message style
- Media selection
- Integration

The majority of students used a suitable framework, but were unable to develop strategy or consider Woodstock's corporate brand. Another disappointing feature was the poor use of the figures that had been provided.

Integrated Marketing Communications Plan

for

Woodstock Furniture Co Ltd

Prepared by

A CIM Student
June 2000

Contents

Executive Summary

Introduction

Context Analysis

Promotional Goals

Marketing Communications Strategy

Promotional Methods

Budget and Management Control

Evaluation

Executive Summary

This marketing communications plan for Woodstock Furniture Company seeks to build on the business and marketing strategies and over the next two years develop the Woodstock corporate brand. Funds are limited and this plan seeks to develop the brand by repositioning it away from the high street competitors as a high quality craftsman brand. This will be achieved by making the brand aspirational and will use a range of promotional tools designed to reinforce the craftsman position and by stimulating word-of-mouth communications.

Introduction

This Integrated Marketing Communications (IMC) plan has been developed for the Woodstock Furniture Co (WFC) based on the information provided in the briefing document. It covers a two year period and is designed to build on the marketing strategy which has already been put into position. WFC needs to develop its corporate brand and this plan sets out the way in which this is to be achieved, the costs and the timing associated with the activities.

Context Analysis

In order to understand the situation facing WFC it is necessary to understand the context within which the communications are to be implemented. The following analysis sets out some of the key communications related issues facing the company.

Business Context

The company's performance has been quite variable over the past few years. Revenue has grown to £1.7m and profits stand at £117,300. Market share is 21% and the corporate goal is to grow at 15% pa. This may be difficult in a static market but with property prices in London and the South East starting to level out more people may decide to withdraw their homes from the market and wait for prices to rise in the future. In the meantime they may choose to refurbish their kitchens. Kitchens are an important room for buyers when they consider a house purchase.

The competition from the high street brands is seen as a threat but in terms of materials, product quality and design they do not attract the more discerning customer, sought by WFC. The promotional materials used by these large brands pose a threat and serve to homogenise the market. As a result of this there has been a change to the organisation's view of its own business. It no longer perceives itself as a manufacturer and installer but as a craftsman based company who design and construct high quality furniture to match and complement the interior of a home. This decision represents a repositioning away from the high street retailer based competition and seeks to differentiate the Woodstock brand. This change in purpose needs to be communicated to relevant stakeholders and acts as the base for this communications plan.

Customer Context

WFC customers are characterised by their wealth. They are affluent and can afford to have kitchens and bathrooms crafted to complement their homes. It is important to them that they appoint companies who attend to detail and who are able to match the decor of their homes. The communications that are recommended here reflect the privacy that the target audience values. The purchase decision represents high involvement so it is important to develop positive attitudes prior to purchase. This will require the development of high levels of trust which needs to be converted into commitment to the WFC brand. The strength of the credibility and subsequent customer satisfaction with their new installation should help provoke positive word of mouth comment. Advocacy can be developed if post purchase communications maintain levels of purchase satisfaction and privacy.

Members of the target market take pride in their homes and have a modern outlook. This is demonstrated by their interest in new technology and innovations generally. It should therefore be quite feasible to communicate with them through the Internet.

The marketing plan specifies that alliances are to be created with other manufacturers in related markets (conservatories, studies) which represent a horizontal dimension. In addition, new markets are to be approached through the development of new relationships with architects and property developers in what is a vertical dimension. This will require suitable communications.

Stakeholders

The brief fails to mention other stakeholders in detail but WFC needs to identify key stakeholder audiences. These may be associated with the new markets (eg trading association for conservatory manufacturers) or financial institutions and venture capitalists in an attempt to attract investment. Communications with these audiences need to reflect the values and performance of WFC rather than product range or terms of business.

Organisational Context

The company needs to update its old systems and procedures and become more efficient. However, the values associated with craftsmanship must not be lost. Rather, they need to be incorporated in the style and format of communications with the various target audiences. One way of doing this is to build on the loyalty and affinity many of the staff have for the organisation. Their knowledge of the market and the organisation can be used to signal high value, prestige and their behaviour harnessed as a strong corporate identity cue.

One of the most critical factors is the small amount of financial resources available for marketing communications.

External Context

The wider external environment is relatively unimportant in this context. It is unlikely that changes in the political arena will impact on the company but changes in the economic conditions (eg changes in capital gains taxation, stamp duty) might affect decisions to invest in kitchen furniture. However, it is felt that promotional materials and the new position should not stress, or even mention price, as this is not a decision criteria for this target audience. Wider social influences are few and technological influences limited to the methods WFC can use to communicate with its target audiences.

Promotional Goals

Three main types of objective can be determined:

1 *Corporate Objectives*

   These refer to the revised mission which repositions the organisation as a craftsman based organisation which designs and builds high quality bespoke furniture. This needs to be understood and accepted by all employees within 3 months and 75% of all strategically significant stakeholders within 6 months.

2 *Marketing Objectives*

   These are that the company must grow at 15% per annum, that prices should be adjusted to reflect the premium position and that new marketing channels (vertical and horizontal based relationships) need to be developed.

3 *Marketing Communication Objectives*

   The marketing communication objectives are to reposition the company and develop a corporate brand which reflects values of craftsmanship.

In order to accomplish this it will be necessary to first raise awareness (60% prompted) amongst the target customer audiences, then build positive attitudes towards the brand. This will be accomplished over the next two years.

In addition, communications need to reach architects and property developers (80% awareness) and links with other carefully selected manufacturers need to be established.

Marketing Communications Strategy

Owning a WFC kitchen should be regarded as a signal of achievement. However, the limited amount of funding restricts the amount and impact that the marketing communications can be expected to deliver. Therefore, a strong pull strategy is not realistic at this stage of development. The main weight of the campaign should be directed to a profile strategy and the generation of word of mouth communications. The essence of the profile strategy is to differentiate WFC on the basis of its total craft approach, employee skills and overall attention to the detail of customer needs. The brand needs to be repositioned as *aspirational* among successful entrepreneurs, sports personalities and other celebrities.

The strategy should be built first around the employees. These people need to be trained in customer service and management so that they carry and reflect the high values of the WFC brand. Whilst this is proceeding we need to reconsider the design elements of our corporate identity to ensure that it conveys the correct values that support the Woodstock brand, in all the ways that we project it (letterhead, workwear, vehicles etc.).

The next stage will involve the development of a suitable web site that seeks to provide information and be capable of collecting information about potential customers. A more extensive and interactive web site will be beyond the current resource levels and should be developed as a separate business strategy, at a later date.

A suitable set of consistent corporate identity cues need to be developed and conveyed through reasonable points of contact with customers and architects.

In order to reach architects and other specifiers a push strategy is also required. This includes appropriate sales literature which must include product specification (capabilities) information. High quality photography is not important, just the accuracy and completeness of the information provided.

Towards the end of the two year period aspects of a pull strategy might be introduced.

Promotional Methods

In order for the corporate brand to become established, a *word of mouth* campaign is to be developed, perhaps through a viral email campaign and selected kitchen based 'parties' (events) at special high profile locations.

Public relations activities are essential and could feed off the 'parties' by placing articles and editorial features about kitchens and related issues, in suitable magazines and newspapers. This is crucial to establish the values of the WFC brand.

Advertising in trade journals will be necessary during the first year. Placement in up-market consumer magazines is recommended towards the end of year 2 or possibly later as the word of mouth campaign may still be running.

Sponsorship may not be possible but should be considered for the longer term. An association with the arts, certain food manufacturers or fashionable yet well designed restaurants may complement the required positioning.

Personal selling remains an important part of the promotional mix. This is necessary not only to finalise customer orders but also to meet architects and to arrange horizontal alliances. In reality, there may only be a few people in the organisation responsible for personal selling but regardless of their status, these people need to be advised of the repositioning, given suitable promotional materials and trained in closing orders to increase the conversion ratio. Selling to architects and specifiers is very different to selling to end user customers. It may be worth considering the recruitment of someone with suitable skills and experience which can then be transferred internally.

Direct Marketing will be useful in the second year as names and addresses of potential customers build. The current format of the brochure needs to be revised especially with the technical data required by the specifiers. The craft approach needs to be reflected in a contemporary style.

It is important that these activities be coordinated, timed and delivered in such a way that the audience perceives a single consistent message, whether this be through the actions of employees or through the web site or sales brochures.

Budget and Management Control

The budget available to WFC is approximately £85,000 for each of the two years of the campaign. This represents 5% of revenue and does not take into account higher margins or increased revenue in year 2. Cash flow needs to be monitored carefully to ensure there is no over commitment to the marketing communications strategy.

PROMOTIONAL TOOL	Q1	Q2	Q3	Q4	Q5	Q6	Q7	Q8
Public Relations	x	X		x	x	x		x
Email Campaign			x	x				
Direct Marketing						x	x	x
Advertising – Consumer								x
Advertising – Trade				x	x	x		
Employee Training & Communications	x	X			x			x
Corporate Literature and Sales Brochures		X				x		
Web Site Development	x	X	x					

Table 1.1 Schedule of Promotional Methods

Evaluation

The campaign should be evaluated not only at the end but also periodically through the campaign's life. The limited number of funds suggests that official recall and recognition techniques will not be possible. However, it should be possible to record informally where and how new customers and architects first heard of WFC. Once the Web Site is up the number of hits and the collection of names, addresses and other materials should be possible.

Finally, the campaign should be tracked against the objectives listed above. It is through some understanding of the level of awareness and the attitudes held about the Woodstock brand that the true worth of the campaign will be understood.

58   APOLLO DATA LOGGERS

Examiner's comments. It was essential in this question to talk about strategic aspects of marcomms, particularly issues on positioning and branding. Students attempting to produce a marketing plan would not be successful here. It is also important to prioritise the communications issues in part a. The use of e-commerce is an important aspect of future marketing communications but students should not forget the traditional methods and the problems that could be associated with its implementation.

To: Board of Directors, Apollo Data Loggers

From: Marketing Manager

Date: December 2000

Re: Future Marketing Communications Strategy

Introduction

This report will investigate our future marketing communications strategy for Apollo Data Loggers (ADL) that will contribute to the achievement of our future marketing objectives. It will begin by identifying the key strategic issues that are pertinent to our success, concentrating on our distribution network and clients. The second part of this report will put forward recommendation for future Integrated Marketing communications (IMC), showing how we can make smarter use of the technologies available.

(a) **Key Strategic Issues**

Several key strategic issues need to be addressed through out our IMC strategy; these will be prioritised at the end of this section to allow us to discus the best resource allocation.

As we know ADL provide a superior product in terms of data logging technology but we have not concentrated our efforts in any way. Since data logging equipment can be used in so many markets then we are spreading our efforts too thinly and our communication is not tailored. Of course we do not have sufficient resource to blitz all potential markets and communicate with them all successfully so it is strategically important to decide which target markets are likely to generate the highest return. A niche marketing approach will allow us to choose the best marcomms methods, media and messages for that particular market- like we do with our products. Above all it will allow us to understand our customers marcomms needs better.

Our product range needs frequent adaptations to meet client needs so that our products are almost bespoke. However profitability and our marcomms activity do not reflect this. Our literature and brochure is often out of date and does not reflect the level of service and technology that we offer our clients

Our turnover per distributor of only around £71,000 with profitability of only 6% suggest that some of our distributors are less important than others and therefore our marketing communications budget should be used wisely, concentrating on those markets and distributors where there is greatest potential.

At present, communication with the end customer is just one way- we receive little feed back other that the ad hoc contact we receive on visits to site and exhibition support. Much of the feedback we receive is via distributors who will act as gatekeepers and interpret the message in a way that reflects their own agenda. It will therefore be important to allow a free flow of information three ways to ensure that distributors and customers have equal say- a "trialogue!" It is important to try and ensure that our main distributors feel that they are in partnership and this will be achieved through better communication.

Presently the message customers and distributors receive is rather fragmented and our use of a very traditional business to business communication mix does not reflect what ADL is about- our product are highly technical and cutting edge and our marcomms should reflect and announce this.

We need to decide what our branding strategy should be- at present we could fall into the trap of being just another equipment supplier but this would suggest competing on price. There are two options.

1   Use a product branding strategy that tries to position a (range of) product for each unique market. This would allow us to serve many different markets at the same time. However this will be expensive and difficult since many of our products are bespoke.

2   Undertake a corporate branding strategy, initially concentrating on a few strategically important markets but telling our stakeholders, including staff here, what ADL is about- superior technological back up and the most effective products and superior service. Then any product or revision that comes from ADL will be seen to have the same values- and distributors will be guided by this principle.

Finally our global presence, likely to increase, must allow the same level of service to our overseas markets as clients get at home. We need smart technology to allow us to achieve this.

To summarise the following priorities need to be taken into account, with the most compelling first,

1   Decision on branding? This will require discussion with all stake holders- internal and external, including key distributors and customers. We probably need to consider a corporate branding approach to reflect our enhanced service orientation and our superior technology and support.

2   Positioning- what do we stand for in the market place and what markets do we want to position ourselves in? Which partners will be key?

3   Marcomms objectives need to be set- these must help us achieve our marketing and corporate objectives.

4   Integrated marcomms- across product and distributors so that unified methods and messages are received.

5   Facilitation of dialogue with customers, distributors and staff

6   Faster communication to all key distributors and customers

(b)   **Future Integrated Marketing Communications**

In order to address the above issues we need to start to move towards a fully integrated marcomms system to pull together the service and product offering and keep all stakeholders informed in a unified way.

Technology could be the key to ensure fast, three way communications even across our global markets.

Extranet

We are already using email systems but in order to offer a more specialized and useful service to our customers and key distributors an extranet system needs to be developed which allows access to

- Up date information as required
- On line ordering and stock control
- Electronic Data interchange offering on line payment systems

This will only be accessible to key account distributors and customers but will allow three-way information and move towards a fully integrated customer relationship management system. Any communication will be recorded, whether by phone, through email or Internet and so our service personnel will know previous customer history at all times and will be able to provide a better service, regardless of point of contact.

Website

This will offer general corporate branding information and we will be able to monitor visitor activity and update the site as necessary. Customers may use this as a first port of call and be signposted to information on their local distributor sites, troubleshooting, ordering etc. Once our chosen markets have been established we can ensure that we are accessible through relevant search engines, possibly considering banner advertising on relevant sites. Press information and shareholder information can also be made available at this port of call.

Intranet

For sales personnel and internal engineering staff to allow access to up to date info on customers, products and services. Fast speedy information, relatively cheaply transmitted is the key here and can help service engineers on site to get the data they receive if mobile telecomm access is also made available.

Laptop and other mobile technology

Sales people can use this to access relevant sales presentations and information at customer sites and distributors will also have access to this relevant technology

CD ROM

Brochures need to be made more up to date. Initially CD ROMs could be supplied for those customers that require this with electronic brochures replacing this technology eventually. A reasonably inexpensive way for information to be supplied and updated to the smaller customers

Database

This could record all customer and distributor activity and behaviour to allow better targeting of marcomms messages in the future. Registration on websites and data capture of source will allow a more focused and relevant approach.

Video Conferencing

To offer the opportunity for customers/ distributors and our own engineers to communicate at the same time.

Traditional Methods

It would be unwise to move to the new methods mentioned above without considering a better use of the more traditional methods like advertising, public relations, direct mail and exhibitions. However these will be made more efficient as we use the technology to measure the effectiveness of this activity and discover the most suitable media for our chosen markets and our positioning strategy. The new communications technology will be a good public relations story. The methods will be used in conjunction with our distributors and all relevant leads and information will be shared with them. Once this partnership has been established then they will commit to us and share costs of advertising and exhibitions.

Conclusion and Final thoughts

This report has made some suggestions of how technology can be used to help achieve amore integrated marcomms strategy. However it must be borne in mind that this move to a fully integrated one-touch CRM system is not without problems.

- Distributors may be suspicious of technology for fear of losing their clients direct to us.

- The ideas above are expensive initially in terms of resource but will eventually speed up and integrate the marcomms process. The process will need to be managed over time.

- The technology needs to be accessible by all key stakeholders.

- Corporate branding needs to guide the use of technology- gimmicks will have a negative effect on our brand and if there are technical hiccoughs then this will reflect poorly.

- Internal marcomms must not be ignored.

However a conscious development towards a CRM system will ensure an integrated marcomms strategy, provided the corporate branding and objectives guide the implementation and an integrated use of the full promotional mix for communication with all stakeholders is taken. Success must be evaluated at all times.

59   BREAKFAST CEREALS

Examiner's comments. This was not an easy question and it was designed specifically to test understanding of strategic issues.

I was pleased that a large number of students displayed some good strategic awareness and tried to answer appropriately. In some cases the depth of response was not suitable but many students did write a great deal and provided genuine insight and understanding. Increasingly, students are becoming aware of the role of positioning, as demonstrated here by trying to relate positioning strategies to each of the brands.

Some students were totally lost and resorted to rewriting much of the information that was in the mini-case – understandable but not very productive in terms of marks. Too few students tackled the SOV statistics. Had they understood the concept they would have achieved high marks.

Overall, students made a good attempt, did better on Question 1(a) rather than Question 1(b) and displayed an increasing awareness of strategic topics.

The Ready to Eat Breakfast Cereals Market

An evaluation
And Strategy

Prepared by
CIM Student
June
2001

Contents

Executive Summary

Introduction

Present Players- An Evaluation

(a)   Kellogg's
(b)   Weetabix
(c)   Cereal Partners

Suggested Marcomms Strategy
Weetabix

Conclusions

Executive Summary

This report looks at the highly competitive ready to Breakfast Cereals market in the United Kingdom, which is presently dominated by three main players- Kellogg's, Weetabix and Cereal Partners.

As the market is in maturity phase an evaluation of the present marketing communications strategies for each company is undertaken which shows how each has responded to the environmental changes including social changes and the power of retailers. It compares the success of each company communications and branding strategies.

The report concludes by offering some suggestions for the marketing communications strategy for Weetabix and stresses that the company must continue to use the brand strengths to maintain and improve current market position and develop their relationships with the retailers and their chosen market segment.

Introduction

The market for ready to eat cereals is very competitive and would appear to be in maturity at the present time with growth for individual companies being possible through product development, better market segmentation or more effective promotion to allow them to steal market share from competitors. The threat of own label, which is growing at 5% per annum, is a major threat and presently only Cereal Partners have benefited by making some own label products. However gaining shelf space is key to success and the dominance of some retail groups in the UK would suggest that a well-developed push strategy is important

There are also many social changes in the market that may be useful in developing successful marketing communications strategies in the future. These include repositioning as an all day snack, trend to healthy eating and the trend to all day 'grazing' rather than eating at mealtimes.

Cereal purchase may well be routine with limited problem solving and switching is a possible option for those on a tight budget. Which could mean branding has a big role to play in helping consumers to choose their product since it allows differentiation, and aids decision-making. It is also important for the manufacturers since it avoids commoditisation of the product.

Each Manufacturer has taken a different approach to their marketing communications strategy, with varying success and these will now be examined in turn.

(a) **Kellogg's**

Kellogg's appear to be largely concentrating on pull and profile strategies. As market leaders (42% share by volume) they aim to continue their dominance through aggressively slashing the price of **some** of their products and increasing their advertising spend. This gives out the message to their market that they are value for money and positions some of their products against the own label market- (and therefore Cereal Partners). 'Why buy own label when you can get the best brand at a great price.' The massive investment in advertising means that Kellogg's are constantly reminding their customers that they are there- very important in this routine buying market.

Although using price as communication can be dangerous in the long term, (by signalling lower quality), it offers short-term benefits to the company and consumer. Once in the habit of buying a Kellogg's product then they would hope to ease the entrance of new products under the same umbrella brand. Not all Kellogg's products will be positioned as value for money- some will rely on unique product characteristics to command a higher price.

However Kelloggs will not be able to over rely on this strategy in the long term and must continue to invest in brand meaning and remember their relationship with the retailers.

Efficiency of existing strategy

Kellogg's share of voice is higher than their share of market, which suggests that some of their spending is wasted. However this large budget, coupled with their family branding strategy may ease the introduction of new products like cereal bars in the future. In fact for the cornflakes brand (spend 8%, market share 9%) their spending appears to be most efficient, they are perhaps relying on their lower prices to maintain market share in this sector.

Message strategy and effectiveness

Their benefit orientation message appears to be successful and is well integrated with their profile strategy and suitable for parents as decision makers who will want to choose a healthy breakfast for their family. However it may well be that this message could be presented by using promotional methods to compliment their advertising e.g. Sponsorship. It is difficult to comment on whether their advertising could be more creative and more effective.

Profile strategy

Kellogg's have adopted a family or umbrella branding strategy that means that they will benefit from economies of scale in terms of advertising spend and the lower prices positions the company as a family champion.

Through their collaborative activities on healthy eating with the government they will be seen as a company that cares for the family (their target market). Raising awareness of the importance of breakfast will help themselves and society as a whole (including their competitors!)

Overall Kellogg's have set themselves as market leaders, focusing on the family with an integrated marketing communications strategy. They must be prepared to consider other strategies such as sales promotion such as 2 for the price of one since this will keep competitors out longer and not forget the retailers through well-designed push programmes.

(b) **Weetabix**

Although not market leader, Weetabix appears to be fairly successful and more efficient than its competitors, with the share of voice matching share of market. It concentrates on a pull strategy and appears to be uniquely using a combination of above and below the line activity to maintain its market share.

As a privately owned company, promotional spend may be seen as a cost and it is important for the share of voice to remain consistent with their share of market. This may mean an increase in expenditure if they wish to grow market share. One of the benefits of private ownership means that the company can concentrate their communications on their customers and retailers, rather than shareholders and the city.

Efficiency of communications

The Weetabix spend appears to be more efficient than their competitors for the following reasons.

(i)   Economies of scale, since they are spending nearly a half of their budget on the key Weetabix product, which is also their company name.

(ii)   Co-branding. Weetabix are able to rely on the profile of their partners like Maxwell House to add value to their brand.

(iii)   Smaller product range so promotional resource not spread too thinly.

(iv)   Use of sales promotion to create action at point of sale and to encourage long term buy in by consumers who wish to reap benefits of the sales promotion.

Message strategy

Weetabix have concentrated on some attribute- based advertising coupled with the message that they offer added value through their sales promotions. This appears to be successful since it differentiates the brand from its competitors. However this reliance on providing added value through sales promotions could cause problems in the long term, if the promotions were to stop. Although the product attributes are unique, the sloppiness of the product makes it unsuitable for grazing and therefore some consideration of the best segment should be considered and the message should emphasise the benefits of rather more, including relevant health benefits

Profile

Weetabix must realise the benefits of a profile strategy to portray brand values to a variety of stakeholders, including retailers, potential partners, staff, suppliers and so on. This will ease progress of new products, maintain awareness and allow some retaliation to Kellogg's 40% increase in ad spend. Their corporate branding strategy offers benefits and disadvantages- if all of their products are seen as similar to the mushy Weetabix product then it will be difficult to enter new markets.

To conclude Weetabix are a successful smaller advertiser who have used their budget wisely to maintain their market share. However since the product attributes are not automatically geared up to attack the growth markets the marketing communication activity must now be more focussed to build a profile of the company brand, which will allow new products to be launched. And will also position the main Weetabix product to the most suitable segment.

(c)   **Cereal Partners**

As a relatively new entrant much of the growth has come from the company support of retailers by supplying own label product, which probably accounts for the lions share of their sales. They have adopted a push strategy by selling own label along with a pull strategy, aiming their individual products at the children in the family (pester power).

As an alliance there may be some issues about which name to choose for new products.

Efficiency

Excluding own label sales the share of voice is much lower than the share of market, apart from their main Shredded Wheat brand. This is probably due to the wide number of individual brands that their spend must support. As price is not seen to be an issue for their brands their profitability may well be higher than the other contenders. This could mean that an increased spend is necessary to compete against the price cutting Kellogg's.

Message

The message for the main brands has been the fun and taste of the product which may not fully take advantage of the research suggesting that healthy eating is becoming more popular. However as this company differentiates itself through its positioning for children then at least this better understanding of segmentation strategy has meant a message integrated with its target market.

Profile

Multi-branding is the strategy chosen by Cereal Partners, which does not allow for the economies of scale reaped by the other players. This will need to be considered in the future. It is interesting that Nestle name is not used- this may due to the poor ethical reputation the company has due to its sales of baby milk in 3rd world countries. Therefore an enhanced profile strategy is needed- internal marcomms may be important to ensure that both parties from the alliance are on board.

To conclude it would appear that by being the most focussed supplier cereal partners have a great opportunity to reap the benefits of higher margins for their branded products to subsidise own label manufacture. They have used brand extensions in the past but these can only go so far without eroding the equity of the individual brand. Their relationship with retailers must be continued through successful relationship building. Their pull strategy needs to be further developed if it is to improve its market share against Kellogg's massive increases in spend.

The following chart summarise the key differences between the three challengers.

	Kellogg's	Weetabix	Cereal Partners
Branding Strategy	Family	Corporate	Multi branding
Target Market	Parents	Everyone!	Children
Message	Health/ convenience	Product and added value	Fun/taste
Main Strategy	Pull and Profile	Pull	Push and Pull
Price	Important	Added Value	Not Important
Spend	High	Low	Low
Efficiency	SOV>SOM	SOV=SOM	SOV>SOM
Promotional Mix	Advertising. PR	Advertising, sales promotion	Advertising

(i) **Suggested Marcomms Strategy for Weetabix**

Kellogg's price and discounting strategy must be considered against Weetabix own strategy of offering more value for the same money through sales promotion and co- branding. The Weetabix approach offers many advantages including:

1   Likely to gain the support of retailers more than price cutting which could compete heavily with own label

2   It can be sustained over a longer time period with less damage to margins

3   It is less expensive and less likely to de-value the brand and may enhance it if partners are chosen carefully

4   There are greater opportunities to advertise the promotions and keep the brand fresh

There are disadvantages, however and consumers may become used to the reward and fail to buy if they have no reward.

In order to counteract the aggressive stance taken by Kellogg's there are a number of strategies that could be considered.

1   **Follow the leader** and cut prices. This would be foolish since the company is likely to loose this battle, having a smaller portfolio of brands and probably less investment

2   To **maintain the existing approach**. Although this has been successful it is likely that without further innovations in terms of communication the company will loose market share to both own label and better-positioned competitors since Kellogg's will outspend Weetabix by nearly 5 to 1.

3   **Build the corporate Brand** through a better profile strategy. This is imperative if new product developments are to be considered. The effective use of PR and sponsorship of events aimed at the young would offer improved recognition and brand value to strengthen their position amongst all stakeholders including retailers. As the young and old can eat the product a link with opinion formers such as health visitors could be beneficial.

4   **Reposition and differentiate**. Weetabix must try to differentiate its product, choosing a specific segment of the market (possibly mothers with very young children) offering it not just as a mushy food but as one which is healthy and nutritious. A focus on a particular group initially will ensure a tighter and more effective marcomms programme. A website offering links to parenting sites might be useful. This tighter focus could also mean a more coherent co-branding strategy could be followed.

5   More **emphasis on push strategies**. By increasing their advertising and below the line activity the brand will command more shelf space. Due to the higher margins it will offer retailers. Advertising should be regular with a slight increase to promote new sales promotions where relevant. This will maintain awareness. Relevant **below the line activity could** include development of loyalty schemes and database building to keep customers from the cradle to the grave.

Conclusions

This report has evaluated the alternative strategies of the three main players in the cereal market. It has offered some brief ideas for Weetabix and concludes that they must be clearer about their positioning. This will allow a stronger brand identity, valued by the customer, and using an integrated marcomms strategy this will allow them to take advantage of some of the changes that are happening in the market place.

60   AP ENGINEERING

> **Examiner's comments.** This is the first time the question has used this format, and the intention was to direct candidates to specific parts of the mini case and not use a marketing communications plan. The question was essentially about corporate branding and IMC. Parts (c) and (e) were the most challenging. Part (c) requires some acknowledgement and understanding of the differences between emotional and rational messages for low and high involvement scenarios, and some creativity is welcome.
>
> Implementation issues for IMC planning are different from development issues and should include aspects on budgeting, timetabling, managing, controlling and evaluating. Target audience choice and strategy development are not relevant at the implementation stage.

> To: Board of Directors
> From: Marketing Communications Consultant
> Date: December 2001
>
> ### Communications Strategies: AP Engineering 2002 and Beyond

This report assesses **suitable marketing communications strategies** that will enable AP Engineering (AP) to move forward with its new approach of total engineering solutions. The report is presented in six main sections, each addressing a specific aspect as follows.

(a) Communications strategy for 2002/3
(b) Justification and explanation for strategy
(c) Suggested promotional tools
(d) Core messages
(e) Issues of implementation and integration.
(f) Conclusions

(a) **Communications strategy for 2002/3**

Cultural and **organisational changes** at the company suggest that one of the first jobs that will be required of the communications is to pull together all areas of the business. This will enable an **integrated approach** and offering to be made, and suggests the importance of **internal communications**. In addition our company will need to tell its existing customers and other **stakeholders** about the new one-stop service now on offer.

The strategy that we should propose is initially one of **profile**. This is relevant when a number of different stakeholders need to be addressed, and the main aim of this strategy is to develop our corporate **brand** and **reputation** for providing a full solution for all engineering needs. A **pull** strategy, aimed at existing customers and new business, will then be used to **raise awareness** of specific services.

(b) **Justification and explanation for strategy**

The reasons for the suggestion of a profile strategy can be summarised as follows.

1   The reorganisation has pulled together **new staff** from a number of acquisitions and new alliances. Profile strategies cover **internal marketing** and this will be vital to ensure that all staff and associates work together, uniting to offer an integrated service.

     Our **mission** and **vision** need to filter through the organisation, and a dialogue set up to ensure that any issues affecting **strategy implementation** are understood. Front line staff need to feel valued, particularly when they are new to AP- they may be feeling vulnerable and unsure of new roles in the enlarged organisation. It can be seen that internal marketing provides an essential role during this time of **change management**.

2   **External audiences** such as **customers** need to be told about our new services, and reassured that the changes will make things easier for them. **Suppliers** may also be an important audience. The combined approach of profile and push will ensure that our **corporate brand** is **repositioned** as an integrated service provider. The existing **core values** of credibility and value for money will be retained, but the **service** element will now be highlighted (generally higher margins for us).

3   **Profile strategies** are particularly important in service industries, where **people** are key to delivering the offering.

4   AP needs to maintain its **external visibility** to ensure that it is considered as a supplier by other influential audiences, such as specifiers and architects.

5   Profile strategies concentrate on building **reputation** and corporate **image**, to allow a later pull strategy to concentrate on specific markets with specific products.

6   Margins have been tight, and a profile strategy can be more **cost effective** in generating awareness.

(c) **Suggested promotional tools**

The primary tools that should be used for implementation of the strategy are as follows.

1   **Internal marketing communication** to include training, staff conferences, intranet facilities and newsletters. The flow of communication needs to be two way. Employees should be encouraged, and even incentivised, to make suggestions, get involved with writing press releases about projects they have worked on and take part in external events.

2   **Video conference facilities** to bring relevant experts into the team when required for internal and external communication.

3   Corporate **web site development** with areas for clients, suppliers, staff and other influential professionals, including the press. This should offer a range of useful information to help customers with their projects.

4   **Direct marketing** to existing customers will explain the changes. This will be highly **targeted**, and explain the impact that our new services will have upon ongoing business.

5   **Personal selling** and **key account management**. As a service industry, the new structure and vision can best be explained through personal contact. Key accounts might be invited to a road show.

6   **Key account management system**. Computer systems should be organised around customers, so that all aspects of the business focus on the customer and **integrate** all activity.

7   **Public relations**. This venture is newsworthy, and AP should encourage editorial coverage to get its corporate message out to customers, suppliers and influencers. AP may wish to set up a **reference programme** which encourages joint PR between the client and AP, using civil engineering and building **journals** and the client's **trade press**. Site visits and speaking on the conference circuit may boost AP's reputation as 'one stop' experts, and ensure that it is the first company that comes to mind when a business project is being considered.

8   **Trade shows** and **advertising** may be considered towards the end of the profile strategy.

A combination of the above tools will implement both profile and pull strategies and build the new corporate brand.

(d) **Core messages**

Although communicating with a number of different stakeholders, a single and **consistent message** will be required to show the simplicity of the new vision and the **benefits** that the integrated service will bring.

As the decision to use AP's service will tend to be **high involvement, rational product appeals** will often work best. This requires longer copy and complex messages. Some symbolism of the **brand** may be useful, to present the new ethos in an easy to remember way. This will be followed by more detailed message content, outlining the **features** and **benefits** of AP's combined services for different stakeholders.

An **example** might be:

"AP- the best specialised staff, coming together for a total solution to engineering problems."

This will give a sense of belonging to staff, and functional benefits can be elaborated on in terms of features and benefits for customers. A new logo, showing parts of a jigsaw coming together, could be used to show this visually. This **branding instrument** could then be used on all marcomms activity.

(e) **Issues of implementation and integration**

Before implanting an integrated marketing communications policy several key issues need to be addressed.

1   **Budgets**- without sufficient resource put behind the strategy, it cannot be implemented. The size of budget will depend on the availability of funds, and the attitude of top management towards seeing this as an **investment** rather than a cost. **Internal markets** must be dealt with first when **allocating** the budget, because we have already seen that the change management must be effective to make the service deliverable. Money spent on communicating the service to the customer and other stakeholders will be wasted if the internal processes are not capable of delivering what is promised.

2   **Cultural differences** and methods of working between new and existing staff will need to be addressed. Training and development will be needed, as well as consultation with staff at all levels.

3   **Management of communications**- should this be undertaken **in house** or via an **agency**? Internal marcomms is a specialised area and consultants could advise on implementation. A senior manager should be empowered with introducing the internal marcomms changes necessary.

4   **Measurement and evaluation**. A decision needs to be made on how and when to measure the effectiveness of the campaign . A number of techniques will be used e.g. internal **focus groups** amongst staff to judge whether the change of culture is working, staff satisfaction **surveys**, editorial coverage assessed to judge whether favourable or not. The measurement will depend on the **objectives** set.

5   **Timing issues**- the project will start with internal marcomms, and then follow through with the external strategies. Budgets will need to be spread, and therefore actions will need to be **prioritised.**

6   Identification of **key influencers** that will need to be brought on board to implement the change strategy e.g. unions, professional membership bodies.

7   Are **computer** and other **systems** capable of the necessary reorganisation around key account management?

8   Are all **managers and staff** behind the new changes? Are they **capable of delivering** the marcomms strategy? What will we do if they will not or cannot implement the changes needed?

9   What is the **procedure** for ensuring that all aspects of the plan are **integrated**? Should a **corporate identity manual** be issued, to guide all areas of the business on the new approach? Are messages to all stakeholders **consistent**?

10   Does the plan **complement** and help achieve corporate and marketing **objectives**?

Conclusions

AP Engineering is entering an exciting new period in its evolution. The company has grown and we will need to become more participative in our approach, so that we can offer our customers a complete engineering service.

This requires a **culture change** and a mix of internal and external communications. Initially a profile strategy will be required, and this report has suggested several tools that might be used to implement this. This will be followed with a more specific pull strategy. A simple message has been suggested to portray the new service and, finally, a list of issues that will need to be considered before we implement the strategy. The future for AP Engineering is looking good, and now the role of marcomms comes to the fore to achieve corporate goals.

Test your knowledge

1   What factors have influenced the development of direct marketing?

2   What matters might you consider when developing the packaging for a new product?

3   List eight criteria against which a model may be evaluated.

4   What is the 'product' in internal marketing?

5   What are the thirteen principles of the British Code of Sales Promotion Practice?

6   What are the advantages of personal selling?

7   List three technological developments that have affected or will affect marketing communications.

8   What are response hierarchy models and what are their drawbacks?

9   What are the six groups in the DMU?

10 List seven methods of determining advertising expenditure.

11 List five types of internal communications.

12 Give some examples of measures of advertising effectiveness.

13 List five factors that influenced the growth of advertising.

14 Explain the mnemonic SMART.

15 Why is it important to study buying behaviour?

16 What are the advantages of press as a medium?

17 What does the British Code of Advertising Practice say about decency and truthfulness?

18 Explain the mnemonic SOSTT + 4Ms.

19 What are the strengths and weaknesses of direct mail?

20 What are the disadvantages of outdoor as a medium?

21 What categories of advertising are specifically covered in the British Code of Advertising Practice?

22 List the main types of segmentation variable.

23 What is the main disadvantage of PR?

24 List ten potential publics.

25 What are the three main ways in which a sales force can be organised?

26 How can sales promotions be evaluated?

27 What formats might be taken by a creative brief for an advertising agency?

28 Give two definitions of direct marketing.

29 What is CAVIAR?

30 What issues and developments are likely to affect marketing communications in the future?

31 List all promotional influences on the customer.

32 Explain Mary Goodyear's five levels of advertising development.

33 What is the TGI and what does it measure?

34 Integration of marketing communications is possible at what three levels?

35 What is a brand? What are four types of brand?

BPP
PUBLISHING

Test your knowledge: answers

1   You might have mentioned the following.

(a)   The disintegration of the nuclear family as the dominant group in the population.
(b)   Technology which allows banks of data to be collected and sorted, especially by retailers.
(c)   The growth in use of credit cards and debit cards.
(d)   The rise in the cost of TV advertising.
(e)   The development of global markets and the breakdown of cultural boundaries.
(f)   Better educated consumers and lower brand loyalty.

2   In brief, design, shape, size, colour, graphics and name.

3   Williams listed eight criteria against which a model could potentially be evaluated, as follows.

(a)	Simplicity	(e)	Explanatory power
(b)	Factual basis	(f)	Prediction
(c)	Logic	(g)	Heuristic power
(d)	Originality	(h)	Validity

4   The product is the marketing strategy and the details of the marketing plan. These must be 'sold' to people in the organisation.

5

(a)	Legality	(h)	Truthful Presentation
(b)	Spirit	(i)	Substantiation
(c)	Fair competition	(j)	Limitation
(d)	Consumer interest	(k)	Suitability
(e)	Consumer satisfaction	(l)	Administration
(f)	Fairness	(m)	Responsibility
(g)	Public interest		

6   (a)   Personal selling contributes to a relatively high level of customer attention since, in face to face situations, it is difficult for a potential buyer to avoid a salesperson's message.

(b)   Personal selling enables the salesperson to customise the message to the customer's specific interests and needs.

(c)   The two-way communication nature of personal selling allows immediate feedback from the customer so that the effectiveness of the message can be ascertained.

(d)   Personal selling allows a larger amount of technical and complex information than could be communicated using other promotional methods.

(e)   In personal selling there is a greater ability to demonstrate a product's functioning and performance characteristics.

(f)   Frequent interaction with the customer gives great scope for the development of long-term relations between buyer and seller, making the process of purchase more of a team effort.

7   Examples are the Internet, digital TV and multimedia.

8   Response hierarchy models attempts to predict the sequence of mental stages that the consumer passes through on the way to purchase. Examples are AIDA (Awareness, Interest, Desire, Action) and the DAGMAR model (Unawareness, Awareness, Comprehension, Conviction, Action).

The drawbacks are that such models do not describe many simple purchases where the consumer may not go through the staged process and that in some situations buyers may go through the stages in a different order.

9   (a)   Users
(b)   Influencers
(c)   Deciders
(d)   Approvers
(e)   Buyers
(f)   Gatekeepers

10   (a)   As much as you can afford   (e)   Experiment and testing
          (b)   Historical basis   (f)   Modelling and simulation
          (c)   Matching competition   (g)   Objective and task method
          (d)   Percentage of sales

11   Possible answers include the following.

          (a)   In-house magazines and employee newsletters
          (b)   Employee relations videos
          (c)   Formal employee communications networks and channels for feedback
          (d)   Recruitment exhibitions/conferences
          (e)   Speech writing for executives
          (f)   Company notice boards
          (g)   Briefing meetings

12   Possible answers are:

          (a)   Number of orders
          (b)   Number of enquiries
          (c)   Responses from creative development research
          (d)   Pre-testing results
          (e)   Tracking studies data (omnibus survey results, or panel research data)

13   Factors include:

          (a)   The growth of settlements
          (b)   The invention of printing
          (c)   The Industrial Revolution
          (d)   The development of national and global businesses
          (e)   The invention of broadcasting
          (f)   The development of advertising agencies
          (g)   The growth in competition

14   SMART is a mnemonic for the qualities of objectives. Marketing communications objectives need to be:
                Specific
                Measurable
                Achievable
                Relevant
                Timed and targeted

15   (a)   The buyer's reaction to the organisation's marketing strategy has a major impact on the success of the organisation.

          (b)   If organisations are truly to implement the marketing concept, they must examine the main influences on what, where, when and how customers buy. Only in this way will they be able to devise a marketing mix that satisfies the needs of the customers.

          (c)   By gaining a better understanding of the factors influencing their customers and how their customers will respond, organisations will be better able to predict the effectiveness of their marketing activities.

16   Press has the following advantages.

          (a)   Nationals reach large numbers of people
          (b)   A variety of contents are available from the deeply serious to the frivolous
          (c)   Copy lead times are generally short
          (d)   A choice of reproduction options (black and white, glossy colour)
          (e)   It may be possible to target special interest groups very closely
          (f)   Readers are loyal
          (g)   Local impact is possible

17   The code's definition of *decency* states that advertisements should not contain any matter that is likely to cause grave or widespread offence in the light of standards of decency and propriety currently acceptable in the UK, or, any material that might be found distasteful because it reflects or gives expression to attitudes or opinions about which society is divided. Whether the latter is the case, the code states that advertisers' should carefully consider the effect that any apparent disregard of the

sensitivities involved may have upon their reputation and that of their product, and upon the acceptability, and hence usefulness, of advertising generally.'

The code states that, as far as *truthful* presentation is concerned, 'No advertisement, whether by inaccuracy, ambiguity, exaggeration, omission or otherwise, should mislead consumers about any matter likely to influence their attitude to the advertised product'. The code makes the distinction between matters of fact and matters of opinion, stating that advertisers should be able to substantiate any material presented as a matter of fact in their adverts and that they should not claim that an account that an advert gives of facts is true when there exists a division of informed opinion on the issue. Matters of opinion must be recognisable as such. Subsequent sections of the code explain in detail how this is to be achieved in specific cases such as political claims, quotation of prices, availability of products and so on.

18   The mnemonic is the one used by Paul Smith to summarise the planning process.

Situation	(Where are we now?)
Objectives	(Where do we want to go?)
Strategy	(How do we get there?)
Tactics	(Details of strategy)
Targets	(Target markets/audiences)
+	
Men	(and women required to do the job)
Money	(financial resources/budget)
Minutes	(timetable of activities)
Measurement	(monitoring effectiveness)

The order of the letters represents the logical order of the planning process.

19   Strengths are as follows.

(a)   The advertiser can target down to individual level.

(b)   The communication can be personalised. Known data about the individual can be used, whilst modern printing techniques mean that parts of a letter can be altered to accommodate this.

(c)   The medium is good for reinforcing interest stimulated by other media such as TV. It can supply the response mechanism (a coupon) which is not yet available in that medium.

(d)   The opportunity to use different creative formats is almost unlimited.

(e)   Testing potential is sophisticated: a limited number of items can be sent out to a 'test' cell and the results can be evaluated. As success is achieved, so the mailing campaign can be rolled out.

(f)   What you do is less visible to your competitors than other forms of media.

There are, however, a number of weaknesses with this medium.

(a)   It does not offer sound or movement, although it is possible for advertisers to send out audio or video tapes, and even working models or samples.

(b)   There is obvious concern over the negative association with junk mail and the need for individuals to exercise their right to privacy,

(c)   Lead times may be considerable when taking into consideration the creative organisation, finished artwork, printing, proofing, inserting material into envelopes where necessary and finally the mailing.

(d)   The most important barrier to direct mail is that it can be very expensive on a *per capita* basis. A delivered insert can be 24 to 32 times more expensive than a full page colour advert in a magazine. It therefore follows that the mailshot must be very powerful and, above all, well targeted to overcome such a cost penalty. (In many cases, though, this is possible.)

20   Disadvantages of outdoor include the limited number of prime sites, possible vandalism, long lead times between buying the space and the advert appearing, inflexibility, and the difficulty of achieving national coverage.

21
(a)	Health claims	(h)	Employment and business opportunities
(b)	Hair and scalp products	(i)	Limited editions of products
(c)	Vitamins and minerals	(j)	Advertisements aimed at children
(d)	Slimming	(k)	Media requirements
(e)	Cosmetics	(l)	Alcoholic drinks
(f)	Mail order and direct response advertising	(m)	Cigarettes and tobacco
(g)	Financial services and products		

22   A list of the main types of segmentation variable is given below.

     (a)   *Geographic, eg* Continent (Europe), Country (United Kingdom), Region (South East), County (Lancashire), Town (Manchester), Postcode (WA14)

     (b)   *Demographic*, eg Age (over sixty). Sex (male, female), occupation etc.

     (c)   *Psychographic, eg* Social class (A B C1 C2 D E), Lifestyle (upwardly mobile), Personality (ambitious)

     (d)   *Behavioural*, eg benefits required (quality, service, price). Usage rate (light, medium, heavy). Loyalty status (strong)

23   The main disadvantage is the loss of control over how the message is presented, or even what the message is. Editors can just as easily present a negative picture as a positive one.

24   Possible answers include the following.

     (a)   Customers - existing, past and potential
     (b)   Members of the public in general
     (c)   The trade and distributors
     (d)   Financial publics - shareholders, the City, banks, institutions and stockbrokers
     (e)   Pressure groups
     (f)   Opinion leaders
     (g)   The media - as a special type of public as well as a channel of communication
     (h)   Overseas governments, EU bodies and International bodies
     (i)   Central and local government bodies, MPs and members of the House of Lords
     (j)   Research bodies and policy-forming units
     (k)   The local community
     (l)   Trades Unions
     (m)   Employees

25   Territorial organisation, product organisation and market/customer organisation.

26   Sales promotions can be evaluated:

     (a)   In terms of take-up (number of coupons redeemed, number of competition entries etc)
     (b)   By means of, say, omnibus surveys to measure awareness
     (c)   Through household panel information or retail tracking information (eg Nielsen's Homescan)
     (d)   By means of *ad hoc* research

27   A creative brief might take the following format.

     (a)   *Background/introduction*

     (b)   *Target market(s):* at the very least, a listing of the target audience characteristics. It could also include an assessment of what audiences currently think about the product or service.

     (c)   *Advertising objectives*

     (d)   *Advertising proposition.* This links with (b) above, and answers the question 'What do we want our audiences to think?' The proposition should be summed up in a short sentence or two, stating in laymen's terms the response that is desired from the audience on seeing the advertising. Some agencies call this the brand promise.

(e) *Support.* This is the backup for the advertising proposition. It would include the information or attributes that might help to produce the desired response. Support might take the form of factual benefits that a product possesses which differentiate it from the competition, or it might include findings from research.

(f) *Tone of voice.* Should the advertising be authoritative, serious, friendly, modern in approach?

(g) *Mandatory inclusions.* Typical examples of these would be 'pack shot must be included', or 'parent company logo must be easily identifiable in end freeze frame.'

28 Possibilities are as follows.

(a) The Institute of Direct Marketing in the UK define direct marketing as 'The planned recording, analysis and tracking of customer behaviour to develop relational marketing strategies'.

(b) The Direct Marketing Association in the US define direct marketing as 'An interactive system of marketing which uses one or more advertising media to effect a measurable response and/or transaction at any location'.

29 CAVIAR stands for Cinema and Video Industry Audience Research, which gives details of cinema-going habits, video viewership and other media usage.

30 Possible answers are:

(a) Shifting demographic profiles
(b) Changes in spending patterns
(c) Improved social values
(d) Fragmentation of the media
(e) Increased levels of technology both inside and outside the home
(f) Globalisation
(g) New regulations
(h) Economic cycles

31 Your list should include the following.

(a) Word of mouth   (h) Corporate image
(b) Sales promotion   (i) Packaging
(c) Public relations   (j) Sponsorship
(d) Merchandising   (k) Advertising
(e) Direct marketing   (l) Personal selling
(f) Exhibitions   (m) Branding
(g) Internal marketing

32 Goodyear identifies five levels of advertising development along a continuum from the unsophisticated to the sophisticated.

(a) At the least sophisticated level of advertising, the emphasis is on the manufacturer's *description* of the product. Messages are factual and rational with much repetition. Product or pack shots take prominence.

(b) At the next level, consumer choice is acknowledged so emphasis switches to the product's *superiority* over the competition (eg products that wash whiter, feel softer).

(c) At the mid point on the continuum, consumer *benefits* are emphasised rather than product attributes. Executional devices may include the use of celebrity endorsements or role models may give demonstrations, for example a dentist endorsing toothpaste products.

(d) At a more sophisticated level, brands and their attributes are well known, so need only passing references (perhaps by way of a brief pack shot or logo). The message is communicated by way of *lifestyle narrative* (eg Gold Blend couple; Bisto family).

(e) At the most sophisticated level, the focus is on the *advertising* itself. The brand is referred to only obliquely, perhaps at a symbolic level (eg Silk Cut; Benson & Hedges). Consumers are believed to have a mature understanding of advertising, and are able to think laterally in order to decode messages.

33   The TGI (Target Group Index) is a national product and media survey which collects information from 24,000 adults each year. The TGI measures the following.

(a)   Heavy to light usage for over 3,000 brands in more than 200 FMCG product fields; additionally, usage of over 450 other brands in banking, building societies, airlines, holidays, cars, grocery and other retail outlets.

(b)   The 1,400 or so brands with more than a million claimed users, broken down demographically and by media.

(c)   The readership of more than 200 newspapers and magazines.

(d)   The weight of viewing of ITV and Channel 4, and half-hourly viewing behaviour.

(e)   The weight of listening to commercial radio.

(f)   The level of exposure to outdoor media and the cinema.

(g)   The full range of standard demographics together with special breakdowns such as terminal education age, and working status.

34   (a)   Integration with business strategy
       (b)   Integration with marketing strategy
       (c)   Integration of the promotional tools

35   'A successful brand is a name, symbol, design or some combination, which identifies the "product" of a particular organisation as having a sustainable differential advantage.' (Doyle)

Four types of brand are as follows.

(a)   *Individual* brand name. This is the option chosen by Procter and Gamble for example, who even have different brand names within the same product line, eg Bold, Tide. The main advantage of individual product branding is that an unsuccessful brand (eg Strand cigarettes) does not adversely affect the firm's other products, nor the firm's reputation generally.

(b)   *Blanket family brand* for all products, eg Hoover, Heinz (originally 'Heinz 57 varieties'). This has the advantage of enabling the global organisation to introduce new products quickly and successfully. Also the cost of introducing the new product in terms of name research and awareness advertising will be reduced (eg Honda lawn mowers).

(c)   *Separate family names* for different product divisions, eg the US based company Sears sells electrical appliances under the name Kenmore, and women's clothing under the Kerrybrook brand. This is obviously the option for the global organisation with 'inconsistent' product lines where the family brand name above is not appropriate. But within each 'family' the advantages identified in (b) still apply.

(d)   The *company* trade name combined with an *individual* product name (eg Kelloggs - Corn Flakes, Rice Crispies etc). This option both legitimises (because of the company name) and individualises (the individual product name). As in (b) above it allows new 'names' to be introduced quickly and relatively cheaply.

Diploma in Marketing

June 2002 paper

9.51 Integrated Marketing Communications

3 Hours Duration

This examination is in two sections.

Part A is compulsory, based on a mini-case and worth 40% of total marks.

Part B has six questions, select three. Each answer will be worth 20 marks totalling 60% of the whole for the paper.

DO NOT repeat the question in your answer but show clearly the number of the question attempted.

DO NOT OPEN THIS PAPER UNTIL YOU ARE READY TO START UNDER EXAMINATION CONDITIONS

PART A

Coffee house culture

The rapid growth of the coffee house market in the UK has brought issues about competition, positioning and overall market development to the attention of those in the market and those considering entry.

Coffee house cafés provide real branded coffee which can be enjoyed in a friendly, relaxed environment. Speciality coffees such as lattes, cappuccinos and espressos, combined with a distinctive café culture, have helped drive the huge growth. Big comfortable sofas, pictures on the walls, a huge range of coffee products and a relaxed ambience have made coffee houses popular. In comparison to bars and public houses, coffee cafés are smaller, more intimate, and softer in style. These cafés represent a safe, neutral area; an alternative place to meet and relax.

Starbucks, Coffee Republic and Costa Coffee are the three main brands in a UK market worth over $300 million. Starbucks is a derivative US brand who have adopted a position that says that Starbucks is about coffee and is 'a home away from home'. It is a place to relax and feel at ease, and this is reflected in their advertising strapline, 'Your passport from home'. The frequent launch of new products (eg new coffees, snacks) is important to Starbucks, who pride themselves not only on the variety of products but also the location of their cafés. Their intention is to be everywhere, rather like the availability of McDonald's restaurants, and to do this they are opening new cafés on a regular basis.

The strapline used by Costa Coffee is 'the home of Italian coffee', and this underlines their positioning. Costa is a pure Italian brand and everything associated with the Costa brand is Italian; even the sandwiches and pastries that are served are Italian. Coffee Republic want to be the customers' preferred choice, based upon the high quality of their coffee and the associated experience expressed through the layout, design and atmosphere of their cafés.

Whilst the three market leaders fight it out for the traditional High Street or Shopping Mall presence, new entrants such as Café Nescafé, Aroma and more recently Café Cadbury, search for new distribution outlets such as banks, hospitals, railway stations and bookshops.

Marketing communications have played an important part in the development of the market. Positioning and branding activities are very important, and as the market grows and eventually matures, different roles will be expected from the marketing communications used by the mainstream players. For example, as the market was developed, it was important to inform and educate the market about café culture and the real coffee experience. Then, as the market became established, marketing communications were required to differentiate the brands, offer clear benefits and establish customer expectations. It is likely that maturity will lead to increasing segmentation, niche markets and sub-positioning.

However, the market is not limited to beverage brands and an established ethnic (or cultural) food group, JTA Foods, who have traditionally presented their products as 'in-home cuisine', see an opportunity to extend their brand by taking it into an 'out-of-home' environment. By developing a chain of branded café outlets in which their branded meals would be available, they will be able to reach new target markets and enhance their brand values. One of the dangers is that the strong brand equity they have built up over the past 20 years might be damaged by this strategy, so market entry and position needs to be considered carefully and then maintained.

Question 1

JTA Foods are associated with a country and food style of your choice.

As marketing communications consultant prepare a report advising JTA Foods with regard to the following questions:

(a) Suggest a suitable positioning strategy for JTA Foods in the UK coffee house market.

(10 marks)

(b) Assuming a limited budget which precludes JTA Foods from using television advertising, which tools of the promotional mix and media might best be used to implement your positioning strategy? Why?   (15 marks)

(c) As the coffee house market matures, appraise the role of marketing communications for the leading brands.   (15 marks)

(40 marks)

PART B - Answer THREE Questions only

Question 2

A high street retailer of health and beauty products has developed a web site, which is to be accessible through interactive television.

(a) Explain how offline and online marketing communications might be used to encourage visitors to visit the site.   (10 marks)

(b) How might marketing communications be used to encourage visitors to return to the site?   (10 marks)

(20 marks)

Question 3

A government report has found that a high proportion of women aged 14-24 believe that smoking is not habitual and that they will be able to give up the habit when they choose.

As the Communication Manager for an organisation that makes nicotine patches, designed to help people give up the smoking habit, suggest ways in which you might attempt to change the attitudes held by this particular segment.

(20 marks)

Question 4

You are the Marketing Manager for a small but rapidly growing airline operating in the low-cost segment. The market is characterised by low fares, fast turnaround and limited in-flight services.

(a) Discuss how you might use marketing communications to differentiate your airline from your competitors, who focus purely low prices.   (10 marks)

(b) Briefly explain the extent to which internal marketing communications could be an important aspect of your airline's marketing communications.   (10 marks)

(20 marks)

Question 5

You are the newly appointed Marketing Manager for a not-for-profit organisation. You wish to introduce integrated marketing communications, (IMC), and are preparing notes for a meeting with colleagues in your department, at which you plan to introduce the idea.

(a) Outline in note form what IMC is. (10 marks)

(b) Evaluate the potential benefits of using IMC in a not-for-profit organisation. (10 marks)

(20 marks)

Question 6

Using examples to illustrate your points:

(a) Appraise the strategic role of advertising in brand building. (10 marks)

(b) It there are insufficient financial resources to support an advertising based strategy, explain an alternative brand building strategy. (10 marks)

(20 marks)

Question 7

Evaluate the extent to which global advertising agencies can provide effective integrated marketing communications for internal clients who demand that communication messages be adapted for local or regional markets.

(20 marks)

Answers

DO NOT TURN THIS PAGE UNTIL YOU
HAVE COMPLETED THE TEST PAPER

Question 1

> **Tutorial note.** It is important that the three sections of this question are easily identified in the answer. A marketing communications plan is not wanted. Some detailed understanding of positioning is essential and an attempt at suggesting a suitable strategy *is required. Note that parts* (b) *and* (c) *carry 15 marks and therefore require more depth of thought. Part* (b) *requires a range of ideas which are justified in terms of target audience, buyer behaviour and linked to the positioning indicated in section a.*
>
> It would be appropriate to use the product life cycle to answer part (c) and consideration should be given to the dynamics of the message, mix, media and agency over time. Repositioning should also be discussed.

To: Board of Directors
        JTA Foods

From: Marketing Consultant
Date: June 2002

Stretching the Brand – JTA Cafes

Introduction

The flourishing but highly competitive branded coffee house market offers many opportunities for JTA to extend its present product based brand into the service industry without eroding the strong brand equity built over the past 20 years. This report will examine one of the critical success factors for entering a new market, namely the role of positioning to differentiate the brand. It will make suggestions for a suitable marketing communications strategy to launch the new venture and finally will assess the changes that will be needed as the market becomes more mature.

(a) **Positioning Strategy**

JTA's success with "in home cuisine" products, specialising in several ranges of ethnic foods including Mexican, Afro – Caribbean, Indian and Malaysian needs to provide the basis for our differentiated offering so that we are perceived away from the existing competitors like Starbucks, Coffee Republic and Costa Coffee.

Positioning is the last stage of the strategic process which starts by segmenting the market and targeting the segment(s) that we are most able to serve. It is likely that our new café will appeal to similar segments as competitors, albeit those with a more developed interest in food. Finally the brand will need to be positioned. This is "the act of designing the company's offering and image so that they occupy a meaningful and distinct competitive position in the target customers' minds" (Kotler). Positioning is about what the buyer thinks of JTA cafes, compared to the competition and so the adoption of a suitable positioning strategy is essential in a market already dominated by some big brands.

There are two main ways in which a brand can be positioned – the first is based on functional attributes for example product attributes, price and quality. JTA's offering will be similar in quality and price to the competition – i.e. premium. It will, however, offer a much more substantial choice in terms of eating, emphasising food compared to the competition who feature coffee and a limited range of biscuits, cakes and snacks. The range will be wider, more authentic and will offer choice ideal for lunchtime, afternoon and early evening and so usage will be different. Customers will benefit because they will have eaten a more substantial meal at JTA . There will also be an opportunity to take away a chilled and ready prepared meal from the café for eating later. This will allow dissociation from the present coffee house players and also other restaurant brands.

The second way is to use more expressive means, particularly important in a service industry. The look, feel, ambience and decor of JTA will be more "ethnic" and exciting with a fusion of tastes offered – somewhat different from the "home away from home" used by Starbucks or Italian design from Costa Coffee. This will be emphasised in the promotion, staff training and the processes used.

A perceptual map could be used to show how the JTA brand will be positioned in comparison to its competitors.

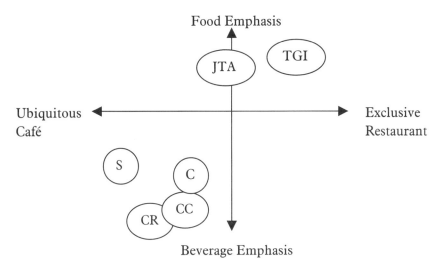

S = Starbucks
CR = Coffee Republic
CC = Costa Coffee
C = Cadbury
JTA = JTA
TGI = TGI Fridays and other restaurants

To summarise JTA will position its cafes away from the existing offerings, nearer to a full service restaurant but with a more casual feel. A mixture of functional and expressive attributes will be used. The following chart summarises the positioning strategies.

Strategy	JTA Approach	Competitors Approach
Product Features	Ethnic Fusion/ Emphasis on food	Light snacks/ Emphasis on beverages
Price/Quality	Premium	Premium
Use	Lunch/Early Evening	Morning/Afternoon
User	Foodies, affluent professionals	Younger, affluent
Product Class Association	Towards restaurant	Café
Benefit	No need to cook, relaxation	Quick refuel & break
Heritage/Cultural symbol	Fusion of cultures. Ambience, design, to reflect this	Italian or American – single culture

(b) **Implementation of Positioning Strategy**

To support the new business launch and help position the brand a variety of integrated marketing communications tools will be used to create awareness, differentiate the offering and encourage visitors to the new cafes. It is assumed that cafes will initially be launched in a limited number of urban environments and therefore a mix of local and national channels will be required. At all times the "ethnic fusion" , "real food" branding message will be presented. The main target markets for the marketing communications include:

- Potential customers – existing JTA in home brand buyers and those new to the brand, possibly affluent professionals with interest in food

- Existing customers – to encourage revisits, stimulate word of mouth and to remind, inform of special events

- Shareholders – to encourage support behind the new venture

- Local audiences including neighbours and council planners – to assure support for new café openings

- Employees and future employees

Above the line – Advertising

Although cost prohibits the use of TV advertising the following media would be beneficial.

- Posters – to be positioned at targeted sites near new outlets, a teaser campaign announcing the new development and then pronouncing the opening and finally reminding (giving directions to outlet)

- Ambient media – a variety of media may be available, e.g. floor posters, scaffolding, building wraps may be use to build awareness and provide directions

- Magazines-advertising in local titles, theatre programmes etc (see PR ideas below)

- Regional Press – to build awareness and carry sales promotion e.g. coupons for free drink with meal to encourage traffic

The above media will need to be carefully selected to give the right audience profile and numbers. Any special events and new menu features will also require support advertising.

- Local Independent Radio advertising may be appropriate to remind customers and programme sponsorship could be considered.

A budget should be made available to support advertising at local events, charity etc.

Below the Line

Sales Promotion

On pack offers will be used to distribute coupons and encourage customers to visit the website to get information on the location and offerings of the new cafes. Sales promotion should convey the concept behind the brand so that the client base are reassured that they will find the same quality and product – but in an out of home environment.

Café users will be given vouchers to encourage revisit and for passing onto friends. These will be diners with similar interests and opinions.

Fliers will be distributed in areas near the café to boost traffic, particularly at less busy times and manage demand.

New recipes (not available in home) can be test marketed at the café's and launched nationally if successful.

Direct Marketing

Invitations to launch events will be sent to local "opinion formers", along with postcards which can be used by these people to send to friends (viral marketing). Word of mouth is an extremely good way of diffusing information quickly and increasing numbers of diners. Leaflet drops will be made during the first few months to raise awareness of the new café and carry sales promotion to encourage a first visit, launch new menus etc.

Loose inserts will piggy back local theatre/venue mailings to encourage before show visits.

Direct marketing is important since it can be more closely targeted to reach the most suitable audience. All sales promotion and direct marketing response will be measured so that promotion is accurately targeted in the future.

Postcode and email details will be collected from café users so that geo-demographic direct marketing can be used to inform customers about new menus, events, openings etc and a loyalty card could be considered.

Suggestion boxes and customer satisfaction surveys will allow the customer to enter into a dialogue with the café operation and improve standards.

E-marketing

The website will be used to give information about location, offer recipe ideas and distribute coupons and leaflets. It will give details about employment opportunities. A community notice board can be developed to encourage a community of users to comment on the café's and promote local events. A special press and shareholder area will be made available.

Email will be used to communicate with registered shareholders, existing visitors, loyalty card holders and encourage revisit, viral marketing opportunities.

Public Relations

Public relations is an extremely important tool since it allows communication with a number of publics and can create greater credibility than advertising. It can use number of media to suit the individual publics.

Press Relations

Press releases can be used to announce planning applications, inform the local people about creation of jobs, launch the café and get local critics to review the café once it is opened. Sponsorships and support for local causes can be announced. National press and business pages will announce the launch to shareholders and generate press interest. As JTA is already well known this new initiative should be worthy of comment. Magazine food writers can be invited to specialist launch events to encourage positive reviews.

Adversarial to be considered along with reader competitions, food articles etc. This will support idea of the cafes having a food orientation rather than beverages.

Sponsorship

Sponsorship of local cultural festivals, dance troupes, employment fairs, food events and so on could be considered and announced via press releases.

Events

After a celebrity opening a number of events should be planned at the café throughout the year to launch new menus, taster sessions, concentrating on the ethnic fusion branding message.

Internal Marketing Communications

Entering the services market means that employees become an extremely important aspect of the marketing mix. Poor service and dining experience can invalidate all of the promotional effort that has gone into differentiating the brand from its competitors. Knowledgeable staff can be empowered to "localise" the service, whilst adhering to brand values. Staff need to be trained to deliver the JTA promise and internal marketing communications will ensure that all have up to date knowledge about promotional and other activities that can affect their work and happiness. Staff turnover can be improved through regular meetings, employee of the month, awards for special service etc. These can be delivered via newsletters, suggestion boxes and team briefings. Unless facilities are given for access then use of intranet etc may not be appropriate at this stage.

Integrated Marketing Communications

All of the above methods are designed to establish dialogue with different publics. As a service industry the extended marketing mix needs to be integrated to ensure that the brand values are consistently upheld throughout the operation. This includes the quality and look of the tangibles like menu design, music, layout as well as staff training and internal processes. As much of the promotion may be undertaken on a local basis a brand manual may be useful to allow staff to take account of local opportunities without damaging the brand values.

All of the above must be consistent with the brand values we wish to promote –i.e. a lively mix of ethnic dishes, real food, freshly prepared, knowledgeable staff, quality and 20 years of experience. JTA is more than a refuelling stop but offers a range of different tastes for snack, lunch or early supper. This will be reflected in the design, message and delivery of the service.

Dynamic Marketing Communications

Encouraging visitors to a café with a brand new and differentiated concept can be relatively easy since novelty value ensures interest especially in initial stages when there is relatively little competition. However as the market matures and new entrants abound maintenance and improvement of business can be a challenge. Trial and adoption by customers becomes slower as they become familiar with the concept. Customers become bored and elderly and this can discourage younger users. Distribution saturation causes the outlets to be too common place and organic expansion becomes less likely. JTA are a relative latecomer into the market place and it should be noticed that there has been some public backlash to companies like Starbucks who are seen as too branded and commercial.

Maturity bring a need to re-tap existing customers and find new markets to stimulate growth. This can be activated through new product development or price competition but the latter can be counter productive as a price war will certainly lead to tighter margins, lower profits and lower quality perception.

The role of marketing communications is therefore important and must change over the product lifecycle. This necessitates a change in the promotional mix, media and message that will be used. It will also mean that the specialist help required from outside agencies will vary although an integrated approach will be needed to ensure brand consistency.

The chart below highlights changes over phases of brand development.

	Introduction	Development	Established	
Communication Role	Awareness,	Differentiate, Inform and Persuade	Remind, Sustain loyalty	Reposition
Marcomms mix	Advertising, PR	Advertising, Branding, Sales Promotion	Sales Promotion, Direct Response	PR, Advertising, Direct Response
Message	We're here	We're different – try us	We're still here	New Proposition for a new market
Media	National media	Local & national media	Internet, Direct Mail, Loyalty card	National

After the established phase the brand may go into decline at which point promotional support will be withdrawn. Alternatively repositioning will be successful and the development phase can begin again.

In order to explain, the DRIP elements will be used to describe the dynamics of the marketing communications for 2 of the main players in the coffee market. **Differentiation** is necessary at the time of introduction and growth of the market place so that Starbucks sees itself as a "home away from home" and Costa Coffee as "Italian" This allows space for both in the market place in the minds of the consumers. Eventually as more competitors enter the market the differentiation may become less clear and so players will need to **remind/reinforce** customers that their position is still unique. Starbucks can do this by re-emphasising their strength in distribution, ensuring that their environment is kept relaxed and comfortable and developing closer links within the local neighbourhood, e.g. throwing street parties and supporting local community events. Costa can use advertising to show the "Italian" nature of their offering and keeping the cafes lively and fashionable, ensuring that they get PR coverage in the smart magazines.

The way in which customers can be kept informed about new developments may reflect their brand values. For example Starbucks may use word of mouth, personal selling, local posters and invitations. Finally customers will wish to be <u>persuaded</u> – firstly to try the coffee shop and then to stay loyal and a variety of direct response tools can be used here, again in keeping with the differentiated offering. The tools used will adapt according to local demand/ competition and some of the larger players may well try to ambush competitor's strategies.

Conclusion

The nature of marketing communications is dynamic and must respond to its changing strategic role. JTA must accept that their plan will need to adapt to the market in order to become and remain successful. This report has emphasised the importance of positioning to differentiate the product offering from a number of strongly branded competitors. A number of ideas for a range of suitable promotional tools to implement the positioning strategy have been discussed and the importance of an integrated approach has been stressed. Finally the need for adaptation as the market matures has been discussed.

It would appear that there is a good opportunity for JTA to stretch its brand into the service market and by introducing a number of JTA cafes it will have a synergistic effect on its existing "in home business".

.ion 2

Tutorial note. Integration of off an on line communication methods is key to a good answer, along with relevant ideas for the stated scenario. A consideration of message and methods to achieve stated objectives can be important.

Beautyspotdotcom

This paper will examine the opportunities that exist for a high street retailer of health and beauty products in developing a web site, accessible through interactive television. Interactive technology has much to recommend it as a marketing communications tool. It can provide information about the retailer and its products to a number of different stakeholders, act as a new channel to market, facilitate sales and supply information to the retailer about the its customers. In short it can create a dialogue between a vast number of customers and the company, a benefit which has been called one to one mass marketing. A successful website can then be used to differentiate our retail operation and add value to the existing brand. Alternatively it can become a stand alone brand. This paper assumes that the website operation will be integrated with the high street offering and will be branded as Beautyspot.com i.e. a bricks and clicks operation.

This paper will consider the role of marketing communication in encouraging visitors to the site and then outline how they will be encouraged to revisit and use the site on a regular basis. Off-line (promotion via non-electronic and non-web based methods) and on-line methods (using the internet, interactive television and other electronic media) will be discussed.

(a) **Encouraging Visitors to the Site**

Off-line Methods

A number of in store promotional opportunities exist. The website address can be promoted in store, on packaging and till receipts. Other **merchandising** tools and sales promotion gimmicks could be used, for example free make up bag or brush carrying website address on spending £10 in store.

Sales advisors could direct customers to the site to obtain further product information.

Direct marketing can be used, for example mail-shot to existing store card holders or loose inserts in a range of health and beauty magazines. This will encourage visitors to look at the site and register for a range of benefits.

Sales promotion to encourage site traffic, including special offers on the website or a competition that requires the entrants to log on to the site. Details of free makeovers or days at a health farm perhaps? Promoted in store or via traditional advertising. All traditional **advertising** will carry the URL, billboard advertising and **ambient** methods including free postcards can be made to be eye-catching and carry a simple message – visit the site. For example a single question can be posed – "Do diets work?" Visit www.beautyspotdotcom to find out.

PR is essential to try and spread the word about the site and inform a wide number of potential users. There are many health and beauty titles, including a range of specialist sports magazines that press releases can be aimed at. For example the web site may well have an area concerning healthy eating and a taste of this can be released in an article which invites readers to find out more by visiting the website Other content e.g. on-line survey results could be offered in printed form for use by editors.

Word of mouth is an important tool and all promotion should try and stimulate this as personal recommendation develops trust in the website. **Branding** consistent with the stores will add on-line security and trust.

On-line

On line communication tools are largely the same as off-line although the consumer will elect on whether to follow the link to the site. The following tools are available:-

Advertising through banner ads, pop up and hyperlinks from complimentary websites or sites known to be frequented by customers similar to our target market. Search engines like google will be useful to provide site direction, using key words such as beauty and health. Interactive TV advertising will also be used to support **PR** activity, programme sponsorship and provision of editorial for on line newsletters and interactive TV.

On line **direct marketing** such as targeted emails and e-viral (an online word of mouth) methods will be used. Opt-in by potential users is essential so that the brand trust is not eroded with Spam.

Incentives such as special offers, broader range availability, special information and good links elsewhere will be highlighted in the message which will tend to be shorter and use direct marketing skills in order to stimulate an immediate visit through a simple click.

On line communication will provide credibility and direction to the site as well as raising awareness.

(b) **Repeat Visits**

After the first visit marketing communications will be needed to encourage return visits by customers. One of the best ways of doing this is to ensure that the site remains informative and interesting and is differentiated from other health and beauty sites by its excellent design, navigation speed and content. In addition the importance of fulfilment, interactivity, dialogue opportunities and excellent service cannot be ignored. Off line brand values need to be delivered on line and the site should offer a good user experience. If users know that content will be regularly updated then their curiosity will encourage a revisit to the site. Site "stickiness" can only be achieved by ensuring that content is interesting, relevant and fun to use.

However customers will need to be reminded to come back to the site and the following tools will be used to arouse site curiosity on a regular basis.

Advertising on and off line, with details of exciting and new content, alongside profile advertising to retain top of mind awareness. Relevant, personalised **E-mails** to past visitors to inform them about new services and site content, using competitions and incentives to encourage revisit. **Text messages** may be considered relevant if the target market agree to use this method. Regular **Sales promotions** e.g. competitions and quizzes, special on line prices and ranges will be used to provide interest and add value to the site and these will be promoted widely. **Order tracking** will be available, along with **Chat rooms** and on line **Community** boards to encourage those with a particular interest to regularly visit. **PR** will continue to help stimulate word of mouth communications and inform consumers about new site content and facilities.

Conclusion

The opportunity to have an on line presence has been taken up by many traditional retailers some with more success than others. An on-line presence should add value to the brand and the importance of encouraging visitors to the site through clever marketing communication programmes has been stressed. Interesting and useful site content is key to getting return visitors but this must be complimented with both on and offline promotions to differentiate, remind, inform and persuade customers about the value of the site. Above all the website must not detract from the brand but reflect and add equity to it.

BPP
PUBLISHING

Question 3

> **Tutorial note.** This question should only be attempted by those with a good theoretical understanding of the components of attitude. The application to the target market and product will bring rewards and full analysis of attributes is useful.

To: Managing Director
        NicoStop Patches

From: Marketing Communications Manger
Date: June 2002

Re: Changing Attitudes

This report investigates the best way to change the attitudes of young female smokers and encourage them to use NicoStop patches as a means to stop smoking. This group of 14 – 24 year olds have traditionally proved difficult to reach since they do not accept that smoking is habitual and believe feel that they can give it up when they choose. They are an important target for us as a business. Attitude change is notoriously difficult and this report will first explain what an attitude is and then suggest a suitable marketing communications strategy for NicoStop.

What is an Attitude?

An attitude is an enduring set of beliefs, generally thought to be made up of three components. These are the cognitive(learn) part i.e. the knowledge and beliefs held, affective (feel) or more emotional elements and co native (do), how they behave aspects. It is sometimes thought that if a company gives information and knowledge about the product, they will like it and this will lead to purchase. The reality though is not always so linear and if we consider cigarette smoking then the young person may well try (do) smoking before forming affective (feel) and cognitive (learn) beliefs about the brand.

As a company we may wish to explore attitudes toward cigarette smoking and also attitudes towards NicoStop patches. They can be positive or negative. We should also explore the attitudes towards the act of buying a patch product. The latter is particularly important for our product since the subjective norm(i.e. what others will think about the act of buying a patch) is likely to be an important influence.

How can we Change Attitudes?

Attitudes are extremely complex and difficult to change but marketing communications will be important in helping the change, along with other aspects of the mix such as intensifying distribution where possible and ensuring that the product looks appealing and actually removes cravings. Several methods of marcomms may be needed which will affect one or more attitude components.

(a) **Attribute approaches**. NicoStop could demonstrate a new attribute such as trendy tattoo designs or longer lasting effects. Salience of a particular attribute may be emphasised – for example the social benefits of quitting smoking rather than the health benefits which our target market have so far ignored. The benefits of saving money by using the patches could also be demonstrated in advertising.

(b) **Brand Associations**. Celebrities could be used to endorse patch use, product placement in popular soaps will help change the subjective norm, emphasising the emotional benefits of use compared to the more rational attribute based beliefs. Our brand could be repositioned to become associated with young people by ensuring that all brand elements appeal – including packaging, distribution and promotional methods (perhaps use sales promotion methods linked with beauty products) and distribution. Music festival sponsorship might increase the association of our brand with the target youth market.

(c) **Change Perception of Competitive products.** NicoStop's competitors include a variety of different brands, use of alternative treatments such as acupuncture, just stopping smoking and also continuing with tobacco. There is already a plethora of data to show the dangers of smoking but the young market have not perceived this as relevant to them – the message needs to be made more relevant. For example many young women may smoke in order to "stay thin" but the perception that smoking is helpful in dieting could be changed with the right message. The message that other methods of stopping are less effective and uncool could be used or we could try and change perceptions towards smoking by emphasising the effects on younger people, rather than the scare "death" tactics which have been used but seem to apply to the older smoker.

(d) **Provide Credibility.** Attitudes towards patches may well suffer from lack of credibility either that the product does not work or that it is not as cool as smoking. PR activity in targeted media will be more credible than advertising and this should be used where possible. To improve credibility information can be given to number of different audiences including health professionals (direct marketing to school and occupational nurses, special website area), pharmacists (personal selling to ensure they carry stock and support sales promotions) and younger people (sponsorship of health information packs). Viral marketing could be used to encourage peer group adoption of the message e.g. postcards, viral email etc. If the user does quit they may wish to tell their friends.

(e) **Change Performance beliefs.** Marketing communications can be used to demonstrate that the product does work, that people like them have used the product with success and that benefits have accrued. For example editorial in magazines giving case histories could be used. Also guarantees could be communicated alongside an emphasis of rational benefits like saving money to buy new clothes, travel, more energy for dancing etc. Positive messages showing boosted self esteem of quitting could be used. Messages showing the numbers who have quit since using NicoStop could be emailed to users on a monthly basis.

(f) **Change Action.** This is the final stage – rewards and other sales promotions could be used (if legal!) to encourage purchase and ensure that our brand of patch is chosen and used over competing products.

Targeted and Relevant Messages

It is important that this target group are treated in a special and relevant way and so the media choice, message and language used will need to be tailored accordingly. Therefore text messaging (perhaps to remind them to change their patch!) or the use of a website based support group could be relevant to this age group, alongside fly on the wall documentaries, sponsorship of Big Brother type competitions, magazine quizzes etc will encourage involvement. In addition messages portraying happier non smokers would gradually erode the association between smoking and fun, sociable occasions (Affective component). Our company could lobby the government to ensure that wide distribution of our products is achieved and that they can be prescribed by doctors. It can support the anti smoking authorities although this should be done in a non branded way – we would not want NicoStop to be seen as a nagging brand but one which is chosen by the youth market as their brand of choice.

Conclusion

Many ideas have been put forward which may help change the cognitive, affective or co native aspect of attitude towards cessation of smoking amongst young females. NicoStop should put support behind the anti smoking lobby and needs to concentrate on ensuring that our brand is the most appropriate for the younger targets. Changing attitudes is extremely difficult and from a commercial point of view it could be argued that the our company will be more successful in the short term by encouraging people to try the product several times before quitting. An understanding of the complex relationship between attitudes and behaviour is important but it is felt that a combination approach suggested here will ensure that NicoStop is the brand of choice for the important young female market.

Question 4

> **Tutorial note**. This question requires an understanding of positioning, differentiation and integration with corporate mission. The question is topical and gives candidates an opportunity to discuss the importance of blending internal and external marketing communications in a service environment.

(a) To: Managing Director
From: Marketing Manager
Date: June 2002

Marketing Communications

Introduction

The low cost airline segment is highly competitive and growing rapidly. However growth is likely to decline as the market becomes saturated. This report will show how investment in targeted marketing communications will differentiate our brand "Flyhigh" from our competitors in order to attract new and keep existing customers. The importance of internal marketing communications will also be assessed.

Differentiation

Sustainable competitive advantage is a strategic approach which requires all areas of the business to pull together to achieve the airline mission and reflect our strengths which will then be communicated to our target markets and delivered efficiently. Our mission is to be the best value for money airline with the best service in the low cost sector. All activities are designed to ensure that costs are as low as possible without cutting service. We issue seat numbers and ensure that individuals are looked after from the moment they order (on and off-line) by a customer service manager. This opens up the possibility to serve business and pleasure markets and be more pro active in communicating with both target markets. Our strap line could be "low cost-more thrills".

The same message will be reinforced through all marketing communications and ordering on line will be acknowledged with a personal email, inviting a dialogue with a named individual at the company. In addition customers will be encouraged to supply information so that their customer service manager on flight will be aware of their needs and allow customer relationship marketing to encourage loyalty.

The job of the marketing communications will be firstly to announce the benefits of our "thrilling" service, via a number of small ads in business and travel pages. Direct marketing will also be used to selected business who regularly travel to airports we serve. In bound telemarketing will support the business and provide access to the customer service people. The message will include price details but not feature them, concentrating on the added value services we offer.

Public Relations will be used where applicable to encourage a positive message is spread by opinion leaders to our target audiences.

Once the customer has travelled we will communicate again, by email, to seek feedback on whether the service was well received and gather more information with regards future potential usage. This information will then be used to generate timely marcomms. A frequent flyer club may be introduced to encourage repeat business from the most fruitful segments.

Costs will be kept low as communication will be targeted, relevant and measured for efficiency.

Marketing communications will be used to Differentiate the service offering, remind customers about the added value, inform them of prices and persuade them to use our airline. Communications will be integrated to ensure that the messages are amplified in all we do and this will reduce costs in the long run.

(b) **Internal Marketing Communications**

The importance of the employee within a service market like ours cannot be under estimated. Customers will feel cheated if employees do not deliver the promise because they are not aware, able or not inclined to do so. Good internal marketing will lead to **transactional benefits**, for example if flight staff are aware of particular customer requirements before they fly and can ensure they have the right resources to accommodate these needs. Speedy internal communications will co-ordinate the actions of all staff, improve the use of resources and direct internal operations to ensure that the company goals are achieved.

In addition to these efficiencies staff who feel valued and know that they are making a difference within the organisation will be motivated and **affiliation benefits** will accrue. High staff turnover is expensive and inexperienced staff may be unable to offer the good service promise in external communications.

Internal communications will therefore allow a dialogue between all staff within the organisation, will be efficient and ensure that staff are enabled at point of service delivery, confident to make the right decision to achieve company and customer satisfaction goals.

Fly high's point of difference is that we will offer better service than the other low cost airlines and we promise that individuals will be looked after by a member of the customer service team, from booking through to flight and thereafter. This requires seamless internal communication and a team approach. This will benefit the staff, now organised round the customer and away from traditional functional lines. Technology can be used to bind together staff in different parts of the world, along with team meetings, training days involving all employees, video conferencing and other more personal methods.

Integration between internal and external messages is very important – if service is promised to customers but employees are being told to reduce costs then a perception gap will emerge.

Conclusion

Within a service industry internal employees are the face of the brand and efficient and effective internal marketing communications will be the lubricant that seals together the promise and delivery and this will differentiate Fly high from other low cost operators.

Question 5

> Integrated Marketing
> Communications at NSPCC
> Briefing Notes
> by
> A. Smith, Marketing Manager

Introductions

Offer welcome and ask for each member to introduce themselves

Introduce self and state marketing background and reason why I have been brought into the team.

State purpose of the meeting is to discuss the nature and value of integrating marketing communications activity and outline the agenda.

> **Draft Agenda**
> Introductions
> What is Integrated Marketing Communications?
> How can it be implemented?
> What are the potential benefits?
> Any Questions?
> AOB
> Date of Next Meeting

What is Integrated Marketing Communications?

This can be seen as the strategic choice of elements of marketing communications that effectively and efficiently inform and influence all stakeholders. It requires that all marketing communications elements are controlled and managed and requires that all communication has been derived from a single and consistent strategy.

This integration can be approached from a number of different levels.

(a) **Promotional Mix**. All elements of our promotional mix should be co-ordinated so that the messages we send out are integrated and consistent. Our collection boxes should carry our branding and our direct marketing should be co-ordinated with our above the line advertising.

(b) **Strategy**. All our operations should need to be integrated vertically and strive towards our corporate mission i.e. to alleviate childhood suffering. This will include fund raising, delivery of services, lobbying external bodies like the government, recruitment of volunteers and so on. Our mission will be translated into marketing goals e.g. to raise £100million which in turn will dictate marketing communication goals – all helping to achieve the mission.

(c) **Internal and External Integration**. Our communication internally must be harmonised with external communication. This is particularly true of service markets like ours where many volunteers are used and it is important that they know how their activities can help achieve our aims. Our volunteers are the human face of our work and must communicate and act in a way which reflects the NSPCC core values. They should be encouraged to communicate back to us whether our strategies are working. Charities have many stakeholders and must communicate with these on a regular basis. These include users of the service, donors, volunteers and professional support workers, many of whom will have different expectations of our work. An integrated approach pulls all of this together.

(d) **Long term approach**. We wish to ensure that our work goes on for as long as necessary and IMC takes a long term view-important so that relationships with our stakeholders continue over time.

Implementation

IMC sounds extremely simple in its approach but implementation within a large charity such as ours is fairly difficult, partly due to the wide number of stakeholders, lack of funds and relatively small numbers of professionally paid staff with knowledge of this approach. Stakeholders may be resistant to the need for integration and a phased development approach is recommended starting with senior professional staff and cascading the plan to all parts of the organisation. Internal marketing communications and training is vital and feedback essential. Each level within the organisation should develop plans for delivering IMC and these plans should be tested, monitored and controlled and good practice amplified.

A starting point will be the co-ordination of the promotional mix used to generate donations – all brand instruments integrated to ensure synergy and economies of scale. This will break down existing barriers between functional areas like direct marketing and corporate brand advertising.

Invite those present to discuss potential methods for starting the process within their own area of activity.

What are the Potential Benefits?

This question will invite comments from the attendees and the following benefits will be teased out.

(a) IMC impacts on **efficiency**, particularly important in charities where costs must be kept to a minimum and maximum funds put into delivering services. IMC is essential if the broad number of communications methods now at our disposal are to be pulled together

(b) Improved internal marcomms ensures a more rapid **flow of information** and can increase the understanding and effectiveness of all stakeholders, improving strategic relationships.

(c) A single message is more **effective**, avoids misunderstanding and wasted effort going into areas which do not support the charity mission.

(d) Internal co-ordination offers affiliation and **motivation** of internal stakeholders, particularly where a true dialogue is set up.

(e) Synergy between marcomms avoids costly **duplication** and ensures a single, **clear consistent brand identity** is put across. There are many active players in the children's charity market and we need to ensure that our cause is differentiated so that donors and volunteers understand why supporting us is so important.

(f) IMC helps develop the **corporate brand** – a method of tangibilising the services we offer. Our full stop logo has many brand associations and acts as shortcut device for our supporters.

(g) IMC ensures that a **systematic, planned and measured approach** is taken and this will help decision making, inhibiting short term actions which may have a negative impact in the long term e.g. inappropriate fundraising tactics.

Any Questions?

As the approach is new comments and questions are invited.

AOB?

Close

Thanks for attendance will be given and the meeting will be called to a close with the important benefits of IMC summarised. IMC will be of great benefit to the NSPCC. This has already started with the excellent full stop campaign but now needs to be further developed and integrated to provide even better communication without huge costs associated. All time and human resources will be maximised. It is important to maintain our image and not to be seen wasting money by our stakeholders.

Suggest it will fit in well with our future and invite ideas and comments to this office for discussion at the next meeting.

Date of Next Meeting

To be agreed.

Question 6

> **Tutorial note**. This question is similar to one used in December 2001 but requires a mix of promotional tools to be discussed in section b. Appraisal of the role of advertising in a strategic way is essential in this question. Examples are required

Building Brands

This essay will discuss a variety of appropriate marketing communications methods that can be used to build brands. It will begin by stating what a brand is and then will appraise the strategic role of advertising in brand building. The essay will consider alternative below the line and other methods for brand development. A number of examples will explain and develop basic principles.

A brand is the mix of intrinsic and extrinsic attributes that combine to create and sustain a positive and enduring impression in the mind of the customer or other stakeholder. Many brands rely on the extrinsic characteristics (e.g. marketing communications, packaging etc) to differentiate themselves from competitor offerings since their intrinsic characteristics are not sufficiently unique. A good example of this would be toilet tissue – most brand are soft and gentle but Charmin (a Procter and Gamble brand) illustrates these characteristics through a cuddly bear, compared to the Andrex puppy favoured by a competing brand.

Marketing communications has an important role to play and because of its visibility. Advertising and above the line methods play an important role.

The role of advertising

Advertising can **differentiate** the brand offering by drawing attention to the intrinsic differences between products. Using certain actors or messages can affiliate the brand with a target market, for example Shredded Wheat's "healthy heart" message using Ian Botham has helped **position** the brand in this growing food sector.

Advertising can be used to **inform** customers about particular brand features. Since advertising is paid for the message is controlled by the sponsor and so the relevant features are communicated without distortion. An example might be magazine advertising for a beauty fluid – the advert will tell us that wrinkles are reduced in appearance by 30% a one sided message that does not invite opposing views.

Advertising can be used to keep out competition. By offering a share of voice that would be costly to match competitors may well decide not to bother with a me too product even if it performs marginally better.

Advertising can be used in a direct way to **persuade** the consumer to try the brand by tangibilising the benefits of the brand. An example here might be Fairy Liquid which shows the extra number of plates that can be washed with one bottle compared to a leading competitor.

Advertising, being relatively cost efficient can allow communication with a wide target market on a frequent basis. This proffers top of mind awareness, important for low involvement products such as soft drinks. The **reminding** and **reinforcing** role is important for many products as the consumer can forget the brand message can be eroded by competing messages if not constantly refreshed and updated.

Advertising is good at creating positive **brand associations**, both functional and symbolic. A good example here might be the difference in advertising between supermarkets – Iceland advertising features the " buy one get one free approach" – a rational and functional benefit whereas Tesco "every little helps" builds a more emotional bond – that Tesco want to help you as a friend.

Advertising can create **added value** to the brand. Guinness is a fine example of this where their clever advertising has given the brand a sophisticated and intellectual image. The Fiat Punto is seen as a clever and cheeky stylish car with the positive associations portrayed in its "Spirito de Punto" advertising.

Below and Through the Line methods

Although advertising does have an extremely important role to play in building brand values not all successful brands have used advertising. Asics are the running shoe of choice to many serious runners based on their technical features presented at point of sale rather than the emotional and intangible characteristics. A gradual trickle down from opinion leaders has been more successful in this market and positioned the brand away from the more fashionable competitors like Nike.

PR such as this can create a more credible brand and add value to the basic message. However the message can be changed and altered by editors and the brand owner has less control over this method.

Sponsorship can develop positive associations, for example a car manufacturer sponsoring a high profile formula one team.,(although it could be argued that this works better in conjunction with above the line advertising support.)

Other brand elements such as packaging, brand name, logo and colour can be used to differentiate the brand. For example the shape of the bottle used by John Paul Gaultier cosmetics is distinctive and positions the brand as a high fashion and serious contender in the market. The olive oil based spread "Olivio" uses its Italian sounding name to add value to the brand with its Mediterranean feel.

Interactive and direct marketing can also be used with limited success to build a brand. It can be cost effective and can be targeted and so if an air of exclusivity is required the use of "special invitations" might endorse this association. A service brand may find that its direct marketing activity is an opportunity to tangibilise the brand values – using recycled paper for an environmental charity for example could work well.

Sales promotion can erode brand values if seen to be associated with gimmicks but occasionally can be used to reinforce them. For example Andrex competition to win a cute toy puppy reinforced brand associations with softness.

Conclusion

Advertising does have an extremely important role to play in developing and building brands as they are often grounded in emotion and advertising can portray this in a controlled , exciting and fun way. However brand building is not the exclusive domain of advertising and the strategic importance will depend on the nature of the brand and the market place. Where budgets are tight a combination of below the line and through the line methods can work equally as well. A small budget does not exclude all advertising and the smart brand owner will wish to ensure the right integration of tools to ensure that the brand is differentiated and positioned in the most suitable way.

Question 7

> **Tutorial note**. This difficult question could be approached in many ways. The product used here is easier to globalise than some other more culture bound products. The role of agencies and their structure are key answer components and better candidates may discuss the contradiction of integrated marketing communication with customisation requirements.

> Global Advertising
> To: IBM
> From: AA Global Advertising
> June 2002

Introduction

This report will evaluate the extent to which our advertising agency can deliver effective integrated marketing communications on behalf of IBM to its global market place. It will outline the following concepts

1 Nature and Scope of IMC
2 The globalisation debate – standardisation v customisation
3 Delivering the chosen strategy
4 A Way Forward
5 Conclusions and Discussion

1 *Nature and Scope of Integrated Marketing Communications*

IBM is a highly sophisticated world wide manufacturer and service provider of computer and e-business solutions. You have taken the global approach of delivering a single message through your strategy of Integrated marketing communications. In your high-tech market which is not so culture bound the simplicity of this approach is appealing, the use of English in printed and electronic media is largely expected and our brand position at the premium end of the market is appropriate worldwide. Most of our clients are aiming to become global players and will be looking for a technology solution that facilitates this approach.

Your change of emphasis from hardware and software to service and solutions now requires more local adaptation for regional markets.

2   *The globalisation debate – standardisation v customisation*

There are many reasons for now taking our globalised approach and adapting this to serve the needs of regional markets. Legal aspects, access to media and other marketing instruments like research are not internationally accessible so the standardised approach may not be appropriate.

The global message suggested that we serve clients looking for big and expensive technology solutions, IBM was seen as unsuitable for companies technically less sophisticated. Sales people were unable to take the message and make it appropriate for customers at the local level and local staff resented concepts in which they felt they had no input. Our shift in emphasis towards solutions and away from technology requires a more personal approach which means a customised approach empathetic to local needs.

3   *Delivering the chosen strategy*

Global agencies such as ours have been ideally suited to IBM as we can co-ordinate all activities from a central point, fully integrating all communications. A single contact for briefing allows you to concentrate on control and evaluation of the campaigns. Speedy response and less duplication benefits budgets and management control.

We also offer expertise in public relations, interactive communications, advertising and below the line activity. Our understanding of your core brand values and ability to undertake worldwide branding research ensures consistency of message delivery.

Our presence in all of your markets throughout the world made us ideal partners since our geographic spread through associates and branches reflect your own international coverage. Your new emphasis suggests that you may be looking for a different service.

4   *Way Forward*

It is important to consider if our international structure is suited to the new approach of adaptation. It is true to say that some global agencies do not fully understand the subtleties of cultural influences on marketing communications and sales campaigns and that a standardised brand message and approach has diminished your relevance in some markets. However our structure and skills enable us to do both jobs – implementation of locally required marketing communication and co-ordination of core messages on a global basis.

Some agencies may not have sufficient local knowledge to take advantage of local media opportunities, specialist skills and tools. Some global agencies offer good reach but poor relevance since decision making is too far removed from operations. This is not the case here – we will ensure that our local partners offer their expertise and knowledge to your local managers and ensure that they can take advantage of local opportunities. Messages will be suited to local conditions. We will still ensure co-ordination and dissemination on your behalf and you will have knowledge of all activities and be able to control these and set objectives.

Your brand position may not be have been appropriate in all regions due to the strength of local competition but we are now able to work on your behalf to use the best available local skills to ensure appropriateness in the future.

5   *Conclusions and Discussion*

BPP
PUBLISHING

It could be argued that truly integrated marketing communications strategies require complete standardisation across regions, message and media and therefore adaptation to suit local markets is not really a possibility. However we have presented here a good solution for IBM that will help them act locally where appropriate but building brand equity and maintain core values throughout the world. Our capability worldwide and agency structure, coupled with our excellent knowledge of your brand will ensure that together we can go forward to a successful future by "thinking global and acting local".

Topic Index

Mr/Mrs/Ms (Full name)

Daytime delivery address

_____

Postcode

Daytime Tel _____

Date of exam (month/year)

CIM Order

To BPP Publishing Ltd, Aldine Place, London W12 8AA

Tel: 020 8740 2211. Fax: 020 8740 1184

email: publishing@bpp.com

online: www.bpp.com

	8/02 Texts	9/02 Kits	Success Tapes (old syllabus)
STAGE 1 NEW SYLLABUS			
1 Marketing Fundamentals	£18.95 ☐	£9.95 ☐	£12.95 ☐
2 Marketing Environment	£18.95 ☐	£9.95 ☐	£12.95 ☐
3 Customer Communications	£18.95 ☐	£9.95 ☐	£12.95 ☐
4 Marketing in Practice	£18.95 ☐	£9.95 ☐	£12.95 ☐
ADVANCED CERTIFICATE OLD SYLLABUS *			
5 The Marketing Customer Interface	£18.95 ☐	£9.95 ☐	£12.95 ☐
6 Management Information for Marketing Decisions	£18.95 ☐	£9.95 ☐	£12.95 ☐
7 Effective Management for Marketing	£18.95 ☐	£9.95 ☐	£12.95 ☐
8 Marketing Operations	£18.95 ☐	£9.95 ☐	£12.95 ☐
DIPLOMA OLD SYLLABUS *			
9 Integrated Marketing Communications	£18.95 ☐	£9.95 ☐	£12.95 ☐
10 International Marketing Strategy	£18.95 ☐	£9.95 ☐	£12.95 ☐
11 Strategic Marketing Management: Planning and Control	£18.95 ☐	£9.95 ☐	£12.95 ☐
12 Strategic Marketing Management: Analysis and Decision (9/02)	£25.95 ☐	N/A	N/A

* Texts and kits for remaining new syllabus items will be available in the spring and summer of 2003.

SUBTOTAL £ ☐

POSTAGE & PACKING

Study Texts

	First	Each extra	
UK	£3.00	£2.00	£ ☐
Europe*	£5.00	£4.00	£ ☐
Rest of world	£20.00	£10.00	£ ☐

Kits/Success Tapes

	First	Each extra	
UK	£2.00	£1.00	£ ☐
Europe*	£2.50	£1.00	£ ☐
Rest of world	£15.00	£8.00	£ ☐

Grand Total (Cheques to *BPP Publishing*) I enclose

a cheque for (incl. Postage)   £ ☐

Or charge to Access/Visa/Switch

Card Number ☐☐☐☐☐☐☐☐☐☐☐☐☐☐☐☐

Expiry date _____   Start Date _____

Issue Number (Switch Only) ☐☐☐☐

Signature _____

We aim to deliver to all UK addresses inside 5 working days. A signature will be required. Orders to all EU addresses should be delivered within 6 working days.

All other orders to overseas addresses should be delivered within 8 working days.

* Europe includes the Republic of Ireland and the Channel Islands.

REVIEW FORM & FREE PRIZE DRAW

All original review forms from the entire BPP range, completed with genuine comments, will be entered into one of two draws on 31 January 2003 and 31 July 2003. The names on the first four forms picked out on each occasion will be sent a cheque for £50.

Name: _____   Address: _____

_____

_____

How have you used this Kit?
(Tick one box only)

☐ Home study (book only)

☐ On a course: college _____

☐ With 'correspondence' package

☐ Other _____

Why did you decide to purchase this Kit?
(Tick one box only)

☐ Have used complementary Study Text

☐ Have used BPP Kits in the past

☐ Recommendation by friend/colleague

☐ Recommendation by a lecturer at college

☐ Saw advertising

☐ Other _____

During the past six months do you recall seeing/receiving any of the following?
(Tick as many boxes as are relevant)

☐ Our advertisement in *Marketing Success*

☐ Our advertisement in *Marketing Business*

☐ Our brochure with a letter through the post

☐ Our brochure with *Marketing Business*

Which (if any) aspects of our advertising do you find useful?
(Tick as many boxes as are relevant)

☐ Prices and publication dates of new editions

☐ Information on Kit content

☐ Facility to order books off-the-page

☐ None of the above

Have you used the companion Study Text for this subject?   ☐ Yes   ☐ No

Your ratings, comments and suggestions would be appreciated on the following areas

	Very useful	Useful	Not useful
Introductory section (Study advice, key questions checklist, etc)	☐	☐	☐
Short questions	☐	☐	☐
Tutorial questions	☐	☐	☐
Examination-standard questions	☐	☐	☐
Content of suggested answers	☐	☐	☐
Test paper	☐	☐	☐
Structure and presentation	☐	☐	☐

	Excellent	Good	Adequate	Poor
Overall opinion of this Kit	☐	☐	☐	☐

Do you intend to continue using BPP Study Texts/Kits?   ☐ Yes   ☐ No

Please note any further comments and suggestions/errors on the reverse of this page.

Please return to: Kate Machattie, BPP Publishing Ltd, FREEPOST, London, W12 8BR

REVIEW FORM & FREE PRIZE DRAW (continued)

Please note any further comments and suggestions/errors below

FREE PRIZE DRAW RULES

1   Closing date for 31 January 2003 draw is 31 December 2002. Closing date for 31 July 2003 draw is 30 June 2003.

2   Restricted to entries with UK and Eire addresses only. BPP employees, their families and business associates are excluded.

3   No purchase necessary. Entry forms are available upon request from BPP Publishing. No more than one entry per title, per person. Draw restricted to persons aged 16 and over.

4   Winners will be notified by post and receive their cheques not later than 6 weeks after the relevant draw date.

5   The decision of the promoter in all matters is final and binding. No correspondence will be entered into.

Sisypl

GH01252145

Michael Richmond

chipmunkapublishing
the mental health publisher

Published by
Chipmunkapublishing
PO Box 6872
Brentwood
Essex CM13 1ZT
United Kingdom

http://www.chipmunkapublishing.com

Chipmunkapublishing gratefully acknowledge the support of Arts Council England.

Acknowledgements

Any acknowledgements here aren't just for those who helped me to write and publish Sisyphusa but also for those who have helped me generally. I'd like to thank: My mum, a gifted teacher and my first reader, without whom I couldn't have written this book; My brother Matthew, for your consistent support, your humour and your invaluable advice in the editing process; Grandma, for your visits, your unconditional love and your relentless optimism on my behalf; Joan, Dr. Prenelle and Dr. Crocker, for your expertise and your humanity; The many caring professionals in the NHS; My family on both sides of the Atlantic for being so understanding of something I know is so hard to understand; Jason Pegler and Chipmunka Publishing for giving me the platform to raise my voice; The talented Temujin Doran and Max Robinson for their pitch-perfect cover illustration; Lastly, to Milo for reminding me how to smile.

Michael Richmond

This book is dedicated to my wonderful parents, Robin and Howard, for your unending love, wisdom, support and patience and for keeping hope alive. To the memory of my hero Arthur Rubenstein, a giant of a man and the best Grandpa and friend imaginable. And to Claire, a guiding light for so many lost in the dark, for your friendship and guidance.

Michael Richmond

Author Biography

Michael Richmond was born in London in 1986. He had a happy childhood, growing up in a loving home with his parents and older brother. He always liked school but was equally occupied with enjoying life with his friends and family and continuing his lifelong romance with Arsenal Football Club. After A-Levels, Michael travelled around India, Southeast Asia and Australasia for 6 months before attending the University of Sussex. He felt in his element being at university and living in Brighton. He was growing, working hard and making wonderful friendships.

However, halfway through his second year of university, in February 2007, he had a very sudden and unexpected onset of what was later diagnosed as Anxiety and Clinical Depression and later still with a form of OCD. Within the space of a week he went from being a very confident and successful student to being unable to leave the house that he was living in with friends in Brighton. Michael had to move back home to his parents' house in London where he has remained ever since.

He has had various talking therapies and medications over the four years that he has been unwell, some of which have been very helpful, others distinctly unhelpful. He began to read avidly after the first year of almost catatonic depression. He has also tried to learn Spanish and Portuguese and has taken up the piano. He wrote Sisyphusa over the course of around eighteen months initially inspired by a strange dream and by the anger he felt after attending a psychiatric day hospital for six months.

Michael has felt a stark rupture in the way in which he has experienced life before and after his breakdown. He is no longer as housebound as he was in the first couple of years, thanks in large part to his Cocker Spaniel puppy Milo who demands constant walks and attention. He has fewer crises, and with the help of his family and caregivers he has learned more effective ways of managing his symptoms. Nevertheless, his situation remains very limited as he feels unable to work or to resume his formal studies, nor does he feel able to be in contact with former friends from school and university or most of his wider family. But he's pleased to be able to share his work with a wider audience and to add his voice to the many thousands fighting against the stigma surrounding mental illness.

Chapter 1

They came in black cloaks, the men from Sisyphusa. Not the white coats you hear of in stories growing up on Fantasy Island. I was living in a rented house on the south coast of the Island. The two-storey red-brick building stood on top of a steep hill on the outskirts of town. There were seven bedrooms, two grimy, unkempt bathrooms and a kitchen that stank of Liquid Escape and stubbed-out cigarettes. We had no living room—our budget could not stretch to such luxuries. We made do with some carefully arranged floor cushions and a second-hand bean-bag placed at the far end of the kitchen. I was living with six other students from South Coast University. We had all met and become friends in the first year and it seemed a natural evolution that we would move off campus together in year 2.

They came for me on a dreary night in February. I was planning a night out at the local Liquidiser to celebrate Loveheart Day with my housemates. On this day lovers young and old must buy their sweethearts all manner of gifts and treats to parade their affection. This left them safe in the knowledge that they weren't obliged to be romantic again until the same time next year. We of number 67 Cossetts Lane decided to enjoy the evening as a group, being mostly sheepish singletons. Loveheart Day was one more chance to imbibe a few gallons of Liquid Escape and lose money on the Electronic Quiz Machine (EQM).

The rest of the clan had gone on ahead. I'd only just woken up after an all-nighter and Wellborn was applying the finishing touches to his hair so we agreed to meet them there. I decided it would be prudent to have a nice hardy dinner before another night of revelry. "In a rush? Ya has ta have a Fasta-Pasta" as the Ad-Verse goes. I slopped the contents of the packet into the Zapper and gave it 30 seconds- time enough to rummage around under the bed for my jacket. It was a silver and black number that set me back 120 coins. I put it on and looked at myself in the mirror, standing in profile. Staring back was a tall, slimmish 20 year-old with short brown hair. My face was protected by patchy brown and red stubble which I had cherished and cultivated ever since it sprouted on my babyish 18-year-old face. Mildly satisfied with my profile I took a closer look. My eyes were blood-shot and glazed from lack of sleep. I stretched the bags under my eyes down over my cheek-bones but was distracted by a huge pimple just below the scar on my forehead.

I moved in closer to the mirror and attacked the enemy with a pincer movement, spraying its guts onto the glass. Victory! I wiped the battlefield with the back of my hand and went to check on my meal. The Fasta-Pasta was ready, so I emptied the packet into a bowl and started wolfing it.

The Hysteria Dominated Tel-aversion(HDTV) was showing Gun Slinga's new song "Homo-Cide". I slumped down on the bean-bag and watched it:

"When I'm cruisin' in ma hood,
In ma fresh new ride,
I pull up at the corner,
And who on my side?
Two fly shorties and one faggot homey,
The dude wearin' pink pretend he don' know me,
I pull out my gat and prepare to collide,
Coz when I see a fag I got to Homo-Cide."

A couple of minutes later I'd had as much of the bowl as I was going to have and flung the rest into the waste bin. The clock on the HDTV read 8:48pm. Drinks time. I shouted up to Wellborn, "Are you done yet?" The diminutive young man couldn't hear me above his stereo. I vaulted up the stairs, three at a time, almost tripping up on the top step. I knocked on the door. He opened up and beamed a smile in my direction.

"Hey Maestro," he said.

"So, are we getting Liquidated or are you gonna do your hair all night, princess?"

"It's all about looking dapper, my man," he grinned.

"Even in a Liquidiser frequented by old men with no teeth and no women?" We both laughed as we strolled around the corner to "The Liquidiser on the Hill" talking about nothing in particular. The I-Spy on the lamppost tracked our movement down the street so we played our usual game with it having play fights and pulling faces at the camera.

The others were all huddled in the corner to the right of the bar waiting for us. Anna and Shovel were sitting down at a table. They seemed to be singing along with the song on the HDTV. Thankfully their voices were out of ear-shot. The others: TT, Shaz and Jr, were already on the EQM. Wellborn offered to buy me my first gallon so I joined the others on the EQM. Twenty minutes and 10 coins later we decided the machine must have been some sort of racket and joined the singers and Wellborn at the table.

Once we'd sat down, TT snatched Shaz's hat off her head and we started throwing it between us. Shaz stretched out her short arms trying to intercept the flying hat but she missed every time. TT cackled, his red eyes bulging like a drunken pirate's. You'd never know he was the oldest of the group. TT stood for something posh, we knew that much, but we never knew exactly what it was.

Unobserved, Anna swooped in, caught the fluffy headwear in mid-flight, and returned it to its rightful owner. She smiled smugly at her unprecedented catching prowess. Shaz pulled the Lime-green hat back over her tangled mop, wiggled her nose to re-arrange her Bes' Specs and grumbled "bastards" as a hint of a smile formed. At that point Jr's Foney started ringing.

It was a sound the rest of us had grown accustomed to since he'd insisted on always keeping the volume on the highest setting. He answered it in his distinctive squeaky voice.

"Ello."

"10 coins says it's his mum or his girl," I whispered to Shovel. He smiled and nodded his head.

"I was just about to. Honest. Like I'd forget. What are you up to anyway?" Jr said, walking outside to escape the blare of the HDTV. Just from that sentence we could deduce that it was Jr's girlfriend berating him for forgetting to call her on Loveheart Day

All of us laughed in unison and the conversation shifted to some other of Jr's past indiscretions. A few hours and countless gallons later we stumbled home. Anna, the designated walker, managed to safely guide us the two-minute walk back around the corner. The previous week when it was just Jr, TT and me (unsupervised), we managed to end up at the wrong house in the wrong street. Jr stood baffled trying desperately to insert his key into the lock when the door opened and an old woman in a nightgown and hair-net stood staring at us, decidedly unimpressed. TT and I burst into laughter and ran away, leaving Jr standing there like a statue with his arm holding the key in the air. He smiled sheepishly, said "Good Evening" and sprinted after us.

Back in the house, we flopped onto the cushions. The HDTV was on an Ad-Verse interval. This one was for the BHS (Beauty Hair-Scanner). It starred Kinky Diva, or was it Wrinkly Diva I always get them mixed up? "Grey hairs getting you down? Looking older than your friends? The Beauty Hair-Scanner is the answer to all of your problems. Just scan the red-light over your head and it will single out any grey hair and zap the critter at the root. Remember, "Look spic' an' spanner with a Beauty Hair-Scanner."

Off.

The HDTV never switches off. The lights went out too. Those were the last lights I was to see for a long time. "It must be the whole electric grid," said Shovel.

We heard footsteps at the front of the house. The front door flew open. It smashed into the wall and the inner handle was lodged into the wall so it stayed open. In strode two huge, shadowy figures. I couldn't make out their faces in the darkness. I was stunned by the sheer size of them. The two monoliths strode slowly down the hall towards us. Our eyes followed them. We were silent. The first figure walked into the room, his face hidden by an overarching hood which plunged it into shadow. Both figures wore the same full-length black cloaks.

"Odis Winston," said the first giant in a monotone.

Silence.

"Odis Winston," he said, louder.

"That's me," I replied stepping forward from the group with a temerity which belied my true emotions.

"You're coming with us."

"Sorry mate, you're not my type!"

I've always used humour at inappropriate times, a bad habit I picked up from my grandfather Abe. The first brute then wrenched me by the arm. His massive, gloved fingers encircled the whole of my right bicep. Jr and Wellborn stepped forward at this point and tried to intercede.

"Hey," said Wellborn. The second figure stepped in front and blocked Wellborn and Jr off. Wellborn fearlessly approached the dark figure but was swatted aside and crashed into the kitchen cabinet. At this point the others raced to our defence, Anna going to Wellborn's aid, and the others attempting to free me from the clutches of the dark intruders. They were similarly dispatched and I was dragged out of the house. I clung to the side of the kitchen doorway but I couldn't contend with the power of my captors.

"Where are you taking me?" "What's happening to me?" "Why are you doing this to me?"

They remained silent. They forced a bag over my head and I felt something strike me on the back of my neck, maybe a metal rod, maybe just his fist.

And then darkness.

Chapter 2

I woke up feeling groggy. I was pulled out of the car by my kidnappers. The bag was ripped off my head but everything was still cloaked in darkness and the cool breeze made me shiver. Stretching as high and as wide as I could see was a towering iron wall. It was plastered with graffiti. Most of it was illegible but the most visible piece said "Lok 'em up 4 life." The henchmen led me to the only doors visible in the entire structure. An I-Spy attached to the wall followed our approach to the doors and flashed as it captured my image. The doors opened automatically and I was led inside. Straight ahead, there stood a tall stone building. Two silhouetted figures were guarding either side of a pair of large wooden doors. Above the doors there hung a sign. I couldn't make out what it said. The swinging light in the foreground kept flickering on and off. Suddenly it stayed on long enough for me to make out what the sign read: SISYPHUSA.

I remembered hearing about Sisyphusa. My father had been taken away there for some months when I was a child. We never talked about it, but I knew I didn't want to go there. Sometimes rumours of Sisyphusa would emanate from the Corporation of Hysteria's Daily Bulletin and the HDTV. Sisyphusa was for people who were different from the rest of the Islanders, people who didn't belong with Normal people and had to be segregated from society. Sisyphusans were the subject of mockery and condescension by the Normal people. That's all I knew.

I became aware of a low snarling sound and then a three-headed dog charged at me out of the shadows. I could smell its rancid breath when suddenly a chain around its torso straightened up and snapped the creature back. It fell to the ground instantly and cowered into the shadows to lick its wounds. An identical beast took its turn to pounce at me from my left. I kicked out to protect myself from the onslaught but it was useless. One of the three heads sank its fangs into my left wrist. Luckily my watch took most of the impact. The glass shattered and the strap was ripped from my arm. I had a deep cut just below the base of my thumb.

The henchman holding my left arm let go and dashed the animal against the stone wall of the old building with consummate ease. He picked up my sagging left side, swiped a card in a slot on the wall and the doors opened. They carried me into the building. The blood started to spurt out of my hand and stained the sleeve of my jacket. We were inside the dimly lit foyer of the building. They walked me past the desk on the right and straight up a spiral stone staircase. I was still feeling woozy and the soles of my boots were no longer meeting the dirty stone steps. Instead, the toecaps were unceremoniously scraped along each and every stair until we exited the staircase at the top and walked through another door.

A dark corridor stretched in front of us, it was impossible to tell how long. On either side of the corridor were an infinite number of metal doors. Eventually the henchman on my right let go of me. He reached down into his pocket and pulled out what looked like a Debt Card. He swiped it through a device with a red light and the light turned green. The door slid open and I was thrown into a cell. At that point I passed out.

I woke up to the bass-line of "Homo-Cide" on the HDTV. Looking around the small room I gradually started to remember how I got there. There was a pain in my right ear. I instinctively reached for it and it felt like something was nailed to my ear. Using piercings on the lobe and all around the outside of my ear, someone had attached some kind of strange Earpiece. I tried tugging at it but it wouldn't budge.

Then I was distracted by a sharp pain in my left wrist. I looked down and saw a mass of dried blood covering my arm. Lodged in the open wound was a shard of glass from my watch. I pulled it out and tossed it onto the floor. The wound began to bleed again. I took off my ruined jacket and laid it on the floor. Standing with my right foot on the hood and wrapping the rest of the jacket around my right arm I pulled my arm up violently. I pulled it up again, harder. The ripped-off hood lay on the floor and the rest of the jacket was still wrapped around my arm. I uncoiled the jacket by spinning my right arm in an anti-clockwise motion and after three revolutions it fell to the floor. I

picked up the hood and wrapped it tightly around my left wrist
and tied it as best I could with the minimal slack available. I saw
at the joint of my forearm someone had given me a tattoo. It
read: "SERVICE USER 108."

I began to survey the room. It was no larger than an
average car. There was no window and the only light came from
the large HDTV screen on the wall. In the corner to the right of
the HDTV was an I-Spy. Facing the HDTV was a scruffy, blue
couch up against the parallel wall. It had yellow sponge showing
through a tear in one of its cushions. I sat down on the other
cushion. To the right of me was a toilet seat in the corner of the
room with a small wash basin next to it. To the left of me was a
bare wall with the only door in it. The door had no handle.
Beside the door was a small metal hatch.

On the hatch someone had scratched "Sisyphusa grub
tastes like shit. Dobbsy." Neatly folded on the floor in front of
the hatch were two dark grey overalls. I picked one up—it had a
black zip from the belly-button up to the neck with the words
"Sisyphusa" and "Service User 108" sewn above the breast
pocket. On the back was written: "Learning To Be Normal
Together." I took off my ripped and bloodied clothes and
replaced them with one of the uniforms.

On the arm of the couch was a remote control. I picked
it up and pressed the "channel down" button. Below HDTV
Music was HDTV Sport. Below HDTV Sport was HDTV Bad
News -"Bad News is Good News." Below HDTV Bad News
was HDTV Entertainment. There was nothing else on so I
switched it back to "Homo-Cide". Just before the song was over
the screen went black. I tried pressing some buttons on the
remote but nothing happened. Then there appeared on the screen
a pale man with grey hair and a grey goatee beard with tiny
bespectacled eyes. He was sat behind a mahogany desk and was
wearing a white shirt with no tie. He began to speak.

"Hello. I am Governor Shade…Welcome to Sisyphusa.
It has been deemed that you are no longer Normal enough to be
on Fantasy Island with the rest of Normal society. But there is
no need to be alarmed. The Climbing Teams at Sisyphusa are
here to help you return to the Island. You will soon become
acclimatised to your surroundings. You are occupying a room in

the main building of the Sisyphusa Compound. In this building are the Service Users' living quarters, the foyer, the wardens' offices, the dining area and the classrooms.

The perimeter of the compound is surrounded by a 100ft iron wall which separates Sisyphusa from the rest of the Island. We will be helping you to learn both how to re-integrate with Normal society and also how to safely traverse the wall. No Service User is allowed to attempt to climb the wall unsupervised. If you are found doing so you will be severely punished. At the end of this message you will be required to take a Weirdness Test using your HDTV and remote. By the end of this test you will be assigned a Weirdness grade. This cannot be changed so be sure to answer the questions with due care and attention.

It is procedure for new arrivals to remain in their rooms until they have completed Solitary Initiation.   Food will be delivered through the hatch and we have provided this HDTV to help you pass the time. You will have occasional visits from wardens who will monitor your progress. There will be, after some time, the opportunity for you to have interaction with immediate family members. Other family members and friends can send you written messages via the HDTV but there is no facility for you to reply.

Finally, we have fitted you with an Earpiece. This will have a voice, much like your own, speaking into it constantly. What the voice says is between you and the voice, and isn't to be discussed with anyone. It may not always be pleasant but it only says things which the device has intercepted from your own brainwaves so you will have only yourself to blame. We look forward to meeting with you in due course."

Immediately the first page of the test flashed onto the screen. The instructions explained that I should work my way down through the questions using the number keys on the remote to rank how much I agreed with each statement, ranging from 1= not at all to 9= absolutely. Questions included, "Do you think you would be better off dead?" and "Has your Weirdness affected your ability to work?" "Do unpleasant thoughts come into your mind against your will so that you are unable to get rid of them?" "Do you avoid social situations for fear of being embarrassed or making a fool of yourself?"

Fearing I would be labelled for life on the basis of my answers, I agonised over every question. Should I second-guess the answers they wanted or attempt to answer truthfully? All the words in the questions began spinning around in my head until I began answering without thinking. When I finally submitted the questionnaire I got an immediate reply informing me that I was Weirdness Grade 2.

The screen went blue for a second and came back on to HDTV Music with Felicity Summer singing "Clothing is for Fat People".

Chapter 3

Solitary Initiation? What does that mean? For how long? They had to be joking. I pounded on the door. "Let me ouuuuut!". I knelt down and pressed my face to the cold floor and shouted through the crack between the door and the floor. "Let me OUUUUUT". No use. I sat with my back up against the door and breathed heavily. Thousands of thoughts raced through my mind in quick succession. 'Why is this happening to me? Who are these people? At least they've given me HDTV Sports! Why do I have to climb a huge wall? Why can't I just leave the way they brought me in? I'm not Weird, am I? I mean, I suppose I am a little, but no one's completely Normal, are they? Maybe they are. Shit.' You only begin to question the meanings of Weirdness and Normality once you've been told that you're Weird.

I crawled to the hatch and slid it up as high as it would go. I tried to squeeze my head through it but I couldn't even get past my forehead. I hollered again: "Helllllooooooo, Helloooooo! I think there has been some kind of misunderstanding. I don't belong here. I'm an ISLANDER. I have rights. I'm NORMAL. If you let me out now, then I promise not to press any charges." No response. My voice echoed down the unfriendly, dark corridor and boomeranged back to me. "Alright that's enough! Get me out of this place. I am not Weird, I am Normal. Whatever's happened you've got your facts wrong and I demand to be released!"

Silence.

I stood up and felt a surge of rage spread throughout my entire body. I began kicking the door, but it was so solid that the contact didn't even make enough noise for me to feel I was making any impact.

My anger increased.

I began hitting the walls, first open-handed and then with a clenched fist. Then I started using both hands. "Aaaarggh". I forgot about my wound.

My anger increased.

I tried to pick up the sofa but it was bolted to the ground. Expecting the sofa to lift easily I had put all of my strength into lifting it and pulled a muscle in my back. My foot slipped forward and I was catapulted to the floor my head rebounding against the wall.

My anger turned to dismay.

I lay there. I turned onto my side, curled up like a foetus and did something I hadn't done since childhood, I began to cry. First it was a sort of pathetic sob, but then, as I replayed in my mind the many calamitous things which had befallen me in the last few hours, it began to crescendo.

I wept, and I wailed, and I yelled, and I sobbed.

I cursed Sisyphusa and I cursed the world. I cursed the all-seeing SkyMaster of the Yes/No books even if I'd never believed in him. This unprecedented outpouring of emotion lasted for a considerable time. Eventually I pulled out the sofa bed, curled up and went to bed with an overwhelming feeling of fear and confusion which would accompany me for many months to come. When I look back on those first few weeks the details blur into each other and time becomes an absurdity. I didn't eat the food they delivered. I talked to no-one—I had no-one to talk to. I tried to pass the time by watching HDTV but I couldn't concentrate. I could barely distinguish between consciousness and my nightmare-haunted sleep. I would have hybrid dreams. During my waking sleep, whatever was on the HDTV would fuse with my troubled subconscious to form the most bizarre scenes. There were flash floods in the north of the Island and a little girl had gone missing in the south but in my nightmares the two separate incidents had merged. I could see out of a window the rescue people zooming around in speedboats with blinding torchlights calling out for the little girl. I turned to my right and she was there, sitting quietly next to me, looking at me quizzically, innocently.

I began to think I was Weird after all. 'Maybe I do belong here?' 'Have I always been like this?' 'It was inevitable that I would end up here.' My fears were worsened by my introduction to the Earpiece. The Earpiece was a uniquely malevolent contraption. Somehow, don't ask me how, it managed to cotton on to my train of thought and twist that thought into the vilest, most disturbing, abhorrent thing imaginable. If allowed to roam free it has the power to imprison you in thought, seemingly forever. For example, one day I was watching HDTV Bad News –"Bad News is Good News"- and a story broke about a Yes/No book Proselytiser who had abused five of his young pupils. The Bad News Instabet icon flashed up along the bottom of the screen saying "Press the red button to place your bet: how long a sentence will the Proselytiser get?" I was very shaken by the story. Of course watching HDTV Bad News is never a barrel of laughs but at this time any story like this made me feel as if the entire world was descending into a pit of corruption and vice.

My cunning saboteur, the Earpiece, began to whisper, "You're glad those children were abused..." "You hope they've been killed..." "In fact, you're the one who killed them..." "You did it..." I knew the Earpiece was a mendacious little bastard. I could never do those awful things. Besides, it was impossible, I hadn't even left that cursed room. But the more I struggled, the louder and fouler the Earpiece fought back. "Of course you killed them..." "You're a disgusting child-killer..." "Always have been..." "You make me sick". Other times, the Earpiece didn't even need stimuli like the Bad News or my own thoughts to fuel its verbal volleys, it just began to attack me out of the blue. "You are pathetic." "Look at you, you make me sick." "It's your fault we're here, you weakling." "Why didn't you fight them off?" "You disgust me." "You are a fat, lazy shit." "You stink." "When was the last time you washed? Shaved? Cut that hair?" "You are so useless, if I were you I wouldn't even bother any more. Look at that piece of glass there." My head involuntarily zoned in on the broken glass from my watch-face lying on the floor. "You can use that. Just end it. You'll never get out of this place anyway. Even if you did you'd be tainted, branded: 'Psycho Sisyphusan.' Not an easy reputation to shake off. You'd never get a job or a wife. Who'd want to marry a Sisyphusan? Just do us all a favour."

I picked up the glass. I pressed it into my fingertip and thought to myself, 'Harder, make it bleed, see what happens...'

I threw it across the room.

Throughout these weeks I received messages on my HDTV from family and friends. My parents and my brother were incredibly supportive and promised to visit me as soon as they were allowed. My dad remembered the Earpiece from his time at Sisyphusa and told me not to argue with it, just to let it say what it wanted and calmly ignore it because I knew that it wasn't true. His words reassured me. He had survived Sisyphusa, maybe I could. My grandparents, Abe and Rifka, sent messages dripping with love and affection.

I also received messages from friends via the HDTV. I knew that they supported me. None of them had been to Sisyphusa, so they couldn't understand the horror but they tried their best. If one of them were taken rather than me, I do not think that I would have known how to comfort them. It hurt that I was not allowed to reply. I would have thanked them for their kind words but asked them to forget me. I wanted to suffer in privacy. With dignity.

I resented all of the Normal people on the Island. Why did I have to be stuck alone in Sisyphusa? I resented that they could go to South Coast University, drink Liquid Escape, have the freedom to enjoy their lives and there I was, an enervated old man of twenty, imprisoned in miserable solitude. Suddenly I realised that things actually mattered just when it was too late.

Everything had its exact time. The food was delivered at the same three times each day. Breakfast 7:00, Lunch 12:30, Dinner 18:00. Breakfast was always something resembling porridge. Lunch and dinner were stew. At first, I didn't eat anything nor did I even bother to get up and wash myself. I used to be someone who never once questioned whether it was worthwhile to get out of bed in the morning. I had always assumed that of course you got out of bed and of course it was worth it. So I was shocked to find myself in the position where it really didn't make any difference whether I got up or not. I lay on the couch watching HDTV interrupted by taunts from the Earpiece until they came and held me down, forcing me to eat.

Some weeks into my incarceration I was watching a football match between The Mercenaries and The Egos when the door slid open. In walked a short woman with jet-black hair tied back tightly in a bun. She paced out three confident strides into the centre of my cell, stopped short and a sentence squeezed out through her pursed lips.

"Service User, I am Warden Shiva. These are for you."

She brought out of her jacket pocket a jar of tablets with a bold label on it: 'CLIMBING PILLS'.

"I don't want your pills," I croaked. "I don't trust you people. How do I know what's in them?"

The warden gripped my shoulder and shot me an icy glare. The feel of another human being was alien and I recoiled. She looked me in the eye. My gaze shot to the floor.

"I assure you, Mr. Winston, no pills, no release, it's as simple as that," she smiled patronisingly at me like some sort of sadistic nursery teacher. "These pills are merely to help you have the energy to climb the wall. Now, you aren't going to be ready to start climbing any time soon, but if we get you started on these, they should begin to take effect within six to eight weeks. Your energy levels will soar and you will be over that fence and back to your life in no time."

"Why do I even need to climb that wall? Why can't you just let me out? And what's the deal with this Earpiece? It's horrible."

"All Service Users must climb the wall. A successful Wall-Climb is proof that you are Normalised and ready to rejoin Island life. As for the Earpiece, that is Sisyphusa policy. All service-users must wear one. It's unfortunate if yours is giving you trouble. Everyone's is different depending on their type of Weirdness. Perhaps you need to try harder at not thinking about whatever it is you're thinking about."

"But it's calling me awful things saying that I'm a murderer and a child-abductor," I spat out, desperate for my caged thoughts to escape my brain.

Warden Shiva looked at me with disgust. "Please don't tell me about the things you think about, I'd rather not be contaminated by your Weirdness. It sounds to me like you have a very disturbed form of the condition, I would imagine that you were probably abused as a child by your parents. Or a teacher maybe. I'll inform the Governor regardless."

I was still trying to process what the warden had suggested. I was in shock, but the bigger shock was what came next. I began to believe that she was right. There was no evidence that it was true, but her confident authority compounded by the continuous stirring of the Earpiece meant that I probably could have been convinced of most things. I no longer trusted my own mind which meant that my ideas of my past, my life and the future were no longer under my control. I was terrified. I wanted to leave right then and there.

"Okay," I told the warden. "I want to climb the wall. Where is it? I'm ready to climb. I'm a good climber."

"Mr.Winston, you are in no fit state to start climbing. Your hand is infected for a start. Regardless, *you* don't decide when you're ready for a Wall-Climb. That comes later."

Knowing I had no power and seeing the two familiar henchmen outside the door, I had no choice but to acquiesce. She handed me the pills and left without another word.

Chapter 4

They drove up the driveway to the gleaming blue and white palace. The small child could barely contain his excitement. He hadn't seen them for a whole year. He spent the entire flight over to the Frontier Empire Mainland pestering his parent. His brother had requested the window seat to be as far away from him as possible. He badgered his father to quiz him. He impatiently waited for his mother to wake up so that she would play card games with him. When the waiting grew tiresome he accidentally poured water on her arm. They were all relieved and exhausted to see the palace.

As the garage door magically opened without prompting, the front door also opened. Out rushed Grandma Rifka. The short, curly-haired lady wasn't wearing her glasses and she squinted as she stepped into the bright sunshine. A toothy smile dominated her face. Knees bent, arms outstretched, she bellowed "Hi, Hi, Hi". Her voice boomed through the thick windows of the rented vehicle. "Hello," his mother replied to her mother at an equal decibel level. The two young boys raced each other to greet the woman. Her arms enveloped them and she attacked the tops of their heads with kisses. "Mwah, Mwah, Mwah. Hello my little boychiks. I missed you so much." They entered the spotless palace as the parents were left to contend with the luggage.

The grandmother led them up the blue-carpeted stairs into the kitchen. She assaulted them with questions.

"So, how was the flight? Any good movies? Did you get any sleep? Did you eat something? No? How about I fix you something? Soup? Chicken Soup? How many Matzoh balls? Two bowls of Matzoh Ball Soup coming right up!"

"Thanks, Grandma," said the boys in unison.

"Grandma. Where's Grandpa?" asked the younger child.

"He's waiting for you in the study."

The boys ran out of the kitchen and passed the landing where they saw their parents struggling up the stairs laden with suitcases.

"*Boys, come and help with your bags!*" *said their mother.*

"*In a minute!*" *shouted the older brother. They ran down the hallway and stopped short at the first door on the left. The door was open. In walked the younger boy followed closely by his brother. On the sofa reading a huge hardback book under a lamp was Grandpa Abe, chief of the clan, a towering, rotund man in his early seventies. He had a balding pate, with a sloping nose which he kindly donated to other generations of his family. As the little rascals ran into the room, he beamed them a broad, welcoming smile, put down his book and reached for his glasses.*

"*Boys, it's so good to see you!*"

"*Didn't you hear us come in, Grandpa?*"

"*No.*" *He clutched them both in a bear hug.* "*How was the flight? Any good movies? Did you get any sleep? You must be exhausted, go have a nap.*"

"*No, Gramps, we're fine*"

"*Okay then, sit down. Now, how's school?*"

The older brother answered first, "*Well I've just finished Class 6 and I'm going into secondary school starting in September.*"

"*Wow. There's no messing around any more. You're gonna be in there with the big boys. Lots more work, lots more reading. Do you feel ready? Good.*"

"*What about me grandpa? I've just finished class 4. We did the Palatine Empire, and the Nilese and, and some other thing from millions of years ago. Ummmmm. Oh yeah...The Just War.*"

Grandpa smiled sadly, "*Excellent, Odis. I'll tell you some stories about the Just War one day. Now, you know of course that we today would be nowhere without the Palatines and the Acropolites, so it's important that you learn all about those civilisations.*"

The travelling family had their soup. They told Abe and Rifka all about their lives back on Fantasy Island. They talked about all of the things that they were going to do during their short time together. The boys wanted to go to the cinema and see all of the new films by Formula Studios and Product

Placement Productions. They wanted to go to the shiny new shopping mall and buy new jackets and boots that you could only get on the Mainland to make all of their friends back on the Island jealous. They wanted to eat pancakes and waffles and microwave popcorn and Nachos and Burgers and Tacos and more Matzoh Ball Soup. They wanted to watch baseball and cartoons and wrestling on HDTV. But above all, they HAD to play poker. The small boy went to sleep that night full of anticipation for the next day. He woke up and could smell the aroma of freshly cooked pancakes straight off the griddle. He waddled sleepily into the kitchen and his grandma, with her hands full of utensils, waved.

"Hi, hi, hi, my little Bubbelah. Sit yourself down and I'll serve you some pancakes and bacon. There's orange juice, and maple syrup, and lemon and sugar on the table."

After everyone had sated themselves, Grandma Rifka took the family to the mall. Abe, as always, sat in his office with his books. They went from store to store. They bought jackets and boots and T-shirts and trousers and hats and underwear and toys and after an hour Rifka was exhausted. They sat down in the food hall and had some Tacos. That night, the boys' aunties and uncles and cousins all came around. The upstairs living room was packed and as noisy as a cock-fight. They played games all night. They started with charades. Then the brave knights in the family gathered for some poker. They took their places around the perfectly circular wooden table. Perhaps the geometry of a perfect circle didn't lend itself to a hierarchical seating plan but everyone knew that wherever the King sat was undoubtedly the head of the table. Grandpa Abe began conducting the ceremonies by dealing out the cards.

"Who hasn't ante'd up? Pair-a-3s. Pair-a-Goric. No help. No help. Rifky's got a Big Ace!(everyone laughed except Grandma.) The bet starts with you, Big As-- I mean Ace."

The small boy was holding his cards tight to his chest. He loved poker. The idea of having 10 whole Mainland Bills on the line filled him with excitement. After the first few hands he started to feel strange. He felt a sharp pain in his stomach and his head began to spin like a roulette wheel. All he could see was a swirling whirlpool of red and black and red and black and red and black and red. The lever of the slot machine was pulled down. The first image was a white Skull and Crossbones on a black flag. The second one matched it. Then the third. A piercing ringing from the machine attacked his eardrums and from the coin dispenser instead of his winnings a wave of burning flames flowed straight towards him. He was alone now. His family had disappeared. It was just him and this huge tidal wave of fire. He ran and ran but it was no use, he couldn't escape. He fell to the floor and turned to face the flame. And he began to throw up. Now there was no longer a flame.

I opened my eyes. I was back in my small windowless cell. I had vomited on my uniform. I felt another bout of rising terror from the bottom of my diaphragm. Clawing myself off the sofa I managed to reach the toilet this time. I was puking up blood. I took a deep breath but the smell that entered my nostrils was too revolting to bear. I felt another convulsion in my stomach. This time there was something else which needed to be purged. I quickly pulled down my trousers and sat on the vomit covered toilet bowl. There was an explosion of pain. A fire hose propulsion of red and brown torpedoed out of me and I began to vomit again, this time into the sink. When I was finally empty, I washed myself and collapsed to the floor.

"Fucking Climbing Pills..."

Chapter 5

"Wake up you lazy pile of shit!" said the Earpiece. I opened my eyes. "Take a good look at yourself. You're disgusting." My overalls were covered in vomit. I climbed out of them. When I stood up, I caught sight of my reflection in the metallic door. I didn't recognise myself. My hair was longer than it had ever been. My complexion was deathly pale, even paler than usual. I had gained weight from all of the inactivity.

"Yep, not just Weird anymore, now you're fat and ugly too," taunted the Earpiece. I yanked at it in frustration.

"Shit!" I yelped. It wouldn't move.

"You'll never get rid of me, fatty," it mocked.

I slid down the door with my back to my alien reflection and began to cry again. It was so strange to suddenly go from being someone who never cried to someone who cried several times a day. A black filter had descended upon the lens through which I saw life. How could I escape this horror? I was powerless. My life was ruined, my freedom had been snatched away from me and I hated everything about myself, an egotistical self-loathing which imagined not only that I was evil but that I must have been the most evil human alive. I would often turn in on myself- find myself talking out loud not sure whether to myself or the Earpiece or neither.

The afternoons in my cell were a desert. The only oasis was the HDTV. Day after day, night after night I watched Aspirati Dog-walking, Aspirati Funeral Live!, Aspirati House-painting, etc. I compared myself to the people my age on HDTV, the ones who could run or sing or kick a ball, and I felt a failure. The Aspirati men were so perfect-looking. They all had ripped torsos, chiselled cheekbones and bulging biceps. How was I ever going to attract an Aspirati type of woman looking like a hobo? It didn't matter that I was stuck in that room by myself. It was the principle. I was afraid of being judged-judged for being Weird, judged for the way I looked, judged for my failure. If people on the Island judged each other by what they do and how they treat people then I would have felt more okay, like I had some control over how I was perceived. But I knew that people were judged by what they owned, what they looked like and how many people knew who they were. Even if I disagreed with those criteria I still felt the same sense of failure and inferiority knowing that I would be judged against these principles by the majority of Islanders. I decided to do what I could to reverse the tide at the very least.

I used the shard of glass to trim my beard, badly. I ripped a strip of clean material from my jacket and wore it as a hair-band. I decided that I would exercise for two hours every day. Firstly I would stretch to warm-up. Then I would jog on the spot for one hour using the Climate Crisis Countdown Clock on the HDTV Bad News channel to time myself. Next I would lie on my back, wedge my feet between the floor and the bottom of the sofa and do 300 sit-ups. After a three-minute breather I did 150 press-ups. I would finish off with 100 lunges and 50 squat-thrusts before another jog just to warm down.

I kept this regime up every day without fail, powering through my natural lethargy and taunts of "What's the point?" and "It's no use," from the Earpiece. I used the HDTV to help with my structure. I never missed The Fantasy Factory: 'Where dreams become reality'- which was the Island's favourite Real-Life show.

And I'd always watch the Bad News at 22:00 to keep in touch with what was happening in the outside world. If ever I fell short of the right number of sit ups or failed to complete my exercises in the allotted time I was liable to break down in tears. My world had become so small that the tiniest things had become huge to me.

One morning I woke up and there in the corner of the screen was the date: April 19th. My 21st birthday. I remembered the dreams I'd had for this day. I was going to throw a huge party. I thought of my friends and all the parties they had been to since my imprisonment. I began to cry. It didn't seem fair that this should be happening to me, that the world was allowed to keep spinning while I was stationary. Turning 21 had coincided with my imprisonment and therefore I would always associate adulthood with misery.

Messages began to flood onto the HDTV. "Happy Birthday Odis, we are so proud of how brave you're being. We can't wait to see you. Love Mum, Dad and Bro." "Happy Birthday, Mate, hope things aren't too bad." "Happy Birthday Ode. Really missing you buddy." "Hey Hun. I really don't know what to say, I miss you loads. I think about you all the time. Happy Birthday. Love Layla." "Happy Birthday my boy, I know that it doesn't feel very happy but you will get through this and there will be plenty more happy days. Grandma sends her love to 'the boy who can do no wrong'. I've always questioned her judgement. She chose me after all. Guess who loves ya kid? Grandpa".

There were more but most of them said the same thing. "Hope you're okay," "Miss you." "Can't wait to see you." I wasn't okay and it wasn't a happy birthday. I should have missed them too, the old Odis would have. The new Odis missed a life he had lost and could never get back. I felt like a soldier who had traded his mundane Island life for his first tour of duty in the Babylonian war.

When messages arrived from family and friends, how could I possibly convey to them the reality which has to be lived to be understood? What words were there to describe my new experience? My old friends could never understand what had happened to me. I didn't even know if I could. All people's identity and view of themselves are constantly changing but most changes are gradual and happen within the usual context of active life and so we take them in our stride, barely stopping to absorb them. I could not cope with the shock of my view of myself and my life being so utterly changed by outside forces that I never knew existed.

The conventions of small talk in correspondence felt meaningless. I hadn't the energy or the ability to reply even if Sisyphusa had allowed it. How hard it is to reconcile yourself to the reality that a door had been slammed shut on the future which you'd always assumed was your right: the easy friendships, the university degree, the high-flying job, the perfect wife, the happy family. Nothing would ever be easy again. None of my old friends understood the extent of my suffering and the annihilation of the Odis they once knew. I could never bear the shame of seeing those people again. As far as I was concerned I had done nothing wrong to become Weird but the fact was I had been taken and that was enough to get people talking. If only some more glamorous or heroic fate had befallen me and not this invisible curse.

My family, however, did understand. My parents sent me messages many times a day offering support, advice, comfort, inspiration. My dad told me how he'd handled his time in Sisyphusa. My brother grasped immediately the gravity of the situation without having been in Sisyphusa. A friend of his had been though and had managed to climb the wall. My brother reminded me of this more than once.

I thought about Layla often. I thought about her short brown hair, her tanned skin and that enigmatic smile, like she was telling herself jokes in her own head. I thought about Layla and I needed her. I had to get back to her, before someone else took my place.

The rest of them would all finish their degrees and I would be stuck in that cell for years and years and years. I'd lost any sense of wonder in the world. It was as if I was haunting my own life. Everything was grey, dull, there was nothing new. I felt I'd been tricked about life. Being taken to Sisyphusa made me question everything and trust nothing. I would sit in my cell and wonder why things were called what they were. Who decided a chair was a chair or a wall a wall?

The pretence had been stripped away from the world around me and life was reduced to a basic struggle for survival devoid of sentiment or solace. It was at times like this when my mind would flit around from worry to worry and I would desperately try to solve each problem I could think of but they wouldn't go away. It was like the plate-spinner I had seen once back home at Sameford Fair- I had to keep every plate spinning no matter how many more were added to the mix.

"Poor little Odis. Boo-Hoo. I've got no friends. I'm a big fat ugly loner. Blah Blah Blah. You really are pathetic, aren't you?" the Earpiece interrupted.

It didn't even wish me happy birthday. One doesn't have birthdays in Sisyphusa. There's a different concept of time. The present is so bad and so empty all you can do is think about the past and the future. But I'd lost all objectivity about the past and had no faith in the future. Existence had become a vacuum, a time-warp where every day was the same. It was a nightmare repeated over and over and over again, where no matter how bad the reality was, in my imagination it could always get worse. I no longer recognised my own thoughts. They say that you're an adult once you turn twenty-one but I honestly couldn't say whether it was adulthood or Weirdness which changed me so irrevocably because they happened at the same time. I whiled away the rest of the day thinking and crying until I finally fell asleep.

Sometime later the door to my cell opened and Warden Shiva walked in.

"I'm here to assess whether you're ready to join a Climbing Team. Have you experienced any side-effects from the Climbing Pills?"

"Nightmares every night…vomiting…diarrhoea then constipation then diarrhoea, then constipation again. I had some hallucinations at first. And sometimes I get these splitting headaches."

"That's normal. We'll up the dose to two a day and if you tolerate that we'll go up to three."

And with that she left.

How many pills would I have to take before they'd let me climb? I didn't want to take them anymore, but what could I do? I would do anything to get over that wall.

Chapter 6

I'd been in solitary confinement for ninety days when I was allowed my first visit. They woke me up at 7am and told me to "be ready in half an hour, your parents are coming." My parents had been sending me messages every single day since my captivity, but I was never able to communicate back. Even if I could reply, what would I say? "Mum, I'm scared," "Dad, I hate life," "If I'm going to be Weird for my entire life, I'd rather be dead." I was so afraid and ashamed of all of the things which the Earpiece was saying to me. In Normal day-to-day life we take for granted an element of control over our minds. With the Earpiece this illusion is gone. I knew that the things it was saying weren't true, but the mere fact that the thoughts were even entering my head made me feel as guilty as if they had been true. I must be a terrible person; evil, dirty, morbid, disgusting, pathetic, at the very least weak.

That's what Normal Islanders think about Sisyphusans. "They're Weird so they belong somewhere else, away from Normal people. They deserve to be mocked and scapegoated." The Daily Bulletin from The Corporation of Hysteria runs a daily story about another Weird person committing rape or murder. I can see the headlines now: 'SICKO SISYPHUSAN IN SERIAL SEX SCANDAL' 'WACKO WEIRDO WASTES WIFE'. It's as if these horrible crimes would make sense if committed by a Sisyphusan. "Oh they used to be in Sisyphusa? Well…that explains it, doesn't it? No Normal person would do what they did"

They say that the punishments aren't hard enough, Sisyphusans should never be let out, "Build Higher Fences!" "Lock 'em up for life!". I know because I used to read the bulletin. I also used to laugh at the comedians on HDTV when they lampooned Sisyphusans and other Weird people. My friends and I would casually call each other Weird as an insult or if any of us did something stupid or eccentric. But now *I* was one of them, *I* was Weird, *I* was a Sisyphusan. Was I right before? Is the Sisyphusan me really Weird or was the Normal me wrong? Which me is the real me?

"Mr.Winston, your parents are here." I went to the sink and splashed cold water over my face. I opened the door and a female warden was there waiting.

"Odis Winston? Follow me."

I followed the middle aged woman down the gloomy corridor. I couldn't help but see that her underwear was wedged down the crevice of her sagging buttocks. She walked uncomfortably for a while, then surreptitiously poked her gloved finger down the crack and scooped the offending material out at the second attempt. She turned around to check if I had seen her indiscretion. When she saw that I had, she looked at me, first with embarrassment but in an instant, remembering her superior status, her expression turned to anger and then disdain. I looked away immediately. I didn't know this woman and she didn't know me, but I felt that her anger and her disdain were totally warranted.

'I don't deserve to be around other people, I don't even deserve to be alive,' I remember thinking as we came to the end of the corridor, 'I wish they would just kill me and donate my organs to people who deserve them.' I could see no point in my life, no point in carrying on. Suddenly there was a high-pitched screeching noise in my Earpiece. I stopped and held my ear, wincing. The sound wasn't coming from the Earpiece's voice. And then I heard some notes played on a piano, it was a song I recognised, some classical piece from a perfume Ad-Verse. As we exited the corridor the music died away.

We descended the spiral staircase and walked past the reception desk. Behind the desk was a blonde woman in her twenties. She was spinning around on her chair. As we walked past she ogled me like a child who hasn't yet learned the art of tact. Her phone rang. "Hello," she answered. "Sisyphusa reception, this is Tina speaking... how may I be of service?" She was attractive in a conventional Daily Bulletin way. Her reaction to me was painful. The kind of woman whom I used to end up in bed with after a night of Liquidising, looked at me like I was the fat man on the dance-floor whom every girl avoids.

The warden led me through some double doors and down another flight of stairs on the left. We entered the first door on the right and there sitting in the room were my parents. The warden announced that we had 30 minutes.

My parents stood up and moved towards me which made me flinch. My mother tried to hug me, but I pulled back immediately. They both sat back down awkwardly. I took the seat across the table from them and stared at the table.

"How are you Odis?"

I didn't answer. I couldn't answer. Thousands of words were queuing up in my head waiting to be uttered but my mouth refused to follow orders. I wanted to tell them that I was afraid. I wanted to tell them that I wanted to go home and back to South Coast. I wanted things to be the way they were. I wanted to be Normal again. But instead I said nothing and kept staring blankly at the table.

"Odis listen to me, son, you are not Weird. There's no such thing as Normal or Weird, they're just labels, constructs. People are all Weird and Normal at the same time, we're all different shades of grey. But you are here now, and as soon as they find you a dose of Climbing Pills that works for you, you'll be over that wall and out of here in no time," said my father.

I looked up at him and he smiled. He hadn't shaved his grey beard or trimmed his hair for a while and he resembled a mad scientist. He looked tired and I felt guilty at the burden I had become to my family. I thought to myself, 'This is the time when I am supposed to become a man. I'm reaching an age when the roles begin to shift and I should be helping my parents, not the other way around. Instead, I am useless to them. As long as I am trapped in this place, I am merely a scar on their lives.'

"Honey, I am so sorry that you've had to come here, especially at such a young age. But we know that you will get out and when you do you will be a stronger and more compassionate person because of it," my mother tried to reassure me.

I slowly turned my head. My mother's head of short brown hair was tilted at a sympathetic angle and her glasses slid down her nose as she smiled. Her brown eyes looked into mine and transmitted a telepathic message which said, "I love you and everything's going to be all right."

But I didn't believe it. I thought, 'You're just saying that because you're my parents and you have to.' I sat there and stewed for a while. Then the Earpiece took hold of me. "Look at your poor, poor parents, burdened with a Weirdo like you for a son. What will the neighbours think? And they say they love you so much. But you don't love anyone, you've got a heart of stone. You're unloving and unlovable. Freak!".

I could feel a tear running down my cheek.

"What's wrong Odis? Let it out. It's better that you talk about it. Are they mistreating you? Are they feeding you properly? Come on what is it?"

"I can't..." I managed to spit out before the tears streamed down my face and I began to sob.

"You can tell us anything Odis. There is *nothing* you could tell us which would make us love you any less," said my mum. She tried to hold back her own tears but when she couldn't I forced myself to stop crying because I couldn't stand the guilt.

"You don't understand. You don't know what it's like. It's so horrible. I'm in a different world. There's no light and no joy. No love, no air, nothing. I feel sick and tired all of the time. And this Earpiece..."

"What's the Earpiece saying, Odis? I was here too, remember? I know what it's like to have an Earpiece. But that Earpiece is just an Earpiece. It's not you," said my father.

"I am you. We are one and the same, you and me. Don't listen to him. You can't tell them what you think about. The murder and the suicide and the rape, they'll think you're disgusting and evil which is what you are. Evil," whispered the Earpiece.

I began to scream and shout. I put my head onto the table and cried into my arms. "I'm never going to get out of here. Never. I just know it. And I'll never get rid of this bloody Earpiece. I hate it. I hate the World."

"The World is neither good nor bad, Odis. What's the Earpiece saying?" my dad asked calmly.

"It's saying that I'm evil and disgusting and weak. It's saying that I want to do terrible things to myself and to other people. It's telling me that I'll never get out of here and that I don't deserve to. I know that none of it is true, but it just won't stop! It never, ever stops!" I screamed in despair and desperation.

The warden walked in flanked by two henchmen.

"Okay, time's up."

"That is not 30 minutes" argued my mum.

"Yes it is. You've over-excited him. You need to leave now."

"We've made him too excited? It's you, you horrible people. You're making his life a misery. You're making all of our lives a misery. Just give us back our son."

"Alright, that's enough. Take him back to his cell," ordered the warden. The two ogres lifted me off my seat and began to drag me away, I struggled to free myself from their grip but it was no use.

My parents shouted after me, "We love you Odis," "You're going to get through this," "Never give up hope."

I wept as the henchmen threw me back into my windowless room. It was hard to see my parents, but they gave me renewed hope. I decided then that I would have to live my life for others until such a time, if it should ever come, that I could begin to live for myself.

Chapter 7

I fell back into the reassuring embrace of my routine after my parents' visit, slightly increasing my level of exercise each day. I needed to push myself as far as I could go. I increased the sit-ups by ten and the press-ups by five. This left me aching all over but I had to be strong enough and prepared enough to climb that wall. Every day was a problem to solve, a block of time to fill. It didn't matter that the exercise wasn't taking the weight off, I had to do it anyway.

I began to draw pictures on the walls of my cell. I used the shard of glass from my watch to scratch pictures into the paintwork. I drew caricatures of Aspirati and people from history who I admired. I also drew pictures of Outlands I had visited when I was eighteen. I drew pictures which helped me to escape from my life. I drew to inspire myself to escape from Sisyphusa. I began to develop a single-minded obsession with my escape.

One day I was watching HDTV Bad News -"Bad News is Good News"- it was leading on a story from the War in Babylonia. The smiling newscasters stopped flirting with each other, changed to their serious faces and announced, "Breaking News: 3 Frontier Empire troops have been killed in a roadside explosion." On the news strap moving horizontally at the bottom of the screen read, "123 Babylonian civilians were killed in a skirmish." The channel's newsreaders were all young and attractive. They had every different hair, skin and eye colour and all spoke with the exact same accent which didn't seem to be from any country in particular.

I sat in my cell and tried to digest the words and images which were being thrown at my brain. This type of news story was a daily occurrence on Fantasy Island. I felt like crying, but the tears didn't materialise. Instead, a feeling of numbness and powerlessness pervaded my body. How are you supposed to deal with such a multitude of suffering when you know full well there's nothing you can do about it? How spoilt and sheltered was I to feel miserable or hard done by when compared to ordinary Babylonians?

I mourned each death as if it were that of a friend. Every story infiltrated the very core of my being, leaving me unshielded from the constant anxiety and despair I felt as each day the world unravelled before my eyes. I had never questioned things like war, death, homelessness or why children are born rich or poor. I suppose I knew about these things, but I never thought about them. I accepted that these were the rules of the game. But things that everyone saw as regular parts of life became terrifying to me. I so wished that I could just slip back into the welcoming embrace of my pre-Sisyphusa certainties.

The previous Bad News story had shown that Chancellor Frown had succeeded Minister Snare as Supreme Leader of Fantasy Island. The Bad News channel distilled the last ten years under Snare into a montage of his "Best Bits". The video showed how he surfed into power on a wave of unprecedented optimism and heralded a new epoch of fairness, prosperity and modern government for the Island. He charmed the people with his self-effacing humour and uncommon sensitivity. He mourned when they mourned, he shared their heroes and he put money in their pockets. But then the world changed and he rushed to join The Emperor to help solve the world's new problems.

Snare and The Emperor announced that they went to war because the Babylonian leader, The General, posed "an immediate threat to the security of the Frontier Empire." This claim was supported by the HDTV Bad News channel and The Daily Bulletin. Hearing of this threat, many people became anxious and angry. "Why do these outsiders want to kill us?" "Well, we should kill them first." The war began.

It didn't take long to overthrow The General and proclaim victory. The General of Babylonia was a vile dictator who had ruled with an iron fist and suppressed or eliminated anyone who opposed him. However, once the Frontier Empire forces had overthrown him, all of the fanatical followers of the Yes/No Book #3 emerged. The Yes/No book #3 is read and followed by hundreds of millions across the world. One group of fanatics read the book back to front and the other reads it upside down and this means that they argue amongst themselves almost as much as they do with the readers of the Yes/No books #1 and #2.

I watched the carnage of the roadside bomb and began to weep and shiver. I was thousands of miles from Babylonia but the death and pain touched me through the HDTV. I felt completely helpless sat in my cell. I felt like I was under attack. I felt so unsure on where I stood—was I for the war or against it? Could I believe that the facts were facts? I didn't know what I believed in but the confident people on my HDTV screen talked with such certainty. I wanted to help people and comfort those in pain but I couldn't. I forgot that even Normal people could feel helpless in the face of unremitting suffering being beamed into their living rooms. I had lost all sense of time and proportionality since being imprisoned. My only experience of the world was through watching my HDTV.

Having at first been a comfort, even a crutch, the HDTV gradually mutated into a source of despair for me, providing the ammunition for my Earpiece to attack me with. Much later I was to discover that HDTV Bad News is like the meat industry: it gets the story raw, decontaminates it of all its dirty components such as facts and truth, then injects it full of preconceived narratives. And like the hygienic headless chicken we buy from MegaMarket, the process takes place behind closed doors leaving the impression that the end product is exactly as nature had intended it.

The extreme, once-in-a-blue-moon type of story that appeared on the rolling news bulletins seemed to me much more common and representative than it really was. The fact that the vast majority of the people on Fantasy Island lived long, mundane lives had utterly escaped my senses. Like when someone commits a terrible murder or sexual assault the newsreader will say the criminal "had a history of Weirdness" as if that's an indisputable causation of violence or criminality. Normal people who've drunk too much Liquid Escape probably committed more crimes than Weird people but that isn't used as an explanation. They don't say "he had a history of being tall, a history of being red-haired, a history of wearing odd socks," either. But they can use Weirdness because people don't understand it so it's perfect to use as a simple, comforting reason as to why someone has committed an awful crime.

My world had become one in which the highs were benchmarked by the glamorous achievements of the Aspiratis and the lows were vivid warning signals in the shape of individual tragic stories from the bulletins, which were a clear and present danger to us all. I changed the channel and watched a comedy programme from the Frontier Empire Mainland on HDTV Entertainment. I saw the perfect Aspirati laughing and joking and I wished that I could be as happy as they were. I lay down, curled up in a ball, with my back to the HDTV screen and tried to fall asleep.

Chapter 8

When I awoke the next morning there was a message on my HDTV. It read: "Odis, I'm sorry to tell you that Grandpa died yesterday. He was sick for a very long time. You know he loved you very much and he would not want his death to hamper your efforts to escape. With love, Mum."

I sat and stared at the ground wondering 'Is this real? It couldn't be. He had just sent me a message a few weeks ago sounding like his old self. Maybe it was a trick they were playing to test me, to mess with my head.' No. "Shut up, you fucking idiot this isn't about you- he's dead, he's gone, you'll never see him again," said the Earpiece. The Earpiece was right. Ever since I'd been in that cell everything was always 'me, me, me', 'I, I, I.' 'How would this affect me?' 'How would I go on?'

I began to cry. Not the shouting and weeping and retching with pain that I had done for so many hours since I'd been in that cell. This was different. I was stunned. 'How am I supposed to cope? What am I supposed to be doing or thinking or feeling?' No-one close to me had ever died before. When I was younger my father's parents had died but I never thought about it much, I was a child and I just followed my parents' lead.

Death on the Island and in the Empire is the only taboo that looms larger than Weirdness. It is a word one often hears in songs or books or jokes or Ad-Verses but is very rarely considered or discussed in its entirety. Many people don't ever consider life let alone death. But in Sisyphusa I would sit and think about death all the time. I feared annihilation- being, then not being. As much pain as I felt in Sisyphusa I feared death and did not seek it as an alternative to my suffering. I had so little control over my mind that every time it was idle, which was often, it would automatically find its way to the most upsetting thoughts.

My subconscious (or was it the Earpiece?) was like the fly that continually flies into the light bulb and burns itself. I'd think of the Grandpa Abe's death, my eventual death, the deaths of everyone I knew, several times a minute spinning round and round, growing and growing with nowhere to go. I didn't expect to be able to solve these problems through thought but as I had nowhere else to go, no-one to talk to and nothing to do, I couldn't get the thoughts out of my head and the harder I tried the more they came back and they became more and more daunting. The Yes/No Books believe that if you follow their particular book then you will never die. I have never followed the Yes/No Books but it would be nice if I could.

It was so final. Suddenly, that message, those few words communicated a reality: I would never see Grandpa Abe again. I tried desperately to remember the last time I saw him, the last time I spoke to him but I couldn't. It had been so long and too much had changed that my memories had all clouded over. Did he know how much I revered him and how much he had taught me? Did he ever know what a force he was in so many people's lives?

I thought about Grandma and how she would cope with the loss. 'Grandma is the strongest person I know' I would think to myself. I was certain that she could cope with almost anything. I wish I could have been there with the rest of my family, not trapped in my cell unable to break free. I had to remember him, mourn him and bury him there, all in my mind, alone in that cold, grey cell as the walls began closing in and the Earpiece had its way with me. I hated those four walls and the people who kept me in them.

Grandpa Abe was the type of hero who usually only appeared in myths and fairy tales. In The Just War, when he was only 19, he was captured by the Bad Men and imprisoned and starved and who knows what else. Did he give up? No. He escaped. Did his trauma ruin his life and the lives of his loved ones? No. He soldiered on, like soldiers do. Because that's what he was: a brave-hearted soldier. The King was dead, and there could be no other.

Chapter 9

I sat up suddenly as the water soaked my head.

"Wakey, wakey, new boy, it's your big day." In front of me stood a short strongly-built man in a Sisyphusa overalls, Service User 49. He wore a broad smile and his green eyes glared mischievously. He put down the glass of water.

"The name's Jude Harris but everyone calls me 'Arry. Pleased to meet ya 108," he said. His accent was just like the one my friends and I spoke with at school. I tentatively shook the hand extended to me. "It's time for you to join a Climbing Team. I'm from Team Recovery. Warden Serky sent me up to fetch ya."

I was utterly silent for what seemed like an uncomfortably long time. Sentences formed in my head but I couldn't spit them out of my mouth.

"You're dressed like me," I eventually got out. "Are you Weird too?"

"I wouldn't say Weird meself. I prefer original," he beamed with pride.

"I've been here for 11 months and 17 days. They took me away…these--these huge men. And they put in here."

"What, you mean them?" he pointed out into the corridor at two henchmen. "They're alright once you get used to 'em. They don't cause you no trouble if you don't cause them none."

"The man with the grey beard came on the HDTV…"

"That's Governor Shade. He runs the gaff."

"And he said something about climbing the wall. And then some wardens have come in and given me these awful pills," I pointed at the half empty jar of Climbing Pills lying on the floor next to the couch. "They make me feel so ill, and the nightmares..."

"Yep. I remember that. My first year was the same. Nightmares, the squits, cried like a baby, I did!" he smiled wistfully as he reminisced.

"First year?? How long have you been here?" I asked, dreading the answer.

"This time…ooooh, must be coming up to three years now."

"This time? You mean you've been here before?"

"Yeah. This is my third. Almost everyone here has been at least once before."

"So, what? You escaped and they caught you again?"

"No nothin' like that. I managed to climb the wall, both times. Almost broke the record, the first time. First sub-3-minute Wall-Climb since Dobbsy."

"Dobbsy? You mean the guy who was in here? This cell, I mean."

"I s'pose so. Wait a minute, how'd you know that?" He looked at me suspiciously.

"He's written on the wall," I pointed out the graffiti on the hatch.

"'Si-sy-phu-sa grub tastes like shit. Dobbsy'," he read aloud slowly. "Hahahahahaha. That's ol' Dobbsy alright. A-hahahahaha. It does an' all. It really does taste like shit. He ain't wrong!" he rubbed his eyes and looked embarrassed. "Right, anyway, what was I saying?"

"About when you got out?" I reminded him.

"That's right. You're a quick one, aintya. We could do with your sort on Team Recovery," he pointed at me and smiled. I forced a pained smile back, out of politeness. "So yeah, they helped me to climb the wall. But after a while, I started getting Weird again and they had to put me back in."

"Had to?" I asked indignantly.

"Well yeah, they can't be 'avin' none of us actin' all Weird out there. It ain't right for the Normal folk on the Island, is it?"

"Tell me more about this Team Recovery then," I said, changing the subject.

"Best team here if you ask me. Best team I been on anyway." He sat down next to me, picked up the remote and started flicking through the channels. "Mind if I sit down? You've got HDTV Music 4, you lucky bastard! They treat the new ones like royalty in this gaff. 'Homo-cide', I love this tune," he starts singing along with the lyrics, "'When I'm cruisin with my hoes, in my RV, I pulled up to my house, And what do I see, the Homo next door, is walkin pas', I pulled out my gat, and buss a cap in his ass.' I love that bloke, he's so cool."

"So Team Recovery…" I prompted him.

"Right yeah. Best team in Sisyphusa. No doubt about it. Warden Serky's Team Leader, nice bird she is too."

"What exactly do you do there?"

"Well. Serky takes us for Normalisation Classes and Climbing Practice every morning. And then from midday til' dinner we go work in the quarry."

"Normalisation Classes, quarry? I don't understand?"

"We have classes every day. They teach us how to be like the Normal Islanders. They teach us why we're Weird and how to stop. Pretty helpful you ask me. As for the quarry, bloody awful place. Hard work it is, but you'll get used to it. You'll soon find out anyway. Let's go downstairs, classes are about to start." He stood up sharply and strode out the door. "You comin'?"

I was rooted to the couch in disbelief. It was all so sudden. I had grown so used to those four walls and then everything was going to change, so many new things and new people. I wasn't myself, I was all fat and dishevelled, no-one would like me. I was afraid. Outside the room wasn't safe. I knew the room. It was my home, my friend. Awful, but safe. I had food, and HDTV, and the toilet, what else did I need?

"Come on."

I snapped out of my anxiety. I had to go, there was no other way. "I'm coming."

We walked down the corridor. I struggled to keep up with his speedy little legs.

"What have you been watching then? On the HDTV," Harry enquired.

"Um, like movies, music, Fantasy Factory, football."

"Oh yeah? What team d'ya follow?" he interrupted. "I'm a Mercenaries man me self".

"South Coast Sharks. They're my local team."

"South Coaster, eh? You'll get on with Ella then, she's from that neck-a-the woods."

"Who's Ella?"

"One of the Service Users in Team Recovery. A right looker an' all if you ask me! Been 'ere years she has." We reached the end of the corridor. SCREEEEEECH. I doubled over, holding my hand over the Ear-piece.

"Earpiece givin' ya grief? Tell the little bugger to 'eff off' that's what I do." The screeching abated and then came the piano music again. I was sure I'd heard my mother play the same song. As we left the corridor, the music trailed off, just as it had the last time.

"What's the Earpiece for anyway?" I asked Harry.

"Keep us on our toes I 'spose? Toes I 'spose. Hehe. Rhymes, dunnit? Nasty bugger though, mine is. Best off just ignorin' it, that's what I say."

"What else is in this corridor, apart from the cells, I mean?"

"That's it. Just the Solitary Initiation Quarters," he corrected me.

"No music room or piano or anything?"

"Nope. Nuffin' like that. Why? Play do ya? Never could carry a tune meself." By this time we had reached the bottom of the stairs and were entering the main foyer. Harry stopped short at the reception desk. He leant on the desk with his elbow and stood there casually waiting for Tina, the receptionist, to finish her call. He looked at her and smiled cheekily then he glanced back at me and winked.

"Sorry, I can't make visiting appointments without Governor Shade's authorisation and he's out of the building presently, but if you call back this afternoon he should be back by then…. Okay… Yes…. I understand…. I know, it must be hard…. Yes… But you'll be able to see him soon…Okay. Bye-bye," Tina slammed down the receiver. "Fuckin' moany old bag. Not my fault she's got a Weirdo for a son!" She looked at Harry with disdain. "What do you want, cretin?"

"Are you addressing me, my precious? I ask of nuffing. It is enough merely to be in your beauteous presence, soaking up the smell of your sweet aroma."

Tina played along but also looked genuinely flattered. "Oh, why thank you, good sir. My aroma 'tis none other than Flanel No.75 from yonder MegaMarket."

Harry took Tina's hand and began kissing it, further and further up the arm. "I would have thought that a dazzling young maiden such as yourself would not need such aid, your natural whiff being enough to drive hundreds of men wild with love," he reached her shoulder and kissed her cheek.

"Hundreds of men?" Tina squawked, pushing Harry away. "What's this hundreds of men about? What are you tryin' to say? I ain't no slag"

"Course not. I never said you was. I was just, you know, playin'." Harry back-tracked nervously, as a lone bead of sweat dribbled down his reddened face. "I know you're a classy bird. Anyone would jump at the chance...I mean....Well, you know...Ummm...Maybe you and me, when I get out of 'ere, we should go out on a date?"

"Me?"

"Yeah."

"And you?"

"Yeah."

"Ahahahahaha. Me. And you. Ahahahaha." Tina was overcome by cackling laughter. "You think I'd ever be caught dead with a Sisyphusan? You must be even Weirder than I thought. Ahahahahahaha".

"Come on." Harry said to me. He led me through the double doors to the left as the laughter continued in the background. He looked embarrassed by the rejection. "I don't even fancy her anyway. She's a bitch, everyone says so. You'll hear. You'll hear 'em say: 'That Tina the Receptionist, she's a right bitch', everyone's at it I'm tellin' ya."

"Well, she certainly didn't seem too pleasant just then."

"No mate, she ain't, trust me. I don't fancy her anyway, never 'ave done. I'm into a more classy type of bird. Now Ella she's real classy, wait til' ya meet her," Harry boasted.

"Are you two involved together?"

"Not yet. But watch this space," Harry prophesied, winking at me and tapping the side of his nose with his right index finger. We had reached a door with a sign on it saying "Normalisation Room 1." "Right, here we are. I'll introduce you to the team." Harry was about to knock on the door and then he turned to me. "Oh yeah, what's your name?"

"Odis. Odis Winston," I replied, nervous about entering a room full of people.

"Funny name innit? I'll call you 108." He knocked on the door.

Chapter 10

There was no answer so Harry opened the door and walked in. Inside was a regular-looking classroom. At the front of the room was a white board with the title "Dealing with Weird thoughts" written in red felt tip. There was a semi-circle of chairs facing the white board almost all of which were occupied by a person dressed in Sisyphusa overalls. Through the large windows at the back of the room I could see more people walking into and out of other smaller buildings also dressed in Sisyphusa overalls like my own, all with the same motto: "Learning to be Normal Together".

All of the eyes in the room fixed on Harry as he dragged me unwillingly in front of the white board.

"This is Otis everyone, the newest member of Team Recovery."

"Odis," I corrected him timidly.

"Sorry. This is Odis everyone."

"Hi, Odis!" everyone greeted in unison with varying levels of enthusiasm.

"Where's Warden Serky?" Harry asked the group.

"She's not here yet. She said she'd be late today, remember?" someone said.

"Come on 108 let's sit over 'ere."

I followed Harry to the only two vacant seats which were side-by-side and we sat down. To the right of me were three blonde ladies who looked almost identical.

"Hiya, I'm Tracey," said the one who was sat next to me. "This is…"

"I'm Stacey."

"And I'm Gracie."

"We're sisters," they chimed, as a strong whiff of Liquid Escape reached me from the women's breath.

"Hi," I mumbled.

"He's a looker isn't he girls?" said the one in the middle.

"You're not wrong there Stace," said Tracey.

"Single are you, Otis?" said Stacey.

"Ummm, no, I had a girlfriend."

"Aaaargh, pity that. You're just Gracie's type you are."

"Ohh shut up Tracey, he is not. You know I like my men dark and muscular-like."

"So how long have you been here…Otis? You don't look like other SUs. If I didn't know better I'd say you were some kind of spy," said Stacey half joking, half serious.

"Eleven months and seventeen days," I replied, ignoring the jibe about being a spy despite feeling affronted at the suggestion that my year of suffering wasn't real and neither was I just because I was perceived as different.

"Oooh we've got a day-counter here ladies. First time, is it?" said Tracey.

"Yes." I replied. I then had my first urge to return to my cell and suffer in silent privacy, with whatever dignity I had left.

"This is our second, isn't it girls?" Tracey said.

"Yeah!" replied the other two.

"Six years, this stretch. Just can't seem to get the knack of that wall can we girls?"

"No!"

"I told you ladies, if you ever want private tutoring from a master I'm always available." Harry offered with a flirtatious grin.

"And we told you, Mr. Jude Harris, if we wanted someone to do nothing but stare at our backsides all day we'd still be with our husbands!" replied Tracey.

"Suit yourselves." Harry leant over and whispered in my ear. "You betta watch out for those old girls they're a right bunch of gossips, never tell 'em anything you don't want the rest of Sisyphusa to know. Know what I mean?" He winked.

"Thanks."

"Any idea where Ella is, ladies?" Harry asked the sisters.

"She's at the Senior Reps Council meeting, she should be in Climbing Practice," said Gracie.

"Course she is. Ta Gracie," said Harry. "Wait til' ya meet her, 108. Ella is something else. Smart and beautiful. The whole package." Harry said to me with his eyes looking skywards in a loving trance.

"Does she know how you feel about her?" I asked.

"Not yet. I'm waiting for the right moment."

"How long have you known her?"

"About ten years."

"Oh."

"Good morning Team Recovery" said the trouser-suited woman as she strode through the door.

"Good morning Warden Serky."

"I see we have a newcomer to the team. You must be Mr.Winston. I'm Warden Serky, I'm your Team Leader," she said as she walked past the white board and deposited various files and folders on her desk. "Mr.Harris, have you introduced Mr.Winston to the group?"

"Yes, Warden Serky."

"Good. Now, Mr.Winston, the Governor has decided that you are now ready to leave Solitary Initiation and begin the Normalisation Process with a view to an eventual Wall-Climb. This decision has been made on the basis of your continued consumption of Climbing Pills and the reduction in your erratic behaviour. I hope you appreciate the opportunity we have given you and you will not waste it. Of course you have your issues as your teammates do but we won't stand for any acting up or grumpiness. I think there will be a few jealous Service Users sitting in this room when I tell them that you are beginning Normalisation after only eleven months of Solitary."

She looked around at the rest of the Service Users as though willing them to react. People began murmuring under their breath, "Eleven months, lucky shit," "These newbies have it easy," "He doesn't know he's born."

"Thank you, Ms. Serky," I felt obliged to say.

"That is Warden Serky," she shot back sternly.

"Umm. Sorry. Warden."

"Warden what?" she demanded.

"Thank you Warden Serky."

"Okay, Team Recovery. Let's begin the class. As you can see, today's topic is "Dealing with Weird thoughts." Weird thoughts are something which every Service User here in Sisyphusa has experienced before. How does it make you feel when these thoughts arise?"

"Scared," answered Gracie.

"No, not scared, guilty," said another voice.

"Angry!" said a huge, bald-headed man sitting in the back of the class, staring blankly at the wall.

"Yes. Angry. Good Mr. Femuz, angry. All good answers but anger is the key. As you all know, anger is the number one cause of all admissions to Sisyphusa. Anger turned inward leads to Weird thoughts, Weird thoughts lead to anger turned outwards and anger turned outwards leads to Sisyphusa."

"But that never happened to me," I blurted out.

"Excuse me, Mr. Winston?" asked Warden Serky.

"When I was taken I hadn't had any Weird thoughts and I was never aggressive or angry towards anyone," I explained.

"Everyone gets angry, Mr. Winston, it's a natural human emotion. You are here to learn how to deal with that anger properly and you'd be best served to do less talking and more listening," she spoke quietly but forcefully.

"But what I'm trying to tell y-"

"Please Mr. Winston this is most irregular. This is your first class, you'd do well to keep quiet and try to learn something. Or else maybe we were wrong in putting you forward for integration? Perhaps you need some more time in Solitary?" she said in a loud, threatening tone.

"No. Please," I said quietly.

"Sorry? What was that? I couldn't hear you?"

"I said I'll keep quiet," I said louder, through gritted teeth.

"I hope so. Anyway, as we were saying, you are all here because of your inability to manage certain emotions such as anger, and fear, and anxiety, and grief, which have all led you to develop Weirdness. Now, as you know, we here at Sisyphusa do not see Weirdness as an incurable illness. We believe that you, with our help, can return to Normality and lead meaningful lives. In the next few months we will be giving you the necessary tools for your eventual Wall-Climb. Each morning, we will have a short session aimed at helping you to adapt to Normal life on the Island, if you make it over the wall.

After this class, Mr. Winston, the team proceeds to the Practice Wall where you will train under wall-like conditions.

Those of you who have done a previous Wall-Climb know the drill and I will be expecting you to support first-time climbers. In order to increase your overall fitness and endurance I have decided to extend your working hours in the quarry by another hour."

"Ahhhhh" "Nooo" "An hour?!" people muttered.

"Excuse me? Am I misunderstanding something? Do you not want to make it over the wall? Because you know what happens to people who don't train hard enough don't you?"

Silence.

"That's what I thought. Now, I know that work in the quarry can be challenging but it is a key component in a successful Wall-Climb. Okay, that's that out of the way, back to dealing with Weird thoughts. Scenario: You're out of Sisyphusa, walking down to the shops and you begin having strange thoughts, what do you do? "

"Warden Serky, Warden Serky," pleaded a dishevelled woman with frizzy grey hair, her arm outstretched to the ceiling.

"Yes, Gloria."

"I would breathe."

"Excellent answer, Gloria," Gloria smiled with nervous relief at the approval she had gained while her teammates scowled at her. "Breathe," the warden continued. "Breathing in and out calmly is an excellent tonic for Weird thoughts. Weird thoughts in through the nose, Normal thoughts out through the mouth," Serky said demonstrating the exercise as she repeated the mantra. "Now the rest of you try."

"Weird thoughts in through the nose, Normal thoughts out through the mouth. Weird thoughts in through the nose, Normal thoughts out through the mouth," the group recited in unison.

"This is ridiculous," the Earpiece taunted. "What will this breathing malarkey achieve? Once a Weirdo always a Weirdo, once a Weirdo always a Weirdo. And there's nothing a bit of poxy breathing is going to change."

"No you're wrong!" I blurted aloud. Everyone stopped chanting immediately and stared at me.

"Excuse me? Mr.Winston, who is wrong?" asked Serky.

"No-one, warden. I'm sorry."

"No, come on Winston, you said it, so someone must be wrong. Am I wrong, Mr.Winston? Are you too good to join the rest of the team's chant?"

"No, warden."

"Yes, you are. It's stupid. They're all stupid. Tell her the chant is stupid. Do it," goaded the Earpiece. 'Maybe he was right, maybe I didn't want to become like them,' I thought to myself.

"No. Stop it!" I shouted, holding my hands over my ears.

"Stop what? This insubordination is unacceptable," said Serky.

"I think it's his Earpiece, Warden Serky. He's not learned to ignore it yet. He was telling me it was giving him trouble earlier," interrupted Harry.

"Is that it, Winston? The Earpiece, is it?" said Serky, in a calmer tone of voice.

"Yes, warden," I answered, on the verge of tears.

"You're new here so I'll give you a tip. Ignore the Earpiece. Don't listen to it. Don't talk back to it. Don't give it more power. And above all, don't let it interrupt my lessons because if it does again you will be back in Solitary before you can say 'Boo-hoo'. Understand?"

"Yes, warden."

The lesson proceeded with more tips on how to ignore Weird thoughts. I watched in amazement as the class followed with rapt attention, taking notes, nodding and even laughing once as Serky dictated to them. The Earpiece continued to hinder my concentration, telling me how stupid and ridiculous they all were. He told me that I was better and smarter than all of those simple Weirdoes. I was upset that I didn't identify with my fellow Sisyphusans and I berated myself for looking down on them. Judging them made me just as bad as everyone else, worse even, because I was Weird myself. The lesson was brought to an end by three loud beeps which echoed around the building and the team stood up and led me to what I assumed would be the Practice Walls.

Chapter 11

We left the main building from the East Exit. A stony path led to a huge warehouse with blacked out windows. The compound was a desolate place. The ground was dusty and littered with pebbles and cigarette butts. People wearing hard hats and carrying pickaxes disappeared into the ground. I could hear a whistle being blown. We entered the warehouse. The entire building was divided down the middle by a wall which reached all the way to the ceiling. On the left side of the divide there were dozens of people in identical uniforms to mine. The majority had their necks craned skywards watching the wall. On the wall were four climbers, spaced ten yards apart. Their partners stood directly below them belaying the rope as each climber inched further up the wall. On the other side of the wall a line of henchmen stood poised behind a row of giant barrels.

"Okay, Team Recovery, we're using Climbing Point 5 today. Get into pairs and form a queue behind the safety line," announced Serky. We walked to the left and skirted around the edge of the warehouse behind the crowd. I looked up at the climber nearest to me as I walked. He was halfway up the wall. The wall increasingly sloped outwards the higher it got. His foot missed its intended foot-hold and he suddenly was dangling just by his hands. I gasped aloud.

"Hahahahaha," several Service Users turned around and sniggered at me. I lowered my head and followed the rest of my team.

"Don't worry 108, you'll get used to it," Harry reassured me. "I was scared shitless first time I came in 'ere but you'll get the 'ang of it in no time. Remember it's not gettin' up there that's the problem it's getting' down what's the 'ard part!" he smiled.

"What do you mean?" I asked.

"You'll see."

We reached the far side of the warehouse and the group crowded around inside the box marked Climbing Point 5 in yellow paint on the floor. Everyone was squabbling over who would partner who. Harry immediately winked at me and tugged me by the sleeve to stand next to him.

"No, you two was together yesterday!" screamed Gracie.

"No we wasn't it was *you* and Stace yesterday remember? I was stuck with Gloria!" Tracey fought back.

"No that was the day before," said Gracie.

"Why don't you go with Ahmed, Gracie, he's dark *and* muscular?" reasoned Tracey. Gracie stormed off in a huff seeking out an alternative partner. After some hustle and bustle the group had organised itself into a line of pairs.

"We have a problem, Team Recovery!" shouted Serky from behind us. Standing next to her was a rather lonely looking Gloria, her eyes fixed on the floor. "Thanks to our new arrival we now have odd numbers. Harris, you will go with Gloria. Winston, you will sit out and watch as it's your first day."

I started walking to the back of the queue secretly relieved that I didn't need to climb the wall.

"Sorry I'm late Warden Serky, the meeting ran over schedule," said a girl running towards Climbing Point 5, tying her hair into a pony-tail as she ran.

"Don't let it happen again, Dietschy. You can go with our new team member, Winston."

Serky pulled me hard by the arm and shoved me towards the girl. We stood side-by-side at the back of the queue. Harry stood looking back ignoring Gloria who was speaking to him, as he tried to catch the eye of the latecomer.

"Hi, I'm Ella," said the girl, extending her hand which was covered with coloured wrist-bands.

"Odis," I replied as I shook it.

"I've never seen you here before. Have you come from another facility?"

"What other facility? Are there other places like this on the Island?"

"They've got them all over the Empire. Wow, you really are new, aren't you?" I blushed with embarrassment but felt impelled to speak.

"They took me. They came to my house and took me, a year ago, and I've been here up in a cell on my own ever since."

"You poor thing. The Initiation is really hard, isn't it? I promise you, it does get better but you need to give it time."

"How long have you been here?"

"Me? I've been here for fifteen years."

"That's impossible, that means they must have taken you when you were what? Five?"

"Ah that's sweet of you to say but no I was fourteen. Been here ever since. Anyway enough about me, where are you from?"

"A little town on the South Coast called Itticar."

"You're kidding, I'm from Sameford," she smiled broadly but her eyes still looked tired and sunken.

"Sameford, I used to go to the Sameford Fair every year when I was a kid." The thought of home brought a shot of comfort and familiarity to my heart.

"They had the best..."

"Sugar-Coated Apples!" We both said it at exactly the same time.

"Wow, that really takes me back," Ella mused. "I used to help my dad out on one of the stalls in the summer holidays. We would have to wake up before sunrise to set up the games and prizes. After half an hour my dad would always say that I could go on all of the rides before everyone else arrived. They had that rickety old roller-coaster that did the loop-the-loop at the end. I would stand outside that ride every morning trying to work up the courage to get on."

"Did you ever manage it?"

"No. I would be able to do it now though, I'm sure I would."

The queue shuffled forward. Up on the wall, Harry was already reaching the top. Gloria struggled to tighten the slackening rope as he scaled. It was as if he knew where every single hold was placed without needing to look. He reached the top and I could see him putting on a helmet and some kind of protective armour.

"Why does he need protective gear to come down the other side when he didn't need it to go up?" I asked Ella.

"Because on the way up there's no-one throwing anything at you," she told me with a solemn expression.

'That explains the henchmen with the barrels,' I thought.

"Why are they doing that?" I asked her.

"Because that's what happens on the real wall. We've got to be prepared. If you make it to the top and start to abseil down the Normal side, they're there waiting for you. They scream and shout at you and throw bricks and stones and darts, anything," she said staring straight ahead blankly.

"How did you survive?"

"Me? I've never been. Somebody I used to know told me," she scrunched a smile using just one side of her mouth forming a dimple.

We began to hear loud thuds reverberating against the other side of the wall.

"What are they throwing at Harry?" I asked with concern.

"Just cricket balls, but with the helmet and body armour they can only bruise you at worst. They have to do it, to prepare us. So you know Jude already, do you?"

"He came to get me from my cell."

"Nice boy, isn't he? I remember when he first came in here. Spotty little kid, all earrings and attitude but we took him under our wing. He's a sweetheart really."

"Are you two together?" I asked, already knowing the answer but more interested in the reaction.

"Jude and me? Great SkyMaster no, he's like my little brother," she said laughing as her dimpled cheeks turned bright red. I felt bad for Harry that his feelings weren't requited but her laugh induced an automatic smile in me which I instinctively suppressed, feeling that I shouldn't smile or didn't deserve to.

Harry appeared a few minutes later nursing a sore leg but feeling energised by his climb. "Not far off my personal best," he told us with pride. His face a picture of contentment which grew more delighted still when Ella greeted him with a hug. "I see you've met 108?" he said as he slow-motion punched my arm.

"Yes, Odis and I are great chums already, both being South Coasters and all," she smiled at me and I was relieved that someone had pronounced my name right first time. The two of them talked for a while about the meeting which Ella had just attended. It turned out each Climbing Team would elect a senior representative to attend a council meeting once a week. At the meeting all of the reps would discuss the conditions and rules of Sisyphusa as well as other formalities such as different teams' climbing dates. Meetings were presided over by selected senior wardens and occasionally Governor Shade. Ella was excited by the developments of that day's meeting.

"We've managed to lobby for orange juice twice a week instead of just water and also we've decided to put forward another proposal to reduce Solitary Initiation for new arrivals." My ears perked up.

"Nice one Ells, you're fightin' our corner as always," said Harry.

"You said *another* proposal, how many have failed?" I enquired.

"This is proposal #72 but I'm quietly confident with this one. We've changed our angle. This is the first time we've argued for shorter confinement on a financial basis. You see, Sisyphusa now holds 108 Service Users with your arrival plus however many are in Solitary right now. With each new arrival spending a year or more in their own cell with their own HDTV and running water, the government is losing money that we argue it doesn't have to. If people were integrated earlier, after say, six months, they'd be sharing the mixed dormitories with one HDTV for a room of 15 or 20 and shared bathroom facilities. More humane-- but more importantly, more cost effective. Like I said, I think we have a chance," she exclaimed with passionate determination.

"So am I going to be moving now?" I asked with controlled excitement.

"Yep. All teams share dorms so that they can study together. You've got the last bed in the room, it's a top bunk mind," Harry informed me with relish.

"Next pair!" bellowed Warden Serky. Without realising it all of the other pairs had done their climb and we were up.

"Don't worry, Odis, I'll climb. You can just handle my ropes. I'll show you how," Ella assuaged my fears. We approached the bottom of the wall and Ella began to put each leg through what looked like a rope nappy.

"Stop, Dietschy," Serky interceded. "Let Winston climb, I'm sure he can handle it can't you, Winston?"

"Yes Warden," I gulped. Ella took off the safety harness and handed it to me.

"You'll be fine," she whispered.

Ella checked I was fully prepared and that my ropes were safely secured.

"Okay good luck."

I looked up. The over-hanging cliff-face came out so far that I stood in its shadow. I couldn't even see the top of the wall from where I stood. I took a deep breath, approached the wall and found two deep handholds on which I could get a firm grip. I then inserted my right foot into a foothold at waist-height and pulled myself up. I could feel Ella quickly tightening my slack. I reached my left hand higher into a small nook and then my right hand even higher into a more solid grip. I had to manoeuvre to the left where I could just about reach a large foothold for my left foot.

"Go on Otis, I was shit my first time too!" one of the sisters screamed encouragement. I hoped that they were talking about climbing.

I began to get the hang of it and managed to move more briskly. My movement and Ella's belaying found a perfect rhythm and I felt exhilarated to be gliding up the wall. I had been so entrapped in my confined cell for so long, this ascent felt like I was flying. Halfway up the wall my left foot slipped and the unexpected shift in weight meant that I lost grip in my left hand and right foot as well. I dangled by my right hand and was spun around slowly almost 180 degrees so that I was looking down at the rest of the team and Warden Serky. To the left I could see that most of the other Service users from the other teams were watching me too.

"Hold on Odis," I think it was Ella who I could hear but it just as easily could have been anyone. I thought of letting go and just giving up and letting Ella lower me down but I didn't want to give Serky the satisfaction. I managed to change my momentum so that I slowly twirled back towards the wall and managed to regain my footing and find a better hold for my left hand. I concentrated everything on each limb at a time and slowed my pace.

As I neared the summit I could hear Harry and Ella below, cheering me on. I couldn't believe that I was doing it. To think how I had felt just that morning. I finally reached my right hand then my left over the top and dragged myself up and toppled over head first. I sat up and rubbed my head. At the top of the 50ft wall there was a 6-foot wide ledge separating the "up wall" from the "down wall." Further along this plateau I could see another climber who'd just reached the top. He reached for the safety gear hanging up straight ahead of him and quickly put it on. He looked at me and snarled, then he faced straight ahead, puffed out his cheeks and climbed onto the ledge holding his rope in his hand and leaned all the way back until he disappeared.

I scurried forward on my hands and knees then I stood up and peered over the edge. The other climber was abseiling down the other side of the wall which was metal and perfectly flat. The henchmen immediately reached into their barrels and began flinging the cricket balls at him at a hundred miles an hour. One just missed him to the right and another came nearer to my direction. I quickly ducked down and sat with my back to the wall as it shook from repeated contact from the balls. I shuffled forward and looked over the other side.

"Odis. I'm untying your rope. You have to pull it up," Ella shouted.

'What the hell? Why are you untying it?' I thought to myself. I turned around and started panting furiously. I sat with my back to the wall I'd just climbed. Straight in front of me I saw body armour and a helmet hanging up. Next to it was a picture and a sign. "Pull up your rope and fasten securely to hook before abseiling," it read. The picture, disconcertingly, showed a stick-man falling haplessly over the wall, clearly having not secured his rope to the hook. I was stuck. I had no choice, I was already up there. I had to get down and there seemed to be only one way down. I figured my best chance was to go when other climbers were going so that they took some of the flak from the henchmen.

I quickly put on the armour which padded the neck, back and buttocks though not enough. I fastened the helmet and guessed that the arms and legs just had to be unprotected. There was also a pair of climbing gloves presumably to avoid rope-burn. I began tugging on my rope furiously. Right hand, left hand, right hand, left hand, I was fighting my own tug of war. The rope came flying over the top. I could see the metal ring where I was supposed to fasten the rope. I unscrewed the carabiner which Ella had used to fasten my rope to her harness and I fastened it to the metal ring which was connected to the wall. I tugged on it twice, hard, to make sure it was secured. I was ready. I waited a minute or so until another climber had reached the top.

A tall skinny man hopped over the wall. He saw me straight away and smiled at me, exposing two missing teeth. I think he could sense my apprehension. He put on the protective gear, pulled up his rope and secured it to the hook like he'd done it a million times. He stood on the ledge then turned to me and saluted sarcastically before falling back fearlessly over the edge to begin his descent.

'It's now or never,' I told myself. I looked over the edge nervously one more time and could see that everyone had gathered on that side of the wall to watch the last of the climbers abseil. I stepped up onto the ledge, rotated around and lingered tremulously. I was panting heavily again until a cricket ball whooshed just past my head. I fell backwards in shock. I snatched quickly for my rope and grasped it. Suddenly I was abseiling. My feet were flat against the iron wall and I began to loosen my slack a bit at a time but not at all smoothly. Cricket balls were rocketing against the wall all around me. I could hear the people below me. Some were cheering in support, the majority were baying for my blood.

I kept on letting out the slack as quickly as I could. Somehow I hadn't been hit yet. I could see the other climber out of the corner of my eye. He'd stopped to nurse a wounded limb of some sort. Our eyes briefly met and he shot me a look of disdain. I looked down between my legs and could see that I was past halfway. I began to get excited. Was I actually enjoying this? I continued to release the slack but then a ball crashed into my left arm and I instinctively let go. I began to free-fall. I tried desperately to slow myself down by grasping the rope with my right arm. I crashed to the floor.

I opened my eyes. Service Users crowded all around me. Ella was holding my head in her arms and Harry gripped my hand in his.

"Am I dead?" I asked.

"You're fine, just a bit battered and bruised," Ella said smiling.

"Mate, that was amazin'! I can't believe you freefell 20ft. But it worked, you beat him!" Harry said in reverence.

"Beat who?"

"Skinny Jim of course, who else?" Harry nodded his head towards the tall, gap-toothed man who I'd shared the wall with. He was being carried away on a stretcher unconscious with what looked like a badly broken arm. "It was the two of you racin' wasn't it?" Harry asked.

"I wasn't racing him. I just wanted to make it down alive, are you crazy?"

"Of course I am. We all are!"

Chapter 12

Just as my backside struck the floor the clock was striking twelve which apparently meant lunch. The mess hall was back in the main building. I limped, struggling to keep up with the rest of the team whose empty stomachs ordered them to rush ahead. Ella slowed down to keep me company. Had I known the food in the mess hall was going to be as revolting as the food I'd had in the cell I wouldn't have bothered. Ella and I were served the last dregs from a filthy cauldron of stew. It was the same lumpy, brown stuff that I'd survived on for the last year. You could see your spoon plunge through the layer of oil which nestled on the surface of the liquid. I sat at a table with Ella, Harry and four other men. Everyone else wolfed down their bowls like it was a gourmet meal. I had my usual couple of spoonfuls and then contented myself with stale bread and water.

Following the meal everyone stayed in their seats. After a while the wardens entered the mess hall holding large bags. Each warden began doling out small white paper bags to members of their team. Warden Serky approached our table. Our table and the two parallel to it were the Team Recovery tables. Serky gave each team member at the table their own bag and then walked off to the other two tables. My small bag had a sticker with "108" printed on it. Inside were capsules of tablets.

"Now that you've joined a team, you get your weeks' worth of Climbing Pills given to you at the beginning of each week," Ella whispered to me, clearly seeing my puzzled expression. Harry and Ella both popped their lunchtime dose with a swig of cloudy water. The packet was a grid of twenty-one small capsules, seven by three, each with a Climbing Pill. The columns of three were headed by the first three letters of that day of the week. I popped the morning and afternoon pills out of their capsules and swallowed them both, making up for missing the morning dose. As I tilted my head back to swallow a gulp of water I looked at the four other men at our table. They had been in the class that morning but remained quiet throughout. They all wore a similar sleepy yet tranquil expression. One of them caught my eye and smiled, exposing a golden incisor. He looked around thirty. He had jet-black hair and thick stubble covered his tanned face.

"Hello, my name is Ahmed," he said in a foreign accent.

"Hello Ahmed, I'm Odis," I extended my hand which he gripped tightly and shook.

"This Abdul, this Khaled, this Mo," he said pointing to the other three men one-by-one as he told me their names. The three men smiled lazily as if they were simultaneously engaged in the same enjoyable dream.

"Pleased to meet you all," I held my hand up in a nervous wave/salute combo. Embarrassed, I quickly lowered my hand and asked the first thing that came into my head.

"Where are you from?"

"Khaled and Abdul is Numis, Me and Mo is Cartajee,"

"Really? I've been to Cartagia on holiday once. Beautiful place," I realised I was speaking loudly and with patronising enunciation and stopped doing so mid-sentence.

"Yes, very beautiful," he said with a nostalgic pride.

"The ruins in El Djeb were particularly memorable," I added, as if I was reading from a travelogue.

"Yes," he looked impressed, "you went to El Djeb?" he asked me with a hint of suspicion.

"Of course," I smiled nervously.

"I from El Djeb," he grinned again. "Most beautiful women in Cartajeea comes from El Djeb!"

"Where's this Al whatsit then? Sounds like my kind of town," Harry said with a mouthful of stew.

"You no want go El Djeb Harry, you go my town, Mousse," said Mo slapping Harry on the back. "I find you nice Moussi wife!" The four men giggled and coughed hoarsely.

"Wait a minute, I never said nothin' about no wife!" Harry looked genuinely frightened. The four men giggled even more, unable to hold it in.

"And does this wife have any say in the matter?" smiled Ella.

"What are you trying to say? That she wouldn't wanna marry me?" said Harry, looking slightly offended.

"Not necessarily, I just feel sorry for the poor girl who would have to put up with your snoring! You keep the whole dorm up half the night!" They all laughed while I absently fretted about sharing a room with a group of strangers. 'Could I cope with this sudden loss of privacy?' My daydream was brought to a sharp end with three loud beeps. All of the Service Users shot up instantly.

"Get a move on, lunch time is over," said one of the wardens itching to exert some power where it wasn't necessary. "Trays to the side, rubbish in the bin!"

"I hope you've recovered your strength from that fall," teased Ella.

"Why?"

"You're gonna need it where you're going!"

She wasn't wrong. I followed the team out of the mess hall and out of the main building. The line of Service Users moved slowly as everyone filed out in ordered silence. I caught suspicious glances from members of other teams including Skinny Jim who was limping and scowling in equal measure. After a hundred or so yards Ella broke off from us and followed a path to the left as did all of the other females.

"I'll see you back at the dorm, Harry. Bye, Odis, good luck."

I began to dread what was coming next. We were moving towards the huge hole. What could it be? More ridiculous extreme sports? Caving? Pot-holing? Death by pick-axe? It was the latter.

All of the men, there must have been fifty at least, walked down into the hole via a flight of creaky wooden stairs. The hole was a quarry, or more like a canyon. It delved deep, several metres deep, into the ground. Inside, wardens wearing yellow hard hats blew whistles and directed Service Users to where their team would be working. The staircase wobbled precariously as the Service Users trudged down each step mechanically. I gripped the one bannister on the left side and continued on slowly. At the bottom I copied Harry and grabbed a hard hat and a pick-axe from the rack that was bolted into the wall on the right-hand side. The axe weighed my arms down instantly. I heaved it up onto my shoulder and we walked across the length of the quarry, which was as long as a football pitch, to where Warden Serky stood waiting for us, whistle in mouth. She gave it one shrill blow, despite the fact that all of the men from the team had gathered around her in perfect silence.

"Good. Listen carefully. Today, we are beginning a new phase of work in the quarry. The Footstool Contract has been fulfilled and we have just received a new order direct from the office of Minister Frown. We...no...*you* have the privilege of providing some of the material to be used for a commemorative monument to be built in the capital city of the Frontier Empire Mainland. The monument will be the sculpted heads of The Emperor and his three under-Ministers as well as our very own former Minister Snare. The Empire predicts that they will need up to 80 tonnes of granite to sculpt the monument, so our unit and others around Fantasy Island have gladly accepted the challenge of fulfilling that request," Serky beamed with pride. I saw her smile for the first time, it looked unnatural. She had gaps between her teeth which made her mouth look like a keyboard.

"Why can't the Empire use their own granite, Warden Serky?" asked a member of the team innocently.

"Because, unfortunately they have run out," the smile faded back to her customary poker-face. "The Mainland ran out of their natural fuels and resources in the last century but as they have done so much to help our small island I'm sure we would agree to help a friend in need, wouldn't we?" the piano-key smile returned.

"Yes, Warden Serky," the sallow-faced Service User replied dutifully.

"Of course you would, we are all happy to do it. Now, let's get to work. It says here you are required to pick-axe lumps of granite 40cm x 40cm in diameter," she announced peering over her glasses to read from a clipboard. "For those of you who don't know, that is approximately the size of this inflatable ball," she pointed to the orange sphere standing just above her knees from the ground. The ball started to blow away as a gust of wind plunged into the quarry.

She ran in her slightly high-heeled shoes after the fugitive balloon and caught up with it just before it collided with a jagged edge which would have burst it. "Okay," she continued unhindered. "Each of you must fulfil a quota of fifteen rocks per day. Once you have quarried your granite, you must wrap one of these sashes around it." She held up a long leather cord which looked like a giant guitar strap. "And you will pull it up the ramp onto the conveyor belt which will transport it into the factory. There, the female Service Users will smooth them down before they are shipped out. I will be stationed under the umbrella at the top of the ramp and will be keeping track of every boulder you have delivered so there will be no skimping. Any questions?"

A dazed silence hung over the entire team. I tried to comprehend the enormity of the task she had just described so casually. Fifteen boulders a day. FIFTEEN. That ramp had to be at least twenty feet long and enormously steep.

"Good. Get to work then. Oh, I forgot, the first Service User to meet his quota will receive a special reward."

A buzz suddenly hummed and murmured through the team. They whispered and speculated as to what it could be. A prize? How could they get excited about some nameless prize? The only thing that would be worth doing this slave-labour for, because it was slave-labour, was freedom.

"Good luck with this one, fatboy," goaded the Earpiece. "You couldn't push that balloon up the ramp let alone a boulder, you pathetic weasel."

He was right. I was totally out of shape, and weak and tired. The other men had already fanned out and had begun pelting away at the granite walls.

"Hop along lardy, don't you want to win the prize? Hahahahaha!" the Earpiece continued.

"Come on 108, over 'ere," Harry ushered me over to a vacant spot of wall next to him. He seemed to be very adept with a pick-axe already.

"The trick is…you've got to start from the top. Make a dent in the middle like this," he flung the sharp tool into the dusty rock, "and then slowly work a semi-circle round both sides. Simple really!" He winked.

I took a practise shot, and then tried to hit that same point. I missed by a foot and dropped the axe after it made a reverberating contact with the unforgiving wall. I picked it up and tried again, this time an inch closer. About an hour later, my overalls were soaked through with sweat but I had almost picked out my first boulder. Harry had just returned from hauling his third up the ramp.

"Nice one, 108. You're gettin' the 'ang of it now. Told you it was easy," Harry encouraged me.

I wrapped the thick part of my leather sash around the back of the boulder and imagined catapulting it through the wall of the compound and escaping. Back in reality, I wrapped the thinner part of the sash around my upper body as if it was the orange and blue backpack I used to carry around at South-Coast University. I attempted to drag it towards the ramp but it wouldn't budge. I dug the balls of my feet into the ground and leant into the sash which was fully taut. It wouldn't budge.

"Told you so. Weakling," the Earpiece chuckled.

I tried again, and it began to inch forward, first a little bit but then one step, then another, it was actually moving, I couldn't believe it. I made it to the bottom of the ramp and had built up the momentum to a brisk walking speed. I stepped up and tried to continue my progress uphill. My feet began to slip on the dusty ground, my legs strained and bent at the knees trying to climb and at the same time maintain balance. I stretched my hands to the ground and clawed for grip, I was climbing on all-fours like a crazed ape.

The boulder was on the gradient and moving slowly upwards leaving a trail in the sand. I began to feel the whole weight of the rock on the thin strip of leather strap digging into my shoulder. I lifted my right hand to my shoulder to readjust the strap but lost balance and fell forwards, face first, into the dirt. The strap slipped from my shoulder and the rock slowly started to slip down the hill erasing my progress. I caught the strap with my hand and gripped it tightly with both hands, and held it facing downhill. I recovered my composure and began to step backwards, up the ramp, dragging the boulder with both hands. The weight pulled down on my shoulder sockets. My feet continued to step back, one painfully slow step at a time, until I reached flat ground and yanked the granite ball up and over the top.

"That's one Winston. You're trailing, you'd better get moving," Serky sat in her chair, an umbrella sheltering her from the sweltering sun, and made a tick on her clipboard. I resisted the urge to scream and rolled the rock up a small metal ramp onto a moving conveyor belt like the ones you collect your luggage from at the airport. The belt carried the boulders on through a giant dog-flap and into the large factory building with a plain corrugated iron façade. I rubbed my sore hands and shoulder and scurried down the hill and back to my pick-axe. I passed Harry, and other Service Users with their eyes on the prize, positively sprinting up the ramp as if they were walking their pet poodle on a leash.

It was the mysterious Mr. Femuz who finished first. I had seen him powering up the hill in seconds with boulders much larger than mine. He had unzipped his overalls revealing a carpet of grey squiggly hairs covering his chest. He tied the sleeves around his waist leaving his bronze torso in the glare of the sun. His huge muscles flexed as he brought his pick-axe smashing down into the quivering granite. He was offered the prize but he ignored it with a sullen expression and trudged back to the main building. Harry gladly received the prize, a Frontier Empire flag lapel pin, and he fastened it immediately to the breast pocket of his overalls. I was last to finish. The sun had died down and just Serky and I remained. When I finally dragged my fifteenth boulder up to the summit, shoulders and hands bleeding from friction burns, the warden said: "Pathetic display, Winston, I'm expecting better tomorrow. I haven't the time to wait around all night for you to finish." And with that she stormed off and I collapsed to the ground.

I re-entered the main building, and followed Tina the receptionist's directions to the Team Recovery dormitory. When I opened the door, the lights were off and everyone was asleep, a loud snore was vibrating from the far corner.

"Odis, is that you?" I followed the voice, too tired to reply. "Over here," the whisper drew me in. A hand fondled my face in the dark and felt my nose. "Ooops, sorry." Ella reached for my hand and led me in the dark. "I heard you'd be coming in late so I waited up to show you where your bed is."

"Thank you," I managed to reply.

"You're over here. You sound pretty tired, you can have the bottom bunk and I'll go on top."

"Thank you, that's very kind." I was in too much pain for a gallant refusal. I heard her scamper up onto the top bunk and I peeled my sweaty overalls off and climbed into the stiff bed.

"Goodnight Odis," she said leaning over the side of the bed.

"Goodnight," I replied already half-asleep.

"And welcome to Team Recovery."

Chapter 13

Days and weeks passed, all of them following the same routine of a short Normalisation class in the morning followed by Climbing Practice, lunch and work in the quarry. I had begun to blank out Serky's morning lessons. Some of the topics she covered included: "Confidence in Normality," "Work = Recovery," and "the Weakness of Weirdness." They all seemed to follow the same thread but were re-packaged, re-condensed for a new hour-long lecture every morning. The majority of the class eagerly jotted down notes while nodding their assent. Mr. Femuz, however, stared into space. His features remained neutral, except for his left eye which would occasionally flit about, surveying the room and its inhabitants while his right eye lay dormant. Ella continued to miss these lessons as she attended more and more meetings, fighting to gain better rights for Sisyphusa inmates, largely a forlorn struggle.

I began to make progress in Climbing Practice. My technique and speed no longer attracted sniggers of derision from the members of other teams. In fact, my times improved to the extent that I had reached the top five best in Team Recovery. One particular session I even managed to get a better time than Harry. Ella congratulated me with a hug and teased Harry playfully, but he failed to see the funny side of it and ignored us both for the rest of that day.

I would talk in whispers with Ella at night while everyone else was asleep, telling her about all of the things that had changed on Fantasy Island since she had been in Sisyphusa. I would tell her what it was like to be at South Coast University and about the friends I'd made there. She would giggle even when I was being serious just like Layla used to. She told me about her childhood, about her mother dying when she was a baby and her dad re-marrying not long afterwards and about her dad having new kids, a new family- one that she didn't feel a part of. That's when she started skipping school, getting into trouble, and eventually she wound up in Sisyphusa. She said she hadn't heard from her dad since. Not one visit, not one message.

She said Team Recovery was her family. Harry and Gloria and the rest, and now me, she added.

At first I would come back from the quarry and she would already be asleep. But I began getting back earlier and earlier and wasn't even finishing last anymore. I wasn't finishing first either. That position was invariably reserved for Mr.Femuz. The work was pure drudgery. For hours every day we had to drag those boulders up that hill. There was a fleeting moment of relief and a sense of achievement when I managed to reach the top. But that feeling soon dissolved into one of demoralisation when I remembered that I'd have to drag countless more, not just that day but for every other day which lay before me in an endless desert of days and weeks and months and years. Maybe the Earpiece was right, what was the point? Why bother? I was doomed.

'No,' I told myself. 'Dad escaped and so did all of the Service Users who had been in and out of Sisyphusa. Remember what Dad said: "The Earpiece is just an Earpiece, it's not you. You'll be over that wall and out of there in no time." I know it's not me, but it's my Earpiece in my ear and I'm stuck with it.' I wanted Dad to be right, I needed to believe him. The nightmare couldn't last forever.

After some weeks of work in the quarry it was announced that for reaching 40 tonnes, the halfway mark of the total quota, we were to be rewarded with a day off. All Service Users were permitted to do as they pleased anywhere within the confines of the compound but were warned that numerous wardens would be patrolling the grounds to monitor behaviour. Harry, the Simons and some of the rest of the team chose to spend the day in the dorm watching an omnibus of Fantasy Factory: "Where Dreams Become Reality." Watching that show was the one thing everyone could agree on. I lay on my bottom bunk, given to me by Ella, watching the first half hour. One of the contestants, a 16 year old ex-prostitute called Alice, was wowing the audience and the pre-Judges with a heart-on-sleeve performance when Ella tiptoed down the ladder and whispered to me, asking if I wanted to go for a walk. I accepted.

"There's somewhere I'd like to show you," she said with a serious expression as we walked out of the main building towards the quarry.

"Okay."

We walked in silence, Ella leading the way. We skirted around the edge of the quarry, past the warehouse with the Practice Wall. Ella stepped off the path and waded through some thick grass, carefully picking a handful of blue and yellow flowers before entering the woods which concealed that part of the compound. I followed her, trying to keep up as branches snapped back in my face after she'd walked through them. She knew the route well, you could tell. Though there was no concrete path, the exact route that she was taking was marked by a muddied track made presumably by her own footsteps.

After a couple of minutes we stepped out of the trees and were in a field of rough grass with overgrown weeds and dandelion clocks. Ella made her way towards an area ahead where the grass was shorter and there they were, dozens of wooden stakes sticking out of mounds of mud- the burial practice of the Yes/No Book #2. Ella walked around the front of the mass of stakes and finally stopped at one in the corner. She dropped to her knees and cleared away some dead flowers and leaves from the mound. She carefully placed the new bunch of flowers and then lifted her fingers to her mouth, kissed them and pressed them to the stake. On the thick rotting plank was carved "Dobbsy". She turned around to me and with a stoical smile tapped the ground next to her. I sat down.

"You would have got along, you and him," she said nodding her head towards the mound. "He was strong, like you."

My Earpiece baulked at the suggestion that I could be strong but I ignored it and tried to continue the conversation. "Were the two of you close?" I asked, knowing the answer.

"The closest," a tear trickled down her sallow cheek and she quickly wiped it away, smiling to fight off the tears. "He's the only person who I ever knew really loved me, who I could trust, you know?"

"Yes."

"He arrived here a couple of years after me. I was sixteen, he was nineteen. We grew up together. Not much of a place to grow up I know but you can fall in love in the worst of situations I guess, can't you? Well, we did anyway. We were so bad for each other, real rebels. I mean we'd egg each other on to do more and more crazy things you know, just for the excitement of it. We'd sneak out at night, set off the emergency alarms during Normalisation Class, trash the other teams' rooms while they were working, it was really exhilarating. A big 'Fuck You' to the wardens, the Governor, everyone. 'If you tell us we're Weird then we're gonna bloody act Weird', that's what we'd say."

"They knew it was us, everyone did. They tried to stop us, separate us. They moved him into a different team, they gave us extra work so we could never see each other, they even stuck us both in Solitary for a couple of months. But none of it worked, we'd always find ways to see each other. When Jude first came we took him under our wing and he would act as a go-between, ferrying messages back-and-forth. Once Jack, that was his first name, sent Jude into my dorm in the middle of the night just for him to say 'Dobbsy says he loves you,' the poor thing looked half asleep. Little Jude didn't mind though, he really looked up to Jack. Ever since Jack left us, Jude's been ever so protective over me, whenever I'm talking to anyone else, even you, he always seems to be keeping one eye on me."

"He just cares about you," I said.

"I know, its sweet I guess, I just wish he knew that I'm a big girl, you know?"

"That you can take care of yourself?"

"Exactly."

There was silence for thirty seconds. "Can I ask…how did he die?"

"I don't mind telling you. That's why I brought you here. I see you as a real friend now, Odis."

"Me too," I quickly spat out.

"That's why I wanted to tell you what happened before someone else does…It was my fault. I killed him."

I could feel my stomach lurch. I knew I shouldn't have got close to anyone. Maybe The Daily Bulletin was right after all—Weird people are the ones who kill.

"It was five years ago. We'd been here for so long and they just wouldn't let us climb. Because of all of the trouble we'd caused, we'd have to sit through the classes and climb the Practice Walls, but when the time came for the teams to climb the wall we were never allowed. 'Maybe next time,' Governor Shade would always say, 'when you've earned it.' They kept on telling us that we had to try harder. If we wanted to be fixed, then we should prove it. We were just kids. Doing things that kids do, you know? They said that we must want to be Weird, that we liked it."

"One day I decided I'd had enough. I'd stolen one of the warden's swipe-cards a few years back so I snuck out of my dorm and got Jack, who was in Solitary at the time. The whole place is shut down at night, no wardens, no Governor Shade. All they have is the henchmen, who are so dumb they barely seem awake half the time, and the Night Warden who no-one had ever seen before. So we managed to evade the henchmen in the corridor of the Solitary Initiation Quarters and then the one who was in the foyer. But when we got to the main entrance the card didn't work, that door must have needed a different card. So I suggested that we climb the wall, this was the only chance we'd ever get."

"What without ropes or harnesses?" I asked.

"No-one gets ropes or harnesses, Odis, not even on the organised Wall-Climbs. They only give you those for practice. Why do you think there are so many?" She pointed at the masses of stakes which surrounded us and I realised how stupid I'd been.

"Oh," that was the only word that I could muster. I felt sick to my stomach.

"Jack never wanted to go. He said it was too dark and that he was afraid something would happen to me. He said that if it did he'd never forgive himself. But I wouldn't leave it. I pleaded with him, I begged, I told him that if he didn't come then he didn't love me at all. I even threatened that I'd go alone and began walking towards the wall. That was when he gave in."

"So we began to climb. He insisted that I went first, he actually thought that if I fell then he would be able to catch me! He was an amazing climber, the best that this place has ever seen, ask anyone."

"That's what I've heard," I said.

"That's why it was so unfair, him not being allowed to climb. He could've made it out, no problem and they knew it. He told me where to put my feet and where not to. It's not like on the nice Practice Wall with perfect handles and footholds. It's all jagged rock and slippery sand, like in the quarry. Jack had to grab my foot once when it slipped out of place, I screamed because I thought I'd fall. That was when the searchlight flashed onto the wall. We froze still, praying that the light wouldn't find us. It skirted around the whole wall, flitting from left to right, up and down, all over the place like a Liquidated firefly. And then it found us and the alarm sounded. The henchmen were out in seconds firing their guns on the wall but we were almost at the top. Bullets hammered into the granite all around us, whipping up puffs of dust and sand into our eyes but somehow we reached the top."

"There'd be no Normal people throwing rocks on the other side because it was the middle of the night and it wasn't an organised Wall-Climb day anyway. We were free, or so we thought. As soon as we both bundled ourselves over the summit of the wall and out of the firing line of the henchmen, I couldn't believe what I saw, just the thought of it still haunts me to this day."

Ella proceeded to describe a monster I'd only previously heard of in comic books. It howled and screeched at the two of them from each of its six heads. Six long, scaly necks squiggled and swayed while the body with its countless legs and huge powerful tail stood rooted to the ground blocking their escape. One of the heads hissed loudly. Its piranha-like teeth jutted out at its prey.

"I was frozen but Jack dragged me up by my arm and positioned me behind him. He picked up a stick and held it still in front of him. We began to edge our way, in-step with each other, along the top. The beast remained still but tracked our movement with its beady eyes. 'Just move slowly behind me, I think we can get round the side of it,' Jack said to me without moving his gaze from the monster for a moment. At the top of the wall there was a relatively flat plateau before coming to the face where we could descend to freedom. The plateau only covers the small part of the wall where the climbs take place. To the right the wall becomes jagged, un-climbable rock and to the left, on the side of the thing there's a cave, where the chain holding it back leads into."

"We continued edging our way around, spotting some space to the right of the creature where we could slip past it and begin climbing down. As we did so, the six viper-like necks all shot forward towards us so close we could feel the heat from its open mouths. They snapped away at us but the chain held it back so we were just out of its reach. We began to move quicker now, realising there was space to pass it where it couldn't reach us, but when we moved into that space the ground suddenly began to shake. I fell to the ground and Jack fell on top of me."

"Out of the ground a deep chasm began to open up which crackled and shook like an earthquake. Then came the noise. A rising rumble began to emanate from deep inside the chasm until it reached the surface, spewing out torrents of water like from a whale's blowhole. Then a cyclonic wind erupted from within and the water tossed round and round creating a whirlpool sucking rocks and sticks and anything else into the chasm. We scrambled to our feet and rushed back to where we'd come from. 'Quick, back over the wall,' Jack shouted at me."

"We climbed backwards over the wall but instantly shots began to rain in on us. We had to climb back up. Jack stood in front of me again, protecting me. We knew we couldn't go back, we had to fight. 'That thing will kill us if we get too close! We can get between them if we veer towards the water,' Jack said. I didn't believe it, I was crying, I was so scared. He gripped my arms and said 'This is it, El, you wanted your freedom, this is our last chance. Are you ready?' I had to say yes. So we moved forward..." She began to sob, her head was in her hands.

"You don't have to carry on, really," I said.

"No I have to tell you," she was full-on crying at that point. "We moved forward and the wind it-it-it took him. I couldn't..." she burst out weeping and put her head on my shoulder.

"It's okay, I understand," I held her head and her neck. Her skinny arms gripped my shoulder blades. I didn't know what to say, I hadn't hugged anyone for over a year.

"We never even got his body. We just buried his things and a photograph." She pulled back and looked at me, still holding my arms, "I held on, I tried to hold on to him, but it was too strong. It was just too strong."

"It wasn't your fault Ella, you can't blame yourself. Blame them. They forced you up there, they shot at you, they stole you from your life and put you here."

"No. It was me, Odis, can't you see? It was my idea to sneak out. I forced him to climb the wall, it's my fault he's dead, if it wasn't for me he wouldn't have died."

"If it wasn't for you Ella, he never would have lived. It sounds like the two of you lived for each other, it sounds like your lives only began the day you met each other. He gave his life to protect *you*. He wouldn't want you to waste his sacrifice by spending the rest of your life blaming yourself, hating yourself. He'd want you to fight, to fight for the freedom that he died fighting for." She stared at me and I stared back. I wasn't frightened by her gaze, it gave me strength. Her cheeks were covered with the trickle-marks of her tears. I put my hands on them and wiped them clean. She eked out a wan smile. She lifted my hands off her face and put them down by my sides, then she stood on her tip-toes and brushed her lips down my cheek.

Suddenly we heard a sound from the bushes. Someone was sniggering. We both turned to where the sound was coming from. The bushes rustled and whoever it was was running away. We chased after them. Ella took the lead again, darting like a predator. Branches and leaves catapulted into my face until we reached another clearing and there, sitting in the long grass, were Ahmed, Khaled, Abdul and a smiling, panting Mo.

Chapter 14

The four men sat in a crescent shape, stooped over so as to be concealed within the long grass. In the middle of the crescent was a makeshift hearth. Four slabs of flat granite formed the base. A small clay pot filled with bubbling water was raised some inches above a fire supported by two bricks.

"What are you doing here?" asked Ahmed.

Mo caught my eye. He winked and grinned as if we shared some naughty secret.

"What are you making?" I asked, changing my gaze back to Ahmed.

"Nothing, nothing. Some tea," he replied uneasily. I looked closer and noticed that on some criss-crossed twigs which lay across the top of the pot, there was a clutch of tiny flowers.

"What's with the flowers?"

"Just, how you say? Erb."

"I've never seem them before," I said suspiciously. The flowers were green and red and the steam from the boiling water made my head whirl.

"They're called Ziziphusa," said Ella. She stared at the men whose dark eyes gazed at the burning embers on the hearth. "They only grow here."

"That smell is so strong. Why are you steaming them?" I asked Ahmed. All four remained taciturn.

"To eat them," Ella answered for them. She switched her glare to me and softened her expression. "You can steam them or boil them or smoke them and suddenly... you aren't here any more. Isn't that right?" she asked the men. They nodded and looked at the ground. "I thought that you'd stopped guys." I could hear the hurt in her voice.

"We tried," said Mo, no longer smiling. "But is too hard. The ZeeZee make it more easy!"

"Not in the long-run, I promise you," said Ella. "It'll just be one more thing you have to beat. You think it makes you happy? You think it takes all your worries away? It doesn't. It can control you. It already does, look, you can't even give it up!"

"Why bother?" interrupted Ahmed sternly. "What else do we have? In your country, far from home and family. Locked up in this place, made to work like slaves for nothing. Everyone know we do ZeeZee. I hear them all talk. They say 'there go flower-eaters', 'addict scum'. Maybe they right, but we no care. ZeeZee take it away. ZeeZee make laugh, make sleep, make forget."

"You don't forget though, do you? You think about home every day. We all do. It's okay to be upset, to cry, to talk to each other about it. But instead you eat it or smoke it away in silence. You promised me you would stop, Ahmed."

"We promise for you. We try for you Ellie, but too hard. No more stop," said Mo sullenly.

"But you know what Governor Shade will do if he catches you!" said Ella close to tears.

"No matter," said Ahmed, with a stoical expression. "Is no matter."

"What will he do?" I asked in a whisper, feeling slightly out of the loop.

"He'll send them home," said Ella.

"Surely that's good, isn't it?" I thought aloud. Ahmed shot me a look of disdain.

"They're political refugees. If they go home they get tortured, at best," Ella told me discreetly.

"And at worst?" Everyone fired back the murderous looks which my stupid question deserved. I thought of something cleverer to say to fill the despondent silence. "Surely, the Governor and the wardens know that the flowers grow here though?"

"Yes."

"So why don't they just get rid of them?" I asked.

"Why would they?" Ella replied. "They keep the Service Users who eat them happy, unrebellious, docile. They'd prescribe them if they could. In fact they do. What do you think is in the Climbing Pills?"

"But they don't make me happy," I told her.

"It's not the same exact flower but they all come from the flowers, the pills they give us. They don't mind us taking it, as long as they can control it."

"So why send them home to die?"

"Why not?" replied Ella. "They're looking for any excuse they can get to send these guys back. They're just waiting for one of them to slip up so they can give their superiors a good reason to send them back. They don't want them here, filling up space, any more than the Normal people on the Island want them," she turned back towards the four men. "And you're giving them that excuse on a plate!"

"I try to stop. Really I do but is too hard. Cold sweat at night, the Earpiece just no stopping and my head go too funny," said Mo.

"I know, I know. The hallucinations, the tremors, the voices, it's awful but it gets better, I promise," Ella reassured him, hugging him tightly.

"You sound like you're speaking from experience," I remarked casually.

"I am," she replied, breaking from Mo to look at me. "I was an addict, I am an addict. You never stop being one. Everyone was doing it here when I first arrived. I was just a kid. I was scared, impressionable, it's no excuse I know."

"You don't have to explain yourself to me," I lied. I did want an explanation. She seemed so strong, so together, my image of her was shattered. "What made you stop?"

"More like who made me stop. It was Jack. He made me feel like I could be somebody without it. He helped me through the bad times, just like we'll help you guys," she turned her attention back to the "Flower-Eaters". "Won't we, Odis?"

"Yes. Of course we will," I smiled. Mo smiled back at me gingerly, the other three men looked far less impressed.

Ella pushed me out of the way, grabbed the cooked Ziziphusa flowers and threw them into the overgrown grass nearby. I was stunned into silence. Meanwhile the "Flower-Eaters" scurried to their feet, straightened out their overalls and stood to attention just as three henchmen, one leading that same beast that bit my arm, burst out of the woods and strode towards us. The two who were unimpeded by the creature approached us first and shoved us to the ground. I looked up and saw the third henchman press a device on his shoulder and mutter something. The henchmen searched Mo's and Khaled's pockets while kneeing them in the back and pushing their faces further into the ground.

"Hey!" Ella complained, rising to her feet. "The rules specifically state that excessive force should only be used when a Service User is being uncooperative!"

The brute searching Mo swivelled off him and swatted her to the floor with the back of his hand in one lethal movement. I jumped up and ran over to see if she was okay but the three-headed dog snapped and snarled towards me so I dropped back to the floor. Ella lifted her bloodied face off the ground and turned towards me, "I'm okay," she assured me. Each one of us was searched and then we waited in silence. It took Serky two, maybe three, minutes to arrive. She marched out of the woods and onto the scene, an unreadable expression on her face.

"Do you have any idea how embarrassing it was for me to receive a dispatch from a colleague informing me that six members of my own team have been found in a restricted zone?" she hissed. None of us responded.

"Well? Do you?"

"I would like to report that I have been assaulted Warden Se-" Ella managed to get out before she received a large boot to the small of her back.

"Assaulted? The only thing that has been assaulted here are our rules, my patience and the reputation of Team Recovery!" Serky responded.

"That's three things," I muttered under my breath. Serky eyed one of the henchmen, tilted her head in my direction and a fist came crashing down into the back of my skull.

"You may have been here a couple of months now, Winston, but I wouldn't feel too comfortable if I were you. Just what are you all doing here?"

"Nothing ma'am."

"Shut up Dietschy!" she roared. "Ali? Hassan? Bin Hamid? Well?"

"Like she says Mrs. We do nothing," Mo lied, badly.

"It doesn't smell like nothing. It smells to me like someone's been cooking up some flowers around here," Serky smiled, surveying our reactions. She motioned to the henchman with the creature. He pulled something from his pocket and held it to each of the three noses one-by-one so that they could all have a good sniff. The animal began to pull at its leash which the henchman proceeded to loosen. The beast tore away, noses to the ground, encircling the perimeter of where we were lying. Each head thought that it picked up the scent in different directions. It scurried around furiously caught in a three-way leadership struggle. It took a matter of seconds before it found the clutch of Ziziphusa flowers that Ella tossed into the field. The henchman pulled in the creature and handed the flowers to Serky.

"Hmmm, smells freshly steamed," she said raising it to her nose deliberately. "I'll remind you all that eating, inhaling and smoking this substance is prohibited. Anyone caught doing so will be punished accordingly. Now are any of you willing to tell me whose this is?"

Silence.

"Very novel of you," she smiled scornfully. "You four," she addressed the others. "Fantasy Island has offered you a safe haven from the evil despots who rule your countries. We gave you jobs, somewhere to live and you repaid us by being Weird yet still we didn't send you home. We have welcomed you here as if you were equal to an Islander and tried to teach you how to be Normal and enjoy our superior Island life. We have persevered in spite of your regrettable command of our language. After all we have given you, this is your gratitude. Well, I shall be informing Governor Shade immediately and I would presume that he will contact the Forced Immigration Authorities forthwith. Do you have anything to say for yourselves?"

Abdul and Khaled stood frozen still, their blank faces looking resigned to the next chapter in their miserable lives. Ahmed's face told a different story. His ears pricked back, his eyes bulged and his dark skin stretched over his cheekbones. Mo, the youngest of the four men, seemed incapable of anger. His expression was one of utter desolation.

"It's mine," I blurted out.

"Excuse me?" Serky looked intrigued.

"It's mine," I uttered in a calm voice after clearing my throat.

"Brave, Mr.Winston. Foolish, but brave nonetheless. Take him to The Pit!"

Chapter 15

I was blindfolded and hauled off by the henchmen. It brought back memories of when I was first taken well over a year earlier. The difference was, by then I knew of the horrors I might face and what my captors were capable of. Talk of The Pit could often be heard in the quarry or mess hall. Specifics were never mentioned, it was more the dread with which it was discussed. The wardens often used it as a threat. If they thought you were slacking off work or stealing food The Pit was all they needed to say and the Service User was back in line. We trudged through the compound in silence. I could feel the uneven ground and the snapping of twigs change to the sandy paths leading back to the main building.

"I don't care whether it was you or not, Mr. Winston, but if it wasn't you you're even more stupid than I thought," Serky said. "Sticking up for those flower-eating Outlanders! I wouldn't go playing the hero around here, it's been tried and failed before. A piece of advice: watch out for yourself and no-one else, because I can assure you that's what Dietschy, those stinking Outlanders and every other Service User here is doing."

I knew we had reached the main building because the muggy heat from outside suddenly turned to breezy air-conditioning. The only place in the compound with air-conditioning was the reception area of the main building where Tina could be heard chattering away, as usual. The reception area could conceivably be mistaken for a wholly respectable and humane establishment--carpeted floors, modern art and hanging chandeliers. Visitors could be duped into thinking that perhaps their loved one 'wasn't in such a bad place after all'.

The dizzying journey up a spiral staircase at first had me thinking I was being taken back to Solitary. But I counted the steps, remembering that it was 71 to Solitary, and we kept on until 95. As we approached step 71 a strange noise, one that I'd heard before, returned to my Earpiece. First the scattered radio signal, then the awful SCREECH which, as we went further and further up the stairs, was replaced by that same beautiful piano melody I remembered my mother playing when I was a child.

At stair 95 I was shoved from the staircase onto the floor. I heard the creaking of a door being opened then I was forcibly bent over and two hands gripped the scruff of my neck whilst another grabbed my feet from the floor. I was thrown forward like a torpedo. I didn't know if I would land on the floor or if my journey would be ended by a brick wall or maybe through an open window though I soon discovered my destination.

I landed chin first on solid stone but I didn't stop. I was descending quickly down some kind of ramp or slide, picking up pace all the time until I finally crash-landed in a heaped on solid ground. I scrambled onto all-fours and took off my blindfold only to find that my re-introduction to sight was something of an anti-climax. The Pit was almost as dark as being blindfolded.

"One month, Winston," Serky's voice echoed down the hole through which I entered. The hatch slammed shut and with it my only source of light was gone. I tried to stand up but smacked my head on the low ceiling and reflexively returned to all-fours. The smell of the place was revolting and made me gag almost instantly. Cautiously, I pawed around in the dark trying to work out the dimensions of my new home. When I sat on the floor and reached for the sky, my arms hit the ceiling without being fully extended, about the height of an eight-year-old child. I could lie down and stretch out my arms and legs without touching any walls. Overall, the area of The Pit was comparable to a chicken pen.

The ground was rock solid but the texture was dusty with some scattered pebbles and stones. I could feel the outlines of bricks in the walls and decided to crawl around to survey the whole space. Feeling around the edges I reached the second corner and the texture of the ground was different, it was softer and raised higher off the ground. When I put weight on my hands they slid down through a gooey substance, like leaving hand-prints in wet mud. The smell in this corner was even stronger and more pungent. I lifted my hands to my nose and instantly began to vomit furiously. I was covered up to the wrist in faeces.

I wiped my hands on the walls and on the floor away from the towering heap of excrement, whilst trying to withhold the geyser of vomit which was travelling up through my insides. I wiped and wiped but the walls and the floor didn't seem to be doing the trick. I slid back as far away from the corner as possible, shuffling back on my bottom to the diagonally opposite corner (which hadn't been used for a toilet). I carefully unzipped my jumpsuit using just my fingertips and pulled off my under-vest, careful to avoid touching my head. I used the vest to wipe my hands clean, as clean as possible.

There was a slight breeze blowing on the back of my neck so I turned around and crawled towards it. Feeling around in front of me, I traced the outline of the hole through which I'd entered. I felt inside the hole and the gradient of the chute I had slid down was extremely steep. The surface of the chute was slippery. It was solid rock but it had a glossy texture which allowed for very little traction. I attempted to climb up it on hands and feet like an ape but slid back down to the bottom after progressing only a few feet.

After many more attempts at this approach I tried another method. With hands and feet on either side of the concrete tunnel, I shuffled upwards, like a spider crawling up a pipe, and reached the top. The slide was at least three or four times the length of my body. At the top, I could see a small square of light - the outline of the hatch. The flat, solid metal of the hatch door was freezing cold. There was no handle, no window, nothing. I began to feel around the whole area haphazardly and my other hand lost its grip on the tunnel. I tumbled helplessly down the chute and landed back in The Pit.

After familiarising myself with The Pit I was filled with a strangely calm acceptance. At first I was alarmed by my lack of panic, 'why weren't the same thoughts running through my head? Wasn't I afraid any more? Had I become brutalised, de-sensitised?' Instead I began to think: 'What else can they do to me that they haven't already done?' I knew that what they wanted was a reaction. They wanted me to scream and shout for mercy- to break me. They wanted me to give up Ahmed and Mo and the rest.

The Earpiece began to blare out: "You're going to die down here," "Down where you belong with another great big pile of shit!" "And all for some grubby Outlanders, you really are a waste of space." I reached up calmly and yanked on the malevolent gadget, past when it hurt, past when I felt the blood pour down my hand and past when my flesh ripped and my ear was deformed. I held the Earpiece out in front of me. The voice carried on. It was speaking, but no longer had an ear to listen to it. The voice began to sound pathetic, weak and ridiculous. I knew it wasn't me, it was nothing to do with me. In the worst of prisons suddenly I had never felt so free. I threw the Earpiece into the corner of The Pit and heard it nestle in the heap of excrement. It was at that point that I knew I was going to get out of there. Out of The Pit and out of Sisyphusa.

Chapter 16

Life in The Pit was without day or night. I drifted in and out of sleep for what felt like hours. After a time, the hatch suddenly opened. I rushed to the hole and my eyes were blinded by the sudden burst of light. A torch shone down the chute.

"108?"

"Yes," I replied in a weak and cracked voice.

"Breakfast."

Something could be heard sliding down the chute and so I braced myself at the bottom hoping to catch whatever it was. A small crate rammed into my midriff and some water splashed up into my face. I felt around inside the crate. There was a small, nearly empty glass of water. I downed what was left immediately. There was also a chunk of hard, stale bread which I scoffed with equal fervour. That was it. I curled back up and fell asleep again.

Some time passed before I awoke again, this time with a sharp pain in my stomach: I needed to use the toilet! I unzipped my overalls, pulled down my underwear and tried to aim everything into the designated corner. I used my shirt again to wipe myself but realised that it wouldn't last anywhere near a month.

In my waking moments I thought of Layla. I tried to imagine where she was right at that moment. A year had passed. Had she forgotten about me? Had she found someone else? In the throes of my infatuation with her I had become a different person. My sense of identity was no longer anchored. Everything was expendable in the pursuit of my obsession. I lived my life to impress another. I suppose I should have just wanted her to be happy, but I didn't—I wanted her to feel pain. I don't know why I wanted her to be hurting. It was unfair that she would never love me the way I loved her. It might have been better if I had died. That way she and my family could move on and I wouldn't have had to suffer the ignominy of everyone knowing that I had become Weird.

The creaking of the hatch and the flash of the torch again woke me up. This time I heard something else slide down the chute.

"108!"

"Yes."

"Secure your tray to the hook." A rope, with a large piratical hook on its end, lay at the bottom of the chute. I fastened it to a metal ring on the side of the crate and it shot back up. It returned almost instantly with my bread and water and this time my dose of Climbing Pills.

I un-hooked the crate, the rope disappeared and the hatch slammed shut. Dinner. This would be my clock. I would stay awake between the breakfast tray and the dinner tray and I would sleep after dinner until breakfast the next morning. I would begin the same exercise regime I had done in the cell: sit-ups, press-ups, squat-thrusts (though the low ceiling prevented my jogging on the spot). I had a plan. 'Time to get back to sleep,' I thought. 'Must keep to the schedule.'

A moustachioed man from the East landed at the young man's feet. The man wore muslin slippers and silk robes with a snaking turban coiled around his head. The stranger summoned the young man forward and they took flight on his magic carpet. They swept over the sandy lands of Lydia, Aram and Babylonia. The Wide-eyed Wanderer felt the sea breeze blow through his hair. They were headed east to tour the lands of the Mauryan Empire.

A red fort took centre stage in a filthy metropolis. The people swarmed around in organised chaos on the streets pleading for a ride on the carpet. It broke the young man's heart that the carpet only had room for two. They shot east and saw a temple overrun by a kingdom of rats. The rodents killed each other and excreted whilst the people worshipped their holy acts. They sailed under the starlit night past a magical golden fort in the middle of the desert. It lit up like a beacon to usher in the ghosts of empires past.

They galloped on the camels down the mountains of the desert while the children screamed out words of an unknown tongue. He saw a city bathed in aquatic blue and rode elephants in the courtyard of a royal palace. They soared over a glistening, ivory tomb at sunrise and he brushed the minarets with his fingertips. He bid a dear farewell to his carpet-man and decided to guide himself the rest of the way. He lay on the praias of the Southwest, dipped into the ocean to race the dolphins then hopped north to the city of the Goddess Mumbadevi where he left through the Gateway Arch never to return.

Next he whizzed past in a magical tuk-tuk through the Land of Sad Smiles. He saw temples of gold, giant statues embossed with jewels and broad-shouldered ladies of the night in a smoggy, noisy city. As the sun set he sailed east to idyllic islands and joined the revellers as they worshipped the full moon in Saturnalian ecstasy.

He trekked through tropical jungles spotting exotic creatures along the way. The elusive tiger lay in the hidden depths of the vast rainforest stalking its prey. A trillion insects crawled under the leaves and the undergrowth. He brushed a giant spider off his arm. Above him he saw a macaque which looked him dolefully in the eye before it started to scrape its protruding bottom against the trunk of the tree. Scratch, scratch, scratch!

I awoke with a start. It had not been the opening of the hatch or a shining light which had woken me this time but instead a distant noise.

Scratch, scratch, scratch.

The Pit was at most times a silent home. The slightest noise would compel one's attention or disturb the most vivid of dreams. The sound was coming from the opposite side, parallel to the "toilet". It sounded like someone sanding a wall down.

Scratch, scratch, scratch.

I worried it could be rats scurrying around. I inched towards the noise cautiously. When I reached the corner I put my ear to the wall. The sound was definitely coming from the other side of the wall. It seemed to be getting louder.

SCRATCH, SCRATCH, SCRATCH.

I could hear dust starting to fall from the wall to the floor. Someone was trying to get in! I shuffled back to the other side of The Pit. I sat in the bottom of the chute, ready to climb up and bang on the hatch. More and more dust and pebbles could be heard trickling to the floor. CRASH. A whole brick smashed to the ground and a light shone through the oblong gap. I wasn't going to wait around to see whoever or whatever it was that was chiselling through that wall. I hastily began to make my way up the chute but all the time I could hear more bricks landing on the floor. CRASH, CRASH, CRASH.

I hurried and hurried, reaching around half way when I felt a sudden, excruciating pain in my backside. My bum went into paroxysms, my legs first straightened up then turned to jelly and lost their grip and I began to roll backwards, down the tunnel, landing on my back with a bump. I opened my eyes and looked up. Standing over me, wearing a helmet with a bright torch attached to it, was an upside-down woman in her late sixties holding a stun gun. The woman smiled, setting off a combination of wrinkles on her face. "Odis Winston?" she asked. "I'm here to help you escape. Now follow me!"

Chapter 17

We snaked through the passageway that the woman had dug. She steamed ahead of me, her speed and agility belying her advanced years- most women her age were already in Assisted Living Facilities (ALFs). The passageway was dank and tight-fitting. I pulled myself along by my elbows while drops of water fell on my head. The woman didn't speak a word or even make a sound. The torchlight from her helmet, the only thing which lighted the passage, edged further and further in front of me until eventually I was left in complete darkness. I kept on and eventually there was light ahead but not as bright as the torch.

I emerged from the tunnel into a small, cosy room. It was dimly lit by a shaded light-bulb on the low ceiling. The string next to the bulb was still swinging. The mysterious woman was dusting the dirt down from her clothes into the fireplace. The back of her overalls were marked with the large Sisyphusa motto- "Learning to be Normal Together." She turned around and faced me, her blue eyes glinting through perfectly round spectacles.

"Would you like a glass of water, Odis?" she asked as she motioned for me to stand up from the ground and sit in one of the two antiquated armchairs which sat facing each other in front of the fireplace.

"How do you know my name?" I asked without getting up from the floor.

"Oh, I know more than that, Odis Winston, aged 21 from Itticar, 2nd year student at South Coast University. Now, fizzy or still?" She stepped over a pile of books and some scattered papers to get to the sink in the corner of the room.

"How do you know all of that?"

"Patience, patience. All in good time, young man. First things first, do sit down and make yourself comfortable and let me get you a glass of water. Fizzy or still?"

"Still, please," I gave in. My preference for still water was a remnant of my childhood aversion to strong flavours. I always preferred juice to fizzy drinks, plain vanilla ice cream to

Sisyphusa

any more flamboyant concoction and a strawberry-flavoured toothpaste right up until my teenage years. I sat down.

"Good," she beamed. Her entire body relaxed and she appeared totally at ease. "Anything to eat? You must be famished with only that stale bread to eat."

"No, I'm fine, thank you. Wait a minute. How do you know what I've been eating?" I stood up sharply and banged my head on the ceiling. "You're one of them aren't you, a warden or something, I know you work for them I can tell by your uniform, tell me the truth!" I accused her loudly whilst rubbing the top of my head.

"Ah, the truth. That old scoundrel? Truth and happiness...the ultimate illusions. Calm down, calm down. Young men these days are so quick to fly off the handle. I said we'd get to all of that business in due course, but first can we not at least pretend to be civilised creatures just for the sake of decency?" she smiled plaintively, so I sat down. I could feel a bump forming on my head. "Thank you," she said with a genuine, serious expression. Then she turned back to what she was doing. "Yes, you must mind your head, I'm sorry for not warning you," she shouted over her shoulder. "I must say you are much better looking in person, though a young man does always look far more becoming with a shorn beard." She brought me a tall glass of water and a cheese sandwich which she had prepared without my even noticing. She sat down in the chair facing me.

"Thank you very much, Mrs.?" I said with an inflection prompting her to offer her name.

"Oh yes of course, how rude of me. Mrs.Orkle, but call me Gwen."

"Thank you Gwen. May I ask, where are we and *who* exactly are you?"

"We are in my home, Mr.Winston, and as I said I am Gwen. I know it's not much, but I feel I've made the best of a bad space. This here is the drawing room," she said proudly indicating the tiny area in which we sat, comprising the two armchairs, the fireplace and the mantelpiece on which sat an old-fashioned radio and some framed photographs. "Over there is the kitchen," she motioned behind her at the sink in the corner, a battered old fridge next to it which made a constant buzzing noise, a toaster oven and some cupboards, drawers, and countertops. "Over there is the W/C, the library and my bedroom," she finished, pointing to three doors each in different parts of the room. The floors were dark grey cement almost completely covered by assorted, un-matching rugs and carpets. There were books, magazines, and papers scattered haphazardly over every surface and spare inch of floor space, but conspicuously, there was no HDTV to be seen.

"Do you live here alone?"

"No, no. Goodness no. That would be miserable, wouldn't it? No, I have Libby and Bastian to keep me company. Libby! Basti!" She yelled. One of the doors she'd pointed to, the one which she called her library, was slightly ajar, and it creaked slowly open. Out poked two ginger cats who sauntered into the room and hopped onto their owner's lap.

"Do you like cats?"

"Yes," I lied. I still hadn't forgiven the species since the neighbours' cat ate my hamster when I was five.

"Well these are the friendliest you're ever likely to meet," she boasted as one silently scowled at me. "Anyway, time to go, kitties," she hastened them on their way and they landed perfectly on the carpet and sprawled out lazily in front of the fire.

"I'm sorry to keep on about it but I really would love to know what's going on. I mean one minute I'm holed up in some awful pit and the next I'm sitting with a nice old lady telling fireside stories. You'll forgive me for being slightly confused," I tried to force the issue.

"Yes, of course, dear. You've every right to be. I suppose I do owe you an explanation. The reason I know so much about you is..." she stood up, "follow me, would you?" She slid on a pair of maroon slippers and led me to the room which the cats came out of. Inside were three long bookshelves, each one entirely filled with books of varying size and colour. In the corner of the room was a desk filled with a panoply of electrical equipment: computers, speakers, keyboards, screens, a mouse and endless wires leading every which way. She walked to the desk, tapped a couple of keys and the largest screen flicked on. It was divided into four separate quadrants, each showing different feeds of live action, all happening inside Sisyphusa. One showed Service Users at work in the quarry, another showed the Practise Walls, one quadrant was black except for a small light in one corner and a strange silhouetted shape in another. The final quadrant pictured a birds-eye view of what looked like a girl sitting crying in a toilet cubicle. It was Ella.

"You're spying on us," I exclaimed indignantly.

"I'd prefer to call it looking out for you," she corrected me.

"That's Ella," I said to myself, walking closer to the screen and touching it with my fingertips.

"The poor girl misses you. Ah, to be young again and have so much life ahead of you, with the luxury to spend all one's time being miserable or finding new ways to court death just to feel alive. You have been getting rather close, the two of you, haven't you? You like her, don't you, please say you do?" she said clasping her hands, one on top of the other, to her heart with a dreamy expression on her face.

"Of course not. I mean, it's none of your business, shame on you watching us all suffer in there like we're contestants on Fantasy Factory. Aren't you a bit old to be behaving like a child?"

"Adults are merely older children, young man. Give them some Liquid Escape and send them to a family reunion and they will all regress into childish behaviours."

"How did you get these pictures anyway?"

"Oh I merely hacked into Sisyphusa's Main Security Network."

"What's that one there?" I asked pointing to the dark quadrant in the bottom left of the screen.

"Why that was you?"

"You've been watching me? You were watching me in that squalid pit for who knows how many hours?"

"And what would you suggest I do? Waltz in there and announce to the Governor and every warden and henchman that I'm getting you out of The Pit? No, I didn't think so. I had to time it in between your meal deliveries."

Then I realised. "But if you're watching The Pit then so are they, which means that they know I'm gone! They're going to find us," I said panicking and rushing towards the door.

"Wrong again, Dearie," she said calmly, not even raising her voice or looking away from the screen. I stopped short at the doorway and turned around. "They're watching this." She pressed another key and the picture in the bottom left corner changed, only slightly. The light from where she had chiselled through the wall had disappeared and a silhouette of a body, my body, appeared lying curled up in the foetal position. "I'm feeding them a video of you sleeping for the last few hours before I came through the wall. They'll be watching that until you go back in."

"Back in? I'm not going back in there."

"Yes you are, young man. Unless you want to give us away completely before we've even got started," I grudgingly accepted her logic.

"Started with what?" I asked her.

"Well, one can't stay in this place forever, can one?!"

Chapter 18

"Ouch!"

"Oh it can't hurt that much, you big softy," said Gwen as she washed my mangled ear. "You've really done a job on yourself here, young man."

"It was the only way to get rid of that bloody Earpiece. The thing was stapled through my ear," I replied.

"I know… I designed it not to be easily taken off," she stopped wiping my ear, stood back a pace and looked at it. "There we are. Much better."

"You designed it?"

"Yes dear, that was my job. 'The Inner Voice 3000' was what it was named in the end. I spent years perfecting the design. It's not a simple thing to fit a Neuro-Function Reading Mechanism into a device the size of a peanut you know?" she stated with pride.

"So you did work for them?"

"I'm afraid so," she smiled. "I was in the employ of the Sisyphusa Institution, in one capacity or another, for thirty-six years. I was a warden for a number of years before I was moved into the research field which had always been my ambition. I wanted to get to the root of what causes Weirdness." She paused to put down the towel she had used to wipe the blood from my ear then she wandered back over to sit in her armchair. "Both my mother and father were taken away to Normalisation camps when I was an adolescent and I never saw them again. It wasn't the same back then, you see. There was no visitation or Climbing Pills, no classes or Wall-Climbs. In those days you were taken and that was it. Locked up for life," she paused for a moment. "They were terribly scared of the effect Weirdness could have on the Normal population. They were not even certain yet that it was not contagious!"

"Contagious? But that's ridiculous!"

"To us *now* maybe. But it's unfair to judge the past by what we know in the present. Science, knowledge, progress…it's about accumulation. The wonderfully irritating thing about conventional wisdom is that it changes. We know the things we know now because of the mistakes and successes of those who have gone before us," she said the last sentence as though she'd had those exact same words spoken to her before.

"So what did you find out? Why am I Weird?" I asked with scepticism.

"Many studies, studies better-funded and more in-depth than my own, have asked that very same question: 'What causes Weirdness?' People have offered very different theories. One thing most learned people agree on is that it involves a certain chemical in the brain, which is why the treatment of what we call 'Climbing Pills' is widespread.

Other than that, the ideas range across the spectrum. Some say it is hereditary and that all families carrying the 'Weird Gene' should be exterminated or at the very least carriers should be sterilised. You can imagine my disagreements with the proponents of this theory. Others say its more social- mere laziness or fraud brought on by an indulgent society. Initially, I wanted answers for myself, but when I saw the way this place, and others like it, operated I wanted to change attitudes towards Weirdness and the treatment of Service Users. I believed that the best way to do this was from the inside so I worked my way up into a research position. If I could prove that Weirdness was not simple laziness or a genetically predestined weakness then perhaps I could change people's approach to Weirdness on Fantasy Island, maybe even throughout the Empire."

"And did you?"

"Did I what, Mr.Winston?"

"Did you find out what causes Weirdness? Why I'm here?"

"I think you'll discover in time that there is no *one* answer for the two questions which you've asked me. However, time is something of a luxury to us at the moment. If you are not back in that hole before the guard delivers your dinner, our plan is somewhat foiled before we've even got to work!"

"What is this plan?" I said in frustration. "I won't go back in there until I get some more answers. Why should I trust you?"

"A fair question indeed," she remarked rising from her seat to pick up one of the identical cats who had ambled back into the room. She sat back down with the cat on her lap, stroking the nape of its neck. "Since I've been watching you on camera, you've struck me as being something of a man of reason. Would you agree?"

"I guess," I answered hoping she'd get to the point.

"Good. Now let's approach your current position from a rational perspective. You have been kidnapped against your will, kept in intolerable conditions, forced into performing back-breaking tasks on a daily basis and if you do not comply with these conditions you are punished brutally. Am I painting an accurate picture thus far?"

"Yes."

"Yet today you met me. I have spirited you away from an undesirable abode, fed you, cleaned your wound and engaged you in a civilised conversation. Still accurate?"

"I suppose so."

"Excellent. Now, from a rational standpoint, in comparison to your experiences of the last year would it not be more prudent for you to take some advice from me? Follow some guidance? Perhaps visit me again? I am not asking that you throw all of your trust behind me instantly, such a request would be *un*reasonable. However, with you being a man of reason, I hope you will accept that were you to, say, adopt a 'trial period' of trust, it would surely be in your best interests." She sat back in her chair, indicating her offer had been extended and that it was my turn to respond. I mulled over what she had said in my head. It was clear she hadn't told me the whole story, yet it was equally clear that she had no intention of doing so.

"I accept."

"Marvellous. Now as I said, time is of the essence. You're going back into The Pit. But first you will need some things. For starters," she stood up and waddled purposefully into a room from which she quickly emerged handing me two small ear-plugs. "For your nose!" she said motioning that I was to stuff a plug up each nostril.

"Thank you," I smiled politely.

"But, more importantly, this," she reached into the pocket of her overalls and brandished a brand new Earpiece.

"No way, not another one," I backed off defensively.

"Worry not. It looks the same, but has an entirely ulterior function. This *is* an Earpiece, but, unlike the other one, which was designed to read and provide a voice for your polar subconscious, this one," she said holding up an identical-looking gadget, "is simply a communication device so that I can speak into your ear. I need to tell you what position to get into in order to match you up to the feed I've been giving them. Also I can tell you when it's safe for you to come back here after your morning bread is delivered tomorrow. Here, try it." She handed it to me and walked into her library. "Stay there."

After a few seconds, a buzzing noise signalled that it was on and I heard her voice speaking into my ear. "Hello, this is Sisyphusa Radio," she announced in a naff Mainland accent. She walked back into the room, still giggling at herself, "Will you wear it?"

"Okay," I agreed tentatively.

"Good, it's important that you do." She took it from me and secured it into my wounded right ear with transparent tape instead of the bolts. "Sorry but it's important that we put it on the same ear in case they notice that it's suddenly changed to your left. Plus it will cover up the cuts on your ear."

"Fine," I said grimacing as she fastened it somewhat roughly. "So you were going to switch my Earpiece all along? If I waited a little longer I wouldn't have even needed to rip it out?"

"I'm afraid so," she said as she showed me a contraption she had invented solely for the painless removal of Earpieces.

"Bollocks," I said to myself wistfully.

"If you're ready, it's time that you left," she said rhetorically as she rushed me towards the hole. "Now you must pile the bricks back up so that the wall appears un-penetrated on their security cameras. I will be watching you."

"Thank you...for everything," I said with my head already in the tunnel.

"You're quite welcome," she assured me.

I followed the damp, claustrophobic tunnel preparing myself to return to its final destination. When I reached The Pit, I crawled over the assortment of bricks around the hole which Gwen had created. The smell of the faeces assaulted me instantly and I reached for the ear-plugs and thrust them, one at a time, up each of my nostrils, I was already getting used to breathing exclusively through my mouth. I sat there for some minutes, re-arranging the bricks back into the wall, while every now and again Gwen would order me through the Earpiece to "move that a little forward" or "no, that doesn't look right."

After my re-creation met her standards she advised me where to lie and in exactly what position, until the guard called me for the dinner delivery. I lay there curled up like a baby, my nose stuffed full of polystyrene thinking back in disbelief over what had just occurred. And then I heard a piano begin to play in my Earpiece. It was that same song which my mother used to play.

Chapter 19

I was awoken once again by the sound of a guard bellowing my Service User number through the hatch in a dull monotone. I instinctively answered, still half-asleep. The bread and water slid down the chute and landed on the ground in front of me. This time the container of water had toppled over completely, its contents spilling over the ground, spreading out in all directions and seeping into the cold surface. The rope slid down. It took another impatient shout from the guard to remind me to attach the crate to the hook so that it could be pulled back up. The hatch closed and darkness returned. I held the rock hard chunk of bread in my hand and deliberated as to whether I was hungry enough to put my teeth through the torment of actually eating it, then:

"No need to eat that rubbish. I'll rustle you up something fresh," a perky voice announced in my right ear. "Just leave it to one side and lie down where I told you to yesterday." I followed her directions. "A little closer to the wall, dear, and don't curl up so tight... a little more to the left...perfect... I've replaced the feed. You're free to come on through."

I took out just eight or nine bricks and piled them neatly to the side in formation so that I could re-place them easily on my return. I squeezed back through the passageway and reached the opening into the living room where Gwen greeted me with a hospitable smile.

"Welcome back. How did you sleep?" she asked as she helped me to my feet and began dusting dirt from my shoulder.

"Not too bad, I suppose, thank you." I replied suddenly realising I still had two bulging ear-plugs protruding from my nostrils and discreetly removing them.

"Your back must be aching. Won't you sit down and I'll get you some water. Fizzy or still?"

"Still, please," I wanted to politely refuse but I was so thirsty.

She fetched us a glass each and we sat down in the two moth-eaten armchairs. "How do you manage to bring in your supplies?" I asked her after a few seconds of silence had passed.

"The furniture and appliances, they were already here. As for the food and drink, I mostly sneak bottled water and sandwiches from the kitchens in the middle of the night when the staff have all gone home. It's only those ogres who are on patrol at night and those knuckle-draggers are simple enough to evade. If there are things which I need from outside the compound I will go on a midnight run every few months. I've garnered a few tricks over the years."

"So what was this place before you lived here? How haven't they found you?" I asked.

"The short answer is: because they don't know that this place exists," I stared at her. "I guess you want the long answer then!" she cleared her throat with a gentle cough. "I managed to persuade a previous Governor to let me use the old library as a research station for my team--hence the plumbing, electricity and fireplace which I no longer use. We would stay holed up here for weeks at a time and even sleep here. After a regime change, the next governor wasn't so keen on research and he decided to shut the project down. As no-one was interested in using the library any more, this place was left abandoned. Over the years, the Institution switched from Governor to Governor, came under ever-changing government departments. So many staff came and went that eventually I was the only person left who even knew that this place existed. All I had to do was sneak back in one night, plaster over the only entrance so that it looked like a blank wall and dig out the passageway from The Pit."

"And you've been here ever since?"

"Ever since."

A beeping noise emanated from the other room. Gwen got up and excused herself.

"What is it? What's that noise?" I asked.

"Come and see if you'd like," she said in a sober voice. She sat down at the desk and pressed some buttons on the keyboard. Instantly the screens which had been showing various different feeds all synchronised to show the same one. A young boy of nine or ten with closely cropped-hair was getting up from the floor. He was in a cell which looked identical to the one in which I had spent most of my first year in Sisyphusa. The boy sat down on a tattered couch and examined his knee which appeared to be badly grazed. It was hard to know for sure but I think he was crying. He looked around the room, studying its layout – it was clear that he'd never been there before.

"A new arrival," said Gwen without taking her eyes off the centre screen.

"But he's so young," I said.

"Yes, they're getting younger and younger," she replied as if she wasn't the slightest bit surprised. "I'm just going to watch him for a few moments, I hope you don't mind. I have to take notes and open a new file. Make yourself at home and we'll talk in a few moments." She assumed a business-like manner and began scribbling some notes onto a pad.

"Okay," I agreed. I sensed she didn't want me watching over her shoulder while she was writing. I turned and wandered towards the back of the room. The Library was much larger than the living room but was almost completely filled with the three towering bookshelves. The ceiling was much higher and the lights far brighter. There was a low humming noise coming from all of the electrical equipment in the corner. I moved slowly down the aisle between the first two bookshelves perusing the ancient-looking, dust-covered books which reminded me of my Grandpa Abe.

My mind returned to the little boy crying in the cell. I wished that I could prepare him for what he was to endure. I thought back to my own arrival and the shock which had lasted for months. 'How much worse must it be for someone half my age?' I peered through the gap between the tops of the books and the shelf above and saw Gwen still scribbling furiously, stopping only to take quick looks at the boy on the screen. I wondered what she had been writing about me when I first arrived. It made me feel uncomfortable thinking about her watching me in such pain for all of those days. 'And she does nothing to stop it. Nothing to help anyone. She just sits there watching all of us, taking notes.'

I felt myself getting angry and decided to take one of the books off the shelf to distract myself. I hadn't read anything since University and even then I wasn't exactly avid. I picked a book at random, a medium-sized red book which, unlike the others, had no title or author on its binding. I sat down on the floor with my chosen book. The cover was coated in a thick layer of dust. I blew it off, though most of it seemed to fly up into my eyes and my nostrils. I managed to fend off a sneeze and wiped my eyes. On the cover was written in a plain black text: "The Travelling Man." There was no mention of an author. I flicked through the book and was surprised to find that it had no pictures to speak of. It seemed to be just hundreds and hundreds of pages of miniscule text. I flipped back to the beginning of the book and opened to the first page. In large bold lettering it read: 'Hereafter tells the tale of the many travels and adventures to the furthest reaches of the globe of Captain Quick, latterly remembered affectionately as The Travelling Man.'

On the next page began Chapter 1. I read on, entranced by the recounting of young Quick's formative years. Whilst his parents tried to usher him into his father's profession he evinced a certain adventurous spirit early on. He left home at seventeen for the big city from where he planned to embark for 'The World and beyond'. Chapter 2 saw him shipwrecked and tantalisingly close to death at such an early stage of the tale. Chapter 3 told of the strange lands in which he found himself meeting fantastical new characters and creatures at each turn of the page.

"What's that one then?" asked Gwen standing over me. I hadn't even noticed her approach.

"The Travelling Man," I told her, closing the book and standing up to put it back on the shelf.

"Oh yes! I love that one. Has he met the Google-oo people yet? They're my favourites, 'Google-oo, Google-oo, what shall we do to you'," she recited, laughing to herself.

"Not yet, no," I smiled, trying to hide my resentment of having plot developments revealed ahead of time.

"Oh, they're brilliant," she smiled nostalgically. "Feel free to carry on reading it."

"No, that's fine," I said, placing it back into its space on the shelf. "I'm not much of a reader. It seems like you are though," I indicated the abundant books.

"Oh, yes, I love to read. But I've run out of new books to read so I just read all of them again."

"You mean you've read every book in this room?"

"Yes," she remarked casually.

"But there must be hundreds!"

"One thousand and one to be exact! They're all very old as you may have noticed, though age has no bearing on quality, does it?" she winked at me. "Now let me see." She kicked a stool out from under the bottom shelf, stood on it and began tracing along the line of books with her index finger pressing her eyes right up to the books to read their titles. "This is the Classics shelf. Behind me is the History shelf and the back shelf is Science and Medicine. Ah!" she exclaimed. She had snatched a huge book from the shelf and swivelled around to face me. "Señor Queso, you must have read this?"

I stared at her blankly.

"Oh well you simply must," she handed it to me and my arms instantly felt its considerable weight. She turned back to the shelf and continued looking. "Hmmm, no, no, no, no, no, no, no, yes! The Arraignment. Now this you must have read?"

I shook my head.

"Honestly. I thought you went to university?"

"I did," I professed.

"Well, what did they have you reading?"

"Business, Economics, Computing, Management, Marketing, lots of things."

"Not that garbage. I mean real reading! Fiction, the Classics, Poetry, History, Philosophy...*Real* reading!"

"They didn't do that in my university."

She stared at me in shock. "Well, that will have to change, won't it?!" She plonked the second book on top of the one I was already holding.

"What do you mean?" I asked.

"I mean welcome back to school, Mr. Winston," she grabbed another book and plopped it on to the top of my growing pile, it was entitled 'Pestilence.'

"What are all of these books about anyway?"

She turned to face me slowly. "These *books* are about love, they are about passion, they are about pain and grief and war and adventure and death. These *books* are about *Life*, Mr. Winston." She inhaled.

"Oh…that's why they're all so long."

She turned back around and proceeded to pass me book after book over her head which I then began to arrange in piles on the floor. Books of every colour, shape and size were ferried to me over her head as she seemed determined to have me read all one thousand and one of them.

Finally, after three huge piles had been constructed, she stepped down from her stool. I smiled at her in relief. She smiled back. Then she kicked the stool across the floor until it stopped just before hitting the second shelf. My heart sank.

"Now for history!"

Four more piles of history books, anthropology books and medical journals about Weirdness then materialised before she was finally satisfied.

"I think that ought to suffice," she said sighing from her exertions.

I looked at the myriad books she intended for me to read and was sure that such a task was impossible to complete in a year, never mind in the time before I had to return to Sisyphusa.

My eyes drifted back to the first shelf. "One more," I said as I reached up and grabbed the medium-sized red book without a title on its binding and placed it on top of the highest pile.

Chapter 20

For three and a half weeks I did nothing but immerse myself in my reading list. I would rush through the passage every morning and barely stop for meal breaks with Gwen. I was determined to work my way through those thousand and one books, it became my sole purpose in life for those weeks, the only thing that kept me alive. Knowledge was no longer a party trick to pull out and impress people with in a Liquidiser. I'd decided it had to become an essential part of my life, a loving pursuit to be nurtured and improved. I became so obsessed with devouring every book that notching each new one up became more important than analysing or enjoying them.

I loved to mix up the order of what I read. One day I would read a novel such as the one I read after I finished 'The Travelling Man'. It was about a magical family who lived in a village deep in the jungle for generations. Whilst they lived and loved and fought and died and everything around them changed, oddly some things never changed. Other days I would veer off in a different direction and read epic accounts of history. I read things about the Frontier Empire which I had never known. It hadn't always been the Frontier Empire, it used to be Fantasy Empire. Our tiny island had owned the entire world, even the Frontier Mainland.

I learnt two crucial mistakes that I and many people on the Island made. The first was accepting that what had happened before and what was going to happen in the future were inevitable and timeless truths not to be questioned. The second was assuming that because we were in the present day that automatically made us smarter, better and wiser than all who had gone before us. The more I read the more I remembered what Grandpa Abe had always said to me since I was a small boy: "Remember, Kiddo, history isn't linear, it's cyclical and the two worst things in this world are greed and tribalism." Finally I began to understand.

I read a book named "Burning Point" about a society where the powerful few forbid the downtrodden many from reading books and instead they burned them all. The people were tranquilised with wall-to-wall screens and drugs. Gwen told me that it was written a long, long time ago, but I was convinced the author must have lived on Fantasy Island.

Every evening after I had finished reading I would sit down with Gwen and discuss the book I'd been reading. First she would insist on getting me a glass of water and also insisted on asking "Fizzy or Still?" even though I always answered still. She explained things I didn't understand or I had missed altogether. I loaded pressure onto my mind to remember all of the important things I was learning. I thought I had to catalogue every word of every sentence of every book, as if there was going to be a mammoth test on life at some unspecified time in the future that I dared not fail. By the end of the three and a half weeks my view of the world had changed utterly.

"I think you're beginning to see, aren't you?" said Gwen.

I nodded but stayed silent. Thoughts raced around my head. I began to wonder how I couldn't have seen it before. I had gone from being accepting in the extreme to questioning in the extreme. Once I began to question life, those questions had become infinite and overwhelming. Why hadn't my family told me about the important things that were in these books? I started to chastise my former self, vilifying him for being so simple and naïve. It was as if I had become my own Earpiece. Gwen saw that I was churning thoughts over and over in my head and so she interrupted:

"Don't beat yourself up. I was only a little younger than you when I realised."

"Eighteen months ago, the world was such a small and simple place for me, I thought I had it all worked out. Back then, I was free, much freer than I am now anyway. I could move around the Island at will, buy what I wanted, talk to whomever I liked, drink as much Liquid Escape as my body would let me. I could even travel across the Empire with my family to see my Grandparents over on the Mainland or visit the Outlands and their quaint habits. I had the world at my feet and yet I thought it was simple. Now, I've been locked up for a year with nothing but my mind, an Earpiece and now you and these books for company. My freedom has been taken from me and

I'm totally isolated and yet somehow I feel I know more about the world than I ever did when I was a part of it all. Oh, I'm talking in circles!"

"No you aren't," Gwen reassured me. "You are making perfect sense, young man. You have learnt a lot in a very short space of time which suggests to me that you knew a lot more already than you thought you did. This world of ours is infinitely large and fiendishly complicated. The ironic thing, however, is that once you come to read and learn more about it, all you realise is quite how much more there is to learn and quite how impossible it is to know everything. It's queer to think that one needs to read quite so many books to realise that one knows nothing."

"I once read somewhere, 'We're all ignorant. Some are just more ignorant than others'. When you get to my age you discover that the trick is not to know everything but rather to be at peace with not knowing. You must always beware of those who claim to know it all, young man, invariably they will know the least. We have always had idiots in the world, the difference now is the extent to which we are forced to listen to them and how celebrated some of them are for everything that they say or do. Time was when power was simply held through violence or the threat of violence. Then force of personality was added to the cocktail to make subjugation taste nicer. There was a brief window of time when novel things like laws, qualifications, expertise, experience and legitimacy were given some import but I am afraid that the poisons of money and fame have seeped into every last particle of this Island."

"I went to university shortly after my parents were taken away. Of course that was before the Education System was completely privatised so they still taught some real subjects. I read and I read, and the more I learned the more it terrified me but once I'd started I couldn't stop. That was when I decided to study Weirdness. A few years after finishing university I came to work here, as I've already told you. And to my eternal shame I believed what I had been taught about Weirdness and I have contributed to much of the Institution which I now so abhor."

"Why?" I asked softly. "Why did you want to work here and do what they do? Why would you invent the Earpiece?"

"I ask myself that same question often, Odis," she looked me straight in the eye when she used my first name. "I believed that this was the way to help people. I knew how much I had suffered when my parents were taken. I wanted to stop that from happening to others. I helped to introduce Climbing Practice and Climbing Pills and Senior Reps Council- things which made Normal society's treatment of Weirdness more humane, things which gave more hope and purpose to Service Users, a little society of their own. A hundred years ago Normal people would pay to come into places like this to watch Weird people for entertainment, did you know that? If you were put in here, that was it, you were in for life. But science helped to change that. We told society that Weirdness is an illness, one that can be cured with pills and exercise and education. But later I realised we were wrong."

"What do you mean?"

"I mean we were wrong. It's rubbish. It's all rubbish. You are not Weird. At least not any more Weird than I am. There's no such thing as Weird, or more accurately there's no such thing as Normal. The Empire has everyone convinced that they are Normal, unless they are Weird or an Outlander. So if you do not fit in you must be hidden away, excluded, locked up, shunned, even laughed at and pelted with stones. It isn't true, it's all to make them feel better, to justify their own Normality and to cement their own status at the top of society. Whatever eccentricity or imbalance some Service Users here may have is vastly enhanced by the way we degrade and lampoon them in our society. 'Service Users'. That's a joke in itself. This is no service. Service Users are not here to 'consume Normality.' This is a prison and whatever you want to call the people imprisoned here will not change the fact that they are prisoners."

"So what can we do about it?" I asked as I could feel the anger boiling up inside of me.

"We can fight back," she replied.

"But how? They're too strong,"

"Hogwash. You've read your history now. No Empire has lasted forever. What happens at the end of 'Burning Point'?" she prodded.

"He meets the group who have memorised the forbidden books. The city burns around them and it's the memorisers who will carry the lessons forward for the next generation," I remembered.

"Right. Your job will be to teach others just as it's my job to teach you. But first this wretched building must burn. And I need you to help me do it," her stare penetrated through my eyes.

"Why me?" I asked, fearful of holding any position of responsibility.

"I've been waiting a long time for you to come along, Odis Winston. I cannot do this alone. I need someone on the inside, a Service User. I need you to be my legs. I will be able to see you on camera and talk to you through your new Earpiece, but it's you who must save the others and escape from this building. I've been watching you for over a year now. I've seen your will-power and stubborn determination in assiduously punishing your body through exercise and quarry-work despite the side effects of the Climbing Pills. I've seen your bravery in sacrificing yourself for those men who were caught flower-eating. Not many of us would do that for people we barely know. And finally, I've seen you read and learn and grow more in a month than I have in 40 years. You might not know it, young man, but there is something slightly special about you."

"Me? You must be joking. I'm as Normal as it gets," I replied. She smiled at me with one raised eyebrow and I suddenly realised the irony of what I had just said.

"Well, not 'Normal' in that sense but well... you know."

"We'll agree to disagree on that then. But are you willing to help me?"

I paused before answering. "Maybe if I just kept my head down and worked on my climbing I could get out of here that way? I just don't want any more trouble than I already have..."

"And what if you do make it over the wall, what then? You're on their files, you'll be back here within a year or two. How many times has your little friend been back here?" she asked.

I assumed she was referring to Harry. I thought back to when he and the Simon sisters were all telling me how many different times they had been taken.

"You don't have to spend your life here. None of you do. I know you care about some of the people here. You can help them to escape. *We* can help them."

"What then? What's the difference which way we escape? You said it yourself, they have me on file. They have all of us on file and they'd find us all again," I argued.

"Very sharp. I thought of that little problem too. That's where you come in. All of your files are part of the System Database which has every current, previous and even some future Service Users throughout Fantasy Island. This database can be accessed by any person with an employee password."

"You used to work here," I interrupted excitedly. "You must have a password. Why don't you just erase every Service Users' details from the database?"

"If only it were that simple. When they retired me they invalidated my old password. Getting access to the database isn't the problem anyway. I managed to hack into their system undetected years ago. Since then I've managed to hack into every security level apart from the top one. That's how I have all of the camera feeds and how I know so much about all of you."

"And only people with a top-level security password can erase Service User files completely?"

"Exactly."

"You said that's where I come in. What can I do? I don't know how to hack into a security database!"

"The only person in this building with top-level security access is…"

"Governor Shade."

"Got it in one. Somehow you're going to have to get that password and then we're in the clear. I'll delete every Service User file in Sisyphusa and you can all escape. Once everyone's out they can mix back in with the rest of the Island or leave the Island altogether, maybe even leave the Empire if you like. And we can burn this building to the ground."

"Aren't you forgetting something?"

"I don't think so." said Gwen.

"The little matter of the Governor, the wardens and, let me see, who am I forgetting? Oh yes… an army of 7ft henchmen and their hungry pets!"

"Oh don't worry about all of that. We'll cross that bridge when we come to it," she answered with a confident wink.

The way she put it made it sound like I didn't have much choice. "Okay, I suppose I'm in," I conceded with a distinct lack of gusto.

"Excellent!" she exclaimed as she shot to her feet. "Let's go in the other room. There's work to do."

I followed her into the library. She opened a drawer and handed me a tiny gadget.

"This is your microphone. Attach it by this clip to the underside of the collar of your Sisyphusa overalls each morning."

"What, you're going to listen to everything I say and everything anyone says to me?"

"It's imperative for the plan."

"No, I refuse. I need to have some moments when there isn't someone watching me or listening to me or berating me through an Earpiece."

"Okay," she said opening another drawer. "This one has an off switch," she smiled as she handed me a different microphone.

That was to be the only time that I had ever made Gwen climb down from a position she had taken. She sat down in front of the large central screen as I stood behind watching. She tapped a few keys and up popped my Island Identification Card photograph.

"This is their file on you," said Gwen.

I began reading the information on the screen:

Name: *Odis Ian Winston*
Age: *21yrs*
Last Known Address: *67 Cossetts Lane, Sector 19, Quadrant C.*
Profession: *Student*

Next of Kin: *Louis and Antonia Winston*
Address: 9 *George Street, Sector 17, Quadrant C.*
Weirdness Grade: *2*
Team: *Recovery*
Team Leader: *Warden Serky*
Current Status: *The Pit*
Minimum Sentence before 1ˢᵗ Wall-Climb Attempt: *7*
years

"Seven years!"

"That's not right," Gwen said as she began flicking through her notebook. She found the page which she'd written my details on. "That's changed. When you were first allowed out of Solitary they entered four years as the minimum sentence. They must have increased it since you were put in The Pit."

"I can't stay in here for seven more years, I'd rather die."

"I'm almost certain that won't be necessary," she smiled. "If we do things my way everyone can leave and never have to come back. Now let me just check something here..." She began browsing through the database. Different files kept on flashing onto the screen. I think I even saw a photo of Harry sporting a Mohican haircut flash up briefly on the screen. My gaze drifted away from the flashing central screen. I scanned the other screens which were showing feeds of live action. I saw Service Users talking in their bunk-beds in the living quarters on one screen. Another screen was a bathroom which had no-one in it. A third showed the huge warehouse with the Practise Climbing Wall which was also completely empty. My vision was then attracted by something moving on the screen in the bottom right-hand corner. It showed a woman walking down a corridor. She opened a door and stopped in front of the wall. She was trailed by a dawdling henchman. It was Serky.

"Where's that?" I asked Gwen.

"What?" she turned her head. "I can't see. What screen are you looking at?"

"Number 9," I read the sticker below the screen. She pressed the number 9 on the keyboard and Serky appeared on the large central screen. She pressed another button.

"Mr. Winston," Serky's voice blared through the speaker below the central screen.

"Shit!" I shouted and began running into the other room.

"Wait!" Gwen commanded. "Have you got your Earpiece and microphone?"

"Yes," I turned and replied.

"Okay," she smiled. "Good luck. I'll be in touch."

I leapt into the tunnel and began scraping and sliding through the mud being sure to dirty up my clothes and my face so I appeared as if I'd been in The Pit the whole time. I could hear her voice screaming my name.

"Mr. Winston, I suggest you wake up!" Serky bellowed. "Unless of course you'd like to stay another month?"

I reached the hole and crawled through.

"Don't forget to replace the bricks," Gwen's voice whispered through the Earpiece.

I placed the bricks silently into formation, filling the hole in the wall.

"Very well," Serky's voice reverberated down the chute. "Another month it is."

"NO!" I croaked. I coughed and cleared my throat acting as if I'd just woken up. "I'm here!" I shouted up through the chute. Silence. Had she left? The hook which they'd used each day to pull up my meal tray came crashing down the chute and landed on the floor at the bottom.

"Grab the hook and you'll be pulled up," said Serky.

I picked up the hook, gripped it tightly and lay on my back in the chute with my head facing towards the top. I was dragged upwards. When I reached the open hatch a henchman lifted me up and flung me out by the scruff of my neck. I landed face down on the floor.

"Welcome back to the land of the living, Mr. Winston," said Serky. I lifted my head a few inches from the floor and saw a pair of perfectly polished black shoes right in front of my nose. "I trust we've seen the last act of heroism from you."

"Yes, Warden Serky."

"Good. Now get up. Go and wash yourself, you're filthy."

"Yes, warden," I couldn't help but smile as I walked behind her turned back. An I-Spy tracked us as we walked down the corridor. I stared into the lens and winked.

"No more looking into the cameras," whispered Gwen. "I'm watching you!"

Chapter 21

Everybody turned to face me as I entered the Team Recovery dormitory.

"Odis!" they all shouted.

"Hi," I replied bashfully. Harry ran up to me first and hugged me tightly. A tuft of his hair tickled me under the chin.

"Welcome home 108!" he said as he slapped me on the shoulder. "Phwooaa, you stink, mate, that Pit is a real shit 'ole innit!"

"Yeah," I blushed as I thought of a room full of people knowing that I'd been sleeping in my own waste for a month. Ella approached me through the crowd and went to hug me but I pulled back worried about the smell. She noticed my hesitation and rubbed my arm instead.

"How are you?" she asked.

"I'm okay," I smiled.

"You must feel awful. It's barbaric that they're still using that place as a punishment in this day and age. We've been lobbying to have it outlawed in the Council for years but the regime overturn it every time. They claim it's the most effective deterrent against insubordination."

"Well it's certainly that!" I assured her. "I'll think twice before crossing Serky again, that's for sure."

"Mr. Odis!" Mo interrupted almost shoving Ella to one side. "You okay!" he came and hugged me as Ella receded into the background. Ahmed was behind him as were Khaled and Abdul. "How can we ever pay you back, Mr. Odis?" said Ahmed extending his hand in gratitude.

"No, please. There's really no need. It was an easy choice. It wouldn't be right for them to send you home to certain death. Anyone would have done the same thing in my position," I assured them.

"No!" Ahmed gripped my hand tightly and fired a bloodshot gaze right into my eyes. "What you did for us was very, very brave. We are in your debt. One day we hope we can somehow pay you back," he finally relinquished his hold on my hand.

"Yes, Yes," agreed the other three men.

"Really, there's no need, so long as there's no more flower-eating from now on?"

"No more," Ahmed replied.

The Simons were all on the same top bunk. Stacey was sitting in front with her legs dangling over the side. Gracie kneeled behind her brushing Stacey's greying blonde hair while Tracey stood up in the background folding strands of Gracie's hair into tin foil.

"Hiya Otis," they screeched in chorus.

"Hello ladies," I ignored their continued failure to learn my real name. "You're all looking very sharp," I said only realising afterwards that "sharp" was a compliment an 80-year-old would use.

"Ooooh, thank you very much," Tracey replied. "You hear that girls? Finally our efforts don't go unnoticed." The sisters cackled feverishly.

"Welcome home, Mr. Winston," Gloria said in a very serious voice. "You'll be pleased to know that I have saved my notes from the Normalisation Classes you've missed and the quota for the quarry work has been fulfilled during your absence."

"Thank you very much, Gloria." I could see in the far corner of the room that the only person who hadn't joined the welcoming party was Mr. Femuz. The huge man was sitting on his bottom bunk with his shoulders hunched over.

As the gathering around me began to disperse I took the opportunity to go and wash myself and put on a fresh set of overalls which were kept in various storerooms in the corridor outside of the dormitory. I returned to the room and went to my bunk where I found Harry and Ella sitting on my bed. I sat down on the floor beside the bed.

"What day is it today?" I asked them.

"Sunday," Ella replied.

"They let you back just in time to start working again tomorrow," added Harry.

"What's on the agenda for tomorrow then?"

"Normalisation as usual in the morning, then climbing, then after lunch it's back in the quarry. Word is there's a new order," Harry informed me.

"Has there always been quarry work here?" I asked.

"Ever since I arrived," Harry answered.

"There wasn't any when I first came," said Ella. "The physical labour was different back then. It was on a much smaller scale. There used to be patches of agricultural land on the main site just like the clearing near the cemetery. Service Users would work the land. It was mostly vegetables. You know: carrots, potatoes, cabbage, that sort of thing. Oh, and there used to be some fruit in the summer. We had gorgeous apples and strawberries. All of the food would be used to feed the Service Users and staff back then, not like now when all of the work we do is for outside contracts," she finished.

"So when did it all change?" I prodded.

"That was when Governor Shade arrived. He said that Sisyphusa had to be run more like a business." She sat up straight and mimicked a dull, nasal voice and circled her thumbs and index fingers around her eyes to signify spectacles. "'This institution has become unprofitable and utterly unsustainable!' That's when we were made to rip up the land and Governor Shade started to receive contracts via the government from the Empire Mainland."

"I've never seen Governor Shade before. Well, except for once when I first arrived. His face appeared on my HDTV screen in my cell," I said.

"Oh what 'Welcome to Sisyphusa,'" Harry now took up the impression. "'Unfortunately it has been deemed that you are no longer Normal enough to be on Fantasy Island. Blah blah blah blah, blah blah blah blah.' Some welcome eh?"

"What's he like then? Have you met him before?" I asked.

"Not individually," said Ella. "He doesn't see Service Users personally. He attends the Senior Reps Council Meeting every so often but he barely says a word. Sometimes when we put a motion forward and the wardens don't know whether or not to accept it they turn to him and he lifts his head up from scribbling to either nod or shake his head."

"What about you, Harry?" I turned to face him.

"Once," he began, milking a dramatic pause for effect. "A few years ago, when Dobbsy was still here, me and him used to sneak around the main building at night. All the wardens had left and the henchmen are so dumb we used to throw rocks and pebbles at 'em and then run an' hide. Just stupid stuff like that. Anyway, this one night, I pull back to launch a stone right at this big ugly one's head and someone grabs me arm from behind. I turn around and it's Governor bloody Shade. So he drags me into his office and gives me the worst dressin' down I've had in me life and if you my old dear you'd know that was really sayin' summin'. Cut a long story short, I spent the next month in The Pit and I decided to stay in the dorm at night after that."

"Where is that then?" I asked.

"What, The Pit? You should know, you've been kippin' there for the last few weeks!" he started laughing but then stopped once he saw Ella's look of disapproval.

"No. Sorry I should have been more specific. Where's Governor Shade's office?" I asked.

"Oh right. That's on the second floor of Tower B," Harry told me, referring to the right of the two towers which flank either side of the main building.

"Why are you so interested in Governor Shade all of a sudden, Odis?" asked Ella.

"No reason," I answered, feigning breeziness. "I guess I just thought it was strange that I haven't seen him in all of the time that I've been here."

"Tell them that you need to use the lavatory," Gwen whispered into my ear.

"Excuse me guys I just need to use the lavatory, I mean, er, go to the toilet." I mumbled.

"Righty-Ho," Harry said in a posh voice. "Toodles." I didn't mind being teased like this but I did begin to feel increasingly adrift, stuck in a no man's land between Gwen and my teammates, between watching Fantasy Factory and reading classic literature. I couldn't unlearn what I had read.

Once I was in the bathroom Gwen began speaking again. "Calm down. You don't need to play detective straight away." I nodded assent. "Don't nod! Someone could be watching you on the I-Spy," said Gwen. I quickly started humming a tune and nodded along with it a couple of times while walking over to the urinal.

"You don't need to press your friends to find out simple details like where the Governor's Office is," she continued. "You have me for that. Your job, for now, is just to settle back into life in Team Recovery. That's all I want from you. Later on we'll begin to worry about the Governor's password. There's no rush. For now just work hard, be a good member of your team and don't arouse suspicion. And do up your flies." I zipped up and washed my hands before re-entering the dorm.

I sat back down by my bed where Gloria had joined the group. "I've brought your notes," she brandished a pile of neatly handwritten notes. "I've copied them from my own originals. I hope you can read my handwriting."

"Thank you," I accepted the papers and sifted through them. "That's so thoughtful of you. Your writing is perfect," I said. Gloria blushed. Headings on the sheets included: 'Breathing Basics,' 'How anger leads to Weirdness,' 'Your parents were probably Weird too,' 'Don't make concessions to Obsessions.' "It looks like I've missed some interesting topics," I lied.

"Ooh yes. The one on anger leading to Weirdness I found particularly helpful," said Gloria before she abruptly walked off to her bunk.

"Thanks again, Gloria."

After a time, everyone had settled in their bunks. Most of the team's eyes were glued to the HDTV as it was the final of The Fantasy Factory XXVII: "Where Dreams Become Reality". The final two contestants were Angel, who was a skinny, emotional blonde girl with a flair for power ballads, up against Mario who had captured the viewers' hearts with his nostalgic crooning. The pre-Judges ramped up the drama, explaining to the contestants that the public would vote after their final performances and the winner could look forward to an illustrious singing career. There was no mention of the runner-up's future prospects. As the two nervy performances were going on, I could hear my teammates whispering to each other about who they should vote for using the HDTV remote. The majority consensus opted for Mario thanks in part to a bloc vote on behalf of the Simon Sisters. Just as Gracie was fiddling around with the remote to place the vote, the picture on the screen disappeared.

"What did you do Gracie?" asked one of her sisters, I think it was Tracey.

"Nothing, I swear. I haven't even touched anything yet," Gracie defended herself.

"Well you must have," said Harry but then the screen came back on. Instead of the Fantasy Factory, it was a newsreader behind a desk with a solemn expression.

"We interrupt all scheduled broadcasts to bring you breaking news," the young woman announced. "A new disease has infiltrated Fantasy Island from the Outlands. The virus, commonly known as 'Pig Plague,' originated from disgruntled farmyard pigs in Nahua who bit their owners. Almost immediately the farmers who had been bitten, began to exhibit strange behaviours. Witnesses have described symptoms including grunting, excessive eating, poor hygiene and in extreme cases public lewdness. It is believed that the virus was carried to the Island via returning tourists and there have been reported cases across the Island. Minister Frown has advised Islanders to remain calm but vigilant and to report any strange behaviour to the helpline at the bottom of your screen." The emergency hotline flashed at the bottom of the screen while images from Nahua showed angry pigs being thrown on pyres and Nahua men and women rolling around in mud making strange noises. "We will now return to your scheduled programme," the newscaster smiled her perfectly white teeth. "Don't panic."

Five minutes later the lights were turned out and everyone went to bed.

Chapter 22

In Normalisation Class the next morning Serky gave us a role-play task. We were told to group ourselves into threes which made it easy for Harry, Ella and me. One of us had to play the sufferer of Weirdness, another had to play their relative whilst the third had to play a henchman who was there to apprehend the "Weirdo." Harry was desperate to play the henchman as he claimed that he had been perfecting his impersonation of them for years. That left Ella and me. She volunteered to play the role of my sister as long as I didn't mind playing the Weird person. I didn't.

Serky announced, as we were rehearsing, that the key to the exercise was "to represent the mature and co-operative way to handle an Apprehension Order." I took this advice on board and decided to play a submissive and resigned victim who went with his kidnapper willingly. In my head there were two warring ideologies with the regime on one side and Gwen on the other. Of course my instincts were with Gwen but in a class under Serky's authority and with a submissive flock surrounding me it was difficult to be confident in my beliefs when I was alone in believing them.

When it came our turn to perform, Ella and I sat at a table pretending to drink tea when Harry burst in with the collar of his baggy overalls pulled up over his head. He let out loud comic grunts. His performance was greeted with howls of laughter from the Simon sisters. He grabbed me roughly round the neck and began to drag me towards the door of the classroom. Ella performed her role brilliantly. "No, don't take him again, I beg you!" she pleaded. "He's only just come back and he takes his pills every day. He's not acted Weird at all, I swear it." She began to sob and cry and grasped at Harry's overalls before collapsing to the floor. "Don't, sis," I said. "It's okay. It's probably for the best. I'll go back and get Normal again and I'll be back in no time."

Ella looked up at me with bemusement and then dropped her head again, shaking it and wiping her tears away. Harry dragged me out of the door.

We re-entered to polite applause. Serky applauded more loudly than the rest.

"Excellent performance, Mr. Winston," she announced to everyone. "That is exactly the way to react to an Apprehension Order. When you are in the throes of Weirdness there is no use in resisting. The best thing is for you to be brought back to a facility with professionals where you can be Normalised. Mr Winston, I see your recent absence has made you see sense."

The three beeps sounded and Ella was the first to run out of the room. I quickly went after her. I called her name, but she didn't stop for me. I finally caught up with her underneath a flight of stairs where she was slumped on the floor, her face and body screwed up and contorted with rage.

"Are you okay?" I asked her. She didn't answer. I crouched down to get closer to her, but she shrugged me off quite forcefully.

"What's wrong?"

"You're wrong," she shot back, glaring at me with disgust. "What was that bullshit in there?" she demanded.

"What bullshit? I thought we were acting?"

"We were… but still, what's happened to you? One little month in The Pit and your spirit is broken? Serky's got you eating out of the palm of her hand now. I thought you were different. Obviously I was wrong." She jumped up, inadvertently crashing her head against the underside of the staircase. "Shit," she shouted as she stormed off.

"Wait," I called.

"Leave her," said Gwen. "It's better, for now, that she thinks she's right. The more important thing is for you to have Serky fooled. You keep her thinking she's broken you and worry about Ella later. She'll forgive you. I think she likes you," Gwen teased. "Either that or she's one hell of an actress!"

Climbing Practice followed. Ella decided to ignore me for the whole session. She went with Gloria and I was partnered with Harry. I'd certainly improved my technique since my first experience. You reach a point where you've been hit by so many balls that you become accustomed to the pain and therefore de-sensitised to it. The trick was to stoop your head as far forward as possible. That way it's practically impossible to be hit on the head, which is, of course, the most painful. The downside of this tactic of course, is that you are looking straight down as you abseil, which at a height of fifty feet is the last place you want to be looking.

Luckily for me, I was just handling the ropes this session while Harry did the climbing. I was supposed to go after him but because Gloria got tangled at the top the whole team got delayed. By the time it was about to be my turn the beeps sounded and we went to the mess hall for lunch.

I was able to catch up with some of the friends I'd previously made from other teams during lunch break. I chatted to my friend Joe whilst waiting in the slow-moving queue. Everyone called him "GI Joe" because he contracted his Weirdness while serving in the army in the War in Babylonia. He welcomed me back with his customary bone-crunching handshake.

"Welcome back, Dizzy." Joe was in the habit of giving everyone nicknames. I don't know where mine came from. "How did lying in yer own shit for a month treat you?"

I fought sarcasm with sarcasm and told him it was fine, but I didn't want to take it up full-time like him.

Harry, Joe and I collected our food and started walking towards our respective team's tables when suddenly I fell forward. My tray crashed to the ground. Slop covered my face and upper body and I turned around to see Skinny Jim with his arm in a sling smiling over me. "Welcome back," he grinned, flashing his rotten teeth.

G.I Joe grabbed Jim round the neck. Jim's two little sidekicks, who were comically squat and obese compared to their leader, started trying to throttle G.I Joe. I saw a warden coming over and told Joe to let go. The warden immobilised Joe and one of his assailants with a Sisyphusa Stun Gun and they both instantly dropped to the floor.

"What's going on here?" asked the warden. Nobody answered. Everyone stared at the floor. I decided to speak.

"It's a misunderstanding, warden. I fell over, but Joe here thought that one of them tripped me up."

By now Joe and Skinny Jim's sidekick were beginning to get back to their feet.

"Is that true?" the warden asked the rest of them. They all nodded. "You all know that there is a zero tolerance policy on fighting here. You're lucky I had my weapon on the lowest setting. If I see any of you involved in any mischief again, it'll be The Pit for a week. Is that clear?" he bellowed.

"Yes, warden," we all replied.

"Now go sit down," he said as he turned away.

I thanked Joe and we dispersed to our tables.

I watched silently as everyone else ate their lunch. I can't say that I was overly dismayed about missing out on the cabbage and anchovy slop.

After lunch the men went to the quarry and the women to the warehouse at the top of the hill. Once we'd made our way down the rickety staircase and into the quarry, we heard Warden Serky make her announcement.

"We have a new assignment in. A new statue of The Carpenter has been commissioned for the Capital City. They want only the best materials for this prestigious project. Therefore extraction will take place solely in the caves. I don't need to tell you how much of an honour it is that we have been given the opportunity to serve the Empire. There will be no slacking and no mistakes. Team Recovery, you will work in Cave #1."

We trudged towards the cave, collecting our helmets and pick-axes along the way. In the background we could still hear Serky assigning the men from the other teams to their respective caves. Harry and I reached the entrance to the cave first. From far away, the inner darkness suggested that the cave went on forever. However, once we stepped inside and switched on our helmet torches, we could see that the cave was actually relatively small. You could nearly reach the ceiling if you tip-toed and you couldn't have parked more than four cars in there. Dripping stalactites protruded from the ceiling. The floor squelched under foot where there were various pools and puddles to navigate.

Harry and Mo began shouting the first words that came to their heads, experimenting with the echo.

"HARRY, Harry, harry!"

"MO,Mo,mo!
"POO, Poo, poo!"

Eventually they ran out of vocabulary. There were ten of us altogether-- the four "Flower-Eaters" as they were called, plus Jacob, Ken, Thomas, Harry, Mr.Femuz, and myself. Jacob, Ken and Thomas were three of the quieter members of the team. Jacob was a very tall and slender man of middling age. His skin was a translucent yellow which made him look perpetually sickly. He had a jet black head of curls which appeared almost perm-like. When he spoke, which was rarely, he did so in a soft well-spoken voice. He often seemed as if he was speaking more to himself than anyone else. I noticed one day at lunch some months ago that he was given a considerably higher dose of Climbing Pills than anyone else which probably meant that he was a Grade 6 but he never spoke about grades or Weirdness.

Ken was slightly younger although his hair had traces of grey in it. He had stubble which was as dark as Jacob's hair. On days when he was clean-shaven he looked a completely different person, though the next day a full layer of stubble would have already grown back. He would never speak unless he was addressed directly. When he was asked a question by the warden in class he would answer in a quiet nasal voice, each word delayed by a painful stutter. He had large bags under his eyes and always looked like he'd just woken up, no matter what time of day it was. Thomas was the oldest. He came from the very north of Fantasy Island which his thick accent betrayed. He had grey hair, a wrinkled forehead and appeared to be in constant physical pain.

We spread out around the cave and began to chip away at the granite walls. After a few minutes of furious pick-axing I began to feel a rumble, a sort of vibration. I stopped work, as did everyone else. But even after we'd all stopped I could hear somebody else hammering hard at the rock somewhere nearby. Thomas was the nearest to the entrance of the cave and went to check where the noise was coming from.

"Hey youse, stop that!" he shouted. The rumbling began to grow stronger. Thomas walked out of the cave to confront whoever it was he was shouting at. Harry and I walked towards the cave entrance as the floor and the ceiling began to really shake. Outside in the light I could see Thomas grappling with someone. They manoeuvred around in a way that revealed who his opponent was. It was Skinny Jim. His two accomplices were, as always, nearby. They were hammering away above the entrance to our cave with their pick-axes. Harry and I reached the entrance but were forced straight back as Thomas was shoved violently into us. We stumbled backwards and Thomas fell to the ground in front of us. We could hear laughter outside of the cave but by now the main noise was the deafening shudders reverberating through both the ground and the ceiling. Suddenly the entrance of the cave collapsed. A pile of rocks had formed in front of us and was completely blocking any way out of the cave.

I was covered in dust and rubble but I was unharmed as was Harry. We both got to our feet and the lights from our helmets illuminated the scene of destruction in front of us. There were huge rocks and boulders everywhere and no sign of Thomas. Then we looked down and saw it. There was a hand poking out from underneath the heap of granite. Thomas was dead.

Chapter 23

"Come on 108, don't just stand there, help me move these rocks," Harry squealed frantically. He was pulling and pushing, even kicking the gigantic boulders but they would not budge. "Come on everyone!" he turned around and screamed. The Flower-Eaters rushed over switching on the flashlights on their hard hats. The immensity of the collapse was further illuminated. It looked as though someone had thrown a grenade into the cave. Not even the slightest ray of sunlight had managed to squirm through the cracks between the rocks.

Jacob and Ken also came over. Everyone began to wrestle with various giant boulders but their efforts were as futile as Harry's. I kneeled down and picked up Thomas's hand. It was floppy and had dry calluses on it. It felt like a hand that had done a life-time of manual work. There was no blood on it, no bruises, but it felt cold and lifeless. I slipped my fingers down his wrist which only just poked out through the meeting of two large rocks. I felt his pulse, or at least where he should have had one. There was nothing.

"It's no use, Harry. He's gone," I said quietly. "There's no pulse."

"What do you know?" he snapped. He didn't cease his furious efforts. "You're not a doctor. We can still get 'im out, maybe we can get it started up again. Come on don't stop!" The others began to tire. Jacob bent over, his hands resting on his knees. The Flower-Eaters sat down on the ground, puffing loudly, trying to catch their breath.

"What are you doing, you idiots. He's supposed to be your friend, isn't he? I thought we were a team?" said Harry. He looked beyond his initial targets but then found a new one. Ten or fifteen metres into the background in the darkness of the cave, Harry's helmet light revealed the silhouetted figure of Mr. Femuz. He was leaning against the wall smoking a cigarette.

"Oi! What are you doin'?" Harry screamed. "Have you got no heart? What are you? A machine?" Mr. Femuz jerked his head ninety degrees and saw that Harry was speaking to him. He stared at him but remained still and taciturn. He turned his head back away from Harry.

"Oi, I'm fuckin' talkin' to you," bawled Harry almost loud enough to make the rest of the ceiling collapse. "What is it with you? You haven't talked ever since you got here. How long have you been here? Four Years? Five? You're a fucking freak." It was hard to tell in the darkness, but I could have sworn Mr Femuz had a wry smile on his face.

"Just leave it Harry. You're upset," I interjected.

"Yeah, I'm upset. I'm upset 'cause this fuckin' Babby bastard is makin' me upset," Harry retorted. 'Babby' was a pejorative term many Islanders directed at the growing numbers of Babylonian refugees, but I'd never heard Harry use it.

"I am not Babylonian. I am Parthian," replied Mr. Femuz firmly but without raising his voice or turning to face Harry. He took another drag on his cigarette and calmly allowed a wave of smoke to flow out of his nostrils and mouth. The smoke floated and rose like a ghost before dissolving into nothingness.

"So what? Who gives a shit anyway? Babby? Parthian? You Book #3ers are all the same anyway," Harry spat out.

"You're out of order, Harry," I shouted. "I know you're upset about Thomas, but you need to just shut up."

"Fuck you. I wasn't talkin' to you anyway," he replied. "What is it with you and Outlanders anyway? First you took a bullet for those flower-addicted losers," he pointed at Ahmed, Mo, Khaled and Abdul whose eyes fell meekly to the ground. "And now you're protectin' Mr. Talkative over here who doesn't even give a shit that Thomas has just died. He's lucky to even be allowed in our country anyway, the cheek of these peasants is fuckin' unbelievable." He began to rant as if he'd memorised whole passages from The Daily Bulletin of The Corporation of Hysteria. He then said to me, but loud enough so that Mr. Femuz could hear it, "Doesn't he have a family to go home to?"

Mr. Femuz took a final drag on his cigarette, flicked it onto the ground and trod on it with his size 14 boot. Then he burst into action. He flew invisibly through the darkness like a shadow and pounced on Harry before he had time to think. He hit him over and over again. I tried to pull him off but he flung back an elbow which connected with my jaw and I fell to the ground. Seeing this, the Flower-Eaters jumped up and went to pull Mr. Femuz off, two on each arm. Harry's face was beginning to look a real mess. They somehow managed to drag him off, Khaled and Abdul were pretty substantial men themselves.

In an instant Mr. Femuz transformed. He shrugged off the Flower-Eaters and strolled calmly back into the darkness. I went over to see Harry. His face was covered in blood. His nose was bleeding, as was his top lip and both of his eyes had puffed up badly. I reached out to see if he was okay.

"Piss off," he gurgled through a mouthful of blood. "I'm fine. The bastard blind-sided me, that's all."

"It looks pretty serious," I said. "Your nose might be broken."

"I said I'm fine!" He hissed as he shoved me in my chest. "I don't want your help. I'm getting out of here anyway. Who's coming?" he asked turning to the others. The Flower-Eaters shook their heads mechanically and avoided eye contact. Jacob and Ken looked at the Flower-Eaters then they looked at me then they looked at Mr. Femuz. Finally they looked back at Harry and nodded their assent.

"Well Odis, are you coming or not?" he asked angrily.

"I think we should wait here. The wardens and henchmen are sure to get us out soon," I replied in as placating a tone as I could muster.

"Suit yourself. Maybe I got you wrong. I think you belong with these freaks." He stormed off past Mr. Femuz and into the dark recesses of the cave. He disappeared down one of the two tunnels. Jacob and Ken scurried after him skirting around Mr. Femuz as far as they could.

"Harry!" I shouted after him, my voice echoing down the pitch black tunnel. "You don't know where you're going! It might be dangerous down there! Be careful!" There was no reply.

I walked past Mr. Femuz towards the tunnel and shouted after them again but again there was no reply. Seeing that I was out of earshot of Mr. Femuz I tried to whisper to Gwen for advice.

"What should I do?" When she didn't reply I fiddled with my Earpiece. It made a fuzzy sound and then went dead. It sucked the life out of my ear like a vacuum. Being in the cave must have interfered with the reception. I decided to stay where I was and wait and hope that the wardens would unblock the cave.

I clicked my jaw from side to side like the carriage of a typewriter which has just come to the end of a line. Mr. Femuz's elbow was certainly made of concrete, but it didn't feel like there was any permanent damage. I walked back and sat on a rock near to where Mr. Femuz was smoking.

"Are you okay Mr. Femuz?"

He nodded.

"I don't agree with what Harry said to you," I told him.

He shook his head in a manner that suggested he didn't care about it.

"So where did you get all of your cigarettes from? I thought they weren't allowed?" I asked.

"Pay warden," he grunted. He offered me the packet which only had two left in it.

"No thanks. I don't smoke. I used to, but only when I was really Liquidated! Is that how you started?"

"No drink in Parthia. Against the law," he said.

"Of course, how stupid of me, I knew that."

There was a short silence. Then he spoke again, "I began to drink when I come here, to the Island."

"Oh really? Do you like it?"

"No I don't like. I hate drink."

"So why did you do it?" I asked.

"Help me to sleep."

"Yes, I understand."

Another silence. It was my turn to break it this time.

"So when did you leave Parthia? After the Revolution?" I asked.

"Yes," he said betraying a trace of surprise. Suddenly he became interested in the conversation. "What you know about Revolution?" he asked me.

"Oh not much," I admitted. It was true, I had only read a little about it in one of Gwen's history books. "I know it was about thirty years ago. I know they got rid of The Leader…"

"Razor," he interrupted.

"Yes, The Razor, that's right. And then they instituted the law directly from the Yes/No Book #3."

"How you know this?" he asked me, sounding bemused.

"I read it."

"I never talk to someone from the Island about my home before," he said.

"That's bad. Well I don't know much but you can talk to me if you like?" I offered. He seemed to think about it for a second. But then he shook his head.

"No. I speak your language very bad, very bad," he said.

"No," I assured him. "You speak well, really well in fact. Better than my Parthian anyway," I smiled. He may have smiled back, I don't know, it was very dark.

"Do people often call you names?" I asked. "Like Babby?"

"Sometimes."

"It must make you angry," I said. "To be confused with people from a country who you fought such a terrible war with."

"Maybe," he said. "But I can't tell difference between accent of people from north of your Island, west of your Island and south of your Island!"

"I suppose you're right," I agreed. Mr.Femuz smoked his cigarette right to its end before stubbing it out against the wall. He took two giant steps towards another large rock across from the one I was sitting on and he took a seat. I waited until he sat down and then asked him another question. "What was your job, back in your country?"

"I was, how you say… Newspaper writer."

"Journalist."

"Yes. Journalist."

"Did you enjoy it?" I asked.

"It was a long time ago," he said dropping his gaze to the ground.

"Please just tell me to mind my own business if you don't want to talk about it," I offered. He continued to stare at the ground in silence, his mind elsewhere. I could hear the Flower-Eaters singing together over by the collapsed entrance to the cave. Mo was screeching in his high-pitched voice while the others hummed a melodic bass-line. "So what was it that made you leave?" I finally asked him.

He didn't budge for some time. Then he lifted his giant left hand to his face and tapped his glass eye three times with his wedding ring. Each tap made a clinking sound like someone tapping on their wine glass to attract a crowd's attention before a speech. "I had to escape," he finally spoke. "I had written against the government and they arrested me."

"What happened? Were you beaten? Tortured?"

He stood up sharply and began pacing back and forth again. "Of course, but that's nothing. I was beaten and tortured just the same when I wrote against The Razor."

"Unbelievable," I said pathetically in my quaint Fantasy Island way. I looked at his ring and said, "I see you're married."

Mr. Femuz stopped pacing. He took a deep breath.

"I'm sorry. It's none of my business," I said.

"NO!" he insisted loudly. "I want to tell you."

With a great effort he regained his composure. "They beat me. I lost my eye. Then they sent me home, but The Guardians watched my house always. They said I could not write any more. And I could not leave the house. My wife, Zahra was her name, she told me I must find a way to escape, to leave Parthia or else they would kill me. I told her I would not leave her but she said 'you must, you must,'" his voice grew louder and he spoke faster as he continued the story. "I promised that I would return when there was another coup. We were so sure that another coup would happen, that the Empire would put The Razor back in power, everyone believed it. So I left." He began to shake his head. "To my shame, I left. Because I was afraid to die, I left like a coward. My wife went home to live with her parents where I believed she would be safe, and my cousin helped get me to the coast. He was a policeman. I managed to get on a cargo ship to Maurya and

139

there I got another ship to Fantasy Island. I have been here ever since. Twenty-eight years."

"I spoke to my wife on the telephone. She found out that she was pregnant only after I left. I could not believe it. I told her I would come back. I didn't care what they tried to do to me, I needed to see the birth of my child. But she insisted that I stayed. I got a job in a restaurant. I could not write because I did not know your language. I tried to save money to send home. I hoped that somehow Zahra might be able to come here. Months passed and the coup didn't happen. Zahra was fired from her job as a teacher. She was harassed by The Guardians. Suddenly she stopped calling. I tried to reach her. Her father answered the phone he began crying and screaming. He called me a coward, a dog. He said Zahra had been killed by a neighbour in the street for refusing to cover herself." Mr. Femuz began to weep loudly. "My beautiful wife and my baby inside of her were beaten to death because I wasn't there."

Chapter 24

The huge giant of a man continued to weep uncontrollably for some time. It was bizarre that he had been so silent for all of the time that I had known him. Why had he opened up to me of all people? I was less than half his age and we had next to nothing in common, not religion, culture, or first language. But the one connection we did have was that we were both there, right there, in that cave, at that precise moment. We were both Service Users, residents of Sisyphusa, held against our will. I wondered how they'd managed to detain him? The henchmen were strong in a clumsy, almost mechanical way, but Femuz was brute force, a titan.

He must have been nearing fifty. What gave it away wasn't any wrinkled skin or physical wear and tear, it was his face. His bushy, black eyebrows, or more accurately eyebrow because they met in the middle, were flecked with grey hairs. His head was completely bald. The sun reflected off of its sweaty surface when we laboured in the quarry. His gait was broad and swift, he would often hold one hand in the other behind his back and pace up and down the dormitory. His mind always seemed to be cast adrift, up in the clouds or at the bottom of the ocean, and always with the same pained expression on his face.

But not then, in that cave, at that moment his thoughts were in Parthia. He had released something which had been bound up inside of him and it kept on coming. The Flower-Eaters hovered in the background. They looked over at Femuz, aware of his pain, but they clearly felt awkward at his outpouring of emotion. They soon slinked off, back into the shadows. So it was left to me. I hesitantly got up and walked over to him. I patted him gently on the shoulder. His head, which hung low in his hands, rose suddenly a couple of inches, surprised at human contact.

"I'm sorry I pushed you to talk, Mr. Femuz," I said softly. "And I'm sorry about your family." He wiped his nose and mouth with his sleeve and rose to his feet.

"It was a long time ago," he said, as if speaking to himself, willing the pain to subside. "Thank you, young man. What is your name?" he asked.

"Odis Winston," I replied.

"My name is Pahla," he said. "Pahla Femuz." His large hand enveloped mine in a handshake. "Now go and be with your young friends. I need to be alone."

"Okay, Mr.Femuz." I walked over to the Flower-Eaters, using my torch to light the ground.

The four men sat in their usual crescent formation. Mo shuffled a couple of inches closer to Khaled to make room for me.

"You okay, Mr. Odis?" Mo asked with concern. "He no give you no trouble?"

"Mr.Femuz? No. He was just a bit upset but everything's fine now."

"Good," said Ahmed. "We no let no trouble happen to you. Especially from no 'Denier of the Sacred Three'," Ahmed looked in the direction of the distant Mr. Femuz and his face screwed up into a knot of disgust.

"What do you mean?" I asked. "What's a 'Denier of the Sacred Three'?"

"He is from Parthia, no? In Parthia they say 'no' to the Sacred Three, the first three keepers of the One True Book. They say only the fourth keeper was sacred and should have been chosen as keeper before The Sacred Three."

"When did all of this happen?" I asked.

"Thousand years ago, some more even," a belligerent Ahmed replied.

"But you both believe in the One True Book?" I asked, still trying to understand.

"Yes, but this is not the point. Many things happen since. Many wars, many dead," he said.

"I understand. But there's no need to hate Mr. Femuz for this just because he's Parthian. You didn't like it when people called you Flower-Eaters. Maybe he doesn't even believe in the Book at all?" I suggested.

"But this is even worse," said Khaled horrified at the very suggestion.

"Well I don't believe in the Book. I don't believe in any of the Yes/No Books," I said.

"What?" asked Mo. "Not even your Book #2?"

"No," I replied.

"Why not?" asked Ahmed.

"I just don't. I never really read them before. I don't think I'd want to believe in only one book. I learn different things from lots of books. Plus, those Books are very old, a lot of things have changed since they were written."

"Some things never change," said Ahmed.

"That's true," I conceded. "So do you think that when I die, I'll go to a bad place like it says in the Books?"

"Maybe?" said Ahmed though somewhat regretfully.

"I no think so," smiled Mo. "As long as you do good things. Like when you helped us."

"Thanks Mo," I smiled back. "Remember some time ago when you said you would do anything for me?" I asked Ahmed. He nodded. "Well, do you think you could give Mr.Femuz a chance? I've spoken to him and I believe he's a good man. If you get to know him and you don't agree, then you're more than welcome not to like him. But it's silly to hate someone before you've even spoken to them."

Ahmed thought for a few seconds but then relented. "Okay, but only because of what you did for us."

"Thank you," I said and I shook his hand.

I sat back down at one end of the crescent and listened to the four men sing songs from their homeland. The songs were not happy ones. I could not understand the words they spoke but I didn't need to. Their voices knitted together in perfect harmony to release a dirge, a lament for home. As I listened I felt transported to Cartagia. I began to feel drowsy and lay back on the unwelcoming ground and drifted off.

The family exited into the barely cooler shadows of the ancient stadium. Its dilapidated walls crumbled like breadcrumbs in the baking heat of the desert. The young boy instantly spotted the two shrewdly positioned men offering camel rides to visitors from the Empire. The two men spotted the little boy and both smiled broadly, beckoning him over with hand gestures. He tugged at his mother's sleeve,

"Can I ride the camel? Please, Mum!?" the boy pleaded in a whining voice he reserved especially for such requests.

"Where?" she asked, looking around for any nearby camel. She looked at the boy's reddening face and splodged a dollop of sunscreen on his forehead and began spreading it around.

"Over there," he pointed with one hand whilst he fought off his mother's wiping with the other.

"Either I do it or you do it," she said referring to the spreading of the sunscreen. The boy began spreading reluctantly. His mother saw the men standing next to two bedraggled camels which looked as though they were as old as the building which they were camped outside. "Must you, Odis?" she asked her son in a tired voice but with a smiling face. Both parents were exhausted. They had been running after the two excited boys in the endless maze of secret passageways in the bowels of the enormous Amphitheatre for the last hour. "Will it absolutely ruin your entire life if you don't get to ride that camel?" she teased the boy.

"Yes," he nodded with the utmost sincerity and seriousness. "Come on, you never let me do anything!" he huffed.

"Oh, yes," she responded playfully. "You're such a deprived child! Whose parents take him on exotic holidays in the Outlands!"

"I am," he tried to withhold a smile. "You never let me do any fun stuff. Dom!" he called after his older brother who walked ahead with their father. "Dom!" he called again.

The older boy turned around with a look of annoyance which suggested that he had ignored rather than not heard the first shout. "What?" he asked disinterestedly.

"Don't you want to ride the camel?" asked the younger boy thinking that a team effort would be the best plan of attack. The older boy shrugged as if he didn't care although Odis suspected he actually did.

"What do you think?" the woman asked her husband.

"Well...do you think it's safe?" he said surveying the unimpressive beasts from afar.

"We could find out how much it costs," she said, as if such a compromise would delay the inevitable.

"Yes!" the boy cried. He ran off straight to the two local men ignoring the pleas from his parents to wait for them. The first man was in charge of the sales pitch. He was short and smiley with grey hair peeking out from beneath his fez.

"Hallo, boy," he said speaking the language of the Empire rather than his mother tongue. "Like to ride camel?" he smiled.

The young boy stared rudely at the abnormally large mole on the man's forehead. His parents and brother arrived and began to take part in the transaction.

"Hello," said the mother. Her Mainland accent always became twice as thick when she engaged in pleasantries with strangers.

"Hallo, Mrs," said the short man. "Like two camel for two boy?"

"Well, how much is it?" she asked.

"Veddy cheap, veddy cheap. I give you special price," the man smiled. "10 dinars for both."

"That does sound good," she said softly to her husband.

"Do you walk alongside while they ride to make sure they don't fall off?" asked the father.

"Yes! No problem," said the man, pretending that he understood the request.

Both boys were hoisted onto their camels by the younger, taller man who one would assume was the small man's son judging by the way in which he commanded him. The young man took two ropes which hung around each of the animals' necks and began to lead them around the stadium.

The boys' parents strolled some paces behind them. The father carried a video camera and filmed the procession. He then turned the camera onto his wife, but as soon as she realised she was being filmed she told him to stop it.

The younger boy was filled with excitement. The shuddering back and forth became rhythmic and exhilarating whilst the animal's spitting and slurping was a hilarious *sideshow. The older boy was similarly enjoying his experience though his camel had stopped briefly to defecate meaning he was slightly trailing his brother. This meant that the young Cartagian couldn't hold both camels' leashes so the young boy's camel continued apace unchecked. When the young boy realised he no longer had a minder, he decided to take advantage of the situation. He began trying everything he could think of to speed up his flagging steed. First he flicked the reins as if he was trying to whip a table cloth from under a laid table. When this failed he began to kick the sides of the aged dromedary. The animal groaned but did not quicken its pace. If anything, it had slowed down. But the mischievous boy wouldn't be denied. When he looked below him at the hump on which he sat, he saw a riding crop tucked underneath the saddle. He immediately pulled it out and slapped the animal on its behind.*

The camel reared up, its two forelegs rose from the ground, then it began running extremely fast in zigzagging lines. Salesmen and visitors alike, of whom there were many milling around outside the amphitheatre, began diving out of the way to avoid the rampaging camel. The boy screamed with fear and delight as the animal bucked and dodged.

But then boy and camel met their match. An old car came driving along the dusty street right in their direction. The driver, adorned in a new pair of sunglasses and singing along to his favourite song on the radio, only noticed the camel at the very last moment. He swerved to avoid it but crashed head-on into one of the columns which supported the ancient structure. The boy was thrown from the camel which then ran off towards the bazaar to wreak more havoc.

Meanwhile the thousand-year-old column, which was due for renovation the next month, could not withstand the force of the crash and it began to crumple and sway. After a few agonising seconds it toppled over sideways into the next column. In this way column fell upon column like dominoes until the whole building began to collapse.

The noise was horrendous. His eardrums burst with the sound of rock smashing rock. The dust, debris and incense from the market stalls swarmed all around like a plague of locusts. And still the columns crashed.

I was awoken by the loud noise of machinery coming from behind the collapsed entrance. The Flower-Eaters began to scream and shout, "Help!" "We're Stuck!" Vehicles began to plough through the mountain of rocks that blocked the mouth of the cave, and chinks of sunlight started to laser into the darkness. We all ran back to avoid the carnage.

After five or ten minutes of work, the rocks were cleared and the henchmen, wardens and Service Users stood in a crowd and gawked at us as we emerged blinking and shielding our eyes from the sun. My captivity was at an end. It was time for me to return to another one.

Chapter 25

When we emerged from the cave we were informed that Skinny Jim and his accomplices had been sent to The Pit for their role in the cave collapse. We also found out that Harry, Jacob and Ken had escaped through a network of tunnels which led them to one of the other caves. Harry acted as if there had been no argument at all. He talked to us all apart from Mr. Femuz whom Harry ignored as if the huge man didn't exist, but I could tell that things were not the same as they had been.

By that time, working hours were at an end. The wardens and henchmen left for the main building and we were left to return to our dormitories when it suited us. The women finished their work in the factory on the hill and Ella, seeing the commotion surrounding the quarry, came down to see what had happened.

She helped the rest of us as we sifted through the rubble looking for Thomas's body. When we found it we carried him to the graveyard and buried him alongside Dobbsy and the others. The whole team helped, even Mr.Femuz, and we all stood in silence while people took it in turns to say something. Ella spoke first, reciting a prayer from the Yes/No book #2. She said that Thomas was in a better place and The SkyMaster and The Carpenter were looking after him as they did everyone. I hated the confidence and certainty that Ella's belief in The SkyMaster gave her when I felt so unconfident and uncertain staring into Thomas's grave. I did feel confident in my reasons why I couldn't share Ella's blind faith but as I had no answers of my own I resented the sense of security believers like Ella had. I imagined how nice it might be to believe.

Gloria, between sniffles, recounted when she and Thomas first met over 20 years ago. She said he was always on time for classes but that once he made fun of her and she didn't like it. She said she forgave him now because he was dead and he could no longer apologise for it.

Harry spoke last. He apologised to Thomas for not being able to save him. But he swore that he would get Skinny Jim back. After Harry finished, the group began to disperse until the only people left at the graveside were Ella and me. Ella had fetched a branch from a nearby tree and had begun to sharpen one end of it with a jagged rock. I saw that she was crying and decided to go and talk to her.

"I'm sorry about Thomas," I said. "There really wasn't anything that could be done."

"That's not what Harry was saying," she said coldly as she wiped her nose with the sleeve of her overalls.

"There really wasn't," I assured her. "He was dead, I felt his pulse."

"I'd rather not talk about it."

"Okay, would you like to talk about what happened this morning?"

"What do you mean? Nothing happened this morning."

She'd never acted this way in the time that I'd known her. She was always so warm, so gentle. But she spoke to me as if we didn't know each other, as if she wasn't paying any attention to what she was saying. She finished carving the branch into a sharp stake before closing her eyes and mumbling a prayer under her breath. After a short while she shuffled along a couple of feet to the side and began tending to Dobbsy's grave. She picked up some dead flowers and pulled out some long grass which was obstructing his stake.

"Why are you ignoring me, Ella?" I asked. "I don't even know what I've done wrong?"

"Nothing. Nothing's wrong. I just want to be alone."

"Of course there's something wrong. But if you don't tell me what it is then I can't help you. This is just what Layla used to do!" I said the last sentence more to myself than to her but she pounced on it.

"I'm not Layla, Odis. And I don't need your help. I'm not a little girl and you don't need to fix me or save me from anything. And you know what? You aren't Jack, and you never will be," she said.

"I know you aren't Layla. I don't want you to be. You're Ella and you're my friend," I took a step towards her but she put a hand up and stopped me. "I was never trying to be Dobbsy, Ella. I wouldn't ever try to be him. I know how special it was, what you two had together. And that's how I feel about Layla."

"It's not your fault," she said almost in a whisper as she shook her head. "It was me. You just reminded me so much of him. I miss him. I think I started to just act like you were him, you know? Oh, what have I done? I'm such an idiot," she beat her forehead with a closed fist.

"No you're not," I said, shocked at how hard she had just hit herself. "Don't be so hard on yourself. It's only natural that you miss him. And, well, we've grown close over these few months and I've found meeting you the only good thing that's come out of this horrible place."

Ella smiled and looked up at me through tearful eyes. "Me too," she said. We hugged. She gripped me very tightly and dug her fingernails into my back. "I'm sorry I've been such a bitch to you today."

"Forget it. It's just been a crap day," I said. "I'm going back to the dorm, are you coming?"

"No, I'm going to stay here for a bit," she smiled.

I left her kneeling at Dobbsy's graveside and could still hear her speaking to him as I walked away. I entered the woods and began to follow the dirt path back to the compound. Kicking the loose branches and crisp fallen leaves I thought about the loud sound that Ella's fist had made as she struck it against her forehead. This was a new side to her. I was familiar with her sensitive side. She would care for the other Service Users and act as a surrogate mother to them, especially the Flower-Eaters and Harry. But I'd never seen her look so vulnerable before. Her tears weren't for the suffering of another this time, they were for herself.

The more I thought about it, the more I realised that she never seemed to be concerned for herself, for her own welfare. She fought on the Council for better rights for Service Users. She helped me settle in after my Solitary Initiation. She helped Mo to read and she even remained admirably patient in her dealings with Gloria which no-one else in the team could do.

I was interrupted in mid-thought by the familiar sound of Gwen in my ear.

"Hello, hello," she exclaimed as if she was testing a microphone before giving a speech. "Mr. Winston, come in, can you hear me?"

"I can hear you," I whispered. I trudged away from the path and into the thick woodland, far enough from the path so that Ella, or anyone else, couldn't see or hear me if they walked past. "Sorry Gwen, I was trapped in a cave all day and the Earpiece must have lost its connection."

"Yes, I heard. A security alert went out over the system and the Service Users have all been talking about it. Are you okay?"

"Yes. I'm fine. But one of the members of the team, Thomas, was crushed by the rocks. He died. We've just buried him," I told her.

She replied, "Yes, I heard that too. His file has already been marked 'deceased'. The perpetrators have been sent to The Pit as I'm sure you're aware."

"That's what I've heard. I just don't know why they would do that. I mean they killed a man!" I said, still in shock at having seen and touched a dead body for the first time.

"'Skinny Jim,' as you know him, is a very disturbed young man. There are things I could tell you about his past that might go some way to explaining his actions, but I wouldn't want to alarm you," she said.

"I think you just have," I replied.

"Oh no, no, nothing too sinister. It might just be better if you stayed out of his way. I imagine he and his friends will be otherwise engaged for a fair few months anyhow. Meanwhile, you will have lots of other problems to be concentrating on, I have your first mission- do you think you're ready?"

"It depends on what I have to do."

"I thought you might say that. It's a very simple task. There are three sisters in Team Recovery who are accorded special privileges by Warden Serky…"

"The Simons," I interrupted.

"Exactly. They are allowed to work at the main reception desk for one day every week. In exchange they are permitted smoking breaks, make-up and cosmetics and most importantly a sense of superiority over their fellow Service Users."

"That's for sure," I agreed. "But what's the mission?"

"Good, you sound keen. The wardens delegate minor responsibilities and privileges to certain Service Users from every team."

"I know. There are those women from Team Restitution who serve the meals and give extra portions to their friends. And then there are the guys from Team Rejuvenation who wash everybody's overalls."

"Right. They also have a number of other Service Users who work as undercover informants, but even I don't know their identities. So what's the point of all this? Why give the Service Users any power at all you may ask?"

"To divide us," I interrupted.

"Yes! To sow the seeds of division, to prevent you from working together. Who causes the most arguments in your Team?"

"The Simons," I answered.

"Who do you think tipped off Serky when Ahmed, Mohamed, Khaled and Abdul were caught eating Flowers?" she asked again.

"The Simons?" I asked.

"The Simons are the most divisive influence in Team Recovery. If you are to lead the Service Users out of Sisyphusa then they must be stopped! But be careful," her triumphal tone morphed into one of foreboding. "Many a man has fallen victim to their charms. You must be mindful not to be lured by their...assets or cowed by their fury. They work on the desk tomorrow. Your job is to persuade them to renounce their privileges, all of their privileges, by any means necessary. Good luck." Her voice cut out.

"Gwen, Gwen," I whispered.

"Yes," she replied.

"I need you to do something for me. I need you to check the databases for someone called Femuz."

"What do you mean Femuz?" she asked. "The chap in your team?"

"Yes, but his child, who would now be twenty-eight, I think, or maybe twenty-nine?"

"Do you have a first name or sex?" she asked.

"No. I don't even know if he or she exists. It's just a hunch. The mother's name was Zahra. Try looking in the Service Users Database for the whole Island and in the whole Empire if you can. Please."

"Okay, I'll have a look," she said sounding decidedly sceptical.

"Odis? Is that you?" A voice shouted through the labyrinthine brush.

"I have to go," I whispered to Gwen. "Someone's coming."

"Yes, who's there?" I shouted back.

"It's me...Ella. What are you doing in there?"

"Wait a sec," I waded back through to the path and joined her. "Just wanted some alone time," I said.

"Odis, you're so polite, you're allowed to admit if you go for a wee in the woods!"

"Well, I just..." I trailed off and looked at her with an embarrassed expression on my face. We walked back to the dormitory together.

Chapter 26

I lay awake most of that night trying to concoct a plan to persuade the Simons not to work for Serky. It seemed impossible. Why would they willingly give up the privileges which gave them so much pride and power? I fell asleep with no such plan prepared.

The next morning I cruised though Normalisation Class in a daze. I gazed at the Simons' empty seats (they were given permission to miss classes to work on the reception desk) and searched my mind for inspiration. Class was over in no time and we were herded into Climbing Practice.

I partnered up with Mr. Femuz, who had increasingly become my favoured companion. There was a lingering tension still simmering between Harry and myself and I opted to leave some space between us which also meant spending less time with Ella. I enjoyed my time with Mr. Femuz. He was far more cultured and well-read than any of the other Service Users but he remained cloaked in the gloom of grief and melancholy, something which I could identify with. He was often silent, but I didn't mind because it gave me time to plot things in my head. We would play chess in the dormitory every day. Mr Femuz had carved a set out of the granite from the quarry. I thought of myself as a good player and arrogantly assumed I would have the better of him but soon discovered the folly of my hubris. I don't remember ever winning a game.

I suddenly had an idea. I told Mr. Femuz to intentionally lose control of my ropes so that I would fall the final few feet of the descent. He asked why I would want to do such a thing. I simply told him that I needed to get out of quarry work that day. At first he refused, not wanting to hurt me but he relented when I told him it was important that he did this for me and that I would tell him why in the coming days. I think he could tell from my expression that this act was part of a larger conspiracy.

When it was my turn to climb I whizzed up over the top of the wall as I had grown accustomed to doing. Missiles rocketed around me ricocheting off the walls and occasionally hitting me. I reached nearer the foot of the wall in a jerky fashion as Mr. Femuz was not an expert at handling the ropes. I was so near to the ground that I feared that Mr. Femuz had changed his mind, but then I heard the sound of the decreased friction between the ropes as I freefell some fifteen feet and crashed to the floor.

I needed only to accentuate my cries of pain a little as most of it was genuine. The other Service Users crowded around me. I clutched my ankle with one hand while I shielded my face with the other. Warden Serky barged her way through the melee and sounded annoyed at the interruption to her lesson.

"What is it?" she demanded. "That was barely a few feet."

"Sorry, Warden Serky," I squeezed out between moans and groans. "I think I've sprained my ankle."

"Well, get up," she said, unimpressed. "Let's see if you can walk on it."

I got up but found that I genuinely did struggle to walk. I limped a couple of steps, wincing with pain. "Sorry, warden, I can't."

"And I suppose you can't do your work this afternoon either?" she asked.

"Sorry ma'am," I said with my head bowed to the ground trying desperately not to betray my delight at a plan well executed.

She shook her head and sneered, "You will never make it in the Normal world, Winston. No-one as weak and stupid as you possibly could. Now get out of my sight. I expect to see you back in Climbing Practice tomorrow. If you are not there, then the whole team goes without lunch for the rest of the week."

I hobbled out of the warehouse and went to the reception desk on the pretext of asking the Simon Sisters whether they had any bandages. I imagined that they would relish the opportunity to play nurse. I was right.

"Oh, you poor darling," cried Tracey. "Come and sit down and we'll see what we can find you." She led me to a chair behind the desk, took my hand in hers and rubbed it whilst her other hand lay on my thigh. Stacey rushed into the backroom where I could hear her rummaging through drawers and boxes.

A muffled cry of "got some!" made its way through the wall. She ran out of the door. "Lift his leg, Gracie," Stacey ordered. Gracie smiled at me and lifted my leg, removing my standard issue Sisyphusa boot and sock and lifted the leg of my overalls way beyond the knee.

"Sorry if I hurt you pet," Stacey winked. She leaned over, her buttoned down overalls revealing her cleavage. Her soft hands wrapped the bandage around my ankle five times before cutting and taping it tightly.

"That should help," Tracey reassured me as she patted my knee. "Now you stay and make yourself comfortable in the back room." They helped me into the large office in the back and sat me down in a comfortable chair. Gracie meanwhile got another chair for me to keep my leg raised up on.

The three sisters busied themselves with their administrative work. Stacey manned the phones. She fielded calls, mainly from Service Users' families and friends trying to get visiting dates. She would palm them off with well-rehearsed delaying tactics insisting that they had just missed the deadline to arrange a meeting for the next visiting day. She would tell them to ring back "in a few weeks" when they would have the new dates.

I wondered how a Service User could deny their fellow captives such cherished contact with their loved ones. It wasn't only that, but Stacey could do it with such dispassionate ease, speaking in clichéd phrases like a mechanical messaging service.

Meanwhile her sisters occupied themselves with paperwork in the back room where I was. They filed what seemed like hundreds of sheets of paper into towering filing cabinets in. They had to use stepladders to reach the top drawers.

Tracey looked up from her desk and eyed me. She smiled cryptically and said to her sister, "Don't he just remind ya of my Billy, Grace?"

Gracie turned her eyes to me and agreed somewhat unconvincingly, "Yeah, I s'pose your right."

"Who's Billy then?" I asked. "He must be a good-looking lad," I joked.

"Of course he is. He's my boy," she trailed off wistfully staring into space as she began to inhabit her nostalgia. "He's about your age," she said as she returned to the present moment. "How old are you?"

"I'm...twenty-one," I hesitated nearly forgetting my own age.

"Yeah, my Billy must be that age by now."

"He's become a man, Trace. Wonder if he's big and strong like Otis here?" Gracie winked furtively as she looked me up and down.

"I expect so. His wanker of a dad was a big enough lug," said Tracey.

"When was the last time you saw him?" I asked.

"Must be around five years ago," she replied as she gathered a stack of papers and tried to align them neatly in a pile. When the pile wouldn't exactly align, her efforts sped up until she banged the vertical and horizontal edges of the pile against her desk before eventually giving up and dumping the pile onto the floor in a heap. "Five years, weren't it, Grace?"

"Yeah, must be. Cos it was just when my Martin died and that's comin' up to five and a half years," said Gracie. "My husband, Martin," Gracie informed me. "Died of cancer."

"I'm sorry."

"Yeah well, life's too short to cry about it. Everything happens for a reason, that's what we always say," she smiled.

Then Stacey entered the room from the reception desk. "Phones ain't ringin' much today. What are you talkin' about?"

"Was just saying how much Otis here reminds us of my Billy," Tracey said, obviously ignoring the mention of Gracie's husband's death.

"D'you think?" queried Stacey. "Maybe. It's hard to say, last time I seen Billy he was only a nipper, not like Otis here."

"Isn't he allowed to visit you, Tracey?" I asked.

"He's allowed. He just don't want to. He ain't forgiven me since they took him away the last time," she said.

"Who took him away?" I asked.

"Social Services...said I weren't a fit mother. Kept being brought back here, was the problem. No-one was there to look after the boy. Young kid like that don't want a Weirdo for a mum does he? A Liquidated Weirdo like me? Even when I was out he was too embarrassed to bring his friends round the house. He said it was cause our flat was too small but I knew it was cozza me," she wiped a tear away with a tissue.

"Don't say that," said Stacey who walked over and put her arm around Tracey. "He loved you to bits. I'll bet next time we get out of here he'll be dying to see you."

"Yeah, *so* dying he ain't visited me once the last two times I've been here? *So* dying he'd rather live with his lazy-arse gamblin' dad!" she began to sniffle and breathe more pronouncedly. "He never forgave me for leaving his dad. Billy always hated Lorraine!"

"Lorraine was Tracey's lesbian life partner," Gracie dutifully informed me in a forced whisper that was audible to the whole room.

"Why d'you always bloody call her that?" said Tracey in a raised voice of exasperation.

"Well that's what you call 'em innit?" Gracie shrugged innocently and looked from me to Stacey for some support.

"Trace prefers it if you call Lorraine her girlfriend. You know that, Grace," Stacey said and Gracie shrugged not believing she'd done anything wrong.

"That's plain wrong that Billy was taken away from you. It's not your fault that you keep being brought here, it's them who are bringing you," I said. Tracey nodded along with what I was saying as if I was articulating something she had long felt. "I know that if it was my mum who had been brought here then I would want to visit her just like my parents came to visit me here, but they haven't been allowed back since."

The Simons looked at each other sheepishly, clearly revealing their own complicity in my parents being denied a visit. I went on as if I hadn't noticed, "When my dad was brought here many years ago they said I was too young to visit him. I remember seeing him being dragged away by the henchmen. I was in a MegaMarket with my parents and we were just getting into a lift when these two huge figures grabbed hold of Dad and ripped him away from our family. We didn't see him again for two years. I'm sure that if Billy could he would want to see you."

Tracey began crying. "That's the point," she blubbed. "He can come and see me. We control who comes and who goes. I've tried to arrange visits hundreds of times but now he doesn't even answer the phone anymore. Lorraine said him and his dad have moved off the estate. I'm sorry that I stopped you from being able to see your parents, Otis. But the wardens say if we stop visits for the others then we'll get visits of our own, and other stuff on top of that."

"That's alright," I said. "But the person who you most want to see in the world has ignored you for five years and look how that has made you feel. Think about all the other Service Users who you're making feel just as awful. Why are you any more entitled to see your loved ones or to wear your make-up or to drink and smoke? We've all been taken just the same as you have, why are you willing to sell us down the river for a few perks from the very people who are keeping you and the rest of us here against our will?"

"I suppose we just thought 'if you can't beat 'em, join 'em," interjected Stacey as Tracey continued to sniffle into her tissue. "We've been coming here a long time. You're just a boy, you don't understand, this is just the way it is. Don't try to change things you'll just end up getting hurt like the others. You want my advice? Keep your head down, don't make friends, get out as soon as possible and pray to heaven you don't get brought back."

"But why have we even been brought here in the first place?" I asked.

"I don't know about you, love," said Tracey, "but all three of us have been coming here for years. So did our mum, and Auntie June. Things just happen the way they happen, I don't ask questions."

"But that's the point. I'm asking the question. I want to know why?"

I suddenly began to worry that whatever I said to the sisters would surely find its way back to Warden Serky.

"Don't you think they should be more clear about what it is that makes us Weird and why it is that we're brought here? Don't they owe us that?"

"I used to think that," said Gracie.

"What made you change your mind?"

"Time, I suppose. It's been such a long time since then. I suppose you just get used to things being the way they are."

"Well, if you ask me," I began, "if I walked down the street and saw you three ladies walking on the other side, do you want to know what I would be thinking?"

"Spill the beans," said Tracey anxiously.

"Well, I wouldn't be thinking 'those three women look Weird', that's for sure. I'd probably be thinking 'I wonder if any of them are single?'"

I couldn't quite believe what I was doing but I was sure that it would appeal to their biggest weakness.

"Stop it!" squeaked Tracey in feigned humility. "We're old enough to be your mother. Anyway, you're not my type! These two are available though," she said pointing to her sisters.

"If we ever get out of this place maybe we could all go out for dinner or something," I offered.

"Somewhere fancy I hope," said Stacey.

"Well, that depends," I said allowing myself to be flirtatious.

"On what?" asked Gracie.

"I need you to do something for me. I need you to stop working for Serky…"

The words left my mouth and the atmosphere instantly died. The vacuum was filled with an awkward silence.

Finally Stacey said "that's impossible."

"Why?" I pleaded.

"You don't understand. Tracey needs the drinks, we all need the smokes and looking good is the only thing which makes us feel good." Stacey looked around furtively and closed the door to the office.

"We have to do what they say," Stacey whispered. "Serky said if we don't then she'll make our time in here a nightmare. Anyway, if we don't take the jobs somebody else will!"

"Not from Team Recovery. You're the only ones who help Serky. Nobody else on the team trusts you, most of them are afraid of you," I said.

The three women looked at each other. The revelation of their own unpopularity seemed crushing to them. They were unaware that their special privileges had turned others against them.

"But I'm not afraid of you. I trust you. I trust that whatever I say to you today will be said in confidence and you won't say a word to anyone. The first time I met you girls in Normalisation lessons, when I was shit scared and messed up by my time in Solitary, you made me feel welcome. I don't think you even know how important you could be to the team. But if you continue to inform on us and side with the wardens, then we can never be a real team. And if we want any hope of surviving and eventually escaping this place, we have a much better chance by doing it together than if we all try to make the best of things going it alone. You have to trust me. If you do your job and quit then I will get us out of here, as a team."

They crowded round each other and whispered for what was only a few seconds. They walked over to me and Tracey announced, "We're in. But on one condition," she smiled. "We get to keep the make-up and smokes we still have left and you have to kiss Gracie!"

"Oi! Shut up, we never said that, that was nothing to do with me," Gracie professed in embarrassment.

"That's two conditions," I said.

"Serky's gonna make our lives hell!" said Stacey.

"You let me worry about her," I said. "You've done the hardest part already. You've decided to do the right thing and once you've won back the trust and affection of the team you're time here will improve no end.

Chapter 27

The next night everyone in the team was in our dorm resting having just returned from work in the quarry. My injured ankle had made the climbing and the quarry-work even more gruelling than usual. I was relieved to finally have my feet up in bed when a familiar piano sonata began serenading my right ear. This of course meant that Gwen wanted to speak to me so I had to find somewhere private to communicate with her. I got up from my bottom bunk to see Ella and Harry both sitting on her top bunk. Ella said "hi" and Harry nodded and smiled perfunctorily. I made an awkward expression to signal that I was going to the toilet. I left the room, ducking under the HDTV trying not to block the screen as the Flower-Eaters and the Simons were engrossed in some Aspirati cooking show.

I entered the corridor. There was an I-Spy swivelling from the ceiling some fifteen yards away. It had a rotation which encompassed the full panorama of the corridor. I walked towards the toilet which was the first door to the left but waited until the I-Spy was filming me. Then when it began to turn to film the other end of the corridor I dashed instead into the closet opposite the toilet where the spare overalls were hanging and closed the door silently behind me.

I crouched down in the darkness and whispered to Gwen,

"Can you hear me?"

"Yes. I have news on your young Femuz," she said getting straight to the point. "The child's name is Zahra, named after the mother."

"Shit! I mean, wow, I can't believe it, I mean it was just a hunch," I said. "How? I mean what happened? Have you spoken to her?"

"Yes. It took some convincing her that I knew where her father was, but once I repeated to her the story that he gave you, she began to cry on the other end of the phone. I told her of the circumstances and she is waiting for him to come and meet her. What happened was that her mother didn't die straight away from the beating. The doctors managed to perform a caesarean before she died. I imagine the child's grandparents didn't want to tell Mr.Femuz the girl was alive. Zahra says that her grandparents brought her up saying that her father had left her mother when she was pregnant to go abroad and that they didn't know where he was."

"Where is she?" I asked.

"She works as a journalist in Lutetia," said Gwen.

"That's great news. He has a daughter! Mr.Femuz is going to be so happy when I tell him!"

"So you are going to tell him?" asked Gwen sounding worried.

"Yes. I have to. He deserves to know," I said.

"But if you tell him about her then you tell him about me and about the plan. Are you prepared to do that?" she asked.

"I trust him, Gwen. He's a good man. I decided that I was going to tell him a while ago, but I was just waiting for the right time and this is it. I need help down here, I'm not going to be able to get everyone out alone," I said.

"On your head be it," Gwen said. "Now for other business. Did you complete your mission?"

"Yes. The Simon Sisters can now be considered trusted members of Team Recovery," I said.

"Excellent. I will get back to you with your next mission shortly. Goodbye."

The Earpiece went dead like she had hung the phone up on me. I opened the closet door just slightly so that I could see through the crack when the I-Spy was facing the other way and when it was I came out of the closet and walked casually back into the dormitory.

I had to wait until the next day before I could speak to Mr.Femuz without anyone else overhearing. The two of us were working side-by-side in the quarry which was the way we had worked every day since the cave collapse. We were still gathering the material for the statue of The Carpenter which The Emperor wanted. Since our cave had collapsed we couldn't quarry the special granite necessary so our job was to help one of the other teams carry their boulders up the hill to the factory conveyor belt.

Mr.Femuz and I latched on to GI Joe's team and they were only too happy to have our help. What Joe said exactly was,

"You can put your feet up or do whatever you want, Dizzy, I don't care, but as long as Mr.Femuz is hauling our rocks, by the time we're finished pick-axing our cave, there'll barely be any left for us to drag up!"

So Mr.Femuz and I wrapped our black sashes around a boulder each and began dragging. Well, he did, mine took a while to get going. Once I was into the swing of things I began to get a rhythm going and could almost keep up with Mr.Femuz, though I think he purposefully slowed his pace for my benefit. On our third rock I decided to tell him.

"Mr. Femuz."

He turned around thinking that I needed help with my boulder.

"No, don't turn around. They'll see we're talking. Just keep looking ahead and listen. I have something important to tell you."

I told him about what happened when I was sent to The Pit. I told him about Gwen and the books, about the history of Sisyphusa and Gwen's research studies on Weirdness. I told him about the special Earpiece that Gwen had given me and the constant contact we were in. I told him we had a plan, a plan to escape, to save the Service Users and to have our files erased and have our freedom. Throughout the story his head didn't turn once. The two times I dared look up to catch a furtive glance at his expression, it hadn't changed, it was that same steely indifference.

But then I told him about his daughter. And when I did that, everything changed. After I'd told him she was alive, she was waiting for him in Lutetia, she was a journalist and her name was Zahra, he stopped short and dropped to his knees. He put his head to my feet and began to weep. But these were no longer tears of mourning like the ones he shed in the cave. These were tears of unadulterated joy. He kept thanking me. I tried desperately to pull him up from the floor as we were beginning to cause a scene. To my relief he eventually stood up, but my relief was short-lived as he then began hugging me and kissing me on both cheeks. I pleaded with him to stop.

"Mr.Femuz, we have to get back to work, the warden is coming over," I said. He didn't seem to be listening, he was in another world. "Please, Mr. Femuz, think of Zahra, if you get sent to The Pit now, we can't escape and you won't be able to see her." Suddenly he snapped out of it. He picked up his sash and began dragging his boulder, only now he was doing it faster than I'd ever seen him before. He was totally re-energised. He flew past the oncoming Warden Serky smiling at her broadly. Before she could stop him, he was halfway up the hill. She stopped me instead.

"What was all of that about, Winston?" she barked.

"All of what, warden?" I croaked as I struggled past her with my boulder.

"Don't give me that, Winston. What was all of that commotion? The feet-kissing and the hugging," she demanded.

"Your guess is as good as mine, Warden," I said. "You know these Outlanders, Weird as they come. Everything to them is either holy or sacred. I was just working, minding my own business and suddenly he starts kneeling at my feet worshipping me like I'm one of his Babby gods!"

Serky narrowed her eyes at me but then turned around and walked back to her station next to the conveyor belt under the cool shade of the umbrella.

Over the next few days I became increasingly worried about the completely altered personality of Mr. Femuz. He had shifted straight away from the taciturn, solitary, anti-social man I had known to one full of energy and conversation. He was teeming with activity. He answered every question in Normalisation classes without even raising his hand, courting the wrath of Warden Serky. His work in the quarry had markedly changed. His power and brute force had always stood out but now added to that was sheer speed and enthusiasm. He was like a dynamo.

But more disconcerting to me than his rediscovered life-force was his unrecognisable personality. I became worried that he would say too much and give us away. I kept remembering

Gwen's words: "On your head be it." It's as if she knew something I didn't.

Now don't get me wrong, I wouldn't want anyone to think that I was insensitive. Of course the man was happy—he'd just discovered that he had a daughter whom he never knew existed. Great joy was to be expected. But it was more than that. I felt like I had really got to know him. I'd spent so much time in his company, often not talking, just working or sitting or eating or playing chess. It was as if we'd found a little sanctuary within all of the chaos and hysteria of Sisyphusa where we could just be quiet and separate. A switch had flicked in him. I felt betrayed. He wasn't like me at all. There wasn't one piece of information from the outside world which would have suddenly made me happy.

When you live in Sisyphusa you are surrounded by emotional extremes. Crying, screaming, fighting, even laughing. But Mr. Femuz wasn't like that. He had been more constant, like me. Even before I came to Sisyphusa I was never someone to fly off the handle. And so my initial induction into life in Sisyphusa when I was in my cell had been a massive shock. I was crying and screaming, attacking inanimate objects and wishing for death. I didn't recognise myself. When I was finally integrated with the other Service Users, even though I was still in despair and mourning for my lost life, I refused to show it. My exposure to the other Service Users and their emotions and hysteria numbed me to my own suffering or at least internalised it.

After hearing about his daughter, Mr. Femuz became hysterical and increasingly hyper. He would talk non-stop, barely pausing for air. He didn't listen to other people's replies when he was having a conversation. He began to take advantage of some of the other members of the team, especially the weaker ones like Gloria and the Flower-Eaters. He would take things from them without asking, knowing that they were too weak to complain. He'd shout them down or interrupt them. I remember once at lunch that he just said to Gloria, "I'm going to take this food from you today, but remind me next week and I'll give you some of mine if I'm not hungry," as he began scraping her meal onto his own plate.

He said it so brashly, so matter-of-factly, he clearly didn't know that he was even being rude. All he saw was that he was hungry and that Gloria had food and she was weak. And sure enough Gloria didn't say anything. In fact she happily obliged. No-one said anything. No-one on the team had even noticed that Mr. Femuz had been acting completely differently to the way he had always been before. I decided at that point I had to say something.

"Don't you realise that what you just did was rude Mr. Femuz?" I asked sternly but still feeling awkward about censuring someone older than myself.

"What?" he said with a face like a confused child. He seemed to wake up from a daze for that split-second and realised he wasn't being himself. But then he quickly returned to the daze, a daze which required no responsibility or conscience. "No, no, no. It's okay. I said I'd give her some next week." And with that he got up and moved to the other end of the table to interrupt a conversation. I had become the teacher who was ruining his fun and he began to avoid me.

Once he'd left, Gloria whispered to me almost inaudibly. "Thank you, Odis. That was the nicest thing anyone's ever done for me."

"What for? Gloria, he took your lunch and he still has it. Why didn't you say something to him?" I asked in a sympathetic voice.

"No, I couldn't. I'm not brave like you. I'd rather avoid any trouble," she said, looking worried and frightened at the thought of conflict. I realised what a different world I lived in to Gloria. For me, telling someone who was stealing from you not to do it wasn't brave, it was just what you do. And speaking up when you saw it happening to someone else wasn't an extraordinary act of kindness, it was just the decent thing to do. Gloria had been cowed and trampled upon for so long that she had little or no self-worth and was thus touched by my intervention.

This made me angry. People were so brutalised and condemned inside of Sisyphusa and out that they'd been taught not to even expect to be treated with decency. That was my job. That was what I had to do. I had to make them hope for more, for some kind of future, for some kind of better life. Whatever the wardens or The Daily Bulletin said we weren't any different to Normal people and we deserved more.

Chapter 28

Mr. Femuz abruptly emerged from his daze a few days later, but he seemed not to have realised that he had changed in any way nor did he remember the way he had treated Gloria and the others. He had not forgotten, however, what I had told him. When we had a chance to speak again he pledged to do whatever it took to escape and promised he would follow me come what may. He continued to thank me for finding Zahra, but I told him, "Don't thank me just don't give us away. Gwen has a plan. I don't know what it is, but when she gives the word we have to lead the Service Users out of Sisyphusa."

"What if they don't follow?" Mr. Femuz asked.

"If Team Recovery are all with us, if we all move to escape as one, then the other teams will follow. Who here doesn't want to escape?" I asked him. He seemed satisfied.

With Mr. Femuz on board and back to his old self, I had to turn my attention to making sure that I had the rest of the team behind me. I decided that it was too risky to tell them all separately about Gwen and the plan- the more people who knew the more likely we were to get caught out. Instead, I had to be sure that Team Recovery trusted me and were beginning to see that they shouldn't accept being kept in Sisyphusa any longer. When the time came, I had to be confident that the others would follow me.

I first began to feel that the momentum was shifting in Normalisation Class, that daily hour of indoctrination where, ever since I had arrived in Sisyphusa, I would seethe with anger while Service Users lapped up the lies and propaganda that Serky would feed them. But this class was different. Things were beginning to change.

The topic of the lesson that day was: "Why are Normal people in charge?" Serky began by outlining the fact that, of course, all of the important jobs and positions on Fantasy Island, and indeed in the rest of the Empire, are held by Normal people- right from Minister Frown down through every doctor, teacher, policeman and warden. She addressed the group, asking,

"Why do you think it is that such important jobs are reserved only for Normal people?"

The class wasn't its usual lively self in recent weeks, fewer people were offering answers in discussion. Eventually Harry, who was sitting alone because Ella was in Senior Reps Council Meeting, volunteered an answer.

"Maybe because we wouldn't be reliable enough to do it?" said Harry, clearly not confident of his answer.

"Good," said Serky. "Would you like to expand on that answer?"

"Ummm," Harry dithered. "Well, for one thing, we might get brought in here if our Weirdness starts playin' up. If, say, Minister Frown was constantly bein' brought in and out of Sisyphusa then who would run the island?" said Harry, clearly proud of the argument he had constructed on the spot.

"Yes. That's true," agreed the warden. "In a job as important as First Minister, regular attendance is crucial. Anybody else?"

Silence reigned. The Simon Sisters, who were back in Normalisation Class having renounced their privileges, were stony-faced. They looked wary of saying anything. Mr. Femuz, following his brief uncharacteristic spell of loquacity, was again a silent spectator in class. The Flower-Eaters watched on. Sometimes, Mo had told me, they struggled to follow the lessons as Serky spoke too quickly for them to understand.

Then out of the silence emerged a soft, unassuming voice. It was Gloria.

"I-I-I don't understand, Warden Serky."

"What don't you understand, Gloria?" the warden asked impatiently.

"Why are all Weird people the same?" she wondered innocently.

"What kind of a stupid question is that?" sneered Serky.

"What I mean is, if Normal people are able to choose to be teachers, wardens, policemen, anything they want, why is it that all Weird people have to be Service Users?" She coughed lightly and I wondered whether she regretted her decision to speak up. But then she appeared to steel herself and continued, "I've been in and out of Sisyphusa, and other places like it, for more than…oooh… thirty years now and I've met a fair few Service Users. Some who have been in and out countless times, like me, others who have been in and out a handful of times and quite a number who have been in once and then never become Weird again," she finished.

"And your point is?" asked Serky.

"I suppose what I'm saying is… I've met a lot of Service Users who have been more than capable of doing all of those jobs, maybe even the First Minister, so I don't understand why the law says that all people who have ever suffered from Weirdness can never do any jobs except maybe work stacking shelves or wiping floors?" In her understated way, Gloria was finished, having had no idea how brave she had just been or how much she had devastated Serky.

"I've never heard anything so ridiculous," said the warden as her face flushed pink. "The fact is, is that, well, Weird people cannot do important jobs. Service User being First Minister! Ha!" she snorted looking decidedly uncomfortable.

An eerie silence settled over the room giving the Service Users time to digest Gloria's argument and the bizarre reaction it had elicited in the warden. Serky, flustered, walked over to her desk and started rifling through the drawers. Eventually she looked up and found all eyes trained on her.

"What?!" she finally erupted. "What are you all staring at? The proposition is just ridiculous," she repeated.

"But why?" asked Stacey. "Gloria's right. There shouldn't be a rule for all Weird people. All of us have different capabilities, we're all individuals. If Normal people have the choice because they all want to do different things, then why don't we? Look at us," she grew louder as she pointed to her two sisters. "We worked here on reception for the last year but if we applied for a secretary job in the outside world we'd get laughed in our faces!"

"And so you should," shot back Serky with a look of disdain. "I gave you the privilege of some extra responsibilities and look what you did, you couldn't handle the job."

"That's not true," chimed in Tracey who always had a visceral, instinctive reaction of anger if she felt she was being misrepresented. "We did everything you said for months. We spied on and cheated Service Users but we won't do it anymore, that's why we left the job."

Serky was furious but she couldn't say anything. She was surprisingly embarrassed about something that everyone knew went on being said aloud in the presence of the very Service Users who were being spied upon.

Ahmed then decided to get involved in the debate, "I used to have job here in this country but then when Sisyphusa say I was Weird they take job away and now I worry if I get out of here I can't get no more work. No work makes me more unhappy and then maybe I do more bad things."

"Don't blame it on us," dismissed Serky. "The fact is, you're an Outlander and even worse you're a Weird Outlander. If I was you I wouldn't expect to be getting a job any time soon."

"What's the fact that he's an Outlander got to do with anything?" said Tracey. "If he can do the job he can do the job!" Tracey looked back at Ahmed and nodded with a determined look of solidarity on her face. The man looked puzzled at first, but soon the hint of a smile emerged on his purple lips.

"Regardless," Serky said, trying to change the subject. "The issue here is why Weird people can't do important jobs and the argument is clear: unreliability, inexperience, poor attendance, lack of authority." Serky wrote each reason down on the white board in bullet-point form as she recited them.

I decided that it was my turn to nudge the argument on. "But how can 'so-called' Weird people gain experience and authority if they are never given the equal chance to hold important positions. I agree with Gloria, the system is unfair." I smiled at Gloria proudly. She returned my smile meekly before becoming too embarrassed.

"What do you mean 'so-called' Weird people," thundered an indignant voice from the other side of the room. It was Harry. "That ain't in question here. If I ain't Weird then why have I been in places like this half my life? You're full of it, 108. Everyone's gettin' too big for their boots in 'ere. I'm all for Service Users' rights but this is gettin' silly. Things just are the way they are and there ain't no use in pretendin' otherwise."

"Mr.Harris is right," Serky interceded. She seemed mightily relieved to have found some support. "Things *are* getting silly now. You all know as well as I do that things are the way they are and for good reason. It just wouldn't work to have such emotionally unstable people in positions of power."

"Who says that Weird people are the only ones who can be emotionally unstable?" interrupted Stacey. "Can't everyone be emotionally unstable at times?"

"I've had just about enough of this insolence from all of you. I have a mind to start sending some people to The Pit. Now, everyone needs to just shut up and take notes, and then maybe, just maybe, you might learn something instead of you all getting yourselves excited about things you don't understand.

The remainder of the session was then played out in silence while we all copied down Serky's arguments which she dictated from the Sisyphusa Warden's Guidebook. The threat of The Pit was clearly more than potent enough to quell any burgeoning uprising, but the seeds of rebellion had been sown.

Chapter 29

The boy was no longer a boy. He had reached the height of a man. Strange tufts of hair had finally begun appearing in strange places—not on his face yet, that still looked like a boy's face. But did he feel like a man? He certainly didn't act like one. He day-dreamed his way through school, counting down the days to the week's apogee: Friday Night.

In Itticar, as in every town and city across the Island, Friday Night was the day when all youngsters worshipped at the altar of Liquid Escape. If you were old enough you would do so at a real place of worship. If you were not, then you found somewhere, anywhere, where you could practise your religion in peace, away from the repressive forces of parents and authorities. Where you did it was not the issue. The crucial components of performing the sacred rites were: your friends, some privacy and an appropriate amount of Liquid Escape.

The boy, I mean man, whatever, had been a regular worshipper for three or four years already, but tonight was a special occasion. He had finally reached the age when he could worship his religion freely, before the gaze of society. And how was he to celebrate such a watershed moment in his young life? By getting Liquidated, of course.

Rather bizarrely, the church where he chose to take his friends to celebrate his birthday was one with an eccentric dress-code: everyone was required to come in school uniform. The friends all congregated outside the church. They queued up with the hordes of other worshippers awaiting admission to spiritual ecstasy. All that was needed was that crucial new accessory he had just obtained, the I.D.

His friends made it in except for the unfortunate two who were not yet old enough, but sacrifices had to be made for the sake of the greater good. The young worshippers gathered at the Liquidiser, wearing their white shirts, striped ties and tight blazers, trying to look aloof. It was paramount that the Liquidation begin immediately or else the true zenith of spiritual awakening could never be reached.

Sisyphusa

After one or two pints, they moved away from the bar and sought the next stage of the sacrament, the dance floor. The dance floor was surely there but it was invisible. It was covered by a heaving mass of humanity all swaying and jumping and shaking to the blasts of music coming from a distant stage that they could barely see. The first-time worshippers were in heaven.

They immediately swarmed into the crowd and lost sight of each other, but that wasn't important, the time had come. It was time to find the other key to the Friday night experience: The Woman.

The boy/man had become separated from his friends. He bumped and barged his way through dozens of other boy/men searching for the scarce pockets of women. Would it be tonight? It would be so perfect if it was tonight on his special day. It had to be perfect, he had waited so long and all of his friends had already done it. A strobe light fell on a group of girls. They were dancing with each other, legs bent beneath them so that their short skirts brushed the floor when they rose up provocatively. The one with the blonde pig-tails is cute. No, she's too Liquidated, it wouldn't be perfect.

He turned back to look for his friend but he was already with a girl. They were slobbering all over each other, grinding up and down and out of time to the music, only taking a breath to pull on the cigarette they were sharing. He's already found one! How does he do it every time? What are you supposed to say before you can start doing that?

He continued walking around the dance floor aimlessly, pretending to no-one, to everyone, that he was looking for his friends, so that he didn't seem desperate. What was he doing? He wasn't with a girl, he wasn't with his friends, and he didn't even have a drink in his hand- at the Church of Friday night this was sacrilege. And this was supposed to be his special day!

He stumbled his way to the Liquidiser. He felt pretty Liquidated already but if he wasn't with a woman and he wasn't with his mates, then he at least needed to be drinking. He bought a pint and sat down in a dark corner. There were a handful of other worshippers in this hidden enclave but they were mainly couples. He sat there drinking, smiling, pretending to have fun, but he felt lonely. Feeling lonely was okay because getting Liquidated is one of those rare things that can equally be an aid to celebration or a companion to misery. Then he looked over to the bar and there she was.

She was his friend from school. At one point, a time full of nervousness and possibility, she was a mere acquaintance. However this potential window is wont to close just as swiftly as it opens. And lo, before he could summon the courage to enact the grand designs of his ambitious imagination, he found himself frustrated with that dreaded label once again: the friend. He had invited her to come and she actually had, he couldn't believe it! He looked away quickly, she mustn't see him staring at her, he had to play it cool. But she looked so beautiful he had to sneak another glance.

She was wearing the same attire as the rest of the schoolgirls in the church but somehow she looked different. Her white shirt wasn't tied up in a knot to reveal her midriff nor were her top buttons undone so that you could see her bra. Her hazel hair was in pig-tails, unlike her normal style, to suit the theme of the church. He saw the profile of her face as she spoke to the Liquid-Server, trying to order a soft drink over the noise. Why did she never drink Liquid Escape?

That Liquid-Server is so lucky to be able to talk to her, to have her smile all to himself. Bastard. The boy/man could just make out that little dimple in her chin and the tiny mole that she had near her mouth. How he wanted to kiss them. He couldn't believe she had come! Shit, she saw him looking at her! Quick, smile! No, not like that, cooler!

She came over and sat down. She wished him a happy birthday and kissed him on the cheek. He blushed but quickly made a joke to diffuse the tension. They talked about the music and the drinks and everything else that made up appropriate church conversation but he yearned for more. He'd talked to her at school and on the Foney so many times that he felt really close to her now, but he wanted even more, he wanted to be even closer. Could this be the night?

He asked if she wanted to dance but she declined politely (as she always did). In a way he was relieved because he hated to dance unless he was really Liquidated. But did that *mean that she didn't like him like that? Probably. But she never dances with any boys, does she? Hope! Just keep on talking to her, keep on being a gentleman like Grandpa Abe says. Don't listen to your friends who say you have to treat them mean if you want it. You don't want a girl who wants to be treated mean anyway. Why would someone want to be treated mean? Surely it was much more logical for her to like you because you were kind to her and would do anything for her.*

His friends, and hers, came and found them. They drank some more Liquid Escape and went to the dance floor en masse. She danced with the girls and he danced with the boys. The two sexes pretended not to be aware of each others' presence, but every thought and every movement was calculated with each other in mind. It was an animal mating ritual in the wild. He watched as her friends began to pair off with his, one-by-one, dancing to the retro music. His friends barely knew her friends, why could they make the transition to dancing so easily when he couldn't? Maybe she knew him too well? That must be it! She knows you too well. You're like her brother, stupid! Who wants to dance with their brother?

He pretended to be dancing. He talked to a friend who couldn't dance with girls either. But he was watching her. Other boy/men he didn't know came over and tried to dance with her. She knew that she would never even consider dancing with any of them but she enjoyed the attention, it gave her confidence. It was nice to know that she could have her pick if she so chose. Everyone wanted to dance with her. Fuck off bastards, you don't get to dance with her! You don't even know her. She's my friend. She's mine. But she's not mine. Ha! Screw you, she doesn't want to dance with you either, it's not just me!

He felt Liquidated. The night wasn't going to end in perfection, the way he had pictured it when he invited her. Time to do something destructive. It was his day, his special day. He swigged the last dregs of his umpteenth bottle of Liquid Escape and clambered onto the stage. The band looked at him with an unimpressed expression. Not another Liquidated stage invader! He raised both of his arms in the air and looked to the ceiling and then closed his eyes breathing in the moment. Jump! Jump! Jump! Jump! His friends were all laughing, admiring, encouraging. He took a run, the crowd beckoned him…they parted, the floor.

He lay on the floor encircled by admirers. His friends congratulated him and then went off to the Liquidiser. But she was there, she stayed. She held his hand, rubbed his forehead and asked if he was okay. The fluorescent lights from the ceiling outlined a shimmering halo round her head, she was an angel. He did make it to heaven after all. The Church of Friday Night was a glorious thing.

"Odis, are you alright?" said a stern whisper. I groggily opened my eyes and a shadowy figured crouched over my bottom bunk. "Odis?"

"What…er…I'm up, I'm up, what is it?" I said.

"You were having a dream," said Ella. "You were saying 'Layla, Layla'!" she smiled.

"Was I? Sorry did I wake you?"

"It's okay. I just thought I'd better wake you before you woke anyone else. You know what the Simons are like if they don't get their eight hours!"

"It's those bloody Climbing Pills-- they play havoc with my sleep. I've got to stop taking them!" I said.

"Yeah, right," said Ella. "They watch us like hawks when they give us those pills!"

"I suppose you're right," I admitted. There was a short silence. Oddly, the silence felt uncomfortable which it never used to between us, but we'd been spending less and less time together.

"So anything exciting?" she asked.

"What?"

"The dream. You sounded pretty *involved*," she winked.

"Oh… I can't remember. You know what it's like with dreams," I said. There was another silence.

"Right well, I guess I'll let you get back to sleep then," said Ella. I couldn't tell whether or not the end of her sentence had an inflection. She seemed to hover briefly, waiting, with an almost doleful expression on her face.

"Okay, thanks," I said, pathetically. She seemed disappointed and rose to her feet slowly.

"Oh, Ella," I whispered.

"Yes," she said bending back down.

"Feel free to give me a kick if I start making any more strange noises!" I said.

"Will do," she smiled.

Chapter 30

The next morning, as soon as I awoke, Gloria told me that there was a message for me on the HDTV. I was excited as I thought that finally, after having no word for many months, a message from my family might have made it through the censors. I pressed the buttons on the remote to take me to the messages and it was an internal message sent from within Sisyphusa. Serky wanted me to report to her office.

I quickly changed into a new set of overalls and washed myself before going to see her. It was seven in the morning and I was still feeling drowsy after a bad night's sleep. Warden Serky's office was on the third floor of Tower B. I began scaling the staircase. I came to the second floor and remembered that when Harry told me his story about being taken to Governor Shade's office he said it was on the second floor. I decided to take a look. I opened the door which led onto a corridor that appeared identical to every other corridor I had seen in Sisyphusa. There were fewer doors on this floor than there were for the dorms or the cells, which I imagined meant that these rooms were far larger.

On the second door there was a large, golden plaque with "**Governor Shade**" written on it. I crept closer to the wooden door until I was so close I could smell the varnish and then pressed my ear to it. I could hear the Governor's voice. When no one replied I assumed that he was speaking on the phone: "…unsatisfactory results…Yes sir, I understand, but our turnover is way up from the last quarter… We are constantly striving to improve our numbers, but I urge you to look at our last Comprehensive Statistical Analysis…Yes sir, but some of the Service Users don't even register on the Weirdness Test. Levels are going up astronomically, we're in a Weirdness epidemic."

It had been clear to me for some time that places like Sisyphusa were no longer used solely for people who had official Weirdness Grades. They were fast becoming the last refuge or dumping ground for the Island's deprived or social outcasts. Afterwards I heard "Yes sir" every now and again and then nothing at all until suddenly there were footsteps heading right for the door. I pulled myself away and walked briskly down the corridor. A voice rang out.

"What are you doing here?"

I turned around slowly and met the face I'd only ever seen on my HDTV screen. Governor Shade was larger in body than his face had suggested. He wore a dark grey suit and tie with a white shirt that matched his ice-white hair. His goatee was closely shaven and meticulously so. He peered at me with tiny piercing eyes.

"I was just looking for Warden Serky's office, sir."

"The warden's offices are on the third and fourth floors, you should have been told that when you were summoned to see her," he said as he turned to lock the door to his office.

"Yes sir, I must have made a mistake. Sorry sir," I said turning around to walk out of the corridor.

"Wait there," he said with the slightly raised voice of a person confident that his every order will be obeyed. "I didn't say that you could go. What does that number say?" he asked referring to the identity number printed on the breast pocket of my overalls.

"108, sir."

"108…and which team are you a member of, Mr.108?" he asked, showing no desire to know my real name.

"Team Recovery, sir," I replied, mournfully regretting my escapade for drawing unnecessary attention to myself and the team.

"Team Recovery," he said in a mimicking voice that someone would use when speaking to a child at primary school. "That's Warden Serky's team, is it not? Oh yes, that's who you said you were on your way to see wasn't it?" he said in a controlled way that made me think he hadn't forgotten it at all but was merely wanting to keep me talking so that he could observe me. He stared at me in silence for ten or fifteen seconds and then said, "Very well, go along. I'll be speaking to Warden Serky about you."

"Yes, sir," I said before walking briskly out of the corridor and up the stairs to the third floor. I knocked on Warden Serky's door. Her shrill voice ordered me to enter. The office was surprisingly small, not much larger than the cell where I spent my first year. The walls were a drab beige colour and the furniture was sparse. She sat behind a metal desk working at her computer. There was a stand with a clutch of perfectly sharpened pencils in it and a picture frame lying face down.

"What took you so long Mr.Winston?"

"Sorry warden, I didn't know what floor your office was on."

She fired me her usual look of disdain, but her features then softened as she moved the conversation on.

"I have an errand I'd like you to run."

Her focus returned to her computer screen and she began moving and clicking the mouse with her right hand. Finally, she let go of the mouse, having found what she was looking for.

"There is a Service User due to be released from Solitary Initiation this morning. I need you to go and pick them up and bring them to Normalisation Class.

"Our Normalisation class?" I asked. "Are they going to be joining Team Recovery, warden?" I asked trying to sound as casual as possible. In reality I was anxious about a new personality joining the team just as I was moulding the dynamic as I wanted it.

"Yes, is there a problem with that?" she asked.

"No. Just wondering."

"Good, I'm glad it meets your approval," she sneered. "Go to Cell Number 4. The henchman on duty knows you're coming and will let you in. Class starts in thirty minutes so try not to get lost!"

I hadn't been back to the cells since Harry had come to collect me from my own Solitary Initiation which was almost a year previously. I walked down the stairs, crossed the reception area and noticed that the Simons had already been replaced on the desk by two Service Users from another team.

The cells were at the top of Tower A. I scaled the spiral staircase and at the top was greeted by a faceless henchman sitting outside the entrance to the corridor. I approached the final stair tentatively and nearly jumped when he stood up. But he was just opening the door. Inside I was greeted by another henchman who showed me the way to Cell Number 4.

I could hear the sounds of the HDTVs blaring away in the cells and there were cries of horror emanating from further down the corridor. "Must be a new one," I thought to myself, surprised at how accustomed I'd become to such awful sounds of suffering and distress.

The henchman stopped outside Cell Number 4. He inserted a card into the slot next to the metal cell-door. I looked at his massive gloved hand and had a flashback to my kitchen and Wellborn being swatted aside like a fly by a similarly gloved hand. I wondered whether it was the same one. There was no way of knowing--they all looked the same. I thought about Wellborn. How was he? Had he forgotten about me? It was a different life.

I had no time to linger in my reverie as the light turned green and the metallic door slid open. The cell was empty. I turned around to ask the henchman where the supposed Service User was but he had already turned around and was lumbering down the corridor back to his station.

The HDTV screen was on the HDTV Kidz channel. On-screen, two pubescent Aspirati youths were frolicking about the streets making fart-noises and scaring elderly people. I reached for the remote control, which was on the arm of the tattered sofa, and muted the programme. As I went to put the remote back in its place I spied a pale, bony elbow caked in dirt poking out from beneath the sofa. As soon as I saw the elbow, it vanished. I knelt down on the ground and put my face sideways to the floor, and there, cowering in the tiny gap under the sofa was an emaciated child.

I couldn't tell whether it was a boy or a girl. The child had long, straggly, unkempt hair and a dirty face. Its blue eyes were like kaleidoscopic marbles and watery from fear. When it saw me it retreated back to the wall like a frightened animal escaping a predator. I froze. I didn't react. I hadn't even seen a child for some two years. I'd almost forgotten they existed. I certainly couldn't remember much of my own childhood. The presence of this child seemed utterly bizarre in the setting of Sisyphusa.

The child was wearing baggy-looking overalls with a logo of a smiling dinosaur on the breast pocket and letters of varying colours spelling out the word Sisy-Junior. It seemed that Sisyphusa hadn't yet mass-produced overalls for a kid quite this small and skinny. A tear at the knee left the material flapping open to expose a nasty cut across a bony knee. Suddenly an image flashed into my mind of being in Gwen's library and seeing that small boy on her camera feed, crying and holding his grazed knee. This was that same boy.

"Hello," I said quietly. The boy didn't answer. He stared at me intently but wouldn't meet my eyes.

"My name's Odis. What's yours?" I asked. The boy didn't move, didn't speak, just stared into space like a blind person. I shuffled closer. The child flinched again and turned his head sharply so that it was facing the wall.

"Sorry, I didn't mean to frighten you. I won't come any closer, I promise. I won't hurt you," I tried to assure him. How could this little kid believe a word I was saying? He'd clearly been through hell for the last year. Neglected, malnourished, isolated with nothing for company but an HDTV, the poor child must have been terrified. And then *I* had appeared, out of the blue. What could I say to get him to trust me? To get him to come with me? What could I offer him? There were no promises that if he came with me and "integrated" with the other Service Users that his nightmare would get any better. I decided to just be honest.

"I know you must be scared," I said calmly. "I was terrified when a stranger came to pick me up from my cell. I was much older than you are now, but I was still scared. These two big, scary men dressed in black cloaks came and took me away from my friends and family. And then when I woke up in a tiny room, like this one, with a funny machine nailed into my ear which started saying nasty, mean things to me and wouldn't stop, I cried and screamed for days but it was useless. Eventually I stopped. I began to lose any hope of ever seeing the people I loved again. But then someone came one morning, not a warden or a henchman with horrible food or wretched pills, but someone different who was dressed just like me, in one of these uniforms." The child slowly turned around. Tears were streaming down his cheeks but he still hadn't made a sound.

I repeated, "My name's Odis. I'm what they call a Service User: someone who's been brought here against their own will, just like you. I'm here to take you away from this cell to live with other Service Users. Would you prefer that instead of staying here all alone?" I asked. The child shook his head from side to side very slightly.

"You must be scared." He nodded. "I was too. But when I was collected I thought, 'Well, even if it gets worse when I leave this room, at least it will be different.' The worst thing about being in one place for so long is the repetition: the same thoughts, the same worries, the same fears, looking at the same spots on the wall and having those spots trigger the same exact thoughts over and over and over again. If you come with me, I can't promise you that everything will be better and easy all of a sudden but it will definitely be different, and you won't be on your own any longer."

The boy slowly inched out from under the sofa and I moved back to give him some space. His overalls were covered in dust and he wore a wan expression as he sat on the sofa lifting his knees to his chin and wrapping his arms around his shins.

"Do...you...have HDTV Kidz?" the boy asked in a crackly, high-pitched voice.

"Ummm, yeah, yes I think we do. We have a screen in our dorm and people can take it in turns to choose what channel they want to watch. I'll have a word with the rest of the guys to make sure you get to watch it whenever you like. Ok?"

The child didn't answer. He appeared to be considering whether or not to come with me. His filthy, bare feet were twitching and were taking it in turns to wrap around each other like a seal's flippers. I waited while he sat there for minutes not saying anything, looking extremely distressed, churning things over in his mind.

Finally, seeing that I was late for Normalisation Class, I asked, "Are you ready to come?" the boy nodded. "Great!" I said. "I'm so glad. What's your name then?"

"Samuel Etch," he said.

Chapter 31

The boy walked two or three paces behind me all the way to the classroom. I explained to him where we were going and told him basic things about the schedule and rules imposed on Service Users. I doubt whether he took any of it in. When we arrived at Normalisation Class, Warden Serky had already begun. I knocked on the door and entered. Serky was standing at the front of the class and I was taken aback to find that Governor Shade, who had never been present at one of our Normalisation Classes before, sat in the corner behind her with one of his legs crossed over the other and a clipboard on his lap.

"Well?" asked Serky, puzzled. I turned around and saw that the boy wasn't standing behind me. He was sitting up against the wall with his knees pressed to his chin and his arms clasped tightly around his shins.

"You have to come in now, Samuel," I whispered. The boy didn't move, didn't look in my direction, didn't even seem to hear anything.

"What is this, Winston?" Serky's terse voice emanated from the classroom.

"Come on, mate," I pleaded with the boy. "You'd better come inside." But still he didn't react. Serky stormed out of the classroom and into the corridor. She immediately saw what the problem was and looked at me with an expression that said 'is that all you're dilly-dallying about?' She yanked the boy up from under his armpits. He didn't struggle or scream but merely flopped into her forceful arms, a body devoid of muscle or bone. Serky plonked him into a vacant chair and went back to the front of the class. I slipped in behind and took a seat between the boy and Jacob, who was asleep.

"As you can see we have a new member of Team Recovery," announced Serky. "He hasn't made a very good start." Raising her voice out of exasperation she said, "I hope the rest of you will show an example to him on how to behave properly. Would you like to tell them your name?" she asked the boy. He didn't answer her but simply sat where Serky had dumped him. She was growing increasingly angry at the child's continued silence.

"The boy's name is written on his uniform, is it not, warden?" asked Governor Shade calmly without lifting his eyes from the clipboard. "His name is 119, nothing more."

"Of course, Governor," Serky replied, chastened. It seemed that the Governor wasn't present merely to keep an eye on a rebellious class but also a faltering warden.

"His name's Samuel," I addressed the other Service Users on the boy's behalf. "Samuel Etch." When I said this, the Governor looked at me impassively and then wrote something down on his clipboard.

"Shut up, Winston... I mean... 108!" exploded Serky with added force. "You heard the Governor." She turned to begin her lesson. The topic for the day was written on the board in large capitals: "THE IMPORTANCE OF DISCIPLINE."

"Who can explain to me what discipline means?" Serky began. The class members were initially slow to get involved in any discussion. The unusual presence of the Governor had everyone on edge, including Warden Serky, who seemed desperate to prove that Team Recovery was full of model Service Users. Eventually Harry answered.

"It basically means doin' what you're told. Either that or somethin' kinky with leather and handcuffs?" he chuckled.

"Behave yourself, Harris," admonished the Warden gently, grateful for a Service User input regardless of its suitability. "Okay, so 'doing what you're told', do the rest of you agree with that?" The rest of us nodded our assent. "Is that all it is? Who is it that's doing the telling?"

"You, warden," answered Harry with his serious face on. "And the Governor," he looked at Governor Shade, but the Governor was scribbling on his pad.

"Right. So what you're saying is in this establishment there are clearly defined roles: the Staff who make the rules, the Service Users who follow them and, if necessary, we have the henchmen on hand to enforce them. Now the second part of our heading for the day is "IMPORTANCE". Why are rules and discipline so important here at Sisyphusa?" Serky asked.

No one answered. Harry seemed in deep thought, while Ella next to him was looking at me searchingly. Gloria raised her hand.

"Yes, Gloria?" Serky pounced with a mixture of relief and trepidation, presumably remembering the unintended mini-rebellion Gloria's last classroom comment precipitated.

"I suppose it's so everyone knows where they stand," Gloria said calmly.

"Would you like to expand on that?" Serky prompted her.

"Well," she paused in thought. "If everyone could do what they wanted, it would be madness. There needs to be people in charge and the rules are there so that we know what you want us to do."

"Does that make sense to the rest of you?" Serky addressed the class again. And again the other Service Users nodded. The Simon Sisters, who were the firebrands of the last heated discussion, appeared limp, while the Flower-Eaters looked terrified to open their mouths. Ella and Mr. Femuz directed furtive glances at me looking for guidance. All it took to rip the courage and team spirit out of the group was the mere silent, disinterested presence of Governor Shade. I had to do something, say something.

"What about self-discipline?" I asked Serky. The Governor looked up at me as I posed the question and squinted his tiny bespectacled eyes. He then turned his head towards Serky and seemed to give her the 'go-ahead' to speak freely.

"What are you referring to?"

"Discipline isn't something which can only be imposed from above. People can also impose it on themselves. Like if someone wants to lose weight they are self-disciplined about exercise or if someone is a student they are self-disciplined about reading," I said.

"Yes, well…," she murmured, not knowing what to say. She looked to the Governor for help who lowered his glasses down the bridge of his nose and peered over the top of them squinting at me.

"Mr…108," he said as soon as he could find the number written on my breast pocket. "The man who gets lost in corridors. I think you may be lost again," he smiled. "Do you know the reason for these classes we have each morning?" he asked as if he attended them regularly himself, whereas he really only received reports about them from the wardens. "I'll tell you," he continued, not allowing me any time to answer his question. "The trick is in the title: Normalisation Class. You, Mr.108, are not a Normal man. You are Weird. And so is everyone else in this room, bar two," he pointed to himself and Warden Serky affectedly. "Society outside does not like you. They do not think that you belong out there with them."

"For hundreds of years we as an Island have locked our Weird people up and thrown away the key. But here you lucky people have a chance. We *give* you the chance for redemption, for reform, for rehabilitation--we give you the chance to Normalise your behaviour and re-join society. I gather this is your first stay with us, so you should ask your teammates here and they will tell you: If you make it over that wall, you are free. Simple as that. You are certified Normal, and, by law, society must accept you until you prove yourself to be otherwise. This is a great opportunity, one which has not been available to people like you in any other era. If I were you, I would take it."

"I would listen to the wardens, work diligently in class, and strive to become as Normal as possible. I would not disagree with my Team Leader or try to be smart or set a bad example for my fellow Service Users. Do you understand?" he asked calmly.

I was seething inside. What was the objective truth that he claimed to know and what gave him the right to impose it on us? How dare he tell us how lucky we were to be kidnapped, locked up, beaten, abused, malnourished and drugged. Had I committed a crime? Had I done anything to deserve such punishment? It was a farce to say that we would be certified Normal if we climbed the wall, everyone knew that in practice we'd be second class citizens.

"Yes sir," I answered through gritted teeth. "Just one thing…"

But before I could continue, a familiar voice piped up in my Earpiece.

"Don't do it," whispered Gwen. "I know what you're thinking, but don't say a word. You're no good to me in The Pit. I need you out there and so does your team. *Don't do it*!"

"Yes?" The Governor said patiently.

"Umm, thank you sir," I mumbled.

"What for?" he asked, arrogantly anticipating the type of sycophancy he was wont to receive on a regular basis.

"For getting my head straight. I was confused."

"You're quite welcome," he replied. He looked at Warden Serky and signalled that she could continue her lesson. She accepted the signal with an embarrassed, crimson face and stuttered her way through a mundane lesson until the beeps sounded.

I took Samuel under my wing for the rest of the day. I showed him how the climbing ropes worked and Serky agreed that he didn't have to do a climb until the next week. The child was so overwhelmed with all that was around him. He received every bit of advice, every word of support with the same sombre, glazed eyes, only moving occasionally to wrap his filthy, bare feet one around the other.

By night time, having stood around and watched myself and Mr. Femuz work at the quarry, the boy was exhausted. I showed him where he could have a wash and gave him a fresh set of overalls. The smallest in the closet were still three sizes too big for him. I set him up in a bottom bunk near the HDTV and he fell asleep watching Alien Skateboarding on HDTV Kidz.

Chapter 32

I had never been more proud of my team than during those first few days after Samuel Etch was integrated. Everyone in the team took it in turns to try to make the boy feel as comfortable as possible. He would always stick close to Mr. Femuz and myself when it came to classes or hard labour, perhaps he gravitated to us because the huge shadow cast by Mr. Femuz's immense brawn combined with my big mouth provided him with exactly the anonymity he craved. In the dormitory he would watch HDTV Kidz religiously, humming along with the songs and mouthing the words of the Ad-Verses. He was entranced by the different toys and the songs that convinced him how much more happy and fulfilled he would be if he could only have that Interactive Darts Simulator 9000. I thought to myself, 'if kids didn't know what they were missing, didn't have a point of reference to yearn for or compare with, wouldn't they be perfectly happy with a cardboard box and a piece of string?' But only box and string makers would be happy with that scenario.

Samuel always had a willing partner in Mo, who would watch anything that was on HDTV, mesmerised as he was by any moving image. But the person who Samuel was most attracted to was Ella. Samuel never talked to anyone, but with Ella he always replied to her calm, gentle questions with a nod or a shake of his straggly-haired head. He would flinch if anyone tried to touch him but he assented every night to Ella tucking him into her bed (which she then shared with the boy) or dressing the wounds he had picked up from his early forays into Wall-Climbing.

Ella was a natural. She was devoted to the child as if he were her own. She told me that she had wished she had someone like a big sister to look after her when she had first arrived at Sisyphusa as a kid. She would always be trawling through her memory, thinking, 'What did I feel like when I was a child?' 'What ways did I find of coping?' She told him stories every night before bed. I remember sitting up and listening to them and they were always about people and places so far away from

Sisyphusa and Fantasy Island that I wondered how they could have come from her own imagination.

In the subsequent days after his arrival Gwen began relaying information to me about Samuel's back-story. It turned out that he was from a rich family in the capital who had connections to the Government. His parents suspected that he had started acting strangely so they arranged for him to be taken on his way home from school.

Little by little Samuel began to say the odd word, mainly just to Ella or myself. One day when Service Users had been given an evening of free time I came back from the quarry to the dorms for a wash. When I went into the room Samuel asked me where Ella had gone because he wanted her to tell him a story. He said that she hadn't come back from the factory like the other women. I told him I had an idea where she might be and that he should wait there and I'd bring her back.

I walked briskly through the deserted grounds following the winding path around the quarry to the woods. It was always that way during free time. Being given free time meant every Service User rushing back to their dorms and arguing over what channel they all wanted to watch on the HDTV.

I entered the forest and for a moment I forgot where I was. It could have been anywhere. I trudged through the undergrowth, the twigs snapped underfoot and I had a sudden panic about how many living organisms I might be killing with each and every footstep. Surrounded by trees and the sound of birdsong I stopped and looked at the evening sky through the canopy and forgot I was in Sisyphusa. I spotted one white blossom tree in the middle of a gang of towering oaks and it looked like a lonely albino being cornered by bullies. The trees didn't know that they were trapped within those walls, the birds weren't imprisoned by anything or anyone. I envied them.

I followed the beaten track to its end and reached the meadow where I saw Ella kneeling in the cemetery. I approached her quietly but she soon heard me and turned around, wiping the tears from her face. I sat down next to her.

"What's up?" I asked.

"Not much," she forced a smile.

"Ella, I can see you've been crying. What's wrong? Is it Dobbsy?" I asked nodding my head towards his grave.

"No, no," she shook her head. She looked down at his grave and ran her fingertips over the grass, smiling. "Do you know what *he* used to say if I was in one of my moods or acting Weird?"

"What?" I smiled.

"'Your life's not as bad as some but worse than others,'" she said imitating what I assumed was Dobbsy's voice.

"And what did you say?" I asked.

"Me? Nothing. That was that. After he said it I snapped out of it and just got on with it, you know. I mean what else can you do?"

"I guess you're right," I agreed. "You know, before I came here I used to think I had so much control over what happened to me. If my parents or teachers tried to tell me what to do, I hated it! I was always striving for freedom, independence, to be an adult and make my own decisions (as long as my parents paid for it!). But then I came here, and I had *no* freedom, *no* control. But it's not just here. I don't think we really have much control anywhere. We don't even have control of our own minds. Before, when I was Normal, I believed, like all Normal people do, that I had an element of control over my own mind but I think that's just an illusion. It's something in our wiring that allows us to get on with things day-to-day. But then you're brought here, and you wake up with one of these nailed in your ear," I pointed to my Earpiece as if it was my old one, "and that's gone. Someone or something else has taken control, an occupier, this sinister voice whose sole aim is to sabotage every single thing that you do."

"Odis, don't," she said putting her hand on my knee. "Let's not talk about it"—meaning the Earpiece—"you know we aren't supposed to."

"See what I mean? These rules. We can't do anything. We're so brutalised we're not even human any more. I mean it's enough to drive people to Weirdness even if they weren't Weird in the first place."

"Just calm down. It's not that bad," she said.

'Not that bad?' I thought. 'Is she serious?'

"If it's so bearable then why are you sitting here crying?" I asked. All of a sudden she couldn't bring herself to look me in the eye.

"It's nothing," she whispered more to herself than to me. She began to rock back and forth and her breathing became more pronounced. "Nothing, nothing, nothing," she repeated, getting louder with each repetition of the word. She started pulling her hair. She dug her fingertips into her skull as if she was trying to drill into her own mind and remove her thoughts by force. All the time she was screaming: "Nothing, Nothing, Nothing."

I put my arm around her but she was too agitated and pushed me away. I cradled her in both of my arms, overpowering her and holding her head to my chest until her breathing started to relax. We sat there for a few minutes not saying anything just swaying back and forth.

"There's something I want to tell you," she finally broke the silence in a crackly voice, her head still pressed tightly to my chest so that she didn't have to look at me when she told me whatever it was that had so upset her. "It's something I've never told anyone."

"If you're sure you want to tell me then you know I will never break that trust," I said.

"I know that, that's not what I'm worried about," her voice quivered as she rode another wave of emotion. "I want you to promise me that you won't hate me, whatever I tell you…"

"Of course I won't hate-"

"No Odis," she interrupted. "You don't know, you just don't know. I want you to swear that whatever I tell you, you won't leave me."

"I swear, Ella. The bond that we have is based on how we've cared for each other in this place. Whatever you did, or think you did, before I met you won't affect how I feel about you." I began to worry in my mind that she may have done something so awful that it would make me think differently of her, but this was Ella, she couldn't be capable of anything so unforgivable.

"Okay," she exhaled, seemingly satisfied with my pledge, and lifted her head from my chest and grabbed both of my hands, holding them tight. Her gaze was at our hands not my face. "Something has happened to me since Samuel arrived. I've begun to think and feel in a way that I haven't for years, not since I first came here. Things are happening, things I don't want to happen, but they're happening again and if I can't stop them then I don't know what I'm going to do," she began crying again.

"What's happening Ella? Tell me," I said.

She steeled herself and wiped her face with her sleeve. She looked at the ground and stroked the grass. "Do you remember the first time I brought you to this place?" she said.

"Yes," I recalled. "You told me about you and Jack [I always called him Jack if I was talking to Ella and Dobbsy if I was talking to Harry.] When you tried to escape."

"Do you remember I told you they never found his body?"

"Yes, but you said you buried a photograph and some of his things, right?" I wasn't guessing, I remembered the conversation word for word.

"That's right. But there was something I didn't tell you," she took a deep breath. "There was someone buried here already." A mournful smile spread across her face. "I say someone," she said in a tone of self-rebuke. "But what do you suppose it is that makes someone a 'Someone'? A 'Someone' should have a name shouldn't they? They should have people who love them? They should have ten fingers and ten toes and they should enter the world screaming and crying and gasping for air shouldn't they? The thing that is buried here isn't, wasn't, a 'Someone'. It was dirty and rotten and Weird just like the person who brought it into this world."

"Did you have a baby, Ella? A miscarriage?"

"It wasn't my fault, I swear it wasn't, it wasn't. It came out like that, I swear it did. Please don't hate me, please, please," she put her arms around my waist and lay her head in my lap while her body began to rock back and forth again.

"Of course I don't hate you," I tried to her reassure her as I stroked her hair. "Why would I hate you? You did nothing wrong, Ella, nothing."

"It just came out like that. It wasn't breathing, I swear, I swear," she kept repeating.

"Were you alone when it happened? Wasn't there anyone to help you?" I asked.

"Nobody knew, nobody," she cried. "They would have taken it away. I was scared. I was only fourteen, I was just a kid."

"And they didn't notice?" I asked.

"It didn't show. It was so tiny when it came out, it can't have been far along. I'd only been here a few months, there was no Solitary Initiation in those days so I was in a dorm. It started to hurt one night so I-I-I came out here into the field and it happened, I knew straight away it wasn't right. I saw it when the sun came up. Its tiny head, and its tiny hands and feet," she was breathing hard. "It didn't even have all its fingers and toes. But I know it was a boy. And so I buried it."

"You poor thing," I said holding her tight. "Fourteen…You're so brave Ella. I'm so, so sorry. And then you just pretended like it never happened?"

"They caught me trying to sneak back into the dorm that morning and I was taken to The Pit."

A seething anger boiled up inside of me. I hated them more then than for whatever they had done to me, more than for what they'd done to Samuel, a child. I wanted to scream and run back to that building and kill Shade and Serky and every warden and henchman I could find. But I didn't. And I couldn't say anything. I just held Ella tighter and told her that everything would be fine. We sat in silence for a while until Ella said:

"There's more, you need to know who the father was."

"You don't have to tell me if you don't want to, Ella. I probably wouldn't know many of the Service Users who were here then anyway," I said.

"He wasn't a Service User," she said coldly, deathly.

"It wasn't a warden? Is he still here, the bastard?" I began to boil up again, my voice rising.

"It wasn't a warden," she said calmly sitting up and looking me right in the eye. "I was already pregnant when I got here…it was my dad."

I couldn't control what happened next. I burst into tears. I hadn't cried in front of any of the other Service Users, but Ella's life was so tragic, so painful, that there was nothing I could say to her, no words of comfort I could give.

I couldn't cope with the situation. I always had something to say but not this time. I crumpled to the ground and covered my face. And then the most bizarre thing happened. Ella began to comfort *me.* She stroked *my* hair. She told *me* it was okay. I couldn't, and didn't want to, contemplate it. I was in awe of her suffering. How could there be anything in the world for me to complain about when there were people like Ella who lived each day with such memories?

We lay entwined in the long grass. Ella's lips were kissing the top of my head and her chest was pressed tightly to me so that her breasts lay under my chin. I had stopped crying but the atmosphere was still suffused with mutual grief and a longing for comfort. Ella began to push her pelvis into my groin. We began to breathe heavily, in unison, as our legs wrapped around each other. I quickly switched off the microphone that was clipped to my collar. Our faces met but our eyes and mouths did not. Her hands began to unfasten my overalls and mine began to undress her.

I looked at Ella's naked body: her supple breasts and hips and her midriff with its faded stretch-marks. But then I saw her arms and wondered how I hadn't noticed. Had she never exposed her arms in all the time that I'd known her? Angry red scars were strewn across both of her arms like tiger's stripes. She saw that I was looking at them and to reassure her that they didn't bother me I kissed both of her arms, and then her chest and then her neck but our mouths never met.

"I've never been with anyone before," she whispered into my ear. "I mean…since…"

"You mean you and Jack?" I whispered back.

"No," she replied. "Jack and I never…I mean since…"

"Oh, Ella."

I thought of telling her that I had never been with anyone without being Liquidated before but any of my hang-ups seemed trivial compared to what Ella had to bear.

She took me with her hand and put me inside of her. Our movement, in tandem, was slow and soft though our breathing grew stronger and louder. My body felt utterly detached from me, knowing itself what to do even if I thought I had forgotten. I felt sensations that had lain dormant for so long that I had begun to believe them extinct but the surest way to establish between dormant and extinct is if there is an eruption. I wasn't left waiting too long for my answer.

After a short time we both lay back and looked up at the evening sky in silence. A great urge had been lifted from my shoulders, my body, not necessarily for Ella and I don't think her necessarily for me but caged urges for a connection, an intimacy with someone human, someone trustworthy, after years without being touched, without being loved. That urge had been set free. We just wanted to feel and act like the young people we still were but hadn't been allowed to be.

"Thank you for listening, Odis," Ella said after some time.

"Of course," I replied.

I think that we both knew that it wasn't love. But it wasn't lust either. It was a single moment in each of our lives when it felt okay to do something…Normal. We walked back to the dorm in silence and both went to sleep in our separate bunks.

Chapter 33

It felt awkward when I saw Ella the next day. Not because of her or what had happened between us, but because when I looked at her, smiled at her, sat near her in Normalisation Class, all I could think about was Layla. It was that same guilt that I had always felt every time I had been with a woman whom I knew I didn't love. It had been so long since I had seen Layla, and I had changed so much in that time that I didn't even know how I felt about her any more. Would I still feel the same way about her if I were to escape and see her again? Would I feel hurt if she had found someone else? Every time I imagined it, I felt as if my heart would implode. She had only existed in the hazy recesses of my memory and imagination for so long that she wasn't real any more. My life was in the world of Sisyphusa, totally separate from the rest of the Island, and I had to separate my new self, my new actions and my new relationships from anything that I may have done or anyone that I may have known before I walked through the doors of Sisyphusa.

Ella acted differently around me too. She was more shy, fawning, submissive. She kept on offering to do things for me: Did I want her to make my bed? Fetch me a glass of water? Watch HDTV with her and Samuel after I had got back from the quarry? If I politely declined, her face would show a hint of rejection as if each time a little piece of her self-worth had disappeared. I felt confused but also repulsed. She could be added to that long line of women who became immediately unattractive to me as soon as they became overly attracted to me. If you don't like yourself, why the hell should somebody else like you? I didn't regret what had happened but I didn't want anything to change between us either. Of course, it did. After a few days of stilted conversation and awkward silences, we eventually just said "hello" or "goodnight" to each other. It's amazing how quickly a friendship can dissolve into nothing when you overstep the boundaries.

I thought at the time that Ella would be thinking and feeling exactly the same as me-- that she was lonely and had pent-up physical urges and that I was somebody whom she could trust. But maybe she had wanted something more, something which I wasn't able to give. The idea of having a relationship with her, in Sisyphusa, was inconceivable to me. My mind was, and had to be, wholly focussed on my work with Gwen and what was in the best interests of the team.

If we were to become a couple it would attract unnecessary attention to us from the wardens—it was inevitable that they would find out. Fraternising between Service Users was completely forbidden. They would do everything in their power to drive us apart, just as they had with her and Dobbsy. My mind was made up. It was the only way. I had to allow the awkward drift and maintain my cold stance for the sake of both of us and for the team as a whole.

No one else on the team suspected a thing. Ella became more quiet and withdrawn, dividing her time between her work on the Senior Reps Council and looking after Samuel and Harry. I resumed my chess games with Mr. Femuz and continued to discuss plans with him but only while we were in the quarry. Mr. Femuz continually badgered me to ask Gwen questions about Zahra: Was she married? Did she have any children? Was she observant of the rules of the Yes/No book #3?

I told him that Gwen wouldn't tell me. And that was the truth. She didn't want anything to distract us from the task that lay ahead and that went for me as well. I knew that she was referring to Ella. I resented how Gwen could go from teasing me about Ella one minute to reproaching me the next. It felt overbearing that she might be watching or hearing everything I did and said. It was almost as if I had replaced one Earpiece with another. Was I not an adult? I craved freedom. But whatever I thought of Gwen interfering, it was irrelevant. Her conclusion about my relationship with Ella was one that I had come to myself anyway.

Some time after this Gwen gave me my next mission. She was confident that I was well on my way to having a strong enough influence over Team Recovery that they would follow my lead once her plan was implemented but that still left the other teams. She advised me to set up a network of allies in each team who would lead their respective groups to follow our plan. We needed one plan that would let us all escape, working together to avoid chaos, but the fewer people who knew that something was going to happen the better. Gwen selected one person from each team whom she considered to be a natural leader.

From Team Re-Activation Gwen suggested G.I Joe which I was delighted with because I was already friends with Joe. From Team Rejuvenation she suggested a woman named Beverley and from Team Restitution a man named Mikey. Finally she came to Team Redemption and I couldn't believe my ears-- she wanted me to recruit Skinny Jim who she said was about to be released from The Pit.

"There's no denying that he is a strong character and possesses leadership qualities," she said. "Anyway the fact is the whole of Team Redemption is completely intimidated by him and they won't co-operate without his say-so. You don't have to be friends with him, you don't have to like him and I certainly don't want you to tell him anything about our plans or give anything away that would implicate you. Use your discretion and be careful." And that was that. She said she would direct me to Beverley and Mikey in the Mess Hall.

Beverley was a tall, thin, mixed race woman with sallow, beige skin and tight Afro hair. I knew which table Team Rejuvenation sat at for lunch and by Gwen's description it was clear who Beverley was, so after we received our Climbing Pills I walked over to the table and approached Beverley. She sat quite apart from the rest of her table and appeared painfully shy when I spoke to her, which made me question Gwen's assessment of her leadership qualities.

"Hello," I said extending my hand. "My name's Odis, I don't think we've met before."

Beverley squinted. "Oh, um, hullo," she said in a nasal voice. "I'm Beverley," she shook my hand without making eye contact and went back to eating her lunch.

"I was wondering if during free time today I could speak with you in private?" I asked her.

Free time had now become a daily half-hour slot on the timetable thanks to furious lobbying by Ella and the other Senior Reps on the Council- perhaps the recent rebellious atmosphere had the staff worried? Some of the other Service Users at the table began to stare at me which only increased Beverley's discomfort. She quickly nodded just to get rid of me.

"Outside the main building after quarry work?"

"Yes, yes, fine," she said hurriedly.

I was walking back to the main building after finishing my quota in the quarry early. No-one else was around so I spoke into my collar to ask Gwen for any further details she had for me about Beverley. As I spoke into my shoulder a warden appeared suddenly from around the side of the Practise Climbing Warehouse.

"Who are you talking to Service User?" asked the small, red-haired man in a stern voice.

My heart pounded as I desperately tried to think of something to say. Was I really going to ruin everything over something so careless? No. I spoke again, not to the warden, but to my shoulder. I argued with myself aloud, "Who am I talking to?" I asked no-one. "Well he's asking me, what should I tell him? Can you tell me your name, at least? If you're going to continually bother me, the least you can do is be polite. Now listen here, I won't have you talk about him like that!" I looked at the warden feigning embarrassment and pointed to my Earpiece. He looked totally unimpressed.

"Are you Grade 6?"

"I'm not," I answered. "But he is," I pointed to my Earpiece again. The warden shook his head angrily and stomped off towards the quarry. For once, being thought to be Weird worked to my advantage.

Beverley was standing outside the entrance to the main building. I invited her to walk with me and we began to talk as we snaked around the narrow dirt paths. Beverley had been in Sisyphusa for 3 years with no successful Wall-Climbs. She was happy to share that she had a Weirdness Grade 5. Once on our own and away from prying eyes she began to loosen up and would occasionally smile ever so slightly.

It didn't take too long for me to discover why it was that Gwen had chosen Beverley to be my ally from Team Rejuvenation. Once we were out of sight of the wardens, Beverley openly criticised the regime in a way that I had rarely heard from any Service User. It turned out that Beverley had once been a warden herself. Some years previously she was thought to be showing signs of Weirdness and the regime forced her to trade in her warden's uniform for a set of Service User overalls. She'd been wearing them ever since.

"You wouldn't believe how easy it was for my colleagues to all turn on me. The first morning I arrived in Normalisation Class as a Service User it was as if I had never even worked there. The past was instantly erased. I was a Service User and as far as they were concerned I always had been," she said. You sensed from her tone that she wished that she was still a warden. She wasn't angry at the treatment of Service Users in principle—no, she was the child in the playground who had been unceremoniously dumped from the cool crowd and was then stuck with the geeks. I had no doubt she would jump at the chance to regain her former status.

But that didn't matter. She had a grievance, one which had been smouldering and gnawing away at her for a number of years, and this seemed to me fertile enough ground to work with.

"That is terrible," I said when she had finished her story. "How long had you been a warden?" I asked.

"Oh, I don't know, four…maybe five years," she replied with a gleam in her tired, sunken eyes which suggested that she hadn't been able to tell her story in all those years and a sympathetic ear had suddenly validated her grudge against the regime.

"And that was it? They said you were Weird and…"

"Yes, yes," she interrupted. "They said I was showing signs of Weirdness but I felt fine. I mean I was very tired at the time but that was it," she said with yet more energy. "Someone had denounced me, I never found out who but I have my suspicions."

"Who?" I asked, urging her on.

"Serky, I just know it was," she said as if she had thought of nothing else since. "She was just a young staffer back then, but she was ambitious. We all used to talk about it: the way she sucked up to the Governor. She would be especially harsh on the Weirdos every time the Governor was looking and she'd always offer to stay longer after hours or to co-ordinate the

Public Rock-Throwing Ceremonies which were supposed to be a senior staff responsibility."

"So she wanted your job?" I prompted.

"Of course she did. Everyone knows she did. You should see the way she looks at me now, with her smug expression, like she's queen bee," Beverley grimaced.

"I bet you'd like to have your revenge on her?" I asked, hypothetically at first, just to test the waters.

"There isn't a day that goes by that I'm not thinking how I can get her back. Get all of them back, those gutless cowards who went along with it are just as bad as she is," said Beverley.

That was enough for me. Beverley had plenty of motive for joining the plan, and just as importantly, she had divulged enough information to me for insurance purposes.

"If that's truly the case then I have the perfect opportunity for you," I said, suddenly changing my voice and demeanour. Beverley was taken aback as the power had shifted from her to me.

"Wh-what do you mean?" she mumbled.

"I mean exactly what I said. If you really want to show them, all of them, how wrong they were to betray you then I can help you, but first I have to know that you mean what you say."

Beverley stood there, dumbstruck. She quickly assessed her options and then said, "I would have to know the details before I committed myself to any scheme. I'm not stupid."

"Fair enough," I conceded. "I can't go into every detail right now. What I can say is that we have a plan in place to seize control of the facility allowing every Service User to escape," I whispered.

"Oh, is that all?" Beverley said sarcastically, beginning to laugh.

"Fine," I interrupted. "Clearly you haven't the ambition for what we're proposing. Let's agree to keep both of our positions quiet and head back to the dorms."

She narrowed her eyes and then said in a measured voice,

"Sorry, I was wrong to laugh, it was just the way you said it. As if it was so simple. What about the henchmen? And the alarm? And no-one would last a day before they were found on the outside anyway. You are aware that someone was killed trying to escape aren't you?" she asked, clearly referring to Dobbsy.

"Yes, but he died climbing over the wall at night, which we all know is suicide. With our plan that won't be necessary. We'll walk straight out the front entrance. As for the henchmen and the alarm, you don't have to worry about that, the less people know the less likely things will go wrong," I said, brazenly hiding my own misgivings about what Gwen's plans were for those two titanic obstacles to our success.

"And what about getting captured straight away even if we do escape?" she asked sceptically.

"We'll have access to everyone's computer records and will delete every Service Users' file from the database. What everyone decides to do from there is up to them."

She stared at me as if she was trying to read from my eyes whether the fanciful plan I was proposing could really work. She was clearly tempted. I knew I needed to seal the deal.

"You don't need to do anything. By the time your job comes around, the plan will have either totally worked and your decision would be a no-brainer, or everything will have gone belly-up and you would be in no way implicated," I told her.

"So why are you telling me anything? What do you need me for?" she asked.

"Your job is crucial even if it will come late in the day," I assured her. "We will have subdued the regime and gained control of the facility, but, with the imposed order gone, there will be chaos. Service Users will be individually making a run for it. They'll be fighting amongst themselves, and a great number, including you, will be wanting to exact revenge on the captured staff." Beverley's eyes suddenly lit up. "But there will be no time for that. We have to work on the assumption that security forces could arrive at any time. And so it's crucial that we are prepared and working in co-operation to leave the compound as soon as the doors open. That's where you come in. You are clearly a leader. What I need is a leader in each team who will be able to quickly and calmly persuade the rest of their team not to go it alone but for us all to leave together. Do you think you could do that?" I asked.

"But I can't tell anyone what's going to happen before hand?"

"No," I said sharply. "That's crucial. No-one can know. It's too risky. When all order is breaking down, if you show that you were expecting it all to happen and you tell them you know what to do, they will listen."

She mulled it over.

"I guess I could do it," she said. "But what about Serky? I want Serky to myself. Otherwise what's the use?"

"Who cares about her? Don't you want your freedom?" I asked, forgetting why it was that Beverley was so aggrieved and assuming that everyone had the same yearning for freedom as I did.

"Screw freedom, I want revenge," she said icily. "No Serky, no Beverley."

"The best way to get your revenge on all of them is to play your role which will contribute to every Service User safely escaping and the collapse of the whole facility, but if it's pure revenge you want then I give you my word that we will find the time for you to confront Serky face-to-face," I promised, although I had no idea how I would keep it.

Beverley was satisfied and we agreed not to speak or even acknowledge each other again until the day before the plan was to be implemented. We walked back to our dorms separately.

Chapter 34

Mikey was exactly as Gwen had described him. Shorn, black hair peppered the back and sides of his otherwise bald head while an even blacker goatee lessened the impact of a protruding chin. Unlike Beverley the week before, Mikey was sitting at the centre of Team Restitution's table in the mess hall. He had a bright, cheerful disposition, with alert eyes and infectious energy. When I approached the table he was just finishing telling his teammates a story.

"…And there I was, stark naked and I c'n tell you it was nae a warm day," he said in a thick accent from the mountainous north of the Island. Some of his teammates laughed, some smiled wearily, but the vast majority stared at me with their pallid, drawn expressions, intrigued, perhaps threatened, by a member of another team entering their territory.

I arranged to meet him during free time the next evening on the pretext that I wanted advice on Wall-Climbing as he was known for being one of the most proficient climbers. I suggested we take a walk around the compound. He was unlike any of the other Service Users I had met. There was either a very acute or slightly dormant sadness which characterised almost every person imprisoned in Sisyphusa. Mikey, though, had the demeanour of someone totally at ease in his own skin and with his predicament.

I told him a little about myself: my name, age, team, Weirdness Grade, and he reciprocated. He was 41 and had only been in Sisyphusa for around a year and a half but he had been in numerous facilities all over the Island since he was a teenager, including previous stays in Sisyphusa. He said that he didn't have a Weirdness Grade, or more accurately, he had been given so many different grades by so many different people over the years that no-one seemed to know how to categorise him any longer.

We then got on to what we were doing in our lives before we were brought to Sisyphusa. I told him that I had been a student which elicited a number of stories from his own university days during his interrupted youth. He never managed to complete a degree but he came across as well-read, erudite and perceptive. More recently, he said, he had been doing odd-jobs for a while, whatever he could get (considering that all employers on the Island had access to the Weirdness history of all job applicants). But then he began to feel a bit strange and decided to check himself in to Sisyphusa. I couldn't believe that there were Service Users who actually voluntarily admitted themselves to Sisyphusa.

"So, what's the story? I know y'aren' interested in ma climbing technique- I've seen you climb and you sure as heck don' need ma advice!"

I'd been rumbled already. It was clear that I couldn't talk my way into his psyche and hunt down his motivations the way that I had with Beverley.

"I won't lie to you. I didn't want to talk about Climbing Practice. I had just heard a lot about you and you sounded like an interesting guy and I just wanted to introduce myself," I told him.

"I thought you were nae going to lie to me? You just seed so yoursel'!"

"What? I'm not lying!"

"This is Sisyphusa, boy-o! No-one just wants to talk. Someone from another team wants to speak to ya, it either means they wanna shag ya or they've got some scheme goin'! I'm hopin' it's the latter?" he smiled not just with his mouth but with his entire face.

I didn't know what to do. I hadn't got to know him enough to find out whether he was suitable, whether he could be trusted. I didn't have any dirt on him for insurance. Gwen had suggested him, I thought to myself. If he's not right then it's her fault. My instincts told me that I should go ahead. I liked him.

"You've seen right through me," I admitted. "There is a plan. I mean I…we have a plan, to escape…"

"Well you're selling it very well so far," he chuckled. "Only joking, tell me about your plan," he prompted me like I was a little kid eager for his approval.

"We're going to overthrow the wardens and free the Service Users," I announced with pride.

"Oh, that old chestnut," he said. "You're old Gwen's newest apostle I take it?"

My heart fell to my feet. "Gwen? Who's th…," I started, but there was no point. "How do you know Gwen?"

"Must have been seven or eight year ago, I were in that Pit and she burrowed her way in like a wee mole. Scared the shite out of me," he reminisced. "Well, if there were any shite left in me, I take it you've vacationed at The Pit before?"

"I don't understand," I said, more to myself than to him. My initial emotion was the pain of a bruised ego. I couldn't believe that I wasn't the first "Inside Man" that Gwen had wanted. I felt like a second choice, a back-up plan.

"I think it were seven year ago, anyway? You can ask Gwen on your thingamajig," he suggested, pointing to my Earpiece.

"Excuse me," I said through gritted teeth. "I'll be right back." He smiled smugly. I walked a few feet away, out of his earshot but before I could pick my bone with her, Gwen's voice said calmly:

"Don't overreact."

"What do you mean don't overreact?" I shouted and then quickly composed myself, not wanting to give Mikey the satisfaction. "You've got me walking around here like your puppet secret-agent and you didn't even think to tell me that half of them already know you!"

"Now you're just being silly. It is only Michael of the current crop."

"Of the current crop? So there were more besides?"

"Yes. One or two. I've been trying to work this plan for ten years. Did you think I had really been waiting this whole time just for someone as magnificent as you? You aren't The Carpenter himself, born to save all of mankind, dear."

"I never said that," I replied. "It's just…well…you could have said something before. I mean, you suggested Mikey yourself. Did you want me to be humiliated?"

"No, no, no, of course not. I just thought that maybe your youthful enthusiasm might re-ignite some fire in him. If you knew about our past, then it would have been one big, male, horn-ramming contest."

She was right, but there was no way that I was going to admit it. "So what happened? Why didn't the two of you go ahead with the plan?" I asked.

"Why don't you ask him? You need to persuade him that it still matters, Odis. That really *is* something that only you can do. Tell him I said 'Haló, Ciamar a tha thu?' He'll understand. Now play nice, you're both good boys. I'll leave you to it." The line went dead.

I trudged back over to a smiling Mikey and garbled the phrase Gwen had relayed.

"Gwen says 'Hallo, karma a tattoo'."

"He-he, you mean 'Haló, Ciamar a tha thu?'"

"That's it. What does it mean?"

"It just means 'Hello, how are ya?' in ma language. Did she say anything else?"

"She just said that we should talk, get to know each other."

"So, I'm guessing you'd like to know why Gwen and I didn't lead the Service Users to the promised land like the ol' wizard in the Yes/No Book #1?" He read my mind again.

"I suppose I was wondering why you didn't want to escape," I replied.

"Escape is your word," he corrected me. "I have no need to escape, Odis, I'm here by choice. I don't choose to be Weird but I am in Sisyphusa of my own accord. When I met Gwen she certainly made an impression on me. Even back then I was quite a lot older than you are now, och I'm really showin' ma age aren't I? I read her books, and I listened to her theories and I learned a lot from her. I agreed with most of what she taught me: there is gross mistreatment of Service Users; the exclusion of Weird people by the rest of society is a huge part of the problem; the Climbing Pills do often do more harm than good. But that's just the way things are and there's nothin' you or me or Gwen can do about it. The problem is too big for us."

'Maybe Mikey was right?' I thought to myself. 'The problems that we were fighting were so endemic, so ingrained, so maddeningly accepted by the majority, perhaps it would always be a losing battle? Maybe each time a Sisyphusa falls ten or twenty more institutions like it spring up in its place, like my acne. But what was the alternative? Should I accept a reality, a world that so entirely repulsed me? Do I blend into the crowd, nod my head in class, saying please and thank you each time I'm degraded and hope to avoid attention?'

"You remind me of myself at your age, Odis," Mikey snapped me out of my reverie. "I wanted to set the world to rights, I thought I had all the answers, and all the world needed to do was listen to me."

"So what happened?" I asked, convinced that he had sold out his former principles.

"I became Weird," he said, for the first time letting down his chirpy guard.

"What does that mean?" I raised my voice in frustration. "Sorry. It's just I'm so tired of hearing that bloody word. I mean what does it mean, really? Is it a way of behaving? A way of thinking? A criminal tendency? Is every Service User in here the same? Or is our only thing in common our predicament? I'm beginning to wonder whether it is just what we call people who don't (or can't) conform to the social norms of the majority of society. Are Mr.Femuz and the Flower-Eaters Weird because they're away from their homeland and their families? Are the Simon Sisters Weird because of poverty? And is Ella Weird because of a traumatic life? What about me? Why am I Weird? Do I seem Weird to you?" I asked him.

"Not especially, no. But it's not about lookin' a certain way. I think it's all of those things that you've mentioned. It is behavior and thoughts and life traumas and displacement and grief and more. It can be lots of things. Is Weird a helpful word for it? No, maybe not. Is everyone here the same and have they all got the same problems? No. But for me Sisyphusa is a sanctuary, a safe-haven. When everything out there in the 'real world' gets on top of me and I can feel myself getting over-heated, I know that I can come here and be with people who won't judge me, where I can do mindless work and just be."

I couldn't believe what I was hearing. Here was this guy who was older, smarter and more together in every way than me, and he *liked* it in Sisyphusa. He liked being told what to do and when. He liked being made to slave away in the quarries and could stand being lectured nonsense in Normalisation

Classes. He had read Gwen's books and agreed with most of what she said and yet he used that education to come to a completely different conclusion from mine. This terrified me.

Was he right and was I wrong? Was Sisyphusa the right place for me to be? Had I somehow become different from everyone outside and would climbing walls and taking notes and sleeping in The Pit make me Normal again? I'd never really given it a chance. Ever since I arrived in Sisyphusa I thought that it was a terrible place and I dreamed of not being there anymore. Had the best way of achieving that been the thing that I had avoided all along? If I had succumbed, mind and body, to authoritarianism would I have "climbed that wall" and been "out of there in no time" like my father had told me in those first few months.

All of this questioning and second-guessing myself was getting me nowhere. I had done what I thought was right. I had followed my instincts and my heart, and in my heart I disagreed with Mikey. Even if there was something that made Service Users different from Normal people, the system was brutal and they had no justification to treat us the way they did. They had to be stopped. And I needed to persuade Mikey to help us.

Chapter 35

We'd reached the end of the dirt path which snaked around the quarry and I asked Mikey if he wanted to come through the woods and sit in the meadow by the cemetery. He said he'd never been there before. He'd overheard other Service Users saying they were going there but he had never known any one buried there and as such had never felt obliged to visit.

Dead leaves crackled under our feet as we trudged through the woods. I hadn't been through the woods since that warm, summer's evening with Ella. The season had changed and the trees looked bare and lifeless, the sky was bleak and the air had an unforgiving chill. I slipped my sleeves over my hands and blew into each one alternately as if I was trying to keep a fire lit in both sleeves simultaneously.

"Stop being such a wimp," Mikey joked. "This is beach weather where I'm from!"

I sat down on the long grass, expecting Mikey to join me but the cemetery immediately attracted his attention. He walked through the graves reading every carved memorial on the assorted stakes. When he had finished he came and joined me.

"This is the third time I've been in Sisyphusa and I can' believe I've never been here," he said.

"I only know of it because one of my teammates brought me here once. I've come back a few times since, sometimes with others, sometimes alone. It's so quiet here you can almost forget where we are."

"I thought I didn't know anyone here but it's nae true. Lookin' through the graves I recognised some names...people from ma previous stays."

"I'm sorry," I told him.

"What for?"

"I'm sorry that you've found out that some of your friends have died."

"Don't be silly, they weren' ma friends. Just acquaintances, ya know," he said, looking uncomfortable. I was reminded of the looks on the faces of all of Mikey's teammates as he was telling his joke when I first saw him. The faces which

either said "not another joke" or just "I wish I wasn't here."
Mikey was smart, he was funny, he was personable, but at the
same time he could be prickly and abrasive, even cutting.

The first thing I noticed about him was how different he
was from all of the other Service Users, the ease with which he
sailed through Sisyphusa as if it were a luxury spa or hotel.
Could it be that his constant joking and confident chit-chat were
a cover for the fact that he had nothing in common with any of
the other Service Users? Could it be that he had no friends?

It sounded like he'd moved around a lot, worked odd-
jobs, been in and out of Weirdness Institutions. With that kind
of life it would be incredibly easy to have never put roots down
anywhere or had relationships. He'd not really mentioned his
family in the whole time that we'd been talking.

"You never mentioned your family, Mikey," I said. "Do
they still live up north?"

"No, no," he said. "No family."

"I'm sorry."

"Don't be. Could be worse. I could have had one and
then lost them. Much better to have never had one, I reckon.
It's like the difference between being born blind and losing your
sight mid-life." It sounded as if Mikey had repeated this analogy
throughout his life every time the subject of family came up.

"So were you an orphan? Were you adopted? You don't
have to tell me, I'm just interested."

"No problem. Ma mam, whoever she was, musta no'
wanted me. Left me at the hospital. Had some foster mams but I
was always gettin' into mischief so they ne'er wanted me too
long. Then when I wa' Removed for the first time…"

"What do you mean 'Removed'?"

"You never heard it before? That's what they call it
when you get taken in, told you're Weird, ya know? They've
started to call it an Apprehension Order now- as if givin' it more
syllables makes it any less unpleasant. So anyway, no-one
wanted to come near me after that. But I was 14 by then so I
was old enough to go my own way. I was on the streets for a
while but then I met someone who helped me out. They took me
in, let me stay with them and set me up with some courses.
Eventually I made it to University but then in my second year I

was Removed again and it's been in and out of places like this ever since."

"That's when I was taken," I told him. "My second year."

"Aye. Pity that. Ah well. Life goes on."

"How can you be so accepting about it? Doesn't it make you angry?"

"Used to. Not any more. What good's it gonna do? We're just a bunch of pricks on a rock, flying through space. We think we're more important than we are!"

"That may well be," I agreed. "But even if that's what you think, does that mean that we shouldn't care what happens to us and the people we love during our short time here? I'm no Yes/No book reader, I don't think there's any great plan or meaning to all of this, but if we use the kind of anti-logic that because we live in a meaningless universe then nothing we do matters we're going to leave the door open to others with beliefs which you and I don't agree with."

"What people that I love? There's no-one and nothin' that I care about. Life's been cruel to me and I'm just trying to get my head down and live out my days in peace. That's what I told Gwen all of those years ago and I haven't changed my mind."

"I'm sorry, I know that I've only just met you but I don't believe you. Do you not care about Gwen? Or the members of your team? You live together, eat together, work together: your team is like a family. And Gwen says that you are at the head of that family which means that you are the only person who can help us."

"I'm not like you, Odis. You're young, you still have hope."

This comment took me aback. Was I the hopeful one? All I had felt those awful years in Sisyphusa was utter hopelessness. Even at that point I would have the same argument with myself every day about whether it was worth getting out of bed and leaving that dorm, knowing that all I had ahead of me was another day hauling granite up that hill, and the next day, and the day after that. But once I was speaking to Mikey, or Beverley, or Mr.Femuz or Ella, there was another

Odis. I was able to stand outside of my own situation and enter into theirs. When I was in theirs I was able to be rational, compassionate even optimistic, things which I was wholly unable to apply to my own predicament. I was an enabler. Perhaps Gwen was right to choose me after all. Not because I was as smart as Mikey, as brave as Dobbsy or as strong as Mr Femuz but because I could see into people, tease out their stories and make them believe in the plan even if I had my own doubts. I was a salesman.

"I have hope for you too," I told Mikey. "It's not easy to have hope. Not when things look as bad as they do for you and me. But we can do something. We can hope. My father used to tell me that 'the only constant in life is change.' No matter how stuck I feel here I can't believe that it will always be this way. In fact things are changing all the time. At first I was in Solitary and I didn't speak a word for over a year. I was convinced that I had lost the ability to talk to other people. But then when Harry came to my cell, and I was integrated into Team Recovery I couldn't believe that I found myself talking to strangers openly, it was so instinctive to want to communicate with people again."

"I've made friends, I met Gwen, I've met you, and I've learned things. I've learned how to hope from others. I've met people who have been here much longer than me, or more times than me or have suffered more traumas in their lives but they are all fighting. I don't know you yet but you give me hope too. When I was first integrated I felt that I didn't have a thing in common with any of the other Service Users. They didn't seem to question anything, or even think about it, they just accepted it."

"So do I, I accept it," Mikey insisted.

"No, I don't think you do. I think you've persuaded yourself to accept it because you think you have no choice. You see their power, and it seems pointless to resist and so did I but Gwen has persuaded me. And it's not because I'm younger than you it's because I believe in her and because I have hope that things can be better, that we can change things and that we can help people. I can accept that you may have lost your hope but I can tell that you haven't lost your affection for Gwen or the desire to help your fellow Service User."

"You are seriously corny, you know that don't you," Mikey's smile returned to his face. "'Your fellow Service User!' You sound like a bloody Levellist. So what is this grand plan of Gwen's then, anyway? Still the same old plan I take it? She stays tight-lipped about the details, you do all the donkey-work and they all live happily ever after?"

"Sounds like you're interested?" I smiled.

"Well I suppose I'm not doing anything else."

"Fantastic," I patted him on the shoulder. "All you need to do is keep Team Restitution calm and lead them to the gates when I give the signal. I will contact you the day before and tell you what the signal is, okay?"

"Just don't fuck it up!"

And with that we shook hands and went our separate ways. As I lay in bed that night I decided that the next day I would speak to G.I Joe in the quarry. I hadn't seen Skinny Jim in the mess hall yet so assumed he must have still been in The Pit. I fell asleep agonizing over how I could possibly get someone like him on board.

Chapter 36

The bass-line of Gun Slinga's latest song reverberated throughout the building. They had opened their cramped student flat up for a party for the first time since they'd arrived as complete strangers at South Coast that year. The Young Man was dressed in black except for a white bow-tie. It was supposed to be fancy dress but he didn't want to wear anything that might have made him look silly so he wore his expensive suit and said that he was "a Gangster".

Shovel and Anna were dressed as a pantomime horse, Wellborn was a caveman, TT was a knight in shining armour, Shaz was a Teddy Bear and Jr wore nothing except for a baby's nappy. They had moved the stereo into the kitchen and hidden all of their valuables, knowing that in all likelihood the party was liable to get out of control.

The Young Man's old friends had made the journey from his home town, jumping at the chance to sample university life. The flat was packed with people, some of whom the flatmates knew and many whom they didn't. The Lion, the Skeleton and the Unicorn were snorting Talking Powder in the corner and the Policeman and the Four Bearded Swordsmen, who were dancing on fast-forward in the middle of the living room, were clearly on Love Tablets.

The Gangster sat in the corner with a Liquid Escape in his hand and a cigarette in his mouth, nodding along with the bass-line. He never used to smoke cigarettes but in recent months he'd felt compelled to accompany every gallon of Liquid Escape he imbibed with a satisfying smoke. He watched his friends dance and he laughed as they all fell over. He took another drag and surveyed the crowd when the Fairy caught his eye. He had met her once before in a Liquidiser. She smiled at him and sat down on his lap.

Meanwhile, Jr was outside on his Foney. Halfway through his heated conversation he dropped it, it broke, he burst out laughing and came back inside where he joined in a drinking game with TT, Shaz and Wellborn. Anna and Shovel were speaking to some Mermaids by the window.

Sisyphusa

*The Gangster and the Fairy clinked their bottles
together and began to talk. She was attractive, with short light
brown hair, bright blue eyes and full, shiny lips. She tapped him
on the nose with her wand and asked if he had any wishes. He
asked if it wasn't Genies who granted wishes. But nevertheless
he told her his wish was that she would come to his party and
that it had already come true.*

*Even though the remark was jokily flirty and they both
knew it, he still wondered why it was that he always acted this
way. He'd done the same thing with that blonde girl last week
and ended up sleeping with her which meant yet another girl on
campus who he would be too embarrassed to talk to when he
wasn't Liquidated.*

*The Fairy noticed his scar and asked him how he'd got
it. Too embarrassed to tell her that he'd fallen out of a tree
when Liquidated he played the Gangster and told her it was from
a knife fight and that she should see the other guy. She laughed
and then took the cigarette from his mouth and put it to her own
lips before taking a long drag and blowing the smoke into the
Gangster's face. He smiled and they began to kiss.*

*Out of the corner of his eye he saw an Angel walk in
with a Clown, a Cat and a Devil. She was resplendent in white;
white shoes, white stockings, low-cut white dress and a golden
halo. She and her friends smiled and joked with each other as
always. They acted oblivious to the rest of the room, their
togetherness serving as a shield. Some people misunderstood
this as arrogance when it was in fact shyness.*

*The Gangster stopped kissing the Fairy. He introduced
the Fairy to the Angel who was polite but quiet, allowing the
Clown and the Cat to make pleasantries with the Fairy. He
looked at the Angel and their eyes met. She smiled at him and as
she did so the dimple in her chin contracted and the tiny mole at
the corner of her mouth curled up.*

*He wondered if she had seen him kissing the Fairy.
Why did it matter? If he couldn't kiss her then why not kiss
whoever else he wanted? But he still kidded himself that there
was a chance. He'd known her all these years, loved her all
these years, but she was still an enigma to him. The relationship
was like that of a fly and a candle: the flame so mesmerizing, so*

alluring, that the fly forgets everything which has gone before. 'This time,' he thinks, 'I won't get burned.'

She'd made her feelings clear that she didn't love him but he couldn't accept it. His imagination was too creative for that. Every smile, every touch, every gift was new proof that her feelings had shifted from affection and companionship to attraction and desire. He would daydream of that perfect watershed moment when he could win her over, prove his worthiness and devotion with some grand gesture- he would take a bullet for her, donate a kidney, something, anything to show her how he breathed for her and her alone. She was so guarded with her feelings which made it easy for anyone to project all of their hopes and dreams onto her because she revealed so little.

The party wore on and everyone became more Liquidated. One of the Gangster's friends from home had thrown up in the kitchen sink but when someone offered him 5 coins to down another gallon he happily took up the offer. A fight broke out in the hallway as Jungle Man saw The Vicar kissing Jungle Woman. After this last straw, campus security broke up the party leaving the obliterated flat to its regular inhabitants plus a few stragglers.

The Gangster's friends from home had passed out in various parts of the flat; one in the bath, one with his head in the toilet, one straddled on the staircase and the rest in the garden. The Gangster himself was sitting in the living room with his flatmates and the Angel who had stayed behind. He had taken the Fairy's Foney number when she offered it but he knew that he wouldn't ring it.

The music was softer now and so was the conversation. They discussed the future and what they all planned to do. The flatmates were all excited that they had already found a house off campus, in Cossetts Lane, and the Angel and her friends happened to have found one just around the corner. The Gangster knew that he would only live with his friends for one more year as he was headed off to study in the Frontier Empire Mainland for a year after that. He would move back in with them when he returned, he thought to himself. Who knows? Maybe he'd study more, get a job and settle there for good? He didn't think too far ahead but he was confident that the future held only good things.

Little by little, his flatmates went off to bed and the Gangster and the Angel were left alone. They decided to go to his room and listen to some music. He turned out the lights and they automatically got into his bed together, as they often did, and pulled the covers over them. Her very presence in his bed intoxicated him. He moved closer to her and put his arms around her, holding her tightly. She accepted his embrace somewhat reluctantly but she knew it was inevitable, they could never find themselves alone in the dark, in his bed, without him needing to hold her. She enjoyed the closeness, the intimacy of his touch when he held her hand. She trusted him implicitly and felt comfortable in his embrace. But, as always, she dreaded that he would try to push too far.

He sensed her boundaries and they talked. They discussed their friends and they argued playfully about which of the two of them was more intelligent. Their years of history afforded them a language, a groove, a dynamic of their own which they automatically assumed as soon as they were alone together. When they were with others they were different. She was more careful of her words and her actions, always aware of who they were with. He played the go-between, helping to direct the conversation and injecting humour to ensure that all parties were socially comfortable.

They both went quiet and again he moved closer. He knew that she would leave soon, she could never spend the whole night with him. He was desperate. Every one of his senses was screaming at him to touch her; he smelt her hair and her fragrant skin, he could hear her breathing tremulously, he could feel her rounded buttocks settled perfectly into his midriff like the last pieces in a jigsaw puzzle.

His desire overcame him and he began to touch her. He moved his fingertips softly up her ribcage and onto her breast, she resisted but when he didn't desist she quickly gave up. He pulled down the straps of her dress and uncovered her bare breasts. He circled the nipple with his index finger then kissed them quickly but it didn't feel right so he quickly withdrew to touching again. She was unreceptive, unresponsive, as if she was a child pretending to be asleep. He wanted her to want him, like the other girls he had been with.

He traced his fingertips down her torso and up the inside of her leg under her dress. This would make her desire him, this always worked with every woman. He felt her knickers pulled up high almost to her belly button and he stroked over the top of them disbelieving in his head where his hand was. He touched her skin on her inner thigh and she shuddered. She could no longer pretend that she was asleep and he could no longer kid himself that this was right.

He knew that he had taken it too far, way too far and a feeling of self-loathing descended over him immediately. He felt disgusting, like a criminal. It couldn't keep on the way it had been for so long, something had to give. He had tried not to love her but every time he saw her he found a new thing to love; her competitiveness, her generosity, her devotion to her family, the way she danced, her innocence, her capricious nature. They couldn't be friends and they couldn't be lovers, their relationship was beyond category. She told him she had to go and he sat in disgraced silence as she covered herself up and departed.

I was woken up by Harry shaking my arm. "Odis, Odis," he said in an uncharacteristically sober tone. I opened my eyes and remembered where I was. "Samuel won't get out of bed. Ella and me 'ave been tryin' to get 'im up and dressed but he won't budge and he won't say anythin'. He just lies there facin' the wall, stiff as a plank."

I got out of bed and walked over to Ella and Samuel's bunk. Ella had swapped places with Ken a few weeks ago to be nearer to Samuel (and further away from me).

She was rubbing his shoulder and whispering in his ear when she saw me coming over. We exchanged awkward smiles like the acquaintances that we'd become. She shook her head as if to say "it's no use, he won't get up."

I sat down next to Samuel's bed and said, "Samuel, it's me, Odis. Are you going to get up? We have to go to class soon and you need to go get washed with Ella and all that." No answer, not even a shrug. His hair had grown so long that he started to resemble a feral child, especially with the vacant, wronged expression which he perpetually wore.

"Sammy," said Harry. "If you don't come to class they're gonna punish ya. One time when I felt too ill to get out of bed they sent the midgets [which is what Harry had begun affectionately referring to the henchmen as] to come and teach me a lesson."

Some of the other members of the team had begun to crowd around the bunk and voice words of support to the boy.

"Be strong, Sammy," said Tracey.

"We'll look after you, Samuel," Mr Femuz offered.

"Don't let them win," said Gloria. "We have to fight, darling, fight every day."

But the child was unresponsive. He was frozen still. The beeps sounded to warn us that we had to be in class and the team members began to drift away from the scene. The team had grown strong in recent months, everyone looking out for each other, supporting each other, but we all knew that there was only so much you could do for another Service User. You entered Sisyphusa alone and you had to live it alone.

We agreed that we would all forfeit our free time and rush straight back to the dorm as soon as our work in the quarry and factory were finished and we told Samuel that we would. Reluctantly, Ella and I were the last to leave the dorm.

Chapter 37

Normalisation Class that day was titled: "How to blend in." Serky went through a bullet-point list from the Sisyphusa Warden's Guidebook of suggestions on how to appear Normal. The list included things like- "Dress appropriately," "Laugh at people's jokes," "Do not cry in public," etc. I can't remember any of the others. The class was quiet. I was thinking about Samuel. I could identify with his not wanting to get out of bed. I remembered back to when I was first integrated into Team Recovery, most days I didn't want to get up either. I knew that all that lay ahead of me was another day of propaganda, missile-strewn Wall-Climbs and back-breaking manual labour. And Samuel was just a child, what could we do for him?

Climbing Practice had been more strenuous in recent weeks. There was a rumour flying around that there was an official Wall-Climb coming soon. Service Users are never told until the last minute when they will be climbing, presumably because the wardens want one hundred percent commitment regardless of whether you have a climb coming up or not. I used to think to myself, 'it's not as if you would slack off even if you didn't have a climb approaching, there are balls flying around you at a hundred miles per hour anyway, it's only you who will get hurt.'

Mr.Femuz and I were still working with G.I Joe and his team since our cave had collapsed. Warden Serky told us that, "Team Recovery would continue to be divided up to work in the other teams until further notice,"—which I think meant that they didn't have the money to repair our collapsed cave. It wasn't the only thing that the regime appeared to be cutting back on. Since the The Great Money Pyramid on the Mainland collapsed, all of the Money Pyramids on the Island and throughout the Empire had begun to collapse as well because apparently they were all intricately linked with a MAD (Mutually Assured Destruction) Clause when they were built. Seemingly very few people were aware of this clause before it happened, least of all me.

The Money Pyramids held all of the currency in the world and the Pharaohs of the Empire, who ran them and were therefore worshipped more than the SkyMaster himself, were permitted by The Emperor and his Ministers to keep and distribute the coins to the public and to the Corporations as the Pharaohs saw fit. As only the Pharaohs had the keys to the Pyramids they had to be allowed to keep the majority of the coins even once most of the coins had been destroyed.

The Emperor said that it would take many years to rebuild the Pyramids and replenish the currency and that everyone in the Empire would have to work together and make sacrifices so that the Empire could return to its former greatness. I wondered if, given that the Pyramids had collapsed, it wouldn't be better to devise a more sensible system in their place but I was no Pharaoh.

In the meantime this meant that coins, now in short supply, had to be spent wisely. The HDTV Bad News channel dedicated much of its time no longer to reporting the deaths of soldiers in the wars but to showing in-depth coverage of the various Pyramids collapsing, the queues of people waiting to collect their remaining coins and the even larger queues of unemployed people who were waiting outside Minister Frown's office to be given a loan. I found out later that the Pharaohs had jumped to the head of the queue and the public were told that they'd have to wait a long time. In between the coverage, Ad-Verses were shown trying to sell products to people which none of them could any longer afford.

Sisyphusa wasn't immune either. The tattered old overalls weren't replaced. The technology used in the Normalisation Classes was no longer updated every month as it used to be. Even some of the wardens just disappeared without explanation, presumably to join the queue outside Minister Frown's office?

Anyway, we were happy to work with G.I Joe and the Team Re-Activation lads. Team Re-Activation was an all-male team made up solely of veterans from the Bactrian and Babylonian Wars. They kept all veterans together because they were thought to have the same Weirdness Grade, Grade 4. They were a well-disciplined, hard-working team as you would imagine from their background, but most of them appeared listless and lost. Large and muscular to a man, the veterans were extremely proficient climbers and quarry-workers, but they seemed especially cowed in the presence of wardens. The henchmen and their missiles were no match for Team Re-Activation's skilful dodging and weaving and held no fear for them but whenever I saw the ex-soldiers being rebuked or disciplined by their Team Leader, Warden Shiva, they looked like frightened little children. I always used to wonder how those huge guys could be so afraid of that tiny little woman.

As I got to know Joe over the years I began to piece together more and more of his story. He dropped out of school when he was sixteen and then couldn't find a job. He began to dabble in Talking Powder and Liquid Escape which he paid for by committing petty crimes. His mother and father were divorced and he'd never met his dad, but when his uncle came home from serving in the army they became close. Joe began to look up to him. He was impressed by his uncle's uniform, the confidence he exuded when he walked through the estate. His uncle would tell him stories of what fun he and his battalion had on operations, the rush you got when you were under fire and the satisfaction you felt when you rid the world of an insurgent.

Joe was decided-- as soon as he turned eighteen he was going to join the army. He loved his country, he knew that, and he was in good shape (as long as he cut down on the Liquid Escape.) He saw the army Ad-Verse on his HDTV which promised a substantial wage and an adventure, something which Joe had always dreamed of. He had never left the Island, or even thought of leaving it. Who could have believed that the first time he would leave the shores of Fantasy Island it would be for Babylonia, a vast desert land on the other side of the world?

He had followed the lead-up to the Babylonian War with interest. When he read in The Daily Bulletin about The General, his threats against the Empire and the way he treated the Babylonians, Joe did not take much convincing that this tin-pot dictator needed to be shown who was boss. And who better to mete out the rough justice than Fantasy Island? The Daily Bulletin has always had a way of convincing people that the Island is rather bigger and more important than it is in reality. Nevertheless, reading about The General made Joe angry. He sounded like a bully and if there was anything that Joe hated it was bullies. When he turned eighteen he enlisted and completed his training. His uncle had served two tours in the Bactrian War, so when Joe received confirmation that he was to be sent to Babylonia he was pleased. He wanted his own war and his own stories to tell.

When Joe first arrived at the base in the middle of the desert, army life struck him as being incredibly boring. It was nothing like as adventurous as the Ad-Verse had portrayed. He and his battalion were stuck doing manoeuvres in the middle of nowhere for two months. They would listen to the radio day after day, hearing reports of what the Mainland troops were doing in Babylon City and they were so jealous. They were missing all of the action. The city had fallen and the war seemed as good as won.

The day finally came when they were given a mission which involved leaving the base. Now Joe would be able to put all of his training and skills to the test. His commander informed the battalion that they were going to a village fifty kilometres away where they had intelligence that insurgents were being given shelter by the local population.

"Insurgent" was an army term for anyone who was fighting against the Empire's war effort. Almost as soon as Babylon City had fallen multiple militias groups had formed and were beginning to fight each other and the Frontier Empire troops. 'Why do they want to kill us?' Joe wondered. They were there to free the Babylonians from The General, who was by that point in hiding.

Joe and his battalion entered the small village under the cover of night which Joe was elated about because it meant that he could try out his state-of-the-art night-vision goggles. They split into groups of five just as they had trained to in drills at the base. Danny, who was the leader of Joe's group of five, told Joe to bring up the rear while he led them into the courtyard of a cluster of small adobe houses.

They entered the first house by force. Women began to scream but Joe, being at the back, couldn't see what was happening. When he got into the tiny house he saw a large, terrified family standing with their hands in the air. There was a middle-aged man and woman, five small children and an elderly lady sitting in the corner who barely acknowledged the soldiers presence. The middle-aged woman was hysterical, and kept screaming but Joe didn't speak "Babby."

Danny was shouting at her to "calm down", saying "we aren't here to hurt you," but they didn't seem to understand. The middle-aged man began to shout at the troops while simultaneously trying to calm down his wife. Danny kept his rifle pointed at the family, ordered Joe to watch the door and the other three to search the premises which was only the room that they were in and a bedroom. All three of the soldiers went into the bedroom.

As the other three searched and Joe kept a vigilant watch over the door a shot was fired in the main room and then came the screams. Joe came into the room and a teenage boy lay on the floor with a bullet in his chest. Danny frantically told Joe that the kid had appeared out of nowhere, snuck up on him. It later became apparent to Joe that the youth had been in the outhouse in the garden and had heard the screams coming from his house and came to the back door to see what all of the commotion was.

The family were now all screaming. The children were crying, the mother was on the floor holding her dead son's head in her arms and kissing it while she rocked him back and forth as though he were a baby. The father was crying as well and began to shout at Danny. The man ripped at his clothes, shouted at the sky and pounded his chest. He then jumped at Danny and the two of them began to wrestle over Danny's gun. It looked like the man was beginning to overpower Danny and was heaving the rifle away from him. "SHOOT HIM!" Danny shouted.

Joe shot him once, in the head, and the man fell to the ground and died instantly. The woman then came at Joe, hitting him and scratching at his face and wailing at the top of her lungs. The other three soldiers came in and detained her and then the five of them went into the garden and frantically discussed what they were going to tell the commander had happened.

Danny said that he had no choice, the boy came out of nowhere and then the dad was trying to kill him. They should just tell the commander that both of them, father and son, were hiding in the bedroom and tried to ambush them. The other three agreed and then they all looked at Joe. He quickly nodded his assent, still in shock at having taking his first life.

Danny said that they couldn't shoot them unless they had had weapons so he and Joe scoured the house for weapons while the other three took the traumatised family outside into the garden. Joe and Danny looked all over the two rooms for guns but couldn't find any so they settled for two knives they found in the kitchen drawer. They looked like they were used for farming or sheep shearing or something like that. Danny took the knives, made a cut down his forearm and put one in the right hand of each of the two corpses. He radioed in to the commander that they had executed two insurgents who had attacked them.

When the rest of the battalion arrived at the scene Danny did all of the talking and explained the story, which was accepted. As Joe left the house and walked through the garden and back to the row of Jeeps on the outside of the village he heard the mother and her children screaming at him and at Danny but he didn't look. He kept his head down, his eyes to the floor and they went back to base.

By the end of his tour Joe was exhausted. The guilt of what he had done had consumed him. He began to hate Babylonia and its people and couldn't wait to return to Fantasy Island where everything would be like it was before he left.

Back home, he would walk around his estate proudly donning his uniform like his uncle did, but it was different. He now realised that other people had never revered his uncle as he did and they didn't look at him that way either. People would welcome him back and say "good on ya" but it was awkward and stilted, even with his mother. She was so relieved to have him home that she would constantly fuss over him, cooking and cleaning for him and buying him gifts but she didn't know what to say.

There were times when Joe wanted to talk to his mother about Babylonia and what it was like but the few occasions when he did his mother would quickly change the subject, thinking that it would be best for him not to dwell on such things. And so he kept it to himself- the guilt, the shame, the confusion about what had happened and how his life had changed so irrevocably.

He re-connected with his old friends from school and they would all congregate at their local Liquidiser every Friday and Saturday night to worship at the altar of Liquid Escape. Since he had been back from Babylonia something had changed. He could no longer laugh at his friends' jokes because they were no longer funny; he'd lost all interest in football and cars and gambling. He felt as if he didn't have anything in common with anyone any more. How could everything still be happening on the Island as if everything was hunky-dory and the war wasn't still going on?

He yearned to have a woman, someone who would love him and take care of him. He wore his uniform out one night hoping that it would attract some attention. But when he scoured the dance floor approaching one girl after another none of them wanted to dance with him or even talk to him. Perhaps it was the uniform but more likely it was him. He had begun to drink three gallons of Liquid Escape a day, even alone at home. But it no longer had the same effect on him. Whereas before it made him happy, confident and energetic now it made him angry, aggressive, paranoid and his body grew out of shape.

He would sit in the park day after day, alone, with a crate of Liquid Escape and try to have conversations with people who walked by. He tried to tell them what was happening over in Babylonia. Those that did stop, which weren't many, either told him that they knew everything already, having read it in The Daily Bulletin or others would accost him for being so Liquidated in a park where children were playing.

It must have been for this reason that one day, when he was sat on his usual bench, two henchmen from Sisyphusa came and took him away. He didn't fight them off or shout and scream. He was happy to be taken away, he hoped they would do something terrible to him like he thought he deserved.

During Joe's time in Solitary Initiation he struggled badly, especially having no access to any Liquid Escape. He became very sick and the Climbing Pills made it worse. He would have terrible nightmares every night where all he could hear was the screaming of the middle-aged woman in that small village in Babylonia as she beat her chest and pulled out her hair. During the day it was the turn of his Earpiece to torment him.

He didn't ever tell me what kind of things his Earpiece would say to him (because of the rule) but he gave the impression it was every bit as bad as the nightmares.

When Joe was integrated, things began to pick up for him. It was such a great relief to him when he found out that Team Re-Activation was made up completely of veterans. He made friends with his teammates instantly. They gave him the nickname G.I Joe (they said everyone had to have a nickname) which he was pleased with. Even though they had all been to either Bactria or Babylonia, one lad had even been to both, they rarely talked about it. It was enough for Joe just to know that he was with other men who had seen similar things, done similar things. It felt like being back in the training barracks again before he was sent away for his first tour.

Joe enjoyed Climbing Practice and the work in the quarry. He quickly regained his physique and he felt pride knowing that he was one of the best climbers and hardest workers. The Normalisation Classes though, were a different story. He didn't enjoy them at all. Team Re-Activation was taught by Warden Shiva who was known by every Service User for being the cruellest and most callous of all the wardens.

Shiva was a disciplinarian which was okay with the lads because that's what they were used to and, in a sense, what they wanted. Unlike the other lads, Joe had started to see things differently. He would tell me, "there's a difference between being a disciplinarian and abusing power." He disliked the way Warden Shiva taunted his teammates, the way she spoke to them dismissively and constantly derided their efforts to Normalise themselves. 'These men have risked their lives for this Island,' he thought to himself, 'who was she to treat them this way?'

Chapter 38

G.I Joe greeted me with a broad smile as I took up a position next to him in the quarry and began to swing my pick-axe. He always seemed happiest when he was smashing something. I hadn't taken as much care thinking over what approach I would take to persuade Joe to join the plan as I had with the others. I thought that somehow he would be easy to enlist, partly because we were already good friends and so he already trusted me, but also because he wasn't as smart as Mikey or as implicated as Beverley. But that's not how it transpired.

I began by initiating a conversation about Warden Shiva. He often came to me when he wanted to air his dissatisfaction with her, so I thought that it would be a good starting point.

"How's it going with Shiva?"

"The Destroyer?" laughed Joe through gritted teeth. It seemed that just the mention of her name made him angry.

"Is that what you're calling her now?"

"That's what we called our tanks out in Babylonia," he smiled. "She may be small but that woman will mow down anything in her path!" He lifted his pick-axe high in the air and brought it down with a hefty clunk. "Gotcha," he said directly to the granite as if it were a certain 5'1 warden. "You'll never guess what that woman did the other day. She made Tiny cry."

Tiny was like Joe's sidekick. He was 6"4 and barrel-chested. Joe looked out for Tiny because he was somewhat slow-witted. Tiny looked up to Joe and was always trying to please him and impress him. I remember one time during Climbing Practice Tiny rigged up Joe's harness especially so that it would be more comfortable to wear. Unfortunately, half way up the wall it came loose and Joe crashed to the floor in a heap.

"What did she do?" I asked Joe.

"I asked Tiny to clear up the climbing equipment after the session was over. I would usually do it myself but Sideways had got a ball in the eye and I was going to give him some first aid back in the dorm. So anyway, five minutes later Tiny comes into the dorm and gets straight into bed and starts bawling. He says Shiva told him to hurry up but you know how he is, he has to do things his own way, everything has its right place and when he gets rushed he flips out. She starts calling him stupid and says she'll send him to The Pit if he doesn't clear it up in thirty seconds."

"So is he alright now?"

"He's in The Pit."

"What do you mean he's in The Pit? I thought you said he came back to the dorm?" I asked.

"She told him to wait there for the henchmen to come and get him."

"And they did?"

"Yep."

"And when was this?"

"Last night."

"Did they say how long he's got?"

"Nope. Probably only a week but a week for Tiny is like a year for anyone else. I fucking hate that woman," Joe snarled as he took another swipe at the rock.

"That's fucked up," I agreed. I always found myself swearing more whenever I was with Joe. "Poor Tiny. I'm sure he'll be alright though, he must have had to put up with some tough situations in the army."

"I guess you're right. Maybe I underestimate him sometimes."

"That was so uncalled for," I thought aloud. "To send someone to The Pit because they didn't clean up some equipment in thirty seconds, that's just gratuitous."

"Well I don't know what 'gratuitous' means but it's bloody harsh, is what it is."

"That's what I meant."

"But that's Shiva, innit? That's how she's been since day one. It was never like that under Warden Charles."

"Who? Beverley?" I asked. Charles was Beverley's surname and I knew that she used to be a warden but I didn't know that she was Joe's Team Leader.

"Yeah, well, I know she's an SU now but I can only call her Warden Charles. Now there was a Team Leader."

"Really? How so?"

"The key to leadership, Dizzy, is knowing when to delegate," Joe now sounded in his element. "Warden Charles never had any less power over us lads but we didn't just fear her we respected her. We knew that she had the authority to punish us but we knew from experience that she wouldn't do it unless we deserved it."

"Give me an example," I said. I was intrigued to find out more about what Beverley was like when she was Warden Charles.

"Okay. Take Sideways. Warden found him with a gallon of Escape, someone must have give it to him on a visit. Does she stick him in The Pit straight away? No. She makes him down the thing in one so he pukes it up all over himself. Genius."

"And did he ever get caught drinking again?" I asked.

"Of course. And that's when you send him to The Pit. When the boy's been warned and he's stupid enough to do it again then he deserves The Pit. The point is, we all knew that the warden would give us a fair deal and the rest of us weren't stupid enough to take liberties. Warden Charles could see that we weren't looking for any trouble. We're all good soldiers and she saw she could use that. She let me take the lead, the army way. The lads would follow my lead in making the bed each morning, making sure their overalls were clean, I would lead them in Climbing Practice and I would direct the work in the quarry. And then they got rid of her."

"Do you think that's why?" I was asking Joe the question but in my mind I had already answered it. The regime didn't like the fact that Beverley was innovating, that she was empowering Service Users to be responsible for themselves and each other. Who knows whether Beverley did it out of altruism, maybe she could just see the opportunity to lighten her workload? But it was clear now: It wasn't Serky's petty ambition which led her to denounce Beverley as being Weird, it was Shade who put her up to it.

"Probably, who knows?" Joe speculated. "But it seems to me that each new warden that comes in is more strict than the last. What's yours like? What's she called again? Perky? Lurgy?"

"Serky."

"That's it," he smiled pretending that he'd genuinely forgotten.

"She's more like Shiva."

"That's the way they make 'em these days. They don't give you an inch. You need to ask permission to scratch your arse. It's checklist this, questionnaire that! Bloody idiots. If they just left it to me I'd have my team in perfect working order."

The two of us had separated a large amount of granite from the wall and so we stopped to gather our haul in our sashes and then we slowly trudged towards the hill. As we walked I continued the conversation.

"I get the feeling that more and more of us are beginning to think that way."

"What do you mean?" asked Joe.

"Things have definitely changed since I've been here. The regime is getting twitchy. That's why they seem to be getting stricter. It's because they feel vulnerable." I changed the subject quickly as we passed a warden. I pretended to be talking about climbing technique.

"I can only go from what I've seen going on in my team," I continued once the coast was clear. "People aren't so afraid to speak up. A few weeks ago in Normalisation, Gloria had a full-on rant about how unfair it was, the way we're being treated. *Gloria!*"

"So what's your point?" asked Joe, sounding wary.

"My point is that there's a rebellious mood in the air," I decided to test the waters.

"Rebellious mood? As in what? A mutiny?" Joe sounded distinctly unimpressed. He was perfectly comfortable mouthing off about the regime to let off steam, but it was clear that his army background had instilled in him a complete aversion to challenging authority. I could see that persuading him wouldn't be as simple as I'd hoped.

"And why not?" I whispered. "Something has to be done, Joe. We can't keep on letting them get away with it."

Joe shook his head. "You really do have a screw loose. Who do you think you are? You need a reality check my man."

We reached the top of the hill and deposited our rocks onto the conveyor belt which led in to the factory. Then we walked back to Team Re-Activation's cave and picked up our axes again.

"I'm serious Joe. We have a plan."

When I told him this Joe no longer looked disappointed or unimpressed he looked terrified.

"A plan? You mean you're serious?" He stopped and turned to face me.

"Get back to work," I told him. "You'll draw attention to us." Joe got back to work on the wall and I got back to work on him. "We're going to overthrow the regime. And we need your help. I need your help."

"No fucking way. Rebel? Me? Never. You can count me out of your little plan. Don't ruin this for me, Dizzy. I've only just got myself straight again. It's not a bad deal here. I mean I'm off the Escape, I've got my lads, I've got work to get on with. I know I complain about Shiva and that but she's not all bad. You need discipline."

"You're not in the army any more, Joe. You aren't working for anything here, you're as good as a slave."

"Fuck you, Dizzy."

"Not just you, Joe. We all are. Can't you see? You, me, Tiny, every one of us. They can do whatever they want to us and no-one gives a damn. They aren't accountable to anyone except whoever gives them their money. We have the opportunity to change things, to show them that they can't get away with treating people this way."

"Did you ever think that maybe this is where we belong?"

"Not once," I lied.

"Well that's nice for you. But I deserve to be here. I deserve to be a slave, to have no rights and no freedom. To tell you the truth, I deserve much worse for what I did to that woman and her family, for what all of us lads did to that country. If Weirdness is our only punishment for what we've done then we've been lucky. Who are we to complain when our boys are dying out there every day, losing arms and legs. And here we are, we have all our limbs and we can climb these walls and drag these rocks but we're too Weird to finish the job we started. It's just weak, there's no other word for it."

"You're contradicting yourself. You make this huge fuss about honour and loyalty and you can never disobey the authority in power, even when it's as abusive as the one here. But on the other hand, here you are trying to blame yourself individually for everything that happened to that poor woman in the village and even everything that's happened to the whole of Babylonia. Did you go over there out of choice because you wanted to travel half way around the world and kill strangers? No. You were sent there because it was your job. And you did the best job that you could. What you did to that family was wrong, worse than wrong, there's no denying it. But you were told by a superior officer to shoot that man. So in your world of following orders what you did was perfectly justifiable. So which way is it? Is your world going to be black and white, right and wrong, your whole life? Or can you try to judge your current situation on its own merits?"

"Well..." Joe started.

"Wait, I haven't finished yet," I interrupted. "One more thing. You can call yourself weak if you like (for what it's worth I think you're the opposite) but don't call those lads weak. Tiny is sat in that shit-hole right now, is he weak?"

"Let me tell you a story. My grandfather was seventeen when he volunteered to fight for the Mainland in the Just War. He served with distinction and was captured by the enemy. Who knows what unspeakable things were done to him? When he came back, he was taught to forget about it because that's what you were supposed to do."

"And so he got on with his life. He got married, had my mother and three other kids then later there were grandchildren. But even after all of that time, the horrors of war can never disappear for good. He was taken away by the men in black cloaks. Whatever happened to him all those years ago had come back to haunt him and they took him away. My Grandpa Abe was no weakling. I've never met a stronger, prouder man. So you can hate yourself and insult yourself but I won't let you insult my grandfather or the rest of your team."

"War-related Weirdness is not weakness. War is inhuman by definition and it's no wonder that it stretches the will of human beings to breaking point. But you don't look like a broken man to me. You're a fighter and fighters adapt. So you've found a groove here. You've worked a nice little position for yourself. But that's not because this place is alright and they've kindly made you feel welcome. You've got yourself back together through your own hard work. No, you've got to think about your men. Is it in their best interests to be here? Is this the best place for Tiny?"

I looked over at G.I Joe at this point and saw that his face had frozen still. He snapped himself out of it and began to hit the granite even harder than before.

"What happened to him?" he asked.

"To who?"

"Your grandfather? Is he still inside?"

"No, he got out. It took him a long time but he managed it. He's dead now. He died while I've been here in Sisyphusa, I got a message from my mum a couple of years back."

"I'm sorry," said Joe. "He sounded like a real soldier."

"He was," I agreed.

"Maybe you are right. Maybe we do need to change things, maybe we need to get Tiny and the rest of the boys out of here," he said as if trying to persuade himself out loud that it was okay to be having such subversive thoughts. "But what then? There's nothing out there for us. We can't enlist again, we're blacklisted. No soldier with Grade 4 Weirdness is allowed to serve again."

"So change that," I told him. "Campaign, fight, set up groups outside to help other soldiers like you guys."

"Maybe you've got an idea there Dizzy. You're not so Dizzy after all! But wait a minute, what are we talking about? They'll catch us as soon as we're out of these walls!"

"No they won't," I reassured him. "I've got someone on the inside. She's got access to the database and the Secure Zones and she'll delete all our files and give us new identities as soon as we're free."

Joe smiled. "You've got it all worked out don'tcha? How is this *Masterplan* of yours gonna work then? "

"You don't need to know that. You just need to know your job. Delegation, remember? The key to leadership... you said so yourself."

He smiled again. "Cocky bastard! Come on then what's my mission?"

"Simple. Just do what you do anyway. Lead Team Re-Activation. All I needed from you was to know that you're on board and that when the plan is implemented and the shit hits the fan you're on my side! When I give you and the other appointed Team Captains the signal all you've got to do is to keep your team calm, make sure all of us are working together and we'll all walk out the front door together."

"Well I don't know how the hell you're expecting to do it but if you do your job then I'll do mine!"

"Excellent" I said.

The men finished work in the quarry at the same time as the women came out of the factory and so we walked back to the dorm as a team. I walked at the front and as I walked I began to congratulate myself for how well the plan seemed to be coming together. Team Recovery had become like a single organism. When one member was struggling the rest would take up the slack. Beverley, Mikey and G.I Joe were all now on board and I was confident in their ability to lead their respective teams.

That only left Skinny Jim whom I assumed was out of The Pit by that point because no-one else could fit in there with Tiny. I would plan my approach for him over the next few days, but I no longer felt apprehensive about it. It felt as though things were falling perfectly into place and that success was almost inevitable.

That was the last thought going through my mind as I was the first to reach the dorm. I pushed the door expecting it to open easily as usual but there was something blocking it. It wasn't completely blocked, but when I pushed harder a sound came from the top of the door. I looked up and I saw that a taut sheet was stretching down from the ceiling, tied around the lamp which hung over the door. The sound was the friction of the sheet against the door as I tried to push it open. Something was weighing the sheet down.

The others had arrived at the door now and Mr.Femuz pushed the door open enough for the rest of us to slip into the room. I was the first to see it. Samuel Etch's lifeless body hanging from the ceiling. His purple face had the same frightened expression that it had had ever since I'd met him.

The following minutes are a blur. There was a lot of crying, a lot of screaming. Harry tried to hold him up by his legs as if he hadn't clearly died hours ago. Harry refused to accept that Samuel was dead. We pulled him away from the body but he shouted that it was our fault and that we never should have left Samuel alone. Ella sat on the floor and stared at the boy's dirty bare feet as his body swayed and dangled. She didn't speak a word for days but somehow she didn't seem shocked, just consumed with loss.

Henchmen and wardens arrived and took the body away seemingly unaffected by the situation- simply another day in Sisyphusa. At that point I wondered why they hadn't known about it sooner. I looked up at the I-Spy in the corner of the room and saw that it had been covered over with a pillow case. I lay awake all night wondering how it was that a ten-year-old child knows to cover up a camera before he hangs himself. I found it strangely comforting that he had spent the last few minutes of his short, unhappy life in privacy.

Chapter 39

The rules stated that we couldn't hold a burial ceremony for a suicide. Instead, Samuel's body was hastily buried by henchmen in an unmarked grave at the back of the cemetery. Over the subsequent days, team members visited the grave and by the end of the week it was covered with flowers, messages and a carved wooden stake. The stake was obviously done by Ella because the inscription was written in her handwriting. It read, "Samuel Etch, cruelly taken from us too early. May he enjoy the peace he deserves in the next life that he was denied in this." Ella spent all of her free time now in the cemetery and seemed to retreat more and more into herself. I could often hear her in the middle of the night, when everyone else was asleep, muttering lines from the Yes/No Book #2. She repeated the same lines over and over again, as she sobbed quietly. I wondered angrily what Ella's SkyMaster had ever done for her but it was all meaningless.

I also noticed some blood seeping through her sleeve one morning and her face was even more pale than usual. I thought of intervening but I didn't. I was grieving for Samuel myself and her grief was too much for me. I began to resent her monopoly on misery and avoided her gaze at all times. Not that she was looking anyone in the eye anyway. She seemed to lurch through her days oblivious of anything or anyone around her. She stopped attending the Senior Reps Council and when Serky addressed her in class she didn't answer her, even when shouted at. Ella's grief was even too much for Serky who refrained from punishing her as she otherwise would have, seemingly frightened of what the silent apparition might do.

Suicides were a huge embarrassment for the regime. Gwen told me that all Weirdness Institutions have their funding decreased for every suicide which they allow to happen. The fine would be even larger if the Corporation of Hysteria were ever to catch wind of the story and publicise it. Whilst a death which takes place during a Wall-Climb is acceptable, a suicide is considered to be a sign of lax security. Precautions had been taken all over the facility to try and avoid them but they were still fairly common.

The year before, our Normalisation Classes were moved to another room whilst renovations were being done in our regular classroom. After a number of weeks we returned to find the room almost exactly as it had been except for two changes. One, the metal coat hangers at the door had been replaced by springy plastic ones. And two, the beam which stretched across the ceiling had been boarded up on either side of it presumably so that some determined Service User didn't string a rope over the top and hang themselves in the middle of his or her lesson. It's somewhat ironic that in all of their meticulous "suicide-proofing" to avoid censure they somehow failed to imagine the relatively simple method which Samuel devised which was to hang himself with a bed sheet from a hanging lamp which even a ten-year-old could reach from the top bunk.

When I spoke to Gwen she sounded very upset. She blamed herself for not paying close enough attention to the security feeds. She had been busy watching the feed from the quarry as she listened to mine and Joe's conversation and hadn't noticed Samuel covering up the I-Spy. When the screen went black she assumed that there was a technical fault and thought nothing more of it until she heard the screams over my microphone. I had never heard Gwen sound fazed by anything before. However, while Gwen seemed able to channel her grief into anger at the regime and used it to redouble her efforts to bring them down it had the opposite effect on me.

I felt the same as I had in the first few months of my Solitary Initiation. I felt hopeless and lost. So much of getting through Sisyphusa is an act and I'd lost the energy or desire to play my part. Life was too cruel to have hope. Why persevere in such a morally ambiguous world with no order or justice? I saw no point in the plan any more. I convinced myself that it was doomed to failure and that it wasn't worth doing anyway because the system was so powerful that it could absorb the destruction of one hundred Sisyphusas and still remain in place. I lost the motivation to be the motivator. When things had got bad in the past I took it upon myself to gee up the team, to galvanise other Service Users, to lead by example but I didn't have the strength to pretend any more.

There was no positive spin that could be put on Samuel's demise. It was horrific and it was permanent and what's more it happened in the room we still had to sleep in. The now broken lamp that hung askew from the ceiling was a constant reminder of Samuel's final despairing act. Each morning when I awoke and saw the lamp it was as if I had been dealt the blow of his death for the very first time all over again, the reality never fully sinking in.

The whole team remained in collective mourning for weeks. After that time it was the Flower-Eaters who first began to emerge from the shadows, especially Mo. Mo's simple faith in life inspired me. I clung to his company day after day, hoping that his outlook might be contagious. Previously, I had either been attracted to more cerebral people like Gwen and Mr. Femuz or emotionally vulnerable people like Ella. It was these people who stimulated me intellectually and helped me to find some meaning in my situation.

But I felt tired of thinking, of constantly analysing myself and others. I wanted to see the world just the way Mo saw it. I wished that I could feel Mo's constancy, his sense that "life goes on" and that bad things are to be expected. Who was to say that I was right and they were wrong? I doubt that any of the Flower-Eaters had read the books I'd read, but did that better equip me to deal with pain and death? Death was the ultimate leveller. Weirdness *could* descend on any of us, Islander or Outlander, Aspirati or warden or Service User, but death is for certain, it *will* come to all of us no matter what.

When you grow up on Fantasy Island, you are taught to expect that life is a dance and the world is your dance floor so when something bad happens to you or someone that you love it comes as a terrible shock. I had become acclimatised to suffering since my arrival in Sisyphusa but I had come to realise that no matter how desperate you thought things were at any given time, they could always get worse.

Mr. Femuz and I climbed with the Flower-Eaters, ate with them, and worked with them in the quarry. We did things at their pace which was considerably slower than that of other

Service Users. I talked to Ahmed about the farm that he grew up on and I spoke to Khaled about his four daughters and his dreams of them being married—they had to be dreams because he had not heard from his family for years. Mo would sing cheerful songs while we worked. It came as a relief to me that they were in another language, one that I couldn't understand. Another language is a completely different way of interpreting the world and I decided that Cartajee was a positive language. I didn't want to know what the songs were about, that would ruin them. I preferred to imagine that they were about happiness and joy and love.

I would idealise the Flower-Eaters' homeland, wilfully ignoring the political instability and poverty and I would focus on the unchanging culture and way of life, the relationship with their natural environment and the beautiful beaches and sand dunes and ancient buildings. Perhaps these things only existed in my imagination. Their homeland was probably as changed and as troubled as mine, if not more. People there were probably no better than people here, all of the faults of our species were probably universal but it helped me to dream of a better place than the one which I was in.

There were also a lot more arguments within the team during this time. Harry exploded at Jacob because he had taken Samuel's pillow only a week after the boy's death. The Simons grew increasingly prickly with the Flower-Eaters who, in their opinion, weren't showing enough grief.

I also lost my temper. My outburst was prompted by a story on the HDTV. One night, all regularly scheduled programming was interrupted for special Bad News coverage, which happened from time to time. By this point I had completely stopped watching the news. In fact I actively avoided it which was difficult considering the ubiquity of HDTV screens in every room in Sisyphusa.

"Our breaking news tonight," said the blonde newsreader. "Sources close to the singer and Aspirati have confirmed that Kinky Diva has been apprehended on suspicion of Weirdness. She had been exhibiting unusual behaviour over the past few weeks and it appears that action has finally been taken for her own safety and the safety of others." Whilst the newsreader continued to read her autocue, a montage of Kinky Diva's career was being shown. By this point I was watching with the others. For some reason I was intrigued by the story.

The footage showed her changing appearance over her short career; her ballooning then deflating weight, her various hair styles, her magically inflating breasts. She, like many Aspiratis, gradually became a caricature of herself, clearly advised to fetishise her humble beginnings and how Normal she was, but woefully oblivious to how detached from reality she had become.

There were pictures of Kinky's three husbands. Her marriages followed the standard 3-Step Aspirati Marriage Plan:

1. ***Merger.*** Kinky is set up by her people with a young male Aspirati of a similar standing in a mutually beneficial venture. The marriage is allowed to fizzle out once it is no longer profitable or one partner outgrows the other.
2. ***Acquisition.*** A more successful Kinky, empowered by her status, is given the chance to choose from a selection of attractive propositions.
3. ***Hostile Takeover.*** By now, with her Acquisition dumped, Kinky is double-platinum and a shark in the dating game. She could give her people any name and they would go and make that man an offer that he could not refuse, and he didn't, at least, until he found out she was Weird.

There were pictures of Kinky being chased by men with cameras and many more pictures of her staring into the camera, pouting, enticing it. It was as if she had found the key to eternal life in that lens or perhaps she was just mesmerised by her own reflection in it. I often wondered why the Aspirati seemed to be so in love with cameras. If they notice a camera trained on them they completely change their expression, assume a different persona. I marvelled at the power of a simple machine to utterly change a personality. Who was watching that was so important to them? Anyone they knew? Their mother? Their children? Their spouses? No. The multitude. The camera represented this mythical illusion which Aspiratis and Ministers referred to as 'The Public.' In their mind, the whole Island was watching and the Island was one, it was homogeneous and it was easily impressionable. It existed to reinforce the Aspiratis' own view of themselves. The newsreader continued, "A spokesperson for Ms Diva has told the Bad News Channel, 'Kinky has been taken to a Special Treatment Facility where she will stay until she has been Normalised. She remains in good spirits and would like to thank all of her fans for their messages and kind wishes.' The newsreader then read another announcement, this time from the Corporation of O'Besity which controlled the food supply throughout the Empire and had recently signed Kinky to promote their brand. "The statement says: 'Following the news that Kinky Diva is in a position of un-Normality at present, the Corporation of O'Besity has taken decisive action to cancel her contract. The Corporation would like to make it clear that we no longer have any association with this person.'"

The newsreader affected her serious face and finished, "We will have pictures of Kinky Diva's arrival at the facility via our HeliSpy soon. Now for your messages: Gerald from Pedantshire says, 'This is just so typical of Kinky's behaviour, what is the world coming to when young girls, including my daughter, are looking up to this basket case? We should sterilise her like we did in the old days.' Whereas Julie from Melodrammington asks, "Who is looking after this poor girl? Where are her parents? This is just awful, get Normal soon Kinky.' Thank you so much for all of your messages we hope to read out some more later so keep them coming in but in the meantime, we will take a short break." The first Ad-Verse was for Kinky Diva's latest album on sale at the Corporation of Hysteria's music store.

What made me angry wasn't the story itself, although I did wonder why it was considered important enough to be the top story or a news story at all. It wasn't even the cynical and shameless reality that Corporations had become the supreme moral arbiter of when an Aspirati had strayed beyond acceptable behaviour. No, what really made me lose it was the reaction of my teammates.

The reaction was a mixed one and could be split into two distinct camps. There were those who were strongly sympathetic towards Kinky Diva: Gracie and Gloria; and then there were those who were harshly critical of her: Stacey, Tracey and Harry. The others either didn't express an opinion or weren't watching.

In the sympathetic camp the argument could be simplified as, "That poor thing. She used to be such a nice, pretty girl, but she's been driven to Weirdness by those awful journalists. I do hope she makes a speedy recovery." The opposing camp's argument could best be summed up by Harry's words, "Ha, she got what was coming to her. She wanted to be an Aspirati but she couldn't hack it and now we're supposed to feel sorry for her? Not me! She's a bloody millionaire!"

You might be thinking which argument it was that led to me losing my temper? The answer is both. I despaired at Gracie and Gloria's emotional connection to the welfare of this utter stranger. Why couldn't they see how unfair it was that because she was an Aspirati, Kinky Diva was taken to a "Special Treatment Facility"? Why did they think that a person who sings songs and appears in Ad-Verses was more important than them? Why was her being Removed, and not all of us being Removed, suddenly an issue that was newsworthy?

And then there was Harry's response. Harry couldn't seem to make any connection between Kinky Diva's Weirdness and his or any of the rest of ours. Because she was an Aspirati, Kinky Diva was fair game and was there to be shot at. Somehow her Weirdness was her own fault and even though Harry, Stacey and Tracey knew of the kind of suffering the Aspirati might have been going through, "it was different."

So I spoke up. "Why the fuck is this even news?" I shouted more at the screen than at anyone in the room. "This girl is just a human girl who has been Removed, like millions are all over the Empire, every year, every day. Why, just because she's an Aspirati, is Weirdness suddenly newsworthy?" It felt as though people had become so de-sensitised to the Corporation of Hysteria's methods of attracting our fly-like attention that there was no sense of priority. If every story is a 'row' or 'scandal' be it the Climate Crisis, the wars or the private life of an Aspirati, how are people supposed to perceive these things as being anything but remote from their own lives? If these issues emerge only as simply packaged narratives to hold people's focus for a couple of days until there is a new story, how can we hope for people to engage in the long-term to address the truly big problems of our time?

The others looked at me but no-one said anything. I didn't often raise my voice or lose my cool and they appeared to be shocked. And then Ella spoke to me for the first time since Samuel's death. "We should be pleased that Weirdness is getting news coverage at all, if it's because of some Aspirati, so be it," she spoke in a measured monotone.

"That's rubbish. So you really believe that 'all publicity is good publicity?' The story here isn't Weirdness; how awful and painful it is, how badly Service Users are treated, how harmful the stigma towards it is. The story here is the next episode in an Aspirati's life, put out for public consumption as if it wasn't a real human being's life but one of those Real Life shows on HDTV. Like last month," I continued, my blood really up. "There was that young Aspirati who died of cancer. Her funeral wasn't just on Aspirati Funeral Live it was on HDTV Bad News and three other channels."

"Who decides what the news is? Why do all of the HDTV channels and all the Dailies cover the same stories? They're attracted to the scene like kids crowding around a fight in the playground, not interested in the cause or the potential fallout of what is happening but easily distracted by the next one kicking off on the other side of the playground. People lined the streets to mourn this woman because she had appeared on Fantasy Factory for a few weeks. Why was her death more tragic than all the other twenty-somethings who died of cancer this year? Those same people, who cried for this dead stranger, their parents or husbands or siblings will die of cancer in a dingy hospital room with no fanfare, no public outpouring, how is that fair?"

I knew that I'd lost my audience—I hadn't won people over to the plan by shouting at them or lecturing them. Most people didn't care about those things like I did. Aspiratis are seen by a minority as gods or icons but by a majority as a bit of fun. I think a smaller minority, including me, feel that the power that is behind them and their influence on the Island are incredibly unfair and damaging. It seems that Island culture's only way of experiencing the vicissitudes of the human condition is through a better-looking, sometimes more talented, often better-connected and largely more desperate focal point: The Aspirati.

What I resented was the way in which we were persuaded by the Corporation of Hysteria and others that the joy or the suffering of an Aspirati is more important than anyone else's. But when those who control the access to reality choose to distort it for their own profit who can compete with that? It seemed that everyone on the Island wanted to be an Aspirati and with more and more channels on the HDTV and less and less good reasons for people to be on it, perhaps they would get their wish. But what happens when there are more Aspirati than viewers?

By this point the newsreader had moved on to the next story, "The Struggles of Minister Frown- how long can his government survive? You decide now on Instabet." Someone changed the channel and I went to sleep early, feeling more alone than I ever had since leaving Solitary.

Chapter 40

Things were stagnant. The fractious atmosphere in the team remained. It would swing between awkward silence and spiky confrontation. The dorm remained a horrible place to be and the sense of togetherness within Team Recovery that it had taken months, even years, to create lay in ruins. I felt powerless to change what I could see happening before my eyes. I couldn't even help myself let alone the team. My sleeping was worse than ever and my appearance began to deteriorate. I began to haunt my own life again as I had for the first year of my stay in Sisyphusa. I barely spoke three words a day. I would come straight back from the quarry every evening and just lie in bed until morning, sometimes twelve hours, sometimes fourteen but I could barely sleep for more than an hour at a time.

I wanted to visit Samuel's grave but I knew that Ella would be there and I had nothing left to say to her. The cemetery was the only place I knew where I could be alone and she occupied it for the free time of every day. I had begun to resent her very presence. I found myself flooded with irritation when I looked at her ashen face, tired with the signs of constant crying. How could she have felt so much for him when he had barely even uttered a word to her? He was a blank canvas that Ella could project all of her own story onto. I could no longer find it within myself to feel compassion for her or anyone else. It was as if Samuel was our child and his death had spelled the death of our relationship.

During the next free time I decided to try to find somewhere else where I could be alone and maybe talk to Gwen. I went to the same woods which led to the meadow and the cemetery. Instead of following the dirt path I went straight through the brush as far as I could until I reached the wall of the Sisyphusa compound. I sat down with my back against the wall and spoke into my microphone.

"Are you there Gwen?" I asked. When I spoke my lips quivered. The attempt to speak a sentence seemed to be all it took for my defences to break down.

"Yes, Odis, I'm here. How are you bearing up?"

"Not well," I said, desperately trying not to cry. "Everything's shit Gwen. It's just so shit!"

"I know it is, I know."

"I don't know what to do Gwen? What am I supposed to do? Tell me, please!"

"What do you mean, *do*?" she asked.

"I mean, it's all fucked, everything. Samuel's dead, the team is in ruins, they're either at each others throats or they've given up. I've failed. There's nothing I can do!"

"You don't have to *do* anything, right now. You just have to *be*. You have to allow yourself and those around you to grieve, Odis. Don't put so much pressure on yourself. I know that I've asked a lot from you these past few months but you must allow yourself some time and some space to rest."

"There's no time," I told her. "What about the plan? My life is wasting away, can't you see? I need to get out of this place soon or I'll never get out. I can feel myself becoming like the rest of them. I've been here too long Gwen, I'm becoming too used to this place. It's like you said, 'less thinking, more doing.' Give me a mission, Gwen, please, I'm begging you."

"Odis, give it some time, maybe just a few days or so, until you get some sleep and you start to feel more like yourself. You're not in the right frame of mind to do anything right now. Things are terrible now, of course they are, but things change. Life is a lot about momentum. No one has a fixed philosophy or unchanging plan even if they think they do. You just fall in and out of grooves, some good and some bad."

"When was the last time I was in a good groove?" I snapped angrily.

"Well no, of course not. Random events will always dictate our paths. But it's how we respond to these events that is the real measure. You will emerge from your suffering a stronger, more compassionate human being, I'm sure of that."

"You're imposing a narrative onto chaos," I sneered dismissively.

"Isn't that true of everything?" she replied instantly. "I'm asking you to trust me again young man. You need to rest, recover and then be ready."

"Please Gwen," I began to cry. "Give me anything, anything. If I can't feel like I'm working towards getting out of here, I'm going to lose it, I mean really lose it. I need this Gwen."

"Leave Team Recovery be," she finally gave in. "Trust in your work. The bonds that you have forged have not disappeared. The team needs time to recuperate and when it does they will be stronger for it. In the mean time, you should concentrate your efforts elsewhere, starting with Skinny Jim, you know that he is out of The Pit?"

Just the mention of Skinny Jim's name increased my heart-rate. Although I would never have admitted it to anyone, I was afraid of him. "Yes I've seen him," I said. I'd seen him the previous day in the mess hall with his two minions. I saw him smiling at me but I didn't have the energy to react. It was clear that his time in The Pit hadn't reformed his character.

"Are you sure that you want this mission, Odis?" asked Gwen, breaking the short silence. "Maybe wait a little while longer?"

"No," I said strongly. "I'm ready now. What do you want me to do? The same as the others?"

"No," she replied. "It's not the same as the others is it? It's very different. I didn't pick Skinny Jim because I wanted to, I picked him because there was no-one else. Unless we want to leave the distinct probability that when we implement the plan Team Redemption will be a hindrance rather than a help then something must be done about Skinny Jim."

"But I can't tell him," I said.

"No, of course not. He cannot be trusted."

"Then what?"

"I don't know exactly, Odis? That's for you to determine when you speak to him. The bottom line is that by the end of your conversation, Skinny Jim must be in no doubt as to who is the most powerful Service User in Sisyphusa. Do you think you can do that?"

"Yes," I answered with a determination that belied my apprehension.

"One more thing Odis," she said softly. "Plant something, cultivate something, give something new life, it might help. Many years ago we used to have allotments on the compound and whenever one of the Service Users did what Samuel did, I would bring a new flower, or seed, or vegetable for the Service Users to plant. Just an idea." She ended the communication. I surveyed the woods around me, looking for something that I could plant. Eventually I spotted a small flower and carefully took some of its seeds, or what I thought were seeds. I buried them in one of the few spots of natural light that squeezed through the thick woodland canopy. I don't know if those seeds ever turned into flowers.

As I trudged back through the thick brush I began to think how I could even approach Skinny Jim. What could I say to him? On what pretence could I possibly arrange to meet with him privately? And even if we did meet, then what? Like Gwen said, he couldn't be trusted. So, what?

I came to a small opening in the woods where the trees weren't so dense and I could hear a sound, it sounded like singing. I followed the noise and found behind a large bush the familiar sight of Ahmed, Khaled, Abdul and Mo. The four men sat in their usual crescent shape in the middle of which was that same set-up of implements which Ella and I had happened upon in the meadow all those many months ago. The small fire boiled the water in the clay pot and above the pot lay a clutch of Ziziphusa leaves steaming away, becoming potent.

The Flower-Eaters looked at me with a guilty expression, like a teenage boy caught watching pornography by his mother. They had been caught. My first reaction was one of great disappointment. The guys had promised me that they would give up, especially since they knew what I had endured in The Pit when I took the rap for them. I wanted to tell them off but then I had a better idea.

"Sorry Mr Odis, so sorry my friend. Is bad but we try to stop," said Mo rather pathetically. The other men said nothing but their looks said it all, especially Ahmed. His expression was that of a man of honour who knew that he had given and broken his word. He was ashamed.

"It's okay guys, I knew it already," I lied. "Just make sure you don't get caught this time, you know what will happen."

The four of them were visibly shocked that I hadn't come down hard on them, it's almost as if they were disappointed- if I wasn't there as a moral compass for them to judge and punish themselves by then was it wrong to eat flowers after all?

"In fact can I have some?" I asked them casually.

Their expressions now turned from shock to terror. "No, no. You must not take. Is bad, very bad. Must not start," said Khaled, terribly serious.

"He's right Odis," said Ahmed. Ahmed still looked embarrassed. He knew that he had no right to lecture me on flower-eating. "You must not eat."

"Do you think it would be my first time? You must be joking." I had experimented with various things before Sisyphusa but never regularly. "Come on guys, just lend me your stuff for a couple of days and I'll give it straight back."

The Flower-Eaters looked decidedly queasy. They stared at each other unsure of what to do. On the one hand they must have been relieved that I hadn't rebuked them although it confused them and left their guilt hanging in the air. On the other hand they clearly didn't want to be responsible for me taking up the same bad habit.

"Guys I only want to try it one time. I'll give the stuff back tomorrow night and I won't ask for it again. Without the pot and the matches I wouldn't be able to prepare it anyway."

They reluctantly agreed to lend me their equipment until the next night as long as I promised them that it was a one-off. To make such a promise was an easy sacrifice because I had no intention to eat any flowers myself. However, I was sure that Skinny Jim was partial to the odd Ziziphusa.

Chapter 41

I didn't want to approach Skinny Jim in the mess hall in case any of my teammates saw me. Since Thomas' death Skinny Jim was hated by everyone in Team Recovery so if they saw me talking to him it would certainly have been looked upon as a betrayal. This left me without too many options but then I remembered the first time I ever saw Skinny Jim—at the top of the Practice Climbing Wall.

So during Climbing Practice I made sure that I was climbing at exactly the same time and pace as Skinny Jim. I was by then a much faster climber than he was so I purposefully held back in order to reach the summit just before he arrived. I quickly unclipped my harness and connected it to a hook and then I hurried over and stood where Skinny Jim was about to climb over the top.

The long, spindly fingers gripped the top of the ledge like a spider's legs and he pulled himself up over the top. When he saw me standing there he exhibited no signs of being surprised or perturbed, he just asked, "What the fuck do you want?"

"To talk, just me and you," I told him.

"We ain't got nuffin' to talk about," he snarled. He barged me out of the way and reached for the protective gear. I grabbed his arm and held it tightly.

"Well I think we do," I told him.

He pushed me in the chest with his other hand and freed himself from my grip. "Don't fuck with me. I'm warning you but just this once. I ain't like no-one you've come across in your world."

"What world is that?"

"I don't know what your world is like but I can tell it ain't like mine."

"I wouldn't be so sure," I told him as I bent down and reached into my sock. "Do they ever do this in your world?" I asked him as I pulled out some Ziziphusa leaves.

He looked at me suspiciously and then he said angrily, "What the fuck are you looking at?" He wasn't looking at me when he said this so I turned around and saw that he was speaking to a climber from one of the other teams who had just reached the top. The small man shook his head sheepishly and quickly scurried over the other side of the wall and began abseiling (completely forgetting to put on any safety gear.)

Skinny Jim turned his focus back to me and said, "So what? The stuff grows all over this place, everyone knows that," he dismissed the clump of leaves in my palm. "If you haven't got the right shit to prepare it then you're basically eating grass."

"Well then it's lucky I've got a pot and matches and I know a place hidden where we can prepare it."

"What's the catch?"

"No catch. Either you want to or you don't but decide now before people start wondering why we're taking so long." He nodded his head. "Meet me at the cemetery during free time today and come alone," I told him. I quickly ran back over to my section of the wall, re-attached my harness, put on my safety gear and abseiled down the wall without getting hit once.

I waited in the cemetery for some time after finishing my work in the quarry. I had almost decided to leave when Skinny Jim finally arrived. I led us away from the graves and into the thick of the long grass, to a secluded spot where I had set up a hearth like the one which the Flower-Eaters used. There, already prepared, was the pot of water raised on stones above a small fire. On top of the pot was a criss-cross of tiny twigs which I then lay the Ziziphusa leaves on and they began to steam from the rising heat of the bubbling water.

I sat down and invited Skinny Jim to do the same. He looked around suspiciously but eventually joined me. Once the flowers looked frazzled I handed them over to Skinny Jim. He looked at the leaves and then he looked at me, "Aren't you doing it too?" he asked.

"No thanks," I replied. "You eat and I'll talk."

"No deal," he shook his head. "You don't eat, I don't eat, simple. You think I'm stupid just because I don't use your fancy words? You could've done anything to these, I know you want me dead."

I'd hoped that I wouldn't have had to join him but I predicted he wouldn't agree to do it unless I did to. I had eaten flowers before, not Ziziphusa but others like them, and I was desperate not to eat any. I had lived for over two years without any Liquid Escape or flowers since I'd been in Sisyphusa. I could easily have got hold of either one of them—plenty of Service Users did—but as soon as I arrived I realised I didn't want any. Liquid Escape, for me, was something I took to have fun, do stupid things and give me the confidence to meet women. In Sisyphusa it would have done nothing for me, just made me feel worse. And that's why I was wary of eating flowers too, but I knew that I had to.

"I don't want you dead, I told you, I just want to talk to you. But if you won't talk to me unless I eat it, then I'll eat it." I chewed and swallowed the soggy leaves. They tasted like spinach but had a strong, burning after-taste which made me cough.

Skinny Jim sniggered. "Amateur," he said under his breath before shovelling a much larger handful into his almost toothless mouth. "It's good stuff," he said with his masticating mouth still full. "Where did you get it?" he asked as he pointed to the pot and matches.

"From someone on my team."

He nodded his head. "Can you feel it yet?" he asked.

"A bit." He offered me some more. "No, I'm alright thanks," I told him.

"What a lightweight," he smiled. "Is that how it goes down in your world? A couple of little leaves and you're good for the night? Does mummy read you a bedtime story before beddy-byes too?" He cackled as he began to pick at his remaining teeth with a twig. Every so often he would spit out large, dark globules right next to where I was sitting.

I said nothing. Instead I grabbed another handful of leaves and ate them without wincing. I began to feel strange almost immediately. My face started to burn to the extent that I began to touch it just to make sure it wasn't on fire. My head was swimming with thoughts and my stomach churned. I looked at Skinny Jim and he appeared different. I suddenly saw him as being very afraid, very insecure. He stared back at me and said, "What are you looking at?"

"A scared little boy," came out of my mouth without my conscious consent.

"What did you say?" he barked as he jumped to his feet and loomed over me in a threatening manner.

"Why are you always so angry?" I asked him, as I suddenly began to giggle uncontrollably. Before I had time to try and stop laughing Skinny Jim's size 11 boot came flying into my chest and I was rocked back onto the ground. I instinctively rolled to one side to avoid more blows which I expected were coming. I got to my feet and ran at him. He was waiting there with his fists primed but I tackled him to the floor and we began to tussle.

First I had him in a headlock then he wriggled out of it and gripped me around the neck with his bony digits. It suddenly dawned on me that I was in a fight. If I wasn't being strangled then I may have felt the urge to start giggling again at the absurdity of it. I had never had a fight in my life nor had I ever imagined that I would, especially not with someone like Skinny Jim who fought dirty like a seasoned veteran.

I managed to extricate myself from his grip with a swift knee to his abdomen and then we both scrambled to our feet. We stood facing each other as the wind began to pick up and swirl through the long grass. I had completely lost the urge to laugh. I gathered my thoughts and reminded myself of what Gwen had told me-"The bottom line is that by the end of your conversation, Skinny Jim must be in no doubt as to who is the most powerful Service User in Sisyphusa."

I stood there panting, looking at the wiry figure in front of me and I remembered what it was that I was fighting for. Skinny Jim represented everything that the regime wanted a Service User to be: self-interested, unquestioning, inarticulate, petty. And despite the fact that he caused trouble, it was exactly the kind of trouble they liked because it caused factions among Service Users and distracted them from seeing the regime as the enemy.

I knew if I wanted to change things, if the plan was to work, then Skinny Jim would have to be taken care of. If Skinny Jim was what stood in the way of everyone else's freedom then it was down to me to do what was necessary to move him out of the way.

"When I'm finished with you," he said, breathing frantically. "You're gonna end up like your little friend." He mimed a hangman's noose being strung around his neck and stuck his tongue out the corner of his mouth, and then he smiled.

It was as if all the anger that had been stored up inside me for so long suddenly exploded. I charged at him and immediately his expression changed. For the first time he looked afraid. He was no longer the aggressor. I was confronting him, and he didn't know how to react because no Service User had ever challenged him before.

I pounced on him and took him to the ground. I began to shower him with blows, to the chin, the face, the chest, the ears. I punched him because of what had happened to my life, I punched him because Samuel was gone, I punched him because of what he did to Thomas. My knuckles were covered with blood, either my own or his which gushed from his nose, his lip and a cut above his eye.

I grabbed him by the scruff of the neck and pounded his head against the ground. "Is this what you wanted? Is this the only language you speak?" I screamed in his face. "Answer me!"

He shook his head from side to side, too afraid to open his eyes or his mouth. He looked pathetic.

"You don't threaten me again, ever! You hear me?" I shouted. "You don't threaten anyone. Your time is over. Finished. I'm in charge now, get it? GET IT?" I pounded his head against the ground again.

"Yes, yes," he cried as a mouthful of blood spluttered down his chin.

"You do what I tell you. Whatever happens, if anything goes down you don't do a thing without my say-so, understand?"

"I understand, I understand."

"Now get up." I grabbed his arm and lifted him to his feet. As I was doing so I saw a figure out of the corner of my eye walking across the far side of the long grass by the cemetery. It was Ella and she was staring straight back at me. She quickly turned away, but I knew that she could see it was me and I was sure she could see that it was Skinny Jim. And because I was grabbing his arm at the moment she looked I could only imagine what kind of betrayal she was accusing me of in her mind.

"Go get yourself cleaned up," I told Skinny Jim without looking at him. He scurried off into the woods like a wounded animal. I waited a couple of minutes and then went back to the dorms.

Chapter 42

I lay awake all night. My muscles ached and my head throbbed. I vowed to myself that I would never again eat flowers. I had to be in control at all times. I felt my mangled knuckles. They stung with each small touch. I wondered whether Skinny Jim was able to sleep, whether his wounds were stinging. I didn't feel any guilt for what I had done to him. In fact the lack of guilt was the only thing which made me feel guilty. My heart felt like it was still beating faster than usual. I wanted desperately to fall asleep. The prospect of working a full shift in the quarry on zero night's sleep didn't bear thinking about.

I can't remember falling asleep that night but I remember waking up the next morning. I was dragged out of my bed by two henchmen. The other housemates were still in their bunks. The ones who had woken up from the commotion looked on in shock as I was taken towards the door. It was reminiscent of the night over two years previously when the henchmen took me away from Cossetts Lane. My teammates, just as Wellborn and Anna and the others had, stared on with the same looks on their faces, knowing there was nothing that they could do.

I was hauled down the corridor and through the reception area. It was barely even light outside. We went up the Tower B staircase to the third floor and stopped outside Warden Serky's office. One of the henchmen gave the door a firm knock which was met with a swift reply,

"Bring him in," the warden said.

Inside the office Serky sat behind her desk. Facing her on a sofa sat Skinny Jim and Warden Eavel, the Team Leader of Team Redemption.

"Sit down," Serky indicated a wooden chair in front of me as the muscles in her face and jaw contorted with anger. I took a seat. "Have you not caused enough trouble since you've been here?"

I stared back at her blankly. I was too tired to put on any act.

Michael Richmond

"Well? Aren't you going to ask me what you're doing here?" Serky shouted.

"He knows," hissed Warden Eavel disdainfully. The small, hunched man's shiny, bald head reflected the bright light into my eyes. "He knows exactly what he's done," he said as he shot me an angry glance. I looked at Skinny Jim whose chin lay on his chest and whose gaze was rooted to the grey carpet.

"Go on, take a good look," said Warden Eavel, who noticed me glancing at Skinny Jim. "Proud of your handiwork? We'll see if you like it, shall we?"

"That's enough, warden," said Serky.

"No, I haven't finished. How would you like it if one of mine did that to one of yours? He won't be able to work all week. I can't reach my targets," said Eavel pointing to Skinny Jim who cut a pathetic figure.

"That's enough now. As your superior I'm telling you to be quiet," Serky said sternly. Eavel sat back on the sofa with a chastened expression on his round, red face.

"What's all this about?" I asked.

"You see what's happened to #54 here," she pointed at Skinny Jim. "Lift up your head #54!" Skinny Jim lifted his head just enough for me to see that one of his eyes was swollen totally shut and his nose was crooked. "We know that you did this #108, there's no point in denying it."

I looked at Skinny Jim who purposefully met my gaze. He stiffly shook his head ever so slightly and his open eye was filled with terror. I could see that he was trying to convey to me that he hadn't told the wardens and I believed him. I began to wonder what they might be planning to do to me. I hoped for a beating (as long as I could still walk and talk I could still carry out the plan.) The last thing I wanted was to be sent to The Pit, I needed my freedom. If I was sent down the whole rebellion would have to be aborted.

"Who told you that?" I asked.

"Never mind that, we just know."

"I want to know who it was. Who's been telling lies about me?"

Serky nodded her head at one of the henchmen standing behind me who clattered me on the head. I instinctively raised my hands to my head to feel if it was bleeding.

"What have you done to your knuckles, Mr.Winston?" asked Serky, who smiled as she looked at my open wounds. There was nothing I could say. "Take him to The Pit," Serky ordered the Henchmen.

"No," I cried, desperately trying to shake off their grip.

"Don't fight them Odis," Gwen said softly in my ear. "It's time for us to meet again." I allowed myself to be taken away with only token resistance. 'At least they'll have to let Tiny out,' I thought to myself as I was taken out of the room and towards The Pit.

The last thing I remember after that was being walked down the corridor outside Serky's office before receiving another, much harder, blow to the back of the head. When I came-to I found myself in familiar surroundings. I opened my eyes but darkness was all around. I was face-down, my head was killing me and the smell of excrement was all-pervasive: The Pit was just as I remembered it.

Soon after regaining consciousness I was contacted by Gwen. She informed me that I had been out of it for a few hours, and she had already changed the feed on the Security System to show recorded footage of me asleep. I found the loose bricks in the wall and took them out one-by-one. I wriggled down the tight passageway, thinking that either it had got tighter or I was getting wider.

When I emerged into Gwen's living room I was immediately greeted by Libby and Bastian, who pranced over to me. Bastian arched his back and rubbed against me while Libby lay on her back expecting me to stroke her ginger belly like I used to do every day when I was reading my books.

"They remember you." Gwen was standing over us with her hands on her hips and her head slightly tilted to one side.

"I should hope so," I said. "The amount of attention I gave them."

"Attention will only get you so far, young man. Feed them, however, and they are yours eternally. Come, come, anyway, do dust yourself down and take a seat. I'll get you some water."

I did as she said and sat in the chair which I had always sat in. Our designated places were an unspoken rule but one which I would never have dared to break.

"Fizzy or Still?" asked Gwen, unaware of her own catchphrase.

"Still, please," I replied. I never had the heart to point out that I hadn't once asked for fizzy. Maybe she knew? Maybe it was just what we did, a familiar ritual to settle into each other's company before getting to work.

Gwen busied herself in the kitchen preparing the drinks while I felt my head. I had two large lumps from the two thumps I'd received from that henchman. The two lumps were so close together that it felt as if a camel was trying to break out of my skull.

"Take a good whack, did you?" asked Gwen as she walked over and handed me my glass of water.

"It's nothing, just a couple of bumps," I assured her.

"Let's have a feel," she got straight up out of her chair having just sat down and her tone of voice suggested that she was peeved at having to do so even though I hadn't asked her to. I pointed to the spot where the camel was residing and she pressed the bumps with her index finger.

"Ouch."

"They got you alright," she giggled. "You do seem to get yourself into some scrapes don't you? Never mind, it'll go down in a few days, as long as you don't have concussion. You don't, do you?"

"I don't think so."

"Good. Now, look around," she ordered. "Do you notice anything different?"

I scoured the cramped room but I didn't see anything different. "What am I looking for?"

"You're looking for change," she replied impatiently. She gave me a few more seconds before losing her patience. "It's the photograph, you oaf! Men never notice anything," she huffed.

I looked closely at the picture in the frame on the mantelpiece. It was of me. I was standing in a rain forest, dripping wet with sweat, leaning against a tree and trying to smile at the camera. I got up and grabbed the frame.

"Where did you get this?" I asked.

"I printed it off your file."

"You mean my Sisyphusa file?"

"Yes."

"What was it doing on there?" I asked angrily.

"Goodness knows. But I thought it was a lovely picture of you. You did used to be a lot slimmer didn't you? And you look so much better without that dreadful beard. Anyway, put it back now."

I stared at it a little longer trying to recognise the person in that picture, his smile, his freedom, his adventure. I rested it back on the mantelpiece and sat down.

"Let's get to work," Gwen said. "First things first, do you think that Skinny Jim will endanger the plan?"

"No," I replied. "I don't think so. At least I didn't think he would be a problem any more until I was sent down here as punishment for the fight. Now I'm not so sure."

"Why not?"

"Because I don't know whether it was him who informed them. For what it's worth I didn't get the impression that it was him. Also, now that I'm down here, for who knows how long, it's possible that he could regain his confidence without me there as a daily reminder of his diminished status."

"Hmmm. You could have a point," Gwen pondered it. "But I don't think so. Imagine it: all of the Service Users are escaping, the other teams are organised and co-operating, he can only choose between organising Team Redemption to join us or leave all of them to go it alone. Skinny Jim is no mastermind. He's a bully. He rules people who are weaker than him, it's all he knows, it's how he survives. I think that when given the choice he will choose to lead his team to escape not just because every one else will be doing it but because he wants to be in charge of his team."

"Okay, if you say so. That's it then, everything's prepared."

"Almost everything," Gwen corrected me.

"The password," I remembered.

"Exactly. But that's the final mission. Once we have access to the top level of the security system we can erase the files of every Service User in Sisyphusa from the Island's Weirdness Database. After that, it'll be safe to escape."

"Once you have the password could you delete all of the Service User files on the whole Database? That way we could free everyone on the Island not just those in Sisyphusa."

"I'm afraid not," she frowned. "The Governor's password only allows you to delete files from his institution. What would be the use in deleting all of those files anyway? Think about it, what would it achieve? Some of the people on the database would be in institutions anyway, and those who weren't wouldn't know that their name had been deleted. They may not even know there's a database at all. It would be nothing more than an administrative nuisance to those who run the system. The worst part of it is the Service Users might not even care if they did know about the database."

"They have never known it any other way and they might not want to escape their situation. You remember the people on your team when you first arrived, don't you?"

"Yes."

"Did they strike you as a group of people who were ready to rise up and fight the system?"

"No," I conceded. "I'm not sure if they all are now either, come to think of it. So what's it all for, Gwen?"

"The plan or life?"

"Both!"

"The point of the plan is to help people. The point of life is much the same but, in truth, there isn't a particular point to it," she shrugged casually. "Just give it a good go."

"But if everyone is so happy with the status quo except us, why bother?"

"Who's happy? I never said happy. Unquestioning? Yes. Uninformed? In cases. Disempowered? Definitely. But I don't see anyone who's happy here. Not even the wardens. The only people who are happy are the people at the very top of society who gain from the order and ideology that places like

Sisyphusa supposedly give the Island. And they only think that they are happy, I very much doubt that many of them are. It's always difficult to know what the right thing to do is Odis, especially when it concerns other people. Some people may think me dreadfully arrogant presuming that I know what's best for such a large group of people but I wouldn't claim to know what's best for them at all. If there is one thing on this earth that I am an expert on then it's Sisyphusa, and there is nothing I'm more sure of than the fact that this place brings no good to anyone who comes into contact with it and it must be destroyed. Do you agree?"

"You know that I do. I just want to do more. The Service Users here are just a drop in the ocean, there must be thousands, hundreds of thousands more on the Island and in the rest of the Empire, I want to help free them all. Don't you?"

Gwen smiled. "Maybe you will."

"We both will, as a team."

She smiled again.

Chapter 43

"So how are we supposed to get hold of this password then?" I asked Gwen.

"Quite simple really," she replied. "A new password is relayed to the Governor from Central Office once a month. That way they retain the power to change Governors at any time without any danger of the records being tampered with by a disgruntled ex-employee. All we have to do is to intercept it."

"And how are we supposed to do that?"

"The password is told to the Governor over the telephone. You are going to sneak into his office and bug the telephone."

"How do you expect me to do that? You can't 'sneak' anywhere in this place without being caught, least of all into the Governor's office!"

"I'm sure that we can get around all that," Gwen replied calmly. "Now come into the library I have something for you."

We got up and walked to the library, the cats zigzagged through our legs to lead the way. I wondered what she had in store for me: A message from home? Some real food? Maybe some more classic literature?

"That should be enough to keep you busy," said Gwen as we walked into the room.

I could see straight away what she was referring to. On her desk sat a pile of books which, on closer inspection, I saw were titled: "Wiretapping for Beginners," "Telephone Technology," "A Guide to Spying," "Breaking and Entering," "Forgive us our Trespasses" and "Telecommunication Surveillance Made Easy."

Gwen was right, they did keep me busy. I struggled through the books she had picked out for me over the following days. Technology had never been my strong point, but when Gwen gave me an old telephone I was able to pull it apart and connect the theory in the books with the practical set-up of the telephone.

I also read about how to pick a lock with a tension-wrench and a paper clip. After I'd studied the mechanics of it, I tried it out on Gwen's bedroom door which she told me was the same type of lock as the Governor's. It wasn't particularly difficult. It required patience more than anything.

I did a number of practice-runs. Gwen would stand-by with a stop-watch and time me as I first picked the lock and then dismantled the phone, connected the recording device to the wires in the receiver and then put the telephone back together. The recording device was a tiny microphone which Gwen taught me how to connect to the wires within the handset of the telephone.

Once connected the device would be powered by the electricity running through the telephone and would transmit all of Governor Shade's telephone conversations directly to Gwen's computer. I managed to steadily improve my practice times over the next couple of days until I was confident of being in and out within three minutes.

Next we addressed the issue of when to break into the office and how to avoid being caught. Gwen said that the call would be arriving early in the morning exactly a week from that day, which was perfect because she had just found out that I was due to be released from The Pit in four days.

The plan was for me to bug the phone the night before the call was to arrive so that the Governor and the wardens would have already left the site for the night. Gwen was able to unlock the dormitory door via the computerised security system. Once it was unlocked I had to sneak out without waking up any of my teammates and make my way to Tower B avoiding the henchmen. Gwen assured me that the I-Spys would not be an issue because she was planning to override the live feeds with recorded footage of empty corridors and stairwells just like she did whenever I left The Pit to visit her.

Gwen declared herself satisfied with the bugging mission and we turned our attention to other matters. She rummaged around in some drawers in the living room and emerged with a large folded piece of paper. She opened it and spread it out on the floor of the library revealing a detailed map of the Sisyphusa Compound. It was time to plan the escape.

I was to follow the regular daily schedule with the rest of Team Recovery upon on my release, then on the third night I was to sneak up to the Governor's office and bug the phone. Gwen would then listen in to the call the next morning and use the password to delete the Service User files and finally give us the go-ahead to rise up.

"You must warn your Team Captains the day before the call arrives," said Gwen.

"What do I tell them? When you get the password and delete the files, what then? There's still the henchmen and the wardens, what do you expect us to do? Just walk out the front door?"

"Well, that is where the buses will be waiting for you, ready to take you away," she smiled. "Don't worry about the henchmen, I promise that I will take care of them. The wardens and the Governor, though, will be your concern. Once I have the password I'm going to wait until all of the Service Users are in the warehouse for Climbing Practice," she pointed at the building on the map which was labelled Practice Climbing Warehouse. "Then I'm going to send a 'Staff Alert' through the system. This will tell all of the wardens and the Governor that there is an SUD (Service User Disturbance) in the Practice Climbing Warehouse. Once they are all in there I will electronically lock the door and you will detain them."

"This is when you must make sure that things don't get out of control. Each Team Captain has to quickly explain the situation to their team and calm them down. There must be no Service User retribution, there will be simply no time for shenanigans. Once they are tied up you and some Service Users whom you trust must lead them as well as all other Service Users to the reception area of the main building. At this point I will use the Governor's password to open the front entrance and all Service Users will board the buses leaving the staff on the side of the road."

"Why can't we just leave the staff in the Practice Climbing Warehouse?" I asked.

"This is why," she said as she stood up and motioned for me to follow her to her bedroom. We entered the small room which consisted of just a small twin bed which was covered with clothes and next to the bed was a small bedside table with a lamp on it. The only other thing in the room was a bundled blanket in the corner. She walked over to this blanket and lifted it up to reveal a huge pile of explosives.

"Holy Fucking SkyMaster!" I exclaimed as my mouth gaped open.

"Indeed," she smiled proudly. "There are others like this safely hidden in the quarry, the factory and the Practice Climbing Warehouse all ready to be detonated simultaneously once the compound has been evacuated. So you see, you must leave the staff out in the street because we don't want any harm to come to anybody, do we?"

I shook my head, still dumbfounded that she had a pile of dynamite next to her bed as she slept. How had she even got hold of it?

"Will you meet us on the bus then?" I asked.

"Yes, yes. I'll be coming out a different way but I will be ready for the great departure," she smiled.

"Is that it then? Everything's planned?"

"Yes, that's everything. We'll go through it a few more times before it's time for you to leave."

Over the next three days we went through the plan over and over again until the order was ingrained. There was also some time for me to do some reading that wasn't related to espionage or burglary. I chose to read a book which Gwen had previously said I wasn't ready for. It was the thickest book out of the entire one thousand and one, but once I'd begun reading it I lost any sense of how long it was. In fact, I wished that it could have gone on forever.

Reading that book made me think that I could imagine how believers might feel when they read the Yes/No Books. The language, the images, the characters, the entire world it invited you to explore, it told the story of what it means to be alive, how much we can suffer and what joy we can feel. I finished the book on the day that I was to leave Gwen's home forever. When I closed the book, after the final page, I felt bereft knowing that I would never read a better book. I felt bereft losing my friends, The Prince and The Count.

"Time to go, young man," Gwen said patting me on the shoulder. I handed her the book. She took it and laid it down on the chair in the living room. "So what did you think? Were you ready?"

I nodded my head.

"I thought so," she smiled. "Do you have your equipment?" I nodded and patted both pockets which held the tension wrench, the paper clip and the bugging device. I kept the mini screwdriver in my sock. We stood across from each other in silence. We knew that they'd be coming to get me any minute and I had to go back to The Pit. Gwen hugged me tightly and didn't let go for some time.

"Good luck," she said.

"We don't need it," I told her. "We have a plan." I snaked back through the passageway, ready to re-enter Sisyphusa for the last time.

Chapter 44

Team Recovery all welcomed me back as I returned to the dorm. I exchanged hugs or handshakes with all of them, all except for Harry and Ella. They sat on their bunks, staring at me.

"G-g-good on you, Odis," said Ken as he patted me on the back.

"Yeah, you really showed him," Tracey added. Clearly the fight between Skinny Jim and me had become common knowledge.

"So everyone knows?" I asked. "Well I'm not proud of what happened, and I don't deserve any of your congratulations. I just lost control."

"That's not what I saw," Ella piped up from the back of the room. She then got off the bunk and walked into the middle of the room. "Why don't you tell them the truth?" she asked aggressively.

"I don't know what you think you saw, Ella, but I am telling the truth," I replied as calmly as I could.

"Aren't any of you wondering," she was now addressing the rest of the team only, "what it was he was doing out there in the long grass with *him*?" She laced the word "him" with as much poison as she could muster for Skinny Jim.

The rest of the team looked at me, not in the threatening way that Ella did, but inquisitively, waiting for answers. I couldn't tell the truth, the plan had to stay secret. I tried to conjure something up but my mind went blank and I began to panic.

"It was for me," announced Mr. Femuz, casually sitting on his bottom bunk, playing a game of chess against himself. Everyone looked to Mr. Femuz for answers. "You all know that this man, Skinny Jim, is a man who can get things, things from the outside. Well, I needed some special medicine and I asked Odis to speak to Mr. Skinny Jim about this."

"And why couldn't you speak to him yourself?" Harry now got involved in the dispute.

"Because if I had met with him, I would not have just beaten him, I might have killed him for what he did to Thomas." Mr. Femuz's performance had gone down a treat. Everyone seemed convinced, everyone except for Ella.

"So why did you end up fighting him?" she asked me directly.

"I went to try to make a deal with him for Mr. Femuz's medicine but then once we got talking he began to boast about what he'd done to Thomas and I just lost it. Why are you acting like this, Ella? You hate Skinny Jim more than anyone. Why are you so worried if he got some of what he deserved?"

"Because I don't believe you, Odis. I saw the two of you in the field together, you were shaking hands. You've turned your back on us, on your team, on Thomas, on Samuel, that's why I had to do it," she was becoming hysterical.

"Do what?" asked Gracie.

"Tell Serky," said Ella cried.

"You did what?" asked Tracey. "You grassed?"

"You can talk," Harry leapt to the defence of Ella. "Everyone knows youse three was working for Serky for months."

"Yeah, but not any more, not for ages," said Stacey. "We've been working for the team."

"So was I," said Ella, who had regained her composure. "I was doing what was best for the team, can't you see? Everything was easier before, before Odis was here. He deserved to go to The Pit, not for beating up Skinny Jim but for all the other things."

"You are not making sense, Mrs.Ella," said Mo calmly. "Mr.Odis is a good man, a good, good man. He is my friend and he is your friend too. He is not lying to us, he did try to make deal with the bad man. This is why he borrowed some of our Zeezee to make swap, yes Mr. Odis?" Mo asked.

"Yes, Mo, that's right," I said calmly.

"I think you owe Odis an apology," said Tracey to Ella.

Ella looked bemused and exhausted by now. "I'm sorry Odis," Ella spoke in a distant monotone and stumbled back to her bed like a zombie.

"Come on, guys, everyone's just tired," I told them all. "It's no big deal, just a misunderstanding. I don't hold it against Ella and I hope she's all right with me. Let's all get back to doing what we do best, working like a team." Everyone loped off to bed and I thanked Mr. Femuz and Mo for their help in resolving the argument before finally going to sleep myself.

The next day I updated Mr. Femuz on everything whilst we worked in the quarry. I told him that I'd met with Gwen and that she'd taught me how to break into the Governor's office and bug the phone. I also told him about the plan we'd devised, what day the escape would take place and the order of how it would unfold. He listened diligently and when I'd finished asked only one question, "What do you want me to do?" I told him that I would need him to help me calm the Service Users down once we'd apprehended the wardens and then to help me escort the wardens and the Service Users to the reception area.

I tried to behave as I usually would the following day but inside I was a mess. The pressure of knowing that something so big was going to happen and that almost no-one else knew about it was making me feel sick. I wanted it to come straight away so that at least I wouldn't have to worry about it any longer.

During Normalisation Class the next day I ripped off three scraps of paper from my Normalisation Diary and wrote on each of them, 'TOMORROW DURING CLIMBING PRACTICE. BE READY.' I scrunched the scraps up into tiny balls and stuffed them into my pocket.

I managed to slip one into Beverley's hand when I walked past her in the Practice Climbing Warehouse. She quickly noticed it was me and put it in her pocket with the minimum of fuss, not even taking the risk to meet my gaze.

In the mess hall at lunch I snuck into the queue directly behind Mikey and subtly nudged his shoulder. He turned around and I directed him to his tray where I had placed the screwed up scrap of paper under the shadow of his bowl. He quickly placed it in his pocket and we both waited for our lunch as if we were strangers.

Finally I could hand G.I Joe his message with less of a need for stealth inside our cave in the quarry. He peeked at its contents in front of me and looked at me nervously. I nodded my head in a business-like fashion and he squared his jaw, puffed out his chest and saluted me as if I were his superior officer.

The whistle sounded, we'd finished our work in the quarry. I walked back to the dorm knowing that, whether the plan failed or succeeded, that was the last time I would ever drag any boulders up their hill for them. Every part of my body ached with fatigue after three relentless years of abused muscles, bruised bones and lacerated skin. If we didn't make our escape the next day, I knew I would die trying.

The dorm was quiet that evening. Tension had floated through the room ever since my return. Ella was still in a confused trance which left Harry as her bulldog to snarl and glare at anyone who dared come near their bunk. I could tell that Tracey still resented Ella for getting me put in The Pit, but the rest of the team were genuinely concerned for Ella. I wondered how she would react in the Practice Climbing Warehouse the next day when the tables were turned and the Service Users had the power. Perhaps that was what she had been fighting for on the Senior Reps Council? But she hadn't been to a council meeting for weeks, not since Samuel had died. I banished thoughts of Ella from my mind—I couldn't worry about her or any individual Service User. I had to think of everyone, and how I could best help us all to escape.

After the lights had been turned out and the others had all fallen asleep I felt myself beginning to doze off until that familiar piano music filled my ear and a soft whisper announced, "The door is open, young man. Don't forget your equipment."

I reached into my pillow case, removed my four pieces of equipment and stuffed them into my pockets. I got out of bed, tiptoed over to the door and opened it as quietly as I could. Once I'd closed it behind me I could hear the lock bolt shut again as Gwen pressed a button on her keyboard.

"Remember, I-Spys are not a problem but henchmen are," Gwen reminded me. "I will try to direct you from up here, but not every angle I have is visible so keep your wits about you. Walk to the end of the corridor and wait for my next instruction."

I walked slowly to the end of the corridor, concentrating intently on placing each foot on the floor in the same motion that a caterpillar slides along a leaf. When I reached the door which led to the reception area I looked through the window and saw the back of a henchman's head. The giant was sitting down guarding the door so I quickly crouched down on the floor and whispered to Gwen, "There's one guarding the door right in front of me, what should I do?"

Gwen had no reason to answer me because I could hear through the door what her plan was, the phone at the reception desk had begun to ring. I stood up slowly and peeked through the window where I could see that the henchman had risen from his chair and was beginning to trudge towards the reception desk, grunting with each step.

"Open the door and walk around the rim of the foyer. Stop at the bottom of the Tower B staircase. Stay in the shadows," Gwen said clearly and calmly.

I opened the door and followed her instructions exactly. I hugged the perimeter of the spacious reception area remembering just in time that Tower B was to the left and Tower A to the right. As I neared the bottom of the spiral staircase the phone suddenly stopped ringing just before the henchman reached the desk. The hulking figure swivelled around with the speed of an ocean liner and trudged back to his post. Inside the bottom of the spiral staircase and out of sight of the henchman, I caught my breath and waited for my next instruction.

"Slowly scale the staircase," Gwen instructed. "There is a henchman standing guard at the entrance to the first floor. You are going to the second floor. Before you reach the top of the stairs you will find an envelope on the penultimate step. Open the envelope and throw its contents as far as you can down the other side of the corridor, once you hear the henchman and his companion following the sound at the other end of the corridor you will be free to continue scaling the stairs. Stop before you reach the second floor."

I wondered what she meant by the 'henchman's companion' but soon enough my question was answered. As I approached the first floor I could hear a snarl and a bark reverberate through the corridor and down the staircase. I knew that it had to be one of those creatures which had attacked me the day I arrived at Sisyphusa. I crawled along on my belly the rest of the way until I found the envelope that Gwen had seemingly stashed in a nook on the penultimate step. I opened the envelope to find two items.

"Throw one down the corridor and keep the other for the way back," Gwen told me. Inside the envelope were two bouncy balls. I put one in my pocket and held the other one in my right hand. I pulled back my arm and flung the ball hard over the top of the steps. As the ball slapped the ground, a siren went off like a giant alarm clock. I peered over the top step and saw the three-headed dog chasing after the noisy ball which flashed fluorescent green and pink every time it bounced. The henchman lumbered slowly after the dog and I took my chance to continue up the staircase to the second floor.

"Proceed to Governor Shade's office, your path is clear," Gwen assured me as I reached the second floor. I entered the corridor and passed several doors before reaching the one with the golden plaque which read '**Governor Shade.**' I got out my tension wrench and my paper clip and proceeded to break in. As I did so I thought back to the first lines of the book Gwen had me read, 'Forgive us our Trespasses': "There ain't gonna be no daily bread, unless you get some coins with a dead man's head."

Chapter 45

The office was bathed in total darkness. I closed the door behind me and felt my way towards the desk where I found a lamp and switched it on. The light revealed a much larger room than I had expected from the tightness of the corridor and the close proximity of the doors. The Governor's neighbours on either side must have had considerably more cramped working conditions.

The beige carpet was fluffy under foot and spotlessly clean. There was a plush set of leather sofas and chairs around a glass coffee table. The largest HDTV Screen I had ever seen hung on the wall above the fireplace. The Bad News Channel was on so I turned up the volume slightly. A young woman was interviewing one of Minister Frown's Deputies.

"How does the government hope to give the public their coins back if they've all been used to refill the Pyramids?" the interviewer asked aggressively.

"I am confident that if we are generous to the Pharaohs, in time, they will return the public's coins with interest. This government has always had the interests of the public at heart and has defended them robustly at every turn," replied the Deputy with forceful, assertive hand gestures.

"Did you have the public's interests at heart when you spent their coins on a conservatory for your mother-in-law eighteen months ago?" The interviewer was referring to a scoop by The Daily Bulletin some months back which uncovered evidence of politicians of varying stripes using the public's tax coinage for their own enrichment.

"I have apologised unreservedly for that," he squirmed. "It was within the guidelines, which were clearly wrong and we have led the way in reforming in a transparent process. There were some clerical errors made in my office and those responsible have been punished severely."

"Don't you think that you should resign?" she pressed him.

"Did you resign, Angela, when you were caught tapping Aspirati's phones?" he fired back, referring to when the interviewer had worked for a different channel that had been asking very different questions.

"This isn't about me, Deputy. The public will want to know how you and your colleagues intend to win back their confidence. Can you guarantee to them that the Pyramids will never be allowed to collapse like this again?" demanded the young woman, desperately trying to simplify a complex issue.

I was beginning to notice how interviewers tried their best to tease out definite policies from the politicians as well as predictions about the future. The politicians fought back with a combination of vague platitudes and condescension. The farce of an interview continued with the interviewer intent on proving that she had the public's interest in mind rather than her big scoop, while the Deputy continued to reply speaking only in Robot to avoid being caught saying anything controversial or true.

I left them to their dance of mutual distrust as my attention was drawn to the wall behind the large mahogany desk. The wall was dotted with framed pictures. I walked over to take a closer look and saw that each one was a photograph. Each picture had Governor Shade with his arm draped around a different person, but not just any person, they were all Aspiratis.

I saw actors, singers, footballers, HDTV presenters. The Governor smiled keenly in each shot but his companions in the photographs never seemed to be showing the same enthusiasm. In fact they all looked rather forlorn and exhausted and that's when I realised why. They were all Service Users, I could see their Earpieces. Each photo was taken in exactly the same place. I knew this because in the background there was a sign which said 'Sunflower Lodge.' It seemed that Governor Shade had previously been the Governor of a Special Treatment Facility.

"Have you started on the phone yet?" asked Gwen.

"No, not yet, I'm just looking around. Can't you see me?" I asked, looking around the walls and ceiling for an I-Spy.

"There's no I-Spy in there. Now stop dawdling and get to work."

"Gwen, have you ever heard of Sunflower Lodge?" I asked.

"Yes. It's a Sisyphusa for rich people." she answered impatiently.

"Did Shade used to work there?"

"Yes, but something happened and he got demoted to Sisyphusa. No-one knows what, but I've heard the wardens saying something about an incident with a Service User. Now that's enough gossip, mind on the job!"

I took a seat at the desk. Everything on the desk was in perfect order, every item in its rightful place and each notepad or pencil sharpener at an exact right-angle. On the desk was another picture frame, though there was no sign in the background of this one, just the Governor standing awkwardly next to a woman with bright blonde hair and large golden earrings. This woman had no Earpiece and was smiling uncomfortably. She didn't appear to be a Service User although she looked just as forlorn and exhausted.

Next to the photograph was the telephone. I got out the screwdriver and the recording device and set to work. I undid the screws in the handset and placed the device next to the receiver. I then screwed it back together and stuffed the screwdriver unthinkingly into the same pocket in which I was keeping the bouncy ball, the tension wrench and the paper clip. I was just getting up to leave when the telephone rang and I leapt out of the Governor's swivel chair, and crammed myself under the desk. The telephone rang a couple of times and I didn't know what to do.

"Aren't you going to answer that?" asked Gwen.

"Is it you?"

"Well, of course it's me, dear, you didn't think I was going to let you leave the room without checking that the blasted thing works, did you?"

I answered the phone and spoke a few words through gritted teeth before Gwen gave me the all-clear that the bug was working and I could make my way back to the dorm. I was to use the bouncy ball again for the henchman and his dog on the first floor and then wait for Gwen to ring the reception telephone again once I'd reached the bottom of the Tower B staircase.

I left the office and walked down the corridor and out onto the stairwell. I slowly crept down the stairs, one step at a time, mindful that the henchman and the creature could be right at the bottom of the stairs. I could hear a noise coming from further down the first floor corridor and chose to step out and throw the bouncy ball down the hall. However when I went to pull the ball out of my pocket I inadvertently pushed the screwdriver out and it fell to the floor. The sound it made wasn't overly loud but the henchman and the creature, twenty metres down the corridor, turned around immediately, like a shark sensing blood in the water.

I instinctively ran down the stairs, hearing the thumping stomps of what was chasing me. I tripped over and fell down the last few steps but regained my footing and was in the reception area. Only thinking of what I was running from I hadn't had any time to consider what I was running towards, and there was the other henchman leaping up from his seat, blocking my route to the Team Recovery dormitory. I ran into the middle of the reception area, now totally unaware of what I was doing but merely trying to get as far away from danger as possible.

As I neared the front desk, another henchman emerged through the door that led to the visiting rooms. My back was against the wall and all I could do was stand and watch as the three henchmen approached me from every direction. The three-headed dog was snapping and snarling, desperately tugging at its leash but the henchmen plodded methodically, closing in around me like a hangman's noose slowly being pulled tight around his victim's neck. I melted down the wall and held my arms aloft as if I could protect myself from what was to come. I could hear the sound of their footsteps draw closer and the creature's grunts growing louder, my eyes covered by my hands.

Then nothing. A long silence followed by a sound like a car backfiring. I peeled my fingers away from my eyes to find that the dim lights in the reception area had gone off and I could see precisely nothing. There was no sound or movement coming from the henchmen who couldn't have been more than a few feet away from me. Another loud noise went off which sounded like a gigantic computer re-booting some distance away and the dim lights came back on to reveal the three henchmen and the guard-dog frozen right in front of me, poised to pounce.

I stood for a moment and stared at them, worried that if I moved they might come back to life. Finally I decided to try to creep away from them, but just as I took my first step they moved. They didn't pounce. Instead, the henchmen's heads and shoulders slumped forward like rag-dolls while the creature collapsed to the floor. 'What on earth was going on?' I thought to myself. And then I had my answer.

A tiny, squeaky giggle could be heard through my Earpiece. The giggle grew louder and louder eventually evolving into full-throated laughter.

"Y-Y-You look like you've seen a ghost," spluttered Gwen before she proceeded to burst into another fit of the giggles.

"Will you please tell me what the hell is going on, right now, and stop bloody laughing at me!" My voice reached a shout as I became angrier over the course of the sentence.

"Hehehe, yes...sorry...of course. They're..." she then broke off but I could hear her giggling in the background away from the microphone. "Sorry, I had something in my throat, where was I? Oh yes, they're machines, dear."

"What?"

"Yes, yes, have a feel of them yourself. I de-powered them now, they're totally harmless."

I went up close to one of the henchmen and warily prodded his torso which was as hard as the granite in the quarry and freezing cold. I lifted his black cloak to find that he wasn't a 'he' at all, but an 'it'. I checked each one of them and found the same thing under each of their clothes: metal and wires. Even the dog's fur could be easily unzipped under its belly to reveal where its batteries were kept.

"But I don't understand?" I cried in stupefaction. "They came to my house and took me away, they've taken me to The Pit and beaten me when Serky told them to, how can it be?"

"Remarkable contraptions aren't they, it must have taken some genius to invent them!" she boasted.

"You again?" I asked in disgust.

"I'm afraid so. They have sophisticated sound and movement sensors, they can follow very basic instructions and can be programmed to collect new Service Users using an

internal satellite navigation system and photographic recognition
of their targets."

"How could you, Gwen? How could you put your mind
to something so awful?" I asked in dejection at my mentor's
fallibility.

"There is no excuse, Odis, I can't even think of a good
lie to tell you. I was one of them, young man. I believed in the
system. I believed that if we got Weirdness sufferers here and
gave them the right pills, the right advice and strong discipline
then it was the best thing for them. I was a young woman when I
joined this place. I was traumatised from having my parents
Removed from my life and I wanted…I needed answers. I found
them here. At Sisyphusa things are very simple, you're either
Weird or you're Normal, and if you're Weird then you need to
be made Normal and there are no lengths that they won't go to to
achieve Normalisation."

"I found my calling, I was good with machines, always
had been. They told me to invent something to collect and guard
the Service Users. I designed them the henchmen and dogs.
They told me to invent a machine to occupy the Service Users'
thoughts so that they wouldn't sabotage their treatment or that of
their fellow Service Users, I designed them the Earpiece. I was
unquestioning, Odis, just like many members of your team are.
It isn't just the Service Users who are institutionalised you know,
the wardens are too. Anyway, that's that then," she ended
matter-of-factly.

"So why didn't you turn the machines off ages ago?" I
asked angrily.

"Because you weren't ready *ages ago*. Because the
Service Users weren't ready to act together *ages ago*. Because
we didn't have the password to erase your files *ages ago*, enough
reasons for you?"

"Well that answers the '*ages ago*' question. But why
did I have to go through the ordeal of sneaking past them and
almost being killed by them this evening when you could have
bloody switched them off?"

"Well, once you turn them off, they do take ever such a
long time to re-boot. You do realise that I'm going to be up half
the night just to have them re-programmed before the staff arrive

tomorrow. Besides it did tickle me to see your face just before I flicked the switch, hehehehehe," she trailed off into laughter and I stomped back to the dorm in a huff. "The door is unlocked, Odis--sleep well, we have a big day tomorrow."

Chapter 46

'Would this be the final night I spent in Sisyphusa?' I lay awake in bed thinking. I can tell you that such a momentous thought with all its implications and possibilities did not invoke a sleep-inducing calm in me. In fact, I barely slept at all. Every time I managed to drift off for a few minutes I would be awoken by a nightmare. There was one where Gwen forgot to turn off the henchmen and one of the dogs ripped my right leg off with its teeth and ran away with it. In another one, I led the Service Users to the main entrance but when the doors opened unaided a blinding light entered into Sisyphusa and a blaze of fire burned a path towards us. There was no escaping it but we tried to run away regardless and as I ran I repeated to myself under my breath, 'I love life and I'm not afraid any more. I love life and I'm not afraid any more.' After this nightmare I decided to stay awake until the alarm rang for everybody else to get up, which was only in another hour.

As the others began to emerge to the blaring sound of the alarm, Mr.Femuz instantly caught my eye and I nodded at him to indicate that I had got the password and the escape was to go ahead as planned. Everyone washed themselves around the two sinks in the bathroom and then put on their overalls. I looked at the motto on the back of Mo's uniform: "Learning to be Normal Together." This motto was ubiquitous throughout Sisyphusa. It was on the stationery, the clothing, around the buildings and the grounds, and yet it is the sole suggestion I came across in the whole time since I had been Removed that there was a sense of solidarity and support. "Learning to be Normal Together" is a promise of collaboration, working as a team, but no matter what the motto said, through their actions the regime showed again and again that theirs was a policy of divide and rule.

As I was putting on my overalls Ella approached me coyly and whispered in a crackly voice, "I'm sorry." She couldn't hold my gaze and her skin was paler than ever, as if all of the blood had been drained from her body.

"It's fine, Ella," I assured her. "As long as you know now that I would never do anything to betray this team, especially not you."

She nodded and allowed a half-smile to escape from her tortured soul.

The subject in Normalisation Class for that day was "Act Normal, Become Normal." Serky played us numerous clips on the HDTV of Normal people doing various Normal things like shopping, dancing, smiling and chatting with other Normal people and working in an office.

We were also shown an Aspi-Doc -- a film in which an Aspirati helpfully explains to the public a given topic by fully immersing themselves in that subject for three days. In this case we had a former Real Life star demonstrate to us how to shop, dance and make small-talk even if you don't feel like it. She ended by saying, "It's so easy, I reckon even Weird people can do it. If all else fails, a little Liquid Escape never hurt anyone!"

My attention drifted away from the HDTV screen to the white board where I spotted the date written in Serky's rigid handwriting--it was my 24th birthday. I had been so focussed on the escape and before that I'd been in and out of The Pit so I'd completely lost any sense of what day or even month it was. Many times I'd forget how old I even was because none of the conventional things that mark time took place in Sisyphusa. Minor details like time and date meant very little.

Nevertheless, I noted the irony that the escape was to take place on the fourth birthday that I had spent in Sisyphusa -- it would be perfectly symmetrical to leave the world on the same date on which I had arrived in it- if anything were to go wrong, that is.

After the films, Serky held a discussion with the team, but she didn't seem her normal energetic, tyrannical self. In fact she hadn't been the same for weeks. She was often distant, even disinterested. She would ask questions but not listen to the answers. She had become more lax, allowing us to have time to chat between ourselves at the end of class but once we were in the Practice Climbing Warehouse or in the quarry (where other wardens were around) she would begin to shout and hurl abuse at us, but it a seemed forced imitation of her former self.

Towards the end of the lesson Gwen contacted me.

"Have just listened to the call and received password," she began, in the militaristic style that G.I Joe and the other Team Re-Activation boys used to communicate with each other in the quarry. "I repeat, HAVE RECEIVED PASSWORD. Will be erasing Service User files shortly and will send out the Service User Disturbance alarm fifteen minutes into Climbing Practice, repeat: 15 MINUTES. Operation Rising Stickleback is about to commence."

I didn't know how she could make jokes at such a time. Beads of sweat started to dribble down my forehead and my heart was palpitating. This was really it—after all the waiting, all the missions, the persuading and cajoling, the suffering, we were finally going ahead with the plan.

The three beeps sounded to signify the end of Normalisation Classes and Serky led us out of the main building. The HDTV in the corridor was showing pictures of an angry crowd of people rioting outside Minister Frown's office. The people were angry with Minister Frown but their signs suggested that it was more than that. They were angry that they had no stake in Island society and were resentful and bitter about the forces which were affecting their lives but left them with no-one to blame and no scope for change. The reporter in the foreground was frantically explaining exactly what every viewer could see with their own eyes. At the bottom of the screen the Instabet icon asked will 'Will Minister Frown last out the week?' The screen suddenly turned off and wouldn't come back on.

We headed towards the winding dirt path that led to the Practice Climbing Warehouse. I could see the other teams walking in single-file ahead of us. We entered the warehouse which echoed with the casual chit-chat of oblivious Service Users. As we passed the other teams' Climbing Points I met the eyes of my Team Captains and gave them each a small nod to indicate that yes, the plan was going ahead.

I glimpsed at the giant clock which hung from the far wall of the warehouse. The second hand ticked around as it was approaching two minutes past the hour...thirteen minutes to go. Team Recovery lined up in pairs in front of the Practice Wall at Climbing Point 5, the furthest point away from the only door.

Mr. Femuz and I skulked to the back of the queue and I began to survey the entire room.

The five teams were lined up behind the five yellow Safety Lines painted on the floor parallel to the foot of the wall. At the head of each line were the five Team Leaders as well as two other wardens patrolling up and down on either side of the wall.

On the other side of the Climbing Wall I couldn't see them but I could hear the intermittent thuds of balls striking against the metal which told me that five henchmen were in their usual positions limbering up for their prey (or programmed to obey their command.) 'So, seven wardens and five henchmen,' I thought to myself. I knew that Gwen would take care of the henchmen. That just left the seven wardens.

Gwen was going to set off the SUD staff alert through the computer system which would bring every staff member to the warehouse, so the key to the whole operation was not to let any of them escape. I whispered to Mr. Femuz that once the clock reached 11.15 he should sprint to the door and stand guard. Once we'd secured the building we could detain the wardens. It would be up to the Team Captains to calm their teams and explain the plan. Then we would need to hide the detained wardens and the bulk of the Service Users on the other side of the wall while Mr. Femuz, myself, G.I Joe and Tiny could wait on either side of the door to detain each staff member that rushed through it.

The first climbers from each team had scaled the wall already and the second group were setting off. The patrolling warden on our side of the wall had reached the door, turned one hundred and eighty degrees and was now heading back towards us. Meanwhile, the second hand on the clock counted down the last thirty seconds to 11.15. Once the warden was near us I gave Mr. Femuz the go-ahead and he sprinted into action running past each team and straight for the door, as the Service Users who noticed looked around at him in bemusement. The patrolling warden had set after him from behind us, but when he ran past me I extended my leg to the side and he fell over it spectacularly.

"Team Captains!" I bellowed as loud as I could. "Detain your wardens!"

"What the hell?" screamed Serky. "Winston you're finished. Henchmen, take him to The Pit!"

"Not this time, Serky," I told the warden as I ran over and grabbed her. I twisted her arms around her back and pushed her face first into the Climbing Wall. The rope which was being used by the active climber, Ken, who was half way up the wall, dangled to the side of me so I grabbed it and tied it around Serky's wrists.

"Come down, Ken," I shouted up to him. "No more climbing today." I turned around and faced the rest of my team who looked horrified by what I'd just done. "Keep an eye on her," I indicated at Serky who had now crumpled to her knees and was swearing at the top of her lungs what she would do to me. "Don't worry guys, trust me, I know what I'm doing. I'll explain everything once the room is secure." I handed the ropes to Ahmed knowing that he would be able to handle Serky even if the rest were too afraid. As I ran away I glanced over my shoulder to see Ahmed stuffing Serky's hair-band into her own mouth to keep her quiet.

I ran past each team to see that Beverley, Joe and Mikey had all detained their wardens and were in the process of calming their teams and explaining what was happening. It looked to be an easy job for Joe who was trusted implicitly by his team, but I could see some team members from Rejuvenation and Re-Activation were boiling over. I had to leave them to take care of it and trust that they would.

The final team was Team Redemption. I ran towards the door where I could see Mr. Femuz grappling with the two patrolling wardens. Out of the corner of my eye I saw that Skinny Jim had not only detained Warden Eavel but had the warden and his whole team sitting calmly on the floor. He looked at me and held his right thumb in the air, desperately seeking my approval which I gave him. I never even told him what to do, he just followed the other Team Captains.

When I reached the door I saw that Mr. Femuz had given the two wardens a beating. They lay sprawled on the ground showing no more desire for a fight.

"Well done," I told Femuz. "Stay here and make sure no-one gets out. I'll be back in one minute with some others to deal with anyone who comes in, okay?" He nodded.

"I see you're having fun," said Gwen in the Earpiece. "I've sent the SUD alert and the staff will start arriving soon, so be prepared. They have no idea what's happening, I've turned off their security cameras, although I am enjoying my own private viewing!"

As I listened I could see the henchmen begin to emerge around either side of the wall. "Gwen, turn off the bloody henchmen!" I shouted.

"Oh crumbs," I heard her say.

The henchmen were approaching both Team Redemption and Team Recovery, some of whom ran away. Others, such as Skinny Jim and the Flower-Eaters, chose to stay and fight. Thankfully they didn't have to because just as the brave Service Users were squaring up to them, the life (or power) disappeared from the henchmen and they stood frozen, heads slumped forward. Crowds of Service Users began to tentatively flock around them, touching them to see what had happened, as if they had encountered some bizarre new species.

"They're machines," I shouted. Everyone turned around and looked at me, dumbfounded including, to my surprise, some of the wardens.

"No, they aren't," bellowed Warden Shiva. "They're just tired. You had better let us go and get back to your work or else they will wake up so-"

"She's lying!" I interrupted. "It's all lies, all of it. Don't listen to them any more. The henchmen were machines all along. I know because I've just had them switched off. I have someone on the inside who has access to their security system and we've been planning this for months. I told Joe, Mikey and Beverley that something would be happening just so that there would be one person who everybody trusts on each team to take charge. Team Redemption Skinny Jim is your Team Captain. The plan is to escape. Our records have been erased from the database and buses are waiting for us outside. I'm sorry that I couldn't tell all of you before but I couldn't risk being found out. I know that some of you don't know me all that well, but you'll at least know someone who does know me and I hope that they'd tell you that I can be trusted."

"I can't explain everything now because the other wardens and the Governor are on their way and we need to capture them and detain them. I need Team Captains, that means you too Ahmed, I need you to lead your warden and your teams around to the other side of the wall and make sure everyone stays quiet. Team Re-Activation, can you come and help Mr. Femuz and me?"

The reaction to my speech was mixed. I could see that some Service Users cheered and whooped for joy at the revelation that they might escape. Others looked very nervous and frightened. Some just appeared numb, unable to process such a sudden change in their routine but everyone seemed to co-operate as they made their way around to the other side of the wall. Perhaps it was because there seemed no alternative as I was the only person who was willing to orchestrate things?

Team Re-Activation, led by G.I Joe, marched to the door and I ran past them to make sure that Mr. Femuz was okay. By this time Mr. Femuz had tied the wardens' jackets around their wrists and was ordering them around the other side of the wall which they followed dutifully.

"Not a bad operation you're running here, Dizzy," Joe's voice boomed cheerfully. "The henchmen power cut was a nice touch, can't say I saw that one coming."

'You and me both,' I thought to myself. "Thanks Joe, good to have you lads on board," I shook hands with each one of the guys and was bear-hugged by Tiny whom I hadn't seen properly since he'd been sent to The Pit. "Okay guys, so let's stand half of us on that side of the door and half on the other side. Wait for them to walk right into the room and then grab them. Tiny, can you get some of the climbing ropes so that we can tie them up?"

As Tiny ran to fetch the ropes from Climbing Point 1 the rest of us split into two groups and hovered on either side of the doors waiting to pounce. Wardens began to arrive, some alone, some in groups of three or four but all wore the same horrified expression when it dawned on them that the Service Users had taken over Sisyphusa. We tied them all together with a long rope like a chain gang while they yelled insults and swore revenge.

The last person to walk through the door was Governor Shade. He strode in looking thoroughly peeved that his morning had been interrupted by what he imagined could only be some minor SUD. But he imagined wrong. As he entered the warehouse I walked out in front of him slowly and faced him.

"What's going on here?" he demanded. He turned around and saw a line of his best wardens bound and gagged and Mr. Femuz and the other titans from Team Re-Activation standing there holding them. The Governor's tiny eyes widened and he quickly bolted for the door but the giants closed ranks and Shade had to stop short and in doing so fell to the floor. He turned around to face me and crawled towards me.

"If you let me go now, I promise that I can keep you out of trouble, you have my word," he pleaded in a quivering voice.

"Too late to turn back, Governor," I told him.

"No," he stuttered. "No, no, it's not too late. You can just let me go, only me, and I'll go home and say that I didn't come in today."

"You're talking nonsense, Governor," I smiled. "Why would we want to let you go? You're the jewel in Sisyphusa's crown, the big boss, the man with all the answers. No, I think we'll keep you, what do you reckon lads?"

Joe laughed and agreed and the others followed suit.

The Governor crawled closer still and tugged at my trousers. "Please, please, don't do anything terrible to me. I was only doing my job."

""Terrible?" I began to shout. "Terrible, like what? Like stick you in a tiny cell for a year? Or send you down a little hole for a month and watch you roll around in your own waste?"

"Or stop you from seeing or speaking to your family?" Tracey shouted from the side of the wall where a number of Service Users had now gathered.

"Or prevent you from being able to work and serve your country," added Joe.

"Or how about we bury you in an unmarked grave so that no-one can even mourn your passing, though I don't think many would with you anyway," I said.

"No, please," he cried. "You're not really going to kill me, are you?"

"Enough of this, Odis, get them to the reception area," Gwen barked into my Earpiece.

"Maybe not, as long as you co-operate," I answered the Governor. "Joe, tie him to the others and you and your team take them to the reception area and wait for the rest of us to arrive."

"Done," Joe replied. He grabbed the Governor, who cut a pathetic figure, and led the bound wardens and Team Re-Activation out of the warehouse.

By this point, sensing that they need no longer hide behind the wall, the rest of the Service Users had gravitated towards the door along with the tied up wardens.

"This is it," I told all of them. "It's time to leave. If any one has anything to ask or complain about, do it now? If anyone doesn't want to leave, say so now."

Everyone was silent. Service Users looked around at each other all expecting someone else to ask or say something.

"Where will we go?" asked one small lady who might have been in Team Restitution or maybe Rejuvenation. "I've been in here for years, I've got no home left outside, no job."

"What about your family, can't you go and see them?" I asked.

"Could do, I suppose. It'd be nice to see my kids but they'll just come and get me again in a few days, it's not really worth the hassle is it?"

"It doesn't have to be that way," I urged. "Our files are deleted. They don't have any more record of our names, where we live or anything about our families. If you're careful you could stay here or if you wanted you could leave the Island altogether," I suggested.

"Leave the Island?" asked Tracey. "This Island is my home, I was born here and I'm sure as hell gonna die here and there ain't no bloody person who's gonna chase me off it. Not me, Otis. I'm gonna walk out of here and get myself home. If someone comes and takes me away then so be it, but I ain't runnin' away from no-one! Come on everyone, let's make a run for it, no-one's gonna stand here and tell me they wanna wait to climb out again."

"Tracey's right," I added. "Even if they come and find us, at least we can say that we tasted real freedom again, without being watched or monitored. What do you say?"

A majority of the crowd cheered and clapped and whistled which was loud enough to drown out those who were still undecided. I went with the majority.

"Everyone follow me to the reception area. Team Captains escort your wardens."

Chapter 47

I kept looking behind me as I led the vociferous throng towards the main building. Some Service Users were skipping along the path intoxicated by the excitement. I could also spy a few who were taunting the restrained, terrified wardens who looked like they thought they were in the hands of wild animals. I considered trying to calm the situation but decided that it would be best to make it to the reception and then out of Sisyphusa as quickly as possible.

We entered the building and made our way to the reception area where Team Re-Activation and the other apprehended staff were gathered. Governor Shade had changed tactics from his pleading and begging, and had begun to barrack me as I entered the room.

"You won't get away with this you, you Weirdo," he shouted. "They'll find you. Oh you better believe they'll find you!"

"Shut him up, will you, Joe," I said, not wanting the Governor's outbursts to further rile the already excitable crowd which was filing in behind me. Joe, misunderstanding my order, proceeded to wallop the Governor, sending him flying into the wall as his expensive Bes' Specs glasses fell to the floor in pieces.

"I meant put something in his mouth to keep him quiet, Joe!"

"I did," he shrugged. "My fist."

The assault on the Governor precipitated the wardens being held by Team Re-Activation to bump and barge their captors despite their hands being fastened behind their backs. The Re-Activation boys reacted by bumping and barging back harder and this melee was the scene which greeted the other four teams as they all squeezed into the foyer.

It didn't take long for the chaos to spread as I could see Beverley charging towards Serky who was still tied up and being held by Ahmed.

"I know it was you, you cow!" Beverley shrieked as she tackled the defenceless Serky to the floor and began clawing and scratching at her face. This single act seemed to lead nearly every Service User to seek out their most reviled member of the regime and reap revenge. I saw Tracey join in attacking Serky and several others went for Warden Shiva. In the pit of my stomach I admit that I too was tempted to navigate the chaos before me and seek retribution on my tormentors.

"Odis, do something," cried Gwen, on the Earpiece. "You must stop this."

"Stop, everyone," I screamed as loud as I could. "Stop what you're doing, this is not the answer!" No-one even noticed that I was there so I climbed on top of the reception desk and picked up the vase of flowers that were on it. I held it high above my head and smashed it onto the floor. Shards of glass flew in every direction and the water and the flowers spread across the floor. Everyone stopped what they were doing and turned towards me.

"Stop this," I pleaded with them. "This isn't going to achieve anything!"

"Who wants to achieve anything? I want revenge!" Beverley argued while she still had a handful of Serky's hair.

"So what, so you beat her up, then what? It might make you feel a little better at first but it won't change what's happened. The thing that you're angry about is what has happened to you, what's happened to all of us. You were Removed just like we were. Maybe it was even harder for you because you knew what it was like from the other side. If you really look deep inside, you'll see that you're angry with them for betraying you but also for taking your freedom. Well, this is it," I pointed at the door which led out of the reception area. "This is our chance at freedom, do you want to waste it by settling a score with these small, pathetic people?"

"We deserve to settle our scores," shouted another Service User with a stubbly chin and missing teeth. "They have to be punished for what they've done! They've treated us like animals, like vermin." The man struck Warden Eavel, who he had been holding, on the back of the neck.

"You're right," I told him. "They do deserve to be punished. There is no punishment that would be too harsh for the things that they've perpetrated against us but the best way to punish them isn't to leave them with a few cuts and bruises, or even broken bones. The best revenge is to leave them tied up outside the walls of their prison and let them watch us drive away to our new lives. We should pity them that they need to spend their lives gaining some sort of satisfaction from being so cruel."

"I want to admit something to you," I raised my voice. "When I first arrived here, I judged you, all of you. I was afraid. I was afraid of being out of Solitary Initiation, I was afraid that you could be dangerous like in the stories from The Daily Bulletin and most of all I was afraid that if you really were Weird then maybe I might be too. But I'm not afraid anymore, in fact I haven't been for a long time. We may be different from the majority, I don't know, but the way they separate us off makes the difference seem so much bigger than it really is."

"We're not Weird. In fact maybe everyone is Weird. We're all Weird and we're all Normal. We aren't Service Users here to consume Normality, we're people, individual people with our own histories and our own needs. In the time that I've spent in Sisyphusa I've met some of the bravest, strongest, most resilient people I could ever wish to meet and you're all an inspiration to me," I searched the crowd for Ella but I couldn't see her anywhere. "That's what they wanted from us. They wanted us to fear each other, fight each other and compete with each other for their approval, but look, we've proven what we can do when we work together. We've beaten them, we're one tiny step away, let's not throw it all away, wasting any more of our time in this awful place."

"What are these great new lives that you're talking about?" a Service User posed sceptically. "Have you watched the Bad News recently? All that's waiting for us out there is unemployment and Pig Plague. Life's hard enough when you're Normal let alone when you're Weird. And that's just to keep us occupied until we're tracked down and Removed again. Not for me, thank you. I'll gladly have my revenge now and then stick around and face the consequences, it'll be worth it just to remember the look on their faces," mused the Service User as he kicked the warden kneeling in front of him with the heel of his boot.

After listening to that Service User I realised that most of the other Service Users didn't care about the same things I did. They weren't pre-occupied with the abstract idea of freedom or angered by their status in society. Most of them just wanted simple, dignified lives whether inside or outside of Sisyphusa. They wanted respect.

Maybe a large number of them were simply followers and they had just gone from following the regime to following me. I didn't know how they would cope in the outside world—I didn't know how I would either after all the time I'd spent held captive. But I was more convinced than ever that they deserved a chance. They deserved a life without Climbing Pills or quarry work, Normalisation Classes or Weirdness Databases. They deserved to taste freedom even if they didn't yearn for it.

"It may well be that things are falling apart outside, but when weren't they?" I began. "At least outside there is the *possibility* of finding something better. We know what it's like in Sisyphusa, we have been here long enough to know that in Sisyphusa things are either shit or unbelievably shit," some Service Users laughed. "I can't promise you that on the outside you'll find a job, avoid suffering and marry your favourite Aspirati," they laughed again. "Part of life is about living with uncertainty. And if there's one thing I *am* certain of it's that our lives will not get any better if we stay in this place."

"He's right," cried the Simon Sisters.

"This is our only chance to leave," added Mikey with more enthusiasm than I'd ever heard him say anything. "If we don' go for it, we'll regret it for the rest of our lives." The Service Users engaged in a collective murmur.

"Who's for leaving?" I asked.

A few hands shot up, mainly from Team Recovery members and Team Re-Activation. Other arms were sheepishly raised until eventually an ocean of Service User hands reached for the sky, even those who had spoken out for staying.

A huge sense of relief settled over me and I turned my attention to getting Gwen to open the door using the Governor's password. Before I could talk to her however, Gwen screamed breathlessly into my Earpiece.

"Odis, quick, the corridor, it's Ella and Harris. They're heading for the…"

Before she could finish her sentence the alarm began blaring and the calm I'd just managed to restore had been lost forever.

Chapter 48

"Stop!" I shouted at the mass of angry Service Users who had quickly rounded upon Harry and Ella in the corridor. Their faces were anything but triumphant following their betrayal. Ella was her usual gaunt shadow, filled with guilt and self-loathing. Harry appeared bemused by everything. Some of the other Service Users began to push and kick at the two hollow figures who did nothing to protect themselves.

I pushed my way through the crowd and managed to act as a shield against the baying mob until they eventually desisted. I looked at the first two friends I had made in Sisyphusa and I could no longer recognise them. The two most confident, welcoming members of Team Recovery were now strangers to me. They could not bear to look me in the eye and instead they stared into the distance.

"Why are you protecting them?" roared one Service User.

"Let us at them," barked another. "They've ruined everything. That alarm means the whole facility has been locked down!"

"Reinforcements will be here any minute," the Governor's battered and bruised face smirked as he announced this. "You might as well go to your dorms now and await your punishment."

"Joe, shut him up will you," I shouted across the room, loud enough to be heard over the piercing alarm. Joe began to lift the sock up and stuff it back into the Governor's mouth.

"No, I meant your way!" I shouted. Joe smiled and fired a straight-right into the Governor's nose which felled him like a chopped down oak.

"Mr. Femuz!" I called out. "Take Harry and Ella over to where the wardens are and tie them up." I apologised softly to my two old friends but they didn't acknowledge me nor did they put up any resistance to being held with the wardens.

"What are you doing?" asked a flabby member of Team Rejuvenation whose name I've forgotten. "Are you just going to let them get away with it?"

"No-one's getting away with anything," I snapped back at the man, irritated that his petty pleas for revenge were disturbing the little thinking time I had. "Gwen," I spoke into my communication device. "Can you still open the door?"

"Who are you talking to?" raged the angry fat man. "Are you a Grade 6?" he asked disdainfully. "I can't believe we're being lectured by a Grade 6!"

"Hey, I'm a Grade 6," shouted an offended Service User.

"Exactly," retorted the fat man. This precipitated a scuffle between the two which I didn't have the time or will to stop.

"Gwen, can you open the door or not?" I asked again impatiently.

"I've been trying to override it but it's no good," she sounded exasperated.

"How long have we got?" I asked.

"The first reinforcements could arrive in fourteen minutes, fifteen if you're lucky," she said. "Are you suggesting…"

"I don't see that we've got any other option," I interrupted.

"What about those who can't climb?" asked Gwen.

I thought for a moment and then I suggested, "We could get the ropes from the practice room and those who can climb without ropes will carry them to the top and pull the others up."

"Excellent idea," she shrieked. "You know there's a problem, though," she realised.

"The Night Warden? But it's before lunch?" I shuddered as I remembered Ella's description of her and Dobbsy's fateful encounter with the six-headed creature.

"Yes, but once the alarm has been activated The Night Warden is on patrol until the alarm is disabled. It mightn't be as bad as you think," Gwen reassured me.

"From what I've heard, the thing sounds impassable."

"Not necessarily. The trick is to avoid the whirlpool and veer more towards the…"

"The six sets of teeth which are all trying to eat us?" I interrupted.

"Precisely," Gwen replied. "The whirlpool would swallow you all whole, you'd be better of taking your chances with Cilla."

"Cilla?"

"That's what I named her," she said. "After my great aunt Cilla. Dreadful woman…a real monster."

"So you made them as well? It seems that the hardest parts about escaping Sisyphusa are avoiding your handiwork."

"Well, at least it shows that I was good at what I did!" she laughed. I did not.

"Are they mechanical like the henchmen? Couldn't you just shut them off?" I asked hopefully.

"I'm afraid not," replied Gwen. "Now that the alarm has been set off I can't override the system any more."

"So we veer towards Cilla, what then?"

"Then you do your best," Gwen said mournfully. "She's a formidable guard dog. But surely it's better to lose some of you passing Cilla than to lose you all in the maelstrom?"

"How can you say 'lose some' so casually, there must be another way?" I pleaded.

"Maybe there is!" she yelled. "I've just had an idea. If I remember correctly, I designed an Emergency Deactivation Switch somewhere on her body. If some of you distracted her while one person snuck around the back of her and flicked the switch then it could work?"

"Fantastic! We'll try anything. As long we can all escape together, anything but going up there knowing that some people won't make it. Where is this switch?" I asked.

"Cilla is a strange contraption," Gwen began. "She has six long, serpent-like necks which I fitted with motion and sound sensors. Her torso is thick and rough, and her twelve legs are based on my childhood dog, Millicent. Now, where did I put that switch?" she asked herself aloud. "Ah yes, it's in the small of the back, just where the torso ends and Millie's legs begin."

"Great, thanks," I said as I ran back down the corridor past the crowd of Service Users who were arguing amongst themselves. Gwen said something back to me but it was impossible to hear it over all the noise. When I reached the reception I ignored all of the people approaching me, firing numerous questions in my direction and instead I headed straight for the desk.

I stood atop the desk again and addressed the whole group as well as I could with the blaring alarm still in full voice. "We can't leave by the door like we planned to," I screamed. "But we can climb the wall." No-one said anything which led me to believe that they hadn't heard me but then I saw them begin to murmur to the people stood next to them.

"People, there's no time," I shouted impatiently. "Either we escape now or we never escape."

"Some of us aren't ready to climb," said one elderly Service User.

"Those who can climb will do so, those who can't, will be hauled up with the ropes," I said. "Joe, can you and Tiny fetch all of the ropes from the Practice Climbing Warehouse and take them to the wall." Joe and Tiny raced out of the building.

There were no more questions, no more complaints which meant that either the majority of the Service Users weren't aware of The Night Warden or they were and they just assumed that it wouldn't be on duty so early in the day.

"Okay everyone," I announced. "Follow me. Bring the wardens and the Governor." The Service Users followed after me with the prisoners in tow. Mr. Femuz brought up the rear with the docile Harry and Ella who were still shell-shocked.

Chapter 49

I stood in the sizeable shadow of the wall and stared up at its summit. Here it was, 'The Great Wall', the reason for all of the sickening pills and missile-interrupted practice climbs. This was the foundation of Sisyphusa, this was what Sisyphusa was for. The ethos was that if you, the Service User, suffered enough, both physically and emotionally, you would have to be tough enough to successfully scale the wall and by extension re-integrate with Normal society.

I wondered, as I scoped out a favourable route up the jagged rock-face, how the wardens, Governor Shade, and all of their superiors all the way up to Minister Frown, could possibly believe that their approach to what they called Weirdness was working, whatever their statistics were telling them. If they thought Sisyphusa, and other places like it, were working then how did they explain the fact that almost all of the Service Users I'd met had returned to Weirdness Institutions multiple times, often within mere weeks of a successful Wall-Climb? It shouldn't suit their penchant for cost-cutting to have to keep dealing with the same Service User over and over again. I had no idea what the solution was but that didn't mean that I couldn't disagree with theirs.

Joe and Tiny arrived at the base of the wall with the ropes at exactly the same time as we did. I took Joe and Mr. Femuz to one side and told them about what was awaiting us at the top: the whirlpool, Cilla and the Emergency Deactivation Switch. Mr. Femuz was stony-faced and unflinching, whereas Joe was almost salivating.

"What's the plan?" he asked excitedly, desperate to have a mission to fulfil.

"What do you think?" I asked him. "This is much more your kind of expertise."

Joe hesitated for a moment, his expression betrayed his apprehension at being trusted with such a strategic and commanding task as opposed to just following orders.

"Well, I suppose it's just a standard ambush procedure," he began tentatively. "I don't know the terrain at the summit," he continued, picking up a nearby twig and drawing a tactical plan on the dusty ground. "But if the target is located on a relatively flat plain then I'd place all of my men here as a decoy," he said, designating a straight line of men to the left and a large dot to represent Cilla. "And I would manoeuvre around the back of the enemy like so," he finished his diagram with a squiggly line rounding Cilla as she approached the others to mark himself.

"What about Mr. Femuz and me?" I asked.

"This is a dangerous mission, Dizzy," he told me gravely. "It's not for civilians. No offence. It would be mine and the rest of the boys' honour if you trusted us with such an important mission."

"Of course I trust you, but…"

"Please, Odis," Joe interrupted. "Let me do this." The only other time I had seen the expression Joe was wearing was when he spoke about his experiences in the war.

"Okay, Joe," I relented. I was uncomfortable with the idea of not being able to have any personal control over events at the top of the wall but Joe was right, they were trained, maybe not for six-headed robots, but they were more cut out for a fight than me.

"What do you want us to do?" I asked.

"We'll climb the wall now, with the ropes. Once we've disposed of the target we'll lower the ropes down and you can start sending the Service Users up."

Joe strode over to his men and informed them of the mission they were about to carry out by drawing another plan on the sand for them. They nodded, some more enthusiastically than others, then they engaged in some form of ceremonial fist-pumping session before each draped a coiled rope over their shoulder and scaled the wall in double-quick time.

I informed the group that the Team Re-Activation boys would just survey the area at the top of the wall before lowering the ropes down for us to follow. All of us were on edge, expecting the government troops to arrive at any second and restore order at Sisyphusa.

"What's taking them so long up there?" asked Tracey.

"The ropes will be down soon," I said, willing it to be true.

In order to tell you what happened atop that wall I'm going to have to do something which I haven't done throughout my account, that is, describe events that I didn't see with my own two eyes. Joe described to me in detail what took place, and I have no reason to doubt the veracity of his description. Here is what he told me:

"The top of the wall was much bigger than I thought it would be. When you get up there you can't see to the other end where you're meant to climb down with huge rocks on one side and mist on the other. The lads advanced through the middle while I hung back.

They came into closer proximity with the misty side and that's when the whirlpool appeared. It started by rumbling and then the ground opened on that side and water rose to the surface and began to circle round and round like a washing machine.

The boys moved away from that side but that's when the enemy emerged from behind the rocks. The target had six heads and all of them moved as if they had minds of their own. The necks extended towards the lads and the teeth snapped at their arms and their heads but they fended them off with sticks and threw rocks at the thing to keep it at bay.

That's when I made my move. I circled far enough around the enemy to be out of range and then I approached it from behind. At first I moved slowly but then I stopped and signalled to my men to act as decoys by charging at it from different directions. This distracted the enemy which gave me the opportunity to charge in from behind and disable it via the Emergency Deactivation Switch. We suffered no fatalities but one man lost two of his fingers and another had a chunk of his leg removed."

The action that Joe described, without emotion, lasted no more than seven or eight minutes by which time we heard the thud of the ropes hitting the ground waiting for Service Users to pull up. There were five ropes lowered down so I told everyone to line up in their teams and for Team Captains to send up Service Users one at a time.

That left the fifth rope free because Team Re-Activation was already at the top so I rounded up the wardens and the Governor and began to send them up one at a time, connecting them with harnesses but leaving their hands tied. Serky, Shiva, Eavel, all of them allowed themselves to be lifted up the wall, not asking why or complaining in any way. It surprised me how quickly, and how easily, the wardens slipped into the role of passive victim. They were unrecognisable from the authoritarian despots they had been when running their own respective teams only as recently as that morning.

The other teams' lines were quickly dwindling as Joe and his team worked at a furious rate. I reached the last member of my group, Governor Shade. I pulled the sock out of his mouth which made him screw up his face, a face which was by that point a bloody mess.

"Do you want to go down with the ship, Captain?" I asked the Governor.

"I am not wedded to this place," the Governor sneered. "This is not my home. That building holds no sentimental value to me, it is just a job. You haven't defeated me or ruined me. I'll find another job as Governor in one of the other hundreds of Weirdness Institutions on this Island or beyond because I can assure you, there are always Weird people in this world who need to be Normalised." He smiled and offered himself up to be lifted up the wall.

I had hated the Governor ever since I first woke up in my Solitary Initiation cell and his face appeared on the HDTV Screen. I'll never forget how his face filled the entire screen, because that's what he was, the face of Sisyphusa, its figurehead. Governor Shade personified the system that he represented but I realised that I had been mistaken in thinking that the Governor was the root of all evil and the mastermind behind my kidnap and imprisonment.

The Governor was a small man. His ambitions were limited. He wanted a nice wage, a car which would allow him to imagine that he was someone important and an institution full of vulnerable people whom he could impose himself upon. The power in the system was not concentrated in people like Governor Shade, they are its puppets. The powerful people are faceless, they don't seek the limelight like an Aspirati or crave petty power like Governor Shade, they are content to live a life in the shadows, spending their fortunes in private.

I attached the Governor to the rope and watched him being lifted up with the smug expression still occupying his battered face. I don't know what happens to a man to give him such an angry, twisted soul but I wish he and his ilk didn't feel the need to inflict it upon others. I was content to let him believe that he had won because I knew that those were the kinds of small victories that he needed. They sustained him. In truth, there was no winner or loser. I realised that there had never even been a personal battle between us, we had merely found ourselves on opposing sides of a system over which neither of us had any real control. I wondered whether knowing of my lack of power or control left me any better off than the Governor?

"Odis!" Ahmed shouted from the Team Recovery line. I ran over to the line past where all of the other teams had been but had vacated. Ahmed was standing with Harry and Ella.

"Odis, they won't come, please tell them," a flustered Ahmed explained to me.

"Okay, Ahmed," I told him calmly. "You've done a good job. You go up now and we'll follow straight after you."

He nodded warily. "You come straight away? I not leave without you."

"I promise, you go now," I assured him. He attached himself to the rope and tugged on it twice to indicate that he was ready to be lifted and off he went.

I looked at my two friends standing in front of me and I wanted to cry. Harry kept on scratching himself and couldn't stand still, he looked like someone who was addicted to Ziziphusa or something stronger. As for Ella, she stood motionless, almost catatonic, seemingly shut off to everything that was going on around her.

"Well, here we are guys," I said trying to sound cheerful but not succeeding. "It's only the three of us left. Are you ready to go?" I asked, my voice cracking.

My question disappeared into the chasm which now existed between myself and my two friends. Ella didn't move a millimetre and Harry continued to scratch and shake so I couldn't tell whether he was shaking his head or if that was just a twitch.

"Come on, guys, you can't stay here, it might not be safe. Come with me and I'll take care of you," I pleaded with them. I tried to pull Ella gently by the arm but she suddenly threw her arms up in the air and began screaming as soon as I touched her. Harry reacted by leaping forward and pushing me towards the wall, making animal noises and speaking gibberish.

"Please, guys," I cried. "Please come. I'm begging you. You can start a new life, no wardens, no walls, no pills, just the three of us." They looked at me as if they couldn't understand what I was saying.

That's when the first explosion happened. The Factory was the first to be detonated. The ground shook beneath our feet as the bomb went off and I could see the building go up in flames in the distance. Plumes of smoke filled the sky and the entire compound was instantly cloaked in a smoke-filled darkness. Then there was a second explosion. This time the noise was more implosion than explosion and rather than the quarry going up in flames instead it collapsed in on itself.

"Come on, guys, we have to go NOW," I shouted. They just stood there in shock watching Sisyphusa crumble around them.

"Let's g-" I began before I was drowned out by the Practice Climbing Warehouse being blown up and ripped apart with debris strewn in all directions. "For fuck's sake, Gwen!" I shouted.

"Odis, come on, let's go," I could hear people shouting from the top of the wall.

I looked up at them and felt rain on my face for what seemed like the first time in years. I began to attach myself to the rope. "Please guys," I said. "This is it, I'm going now, there's still time for you to come with me." They didn't even turn around. I walked up to them and tried to touch Ella's shoulder just to say goodbye but Harry pushed me away. I tugged the rope twice and wiped the tears from my eyes as I watched Harry and Ella sit down and watch the destruction encircling them.

As I was nearing the top of the wall, the explosives in the main building were detonated and the whole thing caught fire and began to fall apart. I knew almost telepathically that Gwen was still inside and that she had always planned it that way. She was as institutionalised as Harry and Ella. She had spent the majority of her life in Sisyphusa and she had made it her life's work first to build it up and later to tear it down. Her mission to undo all of the bad things she had done gave her life meaning and I suppose she thought that she was too old to begin again.

I reached the top of the wall and was helped up by Mr. Femuz. The rain had by then turned into a downpour. I was in tears and he put his arm around me as we watched the whole compound burn. I hoped that Gwen had found redemption and some inner peace in the end. I reached up to my ear, removed the Earpiece which Gwen had fitted me with and threw it as far as I could into Sisyphusa.

Chapter 50

Mine were the last feet to touch the sodden ground having abseiled down the outer wall of Sisyphusa. The outer wall wasn't jagged and uneven like the inner wall. It was smooth, grey concrete which gave the deceptive appearance to passing onlookers that beyond the wall might lay a workplace, a car park, even a school. The surrounds of the compound were sparse and surprisingly quiet. There were no buildings, no cars, no people to pelt us with missiles or put us back in chains, just a lonely tarmac road and barren, untended fields.

It wasn't until some time later that I would find out why it was that no government reinforcements answered the alarm. By that time there were no reinforcements because there was no longer a government. Minister Frown and his clutch of loyal Deputies were hounded out of power by baying mobs and the whole Island fell into chaos. There were no policemen on the streets, patients were left untended in hospitals and the postal service went on strike.

Amidst all this chaos there was one consistent voice of calm leadership. Every night on the HDTV Entertainment channel a fresh-faced young Aspirati told everyone that he could sort out the mess. He told the watching public that he knew them, he knew their struggles and their hopes. He listened sympathetically when he spoke with members of the public in the studio and nodded with a concerned look on his face.

It didn't matter that he had no experience or that his father was the Pharaoh of the Island's largest, and recently destroyed, Money Pyramid. He knew the public and he was just like them. When it came time to elect the next Minister, the people of the Island voted in their favourite Aspirati, via their HDTV remotes, in a landslide victory. The Aspirati marched triumphantly into the government building and hired a cabinet of fellow Aspiratis and Pyramid workers. The ordinary people who voted them in were the ones who were disadvantaged by the new Government's policies but at least they were understood and felt comforted by the idea that someone like them would be running the Island.

On the lonely black tarmac outside Sisyphusa I mentioned how empty the scene was on our escape. There was, however, one person there to greet us. An old man standing next to a giant, rickety red bus was waving his arms and ushering us over. There were two other buses behind us which some of the other Service Users made their way towards. We left the wardens and the Governor on the side of the road, ignored and irrelevant. The Service Users' hope for a new beginning was tangible which meant the burning desire for revenge cooled to a genuine indifference.

The exhausted retinue of Service Users stumbled up the steps of the buses and collapsed into their seats. The old man smiled at each of his passengers and patted them all lightly on the back, uttering, "Fill her up from back to front, please folks. Back to front."

I was the final one to reach the entrance after Mr. Femuz climbed on board ahead of me. I tried to smile at the bus driver but my body felt frozen with grief at losing Gwen and leaving Harry and Ella behind. I tried to climb up the steps but the old man extended his arm across the doorway to block my way.

"Now then, you must be Odis," he smiled.

"How did you know?"

"Gwennie told me you'd be the last one to board. Seems she had your number alright," he chuckled.

"I suppose," I answered glumly.

"Don't be so sad, young man," he patted me on the shoulder. "Gwennie did what she needed to do. I know you'll miss her, I will too, but she did the right thing, you both did. I mean look at that bus, look at what the two of you have achieved together, these people can do whatever they like now."

I felt the tears sliding down my cheeks and rubbed them in embarrassment. "How did you know her?" I asked the old man.

"We go... I mean...went back many, many years, it's not really important. Anyway your seat is up front just behind me," he finished, gently nudging me on board.

I walked up the steps and saw that the Service Users crammed into the bus were all opening envelopes and reading the letters inside of them. I took my seat at the front next to Mr. Femuz who was crying and gesticulating towards the sky.

"Praise The Sacred Fourth!" he exclaimed. "Look, my friend," he showed me. Inside Mr. Femuz's envelope was a passport with a new identity, a letter and photograph from his daughter and a boat ticket to see her in Lutetia.

"That's wonderful," I told him. In the background throughout the entire bus I could hear calls of jubilation as each Service User discovered his or her new identity and other personalised surprises be it a letter from an estranged son or news of families set to be reunited with their husbands and fathers from the Outlands.

"You must open yours," Mr. Femuz implored me. I followed suit and slowly opened the envelope to find a passport with my photograph pasted in it but the name of 'Captain Quentin Quick. Occupation: Travelling Man.' I smiled and remembered back to the medium-sized red book which had no title or author on its binding.

I delved back into the envelope to see if there was anything else but was disappointed to find that there wasn't. I was about to put the envelope away when I noticed that there was something written on the underside of the flap. It read: "Look in overhead compartment."

I stood up uneasily as by that point the bus was in full motion and I had forgotten what it was like to be in a moving vehicle. I opened the hatch and saw a cardboard box which I hastily lifted trying not to fall over as I did so. With the heavy box on my lap I opened it up to find Bastian and Libby stretching as if they'd just had an afternoon nap and then they purred at me. Mr. Femuz and I took one of them on each of our laps and stroked them under the belly and over their arching backs. While stroking under Libby's chin I noticed that she was wearing a collar which she never had before. I also saw that hanging from the collar was a tiny locket. I opened it and unfurled the tiny scroll of paper which had a message that said: "The work is not yet done."

The old man continued driving through the night towards the main city on the Island from where you can reach whatever destination you choose. We all got out wearing our new clothes and clutching our new identities close to us as if they could be taken away at any moment. People began to go their separate ways and I said goodbye to my team, wondering how they would get on but knowing I would never see most of them again.

That was over a year ago now and I haven't met or seen any of them since. I know that Mr. Femuz did meet up with his daughter because he sent a postcard to the first place I stayed in after the escape. But I have moved around several times since then and have fallen out of contact with him. In some ways I miss them, but largely I'm glad that I have no contact with the Service Users of Sisyphusa. I have taken my new identity and travelled far and wide to feel alive in new experiences and forget the old ones. At first I spent much of my time trying to make sense of what had befallen me in my years in Sisyphusa but eventually I accepted that it made no sense at all.

The worst thing to lose, apart from a loved one, is time. I've lost over four years of my life, time that I've lost forever. In fact no, I didn't lose those years. I didn't misplace them or forget where I had put them. That time was forcibly taken away from me through no fault of my own. To experience such a sudden and violent rupture to my previous notion of time, to adapt and to avoid allowing bitterness to totally consume me is a battle that feels like it will last until the end of my life. The scars of Sisyphusa will never leave me, just like the scars on Ella's body and on her mind could never leave her. There is an ever-present sense that you must constantly look over your shoulder, mindful that you can be Removed again at any time.

I have been able to visit my family but only for short spells because I worry that I'll bring trouble upon them and I know that the neighbours have loose lips when it comes to Sisyphusans. I haven't seen any of my old friends. For so much of my time in Sisyphusa I had such a clear idea of home, the physical places and faces, especially Layla's. These images in my mind sustained me. They would be my reward if I could only get through that minute or that day. Now I see that home was nothing but an idea, a fantasy that time had stopped, and that I could return to how things were.

So I stay on the move, travelling all over the Empire and outside of it, trying to affect change. I managed to contact Joe last month and we've been discussing trying to set up a project dedicated to helping veteran soldiers who have been discharged after showing signs of Weirdness. We thought we'd call it 'WarFair'. There is nothing concrete yet but we're hoping to meet in person some time soon.

I've told you my story which is all I can do because no two people's experience of what we call Weirdness, or the places we send Weird people to, are the same. I do wish that the next time you read a report in The Daily Bulletin or see one on your HDTV telling you the latest atrocity committed by an ex-Service User or the drain that these people are on the public coinage that you will remember Ella, Harry, Mr. Femuz and Samuel Etch or the thousands of other Service Users on this Island for whom life is not a Fantasy. These are people who are in extraordinary pain, most of whom never dream of hurting anyone except for perhaps themselves.

Don't forget, it could be you who they come for next, in their black cloaks, in the middle of the night.

Lightning Source UK Ltd.
Milton Keynes UK
UKOW051935150512

192641UK00001B/32/P